Professional Examinati

CW01624911

PART 2

Paper 2.5

Financial Reporting
(UK Stream)

ACCA Study Text

ACCA

Approved Publisher

ftc

FTC Foulks Lynch
A **Kaplan Professional** Company

British Library Cataloguing-in-Publication Data

A catalogue record for this book is available from the British Library.

Published by:

FTC Foulks Lynch
Swift House
Market Place
Wokingham
Berkshire RG40 1AP

ISBN 1 84390 594 9

Printed and bound in Great Britain by William Clowes Ltd, Beccles, Suffolk

Acknowledgements

We are grateful to the Association of Chartered Certified Accountants, the Chartered Institute of Management Accountants and the Institute of Chartered Accountants in England and Wales for permission to reproduce past examination questions. The answers have been prepared by FTC Foulks Lynch.

Contents

		Page
Introduction		**v**
Syllabus and study guide		**vi**
The examination		**xiii**
Study skills and revision guidance		**xv**
Accounting principles, concepts and theory		
Chapter 1	Review of basic concepts	1
Chapter 2	Accounting concepts, accounting theory	23
Chapter 3	Revenue recognition	31
Chapter 4	Accounting for price level changes	41
Regulatory framework		
Chapter 5	The structure of the UK regulatory framework	57
Preparation of consolidated financial statements		
Chapter 6	Group accounting – introduction	71
Chapter 7	Group accounting – intra-group adjustments	93
Chapter 8	Group accounting – the profit and loss account	117
Chapter 9	Group accounting – associates and joint ventures	143
Preparation and presentation of financial statements for limited liability companies and other entities		
Chapter 10	Preparation of financial statements for limited companies	161
Chapter 11	Taxation in financial statements	205
Chapter 12	Stock and long-term contracts	225
Chapter 13	Reporting financial performance	241
Chapter 14	Related parties and segmental reporting	257
Chapter 15	Share capital and reserves	275
Chapter 16	Fixed assets – tangible	299
Chapter 17	Fixed assets – goodwill and intangible assets	323
Chapter 18	Liabilities – provisions, contingent liabilities and contingent assets	345
Chapter 19	Accounting for the substance of transactions	359
Chapter 20	Hire purchase and leasing	371
Chapter 21	Earnings per share	387
Analysis and interpretation of financial statements and related information		
Chapter 22	Analysis and interpretation of financial statements	401
Chapter 23	Cash flow statements	423
Answers to practice questions and exam-type questions		**449**
Index		**509**

Introduction

This is the FTC Foulks Lynch Study Text for Paper 2.5 *Financial Reporting*, and is part of the ACCA series produced for students taking the ACCA examinations.

This new edition has been produced with direct guidance from the examiner. It covers the syllabus and study guide in great detail, giving appropriate weighting to the various topics. Targeted very closely on the examination, this study text is written in a way that will help you assimilate the information easily. Numerous practice questions and exam-type questions at the end of each chapter reinforce your knowledge.

DEFINITION

- **Definitions.** The text defines key words and concepts, placing them in the margin, with a clear heading, as on the left. The purpose of including these definitions is to focus your attention on the point being covered.

KEY POINT

- **Key points**. In the margin you will see key points at regular intervals. The purpose of these is to summarise concisely the key material being covered.

ACTIVITY 1

- **Activities**. The text involves you in the learning process with a series of activities designed to catch your attention and make you concentrate and respond. The feedback to activities is at the end of each chapter.

SELF-TEST QUESTIONS

- **Self-test questions**. At the end of each chapter there is a series of self-test questions. The purpose of these is to help you revise some of the key elements of the chapter. All the answers to these questions can be found in the text.

EXAM-TYPE QUESTIONS

- **End of chapter questions**. At the end of each chapter we include examination-type questions. These will give you a very good idea of the sort of thing the examiner will ask and will test your understanding of what has been covered.

Syllabus and study guide

CONTENTS

- Objectives of the study guide
- Syllabus content
- Study guide
- Examinable documents

Objectives of the study guide

This study guide is designed to help you plan your studies and to provide a more detailed interpretation of the syllabus for Paper 2.5 *Financial Reporting*. It contains both the syllabus and the study guide, which you can follow when preparing for the examination.

The syllabus outlines the content of the paper. The study guide takes the syllabus content and expands it into study sessions of similar length. These sessions indicate what the examiner expects of candidates for each part of the syllabus, and therefore gives you guidance in the skills you are expected to demonstrate in the examinations.

Syllabus content

1 ACCOUNTING PRINCIPLES, CONCEPTS AND THEORY

a The ASB's Statement of Principles for Financial Reporting.

b Agency theory.

c Price level changes, capital maintenance.

2 REGULATORY FRAMEWORK

a Structure of the UK regulatory framework
- i EC directives
- ii Companies Acts.

b Standard setting process: the Financial Reporting Council (FRC) and its subsidiary bodies; the role of the International Accounting Standards Board (IASB).

3 PREPARATION AND PRESENTATION OF FINANCIAL STATEMENTS FOR LIMITED LIABILITY COMPANIES AND OTHER ENTITIES

a Accounting for share capital and reserves
- i issue and redemption of shares
- ii distributable profits.

b Tangible and intangible fixed assets.

c Net current assets.

d Earnings per share.

e Tax in company accounts including
- i current tax
- ii deferred tax.

f SSAPs, FRSs and UITF abstracts as specified in the examinable documents.

4 PREPARATION OF CONSOLIDATED FINANCIAL STATEMENTS

a Definition of subsidiary companies.

b Exclusions from consolidations.

c Preparation of consolidated profit and loss accounts and balance sheets including:
- i elimination of intra-group transactions
- ii fair value adjustments.

d Associated companies, joint ventures.

5 ANALYSIS AND INTERPRETATION OF FINANCIAL STATEMENTS AND RELATED INFORMATION

a Analysis of corporate information.

b Preparation of reports on financial performance for various user groups.

c Preparation and analysis of cash flow statements of a single company.

d Related party transactions.

e Segmental information.

Excluded topics

The following topics are specifically excluded from the syllabus:

- partnership and branch financial statements
- preparing group financial statements involving more than one subsidiary
- piecemeal acquisitions, disposal of subsidiaries and group reconstructions
- foreign currency translation/consolidations, hedging
- financial statements of banks and similar financial institutions
- group cash flows
- schemes of reorganisation/reconstruction
- company/share valuation
- derivative transactions
- accounting for pension costs
- the ASB's Financial Reporting Exposure Drafts and Discussion Drafts/Papers.

Key areas of the syllabus

The key topic areas are as follows:

Accounting principles and concepts, accounting theory

- Statement of Principles.
- Revenue recognition.
- Substance over form.

Preparation of financial statements of limited companies

- Form and content of published financial statements.
- Accounting and disclosure requirements of the Companies Acts and Accounting Standards.

Preparation of consolidated financial statements

- Definitions of subsidiaries: exclusions from consolidation.
- Simple groups.

Analysis and interpretation of financial statements

- Preparation of reports for various user groups.
- Preparation and analysis of cash flow statements.

Other topic areas

Note these may be examined as part of a question within the above key areas or as a substantial part of a separate optional question:

- hire purchase and leasing
- long-term contracts
- earnings per share
- impairment of fixed assets, provisions
- discontinued operations
- goodwill and other intangibles.

Additional information

Candidates need to be aware that questions involving knowledge of new examinable regulations will not be set until at least six months after the last day of the month in which the regulation was issued.

The study guide provides more detailed guidance on the syllabus. Examinable documents are listed in the 'Exam Notes' section of *Student Accountant*.

Study guide

Chapter where covered

1 REVIEW OF BASIC CONCEPTS, STATEMENT OF PRINCIPLES FOR FINANCIAL REPORTING — **1**

- discuss what is meant by a conceptual framework and GAAP
- describe the objectives of financial statements and the qualitative characteristics of financial information
- define the elements of financial statements

Chapter where covered

- apply the above definitions to practical situations
- revision of Paper 1.1 – prepare the final accounts of a company from a trial balance.

2 ACCOUNTING CONCEPTS, ACCOUNTING THEORY — **1, 2, 4**

- outline the concept of 'comprehensive income'
- explain the principle of fair value
- discuss and apply accounting policies
- describe the deficiencies of historic cost accounts (HCA) during periods of rising prices and explain in principle alternatives to HCA.

3 REVENUE RECOGNITION — **3**

- outline the principles of the timing of revenue recognition
- explain the role of the concept of substance over form in relation to recognising sales revenue
- explain and define realised profits
- discuss the various points in the production and sales cycle where it may, depending on circumstances, be appropriate to recognise gains and losses – give examples of this
- describe the ASB's approach to revenue recognition within its Statement of Principles.

4 THE STRUCTURE OF THE UK REGULATORY FRAMEWORK — **5**

- describe the influence of EC directives
- explain the role of the Companies Acts
- outline the Standard setting process and the role of the:
  - Financial Reporting Council (FRC)
  - Accounting Standards Board (ASB)
  - Urgent Issues Task Force (UITF)
  - Financial Reporting Review Panel (FRRP)
- explain the relationship between UK and International Accounting Standards (IASs)/International Financial Reporting Standards (IFRSs).

5 PREPARATION OF FINANCIAL STATEMENTS FOR LIMITED COMPANIES — **5,10**

- state the requirements of the Companies Act regarding:
  - the duty to prepare annual accounts
  - the form and content of the prescribed formats
- prepare the financial statements of limited companies in accordance with the prescribed formats and relevant accounting standards

Chapter where covered

- describe the main issues involved when a company adopts International Financial Reporting Standards (IFRSs) for the first time
- apply the requirements of the IASB to the preparation of financial statements of a first time adopter of International Financial Reporting Standards
- distinguish between small and medium companies and outline the disclosure exemptions relating to these companies.

6 REPORTING FINANCIAL PERFORMANCE I — 13

- explain the need for an accounting standard in this area
- discuss the importance of identifying and reporting the results of discontinuing operations; define discontinuing operations
- distinguish between extraordinary and exceptional items, including their accounting treatment and required disclosures
- prepare a profit and loss account in accordance with the requirements of Financial Reporting Standards.

7 REPORTING FINANCIAL PERFORMANCE II — 13

- explain the contents and purpose of the statement of total recognised gains and losses, linking it to the Statement of Principles and the concept of comprehensive income
- describe and prepare a:
  - note of historical cost profits and losses
  - reconciliation of movements in shareholders' funds
  - statement of movements in reserves
- define prior period adjustments and account for the correction of fundamental errors and changes in accounting policies.

8 SHARE CAPITAL AND RESERVES — 15

- explain the need for an accounting standard on Capital Instruments
- distinguish between debt and share capital
- apply the requirements of relevant accounting standards to the issue and finance costs of:
  - equity and preference shares
  - debt instruments with no conversion rights, and
  - convertible debt
- explain and apply the general requirements to purchase or redemption of shares
- apply the requirements that allow private companies to redeem shares out of capital

Chapter where covered

- discuss the advantages of companies being able to redeem shares
- define and discuss the Companies Acts rules relating to profits available for distribution.

9 FIXED ASSETS – TANGIBLE — 16

- define the initial cost of a fixed asset (including a self-constructed asset) and apply this to various examples of expenditure distinguishing between capital and revenue items
- describe, and be able to identify, subsequent expenditure that may be capitalised
- state and appraise the effects of accounting standards on the revaluation of fixed assets
- account for gains and losses on the disposal of revalued assets
- calculate depreciation on:
  - revalued assets, and
  - assets that have two or more major components
- apply the provisions of accounting standards on Government Grants
- discuss why the treatment of investment properties should differ from other properties
- apply the requirements of accounting standards on Accounting for Investment Properties.

10 HIRE PURCHASE AND LEASING — 20

- distinguish between a hire purchase contract and a lease
- describe and apply the method of determining a lease type (i.e. an operating or finance lease)
- explain the effect on the financial statements of a finance lease being incorrectly treated as an operating lease
- account for operating leases in financial statements
- account for finance leases in the financial statements of lessors and lessees
- outline the principles of the accounting standard on leasing and its main disclosure requirements. Note: the net cash investment method will not be examined.

11 FIXED ASSETS – GOODWILL AND INTANGIBLE ASSETS — 17

- discuss the nature and possible accounting treatments of both internally generated and purchased goodwill
- distinguish between goodwill and other intangible assets
- describe the criteria for the initial recognition and measurement of intangible assets

Chapter where covered

- describe the subsequent accounting treatment, including the principle of impairment tests in relation to purchased goodwill
- describe the circumstances in which negative goodwill arises, and its subsequent accounting treatment and disclosure
- describe and apply the requirements of accounting standards on Research and Development.

12 FIXED ASSETS – IMPAIRMENT OF FIXED ASSETS AND GOODWILL — 17

- define the recoverable amount of an asset; define impairment losses
- give examples of, and be able to identify, circumstances that may indicate that an impairment of fixed assets has occurred
- describe what is meant by an income generating unit
- state the basis on which impairment losses should be allocated, and allocate a given impairment loss to the assets of an income generating unit.

13 LIABILITIES – PROVISIONS, CONTINGENT LIABILITIES AND CONTINGENT ASSETS — 18

- explain why an accounting standard on provisions is necessary – give examples of previous abuses in this area
- define provisions, legal and constructive obligations, past events and the transfer of economic benefits
- state when provisions may and may not be made, and how they should be accounted for
- explain how provisions should be measured
- define contingent assets and liabilities – give examples and describe their accounting treatment
- be able to identify and account for:
  - warranties/guarantees
  - onerous contracts
  - environmental and similar provisions
- discuss the validity of making provisions for future repairs or refurbishments.

14 STOCK AND LONG-TERM CONTRACTS — 12

- review the principles of stock valuation covered in Paper 1.1
- define a long-term contract and describe why recognising profit before completion is generally considered to be desirable, and the circumstances where it may not be; discuss if this may be profit smoothing
- describe the ways in which attributable profit may be measured

Chapter where covered

- calculate and disclose the amounts to be shown in the financial statements for long-term contracts.

15 EARNINGS PER SHARE — 21

- explain the importance of comparability in relation to the calculation of earnings per share (EPS) and its importance as a stock market indicator
- explain why the trend of EPS may be a more accurate indicator of performance than a company's profit trend
- define earnings and the basic number of shares
- calculate the EPS in accordance with relevant accounting standards in the following circumstances:
  - basic EPS
  - where there has been a bonus issue of shares during the year, and
  - where there has been a rights issue of shares during the year
- explain the relevance to existing shareholders of the diluted EPS and describe the circumstances that will give rise to a future dilution of the EPS
- calculate the diluted EPS in the following circumstances:
  - where convertible debt or preference shares are in issue; and
  - where share options and warrants exist.

16 TAXATION IN FINANCIAL STATEMENTS — 11

- account for current taxation in accordance with relevant accounting standards
- record entries relating to corporation tax in the accounting records
- apply requirements of accounting standards on VAT
- explain the effect of timing differences on accounting and taxable profits
- outline the principles of accounting for deferred tax
- outline the requirements of accounting standards on Deferred Tax
- calculate and record deferred tax amounts in the financial statements.

17 ACCOUNTING FOR THE SUBSTANCE OF TRANSACTIONS — 19

- explain the importance of recording the substance rather than the legal form of transactions – give examples of previous abuses in this area
- describe the features which may indicate that the substance of transactions may differ from their legal form
- explain and apply the principles in accounting standards for the recognition and derecognition of assets and liabilities

Chapter where covered

- be able to recognise the substance of transactions in general, and specifically account for the following types of transaction:
  - stock sold on sale or return/consignment stock
  - sale and repurchase/leaseback agreements
  - factoring of debtors.

18 & 19 GROUP ACCOUNTING – INTRODUCTION — 6, 8

- describe the concept of a group and the objective and usefulness of consolidated financial statements
- explain the different methods which could be used to prepare group accounts
- explain and apply the definition of subsidiary companies in the Companies Acts and accounting standards
- describe the circumstances and reasoning for subsidiaries to be excluded from consolidated financial statements
- prepare a consolidated balance sheet for a simple group dealing with pre and post acquisition profits, minority interests and consolidated goodwill
- explain the need for using coterminous year ends and uniform accounting policies when preparing consolidated financial statements
- describe how the above is achieved in practice
- prepare a consolidated profit and loss account for a simple group, including an example where an acquisition occurs during the year and there is a minority interest.

20 GROUP ACCOUNTING – INTRA GROUP ADJUSTMENTS — 7,8

- explain why intra-group transactions should be eliminated on consolidation
- explain the nature of a dividend paid out of pre-acquisition profits
- account for the effects (in the profit and loss account and balance sheet) of intra-group trading and other transactions including:
  - unrealised profits in stock and fixed assets
  - intra-group loans and interest and other intra-group charges, and
  - intra-group dividends including those paid out of pre-acquisition profits.

21 GROUP ACCOUNTING – FAIR VALUE ADJUSTMENTS — 8

- explain why it is necessary for both the consideration paid for a subsidiary and the subsidiary's identifiable assets and liabilities to be accounted for at their fair values when preparing consolidated financial statements

Chapter where covered

- prepare consolidated financial statements dealing with fair value adjustments (including their effect on consolidated goodwill) in respect of:
  - depreciating and non-depreciating fixed assets
  - stock
  - monetary liabilities (basic discounting techniques may be required)
  - assets and liabilities (including contingencies) not included in the subsidiary's own balance sheet.

22 & 23 GROUP ACCOUNTING – ASSOCIATES AND JOINT VENTURES — 9

- define associates and joint ventures, including an arrangement that is not an entity (JANE)
- distinguish between equity accounting and proportional consolidation
- describe the equity and gross equity methods
- prepare consolidated financial statements to include a single subsidiary and an associated company or a joint venture.

24 ANALYSIS AND INTERPRETATION OF FINANCIAL STATEMENTS — 22

- calculate useful financial ratios for a single company or for group financial statements
- analyse and interpret ratios to give an assessment of a company's performance in comparison with:
  - a company's previous period's financial statements
  - another similar company for the same period
  - industry average ratios
- discuss the effect that changes in accounting policies or the use of different accounting policies between companies can have on the ability to interpret performance
- discuss how the interpretation of current cost accounts or current purchasing power accounts would differ from that of historic cost accounts
- discuss the limitations in the use of ratio analysis for assessing corporate performance, outlining other information that may be of relevance.

  Note: the content of reports should draw upon knowledge acquired in other sessions.

  These sessions concentrate on the preparation of reports and report writing skills

25 & 26 CASH FLOW STATEMENTS — 23

- prepare a cash flow statement, including relevant notes, for an individual company in accordance with relevant accounting standards

  Note: questions may specify the use of the direct or the indirect method

Chapter where covered

- appraise the usefulness of, and interpret the information in, a cash flow statement.

27 RELATED PARTIES **14**

- define and apply the definition of related parties in accordance with relevant accounting standards
- describe the potential to mislead users when related party transactions are included in a company's financial statements
- adjust financial statements (for comparative purposes) for the effects of non-commercial related party transactions
- describe the disclosure requirements for related party transactions.

28 SEGMENTAL REPORTING **14**

- discuss the usefulness and problems associated with the provision of segmental information
- define a reportable segment and the information that is to be reported
- prepare segmental reports in accordance with relevant accounting standards
- assess the performance of a company based on the information contained in its segmental report.

Examinable documents

Prior to each sitting of the examination, the ACCA issues Exam Notes setting out which official documents are examinable.

The documents examinable for Paper 2.5 are set out below. We recommend that students read *Student Accountant* to keep up-to-date.

Accounting Standards

Statements of Standard Accounting Practice (SSAPs)

No	*Title*	*Issue date*	*Chapter*
4	Accounting for government grants (revised)	July 1990	16
5	Accounting for value added tax	Jan 1974	11
9	Stocks and long-term contracts (revised)	Sept 1988	12
13	Accounting for research and development (revised)	Jan 1989	17
19	Accounting for investment properties	July 1981	16
	Amendment to SSAP 19	July 1994	16
21	Accounting for leases and hire purchase contracts (amended March 1997)	July 1984	20
25	Segmental reporting	July 1990	23

Financial Reporting Standards (FRSs)

No	*Title*	*Issue date*	*Chapter*
FRS 1	Cash flow statements (excluding group cash flow statements) (revised)	Oct 1996	23
FRS 2	Accounting for subsidiary undertakings	July 1992	6
FRS 3	Reporting financial performance (excluding group aspects)	Oct 1992	13
FRS 5	Reporting the substance of transactions	April 1994	19
FRS 7	Fair values in acquisition accounting	Sept 1994	8
FRS 8	Related party disclosures	Oct 1995	23
FRS 9	Associates and joint ventures	Nov 1997	9
FRS 10	Goodwill and intangible assets	Dec 1997	17
FRS 11	Impairment of fixed assets and goodwill	July 1998	17

No	*Title*	*Issue date*	*Chapter*
FRS 12	Provisions, contingent liabilities and contingent assets	Sept 1998	18
FRS 15	Tangible fixed assets	Feb 1999	16
FRS 16	Current tax	Dec 1999	11
FRS 18	Accounting policies	Dec 2000	1
FRS 19	Deferred tax	Dec 2000	11
FRS 21	Events after the balance sheet date	May 2004	18
FRSSE	Financial Reporting Standard for Smaller Entities	Dec 2001	10
FRS 22	Earnings per share	Dec 2004	21
FRS 25	Financial Instruments: Disclosure and Presentation	Dec 2004	15
FRS 26	Financial Instruments: Measurement	Dec 2004	15

Abstracts

No	*Title*	*Issue date*	*Chapter*
UITF Abstract 4	Presentation of long-term debtors in current assets	July 1992	5
UITF Abstract 5	Transfers from current assets to fixed assets	July 1992	16
UITF Abstract 15	Disclosure of substantial acquisitions (revised)	Feb 1999	17
UITF Abstract 37	Purchases and sales of own shares	Oct 2003	15
UITF Abstract 40	Revenue recognition and service contracts	Mar 2005	12

Other statements

Title	*Issue date*	*Chapter*
RSI Operating and Financial Review	May 2005	10
Statement of Principles for Financial Reporting	Dec 1999	1, 3
IFRS 1 First-time adoption of International Financial Reporting Standards	Jun 2003	5

Notes

1 FRS 1 is examinable for Paper 2.5 but excluding group cash flow statements and cash flow statements involving foreign currency.

2 Students should note that Chapters 1 and 3 of the Statement of Principles are examinable in Paper 1.1. At Paper 2.5, students are expected to be aware of the issues/reasons which have led to the publication of the Statement of Principles, and to be able to discuss the main thrust of the document.

3 Knowledge of International Accounting Standards other than IFRS 1 will not be examinable.

The examination

CONTENTS

- Format of the examination
- Approach to examining the syllabus
- Examination tips
- Answering the questions

Format of the examination

	Number of marks
Section A: one compulsory question	25
Section B: choice of 3 from 4 questions (25 marks each)	75
	100
Total time allowed: 3 hours	

Approach to examining the syllabus

The examination is a three hour paper in two sections. It will contain both computational and discursive elements. Some questions will adopt a scenario/case study approach.

The Section A compulsory question will be the preparation of group financial statements, and may include a small related discussion element. Computations will be designed to test an understanding of principles. At least one of the optional questions in Section B will be a conceptual/discursive question that may include illustrative numerical calculations.

An individual question may often involve elements that relate to different areas of the syllabus. For example a published financial statements question could include elements relating to several accounting standards. In scenario questions candidates may be expected to comment on management's chosen accounting treatment and determine a more appropriate one, based on circumstances described in the question.

Questions on topic areas that are also included in Paper 1.1 will be examined at an appropriately greater depth in Paper 2.5. Some Accounting Standards are very detailed and complex. At Paper 2.5 candidates need to be aware of the principles and key elements of these Standards. Candidates will also be expected to have an appreciation of the need for an accounting standard and why it has been introduced.

Examination tips

- Spend the first few minutes of the examination **reading through the questions**.
- Where you have a **choice of questions**, decide which ones you will do.
- **Divide the time** you spend on questions in proportion to the marks on offer. One suggestion is to allocate 1½ minutes to each mark available, so a 10-mark question should be completed in 15 minutes.
- Unless you know exactly how to answer the question, spend some time **planning** your answer. Stick to the question and **tailor your answer** to what you are asked.
- **Fully explain** all your points but be **concise**. Set out all workings **clearly and neatly**, and state briefly what you are doing. Don't write out the question.
- If you do not understand what a question is asking, **state your assumptions**. Even if you do not answer precisely in the way the examiner hoped, you should be given some credit, if your assumptions are reasonable.
- If you **get completely stuck** with a question, leave space in your answer book and **return to it later.**

- Towards the end of the examination spend the last **five minutes** reading through your answers and **making any additions or corrections**.
- Before you finish, you must fill in the required information on the front of your answer booklet.

Answering the questions

- **Essay questions**: Make a quick plan in your answer book and under each main point list all the relevant facts you can think of. Then write out your answer developing each point fully. Your essay should have a clear structure; it should contain a brief introduction, a main section and a conclusion. Be concise. It is better to write a little about a lot of different points than a great deal about one or two points.
- **Case studies**: To write a good case study, first identify the area in which there is a problem, outline the main principles/theories you are going to use to answer the question, and then apply the principles/theories to the case. Include relevant points only and then reach a conclusion and, if asked for, recommendations. If you can, compare the facts to real-life examples – this may gain you additional marks in the exam.
- **Computations**: It is essential to include all your workings in your answers. Many computational questions require the use of a standard format: company profit and loss account, balance sheet and cash flow statement for example. Be sure you know these formats thoroughly before the examination and use the layouts that you see in the answers given in this book and in model answers. If you are asked to comment or make recommendations on a computation, you must do so. There are important marks to be gained here. Even if your computation contains mistakes, you may still gain marks if your reasoning is correct.
- **Reports, memos and other documents**: Some questions ask you to present your answer in the form of a report or a memo or other document. Use the correct format – there could be easy marks to gain here.

Study skills and revision guidance

CONTENTS

- Preparing to study
- Effective studying
- Revision

This section aims to give guidance on how to study for your ACCA exams and to give ideas on how to improve your existing study techniques.

Preparing to study

Set your objectives

Before starting to study decide what you want to achieve – the type of pass you wish to obtain. This will decide the level of commitment and time you need to dedicate to your studies.

Devise a study plan

- Determine which times of the week you will study.
- Split these times into sessions of at least one hour for study of new material. Any shorter periods could be used for revision or practice.
- Put the times you plan to study onto a study plan for the weeks from now until the exam and set yourself targets for each period of study – in your sessions make sure you cover the course, course assignments and revision.
- If you are studying for more than one paper at a time, try to vary your subjects, this can help you to keep interested and see subjects as part of wider knowledge.
- When working through your course, compare your progress with your plan and, if necessary, re-plan your work (perhaps including extra sessions) or, if you are ahead, do some extra revision/practice questions.

Effective studying

Active reading

You are not expected to learn the text by rote, rather, you must understand what you are reading and be able to use it to pass the exam and develop good practice. A good technique to use is SQ3Rs – Survey, Question, Read, Recall, Review:

1 **Survey** the chapter – look at the headings and read the introduction, summary and objectives, so as to get an overview of what the chapter deals with.

2 **Question** – whilst undertaking the survey, ask yourself the questions that you hope the chapter will answer for you.

3 **Read** through the chapter thoroughly, answering the questions and making sure you can meet the objectives. Attempt the exercises and activities in the text, and work through all the examples.

4 **Recall** – at the end of each section and at the end of the chapter, try to recall the main ideas of the section/chapter without referring to the text. This is best done after a short break of a couple of minutes after the reading stage.

5 **Review** – check that your recall notes are correct.

You may also find it helpful to reread the chapter and try to see the topic(s) it deals with as a whole.

Note-taking

Taking notes is a useful way of learning, but do not simply copy out the text. The notes must:

- be in your own words
- be concise
- cover the key points
- be well-organised
- be modified as you study further chapters in this text or in related ones.

Trying to summarise a chapter without referring to the text can be a useful way of determining which areas you know and which you don't.

Three ways of taking notes:

- **summarise the key points** of a chapter.
- **make linear notes** – a list of headings, divided up with subheadings listing the key points. If you use linear notes, you can use different colours to highlight key points and keep topic areas together. Use plenty of space to make your notes easy to use.
- **try a diagrammatic form** – the most common of which is a mind-map. To make a mind-map, put the main heading in the centre of the paper and put a circle around it. Then draw short lines radiating from this to the main sub-headings, which again have circles around them. Then continue the process from the sub-headings to sub-sub-headings, advantages, disadvantages, etc.

Highlighting and underlining

You may find it useful to underline or highlight key points in your study text – but do be selective. You may also wish to make notes in the margins.

Revision

The best approach to revision is to revise the course as you work through it. Also try to leave four to six weeks before the exam for final revision. Make sure you cover the whole syllabus and pay special attention to those areas where your knowledge is weak. Here are some recommendations:

- **Read through the text and your notes again** and condense your notes into key phrases. It may help to put key revision points onto index cards to look at when you have a few minutes to spare.
- **Review any assignments** you have completed and look at where you lost marks – put more work into those areas where you were weak.
- **Practise exam standard questions** under timed conditions. If you are short of time, list the points that you would cover in your answer and then read the model answer, but do try and complete at least a few questions under exam conditions.
- Also **practise producing answer plans** and comparing them to the model answer.
- If you are stuck on a topic find somebody (a colleague or a tutor) to explain it to you.
- **Read good newspapers and professional journals**, especially ACCA's *Student Accountant* – this can give you an advantage in the exam.
- Ensure you **know the structure of the exam** – how many questions and of what type you will be expected to answer. During your revision attempt all the different styles of questions you may be asked.

Chapter 1
REVIEW OF BASIC CONCEPTS

CHAPTER CONTENTS

1 The notion of GAAP and a conceptual framework
2 The objective of financial statements
3 The qualitative characteristics of financial information
4 The elements of financial statements
5 Recognition in financial statements
6 Presentation of financial information
7 Financial accounting conventions
8 Preparation of the financial statements of a simple business organisation

This chapter introduces the subject of financial reporting and covers most of the content of the ASB's *Statement of Principles for Financial Reporting*, the framework of theoretical principles that the ASB uses to develop its Financial Reporting Standards (FRSs). You may find it useful to return to this material from time to time as you work through the remainder of the text.

This chapter also revises the more traditional accounting concepts that you will already have met in your earlier studies. Lastly, you will revise the preparation of final accounts for a simple business organisation by working through an example.

Objectives

By the time you have finished this chapter you should be able to:

- discuss what is meant by a conceptual framework and GAAP
- describe the objective of financial statements
- describe the qualitative characteristics of financial information
- define the elements of financial statements and apply the definitions
- discuss and apply the requirements of FRS 18
- prepare the financial statements of a company from a trial balance.

1 The notion of GAAP and a conceptual framework

1.1 Generally Accepted Accounting Practice (GAAP)

KEY POINT

GAAP has support among users of financial information, and includes the requirements of accounting standards, the Companies Acts, the Stock Exchange, and other non-legislative accounting treatments.

GAAP is accounting practice which has substantial authoritative support amongst users of financial information. Accounting standards generally represent GAAP but there may be a point in GAAP which is not reflected in an accounting standard.

Thus the boundaries of UK GAAP go beyond the principles contained in accounting standards to include the requirements of: the Companies Acts; the Stock Exchange; other acceptable accounting treatments not incorporated in legislation or quasi-legislation.

1.2 A conceptual framework

DEFINITION

A **conceptual framework** is a coherent system of interrelated objectives and fundamental principles. It prescribes the nature, function and limits of financial accounting and financial statements.

A **conceptual framework** is a coherent system of interrelated objectives and fundamental principles. It prescribes the nature, function and limits of financial accounting and financial statements.

A conceptual framework enables accounting standards and GAAP to be developed in accordance with agreed principles. This has several advantages as follows.

- It avoids 'fire fighting', whereby accounting standards are developed in a piecemeal way in response to specific problems or abuses. 'Fire fighting' can lead to inconsistencies between different accounting standards, and between accounting standards and legislation.
- Lack of a conceptual framework may mean that certain critical issues are not addressed. For example, until recently there was no definition of basic terms such as 'asset' or 'liability' in any accounting standard.
- Transactions are becoming more complex and businesses are becoming more sophisticated. A conceptual framework helps preparers and auditors of accounts to deal with transactions which are not the subject of an accounting standard.

- Accounting standards based on principles are thought to be harder to circumvent. The alternative to a conceptual framework is a prescriptive 'cookbook' approach, based on rules rather than principles. In the 1980s, 'creative accounting' practices were developed which manipulated the view given by the financial statements without actually breaching any regulations.
- It can be argued that a conceptual framework strengthens the credibility of UK financial reporting and the accounting profession.
- A conceptual approach makes it less likely that the standard setting process can be influenced by 'vested interests' (e.g. large companies or particular business sectors).

1.3 The Statement of Principles

KEY POINT

The **Statement of Principles** sets out the concepts that underlie the preparation of financial statements. It is not, however, the only influence on standard setting.

The ASB's conceptual framework is the **Statement of Principles** for Financial Reporting. It sets out the concepts that underlie the preparation of financial statements for external users. It is intended to be relevant to the financial statements of profit-oriented entities, including public sector profit-oriented entities, regardless of their size.

The Statement of Principles is not itself an accounting standard nor can it override the requirements of any existing accounting standard.

In detail, the intended role of the Statement is:

- to assist the ASB in its development of future accounting standards and in its review of existing accounting standards
- to assist the ASB by providing a basis for reducing the number of alternative accounting treatments permitted by law and accounting standards
- to assist preparers of financial statements in applying accounting standards and in dealing with topics that do not form the subject of an accounting standard
- to assist auditors in forming an opinion as to whether financial statements conform with accounting standards
- to help users of financial statements to interpret the information contained in financial statements prepared in conformity with accounting standards
- to provide those who are interested in the work of the ASB with information about its approach to the formulation of accounting standards.

The Statement of Principles is an important influence on the development of standards. However, it is not the only influence on standard setting. The ASB also takes into account legal requirements, cost-benefit considerations, industry-specific issues, the desirability of evolutionary change and implementation issues.

Topics covered in the Statement of Principles

The following topics are covered in the Statement of Principles:

Chapter 1 The objective of financial statements.

Chapter 2 The reporting entity.

Chapter 3 The qualitative characteristics of financial information.

Chapter 4 The elements of financial statements.

Chapter 5 Recognition in financial statements.

Chapter 6 Measurement in financial statements.

Chapter 7 Presentation of financial information.

Chapter 8 Accounting for interests in other entities.

2 The objective of financial statements

2.1 The objective

KEY POINT

The objective of **financial statements** is to provide information about the reporting entity's financial performance and financial position that is useful to a wide range of users.

The objective of **financial statements** is to provide information about the reporting entity's financial performance and financial position, that is useful to a wide range of users for assessing the stewardship of the entity's management and for making economic decisions.

This objective can usually be met by focusing exclusively on the information needs of present and potential investors, the defining class of user.

2.2 Users and their needs

KEY POINT

Investors are interested in information that helps them to assess management effectiveness and to make decisions about their investment.

Investors (providers of risk capital) are interested in information that:

- helps them to assess how effectively management has fulfilled its stewardship role (the safekeeping of the entity's resources and their proper, efficient and profitable use)
- is useful in taking decisions about their investment or potential investment in the entity.

They are, as a result, concerned with the risk inherent in, and return provided by, their investments. They need information on the entity's financial performance and financial position that helps them to assess its cash generation abilities and its financial adaptability.

KEY POINT

Users of financial statements include: **investors, lenders**, **suppliers and trade creditors**, **employees**, **customers**, **governments** and their agencies, and the **public**.

Other users of financial statements, and their information needs, include the following:

- **Lenders** – interested in information that enables them to determine whether their loans will be repaid, and whether the interest attaching to them will be paid, when due. Potential lenders are interested in information that helps them to decide whether to lend to the entity and on what terms.
- **Suppliers and other trade creditors** – interested in information that enables them to decide whether to sell to the entity and to assess the likelihood that amounts owing to them will be paid when due.
- **Employees** – interested in information about the stability and profitability of their employer. They are also interested in information that helps them to assess the ability of their employer to provide remuneration, employment opportunities and retirement benefits.
- **Customers** – interested in information about the entity's continued existence. This is especially so when they are dependent on the entity (e.g. if product warranties are involved or if specialised replacement parts may be needed).
- **Governments and their agencies** – interested in the allocation of resources and, therefore, the activities of entities. They also require information in order to regulate the activities of entities, assess taxation and provide a basis for national statistics.
- **The public** – interested in information about the trends and recent developments in the entity's prosperity and the range of its activities. For example, an entity may make a substantial contribution to a local economy by providing employment and using local suppliers.

2.3 Information required by investors

KEY POINT

Users of financial statements need information on **financial performance** and **position**, **cash generation** and utilisation and **financial adaptability**.

Investors (and other users of the financial statements) need information on four key areas of an entity:

- **Financial performance** – the return it obtains on the resources it controls, the components of that return and the characteristics of those components.
- **Financial position**
  - the economic resources it controls
  - its financial structure
  - its liquidity and solvency
  - its capacity to adapt to changes in the environment in which it operates.
- **Cash generation** and utilisation in its operations, its investment activities and its financing activities. Information on this provides an additional perspective on its financial performance – one that is largely free from allocation and valuation issues.
- **Financial adaptability** – its ability to take effective action to alter the amount and timing of its cash flows so that it can respond to unexpected needs or opportunities.

2.4 The reporting entity

KEY POINT

An entity should publish financial statements if there is a legitimate demand for the information and it is a cohesive economic unit.

An entity should prepare and publish financial statements if:

- there is a legitimate demand for the information that its financial statements would provide
- it is a cohesive economic unit.

The boundary of the reporting entity is determined by the scope of its control.

3 The qualitative characteristics of financial information

3.1 Introduction

DEFINITION

Qualitative characteristics are the attributes that make information provided in financial statements useful to others.

Qualitative characteristics are the attributes that make information provided in financial statements useful to others.

The Statement of Principles identifies four qualitative characteristics (relevance, reliability, comparability and understandability), subject to a threshold quality of materiality, as shown in the diagram below:

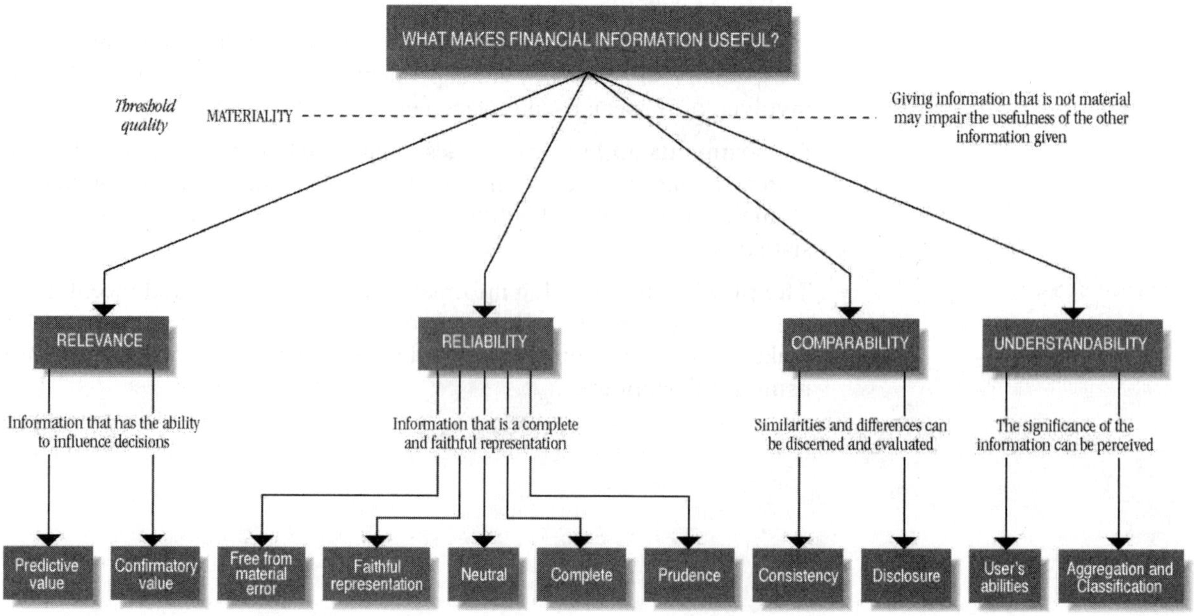

3.2 Relevance of information

KEY POINT

Information is **relevant** if it has the ability to influence the economic decisions of users and is provided in time to influence those decisions.

Information is **relevant** if it has the ability to influence the economic decisions of users and is provided in time to influence those decisions.

Information provided by financial statements needs to be relevant. Where choices have to be made between mutually exclusive options, the option selected should be the one that results in the relevance of the information being maximised – in other words, the one that would be of most use in taking economic decisions.

Information that is relevant has **predictive** value or **confirmatory** value:

- It has **predictive** value if it enables users to evaluate or assess past, present or future events.
- It has **confirmatory** value if it helps users to confirm or correct past evaluations and assessments.

3.3 Reliability

KEY POINT

Reliable information can be depended upon to present a **faithful representation** and is **neutral**, **error free**, **complete** and **prudent**.

Information provided by the financial statements must be **reliable**. Information is reliable when:

- it can be depended upon by users to represent faithfully what it either purports to represent or could reasonably be expected to represent
- it is free from deliberate or systematic bias (i.e. it is neutral)
- it is free from material error
- it is complete within the bounds of materiality
- in conditions of uncertainty, a degree of caution (i.e. prudence) has been applied in exercising judgement and making the necessary estimates.

Faithful representation

If information is to represent faithfully the transactions and other events that it purports to represent, they must be accounted for and presented in accordance with their substance and economic reality and not merely their legal form.

Neutrality

Information must be neutral, that is, free from bias. Financial statements are not neutral if, by the selection or presentation of information, they influence the making of a decision or judgement in order to achieve a predetermined result or outcome.

Completeness

Information must be complete and free from error within the bounds of materiality. A material error or an omission can cause the financial statements to be false or misleading and thus unreliable and deficient in terms of their relevance.

Prudence

DEFINITION

Prudence is the exercise of caution in making judgements about estimates required under conditions of uncertainty.

Uncertainty surrounds many of the events and circumstances that are reported on in financial statements. It is dealt with in those statements by disclosing the nature and extent of the uncertainty involved and by exercising prudence.

Prudence means exercising a degree of caution in making judgements about estimates required under conditions of uncertainty, such that gains and assets are not overstated and losses and liabilities are not understated. The existence of assets and gains requires more confirmatory evidence and greater reliability of measurement than are required for liabilities and losses.

It is not necessary to exercise prudence where there is no uncertainty. Nor is it appropriate to use prudence as a reason for, for example, creating hidden reserves or excessive provisions, deliberately understating assets or gains, or deliberately overstating liabilities or losses. That would mean that the financial statements are not neutral and, therefore, are not reliable.

One of the more controversial parts of the Statement of Principles has been its attitude to prudence. The Statement of Principles views prudence as a desirable quality of financial information, rather than a fundamental concept, and defines it in very different terms from the traditional ones (which are discussed later in this chapter).

3.4 Comparability

KEY POINT

Users must be able to compare financial statements to establish trends and relative performance. Hence, **consistency** and **disclosure** are required.

Users must be able to compare the financial statements of an entity over time to identify trends in its financial position and performance. Users must also be able to compare the financial statements of different entities to evaluate their relative financial performance and financial position. **Consistency** and **disclosure** are therefore required.

Consistency

Consistency is not an end in itself nor should it be allowed to impede the introduction of improved accounting practices. Consistency can be useful in enhancing comparability between entities, but it should not be confused with a need for absolute uniformity.

Disclosure

Users need to be able to identify differences between:

- the accounting policies adopted from period to period
- the accounting policies adopted to account for like transactions and other events
- the accounting policies adopted by different entities.

Disclosure of the accounting policies adopted, and any changes to them, enhances the usefulness of financial statements.

3.5 Understandability

KEY POINT

Understandability depends on **presentation** and **user capability**.

Information needs to be **understandable**; users need to be able to perceive its significance. Understandability depends on:

- the way in which information is presented
- the capabilities of users.

It is assumed that users have a reasonable knowledge of business and economic activities and are willing to study the information provided with reasonable diligence.

3.6 Materiality

KEY POINT

Information is **material** to the financial statements if its misstatement or omission might reasonably be expected to influence the economic decisions of users.

Information is **material** to the financial statements if its misstatement or omission might reasonably be expected to influence the economic decisions of users.

Materiality is a threshold quality that is demanded of all information given in the financial statements.

Information that is material needs to be given in the financial statements. Information that is not material need not be given.

Whether information is material will depend upon the size and nature of the item in question judged in the particular circumstances of the case.

3.7 Constraints on the qualitative characteristics

KEY POINT

Where there are conflicts between the key qualitative characteristics, a trade-off needs to be found.

Conflicts may arise between the key qualitative characteristics. In these circumstances a trade off needs to be found that still enables the objective of the financial statements to be met.

Relevance and reliability

Where there is a conflict between qualitative characteristics, use the information that is the most relevant of whichever information is available.

Conflicts may arise over timeliness. A delay in providing information can make it out of date and less relevant, but reporting on transactions and other events before all the uncertainties are resolved may make information less reliable. Financial information should not be provided until it is sufficiently reliable.

Neutrality and prudence

Neutrality involves freedom from bias. Prudence is potentially biased because it seeks to ensure that gains or assets are not overstated and losses or liabilities are not understated in conditions of uncertainty. It is necessary to find a balance that ensures that deliberate understatement of assets or gains and overstatement of liabilities or losses does not occur.

Understandability

Information that is relevant and reliable should not be excluded from the financial statements simply because it is difficult for some users to understand.

3.8 How the Statement has influenced accounting standards (1)

KEY POINT

The Statement of Principles is influencing the **relevance**, **predictive value** and **reliability** of the information contained in financial statements.

Many of the ideas in the first three chapters of the Statement of Principles have already greatly influenced the recent development of accounting standards.

- Information may be **relevant** because it has **predictive value**. FRS 1 *Cash flow statements* and FRS 3 *Reporting financial performance* both increase the predictive value of financial information. FRS 3 requires reporting entities to analyse results between continuing operations, acquisitions and discontinued operations and to disclose details of unusual and infrequent items of income and expenditure.
- Information is **reliable** if it reports the substance of transactions rather than their strict legal form. FRS 5 *Reporting the substance of transactions* now requires all reporting entities to do this.

4 The elements of financial statements

4.1 Introduction

Seven elements of financial statements are identified, all of which are seen to be interrelated. In order for an item to be included in financial statements, it must fall within one of the definitions of elements.

4.2 Assets

DEFINITION

Assets are **rights or other access** to **future economic benefits controlled by an entity** as a result of **past transactions or events**.

Assets are rights or other access to future economic benefits controlled by an entity as a result of past transactions or events.

Rights or other access

For example, property is only an asset because of the rights (shared or sole) deriving from ownership or the other rights of occupation and use.

Future economic benefits

These are evidenced by the prospective receipt of cash. This could be cash itself, a debt receivable or any item which may be sold. For example, whilst a factory may not be sold (on a going concern basis) it houses the manufacture of goods. When these goods are sold, the economic benefit resulting from the use of the factory is realised as cash.

Controlled by an entity

Control is the ability to obtain economic benefits and to restrict the access of others (e.g. a company being the sole user of its plant and machinery, or selling surplus plant and machinery).

Past transactions or events

The transaction or event must be 'past' before an asset can arise.

4.3 Liabilities

DEFINITION

Liabilities are an entity's **obligations** to **transfer economic benefits** as a result of **past transactions or events**.

Liabilities are an entity's obligations to transfer economic benefits as a result of past transactions or events.

Obligations

These may be legal or not. For example, an entity may have no realistic alternative to refunding the price of goods that fail to meet the expectations of customers, even though there is no legal compulsion to do so.

Obligation implies that the outflow of resources is unavoidable. As long as the entity can choose to avoid the expenditure, costs to be incurred in the future do not represent liabilities.

Transfer economic benefits

This could be a transfer of cash, or other property, the provision of a service, or the refraining from activities which would otherwise be profitable.

Past transactions or events

As for assets, the transaction or event must be 'past' before a liability can arise.

4.4 Ownership interest

DEFINITION

Ownership interest is the residual amount found by deducting all liabilities of the entity from all of the entity's assets.

Ownership interest is the residual amount found by deducting all liabilities of the entity from all of the entity's assets.

Owners invest in an entity in the hope of a return (for example, the payment of dividends). Unlike creditors, owners cannot insist that a transfer is made to them regardless of the circumstances. Their interest is in the assets of the entity after all the liabilities have been deducted.

4.5 Gains and losses

DEFINITION

Gains are increases in ownership interest, not resulting from contributions from owners.

Losses are decreases in ownership interest, not resulting from distributions to owners.

These are counted as two of the seven elements.

Gains are increases in ownership interest, not resulting from contributions from owners.

Losses are decreases in ownership interest, not resulting from distributions to owners.

4.6 Contributions from owners

DEFINITION

Contributions from owners are increases in ownership interest resulting from transfers from owners in their capacity as owners.

Contributions from owners are increases in ownership interest resulting from transfers from owners in their capacity as owners.

Owners contribute to entities by transferring assets, performing services or accepting ownership interest in satisfaction of liabilities. Rights in the ownership interest are usually granted in return for a contribution from owners, such as cash (additional capital) provided to an entity in return for additional shares.

DEFINITION

Distributions to owners are decreases in ownership interest resulting from transfers to owners in their capacity as owners.

4.7 Distributions to owners

Distributions to owners are decreases in ownership interest resulting from transfers to owners in their capacity as owners.

Distributions to owners include dividends and the return of capital. For example, when a company purchases its own shares, this is reflected by reducing the amount of ownership interest.

ACTIVITY 1

Below are listed four situations.

1 M Ltd has paid £3 million towards the cost of a new hospital in the nearby town, on condition that the hospital agrees to give priority treatment to its employees if they are injured at work.

2 N Ltd is the freehold legal owner of a waste disposal tip. It has charged customers for the right to dispose of their waste for many years. The tip is now full, and heavily polluted with chemicals. If cleaned up, which would cost £8 million, the site of the tip could be sold for housing purposes for £6 million.

3 P Ltd has signed a contract to pay its finance director £300,000 per year for the next five years. He has agreed to work full time for the firm over that period.

4 Q Ltd has paid £25,000 to buy a patent right, giving it the right to sole use, for 8 years, of a manufacturing method which saves costs.

For each situation, state whether an asset or a liability is created.

Feedback to this activity is at the end of the chapter.

5 Recognition in financial statements

5.1 Stages of the recognition process

KEY POINT

Recognition involves depiction of the element in words and by a monetary amount and the inclusion of that amount in the financial statement totals.

Recognition involves depiction of the element in words and by a monetary amount and the inclusion of that amount in the financial statement totals.

The **recognition process** has the following stages:

- initial recognition, which is where an item is depicted in the financial statements for the first time (e.g. the purchase of an asset)
- subsequent remeasurement, which involves changing the amount at which an already recognised asset or liability is stated in the financial statements (e.g. revaluation)
- derecognition, which is where an item that was until then recognised ceases to be recognised (e.g. the sale of an asset).

All events that may have an effect on elements of the financial statements should be, as far as possible, identified and reflected in an appropriate manner in the financial statements.

5.2 Recognition and derecognition

KEY POINT

An item is **recognised** if sufficient evidence of it exists and its effect is measurable.

An item is **derecognised** if an event has eliminated a recognised asset or liability or the recognition criteria are no longer met.

If a transaction or other event has created a new asset or liability or added to an existing asset or liability, that effect is **recognised** if:

- sufficient evidence exists that the new asset or liability has been created, or that there has been an addition to an existing asset or liability; and
- the new asset or liability, or the addition to the existing asset or liability, can be measured as a monetary amount with sufficient reliability.

An asset or liability is wholly or partly **derecognised** if:

- sufficient evidence exists that a transaction or other past event has eliminated all or part of a previously recognised asset or liability; or
- although an item continues to be an asset or liability, the criteria for recognition are no longer met.

5.3 Sufficient evidence

KEY POINT

What constitutes **sufficient evidence** is a matter of judgement based on past experience.

What constitutes sufficient evidence? This is a matter of judgement in the particular circumstances of each case. The main source of evidence is experience, including:

- evidence provided by the event that has given rise to the item
- past experience with similar items
- current information directly relating to the item
- evidence provided by transactions of other entities in similar items.

5.4 Measurement

KEY POINT

Recognised items must be capable of being measured at a **monetary amount**.

Items that are recognised must be capable of being measured at a monetary amount. This involves two steps: selecting a suitable measurement basis (e.g. historical cost or current value) for the item, and then determining an appropriate monetary amount on the basis chosen.

5.5 How the Statement has influenced accounting standards (2)

Several accounting standards are based on the ideas in Chapters 4 and 5 of the Statement of Principles. Probably the most important of these are:

- FRS 5 *Reporting the substance of transactions*
- FRS 12 *Provisions, contingent liabilities and contingent assets*
- FRS 25 *Financial Instruments: Disclosure and Presentation*
- FRS 26 *Financial Instruments: Measurement*

These standards use the definitions of assets and liabilities and the recognition criteria set out above and will all be discussed in more detail later in the text.

6 Presentation of financial information

6.1 The principles

KEY POINT

The primary financial statements are the **profit and loss account** and **statement of total recognised gains and losses**, the **balance sheet** and the **cash flow statement**.

Financial statements consist of primary financial statements and supporting notes. The primary financial statements are:

- the statement(s) of financial performance (**profit and loss account** and **statement of total recognised gains and losses**)
- the statement of financial position (**balance sheet**)
- the **cash flow statement**.

The presentation of information on **financial performance** focuses on the components of financial performance and their characteristics.

The presentation of information on **financial position** focuses on the types and functions of assets and liabilities held and on the relationships between them.

The presentation of **cash flow information** shows the extent to which the entity's various activities generate and use cash. In particular it distinguishes between those cash flows that result from operations and those that result from other activities.

6.2 Presentation

KEY POINT

To aid clarity of **presentation**, information should be **aggregated** and **classified**.

Financial statements should communicate clearly and effectively and in as straightforward a manner as possible without loss of relevance or reliability and without unnecessarily increasing the length of the financial statements.

Aggregation and structure

Detail would obscure the message if financial statements reported every single aspect of every relevant transaction and event. Greater knowledge results from an orderly loss of information by aggregation. Aggregating information:

- conveys information that would otherwise have been obscured
- highlights significant items and relationships between items
- facilitates comparability between different entities
- is more understandable to users.

The supporting notes and primary financial statements form an integrated whole. The supporting notes amplify and explain the financial statements by providing:

- more detailed information on items recognised in the primary financial statements
- an alternative view of items recognised in the primary financial statements (for example, by disclosing a range of possible outcomes for a liability that is in dispute, or by disclosing segmental information)
- relevant information that cannot practicably be incorporated in the primary financial statements (for example, because of pervasive uncertainty).

Disclosing information in the supporting notes to the financial statements is not a substitute for recognition. It cannot correct or justify any misrepresentation or omission in the primary financial statements.

Classification

Items that are similar should be presented together and distinguished from dissimilar items. Classification should consider the relationships between different classes of items, for example the relative sizes of profits and capital employed, or of debtors and sales.

Items that are similar or related should be presented in a manner that highlights that similarity or relationship. For example, different kinds of current asset are shown adjacent to each other and current liabilities are usually shown in a manner that highlights their relationship to current assets.

6.3 Accompanying information

KEY POINT

Information accompanying financial statements could include **trend information**, **operating and financial reviews**, **directors' reports** and **statements by the chairman.**

Financial statements are often accompanied by other information, e.g. five-year **trend information, operating and financial reviews, directors' reports** and **statements by the chairman**. This information should not be inconsistent with the financial statements.

The more complex an entity and its transactions become, the more users need an objective and comprehensive analysis and explanation of the main features underlying the entity's financial performance and position. These disclosures (normally included in the operating and financial review) are best presented in the context of a discussion of the business as a whole.

6.4 How the Statement has influenced accounting standards (3)

- FRS 3 *Reporting financial performance* provides users of the financial statements with information that assists them in analysing the components of an entity's financial performance.
- FRS 1 *Cash flow statements* requires separate reporting of cash flows resulting from different activities.
- FRS 25 *Financial Instruments: Disclosure and Presentation* requires analysis of shareholders' funds and long-term debt in the balance sheet.

7 Financial accounting conventions

7.1 Fundamental accounting concepts

DEFINITION

Financial accounting conventions are assumptions which are used to prepare and disclose items in the financial statements.

DEFINITION

Fundamental accounting concepts are the broad basic assumptions which underlie the financial statements of business enterprises.

KEY POINT

Fundamental accounting concepts include the **going concern** concept, **accruals** concept, **consistency** concept and **prudence** concept.

Financial accounting conventions are assumptions which are used to prepare and disclose items in the financial statements. They are also referred to as **concepts** or **principles**.

Fundamental accounting concepts are the broad basic assumptions which underlie the financial statements of business enterprises.

The four accounting concepts below have traditionally been regarded as fundamental.

Going concern concept

In the absence of information to the contrary, it is assumed that the business has an indefinite life. The going concern concept clearly excludes situations where the business is, or may be, going into liquidation in the near future, or where its operations are to be drastically reduced.

Accruals concept

This is sometimes referred to as the matching concept, as it refers to the matching of costs and revenues. Revenue is usually recognised when it is realised. The realisation of revenue is usually taken to mean the date of sale rather than the date when the cash relating to the sale is received. It is thus logical to compare revenue reported in the period with the costs or expenses of earning that revenue. The operating profit determined in this way is supposed to indicate how efficiently the resources of the business have been utilised.

Consistency concept

A business should be consistent in its accounting treatment of similar items, both within a particular accounting period, and between one accounting period and the next.

Prudence concept

Revenues and profits are not reported and recognised in financial statements unless realised. Revenues and profits are not deemed realised until the likelihood of conversion to cash is high. In most cases, this means the date of sale. A business can provide for anticipated bad debts on credit sales as a separate exercise. In contrast, immediate provision is made for anticipated losses, even if such losses are unrealised. An example of the prudence concept is the valuation of stock at the lower of cost and net realisable value.

Where the prudence concept **conflicts** with the treatment required by another concept, it is the former which prevails. In particular, the accruals principle requires expenditure to be carried forward to be matched with related future income. Where there is significant uncertainty surrounding the realisation of this income, the prudence principle applies, and the related expenditure is written off in the period in which it arises.

7.2 FRS 18 *Accounting policies*

DEFINITION

Accounting policies define the process whereby transactions and other events are reflected in financial statements.

Accounting policies define the process whereby transactions and other events are reflected in the financial statements.

FRS 18 sets out the principles to be followed by an entity in selecting its accounting policies. The objective is to ensure that:

- appropriate accounting policies are selected
- the policies adopted are reviewed regularly, and changed when a new policy would be more appropriate
- sufficient disclosures of accounting policies are given.

For example, the accounting policy for the cost of computers might be to depreciate them on a straight line basis over four years to a nil residual value.

Criteria for selecting accounting policies

Accounting policies should be consistent with accounting standards, UITF Abstracts and companies legislation in the overriding objective of giving a true and fair view.

Policies should be judged against the objectives of relevance, reliability, comparability and understandability (as described in the Statement of Principles).

7.3 Accounting concepts

KEY POINT

FRS 18 identifies the **going concern** assumption and the **accruals basis** of accounting as playing a pervasive role in the selection of accounting policies. Entities must prepare financial statements on a going concern basis and on the accruals basis.

FRS 18 identifies two concepts as playing a pervasive role in the selection of accounting policies:

- the going concern assumption
- the accruals basis of accounting.

It appears that prudence and consistency have been downgraded from their 'fundamental' status, and the ASB has been criticised for this. However, prudence is still required as part of the reliability characteristic, and consistency is part of the comparability characteristic, so they have not been shelved completely.

FRS 18 states that:

- An entity should prepare its financial statements on a going concern basis, unless
  - (i) the entity is being liquidated or has ceased trading; or
  - (ii) the directors either intend to liquidate the entity or to cease trading, or have no realistic alternative but to do so.

  Directors should assess whether there are significant doubts about an entity's ability to continue as a going concern.

- An entity should prepare its financial statements, except for cash flow information, on the accrual basis of accounting.

Estimation techniques

DEFINITION

Estimation techniques are the methods adopted by an entity to arrive at estimated monetary amounts in the financial statements.

FRS 18 draws a distinction between accounting policies and estimation techniques. **Estimation techniques** are the methods adopted by an entity to arrive at estimated monetary amounts in the financial statements.

For example, if a fixed asset has a depreciable amount of £5,000 to be written off over five years, different depreciation methods such as straight line, reducing balance, sum of the digits, etc, all represent different estimation techniques. Estimation techniques therefore implement the measurement aspects of accounting policies.

The distinction between accounting policies and estimation technique is important because FRS 3 requires a change in accounting policy to be accounted for as a prior period adjustment (see later chapter of this text), while a change in estimation technique would only be accounted for as a prior period adjustment if it corrected a fundamental error or was required to be so treated by an accounting standard, UITF Abstract or companies legislation.

FRS 18 provides some guidance.

- An entity has previously stated assets at historic cost and it now states them at replacement cost. This is a change in a measurement base and is therefore a change in accounting policy.
- An entity has previously measured the current disposal value of an asset by reference to recent disposals of similar assets and it now does this by reference to prices quoted in advertisements. This is a change in the method of estimation, not a change in accounting policy.

Some accounting standards allow a choice over what is to be recognised For example, SSAP 13 allows development expenditure to be treated as an asset or as an expense. Where there is a choice, that choice is a matter of accounting policy.

A change in the way in which an entity presents particular items is a change in accounting policy. However, if an entity merely presents additional information, this is not a change in accounting policy.

ACTIVITY **2**

Which of the following is a change in accounting policy as opposed to a change in estimation technique?

1 An entity has previously charged interest incurred in connection with the construction of tangible fixed assets to the profit and loss account. It now capitalises this interest.

2 An entity has previously depreciated vehicles using the reducing balance method at 40% per year. It now uses the straight line method over a period of five years.

3 An entity has previously shown certain overheads within cost of sales. It now shows those overheads within administrative expenses.

4 An entity has previously measured stocks at weighted average cost. It now measures stocks using the FIFO method.

Feedback to this activity is at the end of the chapter.

Reviewing and changing accounting policies

KEY POINT

An entity's accounting policies should be **reviewed regularly** to ensure that they remain the most appropriate.

An entity's accounting policies should be reviewed regularly to ensure that they remain the most appropriate. For example a newly issued FRS might require a new policy to be adopted. However, frequent changes to accounting policies would impair the comparability of the financial statements, so should not be undertaken without proper consideration.

Disclosures

The financial statements should disclose:

- a description of important accounting policies adopted
- a description of estimation techniques that are significant and the underlying assumptions
- details of any changes to accounting policies adopted including:
  - (i) a brief explanation of why the new accounting policy is thought more appropriate

(ii) where practicable, the effect of a prior period adjustment on the results for the preceding period, in accordance with FRS 3 *Reporting financial performance*

(iii) where practicable, an indication of the effect of a change in accounting policy on the results for the current period

- details of any changes to estimation techniques, where material
- where an entity falls within the scope of a Statement of Recommended Practice (SORP), the title of the SORP and whether it has been complied with
- any significant doubts about whether the entity is a going concern
- where there has been a material departure from the requirements of an accounting standard, a UITF Abstract, or companies legislation (the 'true and fair view override') there should be:

(i) a clear and unambiguous statement that there has been a departure from the requirements of an accounting standard, UITF Abstract or companies legislation, and that the departure is necessary to give a true and fair view

(ii) details of the treatment that would normally be required and a description of the treatment actually adopted

(iii) the reason why the treatment prescribed would not give a true and fair view

(iv) a description of how the position shown in the financial statements is different as a result of the departure.

7.4 Accounting principles: Companies Act 1985

KEY POINT

The four fundamental concepts appear in the Companies Act 1985 as four of the five 'accounting principles'. The fifth states that in determining the aggregate amount of an item, individual assets or liabilities must be determined separately.

The four traditional fundamental concepts, going concern, accruals, prudence and consistency, are embodied in the Companies Act 1985 as four of the five 'accounting principles'. The fifth principle states that, in determining the aggregate amount of any item, the amount of any individual asset or liability that falls to be taken into account shall be determined separately. For example, when stock is valued at the lower of cost and net realisable value, the value must be determined for separate types of stock and then aggregated. In this way, anticipated losses on one type of stock will not be offset against expected gains on another.

In addition to the five accounting principles, the CA 1985 also requires a general application of the principle of accounting for substance. In deciding how amounts are presented in the profit and loss account and balance sheet, the directors of a company must have regard to the substance of the reported transaction or arrangement. This principle has traditionally been known as the 'substance over form' concept, as explained below.

7.5 Further principles or conventions

KEY POINT

Other conventions include the **entity or accounting unit** convention, the **accounting period** convention, the **stable standard of measurement** convention, **materiality** convention, **objectivity** convention and **substance over form** convention.

Entity or accounting unit convention

The business for accounting purposes is a separate entity quite apart from the owners or proprietors of the business. Separate accounts are maintained for the entity. The term entity or accounting unit usually refers to the business enterprise, but may also refer, for example, to charities and trusts.

Accounting period convention

For accounting purposes, the lifetime of the business is divided into arbitrary periods of a fixed length, usually one year. At the end of each period, usually referred to as the accounting period, two financial statements are prepared as follows:

- the balance sheet, showing the position of the business as at the end of the accounting period, usually on a historical cost basis

- the profit and loss account for the accounting period. Profit or loss is arrived at on the basis of the matching concept.

Some accountants argue that profit can only be meaningfully measured over the lifetime of a business, i.e. the period starting with the date the business is formed and ending with the date the business goes into liquidation. The problem of matching does not arise because the use of arbitrary accounting periods is avoided. There is also certainty of income and expenditure.

In spite of the arbitrary nature of the accounting period convention, it is necessary to strike a compromise between theoretical accuracy and the needs of the financial community. These needs require periodic financial statements which will form the basis of subsequent financial decisions.

Stable standard of measurement convention

Business activity involves the undertaking of all types of transaction. These diverse transactions are expressed in terms of a common unit of measurement, namely the monetary unit. Financial statements prepared on a historical cost basis make the assumption that the pound sterling is a stable monetary unit. This means, therefore, that 20X1 £s can be added to 20X9 £s and a meaningful result obtained.

Example

A company balance sheet states its plant and machinery at cost less aggregate depreciation, made up as follows:

	Cost	*Aggregate depreciation*	*Net book value*
	£	£	£
Assets acquired 20X1	80,000	24,000	56,000
Assets acquired 20X2	100,000	20,000	80,000
Assets acquired 20X3	60,000	6,000	54,000
	240,000	50,000	190,000

If the pound sterling is a stable unit of measurement, the above aggregation is meaningful. But there is a problem: even in periods of gradual inflation, the pound sterling is not a stable unit of measurement. The purchasing power of a 20X2 £ is quite different from that of a 20X1 or 20X3 £. This is a severe criticism of accounts prepared on a conventional or historical cost basis (see later chapter in this text).

Materiality convention

Financial statements should have regard to the materiality of various items, either individually or collectively. The materiality of an item refers to the relative importance of the item in the overall context of the financial statements. An item of expenditure of £10,000 may well be material to a company which makes an annual profit of £50,000, but it is not to a company making an annual profit of £50m.

Objectivity convention

Financial statements should be as objective as possible. Transactions are to be recorded objectively as historical events. This is the main basis of historical cost accounting. Certain aspects of historical cost accounting do, however, represent departures from the objectivity convention. For example, although the depreciation charge is often based on the original cost of an asset (which is objective) it depends also on the estimated useful life and estimated scrap value at the end of that useful life (which is subjective).

Substance over form convention

FRS 5 requires that normally the economic substance of a transaction should be reflected in the financial statements, rather than simply its legal form.

A good example is that of assets acquired on hire purchase terms or under finance leases. Despite the fact that such assets are not owned by the user, a fixed asset is recorded in the user's financial statements.

This convention has now been included in the CA 1985 as a general principle that the directors must have regard to, when selecting the company's accounting policies.

8 Preparation of the financial statements of a simple business organisation

8.1 Revision of key areas and terms used in basic financial statements

Preparation of financial statements is extensively covered in Paper 1.1 and preparation at this level of accounting needs a clear understanding of the techniques learned at the earlier stage.

Layout of the financial statements is important and the correct terminology should be used. Headings such as fixed assets and current assets need to be shown in their correct place on the normal presentation of a balance sheet. The layout and terms used in a profit and loss account can vary more due to the type of business and thus the types of income and expense which it has.

You can revise the terminology by working through the example which follows. The example shows the preparation of financial statements from a trial balance. Other information is given regarding such items as accruals and prepayments, depreciation, stock and bad and doubtful debts.

ACTIVITY **3**

JK Ltd

The following trial balance has been extracted from the ledgers of JK Ltd at 31 March 20X3:

	£	£
Sales (all on credit)		647,400
Stock (1 April 20X2)	15,400	
Trade debtors and creditors	82,851	41,936
Purchases (all on credit)	321,874	
Carriage in	13,256	
Carriage out	32,460	
Electricity	6,994	
Business rates	8,940	
Wages and salaries	138,292	
Postage and stationery	6,984	
Rent	14,600	
VAT control		16,382
PAYE control		4,736
Motor vehicles: at cost	49,400	
depreciation		21,240
Bank deposit account	90,000	
Bank current account	77,240	
Equity shares of £1 each		50,000
Accumulated profits at 1 April 20X2		76,597
	858,291	858,291

The following notes are also relevant:

(1) Stock at 31 March 20X3, valued at cost, was £19,473.

(2) Prepaid rent amounted to £2,800.

(3) Accruals are estimated as follows:

Electricity	£946
Wages and salaries	£2,464

(4) Depreciation on motor vehicles is to be provided at 25% per annum using the reducing balance method.

(5) Accrued interest on the bank deposit account amounts to £7,200.

(6) No interim dividend was paid but in March 20X3 the directors proposed a final dividend of £0.05 per share.

(7) A provision for corporation tax of £30,000 is to be made on the profits for the year.

Required:

(a) Prepare JK Ltd's trading, profit and loss and appropriation account for the year ended 31 March 20X3, in vertical format down to net profit after taxation.

(b) Prepare a statement of the movement on the profit and loss account reserve.

(c) Prepare JK Ltd's balance sheet at 31 March 20X3, in vertical format.

Conclusion

The ASB's *Statement of Principles for Financial Reporting* covers the objective of financial statements, the qualitative characteristics of financial information, the elements of financial statements and their recognition, and the presentation of financial information. It does not have the status of a financial reporting standard but the principles in it have influenced most recent standards.

There are four fundamental accounting concepts: going concern; accruals; consistency; and prudence. The ASB has now issued FRS 18 which is consistent with the Statement of Principles. FRS 18 requires entities to observe the going concern concept and the accruals concept in preparing financial statements. Other important accounting concepts include materiality, objectivity and substance over form.

SELF-TEST QUESTIONS

1 What is GAAP? (1.1)

2 What is the objective of financial statements? (2.1)

3 The ASB's Statement of Principles identifies seven groups of users of financial statements. What are they? (2.2)

4 What are the four qualitative characteristics of financial information? (3.1)

5 What are the seven elements of financial statements identified by the Statement of Principles? (4)

6 Give the Statement of Principles' definition of assets and liabilities. (4.2, 4.3)

7 What conditions must be fulfilled before the effect of a transaction or event can be recognised in the financial statements? (5.2)

8 What are the four primary statements? (6.1)

9 What is an estimation technique? (7.3)

10 What are the five accounting principles embodied in the Companies Act 1985? (7.4)

PRACTICE QUESTION

DWS Ltd

DWS Ltd prepares its accounts to 30 September each year. At 30 September 20X4 its trial balance was as follows:

	Dr	*Cr*
	£	£
Plant and machinery		
– cost	125,000	
– depreciation at 1 October 20X3		28,000
Office equipment		
– cost	45,000	
– depreciation at 1 October 20X3		15,000
Stocks at 1 October 20X3	31,000	
Purchases and sales	115,000	188,000
Returns inwards and outwards	8,000	6,000
Selling expenses	12,000	
Heat and light	8,000	
Wages and salaries	14,000	
Directors' fees	5,000	
Printing and stationery	6,000	
Telephone and fax	6,000	
Rent, rates and insurances	4,000	
Trade debtors and creditors	35,000	33,000
Allowance for doubtful debts at 1 October 20X3		4,000
Bank	3,000	
Petty cash	1,000	
Interim dividend paid	2,000	
Ordinary shares of 50p each		100,000
Share premium account		8,000
General reserve		7,000
Profit and loss account balance at 1 October 20X3		34,000
Suspense account	3,000	
	423,000	423,000

The following additional information at 30 September 20X4 is available:

(i) Closing stocks of goods for resale £53,000

(ii) Prepayments:

- telephone and fax rental £1,000
- rates and insurance £1,000

(iii) Accruals:

- wages and salaries £1,500
- directors' fees 2% of net turnover
- auditor's fees £3,500

(iv) Specific bad debts to be written off amount to £3,000.

(v) The allowance for doubtful debts is to be amended to 5% of debtors, after adjusting for bad debts written off.

(vi) The following book-keeping errors are discovered:

- the purchase of an item of stock has been debited to the office equipment account, cost £1,200
- the payment of £1,300 to a creditor has been recorded by debiting the bank account and crediting the creditor's account.

Any remaining balance on the suspense account is to be added to prepayments or accruals, as appropriate, on the balance sheet.

(vii) The figure in the trial balance for the bank balance is the balance appearing in the cash book, prior to the reconciliation with the bank statement. Upon reconciliation, it is discovered that

- unpresented cheques amount to £3,000.
- bank charges not entered in the ledgers amount to £4,000.

(viii) Depreciation of fixed assets is to be provided as follows:

- plant and machinery 10% on cost
- office equipment $33^1/_3$% on the reducing balance at the end of the year.

(ix) A final dividend of 1.5p per share was proposed during September 20X4.

(x) £10,000 is to be transferred to general reserves.

(xi) Provision of £1,000 for corporation tax is to be made.

Required:

(a) Prepare a trading and profit and loss account for the year ended 30 September 20X4 down to net profit after tax. **(10 marks)**

(b) A statement showing the movement on the profit and loss account reserve for the year ending 30 September 20X4. **(8 marks)**

(b) Prepare a balance sheet at 30 September 20X4. **(7 marks)**

(Total: 25 marks)

For the answer to this question, see the 'Answers' section at the end of the book.

FEEDBACK TO ACTIVITY 1

1 The Statement of Principles defines an asset as rights or other access to future economic benefits controlled by an entity as a result of past transactions or events. M Ltd cannot control the actions of the hospital, nor is it certain that there is access to future economic benefits. Therefore M Ltd does not have an asset.

2 N Ltd controls the tip as the result of a past transaction, but there does not appear to be any access to future economic benefits, as the tip cannot be sold in its present state and no further income can be obtained from it. Therefore the site of the tip is not an asset.

It is possible that N Ltd has a liability for the cost of cleaning up the tip. A liability is an obligation to transfer economic benefits as a result of past transactions or events. In practice, N Ltd may be legally obliged to clean up the tip so that it is no longer in a dangerous condition. If this were the case, there would be a liability of £8 million and a corresponding asset for £6 million.

3 At first sight, the contract between P Ltd and its finance director may appear to give P Ltd a liability. However, the salary is paid as a result of the director's work during the next five years. There is no past event and therefore P Ltd cannot have a liability.

4 It is clear that Q Ltd has acquired rights to future economic benefits (through cost savings) through a past transaction (the purchase) and that it controls the benefits (it has sole use of the method for 8 years). The patent rights are an asset of Q Ltd.

FEEDBACK TO ACTIVITY **2**

These examples are taken from an Appendix to FRS 18. For each of the items, ask whether this involves a change to:

- recognition?
- presentation?
- measurement basis?

If the answer to any of these is yes, the change is a change in accounting policy.

1 This is a change in recognition and presentation. Therefore this is a change in accounting policy.

2 The answer to all three questions is no. This is only a change in estimation technique.

3 This is a change in presentation and therefore a change in accounting policy.

4 This is a change in measurement basis and therefore a change in accounting policy.

FEEDBACK TO ACTIVITY **3**

JK Ltd

(a) **Trading, profit and loss and appropriation account for the year ended 31 March 20X3**

	£	£
Sales		647,400
Cost of sales		
Opening stock	15,400	
Purchases	321,874	
Closing stock	(19,473)	
		(317,801)
Gross profit		329,599
Carriage in	13,256	
Carriage out	32,460	
Electricity (6,994 + 946)	7,940	
Business rates	8,940	
Wages and salaries (138,292 + 2,464)	140,756	
Postage and stationery	6,984	
Rent (14,600 – 2,800)	11,800	
Depreciation on motor vehicles (25% × (49,400 – 21,240))	7,040	
Interest on bank deposit account	(7,200)	
		(221,976)
Net profit before tax		107,623
Tax		(30,000)
Net profit after tax		77,623

(b) **Statement of movement on profit and loss account reserve**

	£
Balance b/f	76,597
Net profit for the year	75,123
Dividend (50,000 × £0.05)	(2,500)
P&L a/c carried forward	151,720

Tutorial note: New legal and accounting regulations now mean that any dividends for the year are not shown in the profit and loss account but instead are shown in the statement of movement on reserves (this will be covered in a later chapter).

(c) **Balance sheet as at 31 March 20X3**

	Cost	*Acc depn*	*NBV*
	£	£	£
Fixed assets			
Motor vehicles	49,400	28,280	21,120
Current assets			
Stock	19,473		
Trade debtors	82,851		
Prepaid rent	2,800		
Interest receivable	7,200		
Bank deposit account	90,000		
Bank current account	77,240		
		279,564	
Current liabilities			
Trade creditors	41,936		
VAT creditor	16,382		
PAYE creditor	4,736		
Accrued electricity	946		
Accrued wages and salaries	2,464		
Corporation tax payable	30,000		
Final dividend proposed	2,500		
		(98,964)	
Net current assets			180,600
			201,720
Financed by			
Ordinary shares of £1 each			50,000
P&L account			151,720
			201,720

Chapter 2

ACCOUNTING CONCEPTS, ACCOUNTING THEORY

CHAPTER CONTENTS

1 **Concepts of income**

2 **The concept of fair value**

3 **The concept of deprival value**

4 **Measurement in financial statements**

This chapter explains a number of theoretical concepts. The most important of these are 'comprehensive income', 'fair value', 'value in use' and 'deprival value'. This is because FRS 3 *Reporting financial performance* is based on the idea of comprehensive income and an increasing number of accounting standards require assets and liabilities to be stated at fair value in the balance sheet. FRS 11 *Impairment of fixed assets and goodwill* and FRS 15 *Tangible fixed assets* use the value to the business model to value fixed assets at their current values. You will study these standards later in the text.

Objectives

By the time you have finished this chapter you should be able to:

- outline the concept of 'comprehensive income'
- explain the principle of fair value
- explain the principle of value in use/deprival value.

1 Concepts of income

1.1 Introduction

KEY POINT

The **comprehensive income** and **current operating performance** concepts are conflicting views of financial presentation.

How should information about income and profits be presented in order to provide users of the financial statements with information about financial performance? There are two conflicting views:

- the **comprehensive income** concept (or the 'all inclusive' concept of profit)
- the **current operating performance** concept (or the 'maintainable earnings' concept).

1.2 The comprehensive income concept

KEY POINT

The comprehensive income concept regards **all gains and losses** as relevant.

All gains and losses, irrespective of their nature, are relevant, and should be reported in the period in which they occur.

'**Net gains**' are the difference between opening and closing shareholders' funds (net assets) after adjusting for capital transactions and dividends.

'**Total income**' includes items such as unrealised gains on revaluation of assets and exchange differences arising on translation of foreign currency items. It is a much wider definition than that for profits or realised gains.

There are several arguments in favour of the comprehensive income approach:

- If certain items are allowed to be omitted from the profit and loss account, preparers of accounts have a means of manipulating the profit figure or smoothing profits over a period of years.
- It is easier to understand a profit and loss account which includes the effects of all transactions in the period. The profit and loss account is also less affected by variations arising from the application of subjective judgement.
- If there is full disclosure of the nature of all transactions, users of the financial statements are able to analyse the performance of an entity for themselves. They can derive an appropriate net profit figure based on their own specific information needs.

1.3 The current operating performance concept

KEY POINT

The current operating performance concept emphasises ordinary **normal recurring earnings**.

The emphasis here is on ordinary, **normal, recurring earnings**.

Only gains and losses which have occurred and which are likely to continue to occur in the future are included in net profit or total income for the period.

'**Total income**' would exclude items such as revaluation gains (whether they were realised or not), extraordinary items and prior period adjustments.

There are also arguments in favour of this approach:

- Most users of financial statements focus on the profit and loss account and the net profit figure. Some users are capable of interpreting financial statements and extracting the information that they need, but many are not. They believe that management should provide them with a profit figure which they can then use to predict future performance.
- If non-recurring items are excluded from the profit and loss account, the profit figure is more comparable, both with that of other entities and with the same entity over time.

1.4 The ASB's view of total income

KEY POINT

The ASB defines gains and losses in terms of changes in assets and liabilities, or ownership interest, and has therefore adopted the comprehensive income approach.

In the previous chapter, we looked at the elements of financial statements in the ASB's Statement of Principles. These interrelate as follows:

- Assets – Liabilities = Ownership interest
- Assets – Liabilities = Contributions from owners + Gains – Losses – Distributions to owners.

In other words, the ASB defines gains and losses in terms of changes in assets and liabilities, or ownership interest. It has therefore adopted the comprehensive income concept. This concept is at the heart of two very important standards, FRS 3 *Reporting financial performance* and FRS 5 *Reporting the substance of transactions*, both of which will be covered in detail later in the text.

2 The concept of fair value

2.1 Introduction

KEY POINT

An increasing number of accounting regulations require or permit the use of fair values.

Traditionally, accounts in the UK have been presented using the historical cost convention, so that assets are stated in the balance sheet at their cost, less any amounts written off (e.g. for depreciation in the case of tangible fixed assets). However an increasing number of recent accounting regulations require or permit certain assets to be stated at their fair value. For example:

- when preparing group accounts using the acquisition method (the only allowable method), the assets and liabilities of an acquired subsidiary must be included in the consolidated accounts at their fair value.
- FRS 7 gives guidance on how the fair values of the assets and liabilities of acquired subsidiaries should be determined.
- The CA 1985 permits financial instruments (e.g. investments in the shares of another company) to be valued in the balance sheet at their fair value.
- The CA 1985 also permits investment properties and living animals and plants (e.g. a herd of cows owned by a farm) to be valued in the balance sheet at their fair value.

2.2 Meaning of fair value

A general definition of fair value is given in FRS 7: 'Fair value is the amount at which an asset or liability could be exchanged in an arm's length transaction between informed and willing parties, other than in a forced or liquidation sale'.

Some more practical guidance can be offered.

- If the item is quoted on an active market, then its fair value is its market value on that market. For example, the shares in large public companies are quoted on the London Stock Exchange. The fair value of 1,000 shares in AB plc quoted at £2 each would be £2,000.
- If the item is not quoted on an active market, but similar items are, then the item's fair value should be determined by reference to these similar items. For example, a company might own 1,000 shares in an unquoted company CD Ltd. If CD Ltd is identical in every way to the quoted company AB plc which has a share price of £2 each, then perhaps the fair value of the shares held in CD Ltd is £2,000.
- If the item is not quoted on an active market, and no similar items can be identified that are quoted, then the fair value must be estimated using a valuation model. For example, a holding of all the shares of EF Ltd, a company with net assets on its balance sheet of £10,000, might also be estimated to have a fair value of £10,000. That would apply the valuation model of valuing a company at the total net value of the net assets on its balance sheet.

ACTIVITY **1**

How would the fair value of the following items be determined?

(a) An investment holding of 5,000 shares in XYZ plc, a large company quoted on the London Stock Exchange.

(b) An office block bought for £2m ten years ago. There are few such office buildings being sold at the moment.

(c) A herd of 200 dairy cows.

Feedback to this activity is at the end of the chapter.

3 The concept of deprival value

3.1 The case for current value accounting

KEY POINT

Traditional cost-based accounting may not report the value of assets in the business, or their sales value or replacement cost.

The objective of financial statements is to provide information about the reporting entity's financial performance and position that is useful to a wide range of users for assessing the stewardship of management and for making economic decisions.

What is wrong with the traditional historical cost basis of measurement used by accountants? Whilst being both easy to ascertain and objective, it fails to relate directly to any of the three decisions that might reasonably be made about an asset:

- Another, similar asset might be purchased. Management need to know the **current replacement cost**, which might have changed substantially since the present asset was purchased at its historical cost.
- The asset might be sold. Management need to know the amount which would be realised from sale, less any costs involved in disposal, i.e. the **net realisable value**. Again, this bears no relationship to historical cost.
- The asset might be used in the business. Management need to estimate the future cash flows arising from the asset and discount these to their present value, i.e. their '**economic value**'. Clearly, there is no relationship with historical cost in this case.

Valuing assets

KEY POINT

Current entry value, **current exit value** and **deprival value** are alternative ways of valuing assets.

There are three ways of valuing assets, other than historical cost:

- **current entry value** (replacement cost) – often referred to as replacement cost and widely considered as a possible basis of measurement to value assets and to determine the cost of items consumed
- **current exit value** (net realisable value) – based on the use of net realisable values if the asset were to be sold
- **economic value** – this is the present value of the cash flows from the use of the asset

Deprival value (value to the business) is defined as the loss a business would suffer if deprived of an asset.

Deprival value has been accepted as being the most relevant for accounting purposes. The ASB has made use of the '**value to the business**' model in its Statement of Principles and in FRSs 11 and 15.

3.2 Deprival value

KEY POINT

Value to the business is the lower of replacement cost and recoverable amount. Recoverable amount is the higher of economic value in use and net realisable value.

To identify deprival value we need to identify all three of the measures of value discussed above: replacement cost, net realisable value and economic value. Then we can identify two important relationships between values:

- the **higher** of net realisable value (**NRV**) and economic value (**EV**) – if management own an asset, they have control over the choice between use and disposal, and if it is economically rational they will choose the option having the highest value – this is known as the **recoverable amount**
- the **lower** of replacement cost (**RC**) and recoverable amount.

This may be portrayed diagrammatically as follows:

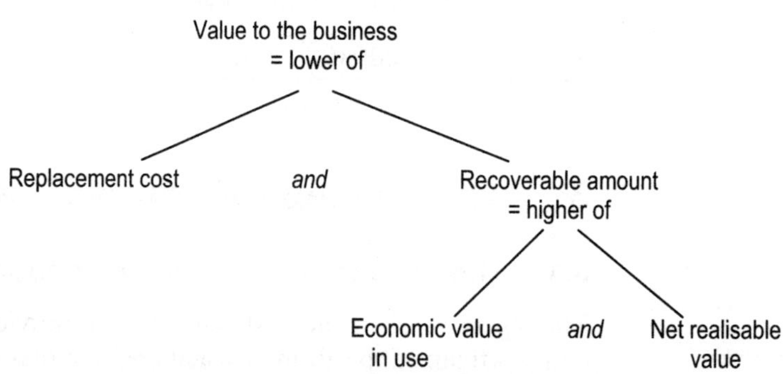

If they are deprived of an asset, management have a choice as to whether or not to replace it. If they are economically rational, they will replace the asset only if they can generate a surplus either by resale or by use.

KEY POINT

The advantage of deprival value is the avoidance of the implicit assumption that assets will be replaced or liquidated.

The main advantage of using 'deprival value' is that the implicit assumptions that assets will be replaced or liquidated are avoided. However, there are a number of arguments against deprival value, including the following.

- The balance sheet may include the total of a number of different valuation bases (RC, NRV, EV), so that the significance of the total assets figure is unclear.
- The basis of this approach is a hypothetical deprival which has not taken place, and there is some debate as to whether this is a satisfactory basis for measuring actual past events.

In the situation where economic value emerges as a measure of deprival value, then this measure is subject to all the practical difficulties involved in the measurement of economic income ie present values of future cash flows.

ACTIVITY **2**

1 Normal business

A company owns a machine with a five-year useful life and no residual value. At 31 December 20X2 the machine is two years old. To buy a brand new machine of the same type at that date would cost £100,000.

If the machine were sold it would fetch about £30,000 but there would be dismantling costs of about £5,000.

It is estimated that the machine could generate cash flows of £40,000 per annum if it were used in the business for the next three years. The net present value of these cash flows is £99,000.

Calculate the deprival value of the asset.

2 Company anticipating closure

Assume that the facts are as in (1) above but that the business is in such a poor state that there are no positive cash flows to be obtained from continuing to use the asset.

Calculate the deprival value of the asset.

3 Company with low NPV

Assume that the facts are as in (1) above but that the net present value of the cash flows associated with the continued use of the asset is £55,000.

Calculate the deprival value of the asset.

Feedback to this activity is at the end of the chapter.

4 Measurement in financial statements

4.1 Introduction

KEY POINT

The ASB concluded that the use of current values for both assets and liabilities provides the information that is most relevant to the decisions of users but no longer suggests that current values should be used in preference to historic cost.

The ASB deals with measurement and valuation issues in Chapter 6 of the Statement of Principles: *Measurement in financial statements.* This chapter has probably been the most controversial part of the Statement of Principles. It changed significantly between the first draft and the final version.

The first draft of the chapter began by contrasting historic cost with the alternatives: a system of measurement based on current values; or adjustments for the effects of general inflation. Accounting for the effects of changing prices is covered in more detail in a later chapter of this text.

The ASB concluded that the use of current values for both assets and liabilities provides the information that is most relevant to the decisions of users, and that practice should develop by evolving in the direction of greater use of current values to the extent that this is consistent with the constraints of reliability and cost. Many commentators interpreted this to mean that the ASB intended to reintroduce a form of current cost accounting.

The ASB subsequently denied this. The final version of the Statement emphasises the need to choose the most appropriate basis of measurement in specific circumstances. It no longer suggests that current values should be used in preference to historic cost.

4.2 The basic principles

KEY POINT

There is a choice between **single** and **mixed** measurement methods; the ASB has accepted the mixed method, so a measurement basis must be chosen for each category of asset or liability.

There is a choice between a measurement system that requires:

- a **single measurement** basis (e.g. historic cost or current value) to be used for all assets and liabilities
- a **mixed measurement** basis to be separately selected for each category of assets or liabilities so that it fits the circumstances surrounding that particular category (for example, the 'modified historic cost' system where some fixed assets are stated at current value while the rest are stated at historic cost).

The ASB has accepted that a mixed measurement system ('modified historic cost') will be used for the foreseeable future.

A measurement basis (historic cost or current value) must be selected for each category of assets or liabilities. The basis selected should be the one that best meets the objective of financial statements and the demands of the qualitative characteristics of financial information, bearing in mind the nature of the assets or liabilities concerned and the circumstances involved.

An asset or liability being measured using the historic cost basis is recognised initially at transaction cost. An asset or liability being measured using the current value basis is recognised initially at its current value at the time it was acquired or assumed.

Subsequent remeasurement will occur if necessary to ensure that:

- assets measured at historic cost are carried at the lower of cost and recoverable amount
- assets and liabilities measured on the current value basis are carried at up-to-date current values.

Such remeasurements are only recognised if:

- there is sufficient evidence that the monetary amount of the asset or liability has changed
- the new amount of the asset or liability can be measured with sufficient reliability.

4.3 Measurement issues

KEY POINT

The value to the business rule should be used to select from alternative measures of current value.

The value to the business rule should be used to select from alternative measures of current value. The current value of an asset is the loss that the entity would suffer if it were deprived of it (deprival value, as described above).

When basing carrying amounts on future cash flows, those cash flows should be discounted.

The only way to determine an appropriate monetary amount for an asset or liability may be through estimates. This is acceptable provided a generally accepted estimation method is used and the measure is supported by a reasonable amount of confirmatory evidence.

4.4 The influence of the Statement of Principles on recent standards

KEY POINT

The ASB wishes to encourage greater use of **current values.**

In later chapters you will be covering Financial Reporting Standards on accounting for tangible and intangible fixed assets. These reflect the ASB's wish to encourage greater use of **current values** and its thinking on **measurement issues**, particularly subsequent remeasurement (revaluation and impairment).

- FRS 7 *Fair values in acquisition accounting* explains how the identifiable assets and liabilities of a subsidiary must be revalued to fair value at the date of acquisition. Goodwill is then accurately measured as the difference between the fair value of the consideration given and the fair value of the identifiable net assets acquired.
- FRS 10 *Goodwill and intangible assets* and FRS 11 *Impairment of fixed assets and goodwill* require that assets are not stated at more than their recoverable amount.

- FRS 15 *Tangible fixed assets* was introduced to overcome many of the problems associated with the modified historic cost basis. It requires that once an asset has been revalued, it must continue to be stated at current value.
- The definition of **recoverable amount** in FRS 11 and the definition of **current value** in FRS 15 are based on the **value to the business** model.

Conclusion

The comprehensive income concept treats net gains as the difference between opening and closing shareholders' funds (net assets) after adjusting for capital transactions and dividends. All gains and losses, irrespective of their nature, are part of an entity's performance, and should be reported in the period in which they occur.

The Statement of Principles states that a measurement basis (historic cost or current value) must be selected for each category of assets or liabilities. Where assets are stated at current value, the value to the business model should be used.

Value to the business (also called deprival value) is the lower of replacement cost and recoverable amount. Recoverable amount is the higher of economic value (also called value in use) and net realisable value.

SELF-TEST QUESTIONS

1 What is the difference between the comprehensive income concept and the current operating performance concept? (1.2, 1.3)

2 How does the ASB define gains and losses? (1.4)

3 What is the general definition of fair value? (2.2)

4 Define deprival value. (3.2)

5 What is the difference between a single measurement basis of valuation and a mixed measurement basis? (4.2)

FEEDBACK TO ACTIVITY 1

(a) Since XYZ plc is quoted on an active market, the current share price is an accurate measure of the fair value. The holding of 5,000 shares should be valued in total as 5,000 times the current share price.

(b) There is currently no active market for such office blocks, so some method of estimation is required. Perhaps a local estate agent or surveyor could give a reasonable estimate of current market value; perhaps there is a government index of price movements on such buildings that could be applied.

(c) There probably is an active market for cows of the age and type that are owned. Each cow can then be valued at its own market value.

FEEDBACK TO ACTIVITY 2

1 Normal business

	£
RC = Gross replacement cost	100,000
Less: Accumulated depreciation $\frac{2}{5}$	40,000
	60,000
NRV = Sale proceeds	30,000
Less: Costs to sell	5,000
	25,000
NPV =	99,000

DV = lower of £60,000 and (higher of £25,000 and £99,000)

Deprival value is the replacement cost of £60,000.

2 Company anticipating closure

	£
RC as before	60,000
NRV as before	25,000
NPV when there are no cash flows	Nil

DV = lower of £60,000 and (higher of £25,000 and nil)

Deprival value is the net realisable value of £25,000.

3 Company with low NPV

	£
RC as before	60,000
NRV as before	25,000
NPV	55,000

DV = lower of £60,000 and (higher of £25,000 and £55,000)

Deprival value is the net present value of £55,000.

Chapter 3
REVENUE RECOGNITION

CHAPTER CONTENTS

1 **The problem of revenue recognition**

2 **Traditional approaches to revenue recognition**

3 **The critical event in the operating cycle**

4 **The ASB's balance sheet approach to revenue recognition**

This chapter explains the principles of revenue recognition. There are a number of ideas and methods that can be used in order to determine whether and when revenue should be recognised in the financial statements.

The ASB's Statement of Principles sets out general principles that should be used to recognise gains and losses, and these can be applied to the problem of revenue recognition. The ASB's approach is different from the traditional methods and has been controversial for this reason.

The ASB's approach has now been included in an FRS by adding a new Application Note at the end of FRS 5.

Objectives

By the time you have finished this chapter you should be able to:

- outline the principles of the timing of revenue recognition
- explain the role of the concept of substance over form in relation to recognising sales revenue
- explain realised profits
- understand and apply the critical event approach to revenue recognition
- describe the ASB's 'balance sheet' approach to revenue recognition.

1 The problem of revenue recognition

1.1 Meaning of revenue

Revenue is the gross inflow of economic benefits during the period arising in the course of the ordinary activities of an enterprise.

KEY POINT

Revenue could apply to the sale of **goods**, **services**, **rent**, **interest** or **dividends**.

The term 'revenue' could apply in any of the following situations:

- the supply of goods on cash or credit sale terms
- the provision of services on cash or credit terms
- rent received from equipment or property hired out
- interest or dividends received on a trade investment.

1.2 Measurement of revenue

KEY POINT

Revenue is measured by the immediate **exchange value** of the goods or services involved.

Revenue is measured by the immediate **exchange value** of the goods or services involved.

- If the sale is a **cash sale**, then the revenue is the immediate proceeds of sale. Allowances may be made for expected returns.
- If the sale is a **credit sale**, i.e. a sale for a claim to cash, then anticipated cash is revenue. Allowances may be made for bad debts.

Allowances for bad debts and returns are usually computed as a separate exercise and disclosed separately. For example, if the anticipated collectable value on sales of £1,000 is £950, some accountants would argue that this should be shown as £950 revenue. Current practice, however, would show £1,000 in the trading account as revenue, and £50 as an expense in the profit and loss account.

1.3 Timing of revenue recognition

A typical operating cycle for a business has several stages. For example, in a manufacturing business:

- **Stage 1**: obtaining an order from a customer for goods prior to manufacture
- **Stage 2**: purchase of goods or raw materials
- **Stage 3**: production of goods
- **Stage 4**: obtaining an order from a customer for goods in stock
- **Stage 5**: delivery of goods to the customer
- **Stage 6**: collection of cash
- **Stage 7**: provision of warranties or after-sales services.

The time taken to complete the operating cycle varies according to the type of business and the particular circumstances. A retail business may have a very short operating cycle, whereas a construction firm might engage in long-term contracts so the operating cycle extends over several years.

Problems arise because financial statements are produced for specific periods, usually 12 months. Accounting periods are not related to the normal operating cycles of businesses. We have to allocate transactions to accounting periods.

There are a number of possible approaches to revenue recognition and these are discussed below.

2 Traditional approaches to revenue recognition

2.1 Realisation

KEY POINT

Before being **recognised** and **reported**, revenue must be **earned** and **realised**, and it must be capable of being **verifiably measured**.

Traditionally, two conditions must be met before revenue can be **recognised** and **reported** in the profit and loss account as follows.

- The revenue must be **earned**, i.e. the activities undertaken to create the revenue must be substantially completed.
- The revenue must be **realised**, i.e. an event has occurred which significantly increases the likelihood of conversion into cash. This also means that the revenue must be capable of being **verifiably measured.**

Realisation is an important principle in accounting. The Companies Act requires that only realised profits can be included in the profit and loss account. The reason for this is to ensure that creditors are paid what is owed to them before profits are distributed to shareholders as dividends. The Companies Act rules for determining distributable profits are covered in a later chapter.

DEFINITION

Profits are realised when an event has occurred (e.g. a sale transaction) which has made the conversion of an asset (e.g. stock) into cash highly probable.

The Companies Act defines realised profits as follows.

'**Realised profits** are such profits which fall to be treated as realised profits in accordance with principles generally accepted with respect to the determination for accounting purposes of realised profits at the time when those accounts are prepared.'

'Generally accepted accounting principles' here are normally taken to mean UK GAAP, i.e. principles in accounting standards, company law and other acceptable accounting treatments.

A more practical definition of realisation for the purpose of revenue recognition is that it takes place when an event has occurred (e.g. a sale transaction) which has made the conversion of an asset (e.g. stock) into cash highly probable. The stock may have been turned into cash or into a highly liquid asset (a trade debtor).

In most cases, realisation is deemed to occur on the date of sale. Thus, the date of the sale transaction is the moment that the revenue is recognised in the financial statements.

2.2 Accruals and prudence

DEFINITION

The **accruals** concept: revenue and costs are accrued, matched with one another so far as their relationship can be established or justifiably assumed, and dealt with in the profit and loss account of the period to which they relate.

The fundamental concepts of **accruals** (matching) and **prudence** are relevant to revenue recognition.

- The **accruals** concept: revenue and costs are accrued (that is, recognised as they are earned or incurred, not as money is received or paid), matched with one another so far as their relationship can be established or justifiably assumed, and dealt with in the profit and loss account of the period to which they relate.
- The concept of **prudence**: revenue and profits are not anticipated, but are recognised by inclusion in the profit and loss account only when realised in the form either of cash or of other assets, the ultimate realisation of which can be assessed with reasonable certainty; provision is made for all known liabilities (expenses and losses) whether the amount of these is known with certainty or is a best estimate in the light of the information available.

DEFINITION

The concept of **prudence**: revenue and profits are not anticipated, but are recognised by inclusion in the profit and loss account only when realised in the form either of cash or of other assets.

Using traditional accounting principles, transactions are allocated to reporting periods according to the principles of matching and prudence. In simple terms, this restates the rule in the paragraph above: revenue is recognised in the same period as it is earned, unless it is unlikely to be realised in the form of cash.

In this view of the accounting process, the focus is on the profit and loss account. The assets and liabilities in the balance sheet have arisen as a result of matching revenue and expenses with the accounting periods to which they relate. For example, stocks are a deferred expense.

ACTIVITY 1

On 1 October 20X1 a company received total subscriptions in advance of £288,000 for 12 monthly publications of a magazine. At the year end, the company had produced and despatched three of the 12 publications. The total cost of producing one issue of the magazine is estimated at £20,000.

Using the traditional approach, how should the company treat the subscription revenue in the accounts for the year ended 31 December 20X1?

Feedback to this activity is at the end of the chapter.

2.3 Problems with the realisation approach

KEY POINT

The **realisation principle** may not be adequate to deal with revenue earned over a **period** of time or as a **continuous** process, or of **barter** or **investment** transactions.

The following are some of the criticisms of the realisation principle:

- In reality, revenue is earned over a period of time. The traditional approach to the timing of revenue recognition may mean that revenue is reported in one period, even though it was substantially earned in an earlier period. For example, some commodities, such as wines or spirits, may take years to produce.
- The realisation of revenue principle conflicts with the continuity of existence (or going concern) concept. Revenue-earning is a continuous process.
- Realisation emphasises the eventual receipt of cash. This appears to mean that barter transactions cannot be recognised. It also causes problems in accounting for some types of investment transaction and has been interpreted to mean that investment income should not be accrued on a time basis. It has been suggested that realisation should be equated with 'reliability of measurement', rather than with 'convertibility to cash'.

2.4 Reporting the substance of transactions

A further problem with the traditional approach to revenue recognition is illustrated by the following situation.

Suppose that A Ltd sells a freehold property to B Ltd in return for £1 million in cash. However, A Ltd has an option to repurchase the property for £1.3 million in five years' time. Income has certainly been realised for A Ltd, because cash has been received, but should it be recognised in the financial statements of A Ltd?

KEY POINT

A traditional approach to revenue may be inadequate to deal with complex situations where the **commercial substance** of a transaction may not be the same as its **strict legal form**.

Because there is an option to repurchase the property, it is possible that the commercial substance of this transaction is not a sale at all, but a loan secured on the property. Although A Ltd no longer legally owns the property, it may still have the same risks and benefits in relation to the property that it would have had if it had continued to be the legal owner. For example, it might still occupy and use the building. If so, A Ltd still effectively has an asset and cannot recognise a sale.

The traditional approach is inadequate to deal with complex situations where the **commercial substance** of a transaction may not be the same as its **strict legal form**. FRS 5 *Reporting the substance of transactions* sets out the principles for dealing with complex transactions such as sale and repurchase agreements.

3 The critical event in the operating cycle

3.1 Possible critical events

Earlier we saw a typical operating cycle for a manufacturing entity. During the operating cycle there will be a point at which most or all of the uncertainty surrounding the transaction will be removed. This is the **critical event** and it is the point at which **revenue can be recognised**.

Stage 1: Obtaining an order from a customer for goods prior to manufacture

Obtaining an order for a large or long-term contract is often a very important event, as it provides evidence that the business is likely to continue to trade. However, the final outcome of the order or contract is normally so uncertain that it would not be prudent to recognise revenue at this stage.

Stage 2: Purchase of goods or raw materials

In most cases, making purchases is a routine occurrence. In many businesses it does not even signify that orders have been obtained or that the goods will be sold. Therefore it is not normally taken to be the critical event.

KEY POINT

In rare circumstances, the obtaining of raw materials is a critical revenue event.

However, there are rare circumstances where obtaining raw materials may be the critical event. This applies where the goods or materials are particularly difficult to obtain. One example is the extraction of precious metals or gems, for example, diamonds. Because there is a ready market, revenue is certain once the item has been obtained.

Stage 3: Production of goods

For most businesses this is another routine event and therefore not critical, because too many uncertainties still remain. It could be argued that the existence of a firm order for the goods would remove some of the uncertainties, but this would almost certainly not be sufficient to justify taking profit at this point. For example, there may be errors in the production process so that the goods are faulty and cannot be sold.

KEY POINT

In long production processes, revenue is recognised in stages.

One possible exception to this is where the production period is long and revenue is recognised in stages during the production period. Long-term construction contracts are one example. The situation where production extends over a long period is discussed further below.

Stage 4: Obtaining an order from a customer for goods in stock

Although most of the uncertainties in the cycle have either been resolved or are reasonably determinable at this stage, most businesses do not treat this as the critical event in the cycle.

KEY POINT

Most businesses treat the **delivery of goods** as the critical event.

Stage 5: Delivery of goods to the customer

Delivery normally coincides with the transfer of legal title to the goods. There are still uncertainties at this point as follows.

- The goods may be returned because they are faulty.
- The customer may not pay for the goods.
- There may be future liabilities under a warranty.

However, most businesses treat this as the critical event and recognise revenue at this point. By this stage, any uncertainties remaining can normally be quantified based on past experience.

KEY POINT

Credit sales would not normally delay revenue recognition, but in some circumstances it may be prudent to recognise revenue at the point of **cash receipt**.

Stage 6: Collection of cash

Where the sale is a cash sale this coincides with delivery of the goods and is treated as the critical event. Where the sale is a credit sale it would be unusual to delay revenue recognition to this point, and to do so would effectively contravene the accruals concept. However, there may be occasions where it is not prudent to recognise revenue until the cash has been received. Examples of this may include sales made to overseas customers, or other sales that are thought to be particularly risky.

Stage 7: Provision of warranties or after-sales services

Collection of cash may not resolve all the uncertainties connected with a sale. A business may have obligations to replace faulty goods or to rectify defects occurring within a certain period. In most cases it is possible to estimate these costs and provide for them at the time of the sale. It would be unrealistic if revenue were not recognised until after the warranty period had elapsed.

A slightly different situation arises where the customer has the right to return goods within a period of time (e.g. three months from the date of sale). There is a strong case for delaying recognition of the sale until this period has elapsed. However, the substance of the transaction should also be considered. If the customer has the right to return goods, but in practice this is either extremely unlikely or has never occurred, then it would be reasonable to recognise the sale before the end of the return period.

KEY POINT

Under the **accretion approach,** revenue is recognised over a period of time, rather than at a particular point in time.

3.2 The accretion approach

The **accretion approach** is an alternative to the critical event approach and is appropriate for certain types of transaction where there is a long production period or where services are supplied over a period of time. Under the accretion approach, revenue is recognised over a period of time rather than at a particular point in time. It may be used in three situations as follows.

Use by others of an entity's resources

The resources are used over a period of time in return for revenue. For example, a company rents out a surplus property from 1 July 20X5 for an annual rent of £20,000 payable in advance. Applying the critical event approach would mean that either the income was recognised at the beginning of the rental period (receipt of cash) or at the end of the rental period (removal of all uncertainties).

However, the rental income accrues over the entire period. The company recognises six month's rent (£10,000) as revenue for the year ended 31 December 20X5, and the remaining £10,000 is included in the balance sheet as a creditor for payments received in advance.

Long-term contracts

Contracts for construction of a major asset, such as a building or a road, normally extend over several months. Under the critical event approach, revenue would not be recognised until the contract was completed, despite the fact that it is earned over the period of the contract and payment is normally received in stages as the contract progresses. The profit and loss account would therefore only reflect the results of contracts completed in the year, not contract activity during the year.

SSAP 9 (which is discussed in detail later in this text) applies the accretion approach to accounting for long-term contracts. Turnover and profit are recognised over the period of the contract. SSAP 9 actually requires a combination of the critical event approach and the accretion approach, because profit cannot be recorded until the outcome of the contract can be assessed with reasonable certainty.

Natural growth and biological transformation

It may be appropriate to apply the accretion approach to production that involves natural growth or ageing. For example, there are market prices available for the various stages of growth of timber and livestock. Revenue could therefore be recognised at these stages.

4 The ASB's balance sheet approach to revenue recognition

4.1 Changes in assets and liabilities

KEY POINT

The ASB's approach to revenue recognition in the Statement of Principles is **balance sheet orientated**. The starting point for the revenue recognition process is always the effect that the transaction or other event involved has had on the reporting entity's **assets** and **liabilities**.

The ASB's basic thinking is set out in the Statement of Principles. The ASB has adopted a very different approach from the traditional one of accruals, prudence and realisation.

The Statement of Principles is **balance sheet orientated.** Gains and losses are defined in terms of changes in assets and liabilities, rather than in terms of matching transactions with accounting periods.

The starting point for the revenue recognition process is always the effect that the transaction or other event involved has had on the reporting entity's assets and liabilities. Assuming that no contribution from owners or transfer to owners is involved:

- if net assets increase, a gain is recognised
- a loss is recognised if, and to the extent that, previously recognised assets are reduced or eliminated.

This has been a controversial area of the Statement of Principles and the ASB has been heavily criticised for departing from the traditional accounting process that is driven by matching and prudence.

The ASB has explained that accounting will continue to allocate the effects of transactions to reporting periods. However, matching is not the main driver of the recognition process. For example, if an entity wishes to carry forward costs to a subsequent period to match revenue being earned in that period, these costs must meet the definition of an asset (and the relevant recognition criteria). In turn this means asking whether the costs to be deferred constitute future economic benefits.

In most cases, this is simply a different view of established accounting practice and most transactions are dealt with in exactly the same way as before. When an entity makes a sale its assets increase, because it has a debtor (access to future economic benefits in the form of cash). Therefore it recognises a gain. The ASB has stated that applying the matching principle will often help in identifying changes in assets and liabilities and recognising gains and losses.

The ASB believes that a balance sheet based approach to revenue recognition is necessary because traditional accounting concepts, such as accruals and prudence, are no longer adequate. They are too simplistic to deal with the complex transactions that have now become common.

ACTIVITY **2**

On 1 October 20X1 a company received total subscriptions in advance of £288,000 for 12 monthly publications of a magazine. At the year end, the company had produced and despatched three of the 12 publications. The total cost of producing one issue of the magazine is estimated at £20,000.

According to the Statement of Principles, how should the company treat the subscription revenue in the accounts for the year ended 31 December 20X1?

Feedback to this activity is at the end of the chapter.

4.2 The critical event in the operating cycle

KEY POINT

The Statement of Principles suggests that the **critical event** approach can be used to determine whether there has been an increase in an entity's assets.

The Statement of Principles suggests that the **critical event** approach can be used to determine whether there has been an increase in an entity's assets and therefore a gain.

In a transaction involving the provision of services or goods for a net gain, the criteria for recognising a gain will be met on the occurrence of the critical event in the operating cycle involved. The critical event in the cycle is usually the point at which there is significant evidence that the gain exists and it is possible to measure the gain with sufficient reliability. It is the point at which changes to assets are recognised.

For most types of transaction, the critical event in the operating cycle occurs when the entity providing the goods or services has fully performed. In practice, this normally occurs when the goods or services have been delivered. However, the critical event could occur at other times in the cycle and there could be more than one critical event. The critical event or events will depend on the circumstances involved:

- If the reporting entity has carried out all its obligations under an agreement except for a few minor acts of performance, the critical event will have occurred. (For example, if there are warranties in respect of faulty goods, the sale is normally recognised when the goods are delivered, even though there is a small chance that the goods could have to be repaired or replaced.)
- If a sale is contingent upon acceptance by the buyer, the critical event will not have occurred if the likelihood of the goods or services not being accepted is significant.
- The reporting entity may be involved in performing a series of significant acts of performance over a period of time. As a result, the operating cycle might best be viewed as involving a series of critical events. A long-term contract to build an asset is usually an example of such an operating cycle. The gain that is expected to be earned on the contract as a whole will need to be allocated among the critical events.

  This is slightly different from the **accretion** approach taken by SSAP 9, which states that revenue is recognised over a period of time, rather than at a particular point in time. The Statement of Principles appears to be proposing a **hybrid** of the two approaches.

4.3 Application Note G to FRS 5

All the discussion in this chapter has concerned theoretical ideas and the non-mandatory Statement of Principles. For some years the ASB has been considering whether to develop an FRS on revenue recognition, which would contain mandatory guidance. In the end the ASB decided against producing a full FRS but, instead, in November 2003 issued an Application Note (known as Application Note G) to be added at the end of FRS 5. This provides mandatory basic principles to be followed in revenue recognition, but falls short of providing comprehensive guidance on this topic.

Basic principles

(a) A seller should recognise revenue under an exchange transaction with a customer when, and to the extent that, it obtains the right to consideration in exchange for its performance.

(b) A seller may obtain a right to consideration when some, but not all, of its contractual obligations have been fulfilled. Where a seller has partially performed its contractual obligations, it should recognise revenue to the extent that it has obtained the right to consideration through its performance.

(c) Revenue should be measured at the fair value of the right to consideration.

You should realise that the ASB is not attempting any large-scale changes to accounting practice in this Application Note. It has continued with the 'balance sheet' approach of the Statement of Principles. Revenue can be recognised when the asset of the right to consideration can be recognised, usually as a debtor at the date of delivery of goods.

Conclusion

Under the traditional approach to accounting for revenue:

- revenue must be both earned and realised before it is recognised and reported in the profit and loss account
- the concepts of accruals and prudence are applied.

The critical event approach recognises revenue at the point in the business's operating cycle at which most or all of the uncertainty surrounding the transaction is resolved. In most cases this occurs when goods or services are delivered.

The Statement of Principles defines gains and losses in terms of changes in assets and liabilities, rather than in terms of matching transactions with accounting periods. If net assets increase, a gain is recognised. Identifying the critical event can help to determine when a gain should be recognised.

This balance sheet approach to revenue recognition has now been confirmed by the ASB issuing an Application Note on revenue recognition to be added at the end of FRS 5.

SELF-TEST QUESTIONS

1 What is the definition of revenue? (1.1)

2 Define realised profits. (2.1)

3 Which two fundamental concepts of accounting have traditionally been used to deal with problems of revenue recognition? (2.2)

4 Which other accounting concept might also be relevant in deciding whether revenue should be recognised? (2.4)

5 What is the 'critical event' in the operating cycle? (3.1)

6 What stage in the operating cycle is normally treated as the critical event? (3.1)

7 Give an example of a situation in which the accretion approach might be used. (3.2)

8 According to the Statement of Principles, when should a gain be recognised? (4.1)

EXAM-TYPE QUESTION

Revenue recognition

The timing of revenue (income) recognition has long been an area of debate and inconsistency in accounting. The operating cycle of enterprises may involve the following stages:

- obtaining an order for goods prior to manufacture
- acquisition of goods or raw materials (including extraction)
- production of goods
- obtaining an order for goods in stock
- delivery of goods
- collection of cash (re credit sales)
- provision of after-sales service or warranties.

Traditionally the 'critical event' approach has been used to determine the timing of revenue recognition. Recently the Accounting Standards Board (ASB) in its 'Statement of Principles for Financial Reporting' has identified 'elements' of Financial Statements. It uses these to determine when a gain or loss occurs.

Required:

(a) In relation to *each* of the above stages in the operating cycle discuss, giving a practical example where possible, the circumstances in which the critical event may be deemed to have occurred at that stage. **(12 marks)**

(b) Discuss the criteria used in the Statement of Principles for determining when gains or losses arise, and how they should be reported. **(5 marks)**

Telecast Industries plc is preparing its accounts for the year ended 30 September 20X7. In May 20X7 it bought the rights to a film called 'Wind of Change'. It paid a fixed fee and will not incur any further significant costs or commissions. It has entered into the following contracts with other parties:

- **Warmer Cinemas plc**

  This is a large company with a chain of cinemas throughout the UK. Warmer Cinemas plc has negotiated the right to screen the film during the period from 1 July 20X7 to 31 December 20X7 in as many of its cinemas and as frequently as it chooses. Telecast Industries plc will be paid 15% of gross box office receipts.

- **Big Screen Ltd**

  This is a small company operating a single cinema. Under the terms of the contract it may screen the film twice a day for the same period as the above contract. It has paid a fixed fee of £10,000.

- **Global Satellite plc**

  This is a satellite TV company that broadcasts to Europe. It paid £4 million in August 20X7 for the right to screen the film ten times at intervals of not less than one month apart during the period from 1 January 20X8 to 31 December 20X8.

Required:

(c) Applying the recommendations in the Statement of Principles, describe how Telecast Industries plc should treat the revenue from each of the above contracts in the accounting year to 30 September 20X7. **(8 marks)**

***Note*:** You are not required to discuss how the cost of the film should be expensed.

(Total: 25 marks)

For the answer to this question, see the 'Answers' section at the end of the book.

FEEDBACK TO ACTIVITY **1**

If we apply the accruals concept to this problem, £72,000 (3/12 × 288,000) should be in the profit and loss account, with the balance of £216,000 being taken to a deferred income account (a creditor) on the balance sheet. This income would be matched with costs of £60,000 (3 months x £20,000).

FEEDBACK TO ACTIVITY **2**

As we have seen, if we apply the accruals concept to this problem, £72,000 (3/12 × 288,000) is recognised in the profit and loss account, with the balance of £216,000 being taken to a deferred income account (a creditor) on the balance sheet.

According to the Statement of Principles, the starting point should be changes to assets and liabilities. As a result of receiving the subscriptions, the company now has a liability. It is obliged to produce and deliver the remaining nine issues of the magazine. However, this liability is not for the deferred income, but for the cost of producing the nine issues, £180,000.

Therefore £180,000 would be recognised as a liability in the balance sheet, while the remaining £108,000 is recognised as revenue. This means that the profit on all twelve issues is recognised at the time the subscriptions are received.

Many commentators believe that this treatment is not prudent.

Chapter 4

ACCOUNTING FOR PRICE LEVEL CHANGES

CHAPTER CONTENTS

1 **Historic cost accounting**

2 **Current purchasing power accounting (CPP)**

3 **Current cost accounting (CCA)**

4 **Capital maintenance concepts**

5 **The ASB's contribution to the debate**

This chapter deals with the complex issues involved in the measurement of income in a period of changing price levels. You will find it takes time to become acquainted with the terminology and the issues involved. There is currently no accounting standard in issue which deals with the topic of changing price levels. However, the ASB has considered these issues in its Statement of Principles.

Most of this chapter is concerned with the two main alternatives to historic cost accounting: current purchasing power and current cost accounting. You will not be asked to perform detailed calculations in the exam, but you will need to understand both systems and be able to explain them in principle.

Objectives

By the time you have finished this chapter you should be able to:

- describe the deficiencies of historic cost accounts
- explain the concepts of current purchasing power, current cost accounting and real terms accounting
- discuss the advantages and disadvantages of the above accounting systems.

1 Historic cost accounting

1.1 The traditional approach

KEY POINT

Traditional cost accounting records transactions at their original **historic cost**.

The traditional approach to accounting has the following features.

- Accounting transactions are recorded at their original **historic monetary cost.**
- Items or events for which no monetary transaction has occurred are usually ignored altogether.
- Income for each period is normally taken into account only when **revenue is realised** in the form of cash or in some form which will soon be converted into cash.
- Profit for the period is found by matching income against the cost of items consumed in generating the revenue for the period (such items include fixed assets which depreciate through use, obsolescence or the passage of time).

These features of accounting have served users well over many years in accounting for the stewardship of the directors. However, in periods in which prices change significantly, historic cost accounts have grave deficiencies.

1.2 The deficiencies of historic cost accounts

KEY POINT

Historic cost accounts take no view of asset **value movements**; profits can sometimes be exaggerated.

- The net book value of fixed assets is often substantially below their current value.
- The balance sheet figure for stock reflects prices ruling at the date of purchase or manufacture rather than those current at the year end.
- Charges made in arriving at profit do not reflect the current value of assets consumed. The effect is to exaggerate profit in real terms. If the profit determined in this way were distributed in full, the level of operations would have to be curtailed.
- No account is taken of the effect of increasing prices on monetary items. For example, the cash tied up in debtors increases even where the volume of operations remains the same.

- The overstatement of profits and the understatement of assets prevents a meaningful calculation of return on capital employed.

As a result of the above, users of accounts find it extremely difficult to assess a company's progress from year to year or to compare the results of different operations.

Example

Company A acquires a new machine in 20X4. This machine costs £50,000 and has an estimated useful life of ten years.

Company B acquires an identical machine in 20X5, except that it buys a machine exactly one year old, with an estimated useful life of nine years. The cost of the machine is £48,000.

Depreciation charges (straight-line basis) in 20X5 are as follows.

Company A	$\frac{1}{10} \times £50,000$	= £5,000
Company B	$\frac{1}{9} \times £48,000$	= £5,333

Net book values at the end of 20X5 are:

Company A	£50,000 – (2 × £5,000)	= £40,000
Company B	£48,000 – £5,333	= £42,667

Both companies are using identical machines during 20X5, but the profit and loss accounts will show quite different profit figures because of adherence to historical cost. Is the comparison of balance sheets and profit and loss accounts for the two companies in 20X5 meaningful?

1.3 Advantages of the historic cost approach

KEY POINT

Historic cost accounting can reduce the element of subjectivity in accounts.

One of the principal advantages claimed for this approach is that it reduces subjectivity to a minimum. Subjectivity refers to the extent to which the accounts can be affected by personal opinion as opposed to verifiable factual information.

In spite of this claim, subjective opinions are extremely important in conventional accounting. The following are examples:

- Revaluation of fixed assets, where the revaluation is actually incorporated into the accounts as opposed to merely being rėferred to in a note to the accounts.
- Depreciation charges require subjective estimates of useful life and estimated scrap value at the end of this useful life.
- Stock may be stated at net realisable value where this is estimated to be less than cost.
- Provision for doubtful debts and obsolete and slow-moving stocks requires subjective opinions, even if these opinions are backed up by reference to factual data.
- Treatment of long-term contracts requires subjective estimations of, for example, expected cost to complete the contract.

Although the use of the historic cost principle has been the chief problem in recent years, the debate may be widened to cover various aspects of the traditional approach.

1.4 Deficiencies of the traditional approach

KEY POINT

Historic cost accounting, whilst being **prudent**, can lead to misleading statements and **bias**.

- As noted above, adherence to original historic costs leads inevitably to the **misstatement** of asset values and profitability. Balance sheets no longer represent a meaningful picture of the economic state of affairs of a business.
- Disregarding items and events for which no monetary transaction has occurred may mean that accounts do not portray the actual economic factors determining the success or failure of the business.
- By recognising only revenue which is realised, changes in wealth that are of benefit to shareholders will be indefinitely disregarded.

- The process of matching expenses with revenue is inevitably **subjective** and possibly pointless, as it is the level and timing of cash flows which determine economic values.
- By taking a **biased** view of the uncertainty associated with a business, its strength and performance are deliberately misrepresented (albeit **prudently**).

1.5 Possible alternatives to historic cost accounting

KEY POINT

Alternative approaches to historic cost accounting centre on **current purchasing power**, **current cost accounting**, or a combination of these.

Despite these limitations, historic cost accounts still prevail because of the past difficulties in finding a suitable alternative.

One alternative to strict historic cost accounting (HCA) is to revalue certain assets, such as property, to its current value but to account for all other assets using HCA as before. This is called the **modified historic cost convention** and produces arguably more relevant information for users. However the basis of asset valuation is inconsistent (some at current value and others at historic cost), so it is not a comprehensive solution to the problem.

The argument for an alternative to historic cost accounting has revolved around the question of whether accounting for the effects of inflation should be directed towards:

1 presenting accounts in the same real terms from one year to another (**current purchasing power** or **CPP**)

2 protecting the operating capabilities of companies (**current cost accounting** or **CCA**)

3 some combination of the two.

Option 1 involves accounting for general price changes. The owners of the business are shareholders who may suffer from general inflation as the purchasing power of their investment in the business declines. Changes in general prices are thus used to record the effect.

Option 2 involves the consideration of specific price changes. Here the perspective of the business as a separate entity is paramount. The effects of price changes on the specific assets owned by the business are therefore used.

The dispute is made more complex by a lack of basic agreement on a definition of 'profit'.

This is best illustrated by a simple example.

Example

Alan sets up in business on 1 January with £1,000, which he immediately uses to buy goods for resale. On 31 January he sells these goods for £1,500. At this date the replacement price of the goods to Alan is £1,200. During January the Retail Price Index (RPI) has risen by 30%.

Solution

In historic cost terms the results of his trading are as follows:

	£
Sales	1,500
Cost of goods sold	1,000
Profit	500

However, if Alan wishes to continue in business at the same level, he must presumably replace the goods he has sold with new stock costing £1,200. If the profit and loss account is to show the amount which can be reasonably distributed while maintaining the operating capability of his business, the profit could more sensibly be stated on a current cost basis as follows:

	£
Sales	1,500
Cost of goods sold (replacement cost)	1,200
Profit	300

But in real terms how much better off is Alan? He began with £1,000 in cash. To maintain his general purchasing power ability he would have needed to have increased this by 30% (rise in the Retail Price Index 1 January to 31 January) to £1,300 by 31 January. In fact, he has £1,500. He is therefore £200 better off in terms of his general purchasing power ability on 31 January than when he started.

The profit could variously be argued to be £500 (**historic cost**), £300 (**current cost**) or £200 (**current purchasing power**). The decision as to which (if any) is the correct figure requires basic agreement as to a definition of profit.

2 Current purchasing power accounting (CPP)

2.1 Concept

KEY POINT

Under CPP, figures are adjusted to show money with the same **purchasing power**. In the UK, the **Retail Price Index** is used.

Under CPP accounting, the accounts are adjusted so that all figures are shown in terms of money with the same **purchasing power**. It is thus necessary to adjust items by means of a general price index. In the UK, the index used for these purposes is the **Retail Price Index** (**RPI**) and items are generally restated in terms of the purchasing power at the end of the financial period.

2.2 Key features

In converting the figures in the basic historic cost accounts into those in the CPP statement, a distinction is drawn between:

- monetary items
- non-monetary items.

DEFINITION

Monetary items are those items whose amounts are fixed by contract or otherwise in terms of numbers of pounds, regardless of changes in general price levels.

DEFINITION

Non-monetary items include such assets as stock, plant and buildings.

Monetary items are those whose amounts are fixed by contract or otherwise in terms of numbers of pounds, regardless of changes in general price levels. Examples of monetary items are cash, debtors, creditors and loan capital.

Holders of monetary assets lose general purchasing power during a period of inflation to the extent that any income from the assets does not adequately compensate for the loss in purchasing power; the converse applies to those having monetary liabilities.

Non-monetary items include such assets as stock and fixed assets. Retaining the historic cost concept requires that holders of non-monetary assets are assumed neither to gain nor to lose purchasing power by reason only of changes in the purchasing power of the pound.

The owners of a company's equity capital have the residual claim on its net monetary and non-monetary assets. The equity interest is therefore neither a monetary nor a non-monetary item.

KEY POINT

CPP accounts are prepared by updating all items in the profit and loss account, and all non-monetary items in the balance sheet, by the **CPP factor**. **Depreciation** is adjusted by reference to the date of the fixed asset acquisition. **Monetary items** are not adjusted.

2.3 The preparation of CPP accounts

You will not be required to prepare CPP or CCA accounts in the exam so we will simply summarise the approach to preparing such accounts which will help you to understand the underlying concepts.

CPP accounts are prepared by adjusting all the amounts in the accounts to reflect the value of money at one point in time. The unit of measurement is the 'CPP unit' rather than the monetary unit. In principle, the CPP unit can be based on the value of money at any point in time. In practice, the value of money at the balance sheet date is used.

CPP accounts are prepared by updating all items in the profit and loss account, and all non-monetary items in the balance sheet, by the **CPP factor**:

$$\text{CPP factor} = \frac{\text{Index at the balance sheet date}}{\text{Index at date of entry in accounts}}$$

Depreciation is adjusted by reference to the date of acquisition of the related fixed asset item.

Monetary items in the balance sheet are not adjusted, because their value in CPP units is their monetary amount.

In the CPP accounts it is necessary to compute a gain or loss from holding monetary items in times of inflation. In principle, this can be found by adjusting all entries in the accounts for each monetary item by the CPP factor, so that the difference between the 'CPP balance' and the actual monetary balance represents the gain or loss on holding that item.

2.4 The advantages and disadvantages of CPP

KEY POINT

CPP has the advantage of being **objective** and a true system of **inflation accounting**; but can be **complex**, can fail to capture specific and general **price divergences**, and CPP units can be **unfamiliar**.

Advantages

- CPP accounting is both simple and **objective**, because it relies on a standard index.
- Because it adjusts for changes in the unit of measurement, it is a true system of **inflation accounting**.
- It measures the impact on the company in terms of shareholders' **purchasing power**.

Disadvantages

The ASB has rejected CPP on three grounds:

- its **complexity**
- its failure to capture economic substance when specific and general **price movements diverge**
- the **unfamiliarity** of information stated in terms of current purchasing power units.

There are other disadvantages:

- CPP does not show the current values (value to the business) of assets and liabilities;
- the RPI is not necessarily appropriate for all assets in all businesses;
- the physical capital of the business is not maintained.

3 Current cost accounting (CCA)

3.1 Introduction

In an earlier chapter we looked at the concept of value to the business, or deprival value. **CCA** is based on the **deprival method** of valuation of assets. In order to reflect deprival values, the balance sheet assets of stock and fixed assets require revaluation.

All other assets and all liabilities are monetary in nature (i.e. they are already stated at current value in HC accounts) and therefore do not need to be adjusted.

The reflection of deprival values on the balance sheet results in additional charges in the profit and loss account to reflect the true cost of using stocks and fixed assets in the production of goods.

ACTIVITY 1

A business has five assets, A to E, for which you are to calculate the deprival value.

	A	*B*	*C*	*D*	*E*
	£	£	£	£	£
Historical cost	100	25	67	500	230
Replacement cost	120	28	60	450	250
Economic value in use	105	30	75	480	220
Net realisable value	110	26	73	505	205

Feedback to this activity is at the end of the chapter.

3.2 A family of techniques

KEY POINT

The **current cost profit and loss account** is charged with the value to the business of assets consumed during the period. The **current cost balance sheet** reflects the current value of stock and fixed assets.

Current cost (or replacement cost) accounting is not a single system of accounting – there are several variants. We will concentrate on general principles, in particular those relating to stock and fixed assets.

- The **current cost profit and loss account** is charged with the value to the business of assets consumed during the period. In particular, the charges for consuming stocks (cost of sales) and fixed assets (depreciation) are based on current rather than historical values.
- The **current cost balance sheet** reflects the current value of stock and fixed assets.

3.3 Fixed assets and depreciation

KEY POINT

In general, property is valued at **market value**. For plant and machinery, **net current replacement cost** is used – i.e. the difference of the **gross replacement** cost and a depreciation provision.

Balance sheet

The general rule is that fixed assets should be included in the balance sheet at their value to the business, i.e. the amount of compensation a company would require if it were deprived of the asset.

In most cases, the value to the business of property is its **market value** on an existing use basis, while for plant and machinery it is **net current replacement cost**.

How is net current replacement cost of plant and machinery calculated? There are three basic stages:

- **Stage 1**: Calculate the **gross replacement cost** (**GRC**) of a new but otherwise identical asset at the balance sheet date.
- **Stage 2**: Allowing for the age of the asset, calculate a **depreciation provision** based on GRC.
- **Stage 3**: **Net current replacement** cost equals 1 less 2, and is shown in the current cost balance sheet.

If GRC cannot be calculated by reference to suppliers' price lists, an alternative is to use specific price indices. These are produced by the Office for National Statistics (ONS).

Example

A company bought an item of plant on 30 June 20X3 at a cost of £4,000. Its expected useful life was ten years, with a nil value at the end. An identical model of plant is no longer available, but you have obtained the following specific price indices which you think are suitable for the purpose:

30 June 20X3	Index = 132
31 December 20X8	Index = 195

Calculate net current replacement cost at 31 December 20X8, assuming the estimated useful life of the asset has not been revised.

Solution

		£
Gross replacement cost at 31 Dec 20X8:	$£4,000 \times \frac{195}{132}$	5,909
Accumulated depreciation:	$\frac{5.5}{10} \times £5,909$	3,250
Net current replacement cost:		2,659

Profit and loss account

The depreciation charge for the current cost profit and loss account must now be calculated. For simplicity, the depreciation charge will be based on the year-end replacement cost of the fixed asset. Current cost depreciation can be based on the average replacement cost during the year, but the arithmetic is a little more complex.

Example

A company acquired a fixed asset on 1 January 20X4 at a cost of £800. Its estimated useful life was five years, with a nil terminal value. A new, but otherwise identical, asset would cost £800 and £960 on 31 December 20X4 and 20X5 respectively.

You are required:

- to prepare the current cost (CCA) and historic cost (HCA) balance sheet extracts at each year end in respect of fixed assets
- to calculate the relevant depreciation charges
- to prepare the relevant fixed asset ledger accounts for 20X5.

Solution

Balance sheets at 31 December

	20X4		*20X5*	
	HCA	*CCA*	*HCA*	*CCA*
	£	£	£	£
Cost	800	800	800	960
Accumulated depreciation (2/5 × £960)	160	160	320	384
	640	640	480	576

Profit and loss accounts

	20X4		*20X5*	
	HCA	*CCA*	*HCA*	*CCA*
	£	£	£	£
Depreciation charge (1/5 × £960)	160	160	160	192

3.4 Stock and cost of sales

The essence of CCA is that, when an item of stock is sold, the proceeds of sale are matched against the current cost of the stock at the date of sale (representing the value to the business of stock consumed).

Example

A company purchased some goods on 31 January 20X2 at a cost of £250. These goods were sold on 31 March 20X2 for proceeds of £320 when the cost of replacing the goods was £272.

Historic cost accounting

Under HCA, proceeds of sale (£320) would be compared with historic cost (£250) to show profit on sale of £70.

KEY POINT

Under CCA accounting, when an item of stock is sold, the proceeds of sale are matched against the current cost of the stock at the date of sale.

Current cost accounting (CCA)

Under CCA accounting, when an item of stock is sold, the proceeds of sale are matched against the current cost of the stock at the date of sale.

	£
Proceeds of sale	320
Current cost of sales	272
Current cost (or operating) profit	48
Current cost of sales	272
Historic cost of sales	250
Realised 'holding gain'	22

ACTIVITY 2

Describe the types of business that would be most heavily affected by the replacement of historic cost accounting with a system based on current values.

Feedback to this activity is at the end of the chapter.

3.5 The advantages and disadvantages of CCA

KEY POINT

The most important advantage of CCA is that it assesses the **current performance** of a business.

Advantages

The ASB has stated that the most important advantage of CCA is its relevance to users who wish to assess the **current state** or **recent performance** of the business.

Under CCA, physical capital is maintained, assets are stated at their value to the business and holding gains are eliminated from profit.

KEY POINT

The main disadvantage of CCA is its greater **subjectivity**.

Disadvantages

The main disadvantages of current value are its possible greater **subjectivity** and lower reliability than historic cost. A further disadvantage is its lack of familiarity.

There may also be practical problems in using current cost accounting, such as the following.

- It is not always easy to obtain an index which is perfectly suitable for measuring the movement in the current cost of a particular type of asset.
- It is often difficult to obtain a suitable market value for specialist items, but indices may be constructed as an alternative.
- There may be no intention to replace an asset
- There may be no modern equivalent asset due to the advance of technology.

It has also been argued that CCA is not a system of inflation accounting as such, because it only adjusts for changes in the value of the assets held, not all assets generally.

4 Capital maintenance concepts

4.1 Principles of accounting for price level changes

The above discussion of CPP and CCA accounting has concentrated on the balance sheet and the valuation of assets. We now need to consider the effect of this approach on the profits that are recognised.

Total gains and losses accruing to the owners in a period equal the difference between the net assets at the beginning and end of the accounting period. The valuation method for recording the net assets therefore determines total gains and losses. However, it is important to distinguish 'profit' from other gains and losses, as users need information about the quality of particular gains and losses, e.g. whether they are realised or relate to assets, essential to the entity's operations, which are likely to be sold.

How profit is determined is affected by the capital maintenance concept which is adopted.

KEY POINT

Capital maintenance concepts can be classified as **physical capital maintenance (PCM)** and **financial capital maintenance (FCM)**.

Capital maintenance concepts can be classified as follows:

- physical capital maintenance (PCM), alternatively known as operating capital maintenance (OCM) – PCM is associated with CCA
- financial capital maintenance (FCM).

FCM can be further divided into '**Money**' **FCM** and **CPP FCM**. CPP FCM is CPP accounting.

Example

A company begins with share capital of £100 and cash of £100. At the beginning of the year one item of stock is bought for £100. The item of stock is sold at the end of the year for £150. Its replacement cost at that time is £120 and general inflation throughout the year is 10%. Any 'profit' is distributed to shareholders at the end of the year.

	Financial capital maintenance		*Physical capital maintenance*
	'Money'	*CPP*	
	£	£	£
Sales	150	150	150
Less: cost of sales	100	100	120
Operating profit	50	50	30
Less: inflation adjustment (alternatively shown by increasing cost of sales to £110)	-	10	-
Profit for year	50	40	30
Dividend	50	40	30
	-	-	-
Capital and non-distributable reserves at year end	100	110	120

The increase in capital and reserves of £10 for CPP is the credit entry for the £10 inflation adjustment. The £20 for PCM is the credit entry for the increased cost of sales. The £20 is known as a 'realised holding gain'.

- It is a gain (the stock was worth more in money terms when it was used in the business compared to when it was purchased).
- It arose purely from holding onto the stock in a period of rising prices.

- It is realised as the product has been sold by the firm.

Under 'money' FCM there is no attempt to adjust for inflation, i.e. the accounts are historic cost accounts.

Under CPP FCM the emphasis is on maintaining the purchasing power of the opening capital. The shareholders require funds of £110 in order to maintain their purchasing power. (£110 buys the same quantity of goods at the year end as £100 at the beginning of the year.)

4.2 Providing equivalent information in a supplementary form

KEY POINT

Supplementary information can be provided by way of '**adjusted earnings statements**'.

Where the profit and loss account is not inflation adjusted, **supplementary information** can be provided in the notes by way of **'adjusted earnings statements'**.

Using the numbers in the example above, the adjusted earnings statement under each method would be as follows:

	CPP FCM	*PCM*
	£	£
Historic cost operating profit (i.e. before dividend)	50	50
Less: Current cost operating adjustments	-	(20)
Less: Inflation adjustment to opening shareholders' funds	(10)	-
Profit/current cost profit	40	30

4.3 Real terms accounting

KEY POINT

Real terms accounting is a further capital maintenance concept based on combining **CPP FCM** and **PCM**.

Real terms accounting is a further capital maintenance concept based on combining CPP FCM and PCM.

There are in fact several variations of real terms accounting but the basic idea is to show the figures as in the PCM statement in the operating profit statement, and to show the inflation adjustment to shareholders' funds in the Statement of Total Recognised Gains and Losses (STRGL).

Thus the figures would be as follows:

Profit and loss account

	£
Sales	150
Less: Cost of sales	120
Current cost operating profit	30
Dividend	30

Statement of total recognised gains and losses

	£
Current cost operating profit	30
Gain from holding stock (i.e. credit entry for the increased cost of sales)	20
Nominal money profit	50
Less: Amount to maintain purchasing power of shareholders' investment	10
Real terms profit	40

As with the CPP FCM concept above, it does not follow that the real terms gain (£40) could be fully distributed if the company wishes to continue in business at the same level of activity. This is because the maintenance of a company's real financial capital does not guarantee the maintenance of its operating capital.

4.4 Choice of capital maintenance concept

KEY POINT

When choosing a **capital maintenance concept**, the **needs of users** and the **nature of the company's business** are the main factors to be considered.

There are two main factors to consider when choosing a **capital maintenance concept**: the needs of users and the nature of the company's business.

The needs of users

Shareholders will generally be interested in maximising the purchasing power of their investment. Thus a financial capital maintenance view may seem the most appropriate choice. (This could be CPP capital maintenance or real terms accounting.)

Managers and employees may consider that the company's major objective is perpetuating its existence by maintaining its ability to produce similar quantities of goods and services as those produced at the present time. This viewpoint is compatible with PCM. But if the company does not maintain its operating capacity, there will be a reduction in the scale of its activities which may mean that employees are made redundant.

Nature of the company's business

CPP FCM or real terms accounting is more suitable for companies in which asset value increases are viewed as an alternative to trading as a means of generating profits. The true measure of the performance of such companies is their ability to produce 'real' profits above the profits which arise from general inflation. The best measure of success here is based on real terms, i.e. opening capital is adjusted by a general index and the change in specific values of assets is assessed.

5 The ASB's contribution to the debate

5.1 Measurement systems

KEY POINT

The historic cost basis has the advantages of **objectivity**, **reliability**, **familiarity** and **understandability;** its main disadvantage is its lack of relevance to the **current state** of the business.

Chapter 6 of the ASB's Statement of Principles considers measurement in financial statements. The first draft of this chapter considered historic cost and the alternatives: a system of measurement based on current values (CCA), and adjustments for the effects of general inflation (CPP).

Although the ASB conceded that the historic cost basis has several important advantages (objectivity, reliability, familiarity and understandability), its main disadvantage is its lack of relevance to the current state of the business, because:

- the balance sheet does not provide an accurate representation of the current financial position
- the profit and loss account reports gains on holding assets when they are realised rather than when they occur: one effect is that no distinction is drawn between gains that have been made in past periods but are realised in the current period and those that are both made and realised in the current period.

The ASB drew the following conclusions.

- The use of current values for both assets and liabilities provides the information that is most relevant to the decisions of users.
- For assets, the appropriate current value is stated according to the value to the business rule. For liabilities, market values may be used.
- A real terms capital maintenance system improves the relevance of information because it shows current operating margins as well as the extent to which holding gains and losses reflect the effect of general inflation. Users of real terms financial statements are thus able to select the particular information they require.

- Accounting practice should develop by evolving in the direction of greater use of current values insofar as this is consistent with the constraints of reliability and cost.

These conclusions were controversial in the first draft because they seemed to suggest that the ASB was planning to reintroduce current cost accounting.

5.2 Choosing a measurement basis

KEY POINT

If both historic cost and current values are reliable, the most **relevant** method should be used. **Current value** is not necessarily less reliable than **historic cost**.

The final version of the Statement of Principles concentrates on the selection of an appropriate measurement basis (historic cost or current value) for each category of assets or liabilities. There is no longer any suggestion that current values are always preferable to historic cost. However, the Statement gives the following guidance on the choice of measurement basis:

- The carrying amounts of assets and liabilities need to be sufficiently reliable. If only one of the measures available is reliable, it should be the one used if it is also relevant. If both historic cost and current value are reliable, the better measure to use is the one that is most relevant.
- Current value is not necessarily less reliable than historic cost. For example, debtors stated at historic cost may need to be adjusted to allow for bad or doubtful debts and this involves a degree of estimation similar to that involved in estimating current values not derived from an active market. The hurdle that a measure must clear to be deemed reliable is set at the same height for current value measures as for historic cost measures.

As we will see later in this text, the ASB still wishes to encourage entities to make greater use of current values.

5.3 Capital maintenance and changing prices

KEY POINT

In almost all cases, the capital maintenance model adopted by an entity will be **financial capital maintenance**.

The final version of the Statement of Principles makes the following points:

- In almost all cases, the capital maintenance model adopted by an entity will be **financial capital maintenance** and ownership interest will be measured in nominal amounts.
- When **general** or **specific** price changes are significant, this approach is open to criticism.
  - **General price changes** can affect the significance of reported profits and of ownership interest. If this problem is acute, profit should only be recognised after adjustments have been made to maintain the purchasing power of the entity's financial capital.
  - **Specific price changes** can affect the significance of reported profits and financial position. If this problem is acute, the user should be informed of the significance of specific price changes for the entity's financial performance and financial position.

Although the ASB has denied that a return to current cost accounting as such is on its agenda, it has evidently not ruled out this possibility if the inflation rate rises in the future.

Conclusion

The debate as to the measurement of revenue, assets and liabilities is made important by the deficiencies of HC accounting in an era of changing prices.

There are two main alternatives to historic cost accounting: current purchasing power (CPP), which reflects the effect of general price changes, and current cost accounting (CCA) which reflects the effect of specific price changes. Neither has been accepted by preparers of accounts.

SELF-TEST QUESTIONS

1. What are the deficiencies of historic cost accounting in a period of rising prices? (1.2)
2. What are the advantages of historic cost accounting? (1.3)
3. What are the two main alternatives to historic cost accounting? (1.5)
4. What are monetary items? (2.2)
5. Why has the ASB rejected CPP accounting? (2.4)
6. Under CCA accounting, which assets on the balance sheet are restated? (3.2)
7. What is PCM? (4.1)
8. What is the capital maintenance concept associated with CCA accounting? (4.1)
9. What is real terms accounting? (4.3)
10. According to the Statement of Principles, which capital maintenance model will normally be adopted by an entity? (5.3)

EXAM-TYPE QUESTION

Barty plc

'The recognition and correct treatment of holding gains in company financial statements are vital for a proper understanding of the position and performance of the business entity.'

Required:

(a) Explain briefly the significance of the treatment of holding gains for the measurement of business profit. **(5 marks)**

(b) Set out the arguments for and against the recognition of holding gains. **(10 marks)**

The following relates to the accounts of Barty plc, a property investment company.

Balance sheet as at 31 December 20X7

	20X7	*20X6*
	£000	£000
Investment properties at market value	14,125	12,579
Other assets	140	421
	14,265	13,000
Called up share capital	2,000	2,000
Profit and loss account	4,720	4,597
Investment property revaluation reserve	7,545	6,403
	14,265	13,000

Profit and loss account for the year ended 31 December 20X7

	£000
Rental income	1,526
Administrative expenses	(160)
Profit before tax	1,366
Taxation	(793)
Profit after tax	573
Dividends paid and proposed	(450)
Retained profit	123

Adjusted earnings statement for the year ended 31 December 20X7

	£000	£000
Net profit after tax for the year		573
Unrealised gains for the year on revaluations of investment properties	925	
Less: Inflation adjustment to shareholders' funds	(520)	
Real holding gains		405
Total real gains		978
Dividends paid and proposed		(450)
Amount retained		528

Notes

- Investment properties are revalued annually at each year end.
- Investment properties were acquired for £621,000 during 20X7.
- The Retail Price Index has risen by 4% during 20X7.

(c) Comment on the adjusted earnings statement prepared by the company.

(10 marks)

(Total: 25 marks)

For the answer to this question, see the 'Answers' section at the end of the book.

FEEDBACK TO ACTIVITY 1

	A	*B*	*C*	*D*	*E*
	£	£	£	£	£
Deprival value	110	28	60	450	220
	NRV	RC	RC	RC	EV

A Since the replacement cost is more than the recoverable amount, the recoverable amount is the loss to the business. This is the higher of the net realisable value and the economic value, which in this case is the net realisable value, £110.

B In this case the replacement cost is less than the recoverable amount, so the business would replace the asset. Therefore the loss to the business is the cost of replacing the asset, £28.

C + D The situation with assets C and D is the same as with asset B: the business would replace the assets, so the losses are the replacement costs, £60 and £450.

E For asset E, the replacement cost is more than the business could gain from owning the asset (the recoverable amount), so the higher of the net realisable value and the present value of future profits is used, that is, £220.

FEEDBACK TO ACTIVITY 2

Businesses with the following characteristics will be most heavily affected by the change to current value accounting:

- large quantities of stock held for long periods of time – the resulting adjustments will impact heavily on the profit and loss account;
- high levels of fixed assets acquired a long time ago – the resulting depreciation adjustment will adversely affect profit;
- large reserves of monetary assets – a charge is made to the profit and loss account to reflect their fall in value when prices are rising;
- large borrowings – a credit is made in the profit and loss account to reflect the beneficial effect of holding borrowing in inflationary times.

Chapter 5

THE STRUCTURE OF THE UK REGULATORY FRAMEWORK

CHAPTER CONTENTS

1 **The legal and regulatory system of accounting**

2 **The bodies involved in the standard setting process**

3 **International Financial Reporting Standards**

4 **IFRS 1 *First-time adoption of IFRSs***

This chapter looks at the work of the bodies involved in the standard setting process. You may already be familiar with these from your earlier studies.

It also looks at the other influences on UK financial reporting, including European Community Directives and the work of the International Accounting Standards Board.

Objectives

By the time you have finished this chapter you should be able to:

- describe the influence of EC Directives
- explain the role of the Companies Acts
- outline the standard setting process and the role of the bodies involved in the standard setting process
- explain the relationship between UK and International Financial Reporting Standards.

1 The legal and regulatory system of accounting

1.1 Introduction

The regulatory framework of accounting is affected by a number of legislative and quasi-legislative influences. This section provides an overview of these influences which can be listed as follows:

- company law
- accounting standards
- EC Directives
- the Stock Exchange.

1.2 Company law

The regulatory framework of accounting is affected by company law in a number of areas.

1 Financial statements of companies must show a 'true and fair view'.

2 Accounting standards issued by the ASB are given legal authority as recognised accounting standards.

3 Prescribed formats for the profit and loss account and balance sheet are required.

4 Detailed disclosures of information are required.

5 A company is limited in the amounts of profits it can distribute to its shareholders.

6 Various provisions have to be satisfied if a company wishes to increase or reduce its share capital.

Items 1 and 2 are dealt with in this chapter. The others are dealt with later in this text.

1.3 The true and fair view

The Companies Act 1985 requires that the financial statements of companies must show a true and fair view. This requirement overrides all other regulatory requirements, including those of accounting standards.

KEY POINT

The requirement for a true and fair view overrides all other regulations. The definition of '**true and fair**' may evolve over time.

There is no absolute definition of '**true and fair**', which is a legal concept. In extreme cases, its meaning may be decided by the courts. It is now widely accepted that the meaning of 'true and fair' **evolves** over time and in accordance with changes in generally accepted accounting practice.

Financial statements that conform with the requirements of the Companies Act and of accounting standards will normally show a true and fair view.

ACTIVITY **1**

Explain why it can be difficult to discharge the duty to present a true and fair view.

Feedback to this activity is at the end of the chapter.

1.4 Accounting standards

KEY POINT

The two types of UK accounting standard are the **Financial Reporting Standards** (FRSs) issued by the **ASB** (Accounting Standards Board), and **Statements of Standard Accounting Practice** (SSAPs) issued by the **ASC** (Accounting Standards Committee).

Accounting standards are authoritative statements of how particular types of transaction and other events should be reflected in the financial statements. Compliance with accounting standards is normally necessary for financial statements to give a true and fair view.

There are two types of accounting standard currently in force in the UK:

- **Financial Reporting Standards** (**FRS**s), issued by the **Accounting Standards Board (ASB)**
- **Statements of Standard Accounting Practice** (**SSAP**s), issued by the **Accounting Standards Committee** (**ASC**), which was the predecessor of the ASB. SSAPs are gradually being withdrawn and replaced by FRSs.

The standard setting process will be examined in more detail later in this chapter.

1.5 EC Directives

KEY POINT

EC Directives require financial statements to be presented in **prescribed formats**; allow certain **exemptions** from the **Companies Acts** for small and medium sized companies, and impose requirements relating to **groups of companies**.

It is the aim of the **European Union** (EU) that its member states will eventually become parts of a single economic entity. To achieve this goal, businesses must operate under the same legal and accounting requirements.

The provisions of the Fourth Directive are contained in Sch 4 CA 1985. The provisions of the Seventh Directive are contained in CA 1989.

Because these EC Directives have been enacted in UK law, all UK companies must comply with them. Other EU members have passed similar legislation.

The EC Directives have influenced UK financial reporting in the following main ways.

- Financial statements must be presented according to **prescribed formats** and must comply with detailed disclosure requirements.
- Small and medium sized companies can take advantage of various **exemptions** from the requirements of the **Companies Acts**.
- Various requirements relating to **groups of companies**, including the definition of a subsidiary and the exemptions from preparing group accounts, are derived from the Seventh Directive.

You will see later in this chapter that the EU has now decided that convergence of European accounting practice will be taken further, with the requirement that all EU listed companies must adopt International Financial Reporting Standards with effect from 1 January 2005. This means that there will be two strands of accounting requirements as far as Europe is concerned:

- listed companies will have to prepare their consolidated accounts in accordance with International Standards
- non-listed companies continue to be governed by the previous company law Directives as implemented in the UK Companies Acts.

1.6 The Stock Exchange

> **KEY POINT**
>
> **The Listing Rules** of the **Stock Exchange** set out the requirements for **listing**, **marketing of securities** and **obligations** of issuers.

The **Stock Exchange** is a market place for trading in the securities of companies. The purpose of **The Listing Rules** publication (known as the '**Yellow Book**') is to set out and explain:

- the requirements which apply to applicants for '**listing**' (i.e. admission to the Official List of the Stock Exchange)
- the manner in which any proposed **marketing of securities** is to be conducted
- the continuing **obligations** of the issuers.

A most important condition for listing is acceptance of the continuing obligations which will apply following admission. These obligations form the basis of the relationship between the issuer and the Stock Exchange, governing the disclosure of information necessary to protect investors and maintain an orderly market.

2 The bodies involved in the standard setting process

2.1 Structure of the UK standard setting process

> **KEY POINT**
>
> The bodies involved in the standard setting process are the **Financial Reporting Council** (**FRC**), the **Accounting Standards Board** (**ASB**), the **Financial Reporting Review Panel** (**FRRP**) and the **Urgent Issues Task Force** (**UITF**).

The current UK standard setting regime was introduced in 1990 and is as follows:

The UK standard setting process

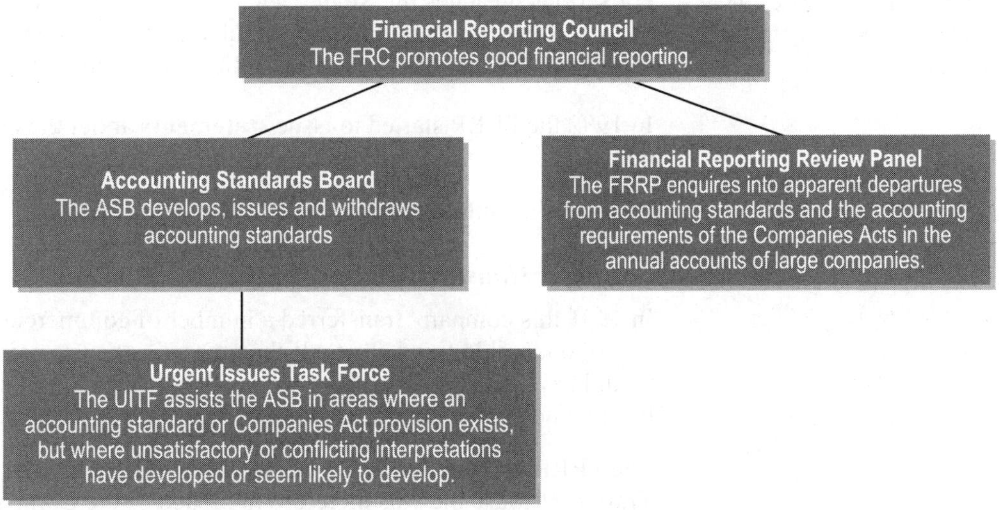

2.2 The FRC

> **KEY POINT**
>
> The **FRC** supervises the standard setting process.

The **Financial Reporting Council** (FRC) guides the standard setting process and ensures that its work is properly funded.

It is the 'political' front to the bodies involved in the standard setting process and produces an annual review which summarises recent events and likely action by the bodies.

The FRC comprises around 25 members drawn from the users and preparers of accounts, and auditors. It has two operating bodies – the **Accounting Standards Board** (ASB) and the Review Panel.

2.3 The ASB

KEY POINT

The aims of the **ASB** are to establish and improve **standards of financial accounting and reporting**, for the benefit of users, preparers and auditors of financial information.

The **ASB** has ten members, including a full-time chairman and a full-time technical director. The part-time members are all well versed in accounting and financial matters.

In July 1991 the ASB issued a short statement of its aims.

Aims

The aims of the Accounting Standards Board (ASB) are to establish and improve **standards of financial accounting and reporting**, for the benefit of users, preparers, and auditors of financial information.

Achieving the aims

The ASB intends to achieve its aims by:

- developing principles to guide it in establishing standards and to provide a framework within which others can exercise judgement in resolving accounting issues
- issuing new accounting standards, or amending existing ones, in response to evolving business practices, new economic developments and deficiencies being identified in current practice
- addressing urgent issues promptly.

2.4 The FRRP

KEY POINT

The FRRP issues **public reports** and **statements** on **departures from accounting standards** by large companies which have been brought to its attention.

The Review Panel has about 15 members and is concerned with the examination and questioning of **departures from accounting standards** by large companies. It does not actively monitor company accounts for possible defects, but investigates matters that are brought to its attention.

For serious breaches the Review Panel has the power to require companies to redraft the offending accounts. For minor faults it is more likely to ask the companies for an assurance that the rules will be complied with in the future.

In 1992 the FRRP started to issue **statements** about the accounts of individual companies.

Examples of **public reports** include the following:

Trafalgar House plc

In 1991 this company transferred a number of commercial properties from current assets to tangible fixed assets. If the properties had remained in current assets, they would have been valued at the lower of cost and net realisable value and this would have reduced pre-tax profits for the accounting period by £102 million.

The FRRP took the view that the accounts did not give a true and fair view and that Trafalgar House plc was therefore in breach of the Companies Act. Initially the directors refused to revise the accounts, but were finally forced to do so when the FRRP applied for a court order. UITF Abstract 5 *Transfers from current assets to fixed assets* was issued in 1992 in order to prevent companies from avoiding a charge to the profit and loss account by transferring unsold trading assets to fixed assets.

Reckitt and Colman plc

Reckitt and Colman plc was forced to alter its 1995 accounts because of inadequate disclosure following an acquisition. The FRRP held that Reckitt and Colman did not explain a valuation adjustment adequately and was therefore in breach of FRS 6 *Acquisitions and mergers* and FRS 7 *Fair values in acquisition accounting*.

Burn Stewart

Burn Stewart, a whisky producer, was forced to increase the disclosures in its 1996 accounts. The FRRP ruled that the company had not complied with FRS 5 *Reporting the substance of transactions*.

So far, all cases have been concluded by voluntary agreement with the directors of the companies concerned; it has not yet been necessary for the Panel to start court proceedings.

2.5 Additional procedures

The Companies (Audit, Investigations and Community Enterprises) Act 2004 has given the FRRP a wider remit for which it has issued revised operating procedures. The FRRP now has the responsibility to:

- review reports under listing rules for compliance
- to take action in relation to these reports by informing the Financial Services Authority of its findings
- review operating and financial reviews for compliance with the Companies Act 1985
- to require companies and certain individuals to produce documents or provide information that it may require for its monitoring function.

2.6 The UITF

KEY POINT

The **UITF**'s role is to assist the ASB in areas where an accounting standard or a Companies Act provision exists, but where **conflicting interpretations** have developed or seem likely to develop.

The **Urgent Issues Task Force** (UITF) is a committee of the ASB comprising a number of people of major standing in the field of financial reporting.

The UITF's main role is to assist the ASB in areas where an accounting standard or a Companies Act provision exists, but where unsatisfactory or conflicting interpretations have developed or seem likely to develop. In such circumstances it operates by seeking a voluntary consensus as to the accounting treatment that should be adopted. Such a consensus is reached against the background of the ASB's declared aim of relying on principles rather than detailed prescription. Thus, within its remit, the UITF is only concerned with serious divergences of current practice or with major developments likely to create serious divergences in the future.

The UITF publishes its consensus pronouncements in the form of documents called UITF Abstracts.

Nothing in the Abstracts issued by the UITF is to be construed as amending or overriding the accounting standards or other statements issued by the ASB.

Scope and application of UITF Abstracts

Consensus pronouncements are applicable to financial statements of a reporting entity that are intended to give a true and fair view of its state of affairs at the balance sheet date and of its profit and loss for the financial period ending on that date. Consensus pronouncements need not be applied to immaterial items.

Compliance with consensus pronouncements

Consensus pronouncements should be considered to be part of the corpus of practices forming the basis for determining what constitutes a true and fair view. Such pronouncements consequently may be taken into consideration by the Financial Reporting Review Panel in deciding whether financial statements call for review.

One of the most important UITF Abstracts is outlined below.

2.7 UITF Abstract 4 *Presentation of long-term debtors in current assets*

The issue

KEY POINT

Where the amount of a long-term debtor is so material that, in the absence of specific disclosure, readers may misinterpret the accounts, the **amount should be disclosed** on the face of the balance sheet.

Both for liabilities and for debtors the Companies Act requires a distinction to be drawn between the amounts payable or receivable within one year and those due to be settled or received after more than one year. Although the distinction is disclosed in the notes for each of the items forming part of debtors, unlike in the case of liabilities it is not required to be carried through to the total of current assets nor to the significant Format 1 sub-total of net current assets (liabilities).

In consequence, there is a certain imbalance between the items that the formats require to be classified under current assets or current liabilities. Examples of long term debtor items include much of the trade debtors of lessors and pension fund surpluses recognised as a prepayment.

UITF consensus

There will be some instances where the amount is so material in the context of the total net current assets that, in the absence of disclosure of debtors due after more than one year on the face of the balance sheet, readers may misinterpret the accounts. In such circumstances **the amount should be disclosed** on the face of the balance sheet.

2.8 The standard setting process

The development of a **Financial Reporting Standard (FRS)** may pass through several stages.

The process normally begins with the issue of a **Discussion Paper**, or a **Discussion Draft**, on which interested parties are invited to comment. Discussion Papers explore an area and set out proposals which, subject to feedback, will eventually form the basis of an FRS.

The next stage is the issue of a **Financial Reporting Exposure Draft (FRED)**. This is the proposed FRS in draft form. Again, interested parties are invited to comment.

After the exposure period has elapsed, the FRED may be revised in the light of any comments received. The FRS is then issued.

2.9 The ASB's work to date

KEY POINT

The **ASB** has focused on preventing '**creative accounting**', developed workable proposals for accounting for '**goodwill**' and worked on **international harmonisation** of accounting standards.

In its first few years of existence the ASB concentrated on preventing abuses and reducing the scope for 'creative accounting'. Early standards included FRS 3 *Reporting financial performance*, which requires extensive disclosure of financial performance and has effectively abolished extraordinary items. It also issued FRS 5 *Reporting the substance of transactions*, which requires entities to account for the economic substance of transactions rather than their strict legal form.

Arguably, one of the ASB's most significant recent achievements has been the issue of FRS 10 *Goodwill and intangible assets*. Accounting for goodwill has been a contentious issue for several years, but it appears that the ASB has managed to produce workable proposals which have gained the support of most users and preparers of accounts.

In recent years, almost all the ASB's work has been influenced by the desire to harmonise UK standards with international accounting standards. This is discussed later in the chapter.

2.10 Has the ASB been a success?

KEY POINT

The **ASB** has been more effective than its predecessor because it is able to issue standards on its **own authority**. Its approach has been underpinned by its **Statement of Principles for Financial Reporting**.

However, the ASB's **balance sheet approach** has received criticism, and some argue that their standards can be **difficult** and **impractical to apply**.

There is general agreement that the **ASB** has been very much more effective than its predecessor, the ASC. One of the reasons for this is that the ASB is able to issue accounting standards on its **own authority** rather than relying on each of the professional bodies to approve and enforce them. It is therefore less susceptible to pressure from particular interest groups.

The ASB consults all interested parties and encourages comment. However, the ultimate content of an FRS is determined by the Board's own judgement, based on research, public consultation and careful deliberation about the benefits and costs of providing the resulting information.

The ASB's approach has been underpinned by the development of its **Statement of Principles for Financial Reporting**, which forms a conceptual framework for UK financial reporting practice. Most commentators support the idea of a conceptual framework and many would argue that the ASB's 'principles based' approach has contributed to its credibility.

However, parts of the Statement of Principles are extremely controversial and the '**balance sheet based**' approach has come in for particular criticism. When the whole Statement was first issued as an Exposure Draft it had such a hostile reception that the ASB issued a second Exposure Draft before proceeding to the final version in 1999.

Critics of the ASB have also attacked it for producing accounting standards which are long, **difficult** to understand and **impractical to apply**. They argue that this leads to financial statements which meet the information needs of investors and analysts at the expense of less sophisticated users.

3 International Financial Reporting Standards

3.1 The International Accounting Standards Board

The **International Accounting Standards Committee** (**IASC**) came into existence in 1973 as a result of an agreement by the leading accountancy bodies of several countries. The IASC developed a suite of International Accounting Standards (IASs) which could be applied in any country in the world.

From April 2001 a new operating structure took effect. The **International Accounting Standards Board (IASB)** is now the standard setting body. It now issues International Financial Reporting Standards (IFRSs) to add to the existing set of IASs.

Countries whose accounting bodies are members of the IASC do not necessarily adopt the IASs and IFRSs issued by the IASC, because many countries have their own national standards. However, a number of countries have adopted IASs and IFRSs, and local standards issued in countries which have not adopted IASs and IFRSs are usually, as far as possible, consistent with IASs and IFRSs.

From now on when IASs and IFRSs are referred to in this text they will be termed simply as IFRSs but this covers the still extant IASs as well.

KEY POINT

The objectives of the IASB are to develop a single set of high quality, understandable and enforceable global accounting standards and to promote the use and rigorous application of those standards.

Objectives of the IASB

The objectives of the IASB are:

- to develop, in the public interest, a single set of high quality, understandable and enforceable global accounting standards that require high quality, transparent and comparable information in financial statements and other financial reporting to help participants in the world's capital markets and other users make economic decisions
- to promote the use and rigorous application of those standards
- to bring about convergence of national accounting standards and International Accounting Standards to high quality solutions.

3.2 The authority attaching to IFRSs

KEY POINT

Neither the IASB nor the accountancy profession can enforce compliance with IFRSs, but IFRSs carry considerable persuasive force worldwide.

Neither the IASB nor the accountancy profession has the power to enforce compliance with IFRSs. Nevertheless, as stated above, some countries adopt IFRSs as their local standards, and others ensure that there is minimum difference between their standards and IFRSs. In recent years the status of the IASB and its standards has increased, so IFRSs carry considerable persuasive force throughout the world.

3.3 The relationship between UK standards and IFRSs

KEY POINT

The ASB supports the IASB. FRSs are formulated with regard to international developments and include a section on the FRS's relationship with the relevant IFRS.

The 1993 **Foreword to accounting standards** states the traditional attitude of the ASB to international accounting standards.

FRSs are formulated with due regard to international developments. The ASB supports the IASC in its aim to harmonise international financial reporting. As part of this support, an FRS contains a section explaining how it relates to the International Accounting Standard (IFRS) dealing with the same topic. In most cases, compliance with an FRS automatically ensures compliance with the relevant IFRS. Where the requirements of an accounting standard and an IFRS differ, the accounting standard should be followed by entities reporting within the area of application of the ASB's accounting standards.

Until recently, it was relatively easy to ensure that most FRSs complied with the requirements of IFRSs. This was because IFRSs in the past were very simple and permitted many alternative treatments. In only a very few cases were there differences between the requirements of a SSAP or FRS and the requirements of an IFRS.

3.4 Recent developments

IOSCO, the **International Organisation of Securities Commissions**, is an influential organisation of the world's stock market regulators, in which the US **Securities and Exchange Commission** (**SEC**) is a key member.

In May 2000 IOSCO agreed to endorse IFRSs for multinational listings in all global markets, subject to some conditions. This means that all stock exchanges will now in theory accept accounts prepared in compliance with IFRSs from overseas companies seeking a listing.

KEY POINT

All EU **listed companies** will be required to prepare their consolidated financial statements in compliance with **IASs**, rather than domestic standards, **from 2005 onwards**.

In June 2002 the EU adopted a Regulation which requires all EU listed companies to prepare their consolidated financial statements in compliance with IFRSs with effect from 1 January 2005. This Regulation (the 'IAS Regulation') has now been incorporated into UK law. The IAS Regulation does not cover the **individual** financial statements of an EU listed company, only the **consolidated** financial statements, and does not cover the accounts of unlisted companies at all. However the UK has decided to permit all these accounts to be prepared either using IFRSs or using UK standards.

There are therefore four possible sets of accounts:

	Parent company accounts	**Group accounts**
Using UK standards	**Companies Act individual accounts** – will be prepared by the large majority of UK unlisted companies	**Companies Act group accounts** – will be prepared by the large majority of UK unlisted groups
Using IFRSs	**IAS individual accounts** – are permitted to be prepared by UK unlisted companies, though most will not take up the option.	**IAS group accounts** – must be prepared by UK listed groups. Are permitted to be prepared by UK unlisted groups, though most will not take up the option.

This study text is concerned with Companies Act accounts, not IAS accounts, so is aimed at the preparation of individual accounts and group accounts in accordance with the Companies Acts and UK accounting standards (SSAPs and FRSs). From the above discussion, you can see that this will apply to the great majority of unlisted companies in the UK.

3.5 How the ASB is responding

KEY POINT

The ASB intends to adopt new IFRSs as they are issued or revised.

As a result of these developments, there is a great deal of pressure for UK accounting standards to be brought into line with IFRSs. Because many IFRSs are being revised at the current time, the ASB does not intend to amend all UK standards immediately. Instead it has announced that it intends to adopt new IFRSs as they are issued or revised. This means that there will be a gradual change, rather than a 'big bang' in 2005.

However, during the last few years, IFRSs have become more detailed and prescriptive, with fewer alternatives permitted. This means that UK accounting practice will have to change significantly in some areas in order to be consistent with IFRSs. We shall be looking at one of these areas, deferred tax, later in this text.

In theory the ASB could still issue standards that are different from IFRSs, for example where it has serious reservations about an IFRS or where there is a need to develop guidance to deal with specific UK issues. In practice the ASB is now committed to international convergence and so this is unlikely.

Instead, the UK accounting profession and the ASB intend to work with the IASB and to influence the international standard setting process in several ways.

KEY POINT

The ASB influences the international standard setting process by working with the IASB. It carries out work on certain international projects and comments on IASB exposure drafts.

- The UK is strongly represented on the IASB, indeed the UK's Sir David Treedie is currently Chairman of the IASB. By commenting on IASB exposure drafts the ASB is able to ensure that the views of the UK accounting profession are known and are passed on to the IASB.
- The ASB is one of several national standard setting bodies that work together to develop a common approach to specific financial reporting problems. Most of the ASB's resources are now directed towards carrying out work on certain international projects and influencing, monitoring and commenting on others.

In March 2004 the ASB accepted that in the medium term there is no case for UK accounting standards to differ from international standards. The ASB's role is to manage the convergence process over the next few years.

4 IFRS 1 First-time adoption of International Financial Reporting Standards

4.1 Introduction

From 2005, International Financial Reporting Standards dominate UK financial reporting. EU Regulations require UK listed companies to apply international standards for periods beginning on or after January 2005. These companies and their subsidiaries will therefore be first time adopters that year. Non-quoted companies have the option to adopt IFRSs, but do not have to.

IFRS 1 sets out the procedures for making the transition from national accounting standards to international standards, and applies to all first time adopters for accounting periods beginning on or after 1 January 2005. This means that for companies that have to make the transition, the task should have been started some time ago.

You may think it odd to include an international standard in this book on UK accounting. However, so many large UK companies will be transferring to using IFRSs from 1 January 2005 that the method of transfer is judged to be sufficiently important to be included in this text. The examiner has stated that IFRS 1 is examinable for the

UK version of Paper 2.5, but that it is the only international standard about which knowledge is specifically required.

4.2 Date of transition: comparative figures

When IFRSs are adopted, they must be applied from the first day of the first accounting period concerned, when there has to be an opening IFRS balance sheet.

Because comparative statements must be published, the opening IFRS balance sheet for an entity adopting IFRSs for the year ending 31 December 2005 will be 1 January 2004, which is the first day of the comparative period. Consequently, for many UK listed companies and their subsidiaries, international standards will have to be applied from the beginning of 2004, and applied for the whole period from 1 January 2004.

For a company with a 31 December year end 1 January 2004 is known as the transition date and 31 December 2005 is the first reporting date.

At the transition date all companies adopting IFRS must prepare a balance sheet which complies with IFRS in force at the first reporting date. This opening IFRS balance sheet must comply with international standards.

(a) It must recognise all assets and liabilities required by international standards and must not recognise any assets or liabilities not permitted by the standards.

(b) All assets, liabilities and components of equity must be re-classified and valued in accordance with international standards.

Any gains or losses arising on the adoption of IFRSs should be recognised directly in retained earnings as at the date of the transition.

ACTIVITY 2

A company which intends to report under IFRS has a year end of 31 March. What is its transition date and what is its first reporting date?

Feedback to this activity is at the end of the chapter.

4.3 Standards to be adopted

Accounting policies for first-time adopters must comply with IFRSs in force at the reporting date. This means that for UK listed companies with a year ending 31 December, international standards in force at 31 December 2005 must be applied to the whole period commencing 1 January 2004. A problem for companies in practice will be that further changes in international standards can be expected before 31 December 2005.

4.4 Areas of difference

As we have seen when a company adopts IFRS there may be assets and liabilities which need to recognised or de-recognised or for which the measurement basis will be different under IFRS than previously reported UK GAAP.

Examples might include the following (all of these will be covered in more detail in later chapters):

- FRS 19 *Deferred Tax* permits the discounting of deferred tax assets and liabilities but IAS 12 does not.
- Under FRS 25 *Financial Instruments: Disclosure and Presentation* redeemable preference shares must be reported as liabilities and convertible instruments must be split between their liability element and their equity element in the balance sheet. These are the same requirements as those of IAS 32 however FRS 25 is only for accounting periods beginning on or after 1 January 2005 therefore these figures will have been reported differently prior to this.

4.5 Reconciliations in the year of transition

Entities must explain how the transition to IFRSs affects their reported financial performance, financial position, and cash flows. The two main disclosures required here reconcile reported equity and profits.

The entity's equity (i.e. shareholders' funds) as reported under previous GAAP must be reconciled to the equity reported under IFRS at two dates:

(1) The date of transition. This is the opening balance sheet date. In our example it is 1 January 2004.

(2) The last balance sheet prepared under previous GAAP. In our example this is 31 December 2004.

The last annual profit reported under previous GAAP must be reconciled to the same year's profit prepared under IFRS. In our example this will be the profit for 2004.

Any material differences in the previous GAAP and IFRS cash flow must also be explained. For UK companies the main difference will be in the definition of cash. The IFRS definition includes cash plus items classified as liquid resources under UK GAAP.

When preparing its first IFRS statements, an entity may identify errors made in previous years, or make or reverse impairments of assets. These adjustments must be disclosed separately.

4.6 Exemptions

IFRS 1 grants limited exemptions in situations where the cost of compliance would outweigh the benefits to the user. For example:

- Previous business combinations do not have to be restated in accordance with IFRSs. This relates to classifying combinations as mergers or acquisitions, fair valuing assets and liabilities, and the treatment of goodwill.
- If it is not possible to establish the cost of an asset, then fair value at the date of transition can be used as deemed cost.
- If a subsidiary adopts IFRSs later than its parent, then the subsidiary may value its assets and liabilities either at its own transition date or its parent's transition date (which would normally be easier).

4.7 Summary of IFRS 1

- In the first IFRS financial statements, all IFRSs in force at the reporting date should be applied to the whole period under review.
- The date of transition to IFRS is the opening balance sheet for the comparative period.
- Any gains or losses arising on transition shall be recognised directly in retained earnings at the date of transition.
- The effects of the transition on equity and profits shall be disclosed.
- There are a few limited and specific exemptions where the cost of compliance would exceed the benefits to the users.

ACTIVITY 3

What would be the advantages of international harmonisation of accounting standards for investors and potential investors?

Feedback to this activity is at the end of the chapter.

Conclusion

The regulatory framework of UK accounting is affected by a number of legislative and quasi-legislative influences:

- company law
- accounting standards
- EC Directives.
- The bodies involved in the UK standard setting process are:
- the Financial Reporting Council (FRC)
- the Accounting Standards Board (ASB)
- the Financial Reporting Review Panel (FRRP)
- the Urgent Issues Task Force (UITF).

All EU listed companies must adopt IASs and IFRSs (both types of standards will be called IFRSs from now on) in their consolidated accounts with effect from 1 January 2005. The influence of IFR Ss on UK accounting is becoming so strong that in the medium term there will be no difference between UK standards and IFRSs.

SELF-TEST QUESTIONS

1 What requirement overrides all others in preparing financial statements? (1.3)

2 Name the four bodies that are involved in the UK standard setting process. (2.1)

3 What is the role of the Financial Reporting Review Panel? (2.4)

4 Outline the stages in the development of a Financial Reporting Standard. (2.8)

5 What are the main objectives of the IASB? (3.1)

6 Can UK companies prepare accounts under IFRSs? (3.4)

PRACTICE QUESTIONS

Question 1: Different bodies

Your managing director has approached you saying that he is 'confused at all the different accounting bodies that are involved in the standard setting process'.

Required:

Draft a memorandum to your managing director explaining the purpose, a description of the type of work and, where applicable, examples of the work to date of the following:

(a) Financial Reporting Council **(3 marks)**

(b) Accounting Standards Board **(4 marks)**

(c) Financial Reporting Review Panel **(5 marks)**

(d) Urgent Issues Task Force. **(3 marks)**

(Total: 15 marks)

Question 2: FRRP

The following is an extract from a press note published by the Financial Reporting Review Panel (FRRP):

Findings of the Financial Reporting Review Panel in respect of the accounts of S plc for the year ended 31 March 2001

The Financial Reporting Review Panel has had under consideration the Report and Accounts of S plc for the year ended 31 March 2001 and has discussed them with the company's directors.

The matters raised by the Panel related to aspects of the company's implementation of Financial Reporting Standard (FRS) 15 *Tangible Fixed Assets*, regarded as standard in respect of financial statements relating to accounting periods ending on or after 23 March 2000.

The company's stated accounting policy in respect of properties was not to provide any depreciation on any given property until approximately ten years before the end of its useful life, from which point the depreciable amount was written off over the remainder of the useful life. In respect of plant and equipment, it was the company's policy not to commence depreciation until the accounting year following that in which the assets were acquired. In the Panel's view, neither of these policies complied with the requirements of FRS 15.

As reported in their Report and Accounts for the year ended 31 March 2002, the directors have accepted the Panel's findings. The directors have amended the 2001 comparative figures by way of prior year adjustment.

Required:

(a) Explain the role of the Financial Reporting Review Panel (FRRP). **(8 marks)**

(b) Explain why the FRRP disagreed with S plc's depreciation policies and explain why it makes this disagreement public. **(7 marks)**

(Total: 15 marks)

For the answer to these questions, see the 'Answers' section at the end of the book.

FEEDBACK TO ACTIVITY 1

The Companies Act does not define the term 'true and fair view' and there is no definition in accounting standards. The Statement of Principles does not address the issue.

Accounting requires the use of judgement. For example, opinion might differ on the life of a particular type of machinery depending on the type of business in which it was used. It is difficult to say which of these values is the true and fair one.

Some accounting standards provide guidance on various matters but still leave room for subjectivity and different interpretations. For example, SSAP 9 allows several methods by which the cost of stock may be estimated.

There are still some areas of accounting which are not covered by accounting standards. Large companies entering into unusual and complex transactions may be particularly affected by this problem.

Users of accounts may have different opinions as to what constitutes a true and fair view and may approach the financial statements from different perspectives. This leads to a further question: to whom should the accounts present a true and fair view?

FEEDBACK TO ACTIVITY **2**

Transition date 1 April 2004. This is the first day of the comparative period.

First Reporting date 31 March 2006

FEEBACK TO ACTIVITY **3**

Investors increasingly make investment decisions on a world-wide basis, because businesses increasingly operate across national boundaries. Therefore investors need to compare the financial statements of companies operating in different countries.

At present most non-domestic investments are made by public investment companies and unit trusts which employ analysts skilled in the examination of financial statements from different countries. An individual investor would have difficulty making an informed investment decision with the present differences in international financial reporting.

Chapter 6

GROUP ACCOUNTING – INTRODUCTION

CHAPTER CONTENTS

1 Introduction to consolidated accounts
2 The different methods which could be used to prepare group accounts
3 The requirements of CA85 and FRS 2 regarding groups of companies
4 Exemptions and exclusions
5 The basic balance sheet consolidation
6 Step-by-step procedure for balance sheet consolidation

In this chapter we begin to consider a major area of the syllabus. We will consider what happens when the activities of a business are conducted not through the medium of a single company, but through a number of companies. Although each company remains a separate entity in law, the economic reality is that they form a combined group. A set of accounts showing the combined results and financial position of the whole group is called a set of consolidated accounts. In this chapter we look at the preparation of a consolidated balance sheet; in a later chapter we tackle the consolidated profit and loss account.

Objectives

By the time you have finished this chapter you should be able to:

- describe the concept of a group and the objective of consolidated financial statements
- explain the different methods which could be used to prepare group accounts
- explain and apply the definition of subsidiary companies in CA85 and FRS 2
- describe the circumstances and reasoning for subsidiaries to be excluded from the consolidated financial statements
- prepare a consolidated balance sheet for a simple group
- explain the need for using coterminous year ends and uniform accounting policies when preparing financial statements.

1 Introduction to consolidated accounts

1.1 What is a 'group'?

Although every company is a separate entity from the legal point of view, from the economic point of view several companies may not be separate at all. In particular, when one company owns enough shares in another company to have a majority of votes at that company's annual general meeting, the first company may appoint all the directors of, and decide what dividends should be paid by, the second company. This degree of control enables the first company to manage the trading activities and future plans of the second company as if it were merely a department of the first company.

KEY POINT

The essential feature of a group is that one company controls all the others **absolutely**.

The first company referred to above is called a '**holding company**' or '**parent undertaking**', and the second is called a '**subsidiary**'. These terms are defined in CA85, discussed later. For the moment it is sufficient to note that the essential feature of a group is that one company controls all the others **absolutely**.

Company law recognises that this state of affairs often arises. It requires further items to be included in the accounts of companies related in this way, including those enacted with the intention of enabling a reader of one company's accounts to identify all the other companies in the group. They also include a requirement that the parent undertaking must produce 'group accounts', showing the results of the whole group, in addition to its usual accounts: S227 (1) CA85.

KEY POINT

'**Consolidated accounts**' are those prepared on the assumption that all the transactions of the group have been carried out by a single equivalent company.

1.2 Normal form of group accounts

Group accounts could consist of a variety of things, but in normal circumstances much the best way of showing the results of a group is to imagine that all the transactions of the group had been carried out by a single equivalent company, and to prepare a balance sheet, a profit and loss account, and (if required) a cash flow statement for that company. These accounts are called '**consolidated accounts**'.

There are four current accounting Standards which are relevant to the preparation of consolidated accounts:

- FRS 2 *Accounting for subsidiary undertakings*
- FRS 7 *Fair values in acquisition accounting*
- FRS 9 *Associates and joint ventures*
- FRS 10 *Goodwill and intangible assets.*

A further accounting standard FRS 8 *Related party disclosures* may affect the presentation of group accounts.

KEY POINT

The parent company prepares consolidated accounts for the group from the individual companies' accounts.

1.3 General procedure

Each company in a group prepares its accounting records and annual financial statements in the usual way. From the individual companies' balance sheets, the parent company prepares a consolidated balance sheet for the group, and likewise a consolidated profit and loss account from the individual companies' profit and loss accounts.

2 The different methods which could be used to prepare group accounts

2.1 Meaning of group accounts

CA85 (as amended) and FRS 2 require a parent undertaking to prepare **group** accounts, which must normally be **consolidated** accounts comprising a consolidated balance sheet and a consolidated profit and loss account. The group accounts must give a true and fair view of the companies included in the consolidation as a whole.

KEY POINT

Group accounts are *any* set of data that gives information about the financial affairs of the group. **Consolidated accounts** are thus just one form of group accounts.

The use of the two terms above – **group accounts** and **consolidated accounts** – implies the terms are not the same. Group accounts can be defined as *any* set of data that gives information about the financial affairs of the group. Consolidated accounts are thus just one form of group accounts.

In most circumstances, consolidation presents group accounts in the most informative way. There are circumstances where consolidation may not be appropriate and CA85 and FRS 2 allow/require non-consolidation. These situations are dealt with later in this chapter.

KEY POINT

Group accounts could be presented under the **entity concept**, the **equity method**, the **proprietary concept** or **separate accounts** for the parent and subsidiary companies.

2.2 Consolidated financial statements under the entity concept

This is by far the most common form of group accounts. Consolidated financial statements are prepared by replacing the cost of the investment in the subsidiary company with the individual assets and liabilities underlying that investment. If the subsidiary is only partly owned, this does not affect the amount of assets and liabilities of the subsidiary which are consolidated, but results in the need to show minority shareholders' interest in those net assets.

The **entity concept** focuses on the existence of the group as an **economic** unit, rather than looking at it only through the eyes of the dominant shareholder group. It concentrates on the resources controlled by the entity.

The two forms of consolidation under this concept are **acquisition** accounting and **merger** accounting. In the past, acquisition accounting has been used in nearly every consolidation, while FRS 6 *Acquisitions and mergers* laid down the very rare circumstances when a genuine merger between two companies could be identified so that merger accounting should be used.

Sentiment against the merger method of accounting is now so strong amongst standard–setters that it is now believed that in the real world no genuine mergers exist. Thus all consolidations should be carried out using the acquisition method and no knowledge of the merger method is required for this exam.

2.3 Group accounts and the Statement of Principles

Chapter 8 of the Statement of Principles, *Accounting for interests in other entities,* sets out the generally accepted principles.

- Single entity financial statements and consolidated financial statements present the reporting entity's interests in other entities from different perspectives.
- In **single entity** financial statements, interests in other entities are dealt with by focusing on the income and capital growth arising from the interest (e.g. dividends received and changes in market value).
- In **consolidated financial statements**, the way in which interests in other entities are dealt with depends on the degree of influence involved.
  - An interest in another entity that involves **control** of that other entity's operating and financial policies is dealt with by incorporating the controlled entity as part of the reporting entity (i.e. by consolidation).
  - An interest in another entity that involves **joint control** of, or **significant influence** over, that other entity's operating and financial policies is dealt with by recognising the reporting entity's share of that other entity's results and resources in a way that does not imply that they are controlled by the reporting entity (e.g. by the equity method).
  - Other interests in other entities (simple investments) are dealt with in the same way as any other asset.
- Although consolidated financial statements are the financial statements of the group as a whole, they are prepared from the perspective of the **parent's shareholders**. As a result, they ultimately focus on the parent's ownership interest in its subsidiaries. The effect on benefit flows of any outside equity interest in the subsidiaries (minority interest) is therefore separately identified.
- Consolidated financial statements reflect the whole of the parent's investment in its subsidiaries, including purchased goodwill.
- A business combination is reflected in the consolidated financial statements in accordance with its character. Therefore, a transaction that is in the character of:
  - **an acquisition** is reflected in the consolidated financial statements as if the acquirer purchased the acquiree's assets and liabilities as a bundle of assets and liabilities on the open market
  - **a merger** is reflected in the consolidated financial statements as if a new reporting entity, comprising all the parties to the transaction, had been formed. (However we have seen that, in practice all business combinations are now to be accounted for as acquisitions.)

3 The requirements of CA85 and FRS 2 regarding groups of companies

3.1 Purpose of consolidated accounts

In this section the statutory and professional requirements for the preparation of group accounts are covered.

KEY POINT

CA85 requires group accounts to be in the form of consolidated accounts which give a '**true and fair**' view.

CA85 requires Companies Act group accounts (i.e. those prepared in accordance with UK standards) to be in the form of consolidated accounts which give a '**true and fair**' view.

FRS 2 *Accounting for subsidiary undertakings* states that the purpose of consolidated accounts is to:

> *present financial information about a parent undertaking and its subsidiary undertakings as a single economic entity to show the economic resources controlled by the group, the obligations of the group and the results the group achieves with its resources.*

The first step, however, is to decide what constitutes a group.

3.2 Definition of subsidiary undertaking

CA89 extended the definition of a subsidiary beyond the previous (CA85) definition to implement the **EC Seventh Directive**. FRS 2 assists in interpreting the legal definition.

The definitions of a subsidiary under the original CA85 applied when either:

- more than 50% of the equity shares were held; or
- there was control over the composition of the board of directors.

These definitions caused difficulties, mainly due to the possibilities of creating a dependent company which was not legally a subsidiary and which could then be used for various 'off balance sheet' activities.

CA89 fundamentally changed the definitions and brought more of these dependent companies into the group accounts. It is important to note that the CA89 definitions for accounting purposes refer to a **subsidiary undertaking** rather than a subsidiary company. A subsidiary undertaking may include a partnership or an unincorporated business.

There are five alternative definitions of a **subsidiary** as follows:

1 the parent holds a majority of the rights to vote at general meetings of the undertaking/company on all or substantially all matters

2 the parent is a member and has a right to appoint or remove directors having a majority of the rights to vote at board meetings of the undertaking/company on all or substantially all matters

3 the parent is a member and has the right to control alone a majority of the rights to vote at general meetings of the undertaking/company pursuant to an agreement with other shareholders

4 the parent has a right to exercise a dominant influence over the undertaking by virtue of provisions in the memorandum or articles or by a lawful contract

5 the parent has the power to exercise, or actually exercises, dominant influence or control over the undertaking, or the parent and subsidiary undertaking are managed on a unified basis.

In the definition above, the existence of a dominant influence is only deemed to apply if the parent has a right to give directions on operating or financial policies and the subsidiary directors are obliged to comply with those directions whether or not they are for the benefit of the subsidiary.

KEY POINT

The definition of a subsidiary is based on **control**, not **ownership**. This reflects the commercial substance of the relationship between parent and subsidiary.

The most important thing to notice about the definition of a subsidiary is that it is based on **control**, not **ownership**. This reflects the commercial substance of the relationship between parent and subsidiary.

3.3 Control

The Statement of Principles discusses the idea of control. Similar definitions are used in standards such as FRS 5 *Reporting the substance of transactions*.

KEY POINT

Control implies the ability to deploy economic resources and to benefit from such deployment.

Control has two aspects:

- the ability to deploy the economic resources involved; and
- the ability to benefit (or to suffer) from their deployment.

To have control, an entity must have both these abilities.

An entity will have control of a second entity if it has the ability to direct that entity's operating and financial policies with a view to gaining economic benefit from its activities. Control will be evidenced in a variety of ways depending on its basis (for example ownership or other rights) and the way in which it is exercised (interventionist or not). Control does not necessarily involve share ownership or voting rights.

3.4 Date of acquisition of subsidiary

The date for accounting for an undertaking becoming a subsidiary undertaking is the date on which control passes to its new parent. This ties in with the control concept being the dominant factor in defining a subsidiary.

3.5 UITF Abstract 15 Disclosure of substantial acquisitions

FRS 6 specifies disclosures that must be given in respect of 'substantial acquisitions'. UITF Abstract 15 clarifies the circumstances in which an acquisition should be classified as substantial. The additional disclosures (the summarised profit and loss account and STRGL of the acquired entity up to the acquisition date) are to be given when either:

- the net assets or operating profits of the acquired entity exceed 15% of those of the acquiring entity; or
- the fair value of the consideration given exceeds 15% of the net assets of the acquiring entity.

3.6 The formats of group accounts

KEY POINT

CA89 states that the formats for an individual company apply and are adapted to groups. '**Minority interests**' appears in the consolidated balance sheet and profit and loss accounts.

CA89 states that the formats for an individual company apply and are adapted to groups in Sch 4A CA85. The following amendments are made to the individual company formats (based upon Format 1):

- '**Minority interests**' appears as a major heading in the balance sheet either immediately after 'Accruals and deferred income' or after 'Capital and reserves'.
- '**Minority interests**' in the profit and loss account appears after the line "profit after tax"

FRS 2 confirms the above disclosures in respect of minority interests.

3.7 Consolidation techniques

CA89 introduced various rules on consolidation accounting into the law. FRS 2 confirms the rules or reduces the choice in some instances.

KEY POINT

Uniform accounting policies should be used when preparing the consolidated financial statements.

There are three main areas, as described below.

Accounting policies

Uniform group accounting policies should be used for determining the amounts to be included in the consolidated financial statements. In exceptional cases different policies may be used, with disclosure.

Clearly, if the aggregate figures are to make sense, they should have been derived using common policies.

KEY POINT

All group companies should have the same year-end.

Accounting periods and dates

The accounts of all subsidiaries to be used in preparing consolidated financial statements should have the same financial year-end and be for the same accounting period as those of the parent company, i.e. coterminous year ends. Where the financial year of a subsidiary differs from that of the parent company, interim financial statements for that subsidiary, prepared to the parent company's accounting date, should be used. If this is impracticable, earlier financial statements of the subsidiary undertaking may be used, provided they are prepared for a financial year that ended not more than three months earlier.

KEY POINT

Intra-group transactions should be excluded from the consolidated financial statements.

Intra-group transactions

In the past, there has been a variety of methods adjusting for the effect of **intra-group transactions.** Such transactions may result in profits or losses being included in the book value of assets in the consolidation. The rules will be covered in later chapters.

4 Exemptions and exclusions

4.1 Introduction

CA89 and FRS 2 recognise certain situations in which either:

- a parent is exempted from preparing group accounts; or
- a subsidiary should or may be excluded from consolidation with the rest of the group.

4.2 Exemptions for intermediate holding companies

KEY POINT

An **intermediate holding company** holds a subsidiary but is itself a subsidiary company.

An intermediate holding company is a company which has a subsidiary but is also itself a subsidiary of another company.

For example:

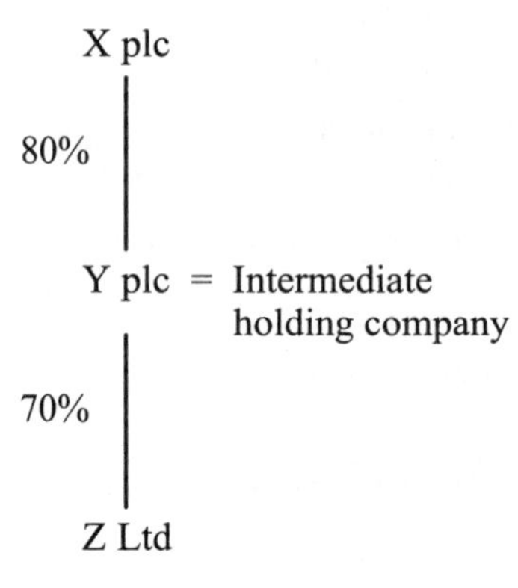

KEY POINT

An intermediate holding company is exempt from the requirement to prepare group accounts under certain conditions.

An intermediate holding company is exempt from the requirement to prepare group accounts if:

- none of its securities is listed anywhere in the European Economic Area (EEA), and
- it is wholly–owned by its parent, or its parent holds more than 50% and notice for the preparation of group accounts has not been served by shareholders owning either more than one half of the remaining shares or 5% of the total shares.

The exemption is conditional on the company and all its subsidiaries being included in a set of consolidated accounts that is either prepared in accordance with the EC Seventh Directive (e.g. as in the CA 1989) or in an equivalent manner. A copy of these consolidated accounts must be filed with the Registrar of Companies together with an English translation, if required.

4.3 Exemptions for small and medium-sized groups

KEY POINT

A parent company need not prepare group accounts if the group is 'small' or 'medium-sized'.

A parent company need not prepare group accounts if the group headed by that parent has less than at least two of the following conditions:

- **annual turnover** – £27.36m gross or £22.8m net
- **balance sheet assets** – £13.68m gross or £11.4m net
- **average employees** – 250.

The '**gross**' figures are those calculated prior to any consolidation adjustments, whereas the '**net**' figures are those after the consolidation adjustments, such as the elimination of intra-group balances, have been made. A company may satisfy the relevant limits on either a net or a gross basis or by a mixture of the two.

The purpose of allowing the calculations to be made using the higher gross figures is to prevent a parent company from having to prepare group accounts in order to discover that it does not need to prepare group accounts.

KEY POINT

The right to exemption from preparing group accounts does not apply to public companies.

The right to the exemption from preparing group accounts does not apply if any company in the group is:

- a **public company**
- an **insurance company**
- a company authorised under the **Financial Services and Markets Act**.

4.4 Excluded subsidiaries

KEY POINT

A subsidiary should only be excluded in **exceptional circumstances**.

Under CA85 there are cases where subsidiary undertakings need not or must not be included in the consolidation. Where all of the subsidiaries fall within the exclusions, group accounts are not required.

FRS 2 is based on the premise that the value of the information provided by the consolidated accounts depends on the extent to which the information about the group is complete, i.e. all undertakings are consolidated. Thus, a subsidiary should only be excluded in **exceptional circumstances**. Where such exceptional circumstances are identified, FRS 2 makes exclusions **mandatory** rather than **optional**.

Materiality

CA85 states that a subsidiary undertaking may be excluded from the consolidation where its inclusion is **not material** for the purpose of giving a true and fair view.

Two or more undertakings may be excluded on these grounds only if they are not material when taken together.

FRS 2 (like any accounting standard) does not deal with immaterial items and therefore does not cover this exclusion.

Severe long-term restrictions

KEY POINT

A subsidiary should be excluded from consolidation where the parent cannot manage it due to **severe long-term restrictions**.

A subsidiary should be excluded from the consolidation where **severe long-term restrictions** substantially hinder the exercise of the rights of the parent company over the assets or management of that undertaking.

Subsidiaries excluded from consolidation are to be treated as **fixed asset investments**. They are to be included at their carrying amount when the restrictions came into force, subject to any write-down for impairment in value, and no further accruals are to be made for profits or losses of those subsidiary undertakings, unless the parent undertaking still exercises significant influence. In the latter case they are to be treated as associates.

Disproportionate expense or undue delay

KEY POINT

FRS 2 states that neither **disproportionate expense** nor **undue delay** can justify excluding a subsidiary.

In CA85 a subsidiary may be excluded from the consolidation where the information necessary for the preparation of group accounts cannot be obtained without disproportionate expense or undue delay. Whether the expense is disproportionate or the delay is undue should be judged in the context of that information to the group accounts.

FRS 2, however, states that neither reason can justify excluding a subsidiary.

Temporary investment

KEY POINT

A subsidiary should be excluded from consolidation where the parent's interest is held **exclusively with a view to subsequent resale**. The investment in subsidiary is shown as a **current asset**.

A subsidiary should be excluded from the consolidation where the interest of the parent company is held exclusively with a view to subsequent resale and the undertaking has not previously been included in consolidated group accounts prepared by the parent company.

The investment in the subsidiary will be shown as a **current asset** at the lower of cost and net realisable value.

Different activities

The original CA85 and FRS 2 permitted subsidiaries that carried on very different activities to their parent, to be excluded from the consolidation, on the grounds that including the subsidiary's different activities would destroy the true and fair view given by the accounts.

Both the CA85 and FRS 2 have now been amended to withdraw this exclusion. It is now recognised that the problem of different activities is better addressed by the provision of segmental analysis of the consolidated figures rather than by excluding the different activities from the consolidation.

Summary

Reason	*CA85*	*FRS 2*	*Treatment*
Immaterial	Optional	Not applicable	-
Severe long-term restrictions	Optional	Mandatory	If restrictions in force at date of acquisition, carry initially at cost. If restrictions came into force at a later date, equity account at date when restrictions came into force. Consider need for provision for impairment in value.
Disproportionate expense or undue delay	Optional	Not permissible	-
Temporary investment	Optional	Mandatory	Current asset at the lower of cost and NRV.

ACTIVITY **1**

Multinational Conglomerate Holdings plc is preparing its group accounts. Which of the following subsidiaries *may be excluded* from consolidation, which *must be excluded*, and which *must be included*? Give a reason in each case.

1 Brighton Pilgrimage Tours Ltd and Portsmouth Happy Holidays Ltd are being sold to another group shortly after the year end. Portsmouth Happy Holidays Ltd has been owned by Multinational Conglomerate Holdings for many years.

Brighton Pilgrimage Tours Ltd was acquired two months before the year end as a small part of the acquisition of another group.

2 MCH (Upriver) Ltd and MCH (Mountains) Ltd are operating in poor countries with bad communications. Both companies have rights over important mineral deposits. If their accounts are to be consolidated, this will delay the preparation of the group accounts. The government of the country where MCH (Mountains) Ltd is operating refuse to allow foreign-owned companies to accept direction from their parents or to pay dividends. Multinational Conglomerate Holdings plc is able to nominate a minority of the directors to the board of MCH (Mountains) Ltd.

Feedback to this activity is at the end of the chapter.

5 The basic balance sheet consolidation

5.1 Worked example

Example

Balance sheets at 31 December 20X4

	P Ltd		*S Ltd*	
	£000	£000	£000	£000
Fixed assets		60		40
Investment in S Ltd at cost		50		
Current assets	40		40	
Less: Current liabilities	20		30	
Net current assets		20		10
		130		50
Ordinary share capital (£1 shares)		100		50
Profit and loss account		30		-
		130		50

P Ltd acquired all the shares in S Ltd on 31 December 20X4 for a cost of £50,000.

You are required to prepare the consolidated balance sheet as at 31 December 20X4.

Approach

The consolidated balance sheet will differ from that of P Ltd's (the parent company's) balance sheet, in that the balance on 'investment in subsidiary account' will be replaced by the underlying net assets which the investment represents.

KEY POINT

The cost of the investment in the subsidiary is effectively cancelled with the ordinary share capital and reserves of the subsidiary.

The cost of the investment in the subsidiary is effectively cancelled with the ordinary share capital and reserves of the subsidiary in calculations known as **consolidation schedules** which are discussed in more detail below. However, in this simple case, it can be seen that the relevant figures are equal and opposite, and therefore cancel directly.

This leaves a balance sheet showing:

- the net assets of the whole group (**P + S**)
- the share capital of the group, which is always solely the share capital of the parent company (**P only**)
- the profit and loss account comprising profits made by the group – in this case we have profits made by the parent company but none made by the subsidiary to bring in to the calculations.

So, by cross casting the net assets of each company, and taking care of the investment in S Ltd and the share capital of S Ltd, we arrive at the consolidated balance sheet given in the solution below.

Solution

P Ltd
Consolidated balance sheet at 31 December 20X4

	£000	£000
Fixed assets £(60 + 40)		100
Current assets £(40 + 40)	80	
Creditors: amounts falling due within one year £(20 + 30)	50	
	—	
Net current assets		30
		—
Total assets less current liabilities		130
		—
Called up share capital (£1 ordinary shares)		100
Profit and loss account		30
		—
		130
		—

Tutorial note: Under no circumstances will any share capital of any subsidiary company ever be included in the figure of share capital on the consolidated balance sheet.

The vertical presentation should be used in the exam, and the headings and format should be in keeping with the requirements of CA85 and accounting standards in so far as the information given allows.

5.2 Goodwill on consolidation

When the investment in the subsidiary costs more or less than the net assets acquired in the subsidiary, there will be a difference between the cost of the investment in the subsidiary and the share capital of the subsidiary.

By modifying the previous example we can tackle this problem.

Balance sheets at 31 December 20X4

	P Ltd		*S Ltd*	
	£000	£000	£000	£000
Fixed assets		60		40
Investment in S Ltd at cost		60		
Current assets	30		40	
Less: Current liabilities	20		30	
Net current assets		10		10
		130		50
Ordinary share capital (£1 shares)		100		50
Profit and loss account		30		-
		130		50

P Ltd acquired all the shares in S Ltd on 31 December 20X4 for a cost of £60,000.

In this case, the cost of the shares in S Ltd exceeds S Ltd's share capital by £10,000. This is the **goodwill on consolidation** or **premium on acquisition**. It represents the excess of the purchase consideration over the fair value of the net assets acquired. The calculation may be set out as a consolidation schedule as follows:

	£000	£000	*Notes*
Cost of investment		60	1
Less: Share of net assets acquired (at fair value)			
Ordinary share capital	50		2
Profit and loss account	-		3
	50		
Group share	× 100%	(50)	4
		10	5

Notes to the calculation

1 The cost of the investment will appear in the balance sheet of P Ltd. If there is more than one investment, details will be given of the cost of individual investments in the question.However for the 2.5 syllabus there will never be more than one subsidiary in a question.

2 We are actually comparing the cost of the investment with the net assets of the subsidiary acquired, as represented by the share capital and reserves of the subsidiary at the date of acquisition.

Remember: **Net assets = Capital + Reserves.**

3 In this case there are no reserves of the subsidiary to consider. However, it is important to note here that the reserves which are taken into consideration in the calculation of goodwill are those at the **date of acquisition** of the subsidiary. Whilst the share capital of the subsidiary is unlikely to have altered since that date, the profit and loss account will have changed.

4 As 100% of the shares in S Ltd were acquired, we compare the cost of the shares with 100% of the net assets of S Ltd. If only a proportion of the shares are acquired, say 90%, we compare the cost of those shares with the appropriate share (90%) of the net assets acquired. This is further illustrated later on in the chapter.

5 The resulting goodwill is dealt with in accordance with FRS 10 *Goodwill and intangible assets*, which requires that purchased goodwill is normally included in

the balance sheet as an intangible asset and amortised (depreciated) over its estimated useful life.

Having first calculated goodwill, the net assets of the parent company and the subsidiary can be cross cast and the consolidated balance sheet completed.

P Ltd
Consolidated balance sheet at 31 December 20X4

	£000	£000
Intangible assets: Goodwill		10
Tangible assets £(60 + 40)		100
Current assets £(30 + 40)	70	
Creditors: amounts falling due within one year £(20 + 30)	50	
	—	
Net current assets		20
		—
Total assets less current liabilities		130
		—
Called up share capital (£1 ordinary shares)		100
Profit and loss account		30
		—
		130
		—

Where the cost of the investment is less than the net assets acquired this is known as **negative goodwill**. It is shown separately on the face of the balance sheet immediately beneath the goodwill heading and written back to the profit and loss account over the periods expected to benefit.

DEFINITION

Goodwill represents the difference between the amount paid to acquire the net assets of a subsidiary and the fair value of those net assets.

Goodwill represents the difference between the amount paid to acquire the net assets of a subsidiary and the fair value of those net assets.

5.3 Reserves

In the examples above, the unrealistic case of a company (S Ltd), where the shareholders' interest consisted solely of ordinary share capital, was considered. Usually, of course, shareholders' interest includes also the profit and loss account reserve. An additional point is that P Ltd may have acquired the controlling interest in S Ltd part way through the year. When looking at the revenue reserves of S Ltd at the year end, a distinction must be made between:

KEY POINT

When considering revenue reserves, a distinction must be made between **pre-** and **post-acquisition reserves.**

- those reserves of S Ltd which existed at the date of acquisition by P Ltd (**pre-acquisition reserves**), and
- the increase in the reserves of S Ltd which arose after acquisition by P Ltd (**post-acquisition reserves**).

When these further complications are included it is advisable to use a standard set of workings in order to prepare the consolidated balance sheet. If you use these workings for all consolidated balance sheet questions they will soon become familiar.

Example

Balance sheets at 31 December 20X4

	P Ltd		*S Ltd*	
	£000	£000	£000	£000
Fixed assets		50		40
Investment in S Ltd at cost		70		-
Current assets	30		40	
Less: Current liabilities	20		10	
		10		30
		130		70
Ordinary share capital (£1 shares)		100		50
Profit and loss account		30		20
		130		70

You are further informed that P Ltd acquired **all** the shares in S Ltd at 30 June 20X4 when the profit and loss account reserves of S Ltd amounted to £15,000. Goodwill is to be amortised over 5 years from the date of acquisition, with a full year's charge in the year of acquisition.

Prepare the consolidated balance sheet at 31 December 20X4.

Solution

(W1) **Establish the group structure**

In this case P Ltd acquired all of the shares of S Ltd therefore P Ltd owns 100% of the shares in S Ltd.

We will need to deal with the goodwill which is effectively computed at the date of takeover. The cost of the investment (£70,000) is compared with the net assets of S Ltd at 30 June 20X4 as represented by ordinary share capital (£50,000) and profit and loss account reserves (£15,000). Note that what we are concerned with are the reserves at the date of acquisition (£15,000) as opposed to reserves at the date of consolidation (£20,000).

Therefore before calculating the goodwill we need a working to determine the net assets of the subsididary at both the date of acquisition and at the balance sheet date.

(W2) **Net assets of Subsidiary**

	At date of acquisition	*At the balance sheet date*
	£	£
Share capital	50,000	50,000
Reserves:		
Profit and loss account	15,000	20,000
	65,000	70,000

The next stage is the calculation of goodwill.

(W3) **Goodwill on acquisition**

	£000	£000
Cost of shares acquired		70
Less: Share of net assets at acquisition (W2)		
£65,000 x 100%		65
		5
Amortisation charge		(1)
NBV of goodwill		4

In addition, a new consolidation schedule, a **consolidated profit and loss account reserve**, is required. The object of this account is to show the accumulated profit of the group at the balance sheet date. Profits made by S Ltd prior to acquisition by P Ltd (pre-acquisition profits) are not regarded as those of the group, whereas profits of S Ltd arising *after* acquisition (post-acquisition profits) *are* regarded as group profits.

Allocate the reserves of S Ltd at the balance sheet date (31 December 20X4) between pre-acquisition and post-acquisition. Pre-acquisition reserves are effectively capitalised, being dealt with in the goodwill consolidation schedule (shown above as (W3)), whereas post-acquisition reserves, together with the present balance on P Ltd reserves, are transferred to consolidated profit and loss account reserves.

(W4) **Group reserves**

	£000
P Ltd: (100%)	30
S Ltd: group share of post-acquisition reserves	
100% x (20 – 15)	5
Less: Goodwill amortised	(1)
	34

The consolidated balance sheet now appears as follows:

P Ltd
Group balance sheet at 31 December 20X4

	£000	£000
Fixed assets:		
Intangible assets: Goodwill (W3)		4
Tangible assets £(50 + 40)		90
Current assets £(30 + 40)	70	
Creditors: amounts falling due within one year £(20 + 10)	30	
		40
Total assets less current liabilities		134
Called up share capital (£1 ordinary shares)		100
Consolidated profit and loss account (W4)		34
		134

5.4 Minority interests

What happens if P Ltd owns only 80% of the ordinary shares of S Ltd? In this case there are said to be minority interests of 20%. What problems does this present?

The main decision to make is whether to consolidate all the net assets of S Ltd, or merely to consolidate the proportion of the net assets represented by the shares held, and the proportion of the reserves which apply to those shares, i.e. consolidate only 80% of the net assets of S Ltd.

The dominant principle is that the directors are preparing accounts of their custody of all the assets under their control, even though there are owners other than the parent company.

Therefore, the generally accepted solution is to consolidate all the subsidiary's net assets and then bring in a **counterbalancing liability** on the consolidated balance sheet to represent that part of the assets which is controlled but not owned.

KEY POINT

A **counterbalancing liability** on the consolidated balance sheet represents the assets which are controlled but not owned. This liability is referred to as '**minority interests**' on the balance sheet.

This liability is presented quite separately in the consolidated balance sheet. It is *not* part of the shareholders' funds. For the purposes of balance sheet presentation, it is referred to as **minority interests** in CA85. It must be shown as a separate main heading on the balance sheet either:

- after **item J** on the Balance sheet format 1 (Accruals and deferred income); or
- after **item K** (Capital and reserves).

Acceptable presentations are therefore as follows:

		£
1	Total assets less current liabilities, say	2,000
	Less: Minority interests	160
		1,840
	Called up share capital	1,500
	Profit and loss account	340
		1,840

		£
2	Total assets less current liabilities	2,000
	Called up share capital	1,500
	Profit and loss account	340
	Minority interests	160
		2,000

The presentation which is *not* allowed is:

	£
Total assets less current liabilities	2,000
Called up share capital	1,500
Minority interests	160
Profit and loss account	340
	2,000

The last presentation implies that minority interests are part of shareholders' funds, which they are not.

Example

Balance sheets at 31 December 20X4

	P Ltd		*S Ltd*	
	£000	£000	£000	£000
Fixed assets		50		40
Investment in S Ltd at cost		70		-
Current assets	30		40	
Less: Current liabilities	20		10	
		10		30
		130		70
Ordinary share capital (£1 shares)		100		50
Profit and loss account		30		20
		130		70

P Ltd acquired 40,000 £1 shares in S Ltd on 30 June 20X4 for £70,000, when the profit and loss account reserves of S Ltd amounted to £15,000. Goodwill is amortised over 6 years from the date of acquisition, with a full year's charge in the year of acquisition.

Prepare the consolidated balance sheet as at 31 December 20X4.

Solution

(W1) **Establish the group structure**

P Ltd owns 40,000 of the £1 shares of S Ltd out of the total share of S Ltd of 50,000. Therefore P Ltd owns 80% (40,000/50,000) of S Ltd.

(W2) **Net assets of subsidiary**

	At date of acquisition	*At the balance sheet date*
	£	£
Share capital	50,000	50,000
Reserves:		
Profit and loss account	15,000	20,000
	65,000	70,000

(W3) **Goodwill on acquisition**

	£
Cost of shares acquired	70
Less share of net assets at acquisition (W2) 80% × £65,000	52
	18
Amortisation (18/6)	(3)
Net book value	15

A consolidation schedule is required to calculate the minority interest in the net assets of the subsidiary.

(W4) **Calculate the minority interest**

	£
Share of net assets at balance sheet date (W2)	
20% x £70,000	14

(W5) **Group reserves**

	£000
P Ltd: (100%)	30
S Ltd: Group share of post-acquisition reserves	
80% x (20 – 15) (W2)	4
Less: Goodwill amortised (W3)	(3)
	31

Note how the reserves of S Ltd are allocated during the consolidation process as follows:

S Reserves
£20,000

20% of reserves at the date of consolidation are allocated to the *minority interest* (20% × 20,000) = £4,000

80% of reserves at the date of consolidation are further divided £16,000

Pre-acquisition reserves, i.e. reserves accumulated at the date of acquisition are included in the *goodwill* calculation (80% × 15,000) = £12,000

Post-acquisition reserves are included in the accumulated profit reserve 80% × (20,000 −15,000) = £4,000

Similarly, the share capital of S Ltd is allocated to the goodwill calculation (the group's share, 80%) and to the minority interest calculation (the minority's share, 20%).

Taking the balances from the consolidation schedules and then adding the other balance sheet items together, the consolidated balance sheet can be constructed as follows:

P Ltd
Consolidated balance sheet at 31 December 20X4

	£000	£000
Fixed assets		
Intangible assets: Goodwill (W3)		15
Tangible assets £(50 + 40)		90
Current assets £(30 + 40)	70	
Creditors: amounts falling due within one year £(20 + 10)	30	
		40
Total assets less current liabilities		145

Called up share capital (£1 ordinary shares)	100
Profit and loss account (W5)	31
Minority interests (W4)	14
	145

This last example includes all the three basic elements of a balance sheet consolidation:

- reserves in subsidiary company
- acquisition of less than 100% of S Ltd's shares
- acquisition earlier than balance sheet date.

Try reworking the example now to make sure you are completely clear on all these points.

6 Step-by-step procedure for balance sheet consolidation

KEY POINT

The routine steps for balance sheet consolidation are:

- shareholdings analysis
- goodwill consolidation schedule
- reserves consolidation schedule
- minority interest consolidation schedule
- consolidated balance sheet preparation.

You should memorise the following step-by-step procedure.

1 Establish the group structure

	%
Group	A
Minority	B
	100

2 Net assets of subsidiary

	At date of acquisition	*At the balance sheet date*
	£	£
Share capital	X	X
Reserves:		
Profit and loss account	X	X
	X	X

3 Goodwill on acquisition

	£
Cost of shares acquires	X
Less share of net assets at acquisition (W2)	X
	X
Less: Amortisation	(X)
Net book value	X

4 Minority interest consolidation schedule

Minority interest	£
Share of net assets at the balance sheet date (W2)	X

5 *GroupReserves*

	£
P Ltd ((100%)	X
S Ltd – group share of post-acquisition reserves	X
Less: Goodwill amortised (from step 3)	(X)
	X

6 *Prepare the consolidated balance sheet*

The consolidated balance sheet comprises:

- balances on consolidation schedules (steps 3 to 5 above); *plus*
- items in original balance sheets not transferred to consolidation schedules.

ACTIVITY 2

The summarised draft balance sheets of a group at 31 December 20X4 were as follows:

	P Ltd	*S Ltd*		*P Ltd*	*S Ltd*
	£	£		£	£
Sundry assets	106,000	34,500	Share capital (£1 ord.)	100,000	20,000
Investment in S Ltd			Profit and loss account	22,000	6,500
(shares at cost)	27,000	-	Creditors	11,000	8,000
	133,000	34,500		133,000	34,500

Prepare the consolidated balance sheet for each of the following alternatives.

1 P Ltd acquired all the shares in S Ltd on 1 January 20X4, when S Ltd had profit and loss account reserves of £6,000.

2 Facts as in 1 above, except that only 16,000 ordinary shares in S Ltd were purchased for £27,000.

Goodwill is amortised over 10 years from the date of acquisition.

Feedback to this activity is at the end of the chapter.

Conclusion

When the activities of a business are conducted through a number of different companies, it is normal to prepare group accounts *in addition to* the individual accounts prepared by each company.

The usual form of group accounts is 'consolidated accounts'. Under this method, the activities of all the group companies are represented as being, in effect, those of a single entity (the group).

CA85 and FRS 2 state that an undertaking is a subsidiary of a parent when that parent controls its operating and financial policies. Control normally results from a majority shareholding, but can arise in other ways.

The basic procedure for preparing a consolidated balance sheet is to add together the assets and liabilities shown in the accounts of each individual company. However, adjustments are necessary to deal with:

- goodwill on acquisition
- minority interests.

SELF-TEST QUESTIONS

1 What form do group accounts normally take? (2.1)

2 According to the Statement of Principles, what determines the way in which interests in other entities are dealt with in the financial statements? (2.3)

3 What is the definition of a subsidiary undertaking? (3.2)

4 What are the size criteria for 'small' and 'medium-sized' groups? (4.3)

5 State the four circumstances in which subsidiaries may be excluded from consolidation under the Companies Act 1985. (4.4)

6 When a subsidiary is a temporary investment, how should it be shown in the consolidated accounts? (4.4)

7 What is represented by the excess of the price paid over the fair value of the identifiable net assets acquired? (5.2)

8 Why must a distinction be drawn between a subsidiary's pre-acquisition and post-acquisition reserves? (5.3)

PRACTICE QUESTION

Subsidiary company

CA85, before amendment by CA89, defined a subsidiary company as follows: 'S Ltd is a subsidiary of H Ltd if:

1 H Ltd is a member of S Ltd (or a subsidiary of H Ltd is a member of S Ltd) and H Ltd controls the composition of the board of directors of S Ltd, or

2 H Ltd holds more than half the equity share capital (by nominal value), or

3 S Ltd is a subsidiary of a subsidiary of H Ltd.

The equity share capital is that capital which has more than a fixed interest in distributions (by dividend or on winding up).'

Required:

(a) Define a subsidiary company for the purposes of preparing group accounts under CA89.

(b) State what you consider to be the faults in the old CA85 definition. **(10 marks)**

For the answer to this question, see the 'Answers' section at the end of the book.

FEEDBACK TO ACTIVITY 1

1 Brighton Pilgrimage Tours Ltd must be excluded from consolidation because it is a subsidiary held for subsequent resale.

Portsmouth Happy Holidays Ltd is not a subsidiary held exclusively for subsequent resale, since it has been owned for many years, and so it must be included in the consolidated accounts.

2 The accounts of MCH (Upriver) Ltd are material, because of the mineral deposits. Although the Companies Act 1985 could allow this company to be left out of the group accounts because of undue delay, FRS 2 rules that for a material subsidiary, no delay could be undue, and the subsidiary must be included.

MCH (Mountains) Ltd is operating in a country where the parent company's rights are restricted. On the facts given, these probably amount to severe long-term restrictions. Therefore, according to FRS 2, this subsidiary must not be included in the consolidated accounts.

FEEDBACK TO ACTIVITY 2

Note: Your balance sheets should be prepared in vertical format. The examiner will occasionally give you 'draft' horizontal balance sheets as in the question, but your solution should always accord with best practice.

1 Establish group structure

	%
Group	100
Minority	-
	100

2 Net assets of subsidiary

	At date of acquisition	*At the balance sheet date*
	£	£
Share capital	20,000	20,000
Profit and loss account	6,000	6,500
	26,000	26,500

3 Goodwill on acquisition

	£
Cost of shares acquired	27,000
Less: share of net assets at date of acquisition (W2) 100% x 26,000	26,000
Goodwill	1,000
Amortisation charge	(100)
	900

4 Minority interest

There is no minority interest at the balance sheet date as P Ltd owns 100% of the shares of S Ltd

5 Group reserves

	£
P Ltd (100%)	22,000
S Ltd – group share of post-acquisition reserves 100% (6,500 – 6,000)	500
Less: Goodwill amortised	(100)
	22,400

P Ltd Group
Consolidated balance sheet at 31 December 20X4

	£
Goodwill (W3)	900
Sundry assets	140,500
Creditors	(19,000)
Total assets less current liabilities	122,400
Called up share capital	100,000
Profit and loss account (W5)	22,400
	122,400

1 Establish group structure

	%
Group	80
Minority	20
	100

2 Net assets of subsidiary

	At date of acquisition	*At the balance sheet date*
	£	£
Share capital	20,000	20,000
Profit and loss account	6,000	6,500
	26,000	26,500

3 Goodwill on acquisition

	£
Cost of shares acquired	27,000
Less: share of net assets at date of acquisition (W2) 80% x 26,000	20,000
Goodwill	6,200
Amortisation charge	(620)
	5,580

4 Minority interest

	£
Share of net assets at balance sheet date 20% × £26,500 (W2)	5,300

5 Group reserves

	£
P Ltd (100%)	22,000
S Ltd – group share of post-acquisition reserves 80 × (6,500 – 6,000)	400
Less: Goodwill amortised	(620)
	21,780

P Ltd Group
Consolidated balance sheet at 31 December 20X4

	£
Goodwill (W3)	5,580
Sundry assets	140,500
Creditors	(19,000)
Total assets less current liabilities	127,080
Called up share capital	100,000
Profit and loss account (W5)	21,780
Minority interest (W4)	5,300
	127,080

Chapter 7

GROUP ACCOUNTING – INTRA-GROUP ADJUSTMENTS

CHAPTER CONTENTS

1 Inter-company items

2 Preference shares and debentures in subsidiaries

3 Dividends and debenture interest of subsidiaries

This chapter covers the treatment of intra-group items. Individual group companies may trade with one another, but because a group is a single economic entity, the effects of these transactions must be eliminated on consolidation, so that the financial statements only include the effects of transactions with third parties. A group cannot trade with itself.

Objectives

By the time you have finished this chapter you should be able to:

- explain why intra-group transactions should be eliminated on consolidation
- account for the effects of intra-group trading and other transactions including:
- unrealised profits in stock and fixed assets
- intra-group loans and interest, and other intra-group charges
- intra-group dividends.

1 Inter-company items

1.1 Introduction

The individual balance sheets of the parent company and subsidiary companies are likely to include inter-company items, i.e. amounts owing between the group companies. These inter-company items must be eliminated when the consolidated balance sheet is prepared, in order to show the proper position of the economic unit, the group.

1.2 Current accounts

KEY POINT

Items in transit may cause current accounts not to agree. Adjusting entries are then required.

At the year end, current accounts may not agree, owing to the existence of **in-transit items** such as goods or cash. The usual rules are as follows:

- If the goods or cash are in transit between the parent company and the subsidiary, make the adjusting entry to the balance sheet of the parent company, irrespective of the direction of transfer, i.e.

  Dr: Cash in transit
  Cr: Current account with subsidiary

KEY POINT

Adjust the books of the **recipient**, unless the goods are in transit between the parent company and subsidiary, when the adjusting entry should be made to the **parent's balance sheet**.

Note: This is for the purpose of consolidation only.

- Once in agreement, the current accounts may be contra'd and cancelled as part of the process of cross casting the upper half of the balance sheet. This can be achieved, along with any other adjustments, as a working paper which would show:
  1 the upper half of the balance sheets of each company
  2 all adjustments to these figures along with cancelled inter-company items
  3 the final figures which will appear in the upper half of the consolidated balance sheet, resulting from the cross casting of items in 1 and 2 above.

EXAM HINT

It is useful to use the balance sheets given in the exam to form the working paper.

However, as this working paper would take time to generate in an exam, it is useful to use the balance sheets given in the exam paper itself to form this working paper.

Example

Balance sheets at 31 December 20X4

	P Ltd	*S Ltd*
	£	£
Investment in S Ltd (at cost)	19,000	
S Ltd current account	10,000	
P Ltd current account		(9,000)
Cash at bank	10,000	23,000
Sundry net assets	41,000	16,000
	80,000	30,000
Share capital (£1 ord.)	50,000	10,000
Profit and loss account	30,000	20,000
	80,000	30,000

P Ltd bought 7,500 shares in S Ltd on 1 January 20X4 when the balance on the profit and loss account reserve of S Ltd was £12,000. The current account difference has arisen as a cheque sent by S Ltd to P Ltd on 30 December 20X4 was not received by P Ltd until 3 January 20X5.

Goodwill is amortised over five years from the date of acquisition, with a full year's charge in the year of acquisition.

Prepare the consolidated balance sheet at 31 December 20X4.

Solution

An adjustment for cash in transit has to be made before the consolidation can be completed. An extra step is therefore required in the consolidation procedure; it is a good idea to make this sort of adjustment early on so that it is not forgotten.

Step 1: Shareholdings in S Ltd

	%
Group	75
Minority	25
	100

Step 2: Adjustments

Cash in transit:		
Dr: Cash in transit	£1,000	
Cr: S Ltd current account		
(P's balance sheet)		£1,000

Cancel the current accounts which are now in agreement. (**Note:** At this stage the top half of the consolidated balance sheet can nearly all be completed – **a useful tip for the exam room when time is of the essence.**)

		P Ltd	*S Ltd*	*Group*
		£	£	£
Investment in S Ltd (at cost)		19,000		
S Ltd current account		~~10,000~~		
P Ltd current account			~~9,000~~	
Cash at bank		10,000	23,000	**33,000**
Cash in transit	**1,000**	–		**1,000**
Sundry net assets		41,000	16,000	**57,000**
		80,000	30,000	

Step 3: Net assets of subsidiary

	At date of acquisition	*At the balance sheet date*
	£	£
Share capital	10,000	10,000
Profit and loss account	12,000	20,000
	22,000	30,000

Step 4: Goodwill

	£	£
Cost of shares acquired		19,000
Less share of net assets at acquisition 75% × £22,000 (W3)		16,500
Goodwill		2,500
Amortisation charge		(500)
		2,000

Step 5: Minority interest

	£
Share of net assets at balance sheet date (W3) 25% × £26,000	6,500

Step 6: Group Reserves

	£
P Ltd (100%)	30,000
S Ltd - group share of post-acquisition reserves 75% (20,000 – 12,000)	6,000
Less: Goodwill amortised	(500)
	35,500

Step 7:

P Ltd
Consolidated balance sheet at 31 December 20X4

	£
Goodwill (W4)	2,000
Cash at bank (10,000 + 23,000)	33,000
Cash in transit (W3)	1,000
Sundry net assets	57,000
	93,000
Called up share capital	50,000
Profit and loss account (W6)	35,500
Minority interest (W5)	7,500
	93,000

KEY POINT

Disagreements between the current accounts of a group require adjustment before consolidation.

When current accounts between members of a group disagree as a result of cash in transit, the balance sheets show the correct position from each individual company's point of view, but adjustment is required before the consolidation can be performed. The two current accounts will then cancel as the balance sheets are cross cast.

1.3 Profits

KEY POINT

Profit loading on closing stock can be **unrealised** from a group viewpoint.

Where goods have been sold by one group company to another at a profit and some of these goods are still in the purchaser's stock at the year end, then the profit loading on these goods is **unrealised** from the viewpoint of the group as a whole. This is because we are treating the group as if it is a single entity. No one can make a profit by trading with himself. Until the goods are sold to an outside party there is no realised profit from the group perspective.

Wholly-owned subsidiary

KEY POINT

For trade with a wholly-owned subsidiary, adjust for unrealised profit either as a **double entry** or by **adjusting the parent's balance sheet**.

Where goods are sold by S Ltd (a wholly-owned subsidiary) to P Ltd (its parent company), or by P Ltd to S Ltd, and some of the goods are in stock at the year end, there are two steps:

- calculate the **unrealised profit** in closing stock
- make the consolidation adjustment for the unrealised profit, either as a **double entry** prior to drawing up the consolidated balance sheet:

  Dr: Consolidated profit and loss account reserve
  Cr: Consolidated stock

  or by making the **adjustment to P Ltd's balance sheet** in the consolidation working papers, as was done with cash in transit:

  Dr: Profit and loss account reserve
  Cr: Stock
  (in P Ltd's balance sheet).

Either method reduces stock to cost and removes unrealised profit from the group reserves. The second option is the most efficient in an exam as it is less likely to be forgotten.

Partly-owned subsidiary

Suppose P Ltd owns 90% of S Ltd. During the year S Ltd sells goods to P Ltd at cost plus 25%. At the year end the closing stock of P Ltd includes £8,000 of goods, at invoice value, acquired originally from S Ltd. What adjustments are required in the consolidation working papers?

In the past this was an area in which opinions differed. CA89 requires intra-group profits to be eliminated, but where a subsidiary is partly owned, it allows the elimination to be either of the whole of the profit or in proportion to the group's shareholding in the subsidiary.

KEY POINT

FRS 2 requires that profit or losses on any intra-group transactions should be eliminated from consolidated accounts.

FRS 2 removes the choice as to who should suffer the deduction of intra-group profit. Profit or losses on any intra-group transactions should be **eliminated in full**. The elimination should be set against the interests held by the group and the minority interest in proportion to their holdings in the undertaking whose individual financial statements recorded the eliminated profits or losses.

Thus, sales from the parent company to the subsidiary produce profits in the parent. Any unrealised profits should be charged against the group. Sales from the subsidiary to the parent company produce profits in the subsidiary company. The unrealised profits should be split between the group and the minority.

Returning to the example, the *total* unrealised profit is:

$$\frac{25}{125} \times £8{,}000 = £1{,}600$$

Note: The denominator in the fraction. The £8,000 is at *selling* price to S Ltd, i.e. 100 + 25.

Consolidated stock must be reduced (credited) by £1,600; the minority interest will be reduced by its share of this (10% × 1,600), £160, and the remaining 90%, £1,440, will be borne by the group as a reduction in group reserves.

This may be achieved by means of a consolidation adjustment put through prior to drawing up the balance sheet.

	£	£
Dr: Consolidated revenue reserves		
90% × 1,600	1,440	
Dr: Minority interests		
10% × 1,600	160	
Cr: Consolidated stock		1,600

If P Ltd had sold the goods to S Ltd the journal entry required would be the same as that in 'Wholly-owned subsidiary' above.

KEY POINT

Profits on intra-group transactions are **unrealised** from a group viewpoint.

Profits made by members of a group on transactions with other group members are quite properly recognised in the accounts of the individual companies concerned. But in terms of the group as a whole, such profits are **unrealised** and must be eliminated from the consolidated accounts as a consolidation adjustment.

Example

Balance sheets at 31 December 20X4

	P Ltd	*S Ltd*
	£	£
Investment in S Ltd (at cost)	75,000	
Stock	12,000	5,000
Other net assets	83,000	95,000
	170,000	100,000
Share capital (£1 ord.)	50,000	40,000
Profit and loss account	120,000	60,000
	170,000	100,000

P Ltd acquired 32,000 shares in S Ltd on 1 January 20X4 when the balance on the profit and loss account of S Ltd was £50,000. During the year, S Ltd sold goods to P Ltd for £80,000 making a standard mark up of 25%. At 31 December 20X4, P Ltd included £5,000 in its stock value as the price paid for goods purchased from S Ltd.

Goodwill is amortised over 3 years from the date of acquisition, with a full year's charge in the year of acquisition.

Prepare the consolidated balance sheet at 31 December 20X4.

Solution

Step 1: Shareholdings in S Ltd

	%
Group	80
Minority	20
	100

Step 2: Adjustments

Unrealised profit on stock:

$$5{,}000 \times \frac{25}{125} = £1{,}000$$

S Ltd sold the goods and made the profit, therefore we shall make a consolidation adjustment to the balance sheet of S, so that both the group and the minority will bear their share of the provision for unrealised profit.

	P Ltd	*S Ltd*		*Group*
	£	£		£
Investment in S Ltd (at cost)	75,000			
Stock	12,000	5,000	**– 1,000**	**16,000**
Other net assets	83,000	95,000		**178,000**
	170,000	~~100,000~~	**99,000**	
Share capital (£1 ord.)	50,000	40,000		
Profit and loss account	120,000	60,000	**– 1,000**	
	170,000	~~100,000~~	**99,000**	

Step 3: Net assets of subsidiary

	At date of acquisition	*At the balance sheet date*
	£	£
Share capital	40,000	40,000
Profit and loss account	50,000	60,000
	90,000	100,000

Step 4: Goodwill

	£	£
Cost of shares acquired		75,000
Less share of net assets at acquisition date 80% x £90,000		72,000
Goodwill		3,000
Amortisation charge		(1,000)
		2,000

Note: This calculation is unaffected by the provision for unrealised profit as the net assets of S Ltd at the date of acquisition are sold.

Step 5: Group reserves

	£
P Ltd (100%)	120,000
S Ltd: 80% [(60,000 – 1,000)* – 50,000]	7,200
Less: Goodwill amortised (W4)	(1,000)
	126,200

Step 6: Minority interest

Share of net assets at balance sheet date	
20% × £100,000 (W3)	20,000
Less unrealised profit in stock (W2)	
20% × 1,000	(200)
	19,800

* the revised reserves figure, as reduced by the provision for unrealised profit.

Step 7:

P Ltd
Consolidated balance sheet at 31 December 20X4

	£
Goodwill (W4)	2,000
Stock (12 + 5 – 1) (W2)	16,000
Other net assets (83 + 95)	178,000
	196,000
Called up share capital	50,000
Profit and loss account (W5)	126,200
Minority interest (W6)	19,800
	196,000

Statement of accounting policies – Stock

Provision has been made for the whole of the unrealised profit on stock.

ACTIVITY 1

Parent plc owns all the shares in Subsidiary Ltd. At the year end, Parent plc has in stock goods purchased from Subsidiary Ltd for £6,000. These goods have cost Subsidiary Ltd £4,500 to manufacture. A further £2,000 worth of goods at invoice price (£1,500 at cost to Subsidiary Ltd) were sent by Subsidiary Ltd to Parent plc just before the year end, but have not yet reached Parent plc. The total value of stocks in the books of Parent plc and Subsidiary Ltd are:

	£
Parent plc	30,800
Subsidiary Ltd	24,600

Calculate the value of stocks for the group balance sheet.

Feedback on this activity is at the end of the chapter.

1.4 Transfers of fixed assets within the group

KEY POINT

Transfers of fixed assets within the group require adjustments to be made to recreate the situation prior to the sale.

One group member may sell fixed assets to another group member. The problems involved are similar to those considered above. Adjustments must be made to recreate the situation that would have existed if the sale had not occurred:

- there would have been no profit on the sale
- depreciation would have been based on the original cost of the asset to the group.

Example

At the beginning of the year, S Ltd (60% owned by P Ltd) sells goods costing £20,000 to P Ltd. P Ltd pays £25,000 for the goods and uses them as fixed assets, depreciating over five years with a nil scrap value at the end of the period using the straight line basis.

Solution

There are two points here:

1 There is an unrealised profit of £5,000 in the transfer price of the fixed asset.

2 During the first year in which the fixed asset is used, P Ltd is incurring a depreciation charge of 20% of £25,000 or £5,000. Had the goods been transferred at cost, the depreciation charge would have been only £4,000. This, of course, works in the opposite direction to 1 from the group's viewpoint.

Step 1: Calculate the cost and accumulated depreciation on the transferred asset as it stands in the balance sheet.

	Per balance sheet £
Cost	25,000
Accumulated depreciation	5,000
NBV	20,000

Step 2: Compare these figures with how the fixed asset would appear had there been no transfer (i.e. how the asset should appear).

	Per balance sheet	*Should be*
	£	£
Cost	25,000	20,000
Accumulated depreciation	5,000	4,000
	20,000	16,000

Step 3: Calculate the adjustments required.

	Per balance sheet	*Should be*	*Adjustment*
	£	£	£
Cost	25,000	20,000	5,000 (1)
Unrealised profit			
Accumulated depreciation	5,000	4,000	1,000 (2)
Depreciation overcharge			
NBV	20,000	16,000	

Step 4: Deal with the adjustments.

1 Unrealised profit on transfer. A provision for unrealised profit will be made, which reduces the cost of the fixed asset from its transfer value to the original cost to the group. The debit will either be wholly to consolidated reserves or shared between the group and minority interest depending upon where the original profit was recorded. In this case:

	£	£
Dr: Consolidated profit and loss account (60% × 5,000)	3,000	
Dr: Minority interest (40% × 5,000)	2,000	
Cr: Fixed asset cost (provision for unrealised profit)		5,000

2 Each year the provision for unrealised profit will be reduced by £1,000 to adjust for the excess depreciation charged. The consolidated reserves, and minority interest when appropriate, will be credited. After five years, at the end of the useful life of the asset, the provision for unrealised profit will be fully written back. In this particular case, the depreciation is charged in P Ltd, and therefore the profit adjustment is wholly attributable to the group:

	£	£
Dr: Provision for depreciation (provision for unrealised profit)	1,000	
Cr: Consolidated profit and loss account		1,000

Again, these adjustments can be carried out using the balance sheets given in the question as working papers, if preferred. The double entries would be:

	£	£
1 Dr: Profit and loss account	5,000	
Cr: Fixed asset cost		5,000

In the balance sheet of the company which made the profit on transfer (S Ltd in this case).

	£	£
2 Dr: Provision for depreciation	1,000	
Cr: Profit and loss account		1,000

In the balance sheet of the company which is depreciating the asset.

These adjusted figures would then be picked up for the calculation of group reserves and minority interest and would give the same overall effect.

Step 5: The fixed assets section of the balance sheet will show:

	Cost	*Depn*	*NBV*
	£	£	£
Fixed assets:			
Plant (25,000 – 5,000)	20,000		
(5,000 – 1,000)		4,000	16,000

2 Preference shares and debentures in subsidiaries

2.1 Preference shares in a subsidiary company

KEY POINT

As **preference shareholders** are generally only entitled to repayment of their share capital but **ordinary shareholders** are entitled to their share of any profits in addition, this affects the consolidation schedules.

As a *general* rule, **preference shares** held by one company in another are irrelevant in determining whether the parent company/subsidiary company relationship exists.

The treatment of holdings in preference shares reflects the entitlement of preference shareholders to participate in profits on the winding up of a company. Generally, preference shareholders are only entitled to repayment of their share capital, whereas ordinary shareholders are entitled to their share capital *plus* their share of any profits. This affects the calculations and the consolidation schedules as detailed below.

Shareholdings in S Ltd

	Ordinary shares	*Preference shares*
	%	%
Group	A	C
Minority	B	D
	100	100

The % holdings of each type of share is calculated.

Goodwill on consolidation

	£	£
Cost of investment (ordinary + preference shares)		X
Less share of net assets acquired		
A% × (ordinary shares + profit and loss) at date of acquisition		(X)
Preference share capital	X	
Group share	× C%	
		(X)
		X

KEY POINT

The group shareholding percentage in ordinary shares is applied to ordinary share capital and reserves. The group shareholding percentage in preference shares is applied to the preference share capital.

The group shareholding percentage in ordinary shares is applied to the ordinary share capital and reserves, whilst the group shareholding percentage in preference shares is applied just to the preference share capital.

Reserves

The calculation is performed as usual, taking the ordinary shareholding percentage (A%) of the subsidiary's post-acquisition profits.

Minority interest

	£	£
Net assets of S Ltd attributable to ordinary shareholdings:		
Ordinary share capital	X	
Profit and loss account	X	
	X	
Minority share	× B%	
		X
Attributable to preference shareholdings:		
Preference share capital	X	
Minority share	× D%	
		X
		X

Again, share capital and reserves are split between those attributable to ordinary shareholdings and reserves and those attributable to preference shareholdings. The minority interest in each is then found separately.

Example

The draft balance sheet of S Ltd at 31 January 20X5 is as follows:

	£		£
Net assets	180,000	Ordinary share capital	100,000
		Profit and loss account	30,000
		Preference share capital	50,000
	180,000		180,000

At 31 January 20X5 P Ltd has reserves of £150,000 on the profit and loss account. P Ltd acquired 70% of the ordinary share capital of S Ltd at a cost of £90,000 when the reserves of S Ltd amounted to £10,000, and 40% of the preference share capital at a cost of £22,000 when the reserves of S Ltd amounted to £15,000. Goodwill has been fully amortised.

Show the consolidation schedules and shareholdings in S Ltd workings.

Solution

Shareholdings in S Ltd

	Ordinary shares	*Preference shares*
	%	%
Group	70	40
Minority	30	60
	100	100

Goodwill

	£	£
Cost of investment (90,000 + 22,000)		112,000
Less: Share of net assets of S Ltd at the acquisition date		
Ordinary share capital	100,000	
Profit and loss account	10,000	
	110,000	
Group share	× 70%	
		(77,000)
Preference share capital	50,000	
Group share	× 40%	
		(20,000)
Goodwill – fully amortised		15,000

Reserves

		£
P:		150,000
S:	70% (30,000 – 10,000)	14,000
Less:	Goodwill amortised	(15,000)
		149,000

Minority interest

	£	£
Net assets of S Ltd		
Attributable to ordinary shareholdings:		
Ordinary share capital	100,000	
Profit and loss account	30,000	
	130,000	
Minority share	× 30%	
		39,000
Attributable to preference shareholdings:		
Preference share capital	50,000	
Minority share	× 60%	
		30,000
		69,000

Tutorial notes

- The revenue reserves of S Ltd at the date of P Ltd's purchase of the preference shares are irrelevant.
- What would happen if P Ltd owned 70% of the ordinary share capital of S Ltd, but none of the preference share capital? In this case, all the nominal value of the preference capital would be dealt with in the minority interests account. Hence, it is quite possible to have the apparent contradiction of crediting the minority interests account with the majority of preference share capital.

2.2 Debentures in a subsidiary company

Debentures are also irrelevant for the purpose of determining the parent company/subsidiary relationship.

Procedure

KEY POINT

The nominal value of **debentures** held by the parent company is cancelled with that same value of debentures of the subsidiary.

- The nominal value of debentures held by the parent company is cancelled with that same value of debentures of the subsidiary when the balance sheets are cross cast. This leaves the debentures of the subsidiary, held by outsiders, in the balance sheet.
- Preference shares of the subsidiary company *not* held by the parent company are included in the minority interest on the consolidated balance sheet. Debentures held by outsiders are shown separately on the consolidated balance sheet – they are *not* part of the minority interest.

ACTIVITY **2**

Maximus Ltd acquired 90,000 £1 ordinary shares, 50,000 £1 preference shares and £10,000 debentures in Minimus Ltd on 30 June 20X1.

The balances in the books of Maximus Ltd and Minimus Ltd as at 31 December 20X4 were as follows:

	Maximus Ltd	*Minimus Ltd*
	£	£
Fixed assets, at cost	450,000	280,000
90,000 ordinary shares in Minimus Ltd, at cost	185,000	-
50,000 preference shares in Minimus Ltd, at cost	55,000	-
£10,000 debentures in Minimus Ltd	10,000	-
Current assets	200,000	143,500
	900,000	423,500
Ordinary shares of £1	500,000	120,000
8% non-cumulative preference shares of £1	-	80,000
7% debentures	-	40,000
Capital reserve	50,000	30,000
Profit and loss account	150,000	66,000
Provision for depreciation	70,000	55,000
Creditors	130,000	32,500
	900,000	423,500

You are also given the following information:

- The capital reserve and profit and loss account reserve of Minimus Ltd as at 30 June 20X1 were £12,000 and £30,500 respectively.
- The stock of Minimus Ltd at 31 December 20X4 includes £22,800 in respect of goods purchased from Maximus Ltd. Maximus invoices Minimus at cost plus 20%.
- Goodwill is amortised over five years from the date of acquisition with a full year's charge in the year of acquisition.

You are required to prepare the consolidated balance sheet of Maximus Ltd and its subsidiary Minimus Ltd as at 31 December 20X4. Workings should be shown.

Feedback to this activity is at the end of the chapter.

3 Dividends and debenture interest of subsidiaries

3.1 Introduction

In dealing with consolidations which involve one group company paying a dividend or interest instalment to another group company, it is easy to get confused, especially if the information given includes one or more dividends incorrectly or incompletely treated. We need to determine, for each dividend or interest instalment:

- what entries should have been made by each company involved
- what entries have actually been made
- the entries to correct or complete the treatment

and then continue with the consolidation.

3.2 Dividends – the correct treatment

If the dividend is paid by the year end:

Paying company:
Dr: Profit and loss account ('Dividend paid')
Cr: Cash

Receiving company:
Dr: Cash
Cr: Profit and loss account ('Dividend received')

On consolidating the balance sheet, no adjustment will be required.

If the dividend is declared but not paid at the year end:

Paying company:
Dr: Profit and loss account ('Dividend payable/proposed')
Cr: Proposed dividend/Declared dividend (a creditor)

Receiving company:
Dr: Dividend receivable (a debtor)
Cr: Profit and loss account ('Dividend receivable')

KEY POINT

On consolidating the balance sheet, a cancellation must be made between the current asset, 'dividend receivable' and the 'proposed dividend'.

On consolidating the balance sheet, a cancellation must be made between the current asset, 'dividend receivable' as shown in the receiving company's books and the 'proposed dividend' shown in the paying company's books. If only part of the dividend is payable to the other group company, then that part payable to outsiders must be shown as a current liability in the consolidated balance sheet with the heading 'dividend payable to minority shareholders'.

3.3 Dividends not accrued

Where the correct entries have not been made in the books of the company, the general procedure is to make entries in the balance sheet working papers to give effect to the missing entries and, if necessary, to reverse any wrong entries.

Example

Upminster Ltd acquired 80% of the ordinary share capital of Barking Ltd several years ago when the balance on the profit and loss account of Barking Ltd was £12,000.

Their respective draft balance sheets at 31 December 20X4 are as follows:

	Upminster Ltd	*Barking Ltd*
	£	£
Fixed assets	100,000	92,000
Investment in Barking Ltd	55,000	-
Current assets	45,000	31,000
	200,000	123,000
Ordinary share capital	100,000	50,000
Preference share capital	-	10,000
Profit and loss account	80,000	42,000
Proposed dividend	-	10,000
Sundry creditors	20,000	11,000
	200,000	123,000

Upminster has not made any entry for the dividend receivable from Barking for its share of the £10,000 ordinary dividend that Barking declared in December 20X4. A proposed preference dividend of £2,000 by Barking Ltd has not been accounted for by either company. Upminster Ltd purchased 30% of the preference shares for £3,500 some years ago.

Goodwill has been fully amortised.

Prepare the consolidated balance sheet at 31 December 20X4.

Solution

Step 1: Shareholdings in Barking Ltd

	Ordinary shares	*Preference shares*
	%	%
Group	80	30
Minority	20	70
	100	100

Step 2: Adjustments

1 Proposed preference dividend by Barking Ltd:

Dr: Profit and loss account	£2,000	
Cr: Proposed dividend		£2,000

2 Dividends receivable by Upminster:

Dr: Dividends receivable (ordinary: 80% × 10,000)	£8,000	
Dr: Dividends receivable (preference: 30% × 2,000)	£600	
Cr: Profit and loss account		£8,600

Cancel dividends receivable/payable when the upper half of the balance sheet is cross cast.

Working paper

		Upminster Ltd		*Barking Ltd*		*Group*
		£		£		£
Fixed assets		100,000		92,000		**192,000**
Investment in Barking Ltd		55,000		–		
Current assets		45,000		31,000		**76,000**
Dividends receivable	**(2) ~~8,000~~** **(2) –~~600~~**					
		200,000		123,000		
Ordinary share capital		100,000		50,000		
Preference share capital		–		10,000		
Profit and loss account	**(2) + 8,600**	80,000		42,000	**(2,000) (1)**	
(Proposed dividend) becomes:						
Dividend payable to minority shareholders		–	**2,000**	**~~10,000~~**	**~~+ 2,000~~ (1)** **1,400**	**3,400**
Sundry creditors		20,000		11,000		**31,000**
		200,000		123,000		

Tutorial note

These amendments may be made to the balance sheets given in the question as this ensures they are not forgotten. However, it is important that your *answer* also shows these amendments, hence the figures bracketed in the schedules and balance sheet following.

Step 3: Goodwill

	£	£
Cost of investment		55,000
Less: Share of net assets at acquisition		
Ordinary share capital	50,000	
Profit and loss account	12,000	
	62,000	
Group share	× 80%	
		(49,600)
Preference share capital	10,000	
Group share	× 30%	
		(3,000)
Goodwill – fully amortised		2,400

Step 4: Group reserves

	£
Upminster Ltd: (80,000 + 8,600)	88,600
Barking Ltd: 80% (42,000 – 2,000 – 12,000)	22,400
Less: Goodwill amortised	(2,400)
	108,600

Step 5: Minority interest

	£	£
Net assets attributable to ordinary shareholdings		
Ordinary share capital	50,000	
Profit and loss account (42,000 – 2,000)	40,000	
	90,000	
Minority share	× 20%	
		18,000
Attributable to preference shareholdings		
Preference share capital	10,000	
	× 70%	
		7,000
		25,000

Consolidated balance sheet of Upminster Ltd and its subsidiary, Barking Ltd as at 31 December 20X4

	£	£
Fixed assets:		
Tangible assets (100 + 92)		192,000
Current assets (45 + 31)	76,000	
Creditors (amounts falling due within one year):		
Sundry creditors (20 + 11)	31,000	
Dividend payable to minority shareholders	3,400	
	34,400	
Net current assets		41,600
Total assets less current liabilities		233,600
Capital and reserves:		
Called up ordinary share capital allotted and fully paid	100,000	
Reserves – profit and loss account	108,600	
		208,600
Minority interests		25,000
		233,600

3.4 Debenture interest payable by a subsidiary

The procedure for dealing with debenture interest payable is exactly the same as for ordinary or preference dividends payable by a subsidiary. The *only* difference is in the description of the group liability to pay debenture interest. This liability has nothing to do with minority shareholders – it is simply a creditor like any other.

Conclusion

If a group company makes profits on transactions with other group members, from the perspective of the group as a whole, such profits are **unrealised** and must be eliminated from the consolidated accounts as a consolidation adjustment.

Where a parent holds debentures and/or preference shares in a subsidiary, as well as equity shares:

- preference shares of the subsidiary company *not* held by the parent company are included in the minority interest on the consolidated balance sheet
- debentures held by outsiders are shown separately on the consolidated balance sheet – they are *not* part of the minority interest.

Intra-group dividends must be cancelled on consolidation. Only dividends payable to minority interests are shown as a current liability in the consolidated balance sheet.

SELF-TEST QUESTIONS

1 How are current account balances between the parent and the subsidiary treated when drawing up a consolidated balance sheet? (1.2)

2 How does FRS 2 require that unrealised profits in year end stocks should be accounted for? (1.3)

3 If P holds 100% of S's ordinary shares but only 10% of S's preference shares, is S still a subsidiary of P? (2.1)

4 How is the minority interest calculated where a parent holds preference shares as well as ordinary shares in a subsidiary? (2.1)

5 Where a parent holds debentures in a subsidiary, how are debentures treated in the consolidated balance sheet? (2.2)

6 What is the correct accounting treatment for intra-group dividends declared during an accounting period? (3.2)

PRACTICE QUESTION

Pixie and Dixie

On 1 January 20X7, Pixie Ltd acquired the following shareholdings in Dixie Ltd. At the date of both acquisitions, the accumulated profits of Dixie Ltd amounted to £20,000.

	Number of shares	*Cost of investment*
		£
£1 Ordinary shares	37,500	58,000
£1 Preference shares	16,000	15,000
		73,000

The balance sheets of the two companies at 31 December 20X9 were as follows:

	Pixie Ltd	*Dixie Ltd*
	£	£
Ordinary share capital	200,000	50,000
7% Preference share capital	-	40,000
Profit and loss account	120,000	38,000
Sundry creditors	56,100	22,100

Proposed dividends:		
Ordinary	20,000	2,500
Preference	-	1,400
	396,100	154,000
Fixed assets	210,000	110,600
Current assets	113,100	43,400
Investment in Dixie Ltd	73,000	-
	396,100	154,000

Current assets of Pixie Ltd include £42,000 of goods acquired originally from Dixie Ltd. Dixie Ltd invoiced these goods at cost plus 20%.

Pixie Ltd has not accounted for dividends receivable from Dixie Ltd.

Goodwill is amortised over 4 years from the date of acquisition, with a full year's charge in the year of acquisition.

Required:

Prepare the consolidated balance sheet of Pixie Ltd and its subsidiary as at 31 December 20X9. **(20 marks)**

EXAM-TYPE QUESTION

Pillar plc

On 1 April 20X8 Pillar plc acquired 90% of the equity shares in Steeple Ltd. Steeple Ltd's retained profits at the date of acquisition were £2,640,000.

Balance sheets as at 31 March 20X9

		Pillar plc		*Steeple Ltd*	
		£000	£000	£000	£000
Fixed assets					
Intangible – Software			-		2,520
Tangible:					
Property		720		1,080	
Plant and equipment		1,824		1,308	
Investments	– equity in Steeple Ltd	5,036		-	
	– others	214		252	
			7,794		5,160
Current assets					
Stock		863		672	
Debtors		629		394	
Steeple Ltd current account		90		-	
Cash		24		-	
		1,606		1,066	
Creditors: amounts falling due within one year					
Trade creditors		570		566	
Pillar plc current account		-		72	
Taxation		274		210	
Operating overdraft		-		32	
Dividend payable		120		-	
		964		880	

Net current assets		642		186
Creditors: amounts falling due after more than one year				
Government grants		(276)		(240)
Net Assets		8,160		5,106
Share Capital and Reserves:				
Ordinary shares of £1 each		2,400		1,800
Share premium	2,400		600	
Retained earnings	3,360	5,760	2,706	3,306
		8,160		5,106

The following information is relevant.

(i) The software of Steeple Ltd represents the depreciated cost of the development of an integrated business accounting package. It was completed at a capitalised cost of £2,880,000 and went on sale on 1 April 20X8. Steeple Ltd's directors are depreciating the software on a straight-line basis over an eight-year life (i.e. £360,000 per annum). However, the directors of Pillar plc are of the opinion that a six-year life would be more appropriate as sales of business software rarely exceed this period.

(ii) At the date of acquisition Pillar plc sold an item of plant to Steeple Ltd for £240,000. This plant had cost Pillar plc £200,000. Steeple plc has charged depreciation of £24,000 on this plant since it was acquired.

(iii) The stock of Pillar plc on 31 March 20X9 contains goods at a transfer price of £30,000 that were supplied by Steeple Ltd who had marked them up with a profit of 25% on cost.

(iv) On 31 March 20X9 Steeple Ltd remitted to Pillar plc a cash payment of £18,000. This was not received by Pillar plc until early April.

(v) Consolidated goodwill is amortised over a five-year life.

Required:

(a) The Consolidated Balance Sheet of Pillar plc for the year ended 31 March 20X9. **(20 marks)**

(b) Suggest reasons why a parent company may not wish to consolidate a subsidiary company, and describe the circumstances in which non-consolidation of subsidiaries is permitted. **(5 marks)**

(Total: 25 marks)

For the answers to these questions, see the 'Answers' section at the end of the book.

FEEDBACK TO ACTIVITY **1**

The group stocks, at cost, are £55,400.

If your total stock value came out at £55,900, you may not have remembered to value the stock in transit at cost to Subsidiary Ltd. The unrealised profit in the stocks which Parent plc held at the year end is £1,500 (£6,000 invoiced price less £4,500 cost to Subsidiary Ltd).

	£	£
Stock in Parent plc:		
Cost	30,800	
Less unrealised profit	(1,500)	
		29,300
Stock in Subsidiary Ltd at cost		24,600
Stock in transit, at cost		1,500
		55,400

FEEDBACK TO ACTIVITY **2**

Step 1: Shareholdings in Minimus Ltd

	Ordinary shares	*Preference shares*
Group	3/4 (75%)	5/8 (62.5%)
Minority	1/4 (25%)	3/8 (37.5%)

Step 2: Adjustments

1 *Unrealised profit on stock* $= \frac{20}{120} \times £22,800$

$= £3,800$

The profit was made by Maximus Ltd, therefore put through a consolidation adjustment on the balance sheet working paper of Maximus Ltd.

2 *Cancel debentures*

The working paper comprises the balance sheets given in the question, as adjusted and cross cast to give the upper half of the consolidated balance sheet.

		Maximus Ltd		*Minimus Ltd*	*Group*
		£		£	£
Fixed assets, at cost		450,000		280,000	**730,000**
90,000 ordinary shares in Minimus Ltd		185,000			
50,000 preference shares in Minimus Ltd at cost		55,000			
£10,000 debentures in Minimus Ltd		~~10,000~~			
Current assets	**(3,800)**	200,000		143,500	**339,700**
		900,000		423,500	
Ordinary shares of £1		500,000		120,000	
8% non-cumulative preference shares of £1		–		80,000	
7% debentures		–	**30,000**	~~40,000~~	**30,000**
Capital reserve		50,000		30,000	
Profit and loss account	**(3,800)**	150,000		66,000	
Provision for depreciation		70,000		55,000	**125,000**
Creditors		130,000		32,500	**162,500**
		900,000		423,500	

Step 3: Goodwill

	£	£
Cost of investment (185 + 55)		240,000
Less: Share of net assets at acquisition		
Ordinary share capital	120,000	
Capital reserve	12,000	
Profit and loss account	30,500	
	162,500	
Group share	× 75%	
		(121,875)
Preference share capital	80,000	
	× 62.5%	
		(50,000)
Goodwill		68,125
Amortisation charge (68,125 ÷ 5 × 4)		(54,500)
		13,625

Step 4: Group reserves

		£
1	Consolidated profit and loss account	
	Maximus Ltd: per question	150,000
	Unrealised profit on stock	(3,800)
	75% (66,000 – 30,500)	26,625
	Less: Goodwill amortised	(54,500)
		118,325

		£
2	Capital reserve	
	Maximus Ltd	50,000
	Minimus Ltd 75% (30,000 – 12,000)	13,500
		63,500

Tutorial note

All reserves are dealt with in the same way. The only difference is that goodwill is amortised through the profit and loss account rather than any other reserve.

Step 5: Minority interest

	£	£
Net assets of Minimus Ltd attributable to ordinary shareholdings		
Ordinary share capital	120,000	
Capital reserve	30,000	
Profit and loss account	66,000	
	216,000	
Minority share	× 25%	
		54,000
Attributable to preference shareholdings		
Preference share capital	80,000	
Minority share	× 37.5%	
		30,000
		84,000

Step 6: Prepare the consolidated balance sheet

Consolidated balance sheet of Maximus Ltd and its subsidiary, Minimus Ltd at 31 December 20X4

	£	£
Fixed assets:		
Intangible assets:		
Cost	68,125	
Amortisation	54,500	
		13,625
Tangible assets:		
Cost	730,000	
Depreciation	125,000	
		605,000
		618,625
Current assets	339,700	
Creditors (amounts falling due within one year)	162,500	
Net current assets		177,200
Total assets less current liabilities		795,825
Creditors (amounts falling due after more than one year)		
7% debentures		(30,000)
Minority interests		(84,000)
		681,825
Capital and reserves:		
Called up ordinary share capital		500,000
Capital reserves		63,500
Profit and loss account		118,325
		681,825

Chapter 8

GROUP ACCOUNTING – THE PROFIT AND LOSS ACCOUNT

CHAPTER CONTENTS

1 **Consolidated profit and loss account**

2 **Consolidation working papers**

3 **Cancellation of intra-group transactions**

4 **Fair values in acquisition accounting**

This chapter covers the consolidated profit and loss account, including the treatment of intra-group transactions and the situation where a subsidiary is acquired part-way through the year (a mid-year acquisition).

It also covers FRS 7 *Fair values in acquisition accounting*. This is an important standard because it enabled the ASB to prevent 'creative accounting' abuses that had previously been widespread.

Objectives

By the time you have finished this chapter you should be able to:

- prepare a consolidated profit and loss account for a simple group
- explain the nature of a dividend paid out of pre-acquisition profits
- account for the effects of intra-group trading in the profit and loss account
- explain why it is necessary for both the consideration paid for a subsidiary and the subsidiary's identifiable assets and liabilities to be accounted for at their fair values when preparing consolidated financial statements
- prepare consolidated financial statements dealing with fair value adjustments.

1 Consolidated profit and loss account

1.1 Basic form of consolidated profit and loss account

KEY POINT

Consolidated profit and loss accounts are prepared by combining the information given in the individual companies' accounts, after adjustments.

Just as the profit and loss account of a single company shows the results of the year's trading of that company, so the consolidated profit and loss account shows the results of trading in the year by the parent company together with its subsidiaries.

Consolidated profit and loss accounts are prepared by combining the information given in the profit and loss accounts of the individual companies, after making any adjustments that may be necessary to eliminate inter-company items, unrealised profits and so on.

Consolidated profit and loss accounts have an underlying form as follows:

Section	*Purpose*
A	To show the results achieved with the assets under the directors' control.
B	To show how much of the net gains shown in Section A accrue to parent company shareholders, and how much to others.
C	To show how the directors intend to dispose of the gains accruing to parent company shareholders.

At **Section A** we will show the whole of turnover, cost of sales, gross profit, ... taxation, and profit or loss on ordinary activities after taxation (or equivalent Format 2 items).

At **Section B** we will show a deduction for minority interests' share of the profits of subsidiaries not wholly owned by the group.

At **Section C** we will show dividends, capitalised profits (if any), retained profits or transfers to reserves.

Extraordinary items, if any, are shown net of any minority share between Sections B and C.

KEY POINT

From turnover to profit on ordinary activities after taxation, all the figures are for the *whole* of the operations controlled by the parent company directors, the share of the minority shareholders is deducted later.

The usual layout will be illustrated in examples later in this chapter; for the moment the main point to appreciate is that at Section A, all the figures are for the *whole* of the operations controlled by the parent company directors, the share of the minority shareholders is deducted later.

1.2 Subsidiary owned for the entire year

In this section we will prepare a consolidated profit and loss account for a group with a subsidiary that has been owned for the entire year under consideration.

Example

P Ltd acquired, several years ago, the entire ordinary share capital of S Ltd. Their results for the year ended 30 November 20X4 were as follows:

	P Ltd	*S Ltd*
	£	£
Turnover	8,500,000	2,200,000
Total costs	7,650,000	1,980,000
Trading profit before taxation	850,000	220,000
Taxation	400,000	100,000
	450,000	120,000

Prepare the consolidated profit and loss account for the year ended 30 November 20X4.

Solution

The consolidated profit and loss account is arrived at by a simple '**combining exercise**'.

Consolidated profit and loss account for year ended 30 November 20X4

	£
Turnover	10,700,000
Total costs	9,630,000
Group profit on ordinary activities before taxation	1,070,000
Tax on profit on ordinary activities	500,000
Profit for the year retained	570,000

1.3 The effect of a minority interest

KEY POINT

If the parent company owns only a proportion of the shares of a subsidiary, this does *not* affect turnover and cost of sales.

What happens if, in the previous example, P Ltd acquired only 75% of the share capital of S Ltd?

This does *not* affect group turnover and costs . They remain the same, as we wish to show the total income under the control of the parent company.

The minority shareholders' interest in the subsidiary's profit is shown after the group tax charge. The calculation is 25% × £120,000 = £30,000.

ACTIVITY **1**

Now prepare the consolidated profit and loss account for the company in the previous example assuming a 25% minority interest.

Feedback to this activity is at the end of the chapter.

1.4 Revenue reserves brought forward

KEY POINT

The consolidated profit and loss account reserve brought forward consists of the parent's balance plus its share of the subsidiary's post-acquisition retained profits, less goodwill amortised.

So far we have carefully avoided the problem of revenue reserves brought forward from the previous year. As far as the **consolidated** profit and loss account is concerned, the balance brought forward consists of:

- P Ltd's *own* profit and loss account balance brought forward; and
- P Ltd's share of the **post-acquisition** retained profits of S Ltd; less
- goodwill amortised as at the beginning of the period.

ACTIVITY **2**

Facts as in the previous activity, but you are provided with additional information as follows:

- Profit and loss account balances brought forward at the beginning of the year amounted to £2,300,000 for P Ltd and £400,000 for S Ltd.
- P Ltd acquired the shares in S Ltd when the revenue reserves of S Ltd amounted to £100,000.

Calculate the brought forward and carried forward figure for the consolidated profit and loss account reserve. Ignore goodwill.

Feedback to this activity is at the end of the chapter.

1.5 Inter-company dividends – ordinary shares

KEY POINT

Investment income of the parent may include **ordinary dividends** from subsidiaries, and income from trade investments. Inter-company dividends are **eliminated on consolidation**.

Most complications in preparing consolidated profit and loss accounts arise because of **dividends** paid from one company to another.

Investment income of the parent company may, for example, include:

1 **ordinary dividends** received (or receivable) from subsidiaries

2 income from trade investments.

Only 2 is shown separately as income in the consolidated profit and loss account, inter-company dividends being **eliminated on consolidation**.

The subsidiary in a group will often pay dividends in order to transfer surplus cash to the parent company. No net profit or loss accrues to the group in the process.

ACTIVITY 3

The profit and loss accounts for P Ltd and S Ltd for the year ended 31 August 20X4 are shown below. P Ltd acquired 75% of the ordinary share capital of S Ltd several years ago.

	P Ltd		S Ltd	
	£	£	£	£
Turnover		2,400,000		800,000
Total costs		2,160,000		720,000
Trading profit		240,000		80,000
Investment income:				
Dividend received from S Ltd	1,500			
Dividend receivable from S Ltd	6,000			
		7,500		-
		247,500		80,000
Taxation		115,000		38,000
		132,500		42,000
Dividends:				
Paid	-		2,000	
Proposed	60,000		8,000	
		60,000		10,000
Retained profit for the year		72,500		32,000

Prepare the consolidated profit and loss account. Ignore goodwill.

Feedback to this activity is at the end of the chapter.

1.6 Inter-company dividends – preference shares

KEY POINT

The minority interest in the ordinary shares and the minority interest in the preference shares are calculated separately. The minority interest in preference shares is applied to the preference dividend only.

The main complication here is the calculation of the minority interests in the profits of the subsidiary. It is essential to keep quite clear:

- the minority interests in the **ordinary shares**
- the minority interests in the **preference shares**.

Example

- P Ltd acquired 80% of the ordinary share capital and 40% of the preference share capital of S Ltd many years ago. The profit and loss account of S Ltd for the current year was as follows:

	£	£
Sales		2,700,000
Total costs		2,300,000
		400,000
Taxation		140,000
		260,000
Dividends:		
Preference	10,000	
Ordinary	80,000	
		90,000
Retained		170,000

Compute the minority interests.

Solution

	Total	*Minority interests*
	£	£
Profit after taxation (S Ltd)	260,000	
Less: Preference dividend	10,000	(60%) 6,000
Available for ordinary shareholders	250,000	(20%)50,000
Total		56,000

The minority interests' share of the profits of S Ltd amounts to £56,000.

The preference dividend normally represents the full entitlement to profits of the preference shareholders. The ordinary dividend, however, represents how much of the remaining profits will be paid to the ordinary shareholders or retained (for their ultimate benefit) within the company. Therefore, the deduction of the preference dividend from the total profits available to shareholders in S Ltd merely represents the total profits accruing to one class of shareholder. The ordinary dividend does not represent this and, therefore, is not relevant to the calculation.

1.7 Additions to the group during the current year

KEY POINT

Pre-acquisition items should be excluded from group figures.

The main problem here is how to deal with the pre-acquisition profits of the new subsidiary. The approach is to exclude the pre-acquisition items of the subsidiary from the relevant group figures. Therefore the profit and loss account figures for S Ltd are time apportioned and only the post acquisition element is included in the group profit and loss account.

ACTIVITY **4**

The trading results of P Ltd and S Ltd for the year ended 31 July 20X4 were as follows:

	P Ltd	*S Ltd*
	£	£
Turnover	1,430,000	600,000
Total costs	1,160,000	504,000
Trading profit	270,000	96,000
Less: Taxation	135,000	48,000
Retained profit	135,000	48,000
Reserves brought forward	900,000	200,000
	1,035,000	248,000

P Ltd acquired 75% of the ordinary share capital of S Ltd on 28 February 20X4. Assume that profits are earned evenly over the year. Prepare the consolidated profit and loss account. Ignore goodwill.

Feedback to this activity is at the end of the chapter.

1.8 Pre-acquisition dividends

KEY POINT

Pre-acquisition dividends may be treated as a return of part of the **cost of investment** or as **investment income**.

A **pre-acquisition dividend** is a dividend paid to a parent company by a subsidiary out of pre-acquisition profits. There are two possible ways of accounting for pre-acquisition dividends in the accounts of the parent and in the consolidated accounts.

1 Treat the dividend as a return to the parent company of part of the **cost of its investment** (i.e. a reduction in the carrying value of the parent's investment in the subsidiary). This is the traditional view of pre-acquisition dividends. The reasoning for it is that only post-acquisition profits can be treated as profits of the group and therefore only dividends paid out of post-acquisition profits can be treated as income. A further argument for this treatment is that a dividend paid out of pre-acquisition profits reduces the value of the parent's investment in the subsidiary to less than cost.

2 Treat the dividend as a realised profit in the hands of the parent (i.e. as investment income). The rationale for this treatment is that the payment of a pre-acquisition dividend does not cause an impairment in the value of the parent's investment in the subsidiary. Therefore no write-down is necessary.

EXAM HINT

The examiner will specify the policy in respect of pre-acquisition dividends.

The first of these two methods is the one that is normally used but the examiner has said that **examination questions** will specify the company's policy in respect of pre-acquisition dividends.

Example

The facts are the same as in the Activity above, except that on 1 March 20X4 S Ltd pays a dividend of £12,000. Show the journal entry for recording the dividend received in the books of P Ltd and calculate consolidated reserves at 31 July 20X4 assuming that:

1 the dividend is treated as investment income

2 the dividend is treated as a return of the cost of the investment.

Solution

Note: In the consolidated profit and loss account, investment income received by P Ltd is cancelled against the dividend paid by S Ltd.

1 Investment income

Journal entry:

Dr: Cash (75% × 12,000)	£9,000	
Cr: Investment income		£9,000

Consolidated reserves:	£	£
P Ltd (1,035,000 + 9,000)		1,044,000
S Ltd: at the year-end (248,000 – 12,000)	236,000	
at acquisition (200,000 + 28,000)	(228,000)	
	8,000	
Group share (75%)		6,000
		1,050,000

The dividend is treated as occurring post-acquisition, although it is paid out of pre-acquisition profits.

2 Return of cost of investment

Journal entry:

Dr: Cash (75% × 12,000)	£9,000	
Cr: Cost of investment		£9,000

Consolidated reserves:	£	£
P Ltd		1,035,000
S Ltd: at the year-end (248,000 – 12,000)	236,000	
at acquisition (200,000 + 16,000)	(216,000)	
	20,000	
Group share (75%)		15,000
		1,050,000

1.9 Calculating the pre-acquisition dividend

KEY POINT

If the dividend has to be divided between the pre- and post-acquisition periods, use either **time apportionment** or consider **pre- and post-acquisition reserves**.

In the example above, it was clear that the whole of the dividend was paid out of pre-acquisition profits. However, in some cases, the dividend has to be apportioned between the pre- and post-acquisition period. There are two ways of doing this:

1 **time apportionment**

2 take the pre-acquisition dividend to be the portion of the dividend that cannot have been paid out of **post-acquisition reserves**.

Example

The facts are as in the previous example, except that S Ltd proposed a final dividend of £24,000 on 31 July 20X4.

Method 1

	Total	*Pre-acq (7/12)*	*Post-acq (5/12)*
	£	£	£
Profit for the year	48,000	28,000	20,000
Dividends proposed	(24,000)	(14,000)	(10,000)
	24,000	14,000	10,000

Method 2

	Total	*Pre-acq*	*Post-acq*
	£	£	£
Profit for the year	48,000	28,000	20,000
Dividends proposed	(24,000)	(4,000)	(20,000)
	24,000	24,000	-

EXAM HINT

The examiner should indicate the required method in respect of pre-acquisition dividends.

Method 1 is the traditional method and probably the most correct theoretically. Method 2 has the advantage of minimising pre-acquisition dividends and is normally favoured by those who argue for the 'modern' treatment of pre-acquisition dividends. Again, the **examiner** should give some indication of which method is required.

1.10 Legal requirements – parent company's profit and loss account

There is one dispensation offered by CA85 of which advantage is widely taken – the ability of a company not to publish its own profit and loss account.

Ordinarily, a parent company (not being a wholly owned subsidiary) must publish:

- its own balance sheet
- a consolidated balance sheet
- its own profit and loss account
- a consolidated profit and loss account.

KEY POINT

A parent company need not publish its own profit and loss account if group accounts have been prepared in line with CA85 and its profit is disclosed in a balance sheet note.

A parent company may dispense with the need to publish its own profit and loss account (S230 CA85), provided that:

- the company has prepared group accounts in accordance with CA85
- the notes to the parent company's **individual** balance sheet show the amount of the parent company profit or loss for the financial year
- the company discloses that it is taking advantage of this exemption.

The profit or loss for the financial year is the profit or loss after all income, expenses, taxation and extraordinary items but before appropriations for dividends or transfers to reserves.

2 Consolidation working papers

The following example brings together the principles explained in the previous sections. It illustrates an approach that can be taken to show sufficient detail to support the figures computed for the published consolidated profit and loss account. For many of the required figures, the consolidated figure is no more than the addition of the parent and subsidiary companies' figures, and thus a 'master' schedule is used to show the additions made.

Example

The draft profit and loss accounts for the year ended 31 March 20X7 of the companies in a group are as follows:

	Tyndale Ltd	*Luther Ltd*
	£	£
Turnover	216,300	126,000
Cost of sales	136,269	79,380
Gross profit	80,031	46,620
Administrative expenses	(21,630)	(12,600)
Income from shares in group companies	6,048	-
Net profit before taxation	64,449	34,020
Taxation	28,119	16,380
Net profit after taxation	35,330	17,640
Dividends	20,000	10,080
Transfer to reserves	15,330	7,560
Reserves brought forward	36,728	23,940
Reserves carried forward	52,058	31,500

- Luther Ltd has an issued share capital of 100,000 ordinary shares of £1 each. Tyndale purchased 60,000 of these two years ago when the balance on Luther Ltd's reserves was £16,380. Goodwill of £10,000 arose on the acquisition.

Goodwill is amortised over five years from the date of acquisition with a full year's charge in the year of acquisition.

Prepare the consolidated profit and loss account for the year ended 31 March 20X7.

Solution

Reconciliation of intra-group dividends

	£
Per Tyndale, received	6,048
Should agree with:	
Luther, paid £10,080 × 60%	6,048

Therefore, no adjustments are required.

Master schedule

Group details	*Tyndale Ltd* P	*Luther Ltd* 60% 12 months	*Adjustments*	*Consolidated*
	£	£	£	£
Turnover	216,300	126,000		342,300
Cost of sales	(136,269)	(79,380)		(215,649)
Administrative expenses	(21,630)	(12,600)	(2,000)	(36,230)
Investment income	-	-		-
Taxation	(28,119)	(16,380)		(44,499)
Net profit after taxation	30,282	17,640	(2,000)	45,922
Minority interests (40%)	-	(7,056)		(7,056)

Note: The consolidation adjustment represents the amortisation of goodwill (10,000 ÷ 5).

Calculation of reserves brought forward

	£
Tyndale	36,728
Luther 60% × £(23,940 – 16,380)	4,536
Less goodwill amortised:	
Luther (10,000 ÷ 5)	(2,000)
	39,264

The consolidated profit and loss account can now be prepared.

Tyndale Ltd and its subsidiaries
Consolidated profit and loss account for the year ended 31 March 20X7

	£
Turnover	342,300
Cost of sales	215,649
Gross profit	126,651
Administrative expenses	(36,230)
Profit on ordinary activities before tax	90,421
Tax on profit on ordinary activities	44,499
Profit on ordinary activities after tax	45,922
Minority interests	7,056
Net profit after tax attributable to shareholders of Tyndale Ltd (Note 1)	38,866
Dividends	20,000
	18,866

Statement of reserves

	£
At 31 March 20X6	39,264
Retained profits for the year	18,866
At 31 March 20X7	58,130

Note

1 Net profit after taxation attributable to shareholders of Tyndale Ltd

Tyndale Ltd has taken advantage of the legal dispensation not to publish its own profit and loss account. Its net profit after taxation is £37,794.

Explanatory notes

- The master schedule is drafted with a column for each company and a 'consolidated' column. The group structure is summarised at the head of each column.

  The meaning of the notes is that Tyndale is the parent company and Luther is 60% owned for the whole of the present year.

- In any example with intra-group dividends, begin by reconciling the amounts receivable by the parent company with the amounts payable by the subsidiary. This may reveal errors or omissions in accounting for the dividends and, if so, they should be corrected before beginning the consolidation.

  KEY POINT

  Under no circumstances do dividends of subsidiaries ever appear in the consolidated profit and loss account.

  Under no circumstances whatever do dividends of subsidiaries ever appear in the consolidated profit and loss account. As discussed previously, their only effect on consolidated reserves is to alter their composition and thus alter the figures in the consolidated statement of reserves of the group.

- For items from 'turnover' to 'net profit after tax' (from ordinary activities), we enter:

  – for **parent company**: the full amount

  – for **subsidiaries owned throughout the year**: the full amount

  - for **subsidiaries acquired during the year**: the amount representing post-acquisition transactions.

- The figure of £45,922 net profit on ordinary activities after tax completes Section A of the consolidated profit and loss account, and it represents the total profit from ordinary activities that the directors have obtained by using the assets that they control.

  However, not all of this will accrue to the shareholders of Tyndale Ltd and now, in Section B of the account, the amount that accrues to the minority shareholders in the subsidiary will be deducted.

  In this case as the subsidiary only has ordinary shares, it is easy to calculate the minority share. It is simply the minority shareholders' fraction of the ordinary shares, multiplied by the last figure, net profit after tax, in the column for the subsidiary.

  The resulting subtotal is the amount of profit from ordinary activities that accrues to the parent company shareholders, and it completes Section B of the account.

- Group reserves brought forward consist of:
  - all the parent company's profit
  - plus the group share of the subsidiary's post-acquisition profits
  - less goodwill amortised up to the beginning of the current accounting period.

- Once the master schedule has been filled in, the actual consolidated profit and loss account can be written out, using the figures from the 'consolidated' column. The account should follow the statutory formats. Minority interests are required, under the group accounting provisions of CA85, to be shown immediately after profit on ordinary activities after taxation.

- The note to the accounts gives the information required by S230 CA85 when a parent company does not publish its own profit and loss account. The figure is the parent company's own net profit before dividends taken from its own profit and loss account. Beware, though, as the parent company's own profit should include any dividends receivable from subsidiaries; if these have not been included in the profit and loss account given, you must add them in for the purpose of this note. Strictly speaking, this would be a note to the parent company's individual balance sheet, rather than to the consolidated profit and loss account. In practice, the disclosure is often shown in this way.

3 Cancellation of intra-group transactions

3.1 Introduction

In the previous chapter on group accounts we dealt with the treatment of unrealised profits on stock arising from intra-group trading. In consolidating the profit and loss accounts a rather more involved adjustment is required.

If in a certain year:

- A Ltd buys a stock item for £60
- A Ltd sells it to B Ltd for £80, B Ltd being a member of the same group as A Ltd
- B Ltd still holds the item at the balance sheet date

then the profit and loss accounts of the two companies will include, in respect of these events:

	A Ltd	B Ltd
	£	£
Turnover	80	-
Cost of sales	60	-
	—	
Gross profit, and hence every other profit and loss account subtotal	20	-
	—	

This £20 is the unrealised profit whose cancellation in the balance sheet was discussed before. In the consolidated profit and loss account we must also eliminate the £80 and £60 as the profit and loss account of a single company that had carried out the same transactions as A Ltd and B Ltd would contain no entries at all in respect of it.

What if B Ltd had sold the item for £95 by the balance sheet date? The profit and loss accounts of the two companies would then have shown:

	A Ltd	B Ltd
	£	£
Turnover	80	95
Cost of sales	60	80
	—	—
Gross profit (and other subtotals)	20	15
	—	—

Both companies have realised their profits and so these should not be adjusted. However, a single equivalent company would show in its profit and loss account:

	£
Turnover	95
Cost of sales	60
	—
Gross profit (and other subtotals)	35
	—

In this case we need eliminate only the £80 from turnover and the £80 from cost of sales in order to establish the correct turnover and cost of sales figures.

In either case the adjustment is conveniently carried out by means of an extra column in the master schedule.

3.2 Effect on minority interests

KEY POINT

If unrealised profit originally arose in the subsidiary, the minority interests must be adjusted for their share in the unrealised profit.

If the **unrealised profit** originally arose in the subsidiary, the minority interests must be adjusted for their share in the unrealised profit. However, this is an adjustment made in calculating their share of post-tax profits; in the first instance all the unrealised profit must be eliminated to determine the correct amount of gross profit earned by the group trading as if it were a single entity.

Example

The profit and loss accounts of Entry Ltd and Exit Ltd for the year ended 31 July 20X7 are as follows:

	Entry Ltd	*Exit Ltd*
	£	£
Turnover	6,956	3,290
Cost of sales	3,108	1,470
	——	——
Gross profit	3,848	1,820
Administrative expenses	(1,184)	(560)
Income from shares in group companies	140	
	——	——

Net profit on ordinary activities before taxation	2,804	1,260
Tax on profit on ordinary activities	1,258	595
Net profit after taxation	1,546	665
Dividends	800	350
Profit transferred to reserves	746	315

Statement of reserves

	Entry Ltd	*Exit Ltd*
	£	£
As at 31 July 20X6	797	3,955
Retained profit	746	315
As at 31 July 20X7	1,543	4,270

Further information

- On 1 August 20X5 Entry Ltd acquired 6,000 of the issued 10,000 ordinary shares and 2,000 of the issued 5,000 7% preference shares of £1 each in Exit Ltd. At that date the reserves of Exit Ltd were £980. Goodwill of £2,000 arose on the acquisition.
- In the year ended 31 July 20X7 Entry Ltd sold to Exit Ltd goods costing £500 for £625 (20% profit margin).
- At 31 July 20X7 Exit Ltd had sold 40% of these goods for £300.
- Goodwill is amortised over five years from the date of acquisition.

Prepare the consolidated profit and loss account of Entry Ltd and its subsidiary for the year ended 31 July 20X7.

Solution

Reconciliation of dividends

Expected preference dividends of Exit = £5,000 × 7%
= £350

Therefore, no ordinary dividend is paid or proposed by Exit.

Entry's share = £2,000 × 7%
= £140

Therefore, no adjustment is required.

Rules for dealing with inter-company trading

1 Eliminate from sales *all* inter-company sales at the selling price. Therefore deduct £625.

2 Compute unrealised profit in goods not sold, i.e. the same calculation as for the consolidated balance sheet.

Closing stock re goods sold from Entry to Exit:
60% × £625 = £375

Unrealised profit:
20% × £375 = £75

or
60% × (625 – 500) = £75

3 Cost of sales is reduced by the amount of the inter-group sale (£625) but the unrealised profit (£75) must be added into the cost of sales figure.

Therefore the reduction in cost of sales is (£625 – £75) = £550.

Thus if there are no unrealised profits, cost of sales is reduced by the same amount as sales.

The figures shown/computed in 1 to 3 can now be transferred to the consolidation schedule.

As the sale was made by the parent company there is no adjustment to minority interests required (see 'Tutorial note' below minority interests).

Master schedule

	Entry Ltd	*Exit Ltd*	*Adjustments*	*Consolidated*
Group details	*P*	*60%*		
		12 months		
	£	£	£	£
Turnover	6,956	3,290	(625)	9,621
Cost of sales	(3,108)	(1,470)	550	(4,028)
Gross profit	3,848	1,820	(75)	5,593
Administrative expenses	(1,184)	(560)	(400)	(2,144)
Taxation	(1,258)	(595)	-	(1,853)
Profit after taxation	1,406	665	-	1,596

Minority interests

		Minority interest	*Minority interest*
	£	%	£
Minority interest:			
Profit after tax	665		
Preference dividend	(350)	60	210
To ordinary shareholders	315	40	126
			336

Tutorial note

If the unrealised profit on inter-company trading originally arose in the subsidiary, the minority interests' share in profits would be reduced by:

40% × £75 = £30

£306 would thus be shown in the consolidated profit and loss account. Note in particular that the unrealised profit of £75 would still have to be deducted to arrive at consolidated gross profit.

Reserves brought forward

	£
Entry Ltd	797
Exit Ltd (60% × (3,955 – 980))	1,785
Goodwill amortised (2,000 ÷ 5)	(400)
	2,182

Entry Ltd and its subsidiary
Consolidated profit and loss account for year ended 31 July 20X7

	£
Turnover	9,621
Cost of sales	4,028
Gross profit	5,593
Administrative expenses	2,144
Profit on ordinary activities before taxation	3,449
Tax on profit on ordinary activities	1,853
Profit on ordinary activities after taxation	1,596
Minority interests	336
Profit attributable to shareholders in Entry Ltd	1,260
Dividends	800
Profit transferred to reserves	460

Statement of reserves

	£
As at 31 July 20X6	2,182
Retained profit for the year	460
As at 31 July 20X7	2,642

3.3 Transfers of fixed assets

KEY POINT

Transfers of **fixed assets** between group companies require adjustments to show the profit and loss account as it would have been without the transfers.

Transfers of **fixed assets** between group companies also affect the consolidated profit and loss account. Adjustments are needed in order to show the profit and loss account as it would be if the transfer had **not taken place**.

- Any profit or loss arising on the transfer is **eliminated**.
- The **depreciation charge** is adjusted so that it is based on the cost of the asset to the group.

Example

On 1 January 20X0, P Ltd sold a fixed asset to S Ltd for £25,000. The asset originally cost £20,000 and at the date of the transfer it had a net book value of £15,000. Both companies depreciate fixed assets at 20% on cost per annum. P Ltd owns 75% of S Ltd.

Solution

P Ltd has recorded a profit on disposal of £10,000 (25,000 – 15,000). This must be eliminated in the consolidated profit and loss account.

The depreciation charge for the year (in the books of S Ltd) is £5,000. If the transfer had not taken place, the depreciation charge in the books of P Ltd would have been £4,000. The depreciation charge must be reduced by £1,000.

The double entry is:

Dr: Profit on sale of fixed assets		£10,000	
Cr:	Depreciation expense		£1,000
Cr:	Fixed assets (net book value 20,000 – (10,000 + 1,000))		£9,000

The minority interest must be adjusted for the minority's share of the reduction in depreciation, as this was recorded in S Ltd's books:

Dr: Minority interest (profit and loss account) (25% × 1,000)	£250	
Cr: Minority interest (balance sheet)		£250

3.4 Intra-group interest

KEY POINT

Intra-group interest must be eliminated **on consolidation**.

Where a parent company makes a loan to a subsidiary company, the resulting **interest** represents an expense in the subsidiary shown under the heading 'interest payable and similar charges'. The parent company will include the interest under the heading 'income from other fixed asset investments' (where the loan is long term).

On consolidation both these amounts must be eliminated by making an appropriate entry in the adjustments column in the consolidation schedule.

4 Fair values in acquisition accounting

4.1 Introduction

DEFINITION

Fair value is the amount at which an asset or liability could be exchanged in an arm's length transaction between informed and willing parties, other than in a forced or liquidation sale.

In order to account for an acquisition, the acquiring company must measure the cost of what it is accounting for, which will normally represent:

- the **cost of the investment** in its own balance sheet
- the amount to be allocated between the **identifiable net assets** of the subsidiary and **goodwill** in the consolidated financial statements.

Fair value is the amount at which an asset or liability could be exchanged in an arm's length transaction between informed and willing parties, other than in a forced or liquidation sale.

KEY POINT

The subsidiary's identifiable assets and liabilities are included in the consolidated accounts at their **fair values**.

The subsidiary's identifiable assets and liabilities are included in the consolidated accounts at their fair values for the following reasons:

- Consolidated accounts are prepared from the perspective of the group, rather than from the perspectives of the individual companies. The book values of the subsidiary's assets and liabilities are largely irrelevant, because the consolidated accounts must reflect their **cost to the group** (i.e. to the parent), not their original cost to the subsidiary. The cost to the group is their fair value at the date of acquisition.
- **Purchased goodwill** is the difference between the cost of an acquired entity and the aggregate of the fair values of that entity's identifiable assets and liabilities. If fair values are not used, the value of goodwill will be meaningless.

4.2 Objective of FRS 7

KEY POINT

The objective of **FRS 7** is to ensure that assets and liabilities are **recorded at fair values** on acquisition and that subsequent gains are recorded as part of the **post-acquisition** group performance.

The objective of FRS 7 is two-fold:

- to ensure that when a business entity is acquired by another, all the assets and liabilities that existed in the acquired entity at the date of acquisition are recorded at fair values reflecting their condition at that date
- to ensure that all changes to the acquired assets and liabilities, and the resulting gains and losses that arise after control of the acquired entity has passed to the acquirer, are reported as part of the post-acquisition financial performance of the acquiring group.

4.3 Reasons why the FRS was needed

FRS 7 was intended to solve two main problems.

- For acquisition accounting CA 1989 and FRS 2 require the cost of investment to be based on the **fair value** of the consideration given. The subsidiary's identifiable assets and liabilities must be included in the consolidated accounts at their **fair values**, but before FRS 7 was issued there was very little guidance as to how fair values should be determined.
- During the 1980s, one of the more common 'creative accounting' abuses concerned the valuation of assets and liabilities of subsidiaries at the date of acquisition.

An acquiring company would set up a large provision for future reorganisation costs/operating losses among the net assets acquired. Setting up the provision had no effect on profits; it increased the purchased goodwill figure, so increased the amount debited directly to reserves on acquisition. (Before the issue of FRS 10, immediate elimination against reserves was the preferred method of accounting for goodwill.) However, after acquisition, losses or costs that would have been charged against profits could then be charged directly against the provision, thus increasing the reported profit figure. The larger the provision, the higher the reported profits figure could be; many UK companies appeared to be abusing this principle in the 1980s and setting up large contingent provisions for expenses that were not known at the date of the acquisition. FRS 7 effectively prohibited this practice.

4.4 Requirements of FRS 7

The FRS's main requirements are as follows.

- The assets and liabilities recognised in the allocation of fair values should be those of the acquired entity that existed at the date of acquisition. They should be measured at fair values that reflect the conditions at the date of acquisition.
- The liabilities of the acquired entity should not include provisions for future operating losses. Changes in the assets and liabilities resulting from the acquirer's intentions or from events after the acquisition should be dealt with as post-acquisition items. Similarly, costs of reorganisation and integrating the business acquired should be dealt with as post-acquisition costs and should not affect the fair values at the date of acquisition. (This prohibits the 'creative accounting' practices described above.)
- Fair values should be based on the value at which an asset or liability could be exchanged in an arm's length transaction. The fair value of monetary items should take into account the amounts expected to be received or paid and their timing.
- Unless they can be measured at market value, the fair values of non-monetary assets will normally be based on replacement cost, but should not exceed their recoverable amount as at the date of acquisition.

KEY POINT

FRS 7 describes how to determine fair values for particular categories of assets and liabilities.

The FRS also describes how to apply the required principles to determine fair values for particular categories of assets and liabilities, including fixed assets, stocks, pension schemes, deferred taxation and long-term receivables and liabilities. These are dealt with in more detail below.

4.5 Allocation of fair values to assets and liabilities

Tangible fixed assets

The fair value of a tangible fixed asset should be based on:

- market value, if assets similar in type and condition are bought and sold on an open market; or
- depreciated replacement cost.

The fair value should not exceed the recoverable amount of the asset.

Intangible assets

The fair value should be based on the asset's replacement cost, which is normally its estimated market value.

Stocks and work-in-progress

Stocks that the acquired company trades on a market in which it participates as both a buyer and a seller should be valued at current market prices. Other stocks should be valued at the lower of replacement cost and net realisable value.

Quoted investments

Quoted investments should be valued at market price.

Monetary assets and liabilities

The fair value should take into account the amounts expected to be received or paid and their timing. Fair value should be determined by reference to market prices, where available, by reference to the current price at which the business could acquire similar assets or enter into similar obligations, or by discounting to present value.

Contingencies

Contingent assets and liabilities should be measured at fair values where these can be determined (reasonable estimates of the expected outcome may be used).

Pensions and other post-retirement benefits

The fair value of a deficiency or (if it is reasonably expected to be realised) a surplus in a pension or other post-retirement benefits scheme should be recognised as a liability or an asset of the acquiring group.

Deferred tax

Deferred tax assets and liabilities recognised in the fair value exercise should be determined by considering the enlarged group as a whole.

ACTIVITY 5

X plc acquired 80% of the ordinary share capital of Y Ltd on 30 September 20X4 for £320,000.

The net assets of Y Ltd at that date had a book value of £350,000.

The following information is relevant:

- Y Ltd's freehold factory is included in the accounts at £100,000 and no adjustment has been made to recognise the valuation of £120,000 put on the property when it was professionally revalued on 15 September 20X4.
- The fair value of Y Ltd's stock at 30 September 20X4 is estimated to be £4,000 less than its book value at that date.
- In August 20X4 Y Ltd announced a decision to close down a small workshop with the loss of some jobs. The net costs of closure are estimated at £10,000. No provision has been made at 30 September 20X4.

What is the goodwill arising on the acquisition of Y Ltd?

Feedback to this activity is at the end of the chapter.

4.6 Investigation period and goodwill adjustments

KEY POINT

It might be necessary to use provisional fair values in the first post-acquisition financial statements of the acquirer. Any necessary adjustments to these should be made by the date of the next full financial statements.

Because the 'fair value exercise' is complex, it might be necessary to use **provisional values** in the first post-acquisition financial statements of the acquirer. Any necessary adjustments to these provisional values should be made by the date that the financial statements for the **first full financial year following the acquisition** are approved by the directors. There must also be a corresponding adjustment to **purchased goodwill**.

Thereafter, any adjustments should be recognised in the profit and loss account as they occur. The exception to this is the correction of fundamental errors, which should be treated as prior period adjustments as required by FRS 3.

4.7 Fair value of the cost of acquisition

KEY POINT

Acquisition costs are the sum of cash paid, fair values of other purchase considerations and acquisition expenses.

The **cost of acquisition** is:

- the amount of **cash** paid; plus
- the fair value of other **purchase considerations** given by the acquirer; plus
- the **expenses** of acquisition.

FRS 7 requires the following with regard to the costs of acquisition.

- When settlement of cash consideration is deferred, the amount expected to be payable should be discounted to its present value. The discount rate used should be the rate at which the acquirer could obtain a similar borrowing.
- When the amount of purchase consideration is contingent on one or more future events, the cost of acquisition should include a reasonable estimate of the fair value of amounts expected to be payable in the future. The cost of acquisition (and therefore the goodwill arising) should be adjusted to reflect changes in this estimate until the amount payable is known with certainty.
- Fees and similar incremental costs incurred directly in making an acquisition should be included in the cost of acquisition. (These might include fees paid to merchant banks, accountants, legal advisers, etc.)
- Issue costs of shares are not included in the cost of acquisition. These are deducted from the proceeds of the issue, as required by FRS 4 (see later chapter in this text).
- Internal costs and other expenses that cannot be directly attributed to the acquisition cannot be included in the cost of acquisition. They are charge to the profit and loss account.

4.8 Negative goodwill in the consolidated financial statements

KEY POINT

Negative goodwill arises where an entity is purchased for less than the total fair values of its identifiable net assets.

KEY POINT

FRS 10 requires that negative goodwill should be recognised on the face of the balance sheet immediately below the goodwill heading.

As we have seen in an earlier chapter, negative goodwill arises where an entity is purchased for less than the total fair values of its identifiable net assets.

The Examiner may ask you to account for negative goodwill in the consolidated financial statements.

FRS 10 requires the following accounting treatment.

- Negative goodwill should be recognised and separately disclosed on the face of the balance sheet, immediately below the goodwill heading and followed by a subtotal showing the net amount of the positive and negative goodwill.
- Negative goodwill up to the fair values of the non-monetary assets (e.g. fixed assets) acquired should be recognised in the profit and loss account in the periods in which the non-monetary assets are recovered, whether through depreciation or sale.
- Any negative goodwill in excess of the fair values of the non-monetary assets acquired should be recognised in the profit and loss account in the periods where the benefit is expected to be felt.

ACTIVITY **6**

On 1 October 20X7, Alpha plc purchased the entire share capital of Omega Ltd for £12 million in cash.

The summarised balance sheets of the two companies at 30 September 20X8 are:

	Alpha plc		*Omega Ltd*	
	£000	£000	£000	£000
Fixed assets				
Tangible assets		17,130		13,500
Investment in Omega Ltd		12,000		
Current assets				
Stocks	4,820		3,600	
Trade and other debtors	5,600		2,530	
Cash	–		1,705	
	10,420		7,835	
Creditors: amounts falling due within one year				
Trade and other creditors	6,560		2,635	
Bank overdraft	770		–	
Taxation	2,820		1,200	
Proposed dividends	2,000		–	
	12,150		3,835	
Net current assets (liabilities)		(1,730)		4,000
Net assets		27,400		17,500
Capital and Reserves				
Ordinary shares £1 each		17,000		10,000
Reserves:				
Profit and loss account		10,400		7,500
		27,400		17,500

The following information is relevant.

(i) The book values of the net assets of Omega Ltd at the date of acquisition were considered to be a reasonable approximation to their fair values. Omega Ltd's tangible fixed assets are all non-monetary and had a fair value of £12 million and a remaining life of five years at the date of acquisition (straight-line depreciation is used). At this date Omega Ltd's only other non-monetary asset was its stock which had a fair value of £3 million. All of this stock had been sold by the company's year end.

(ii) The profits of Omega Ltd for the year to 30 September 20X8 were £4 million. No dividends have been paid during the year.

Required:

Prepare the Consolidated Balance Sheet of Alpha plc as at 30 September 20X8.

Feedback to this activity is at the end of the chapter.

Conclusion

As with a consolidated balance sheet, the basic procedure for preparing a consolidated profit and loss account is simply to add together the profit and loss accounts for the individual companies within the group.

A convenient way to do this is by means of the master schedule illustrated in this chapter. On this schedule you can enter adjustments for:

- inter-company transactions (including trading transactions, disposal of assets and payment of dividends and interest by subsidiaries to the parent company)
- minority interests.

The assets and liabilities of an acquired subsidiary must normally be included in the group accounts at their fair value. FRS 7 sets out the rules for arriving at this.

SELF-TEST QUESTIONS

1 In general, how is the consolidated profit and loss account prepared? (1.1)

2 If a parent and a 75% owned subsidiary both have turnover of £100,000, is consolidated turnover £200,000 or £175,000? (1.3)

3 How are revenue reserves brought forward calculated? (1.4)

4 Where there are inter-company dividends on preference shares, how are these treated in the consolidated profit and loss account? (1.6)

5 How can pre-acquisition dividends be treated in consolidated accounts? (1.8)

6 When can a parent dispense with the need to publish its own profit and loss account? (1.10)

7 How is intra-group interest treated in the consolidated profit and loss account? (3.4)

8 Define fair value. (4.1)

9 What are the requirements of FRS 7 concerning the treatment of provisions for future operating losses in an acquired subsidiary? (4.4)

10 What is the fair value of the cost of acquisition? (4.7)

PRACTICE QUESTION

N and S

N plc acquired 60% of the ordinary shares of S Ltd several years ago when the reserves of S Ltd were £80,000. N plc also acquired 20% of the preference shares of S Ltd on the same date.

The summarised profit and loss accounts of the two companies for the year ended 30 September 20X7 are as follows:

	N plc		*S Ltd*	
	£000	£000	£000	£000
Sales		4,500		1,100
Cost of sales		2,320		620
Gross profit		2,180		480
Expenses		1,400		220
Trading profit		780		260
Investment income		52		
Profit before taxation		832		
Taxation		200		80
Profit after taxation		632		180
Dividends paid:				
Ordinary	140		20	
Preference	15		10	
Dividends proposed:				
Ordinary	280		60	
Preference	15		10	
		450		100
Profit retained		182		80
Reserves brought forward		600		250
Reserves carried forward		782		330

N plc sold goods to S Ltd during the year at an invoice price of £250,000. The goods were invoiced at cost + 25%. Of these goods, one half were still in S Ltd's stock at the end of the year.

Required:

Prepare the consolidated profit and loss account for the year ended 30 September 20X7. Ignore goodwill. **(14 marks)**

EXAM-TYPE QUESTION

Greenhouse plc

Greenhouse plc is engaged in the paper-making industry and has one subsidiary Airedale plc. Greenhouse plc owns 60% of the voting shares of Airedale plc which were acquired on 1 September 20X2, when the profit and loss account balance of Airedale was £1.4 million. The draft profit and loss accounts for the year ended 31 August 20X4 were:

	Greenhouse plc		*Airedale plc*	
	£000	£000	£000	£000
Turnover		15,050		12,340
Cost of sales		(12,679)		(10,622)
Gross profit		2,371		1,718
Dividend income		280		64
		2,651		1,782
Distribution costs	1,042		824	
Administrative expenses	946		307	
		(1,988)		(1,131)
Net profit before tax		663		651
Corporation tax		(268)		(96)
Net profit after tax before dividends		395		555

(a) Greenhouse plc has declared (but not yet paid) a final dividend of 5p per ordinary share. Airedale plc has already paid an interim dividend of 10p per ordinary share on 1 May 20X4 and does not propose to pay a final dividend. The issued share capital of Greenhouse plc is 600,000 ordinary shares of 50p each and of Airedale plc is 200,000 ordinary shares of £1 each. Greenhouse plc accounts for dividends received on a cash basis.

(b) The profit and loss account balances at 1 September 20X3 were £1.75 million for Greenhouse plc and £1.6 million for Airedale plc.

(c) Airedale plc occasionally trades with its parent company. During the year Greenhouse plc had purchased goods amounting to £275,000 from Airedale plc, and Airedale plc had purchased goods from Greenhouse plc amounting to £450,000. These transactions had occurred early in the financial year and none of these goods remained in stock at the financial year end. Inter-company sales are charged at cost plus 25% profit.

(d) Goodwill of £300,000 arose on the acquisition. It is group policy to amortise all goodwill over five years from the date of acquisition.

Required:

(a) Prepare the consolidated profit and loss account for the year ended 31 August 20X4 for Greenhouse plc. **(15 marks)**

(b) Calculate the figure for the group's profit and loss account which would appear in the consolidated balance sheet of Greenhouse plc as at 31 August 20X4. **(5 marks)**

(Total: 20 marks)

For the answers to these questions, see the 'Answers' section at the end of the book.

FEEDBACK TO ACTIVITY **1**

Consolidated profit and loss account for year ended 30 November 20X4

	£
Turnover	10,700,000
Total costs	9,630,000
Group profit on ordinary activities before taxation	1,070,000
Tax on profit on ordinary activities	500,000
Profit on ordinary activities after taxation	570,000
Minority interests (25% × 120)	30,000
Profit for the year retained	540,000

FEEDBACK TO ACTIVITY **2**

	£
Brought forward	
P Ltd	2,300,000
S Ltd 75% × £(400,000 – 100,000)	225,000
	2,525,000
Retained for the year	540,000
Carried forward	3,065,000

It is important to note that the calculation of retained profits brought forward is of the same form as the calculation of group reserves in the balance sheet. To demonstrate that this is so, here are extracts from the working papers for the balance sheet consolidations at 30 November 20X3 and 30 November 20X4.

Consolidated profit and loss account reserves, at 30 November 20X3:

	£000
P Ltd	2,300
S Ltd 75% (400 – 100)	225
	2,525

Consolidated profit and loss account reserves, at 30 November 20X4:

	£000
P Ltd*	2,750
S Ltd 75% (520 – 100)*	315
	3,065

*Reserves of the two companies at the end of the year are as follows:

	P Ltd	*S Ltd*
	£	£
Retained profit brought forward	2,300,000	400,000
Retained profit for the year	450,000	120,000
Retained profit carried forward	2,750,000	520,000

FEEDBACK TO ACTIVITY 3

The main point to remember is that inter-company dividends must be eliminated. Furthermore, as far as the minority's share of the subsidiary's current year profits is concerned, the object of the consolidated profit and loss account is to show the minority's share of the profit after taxation, and *not* how this figure is split between dividends and retained profit.

Minority interests in profit of subsidiary are 25% × £42,000 = £10,500.

Consolidated profit and loss account for year ended 31 August 20X4

	£
Turnover (2,400 + 800)	3,200,000
Total costs (2,160 + 720)	2,880,000
Group profit on ordinary activities before taxation	320,000
Tax on profit on ordinary activities (115 + 38)	153,000
Profit on ordinary activities after taxation	167,000
Minority interests	10,500
Profit after taxation attributable to P Ltd	156,500
Dividend proposed by P Ltd	60,000
Profit for the year retained	96,500

FEEDBACK TO ACTIVITY 4

Consolidated profit and loss account for year ended 31 July 20X4

	£
Turnover £(1,430,000 + (5/12 × 600,000))	1,680,000
Total costs £(1,160,000 + (5/12 × 504,000))	1,370,000
Profit on ordinary activities before taxation £(270,000 + (5/12 × 96,000))	310,000
Tax on profit on ordinary activities £(135,000 + (5/12 × 48,000))	155,000
Profit on ordinary activities after taxation	155,000
Minority interests £(25% × 5/12 × (96,000 – 48,000))	5,000
Profit for the financial year	150,000
Reserves brought forward	900,000
Reserves carried forward	1,050,000

Note: The reserves brought forward can only consist of P Ltd's reserves, as S Ltd was not a subsidiary at that date.

FEEDBACK TO ACTIVITY 5

Adjust the value of Y Ltd's net assets at 30 September 20X4 to fair value

	£
Net assets per question	350,000
Revaluation of property	20,000
Write-off of stock	(4,000)
Provision for reorganisation costs*	(10,000)
	356,000

(***Note:*** Since Y Ltd made the decision to close, and the decision was announced before the date of acquisition, this is a valid provision.)

Calculate goodwill

	£
Fair value of consideration	320,000
Net assets acquired 80% × £356,000	284,800
Goodwill arising	35,200

FEEDBACK TO ACTIVITY 6

Consolidated balance sheet of Alpha plc as at 30 September 20X8

	£000	£000
Fixed assets		
Intangible:		
Negative goodwill (W1)		(960)
Tangible		30,630
		29,670
Current assets		
Stocks	8,420	
Trade debtors	8,130	
Cash	1,705	
	18,255	

Creditors: amounts falling due within one year		
Trade creditors	9,195	
Bank overdraft	770	
Taxation	4,020	
Proposed dividends	2,000	
	15,985	
Net current assets		2,270
Net assets		31,940
Capital and reserves		
Ordinary share capital		17,000
Profit and loss account (W2)		14,940
		31,940

Workings

	£000	£000
(W1) Negative goodwill:		
Cost of investment		12,000
Share capital	10,000	
Pre acquisition profit (7,500 – 4,000)	3,500	
		(13,500)
Negative goodwill		(1,500)
Less: recognised in profit and loss account (5,400/15,000 × 1,500)		540
		(960)

Total non-monetary assets in Omega Ltd are £15 million (3,000 + 12,000)

Non monetary assets recovered in period:	
Stock (sold)	3,000
Tangible fixed assets (depreciated) (12,000 ÷ 5)	2,400
	5,400

(W2) Profit and loss account:	£000
Alpha plc	10,400
Post acquisition in Omega Ltd	4,000
Realised element of negative goodwill (see W1)	540
	14,940

Chapter 9

GROUP ACCOUNTING – ASSOCIATES AND JOINT VENTURES

CHAPTER CONTENTS

1 Associated undertakings
2 Joint ventures
3 Alternative methods of showing an investment in another company
4 Accounting for associates – the equity method
5 Accounting for joint ventures
6 Disclosure requirements for associates and joint ventures

So far, we have only considered subsidiaries, that is, undertakings that are controlled by the parent. In this chapter we look at situations where a company may not be able to exercise control over an investee company, but can influence its operating and financial policies. An entity over which an investor can exercise significant influence is called an associate. A joint venture is an entity which is jointly controlled by one or more other entities.

This chapter shows how to determine whether an entity is an associate or a joint venture, and how to account for associates and joint ventures in the consolidated financial statements.

Objectives

By the time you have finished this chapter you should be able to:

- define associates and joint ventures, including an arrangement that is not an entity
- distinguish between equity accounting and proportional consolidation
- describe the equity and gross equity methods
- prepare consolidated financial statements to include a single subsidiary and an associated company or joint venture.

1 Associated undertakings

1.1 Introduction

Where a company owns more than 50% of the voting share capital of another company, CA85 requires group accounts. The law in effect recognises the control which a parent company may exert over a subsidiary company and the existence of an economic unit, the **group**. If a parent company's accounts were to show only dividends received or receivable from subsidiaries, the shareholders of the parent company would not be given sufficient information regarding the underlying profitability of the unit, the group. Consequently, group accounts normally include the parent company's share of the post-acquisition profits of subsidiaries as we have seen in the last few chapter.

KEY POINT

CA89 introduced into law the requirement for **associated undertakings** to be included in group accounts under the **equity** method.

However, if a company, P Ltd, which has subsidiaries, owns (say) 40% of the ordinary share capital of another company, A Ltd, then A Ltd does not come within the legal definition of a subsidiary company. P Ltd *may* nevertheless be able to exert considerable influence over A Ltd. It would thus seem sensible to allow P Ltd to show information in its accounts about its share of the profits of A Ltd.

FRS 9 provides rules for accounting for associated companies, i.e. companies which fall into the position described above.

CA89 introduced into the law the requirement for **associated undertakings** to be included in group accounts under the **equity** method. The equity method is the method detailed by FRS 9.

The term **undertakings** includes companies and unincorporated businesses. As CA89 requires the word 'undertaking' to be used in the published accounts, the rest of this section will follow the CA89 terminology, where it is sensible to do so.

1.2 What is an 'associated undertaking'?

Company law

KEY POINT

Where an investor holds 20% or more of the shares of another undertaking, it is presumed that this is a **participating interest**.

KEY POINT

An **associated undertaking** is an undertaking in which an undertaking included in the consolidation has a **participating interest** and over whose operating and financial policy it exercises a significant influence.

An associated undertaking will come within the definition of a **participating interest** in the investing company's **individual** accounts.

A **participating interest** is an interest held in the shares of another undertaking, held for the long term, with a view to exercising control or influence to secure a benefit to the investor's own activities. Where an investor holds 20% or more of the shares, there is a presumption that this is a participating interest.

In the group accounts participating interests are split into **interests in associated undertakings** and **other participating interests**.

An **associated undertaking** means an undertaking in which an undertaking included in the consolidation has a **participating interest** and over whose operating and financial policy it exercises a significant influence, and which is not:

- a **subsidiary** undertaking, or
- a **joint venture** dealt with in the group accounts by proportional consolidation.

Note: only **unincorporated** undertakings can be dealt with using proportional consolidation.

Where an undertaking holds 20% or more of the voting rights in another undertaking, it is presumed to exercise such an influence over it unless the contrary is shown.

To summarise, most participating interests are associated undertakings. The difference between the two terms mainly relates to the type of share capital held.

- A participating interest arises when 20% of **any** type of share capital is held.
- An associated undertaking requires a 20% or more **equity** voting shareholding.

1.3 FRS 9

DEFINITION

FRS 9 defines an **associate** as an entity in which another entity has a **participating interest** and over whose policies the investor exercises a **significant influence.**

DEFINITION

FRS 9 defines a **participating interest** as an interest held in the shares of another entity to secure a contribution to the investor's activities by the exercise of control or influence.

The FRS 9 definition is quite complex, but is essentially similar to the company law definition.

An **associate** is an entity (other than a subsidiary) in which another entity (the investor) has a **participating interest** and over whose operating and financial policies the investor exercises a **significant influence**.

A **participating interest** is an interest held in the shares of another entity on a long-term basis for the purpose of securing a contribution to the investor's activities by the exercise of control or influence arising from or related to that interest.

The exercise of **significant influence** means that the investor is actively involved and is influential in the direction of its investee through its participation in policy decisions covering aspects of policy relevant to the investor, including decisions on strategic issues such as:

- the expansion or contraction of the business, participation in other entities or changes in products, markets and activities of its investee; and
- determining the balance between dividend and reinvestment.

The main thing to note is that the emphasis of the FRS 9 definition is different from that in CA89. Under CA89, a holding of 20% or more is presumed to be an associate unless it can clearly be demonstrated otherwise. SSAP 1 (which preceded FRS 9) used a similar definition. In practice, this meant that the 20% threshold was normally the only factor taken into account, so that many investments were treated as associates when the investee did not actually exercise significant influence.

KEY POINT

Under CA89, a holding of 20% or more is presumed to be an associate unless it can clearly be demonstrated otherwise. The FRS 9 definition centres on the substance of the relationship between the parties.

The FRS 9 definition centres on the actual substance of the relationship between the parties (i.e. whether significant influence is exercised in practice) rather than its strict legal form (the size of the shareholding).

An investing company's ability to exercise significant influence may depend on the other shareholdings as well as its own. For example, if A Ltd holds 30% of the shares in B Ltd, but the remaining 70% of the shares in B Ltd are held by C plc, then A Ltd is extremely unlikely to be able to exercise significant influence over B Ltd.

However, in questions you should assume that a shareholding of between 20% and 50% is an **associate** unless you are given information which suggests otherwise.

EXAM HINT

In questions you should assume that a shareholding of between 20% and 50% is an **associate** unless you are given information which suggests otherwise.

Summary

A company is an associated undertaking if the investing company exercises significant influence over it. A shareholding of between 20% and 50% normally gives significant influence.

ACTIVITY 1

Which of the following investments of Gamma Trust plc should be treated as associated undertakings? Assume that all shares carry equal voting rights.

1 19% of the equity shares in Goose Ltd. Gamma Trust plc is the largest shareholder, has a director on the board, and provides management expertise to this rapidly growing company.

2 22% of the equity share capital of Delta Traders plc, a company in the same line of business as most of Gamma Trust plc. In the past there has been an unsuccessful bid for Delta Traders plc by Gamma Trust plc. Gamma Trust plc has no director on Delta Traders plc's board, and its views on the management of Delta Traders plc are neither sought nor accepted. The majority shareholders use their combined voting rights to keep any nominee of Gamma Trust plc off the board, and to prevent any motion proposed by Gamma Trust plc from being passed at general meetings.

3 21% of the equity share capital of Nova Manufacturers Ltd. This shareholding was recently increased from 10%, as the young company is expanding rapidly. The company's business is not within Gamma Trust's core business range, and Gamma Trust hopes to sell its investment within the year.

4 47% of the equity share capital of Alpha Wholesale Ltd. The other shareholders are split between various small investors. Gamma Trust plc nominates seven of the ten directors on the board of Alpha Wholesale Ltd, under a written agreement between the two companies.

Feedback to this activity is at the end of the chapter.

1.4 Types of associated undertaking situations

KEY POINT

The accounting treatment varies depending upon whether the investing company has subsidiaries.

The accounting treatment varies depending upon whether the investing company:

- has subsidiaries and is thus obliged to prepare group accounts anyway, or
- has no subsidiary.

In most cases the investing company has subsidiaries and thus prepares group accounts. This situation is covered here.

ACTIVITY 2

What are the headings in the CA85 group accounts formats for the balance sheet and the profit and loss account which are used for associated undertakings?

Feedback to this activity is at the end of the chapter.

2 Joint ventures

2.1 Introduction

DEFINITION

FRS 9 defines a **joint venture** as an entity in which the reporting entity holds an interest, and which is **jointly controlled** by the reporting entity and by one or more other venturers under a contractual arrangement.

DEFINITION

A **joint arrangement that is not an entity** is a contractual arrangement under which the participants engage in joint activities that do not create an entity because it would not be carrying on a trade or business on its own.

The term 'joint venture' is used very widely in practice to cover all types of jointly controlled activity. Jointly controlled operations, assets and entities may all be described as joint ventures. FRS 9 defines 'joint venture' in a much narrower sense.

A **joint venture** is an entity in which the reporting entity holds an interest on a long-term basis, and which is **jointly controlled** by the reporting entity and by one or more other venturers under a contractual arrangement.

A reporting entity **jointly controls** a venture with one or more other entities if none of the entities alone can control that entity but all together can do so, and decisions on financial and operating policy essential to the activities, economic performance and financial position of that venture require each venturer's consent.

A **joint arrangement that is not an entity** is a contractual arrangement under which the participants engage in joint activities that do not create an entity because it would not be carrying on a trade or business of its own.

2.2 Distinguishing joint ventures from joint arrangements

KEY POINT

For an investment to qualify as a joint venture, there must be a separate **entity** which carries on a **trade or business of its own**.

For an investment to qualify as a joint venture, there must be a separate **entity** which carries on a **trade or business of its own**.

This means that the joint venture must have some independence to pursue its own commercial strategy and it must generally be able to buy and sell on the same terms as are available in the market.

FRS 9 provides further examples of indications of when a joint arrangement is not carrying on a trade or business of its own:

- the participants derive their benefit from products or services taken in kind rather than by receiving a share in the results of trading
- each participant's share of the output or result of the joint activity is determined by its supply of key inputs to the process producing that output or result.

KEY POINT

A joint arrangement to carry out a single project is unlikely to meet the definition of a joint venture.

A cost or risk sharing means of carrying out a process in the participants' own trades or businesses (e.g. a joint marketing or distribution network or a shared production facility) is not a joint venture.

A joint arrangement to carry out a single project is unlikely to meet the definition of a joint venture.

ACTIVITY 3

1 A (a builder) and B (an estate agent) together buy a house which they let to tenants. A is responsible for the initial refurbishment and maintenance of the house and B finds the tenants and collects the rents. A and B each take an agreed share of the rental income from the house.

2 A and B enter into an agreement to manufacture and sell a new product. They set up a company which carries out these activities. A and B each own 50% of the equity share capital of the company and are its only directors. They share equally in major policy decisions and are each entitled to 50% of the profits of the company.

Are these two joint activities joint ventures or joint arrangements?

Feedback to this activity is at the end of the chapter.

3 Alternative methods of showing an investment in another company

3.1 Consolidation, equity accounting and proportional consolidation

KEY POINT

Consolidation reflects the fact that the parent controls 100% of the assets and liabilities of the subsidiary, even though it may not actually own 100% of the equity shares.

Consolidation is used to account for a parent's investment in a subsidiary in the group accounts. Consolidation reflects the fact that the parent controls 100% of the assets and liabilities of the subsidiary, even though it may not actually own 100% of the equity shares.

Consolidation would not reflect the substance of an investor's relationship with an associate or a joint venture, because the investor does not control 100% of the assets and liabilities. Nor would it be appropriate to treat these as simple investments (i.e. by including the investment at cost in the group balance sheet), because this would not reflect the fact that the investor can exercise significant influence.

There are two potential methods of accounting for investments in associates and joint ventures in the group accounts.

KEY POINT

Equity accounting and **proportional consolidation** are the two potential methods of accounting for investments in associates and joint ventures.

Under the **equity method**, accounts record the share of profits attributable to the investing company from the investee and the company's **share** in the net assets of the investee. Thus, minority shareholders' interests in the net assets are not shown.

In the **proportional consolidation method**, the share of individual assets and liabilities of the investee are included in the relevant totals. Again, minority shareholders' interests in the net assets are not shown.

3.2 The equity method

KEY POINT

The **equity method** allows the group balance sheet to record the current share of net assets of the associate.

The **equity method** allows the group balance sheet to record the current share of net assets of the associate but does not mislead the user into thinking that the associate is a part of the group as the assets are not combined with the group assets.

It is used in three situations:

- associates under FRS 9
- exclusion of subsidiaries from consolidation under FRS 2 (see earlier chapter)
- joint ventures under FRS 9 (with additional disclosures).

The main disadvantage of the equity method is that it fails to reveal the underlying assets and liabilities. This is why it is not regarded as a valid method of showing group accounts in the majority of situations, and it is therefore only used when, for some reason, consolidation is regarded as inappropriate.

3.3 The proportional consolidation method

KEY POINT

The **proportional consolidation** method shows the group's share of the underlying assets and liabilities.

The **proportional consolidation** method has the advantage of showing the group's share of the underlying assets and liabilities.

However, it does not clearly distinguish the assets of the investee from those of the group. This treatment implies that the investing group can control the assets and liabilities of the investee. Therefore proportional consolidation would be potentially misleading if it were used for an associate.

Some commentators believe that proportional consolidation should be used to account for joint ventures. They argue that because joint control means a sharing of risks and rewards it gives a higher level of influence than mere significant influence. It is therefore appropriate to recognise the venturer's share of individual assets and liabilities. Proportional consolidation would give a better representation of the economic substance of the investment and it is argued that this would also be consistent with the requirements of FRS 5 (recognition of interests in assets).

KEY POINT

Under CA89 proportional consolidation can only be used for **unincorporated** joint ventures.

The ASB considered proportional consolidation for joint ventures, but rejected it on the grounds that it would be inconsistent with the accounting treatment of both associates and subsidiaries. It argues that in most cases, the venturer controls an interest in the joint venture, rather than its share in individual assets and liabilities.

Proportional consolidation would also be inconsistent with the requirements of the Companies Act in most cases. Under CA89 proportional consolidation can only be used for **unincorporated** joint ventures.

4 Accounting for associates – the equity method

4.1 Equity accounting in the consolidated balance sheet

KEY POINT

Equity accounting brings an investment into its investor's financial statements initially at its cost, identifying any goodwill arising.

The investment in the associate is stated at cost plus group share of retained post-acquisition profits, less goodwill amortised.

Equity accounting is a method of accounting that brings an investment into its investor's financial statements initially at its cost, identifying any goodwill arising. The carrying amount of the investment is adjusted in each period by the investor's share of the results of its investee less any amortisation or write-off for goodwill, the investor's share of any relevant gains or losses, and any other changes in the investee's net assets including distributions to its owners, for example, by dividend.

The investment in the associate is therefore stated at

- **cost**; plus
- group share of **retained post-acquisition profits**; less
- **amounts written off** (e.g. goodwill amortised).

Assuming goodwill has been fully amortised, this will be equal to the investing company's share of net assets in the associate.

Example

H plc acquired 25% of the ordinary share capital of A plc for £640,000 some years ago when the profit and loss reserves of A plc stood at £720,000. Goodwill arising on the acquisition has been fully amortised. H plc appointed two directors to the board of A plc and the investment is regarded as long term. Both companies prepare accounts to 31 December each year.

The summarised balance sheet of A plc on 31 December 20X4 is as follows:

	£000
Sundry net assets	2,390
Capital and reserves:	
Called up share capital	800
Share premium	450
Profit and loss account	1,140
	2,390

A plc has made no new issues of shares nor has there been any movement in the share premium account since H plc acquired its holding.

Show at what amount the investment in A plc will be shown in the consolidated balance sheet of H plc as on 31 December 20X4.

Solution

Investment in associated undertakings

$$25\% \times £2,390,000 = £597,500$$

This figure could also be calculated as:

	£
Cost	640,000
Share of post-acquisition profits (25% × (1,140 – 720))	105,000
Less: Goodwill amortised (W1)	(147,500)
	597,500

Working

(W1) **Goodwill**

	£	£
Cost		640,000
Less: Share of net assets at acquisition		
Share capital	800,000	
Share premium	450,000	
Reserves	720,000	
	25% × £1,970,000	(492,500)
Goodwill – fully amortised		147,500

4.2 Effect on total reserves

KEY POINT

Group reserves will be increased by the group share of **post-acquisition reserves** and decreased by any **goodwill amortised**.

Total reserves in the published accounts will be changed in two main ways due to the equity accounting of the associate.

- Reserves will be increased by the group share of **post-acquisition reserves**.
- Reserves will be decreased by any **goodwill amortised**.

The consolidation schedule for group reserves will include these two items in respect of associated undertakings as shown below:

Consolidated profit and loss account reserve

	£'000
H:	X
S: S% (now – acquisition)	X
A: 25% (now – acquisition) (1,140 – 720)	105
Less: Goodwill amortised	
S:	(X)
A:	(147.5)
	X

4.3 Equity accounting in the consolidated profit and loss account

KEY POINT

The consolidated profit and loss account includes the group share of operating profit, exceptional items, interest and taxation.

The **group share** of the following are brought in:

- operating profit
- exceptional items
- interest receivable
- interest payable
- taxation.

Amortisation of goodwill arising on acquisition of an associate should be deducted from the group share of operating profit and should be separately disclosed.

Example

Following on from the facts in the above section, the consolidated profit and loss account of H plc (before including any amounts for A plc), and the profit and loss account of A plc for the year ended 31 December 20X4 are as follows:

	H plc	*A plc*
	£000	£000
Turnover	11,000	4,000
Cost of sales	(6,500)	(3,000)
Gross profit	4,500	1,000
Distribution costs	(1,000)	(500)
Administrative expenses	(700)	(300)
Operating profit	2,800	200
Interest receivable	300	200
Interest payable	(100)	(100)
Profit on ordinary activities before taxation	3,000	300
Taxation	(1,200)	(60)
Profit on ordinary activities after taxation	1,800	240
Minority interests	(300)	–
Profit attributable to the group	1,500	240
Dividends proposed	(300)	(50)
Retained profit for the year	1,200	190
Retained profit b/f	6,300	950
Retained profit c/f	7,500	1,140

Prepare the consolidated profit and loss account for H plc for the year ended 31 December 20X4.

Solution

	£000	£000
Turnover		11,000
Cost of sales		(6,500)
Gross profit		4,500
Distribution costs		(1,000)
Administrative expenses		(700)
Group operating profit		2,800
Share of operating profit in associates (25% × 200)		50
Interest receivable:		
Group	300	
Associates (25% × 200)	50	
		350

Interest payable:		
Group	100	
Associates (25% × 100)	25	
		(125)
Profit on ordinary activities before taxation		3,075
Taxation		
Group	1,200	
Associates (25% × 60)	15	
		(1,215)
Profit on ordinary activities after taxation		1,860
Minority interests		(300)
Profit attributable to the group		1,560
Dividends		(300)
Retained profit for the year		1,260
Retained at 1 January 20X4 (W1)		6,210
Retained at 31 December 20X4		7,470

Working

(W1) **Retained profit b/d**

	£000
H plc	6,300
A plc 25% (950 – 720)	58
Less: Goodwill amortised (per previous example)	(148)
	6,210

4.4 Transactions between the group and the associate

Trading transactions and/or loans may be made between member companies of the group (i.e. parent company and subsidiaries) and the associate. As the associate is not consolidated, it follows that these transactions are not cancelled out. For example, a loan made by the parent company to an associate will remain as a loan on the consolidated balance sheet (as an asset). The liability recorded in the associate's balance sheet will merely reduce the net assets (which are recorded as one figure – share of net assets – on the consolidated balance sheet).

KEY POINT

If there is unrealised profit at the balance sheet date, FRS 9 requires an adjustment for the group's share.

An adjustment will only be required if there is unrealised profit at the balance sheet date, e.g. if stocks exist as a result of the trading between the associate and the parent. FRS 9 requires an adjustment for the group's share of the unrealised profit. The elimination should be taken in the consolidated profit and loss account against either the group or the associate, according to which of them recorded the profit on the transaction. The adjustment in the balance sheet should be made against:

- **consolidated stock** (if the unrealised profit is in respect of part of this stock)
- **investment in associate** (if the stock is in the associate).

4.5 Applying the equity method – further points

KEY POINT

The investor's share of the total recognised gains of its associates should be included in the STRGL.

Statement of total recognised gains and losses

The investor's share of the total recognised gains of its associates should be included in the STRGL. If the amounts are material, they should be shown separately under each heading either in the statement or in a note to the statement.

General principles

- The consideration paid for the acquisition and the goodwill arising should be calculated using fair values.
- The investor and the associate should apply the same accounting policies.
- The accounts of the associate should have the same financial year-end as those of the investor. If this is impracticable, earlier financial statements of the associate may be used, provided they are prepared for a financial year that ended not more than three months earlier.
- The date on which an investment becomes an associate is the date on which the investor begins to hold a participating interest and to exercise significant influence.
- The date on which an investment ceases to be an associate is the date on which the investor ceases to hold a participating interest and to exercise significant influence.

5 Accounting for joint ventures

5.1 Joint arrangements that are not entities

KEY POINT

Participants in a **JANE** should account for their own assets, liabilities and cash flows.

Participants in a joint arrangement that is not an entity (known as a **JANE**) should account for their own assets, liabilities and cash flows, measured according to the terms of the agreement governing the arrangement.

5.2 Joint ventures

In the investor's **individual financial statements**, investments in joint ventures should be treated as fixed asset investments and shown either at cost, less any amounts written off, or at valuation.

KEY POINT

The **gross equity method** is a method under which the investor's share of the aggregate **gross assets and liabilities** is shown on the face of the balance sheet.

In the **consolidated financial statements** joint ventures should be included using the gross equity method.

The **gross equity method** is a form of equity method under which the investor's share of the aggregate **gross assets and liabilities** underlying the net amount included for the investment is shown on the face of the balance sheet. In the profit and loss account, the investor's share of the investee's turnover is noted.

This means that the treatment is the same as for associates, but with additional disclosure:

- the investor's share of **turnover** is shown in the consolidated profit and loss account (but not as part of group turnover)
- the investor's share of the gross assets and liabilities is shown in the consolidated balance sheet (instead of the investor's share of the net assets).

KEY POINT

Joint ventures are included in the consolidated financial statements using the gross equity method.

FRS 9 has effectively prohibited the use of proportional consolidation for joint ventures. However, it could be argued that the gross equity method is a compromise between the equity method and proportional consolidation.

Example

FRS 9 includes illustrative examples of ways of disclosing information about joint ventures. Example 1 from FRS 9 is shown below. Note that the example also includes associates.

Consolidated profit and loss account

	£m	£m
Turnover: group and share of joint ventures	320	
Less: share of joint ventures' turnover	(120)	
	—	
Group turnover		200
Cost of sales		(120)
		—
Gross profit		80
Administrative expenses		(40)
		—
Group operating profit		40
Share of operating profit in		
Joint ventures	30	
Associates	24	
	—	
		54
		—
		94
Interest receivable (group)		6
Interest payable		
Group	(26)	
Joint ventures	(10)	
Associates	(12)	
	—	
		(48)
		—
Profit on ordinary activities before tax		52
Tax on profit on ordinary activities*		(12)
		—
Profit on ordinary activities after tax		40
Minority interests		(6)
		—
Profit on ordinary activities after taxation and minority interest		34
Equity dividends		(10)
		—
Retained profit for group and its share of associates and joint ventures		24
		—
* Tax relates to the following:		
Parent and subsidiaries	(5)	
Joint ventures	(5)	
Associates	(2)	

Consolidated balance sheet

	£m	£m	£m
Fixed assets			
Tangible assets		480	
Investments			
Investments in joint ventures:			
Share of gross assets	130		
Share of gross liabilities	(80)		
		50	
Investments in associates		20	
			550
Current assets			
Stock		15	
Debtors		75	
Cash at bank and in hand		10	
		100	
Creditors (due within one year)		(50)	
Net current assets			50
Total assets less current liabilities			600
Creditors (due after more than one year)			(250)
Provisions for liabilities			(10)
Equity minority interest			(40)
			300
Capital and reserves			
Called up share capital			50
Share premium account			150
Profit and loss account			100
Shareholders' funds (all equity)			300

6 Disclosure requirements for associates and joint ventures

6.1 All associates and joint ventures

- For each associate or joint venture included in the financial statements of the investing group, disclose the following:
  - name
  - proportion of the issued shares in each class held by the investing group
  - accounting period or date of the financial statements used, if different from those of the investing group
  - an indication of the nature of its business.
- Disclose any notes relating to the financial statements of associates that are material to understanding the effect on the investor of its investments.

- Indicate the extent of any statutory, contractual or exchange control restrictions on the ability of an associate to distribute its reserves.
- Disclose the amounts owing and owed between the investor and its associates or joint ventures, analysed into amounts relating to loans and amounts relating to trading balances.
- Where an investor which holds 20% or more of the voting rights of another entity does not treat it as an associate, a note should explain the reasons for this.

6.2 Detailed disclosures where associates and joint ventures are material to the investing group

As we have seen, one of the disadvantages of the equity method is that it only provides limited information about associates and joint ventures. In particular, only one figure is included in the balance sheet, representing the group share of the associates' net assets. It is possible for material liabilities to be hidden in this figure, enabling investors to use equity accounted entities as a form of off balance sheet finance.

KEY POINT

FRS 9 requires additional disclosures where size thresholds are exceeded.

For this reason, FRS 9 requires additional disclosures where size thresholds are exceeded. The thresholds are applied by comparing the investor's share for its associates or joint ventures of *any* of the following:

- gross assets
- gross liabilities
- turnover
- operating results (on a three-year average)

with the corresponding amounts for the investor group (excluding associates and joint ventures).

KEY POINT

Where the *aggregate* of the investor's share in its associates or its joint ventures exceeds a **15% threshold** with respect to the investor group, the group share of certain items is required to be disclosed.

Where the *aggregate* of the investor's share in its associates or its joint ventures exceeds a **15% threshold** with respect to the investor group, a note should give the aggregate of the investor's share in its associates of the following:

- turnover (associates only; for joint ventures it must always be disclosed)
- fixed assets
- current assets
- liabilities due within one year
- liabilities due after one year or more.

KEY POINT

Where the investor's share in any *individual* associate or joint venture exceeds a **25% threshold** with respect to the investor group, additional details are required to be disclosed.

Where the investor's share in any *individual* associate or joint venture exceeds a **25% threshold** with respect to the investor group, a note should name that associate or joint venture and give its share of each of the following:

- turnover
- profit before tax
- taxation
- profit after tax
- fixed assets
- current assets
- liabilities due within one year
- liabilities due after one year or more.

ACTIVITY **4**

You are provided with the following information about H plc and its associated undertaking, A Ltd, for the year ended 30 June 20X8.

	H plc	*A Ltd*
	£'000	£'000
Turnover	110,000	60,000
Operating profit	30,000	16,000
Profit before tax	25,000	12,000
Taxation	10,000	4,000
Profit after tax	15,000	8,000
Fixed assets	250,000	160,000
Current assets	40,000	24,000
Creditors due within one year	45,000	24,000
Creditors due after more than one year	110,000	40,000

H plc holds 25% of the equity share capital of A Ltd.

Show the additional disclosures required in respect of A Ltd in the consolidated financial statements of the H plc group for the year ended 30 June 20X8.

Feedback to this activity is at the end of the chapter.

Conclusion

An associate is an entity in which another entity has a participating interest and over whose operating and financial policies the investor exercises a significant influence. Associates are included in the consolidated financial statements using the equity method of accounting.

A joint venture is an entity in which the reporting entity holds an interest on a long-term basis and is jointly controlled by the reporting entity and one or more other entities. Joint ventures are included in the consolidated financial statements using the gross equity method.

SELF-TEST QUESTIONS

1 What is a participating interest? (1.2, 1.3)

2 How does FRS 9 define an associate? (1.3)

3 Define a joint venture. (2.1)

4 What is the difference between the equity method and proportional consolidation? (3.1)

5 The equity method is used in three situations. What are they? (3.2)

6 At what amount is the investment in an associate stated in the consolidated balance sheet? (4.1)

7 How are the results of an associate dealt with in the consolidated profit and loss account? (4.3)

8 How should a JANE be treated in the consolidated financial statements? (5.1)

9 What is the gross equity method and when is it used? (5.2)

10 What information must be disclosed where the investor's share in an individual associate or joint venture exceeds a 25% threshold with respect to the group? (6.2)

PRACTICE QUESTION

H, S and A

You are given the following abbreviated profit and loss accounts of three companies, H Ltd, S Ltd and A Ltd. H Ltd acquired an 80% holding in S Ltd paying £6,000 for goodwill when the reserves of S Ltd amounted to £40,000. H Ltd acquired a 25% holding in A Ltd at a cost of £81,200, when the reserves of A Ltd amounted to £32,000. A Ltd is an associated company with a share capital of £250,000 (ordinary shares).

Profit and loss accounts for the year ended 31.12.X5

	H Ltd	*S Ltd*	*A Ltd*
	£	£	£
Trading profit	800,000	100,000	140,000
Investment income	5,000	-	-
UK Corporation tax	(400,000)	(50,000)	(70,000)
	405,000	50,000	70,000
Dividend paid	103,000	-	8,000
	302,000	50,000	62,000
Balance b/d	2,000,000	130,000	100,000
Balance c/d	2,302,000	180,000	162,000

Investment income of H Ltd comprises:

	£
Dividend from A Ltd	2,000
Dividend from trade investment	3,000
	5,000

Required:

(a) Prepare a consolidated profit and loss account for the year ended 31.12.X5 which complies with standard accounting practice

(b) Show the extracts in the consolidated balance sheets as at 31.12.X4 and 31.12.X5 relating to the investment in the associated company.

All goodwill has been fully amortised at 1.1.X5. **(20 marks)**

EXAM-TYPE QUESTION

J plc

The balance sheets of J plc and its investee companies, P Ltd and S Ltd, at 31 December 20X4 are shown below:

Balance sheets at 31 December 20X4

	J plc		*P Ltd*		*S Ltd*	
	£'000	£'000	£'000	£'000	£'000	£'000
Tangible fixed assets						
Freehold property	1,950		1,250		500	
Plant and machinery	795		375		285	
		2,745		1,625		785
Investments		1,500		-		-
Current assets						
Stock	575		300		265	
Trade debtors	330		290		370	
Cash	50		120		20	
	955		710		655	

Creditors: due within one year						
Bank overdraft	560		-		-	
Trade creditors	480		300		275	
Proposed dividends	200		50		25	
	1,240		350		300	
Net current (liabilities)/assets		(285)		360		355
Creditors: due after one year						
12% debentures		(500)		(100)		-
		3,460		1,885		1,140
Share capital (£1 ordinary shares)		2,000		1,000		750
Profit and loss account		1,460		885		390
		3,460		1,885		1,140

Additional information

1 J plc acquired 600,000 ordinary shares in P Ltd on 1 January 20W9 for £1,000,000 when the reserves of P Ltd were £200,000.

2 At the date of acquisition of P Ltd, the fair value of its freehold property was considered to be £400,000 greater than its value in P Ltd's balance sheet. P Ltd had acquired the property in January 20V9 and the buildings element (comprising 50% of the total value) is depreciated on cost over 50 years.

3 J plc acquired 225,000 ordinary shares in S Ltd on 1 January 20X3 for £500,000 when the reserves of S Ltd were £150,000.

4 P Ltd manufactures a component used by both J plc and S Ltd. Transfers are made by P Ltd at cost plus 25%. J plc held £100,000 stock of these components at 31 December 20X4 and S Ltd held £80,000 at the same date.

5 It is the policy of J plc to write off goodwill over a period of five years.

6 No entry has been made in the books of J plc for the dividends receivable from P Ltd or S Ltd at 31 December 20X4.

Required:

(a) Prepare a working schedule detailing all the necessary adjustments for 1 to 6 above. **(25 marks)**

(b) Prepare, in a format suitable for inclusion in the annual report of the J Group, the consolidated balance sheet at 31 December 20X4. **(5 marks)**

(Total: 30 marks)

Tutorial note

This is a longer question than you would expect to find in the exam as questions in the exam are only 25 marks. However it is a good practice question with plenty of adjustments to be made.

For the answers to these questions, see the 'Answers' section at the end of the book.

FEEDBACK TO ACTIVITY 1

1. Goose Ltd is an associated company, despite Gamma Trust plc holding less than 20% of the shares, because of the significant influence Gamma Trust has over the management.
2. Delta Traders plc is not an associated company since, unusually for such a large shareholding, Gamma Trust plc has no real effective influence over Delta Traders plc. Gamma Trust plc has to explain the special circumstances clearly in a note to the accounts.
3. The investment in Nova Manufacturers Ltd is not for the long term. Therefore, even though Gamma Trust may currently have a significant influence, Nova Manufacturers is not an associated company.
4. Alpha Wholesale Ltd is a subsidiary, not an associate, of Gamma Trust plc, since Gamma Trust plc's control over the board of directors and the written agreement give it effective control.

FEEDBACK TO ACTIVITY 2

In the balance sheet under Fixed Asset Investments:

- 'Interests in associated undertakings'.

In the profit and loss account after arriving at operating profit:

- 'Income from interests in associated undertakings'.

FEEDBACK TO ACTIVITY 3

1. This is a joint arrangement that is not an entity because:
   - no separate entity exists
   - the arrangement is a single project
   - it appears to be simply a means of carrying out A and B's own businesses.
2. This appears to be a joint venture because:
   - there is a separate entity
   - the entity appears to be carrying out a business of its own
   - the participants share in the profits of the business.

FEEDBACK TO ACTIVITY 4

Additional disclosures for associates

	£000	£000
Share of turnover of associates (25% × 60,000)	15,000	
Share of assets:		
Share of fixed assets (25% × 160,000)	40,000	
Share of current assets (25% × 24,000)	6,000	
		46,000
Share of liabilities:		
Liabilities due within one year (25% × 24,000)	6,000	
Liabilities due after more than one year (25% × 40,000)	10,000	
		(16,000)
Share of net assets		30,000

Working

H plc's share of the total assets of the associate exceeds 15%. (Note that the disclosures have to be made if *any* of the thresholds are exceeded.)

Turnover $\frac{25\% \times 60{,}000}{110{,}000} = 14\%$

Operating profit $\frac{25\% \times 16{,}000}{30{,}000} = 13\%$

Total assets $\frac{25\% \times 184{,}000}{290{,}000} = 16\%$

Total liabilities $\frac{25\% \times 64{,}000}{155{,}000} = 10\%$

Chapter 10

PREPARATION OF FINANCIAL STATEMENTS FOR LIMITED COMPANIES

CHAPTER CONTENTS

1 Company law
2 The balance sheet
3 Notes to the balance sheet – fixed assets
4 Notes to the balance sheet – current assets and liabilities
5 Preparing a balance sheet in accordance with the prescribed formats
6 The profit and loss account formats
7 Notes to the profit and loss account
8 Preparing a profit and loss account in accordance with the prescribed formats
9 The directors' report
10 Small and medium sized companies
11 Operating and financial review (OFR)

The Companies Act 1985 requires that Companies Act accounts are presented in a standard format and it also sets out a number of disclosures that are required. This chapter covers these presentation and disclosure requirements, which are frequently examined.

Do not be put off by the volume of detail in this chapter. You will gradually acquire the required knowledge by tackling published accounts as you progress through your studies. Refer back to this chapter regularly and you will find that knowledge of the detailed provisions will become familiar to you.

Objectives

By the time you have finished this chapter you should be able to:

- state the requirements of the Companies Act regarding: the duty to prepare annual accounts; the form and content of the prescribed formats; the main provisions of Company law
- prepare the financial statements of limited companies in accordance with the prescribed formats
- distinguish between small and medium companies and outline the disclosure exemptions relating to these companies.

1 Company law

1.1 The legal background to limited companies

A hundred years ago, it was very difficult for shareholders to obtain an accurate assessment of a company's financial position, since very little information was required by statute to be disclosed to them. A series of Companies Acts have been issued since then to improve the shareholders' rights to information.

The Companies Act 1985 and the Companies Act 1989 now require that every company produce financial accounts to the shareholders at regular intervals. They lay down detailed requirements concerning the presentation of company accounts and the disclosure of information to shareholders.

The following pages set out the minimum disclosure requirements of the **Companies Act 1985** (as amended by the **Companies Act 1989** and by later **Statutory Instruments**) in so far as they relate to the balance sheet, the profit and loss account and the directors' report. Some very detailed provisions have been omitted.

1.2 The duty to prepare annual audited accounts

KEY POINT

A **profit and loss account** and **balance sheet** must be prepared every year.

The directors are responsible for presenting to the company in general meeting a **profit and loss account** and **balance sheet** within 18 months of incorporation, and subsequently at least once in every calendar year. For a public company, the accounts must be made up to a date not more than seven months before the date of the annual general meeting (AGM).

The general rule is that accounts laid before the company must contain a report by the **auditors** in which they are required to state (amongst other things) whether, in their opinion, the company's balance sheet and profit and loss account have been prepared in accordance with the provisions of the Companies Act 1985. Small companies (those with turnover less than £5.6m and assets less than £2.8m, see later in this chapter) are exempted from having to appoint auditors.

1.3 Choice of financial reporting framework

An unlisted company (other than a charity) must choose whether to prepare its accounts in accordance with UK standards or in accordance with IASs. Charities do not have a choice; they must follow UK standards.

After switching to preparing IAS accounts, a company can only switch back to UK standards if there is a change in circumstances (e.g. the company's parent company ceases to be listed).

The rest of this chapter assumes that accounts are being prepared in accordance with UK standards, what are called 'Companies Act accounts' in the CA 1985.

1.4 The use of prescribed formats

KEY POINT

CA85 Schedule 4 allows a choice of one each from **two** balance sheet and **four** profit and loss account formats.

CA85 Schedule 4 allows a choice of format of one from **two balance sheet formats** and one from **four profit and loss account formats**. This text follows Format 1 for each, since they are by far the most commonly used in the UK.

Balance sheet Format 1 is a continuous vertical format. Format 2 sets out firstly all assets, followed by all liabilities, which would allow for a horizontal format.

The different profit and loss account formats give different information:

- Format 1 analyses costs on an operational basis.
- Format 2 analyses costs by type of expenditure.
- Formats 3 and 4 allow the presentation of profit and loss accounts in horizontal format and will not be further considered here since they would not normally be used by UK companies.

The formats used in group accounts will be considered later in the text.

1.5 Accounting concepts in company law

KEY POINT

The fundamental concepts are embodied in CA85 as four of the five '**Accounting Principles**'. The fifth principle – **aggregation** – states that in determining the aggregate amount of any item, the amount of any individual asset or liability that falls to be taken into account shall be determined separately.

The traditional fundamental accounting concepts (going concern, accruals, consistency and prudence) are embodied in CA85 as four of the five 'Accounting Principles' that must be applied. The fifth principle – **aggregation** – states that in determining the aggregate amount of any item the amount of any individual asset or liability that falls to be taken into account shall be determined separately. For example, when stock is valued at the lower of cost and net realisable value, the value must be determined for separate types of stock and then aggregated. In this way, anticipated losses on one type of stock will not be offset against expected gains on another.

1.6 Accounting rules for assets in company law

CA85 Schedule 4 contains accounting rules as to the amount at which assets are stated in financial statements of companies. There are no statutory accounting rules for the measurement of liabilities in general.

KEY POINT

Companies may use either **historic cost** or **alternative** accounting rules. Additionally, financial instruments may be stated at fair value.

There are three sets of rules:

- the general rule is that companies should adopt historic cost accounting, as explained in the **historic cost** accounting rules
- however, any individual assets can be stated at current cost or market value, using the **alternative** accounting rules
- finally, any financial instruments (e.g. cash, debtors, creditors or investments in shares) can be stated at fair vale, using the **fair value** accounting rules. These rules also apply to investment properties and to living animals and plants.

Accounting rules

Accounting rules relate to the amount at which **assets** are stated in accounts.

HISTORIC COST ACCOUNTING RULES

Assets should be stated at the **purchase price** or **production cost**.

Modifications to stating assets at purchase price/production cost:

Fixed assets

Reduce cost by provisions for depreciation with special rules for development costs and goodwill.

Current assets

Reduce cost to net realisable value if NRV is lower.

ALTERNATIVE ACCOUNTING RULES

Any of the following assets may be stated at alternative amounts:

Fixed assets

- Tangible fixed assets: market value (at last valuation date) or current cost.
- Intangible fixed assets (except goodwill): current cost.
- Investments: market value (at last valuation date) or any other appropriate basis.

Current assets

- Investments: current cost.
- Stock: current cost.

FAIR VALUE ACCOUNTING RULES

Any of the following may be stated at fair value:

- financial instruments
- investment property
- living animals and plants

DEFINITION

Purchase price is the actual price paid plus any incidental expenses. **Production cost** includes raw materials, consumables and direct production costs.

Purchase price is the actual price paid plus any expenses incidental to the acquisition and includes any consideration (whether in cash or otherwise) given in respect of an asset.

Production cost includes raw materials, consumables and direct production costs. A reasonable proportion of indirect production costs and interest on capital borrowed to finance production of the asset may also be included. In the case of a current asset, distribution costs may not be included in production costs.

2 The balance sheet

2.1 Format 1 – the vertical balance sheet

KEY POINT

Items with a **capital letter** or **roman numeral** must be shown on the face of the balance sheet and must be shown in the order in which they are dealt with in Format 1.

The letters and numbers by each item do not have to be shown in the accounts, but they are relevant in determining which items have to be disclosed on the **face** of the balance sheet and which items may, in certain circumstances, be disclosed in the supporting notes.

Items with a **capital letter** or **roman numeral** must be shown on the face of the balance sheet and must be shown in the order in which they are dealt with in Format 1. There are, however, two exceptions to this:

- **materiality**; para 86 states that amounts which are not material in the particular context of any provision of Sch 4 may be disregarded
- certain items, A, D and J, may be shown elsewhere and will thus have the status of items designated with an arabic numeral (see notes 1, 6 and 10).

The position of those items assigned **arabic numerals** is more complicated. These items **must** be rearranged or adapted where the special nature of the company's business requires it. In addition, these items *may* be combined if either:

- the individual amounts are not material to assessing the state of affairs; or
- the combination of items facilitates that assessment.

In the case of the latter point, the individual amounts must be disclosed in a note to the accounts.

All assets must be shown under the head of fixed or current assets. Fixed assets are defined as those assets intended for use on a continuing basis in the company's activities. Any other asset is a current asset.

Miscellaneous rules:

- any item may be shown in greater detail
- additional headings may be added for items not otherwise covered
- corresponding amounts must be shown for the previous year, and these amounts must be comparable to the current year's figures.

Format 1 is reproduced below:

A Called up share capital not paid (1)

B Fixed assets

I Intangible assets
1 Development costs
2 Concessions, patents, licences, trade marks and similar rights and assets (2)
3 Goodwill (3)
4 Payments on account

II Tangible assets
1 Land and buildings
2 Plant and machinery
3 Fixtures, fittings, tools and equipment
4 Payments on account and assets in course of construction

III Investments
1 Shares in group undertakings
2 Loans to group undertakings
3 Participating interests
4 Loans to undertakings in which the company has a participating interest
5 Other investments other than loans
6 Other loans
7 Own shares (4)

C Current assets

I Stocks

1 Raw materials and consumables
2 Work in progress
3 Finished goods and goods for resale
4 Payments on account

II Debtors (5)

1 Trade debtors
2 Amounts owed by group undertakings
3 Amounts owed by undertakings in which the company has a participating interest
4 Other debtors
5 Called up share capital not paid (1)
6 Prepayments and accrued income (6)

III Investments

1 Shares in group undertakings
2 Own shares (4)
3 Other investments

IV Cash at bank and in hand

D Prepayments and accrued income (6)

E Creditors: amounts falling due within one year

1 Debenture loans (7)
2 Bank loans and overdrafts
3 Payments received on account (8)
4 Trade creditors
5 Bills of exchange payable
6 Amounts owed to group undertakings
7 Amounts owed to undertakings in which the company has a participating interest
8 Other creditors including taxation and social security (9)
9 Accruals and deferred income (10)

F Net current assets (liabilities) (11)

G Total assets less current liabilities

H Creditors: amounts falling due after more than one year

1 Debenture loans (7)
2 Bank loans and overdrafts
3 Payments received on account (8)
4 Trade creditors
5 Bills of exchange payable
6 Amounts owed to group undertakings
7 Amounts owed to undertakings in which the company has a participating interest
8 Other creditors including taxation and social security (9)
9 Accruals and deferred income (10)

I Provisions for liabilities

1 Pensions and similar obligations
2 Taxation, including deferred taxation
3 Other provisions

J Accruals and deferred income (10)

K Capital and reserves

I Called up share capital (12)

II Share premium account

III Revaluation reserve

IV Other reserves

1 Capital redemption reserve
2 Reserve for own shares
3 Reserves provided for by the articles of association
4 Other reserves

V Profit and loss account

Notes on the balance sheet formats

(1) Called up share capital not paid (Items A and C.II.5).

This item may be shown in either of the two positions given.

(2) Concessions, patents, licences, trade marks and similar rights and assets (Item B.I.2). Amounts in respect of assets shall only be included in a company's balance sheet under this item if either:

- the assets were acquired for valuable consideration and are not required to be shown under goodwill; or
- the assets in question were created by the company itself.

(3) Goodwill (Item B.I.3).

Amounts representing goodwill shall only be included to the extent that the goodwill was acquired for valuable consideration.

(4) Own shares (Items B.III.7 and C.III.2).

The nominal value of the shares held shall be shown separately.

The UITF argues that a holding of one's own shares does not meet the definition of an asset, since there are no future economic benefits from holding one's own shares. Therefore, an investment in own shares should not be reported as an asset using line B III 7 or C III 2 but should be shown as a deduction from shareholders' funds.

(5) Debtors (Items C.II.1 to 6).

The amount falling due after more than one year shall be shown separately for each item included under debtors.

(6) Prepayments and accrued income (Items C.II.6 and D).

This item may be shown in either of the two positions given.

(7) Debenture loans (Items E.1 and H.1).

The amount of any convertible loans shall be shown separately.

(8) Payments received on account (Items E.3 and H.3).

Payments received on account of orders shall be shown for each of these items in so far as they are not shown as deductions from stocks.

(9) Other creditors including taxation and social security (Items E.8 and H.8).

The amount for creditors in respect of taxation and social security shall be shown separately from the amount for other creditors.

(10) Accruals and deferred income (Items E.9, H.9 and J).

The two positions given for this item at E.9 and H.9 are an alternative to the position at J, but if the item is not shown in a position corresponding to that at J it may be shown in either or both of the other two positions (as the case may require).

(11) Net current assets (liabilities) (Item F).

In determining the amount to be shown for this item any amounts shown under 'prepayments and accrued income' shall be taken into account wherever shown.

(12) Called up share capital (Item K.1).

The amount of allotted share capital and the amount of called up share capital which has been paid up shall be shown separately.

2.2 The balance sheet – an example of presentation

In the example which follows, the financial statements for Seaton plc are given under the **CA85 Disclosure and accounting requirements**. The example is annotated by tutorial notes (which would not, of course, appear in a set of published accounts) giving the full disclosure and accounting requirements of the Companies Act.

Seaton plc
Balance sheet at 31 December 20X4

	20X4	*20X3*
	£'000	£'000
Fixed assets		
Intangible assets	153	101
Tangible assets	1,986	1,753
Investments	29	33
	2,168	1,887
Current assets		
Stocks	1,637	1,598
Debtors	2,079	1,635
Investments	126	39
Cash at bank and in hand	75	41
	3,917	3,313
Creditors: amounts falling due within one year	3,010	2,980
Net current assets	907	333
Total assets less current liabilities	3,075	2,220
Creditors: amounts falling due after more than one year	910	495
Provisions for liabilities	27	13
	937	508
	2,138	1,712
Capital and reserves		
Called up share capital	1,500	1,500
Share premium account	23	23
Revaluation reserve	25	25
Other reserves	67	67
Profit and loss account	523	97
	2,138	1,712

The accounts were approved by the directors on 3 March 20X5

Colyn Seaton, *Director*

2.3 Approval and signing of accounts

KEY POINT

A company's accounts and directors' report must be **approved** by the board of directors. The company's **balance sheet** and **directors' report** must be signed on behalf of the board by a director.

A company's individual (and consolidated) accounts must be approved by the board of directors. The company's individual balance sheet must be signed on behalf of the board by a director. The copy of the balance sheet which is sent to the registrar of companies must also be signed by a director but not necessarily the same director.

The directors' report must be approved by the board of directors and signed on behalf of the board by a director or the secretary of the company. (The directors' report is dealt with later.)

3 Notes to the balance sheet – fixed assets

3.1 Introduction

Accounting policies must be stated where relevant. Except for small and medium companies (defined later) it should also be stated whether the accounts have been prepared in accordance with applicable accounting standards, and particulars of any material departure from those standards and reasons for it shall be given.

Assets are to be shown as fixed assets if they are intended for use on a continuing basis in the company's activities. All other assets are to be shown as current assets.

3.2 Intangible fixed assets

KEY POINT

Intangible fixed assets include **development costs**, **concessions**, **patents**, **licences** and **trademarks**, and **goodwill**.

	20X4	*20X3*
	£000	£000
Development costs	73	31
Concessions, patents, licences and trade marks	26	13
Goodwill	40	50
Payments on account for intangible assets	14	7
	153	101

Development costs

Development costs relate to a special project for the manufacture, design and marketing of a new range of products. Development commenced in 20X2 and was concluded during the year. Sales commenced during the current year. The costs are being written off over the five year expected life of the new product range.

	£000
Cost:	
At 1 January 20X4	31
Additions	60
At 31 December 20X4	91
Accumulated amortisation:	
At 1 January 20X4	–
Provision for the year	18
At 31 December 20X4	18
Net book amount at 31 December 20X4	73
Net book amount at 31 December 20X3	31

Give reasons for capitalising development costs and the period over which they are being written off.

Concessions, patents, licences and trade marks

	£000
Cost or valuation:	
At 1 January 20X4	28
Additions	23
Disposals	(5)
At 31 December 20X4	46
Accumulated amortisation:	
At 1 January 20X4	15
Provision for the year	9
Disposals	(4)
At 31 December 20X4	20
Net book amount at 31 December 20X4	26
Net book amount at 31 December 20X3	13

See rules for tangible assets.

Goodwill

	£000
Cost:	
At 1 January 20X4 and 31 December 20X4	50
Accumulated amortisation:	
At 1 January 20X4	–
Provision for the year	10
At 31 December 20X4	10
Net book amount at 31 December 20X4	40
Net book amount at 31 December 20X3	50

The goodwill arose on acquisition of the partnership business of Seapound & Co in 20X3 and was equal to three times the average profits of that partnership during its last five years of trading. It is being written off in equal instalments over five years, being its estimated useful economic life.

Goodwill is to be written off over a period not exceeding its useful economic life. The reasons for choosing the write-off period must be stated.

3.3 Tangible fixed assets

	Land and buildings	*Plant and machinery*	*Fixtures, fittings, tools and equipment*	*Payments on account and assets in course of construction*	*Total*
	£000	£000	£000	£000	£000
Cost or valuation:					
At 1 January 20X4	871	998	207	27	2,103
Additions	74	809	25	13	921
Disposals	–	(23)	(5)	–	(28)
At 31 December 20X4	945	1,784	227	40	2,996
Includes assets valued in 20X1:					
At 31 December 20X4	461	29	–	–	490
At 31 December 20X3	461	29	–	–	490
Accumulated depreciation:					
At 1 January 20X4	33	292	25	–	350
Provision for year	11	622	27	8	668
Disposals	–	(4)	(4)	–	(8)
At 31 December 20X4	44	910	48	8	1,010
Net book amount:					
at 31 December 20X4	901	874	179	32	1,986
at 31 December 20X3	838	706	182	27	1,753

The net book amount of land and buildings comprises:

	20X4	20X3
	£000	£000
Freehold	629	555
Long leasehold	129	129
Short leasehold	143	154
	901	838

Fixed assets – accounting principles

KEY POINT

Tangible fixed assets include:

- land and buildings
- plant and machinery
- fixtures, fittings, tools and equipment
- payments on account and assets in the course of construction.

These also apply to investments which are fixed assets.

- Normally fixed assets should be stated at purchase price or production cost, less provisions for depreciation or impairment where appropriate. Interest on capital borrowed to finance the manufacture of an asset may be capitalised. Current cost accounting or the revaluation of specific assets is, however, permitted, but historic cost equivalents must be shown in the notes.
- The depreciable amount of assets with limited useful economic lives must be written off systematically over those lives.
- Tangible assets may be carried at a fixed amount where they are constantly being replaced and are neither material to the company nor subject to material variation in quantity or value (such as tools).

3.4 Fixed assets – disclosure

KEY POINT

Movements must be shown for **revalued amounts**, **additions**, **disposals** and **transfers**. **Cumulative depreciation** and provisions for **impairment losses** must also be shown.

Movements must be shown on each of the four categories (they may be shown in notes) giving **cost** or **revalued amount** (whichever is appropriate), **additions**, **disposals**, **transfers** and any **revision of revalued amount**. Movements on **cumulative depreciation** and provisions for **impairment losses** must also be shown, including provision for the year, the effect of disposals and any other adjustment.

Valuation of fixed assets

Where fixed assets are included at a valuation the notes must disclose the following:

- the years (so far as they are known to the directors) in which the assets were valued and, for each year, the value of the assets involved
- for assets which have been valued during the financial year, the names of the persons who valued them or particulars of their qualifications and, in either event, the bases of valuation adopted
- all historic cost information that would be required if there were no valuation.

Land and buildings

There must be disclosure of the division between freehold and leasehold interests for amounts shown in the balance sheet or its related notes in respect of land and buildings. Leasehold interest must be further subdivided between long leases (unexpired terms of 50 years or more) and short leases (unexpired terms of less than 50 years).

3.5 Investments

	1 Jan 20X4	*Additions*	*Disposals*	*31 Dec 20X4*
	£000	£000	£000	£000
Listed shares (market value £28,500) (£31,000 in 20X3)	24	1	5	20
Unquoted investments in shares	8	–	–	8
Loans	1	–	–	1
	33	1	5	29

Fixed asset investments – presentation

The investments must be analysed into seven categories as follows:

1 shares in group undertakings

2 loans to group undertakings

3 participating interests

4 loans to undertakings in which the company has a participating interest

5 other investments other than loans

6 other loans

7 own shares.

***Note*:** In the example, only categories 5 and 6 are represented.

KEY POINT

For each category of investment there must be **disclosure of the book amount** of listed investments. Accounting principles are as for tangible assets.

For each category of investment there must be disclosure of the **book amount of listed investments**.

The market value of listed investments in each category must be given by way of note where it differs from the balance sheet amount. The Stock Exchange value of any investment must be disclosed where a market value has been taken which is higher than the Stock Exchange value.

Accounting principles for investments

Accounting principles are generally as for tangible assets, except that the purchase price of fungible assets (i.e. those which are indistinguishable from one another) may be calculated using an appropriate method such as FIFO, LIFO or weighted average, and investments that are financial instruments may be stated at fair value, where the fair value can be determined reliably. Where any financial instruments are stated at fair value, disclosure must be given of any valuation techniques used, and the fair value of the items in each category of financial instrument. Similar disclosures are required of any investment properties or living animals and plants that are stated at fair value.

Provision for diminution in value may be made where an investment has fallen in value even though the fall may be temporary. Such a provision must be written back to the extent that it is no longer necessary.

Definitions of investments

Group undertakings are a parent company, subsidiary undertakings or fellow subsidiary undertakings.

A participating interest is an interest held in the shares of another undertaking, held for the long term, with a view to exercising control or influence to secure a benefit to the investor's own activities. Where an investor holds 20% or more of the shares, there is a presumption that this is a participating interest.

4 Notes to the balance sheet – current assets and liabilities

4.1 Accounting principles

KEY POINT

Current assets are stated at purchase price or production cost except where net realisable value is lower.

General rules for current assets are as follows.

- They are stated at purchase price or production cost (defined above), except where net realisable value is lower.
- Provisions to reduce to net realisable value must be written back if the reasons for which they were made have ceased to apply.

4.2 Stocks

	20X4	*20X3*
	£000	£000
Raw materials and consumables	437	505
Work in progress	306	281
Finished goods and goods for resale	871	803
Payments on account	23	9
	1,637	1,598

Stocks – accounting principles

Purchase price or production cost may be determined by FIFO, LIFO, weighted average or some similar method. The method chosen must be one which appears to the directors to be **appropriate** in the circumstances of the company. However, the use of LIFO would not normally be permitted by accounting standards. Any **material difference** between cost calculated by one of these methods and market value or replacement cost or, if more appropriate, the most recent actual purchase price must be disclosed in the notes.

KEY POINT

The stock accounting method must be the most **appropriate** to the company. Any **material difference** between the balance sheet amount and the replacement cost or purchase price must be disclosed.

Stocks may be included at current cost.

Raw materials and consumables may be carried at a fixed amount where they are constantly being replaced and are neither material to the company nor subject to material variation in quantity or value.

Disclosure

Any material difference between the balance sheet amount of stocks and replacement cost or, if more appropriate, the most recent actual purchase price must be disclosed for each category of stock.

4.3 Debtors

	20X4	*20X3*
	£000	£000
Trade debtors	1,327	1,191
Other debtors	408	250
Prepayments and accrued income	344	194
	2,079	1,635

KEY POINT

Debtor categories include **trade** debtors, amounts owed by **group undertakings** or those in which the company has a **participating interest**, unpaid **share capital**, **prepayments** and **accrued income**.

Debtors – presentation

Amounts falling due after more than one year must be shown separately for each item.

There are six categories of debtor as follows:

- **trade** debtors
- amounts owed by **group undertakings**
- amounts owed by undertakings in which the company has a **participating interest**
- other debtors
- called up **share capital not paid**
- **prepayments** and **accrued income**.

Notes

- Called up share capital not paid may be shown as the first item on the balance sheet, before fixed assets, if preferred.
- Prepayments and accrued income may be shown as a separate category, after cash at bank and in hand, if preferred.

4.4 Investments

KEY POINT

Investments disclosed as **current assets** are shown at the lower of cost and market value. The accounting principles are generally as those for current assets; they may be stated at **current cost**.

All investments disclosed as current assets are in shares listed on a recognised Stock Exchange and are shown at the lower of cost and market value. The aggregate market value is £143,000 (20X3 £45,000).

Investments – presentation

There are three categories (these may be shown in notes) as follows:

- shares in group undertakings
- own shares
- other investments.

Accounting principles

As for **current assets** generally, but purchase price of similar investments may be calculated using an appropriate method such as FIFO, LIFO or weighted average.

Investments may be stated at **current cost** under the alternative accounting rules, or at **fair value** under the fair value accounting rules.

Disclosure

In any case where cost is calculated using the methods appropriate for fungible assets, any material difference from market value or, if more appropriate, the most recent actual price must be disclosed.

Details must be disclosed of any financial instruments that are stated at fair value.

KEY POINT

Creditors: amounts falling due within one year include debenture loans; bank loans and overdrafts; trade creditors; taxation and social security; proposed dividends; other creditors; accruals and deferred income.

4.5 Creditors: amounts falling due within one year

	20X4	*20X3*
	£000	£000
Debenture loans	200	–
Bank loans and overdrafts	20	20
Trade creditors	1,281	1,007
Taxation and social security	35	11
Proposed dividends	30	–
Other creditors	62	613
Accruals and deferred income	1,382	1,329
	3,010	2,980

Creditors: amounts falling due within one year – presentation

There are nine categories illustrated in the formats in CA85. These are expanded as follows to include other items which, if they arose, would require to be shown separately:

- debenture loans (showing convertible loans separately)
- bank loans and overdrafts
- other loans
- payments received on account (if not shown as deductions from stocks)
- trade creditors
- bills of exchange payable
- amounts owed to group undertakings
- amounts owed to undertakings in which the company has a participating interest
- taxation and social security
- proposed dividends
- other creditors
- accruals and deferred income.

Accounting principles

Where the amount owing to a creditor is greater than the value of the consideration received (e.g. discount on issue of a debenture loan) the difference may be treated as an asset (rather than written off at once). The difference must be written off by a reasonable amount each year and be completely written off before repayment of the debt. The current amount not written off must be shown separately in the balance sheet or in the notes.

The **accruals concept** should be followed.

Notes

- Indicate loans which are secured on the company's assets without necessarily specifying which assets.
- Show proposed dividends at the net cash amount payable to the shareholders.

4.6 Creditors: amounts falling due after more than one year

	20X4	*20X3*
	£000	£000
Debenture loans	100	300
Bank loans and overdrafts	29	115
Other loans	224	24
Taxation and social security	400	23
Deferred income	157	33
	910	495

Debenture loans

Interest is payable at a rate of 10% p.a. The loans are redeemable in 20X9. £200,000 of the long-term debenture loans outstanding in 20X3 are redeemable during 20X5 and are included in arriving at net current assets.

Other loans

	20X4	*20X3*
	£000	£000
Medium-term (repayable within five years from the current balance sheet date)	15	15
Long-term	209	9
	224	24

The long-term loan is from Seascrew Finance plc. It is repayable on demand after 20X8, and carries a rate of interest of 18% p.a. The loan is secured by a floating charge on the undertaking, property and assets of the company.

Creditors: amounts falling due after more than one year – disclosure

Presentation should be as for **current liability creditors**.

KEY POINT

Presentation of creditor amounts falling due after more than a year should be as for **current liability creditors.**

Debentures and loan stocks

Where **debentures** or any form of **loan stock** have been issued during a financial year, there must be shown:

- the **classes** of debenture issued
- for each class, the **amount issued** and the consideration received.

Where any of the debentures are held for the company by a nominee or trustee, the nominal amount of the debentures and the amount at which they are carried in the company's accounting records must be disclosed.

All creditors

For each item under creditors show the aggregate of both:

- **non-instalment debts** that fall due for repayment after five years; and
- **instalment debts**, some of which fall due for payment after five years.

The terms of repayment and the rate of interest payable should be shown for each debt which falls to be taken into account in the above disclosure. However, it will be sufficient to provide a general indication of repayment terms and interest rates if compliance with this requirement would result in a statement of excessive length.

For each category of creditors, there must be shown the amount for which **security** has been given and an indication of the nature of the security.

4.7 Provisions for liabilities

	20X4	*20X3*
	£000	£000
Pensions and similar obligations	16	2
Taxation, including deferred taxation	8	8
Other provisions	3	3
	27	13

Pensions and similar obligations:	
At 1 January 20X4	2
Transfer from profit and loss account	14
At 31 December 20X4	16

The **taxation provision** is wholly in respect of deferred taxation. There has been no movement on this account during the year.

DEFINITION

Provisions are amounts retained for any clearly defined liability which either is likely to be incurred, or is certain to be incurred but uncertain as to amount or date on which it will arise.

KEY POINT

Any **movements** in **provisions** for liabilities, and the particulars of **pension provisions**, must be disclosed.

Notes

- **Movements**. Where there is a movement on any provision for liabilities (other than a transfer from a provision for the purpose for which it was established) there must be disclosure of the movements on that provision, consisting of:
  - the amount at the beginning and the end of the year
  - transfers to or from the provision during that year
  - the source and application of the amounts transferred.

  Corresponding amounts need not be given.
- **Pensions**. Particulars must be given of any pension commitments which have been provided for under 'provisions for liabilities' and of any pension contributions for which no provision has been made. Separate particulars are required of any commitment which relates wholly or partly to pensions payable to past directors.

Provisions are amounts retained for any liability the nature of which is clearly defined and which either is likely to be incurred, or is certain to be incurred but uncertain as to amount or date on which it will arise.

Deferred taxation, which is not defined in the Act, is expected to be treated as a '**provision**' since it is likely that there will be some uncertainty regarding the amount required. Other tax 'provisions' are likely to be classified as 'creditors' unless there is some uncertainty as to either the amount of the liability or the date on which it will arise.

4.8 Called up share capital

	20X4	*20X3*
	£000	£000
Allotted and fully paid:		
Ordinary shares of £1 each	1,200	1,200
6% cumulative preference shares of 50p each	300	300
	1,500	1,500

DEFINITION

Called up share capital is the aggregate amount of calls made on shares, share capital paid up without being called and share capital to be paid on a specified future date under the terms of allotment.

Called up share capital – disclosure

The amount of allotted share capital and the amount of called up share capital which has been paid up must be shown separately.

The authorised share capital and, where there is more than one class of shares, the number and aggregate nominal value of each class allotted must be disclosed.

Where shares have been allotted during a financial year there must be shown:

- the class of shares allotted
- for each class, the number allotted, their aggregate nominal value and the consideration received.

If there are any redeemable shares, there must be disclosed:

- the earliest and latest dates of redemption
- whether the redemption is obligatory or at the option of the company
- whether any premium is payable on redemption.

If any fixed cumulative dividends on shares are in arrears, there must be shown:

- the amount of the arrears
- the period for which the dividends are in arrears (by class of shares).

Called up share capital is the aggregate amount of calls made on shares, share capital paid up without being called and share capital to be paid on a specified future date under the terms of allotment.

Allotted share capital is not defined but is presumed to be the full nominal value of shares allotted.

4.9 Reserves

Profit and loss account

	£000
At 1 January 20X4	97
Currency translation differences	(28)
Amount set aside from profit for the financial year	454
At 31 December 20X4	523

The profit and loss account balance and the other reserves are wholly distributable.

Revaluation reserve – presentation

An alternative name may be used such as **current cost reserve**.

Revaluation reserve – accounting principles

Surpluses or deficits which arise from stating assets at market value or current cost must be taken to the revaluation reserve.

An amount may be transferred from the revaluation reserve to the profit and loss account if the amount was previously charged to that account and represents realised profit.

An amount may be transferred from the revaluation reserve on capitalisation by means of a bonus issue of shares.

Revaluation reserve – disclosure

The treatment for tax purposes of amounts taken to revaluation reserve must be disclosed.

KEY POINT

All **movements** on reserve accounts are to be shown in notes. It is advisable to indicate whether reserves are considered to be **distributable** or otherwise.

Movements on revaluation reserve are to be shown in notes.

Other reserves – disclosure

There are four categories:

- capital redemption reserve
- reserve for own shares
- reserves provided for by the articles of association
- other reserves.

All **movements on reserve accounts** must be shown. It is advisable to indicate whether reserves are considered to be **distributable** or otherwise.

4.10 Other balance sheet notes

KEY POINT

Other balance sheet notes may include disclosure on the **security** for the indebtedness of others; **contingent liabilities** and **financial commitments**, and **transactions** and arrangements in which **directors** have a **material interest**.

Security for the indebtedness of others

Any charge on the assets of the company to secure the liabilities of another person must be disclosed including, where practicable, the amount secured.

Contingent liabilities and financial commitments

For any contingent liability not provided for in the accounts, there must be shown:

- the amount or estimated amount of the liability
- its legal nature
- details of any security provided in connection with the liability.

As regards commitments for capital expenditure, there must be shown the amount of contracts for capital expenditure which have not been provided for in the accounts.

Any other financial commitments which have not been provided for in the accounts and which are relevant to an assessment of the company's state of affairs must be disclosed.

Any security, contingent liability or commitment which has been entered into on behalf of a group undertaking must be shown separately. Any such disclosure must distinguish between commitments on behalf of:

- a parent company or a fellow subsidiary undertaking
- a subsidiary undertaking.

Transactions and arrangements in which directors have a material interest

The name of the director and the nature of his interest must be disclosed, together with the value of the transaction or arrangement. Service contracts are excluded, and also transactions or arrangements which do not at any time exceed the lower of £5,000 and 1% of net assets as at the year end.

5 Preparing a balance sheet in accordance with the prescribed formats

5.1 Approach to computational questions

Computational balance sheet disclosure questions do not generally specify a particular format to be used and thus Format 1 should be followed.

Allow a whole page for the balance sheet, a page for the notes and a separate page for the workings.

Few workings will be required as the notes to the accounts can often act as workings as well. For example, a fixed asset note per CA85 requires an analysis of each major type of fixed asset showing brought forward figures, additions and disposals for both cost and depreciation. Thus the working out of the year end figures for fixed assets is effectively done by producing the note.

EXAM HINT

When presenting the balance sheet, leave some space between the various parts and allow for the later insertion of figures that you may have forgotten to include. Examiners will not deduct marks if there is a lot of 'white space' but will if the statement is so cramped as to be illegible.

When presenting the balance sheet:

- write out a heading in full.
- use the same narrative as in the CA85 format.
- leave some space between the various parts and allow for the later insertion of figures that you may have forgotten to include. Examiners will not deduct marks if there is a lot of 'white space'. They will deduct marks if the statement is so cramped as to be illegible.

Much use can be made of the combination provisions of the CA85 to show a summarised balance sheet and the detailed figures in the notes. For example:

Approach 1

Face of balance sheet

	£
Creditors: amounts falling due within one year	300,000

Notes to the accounts

Creditors: amounts falling due within one year:	
Bank overdraft	160,000
Trade creditors	120,000
Accruals	5,000
Proposed dividend	15,000
	300,000

Approach 2

Face of balance sheet

	£
Creditors: amounts falling due within one year:	
Bank overdraft	160,000
Trade creditors	120,000
Accruals	5,000
Proposed dividend	15,000
	300,000

EXAM HINT

Approach 1 is often neater and makes it easier to add in missed out creditors. However, **Approach 2** involves less writing. It is helpful to allow **two or three columns** for the figures on the balance sheet.

The advantages of Approach 1 are as follows:

- it is often neater
- it is easier to add in missed out creditors without the end result being cramped.

The advantage of Approach 2 is that less writing is involved. The choice really depends on how tidy and methodical you are.

It is helpful to allow two or three columns for the figures on the balance sheet (comparative figures are rarely required). An example balance sheet (based on Seaton's that was introduced earlier) is reproduced below to show a suggested layout for examination purposes.

Seaton plc

Balance sheet at 31 December 20X4

	Notes	£000	£000
Fixed assets:			
Tangible assets	(1)		2,139
Investments	(2)		29
			2,168

Current assets:			
Stocks	(3)	1,637	
Debtors	(4)	2,079	
Investments	(5)	126	
Cash at bank and in hand		75	
		3,917	
Creditors: amounts falling due within one year	(6)	3,010	
Net current assets			907
Total assets less current liabilities			3,075
Creditors: amounts falling due after more than one year	(7)	910	
Provisions for liabilities	(8)	27	
			937
			2,138
Capital and reserves:			
Called up share capital	(9)		1,500
Share premium account			23
Revaluation reserve			25
Other reserves	(10)		67
Profit and loss account	(10)		523
			2,138

The accounts were approved by the directors on 3 March 20X5

Colyn Seaton

Director

ACTIVITY **1**

Small plc

Small plc is a quoted company with an authorised share capital of £250,000, consisting of ordinary shares of £1 each. The company prepares its accounts as on 31 March in each year and the trial balance, before final adjustments, extracted on 31 March 20X5 was as follows:

	£	£
Ordinary share capital, issued and fully paid		200,000
Retained profits as at 1 April 20X4		61,000
6% Debenture stock (secured on leasehold factory)		60,000
Leasehold factory:		
Cost at beginning of year	200,000	
Accumulated depreciation at beginning of year		76,000
Plant and machinery:		
Cost at beginning of year	80,000	
Accumulated depreciation		30,000
Additions in year	10,000	
Creditors and accrued expenses		170,000
Stock as at 31 March 20X5	160,000	
Debtors	100,000	
Prepayments	80,000	
Balance at bank	90,000	

Profit for the year (subject to any items in the following notes)		111,000
Sale proceeds of plant		12,000
	720,000	720,000

You ascertain that:

- The debenture stock is repayable at par by six equal annual drawings starting on 31 December 20X5.
- The lease of the factory has 56 years remaining at 31 March 20X5.
- Annual depreciation is calculated as follows.
  - Leasehold factory: 2% on cost.
  - Plant and machinery: 20% reducing balance on NBV as at 31 March 20X4 plus additions less disposals in the year.
- Plant disposed of originally cost £16,000. Accumulated depreciation is £3,200.
- Stock has been valued consistently at the lower of cost and net realisable value.
- A dividend of 20% was proposed on 27 March 20X5.
- The directors have placed contracts for new plant costing £5,000. These have not been provided for, but should be disclosed.

You are required to prepare in a form suitable for publication and in conformity with the provisions of CA85, the balance sheet as on 31 March 20X5 together with accompanying notes.

Feedback to this activity is at the end of the chapter.

6 The profit and loss account formats

KEY POINT

Format 1 is the '**operational**' profit and loss statement and Format 2 is the '**type of expenditure**' statement.

6.1 The formats

The two vertical formats are reproduced below. Format 1 is the '**operational**' statement and Format 2 is the '**type of expenditure**' statement. Format 1 is the more common.

Profit and loss account – Format 1

1 Turnover.
2 Cost of sales (14).
3 Gross profit or loss.
4 Distribution costs (14).
5 Administrative expenses (14).
6 Other operating income.
7 Income from shares in group undertakings.
8 Income from participating interests.
9 Income from other fixed asset investments (15).
10 Other interest receivable and similar income (15).
11 Amounts written off investments.
12 Interest payable and similar charges (16).
13 Tax on profit or loss on ordinary activities.
14 Profit or loss on ordinary activities after taxation.
15 Extraordinary income.

16 Extraordinary charges.

17 Extraordinary profit or loss.

18 Tax on extraordinary profit or loss.

19 Other taxes not shown under the above items.

20 Profit or loss for the financial year.

Profit and loss account – Format 2

1 Turnover.

2 Change in stocks of finished goods and in work in progress.

3 Own work capitalised.

4 Other operating income.

5 (a) Raw materials and consumables.
(b) Other external charges.

6 Staff costs:
- Wages and salaries
- Social security costs
- Other pension costs

7 (a) Depreciation and other amounts written off tangible and intangible fixed assets.
(b) Exceptional amounts written off current assets.

8 Other operating charges.

9 Income from shares in group undertakings.

10 Income from participating interests.

11 Income from other fixed asset investments (15).

12 Other interest receivable and similar income (15).

13 Amounts written off investments.

14 Interest payable and similar charges (16).

15 Tax on profit or loss on ordinary activities.

16 Profit or loss on ordinary activities after taxation.

17 Extraordinary income.

18 Extraordinary charges.

19 Extraordinary profit or loss.

20 Tax on extraordinary profit or loss.

21 Other taxes not shown under the above items.

21 Profit or loss for the financial year.

Notes on the profit and loss account formats

(14) Cost of sales: distribution costs: administrative expenses (Format 1, items 2, 4 and 5).

These items shall be stated after taking into account any necessary provisions for depreciation or diminution in value of assets.

(15) Income from other fixed asset investments: other interest receivable and similar income (Format 1, items 9 and 10; Format 2, items 11 and 12).

Income and interest derived from group companies shall be shown separately from income and interest derived from other sources.

(16) Interest payable and similar charges (Format 1, item 12; Format 2, item 14).

The amount payable to group companies shall be shown separately.

(17) Format 1

The amount of any provisions for depreciation and diminution in value of tangible and intangible fixed assets that needs to be shown under item 7(a) in Format 2 shall be disclosed in a note to the accounts where the profit and loss account is prepared by reference to Format 1.

KEY POINT

Every profit and loss account must show the company's **profit** or **loss** on ordinary activities before taxation. The profit and loss account may **rearrange** or **combine** items if necessary.

6.2 Comments on the profit and loss account

- As there are no alphabetical or roman numerals assigned to items in the profit and loss account, none of these items has to be disclosed on the face of the profit and loss account. However the CA 85 does specifically require that every profit and loss account must show the company's profit or loss on ordinary activities before taxation, despite this not appearing anywhere on the statutory formats.

The extent to which items included in the formats need to be disclosed on the face of the profit and loss account is subject to the same principles as the balance sheet:

- items must be **rearranged** or **adapted** where the special nature of the company's business requires such adaptation
- items may be **combined** if either:
  - the individual amounts are not material to assessing the profit and loss of the company; or
  - the combination of items facilitates the assessment of the profit and loss of the company.

  In the latter case, the individual amounts of the combined items must be disclosed in a note to the accounts.

The information disclosed in Formats 1 and 2 is not exactly equivalent. For example, gross profit is not shown in Format 2. It should be also noted that although format 1 does not include items such as staff costs, such items are required to be disclosed as part of the general disclosure provisions (dealt with later).

You will see later, when studying FRS 3, that extraordinary items have now effectively been outlawed, so items 15 to 18 (Format 1) and items 17 to 20 (Format 2) in the statutory profit and loss accounts would not now be used.

The Arabic numerals themselves are *not* disclosed in the profit and loss account.

6.3 The profit and loss account – an example of presentation

Seaton plc
Profit and loss account for the year ended 31 December 20X4

	20X4	*20X3*
	£000	£000
Turnover	4,910	3,505
Cost of sales	(2,475)	(1,210)
Gross profit	2,435	2,295
Distribution costs	(716)	(946)
Administrative expenses	(756)	(1,198)
Other operating income	13	7
Income from fixed asset investments	4	6
Other interest receivable and similar income	15	5
Interest payable and similar charges	(85)	(57)
Profit on ordinary activities before taxation	910	112
Tax on profit on ordinary activities	386	22
Profit for the financial year	524	90

Tutorial note

You will notice that the statutory formats end with the profit or loss for the financial year. Traditionally dividends have then been deducted for the year to show the profit retained for the year. This is traditional UK reporting practice, but is not required by the CA 85. The requirement to show dividends as a separate item in the profit and loss account has been removed from the CA85 by a Statutory Instrument. The dividends for the year however are required to be shown in the Reconciliation of movement in shareholders funds in accordance with FRS 3 (see later chapter in the Text).

7 Notes to the profit and loss account

EXAM HINT

The detailed **disclosure requirements** for the profit and loss account are best learnt by memorising the **statutory formats** and then using each caption as a mental 'peg' on which to hang the information disclosed by notes.

Note: Not all these notes are cross referenced directly to the profit and loss account. Accounting policies are required to be disclosed where relevant.

7.1 Segmental information

	Turnover	
	20X4	*20X3*
	£000	£000
Class of business:		
Seaton	2,378	1,650
Seatex	1,831	1,583
Seatan	701	272
	4,910	3,505

	Turnover	
	20X4	*20X3*
	£000	£000
Geographical market:		
United Kingdom	2,490	2,112
United States of America	1,012	989
Europe	987	182
India	151	63
Australia	270	159
	4,910	3,505

Turnover and profit – disclosure

Notes must show turnover broken down by classes of business and by geographical markets, having regard to the manner in which the company's activities are organised, in so far as these classes and markets differ substantially.

SSAP 25 contains additional requirements for larger companies to disclose the segmental breakdown of profits before tax as well as turnover.

Classes or markets which do not differ substantially must be treated as one class or market. Immaterial amounts may be combined with those of another class or market.

This segmental information may be omitted if disclosure would be seriously prejudicial to the company's interests. The fact that such information has not been disclosed must be stated in the notes.

7.2 Profit on ordinary activities before taxation

	20X4	*20X3*
	£000	£000
Profit before taxation is stated after the following amounts:		
Depreciation and amortisation	701	450
Auditors' remuneration	28	22

KEY POINT

The amount of profit or loss on ordinary activities before taxation must be shown on the face of the profit and loss account.

Profit before taxation – presentation

Surprisingly this heading does not appear in any of the formats but, nevertheless, CA85 specifies that the amount of **profit** or **loss** on ordinary activities **before taxation** must be shown in the profit and loss account.

Note: CA85 specifies that cost of sales, distribution costs and administrative expenses must include any necessary provisions for depreciation or diminution in the value of assets.

Depreciation and other amounts written off tangible and intangible fixed assets

The accounting principles are as follows:

- The depreciable amount of assets with limited useful economic lives must be written off systematically over those lives.
- Provision for diminution in value must be made if any reduction in value is expected to be permanent, or written back to the extent that it is no longer necessary.
- Goodwill is to be written off over a period not exceeding its useful economic life.
- Development costs, where capitalised, are to be written off over a period which must be stated in the notes.

Auditors' remuneration

Amounts must be disclosed for fees (including expenses) paid to the auditors both for audit work and for non-audit work.

7.3 Directors' emoluments

The statutory rules for disclosure of directors' remuneration come from two sources.

(a) Listed companies must follow the Directors' Remuneration Report Regulations 2002, a statutory instrument requiring listed companies to include a detailed report on directors' remuneration in the annual report and to obtain shareholder approval for it.

(b) Non-listed companies must follow the general requirements of the Companies Act 1985.

Rules for listed companies

Listed companies must include a separate detailed report on directors' remuneration in the annual report, and must put a resolution on the report to shareholders at each annual general meeting. The contents of the report comprises both information subject to audit and information not subject to audit.

Information subject to audit

- For each director, the following must be disclosed:
  - total salary and fees paid or receivable
  - total bonuses paid or receivable
  - total expense allowances
  - total compensation for loss of office paid or receivable
  - total non-cash benefits receivable (excluding options and long-term incentive schemes)
- For each director, details of share options and long-term incentive schemes must be given
- For each director, entitlements under pension schemes must be disclosed.

Information not subject to audit

- The names of the members of the remuneration committee.
- A statement of the company's policy on directors' remuneration.
- A performance graph enabling shareholders to assess the company's performance relative to the market. This should be a line graph showing details of the company's performance for the last five financial years, comparing the company's total shareholder return against an appropriate index.
- Details of the service contract of each director.

Rules for non-listed companies

The disclosures required by the CA 85 are illustrated below:

	20X4	*20X3*
	£000	£000
Aggregate emoluments	225	114
Gains made on exercise of share options	10	8
Amounts receivable under long-term incentive schemes	10	5
Company pension contributions to money purchase schemes	25	20
Compensation for loss of office	45	–
Sums paid to third parties for directors' services	–	3
	315	150

Retirement benefits are accruing to six directors under a money purchase pension scheme and to two directors under a defined benefit scheme.

The highest paid director received emoluments as follows:

	20X4	*20X3*
	£000	£000
Aggregate emoluments, gains on share options exercised and benefits under long-term incentive schemes	47	21
Company pension contributions to money purchase scheme	-	-
Defined benefit pension scheme:		
Accrued pension at end of year	20	17
Accrued lump sum at end of year	50	40

Directors' emoluments – disclosure required by CA 85

KEY POINT

Directors' emoluments must be fully disclosed. Where the combined total of directors' emoluments exceeds **£200,000**, additional information must be given in respect of the **highest paid director**.

The following aggregate amounts must be disclosed:

1 Emoluments paid to or receivable by directors in respect of qualifying services (i.e. services as a director of the company). Emoluments include salaries, fees and bonuses, taxable expense allowances, estimated money value of any other benefits and any amounts paid in respect of the director accepting office as a director.

2 Directors' gains on the exercise of share options.

3 The aggregate of the following:

- the amount of money paid to or receivable by directors under long-term incentive schemes in respect of qualifying services; and
- the net value of assets (other than money and share options) received or receivable by directors under such schemes.

4 Any company contributions paid to a pension scheme in respect of directors' qualifying services.

5 Number of directors who are accruing benefits under:

- money purchase pension schemes
- defined benefit pension schemes.

Where the combined total of directors' emoluments, gains on the exercise of share options and amounts receivable under long-term incentive schemes – 1, 2 and 3 – is **£200,000** or more, the following additional information must be given in respect of the **highest paid director**:

- **emoluments** (including gains on the exercise of share options and amounts receivable under long-term incentive schemes)
- company contributions paid to a **pension scheme**
- **accrued retirement benefits** (where the highest paid director is a member of a defined benefit scheme).

7.4 Staff costs – employees

	20X4	*20X3*
	£000	£000
Staff costs:		
Wages and salaries	1,600	1,885
Social security costs	235	280
Other pension costs	187	125
The average number of people employed by the group during the year was:		
United Kingdom	55	82
United States of America	38	42
Europe	47	25
India	30	20
Australia	35	29

Staff costs – disclosure

KEY POINT

Staff costs should disclose **wages** and **salaries**, **social security** and **pension** costs. The **average number** of employees in the financial year should be shown.

Under staff costs, disclose:

- wages and salaries
- social security costs
- other pension costs.

Also disclose the **average number** of employees during the financial year and the average number employed within particular categories, as determined by the directors.

The analysis above might alternatively have been given by class of business, or by qualification of employee. The average number is determined by summing the total number of employees each month throughout the year and dividing by 12.

7.5 Income from fixed asset investments

Within the headings 'Income from other fixed asset investments' and 'Other interest receivable and similar income', the income and interest derived from group companies should be shown separately.

7.6 Interest payable and similar charges

	20X4	*20X3*
	£000	£000
Interest payable on bank loans and overdrafts	80	52
Interest payable on other loans	5	5
	85	57

KEY POINT

Separate disclosure is required of **interest payable** on secured or unsecured **loans**.

Interest payable and similar charges – disclosure

Separate disclosure is required of the amount of interest payable on, or similar charges in respect of:

- bank loans and overdrafts
- loans of any other kind, whether or not secured.

7.7 Tax on profit on ordinary activities

	20X4	*20X3*
	£000	£000
Taxation on the profit for the year:		
UK corporation tax at 30%	356	19
Relief for overseas tax	(15)	(10)
	341	9
Overseas tax	45	13
	386	22

KEY POINT

Special circumstances affecting the liability in respect of profits, income or capital gains must be disclosed, and the amounts for **corporation tax** and **income tax** in the UK, and **foreign taxes**.

Tax on profit on ordinary activities – disclosure

Special circumstances affecting the liability in respect of profits, income or capital gains for the current year or succeeding years must be disclosed.

Also disclose amounts included in tax on profit or loss on ordinary activities for:

- UK corporation tax
- UK corporation tax before double taxation relief
- UK income tax
- foreign taxes on profits, income and (if charged to revenue) capital gains.

7.8 Other items

Reserves and dividends

The following must be disclosed in a note:

(a) any transfers to or from reserves for the year

(b) the aggregate dividends paid in the year (other than those for which a liability existed in the preceding balance sheet)

(c) the aggregate dividends that the company is liable to pay at the balance sheet date, and

(d) the aggregate dividends proposed before the date of approval of the accounts, but not disclosed under (b) or (c) above.

DEFINITION

Exceptional items are those within the normal activities of the business which require disclosure on account of their abnormal size. These should be disclosed in arriving at the profit on ordinary activities.

Prior period adjustments arise during the accounting period but apply to prior years. Their effect must be shown on the balance of retained profit brought forward.

Exceptional items

Exceptional items are those within the normal activities of the business which require separate disclosure on account of their abnormal size or incidence, e.g. large bad debts, stock write-offs and losses on long-term contracts. They should be disclosed in arriving at the profit on ordinary activities.

Prior period adjustments

Prior period adjustments arise during the accounting period but apply to prior years. They arise fairly rarely, on a change of accounting policy and on the correction of fundamental errors. Their effect must be shown on the balance of retained profit brought forward.

ACTIVITY **2**

Jot down notes explaining which of the items below would require to be separately disclosed in notes to the profit and loss account.

1 Audit fee – £6,000.

2 Auditors' expenses – £250.

3 Bad debts – £6,000.

4 Auditors' preparation of taxation computations – £200.

5 Rent of office accommodation – £1,000.

6 Capital expenditure of £20,000 authorised by directors, but no contract placed.

Feedback to this activity is at the end of the chapter.

8 Preparing a profit and loss account in accordance with the prescribed formats

8.1 Approach to computational questions

EXAM HINT

In computational questions, the most common notes that are required are **detailed expenses**, **directors' emoluments**, **details of tax charges** and **earnings per share**.

Most computational questions do not specify a particular format to be used. Format 1 is generally the easiest.

Allow a whole page for the profit and loss account and a page for the notes to the profit and loss account. A working paper may also be needed to show how the various costs given in the question have been allocated to cost of sales, distribution costs and administrative expenses. There are no definitions in the Companies Acts of these cost headings and so, provided a working is submitted which is clear, any reasonable allocation of costs will be marked as correct.

It is important, however, to keep the notes to the accounts on a separate page to the workings. In the notes to the accounts, you are trying to reproduce information in a published document. The most common notes that are required are as follows:

- **detailed expenses**
- **directors' emoluments**
- **details of tax charge**
- **earnings per share**.

When presenting the profit and loss account, use the same principles as for the balance sheet.

- Write out a heading in full.
- Use the same narrative as in the CA85 format.
- Leave some space between various parts and allow for the later insertion of figures that you may have forgotten to include.

In addition, a separate statement of reserves at the foot of the profit and loss account for the year, or in a note to the accounts, is the clearest way to compute the year end reserves for the balance sheet. This method also ensures compliance with the CA85 disclosure requirements (the CA85 requires an analysis of each reserve).

A suggested layout is as follows:

	Share premium	*Revaluation Reserve*	*Plant replacement*	*Profit and loss account*
	£	£	£	£
As at 1 Jan 20X1	Nil	20,000	Nil	90,000
Profit for the year				89,000
Dividend paid and proposed				(10,000)
Revaluation		30,000		
Issue of shares	40,000			
Transfers			15,000	(15,000)
As at 31 Dec 20X1	40,000	50,000	15,000	154,000

A further advantage of the layout is that further reserves can be added as you progress through the question.

8.2 The profit and loss account – Format 2

KEY POINT

In Format 2, include **factory costs** under 5(b) and **administrative costs** under 8. A **change in stock** (item 2) is added to **turnover**.

The layout of Format 2 needs to be known and occasionally there may be a requirement to use this method. Most cost headings are easily understood, the exceptions being item 5(b) – other external charges and item 8 – other operating charges. Neither term is defined but a sensible split would be to include **factory costs** under 5(b) and **administrative costs** under 8.

Item 2 – **change in stocks** of finished goods – requires some explanation.

An increase in stocks of finished goods and work-in-progress is added to **turnover**. The presentation implies the increase is 'quasi-income'. The presentation may be most appropriate for an organisation offering professional services. Work-in-progress at the year end represents costs which will be billed (i.e. produce income) in the next year.

A decrease in stocks of finished goods and work-in-progress is a deduction from turnover.

Note that stocks of raw materials are not included in this line – they are instead added to or deducted from raw material expenditure for the year. As no production had been started on this type of stock, it is not appropriate to treat it as 'quasi-income'.

Example

An extract from the trial balance of Production Ltd as at 30 September 20X3 is given below:

	£	£
Turnover		900,000
Stocks:		
Raw materials	40,000	
Work-in-progress	70,000	
Finished goods	60,000	
Raw materials	300,000	
Wages	200,000	
Production overheads	80,000	
Administration salaries	100,000	
Office rent and rates	20,000	

Closing stocks are:

Raw materials	30,000
Work-in-progress	62,000
Finished goods	80,000

Format 1

The Format 1 profit and loss account is as follows:

Profit and loss account for the year ended 30 September 20X3

	£
Turnover	900,000
Cost of sales (working)	578,000
Gross profit	322,000
Administrative expenses (working)	120,000
	202,000

Working

Allocation of costs	*Cost of sales*	*Administrative*
	£	£
Opening stocks:		
Raw materials	40,000	
Work-in-progress	70,000	
Finished goods	60,000	
Raw materials	300,000	
Wages	200,000	
Production overheads	80,000	
Administrative salaries		100,000
Office rent and rates		20,000
Closing stocks:		
Raw materials	(30,000)	
Work-in-progress	(62,000)	
Finished goods	(80,000)	
	578,000	120,000

Format 2

The Format 2 profit and loss account is as follows:

Profit and loss account for the year ended 30 September 20X3

	£	£
Turnover		900,000
Change in stock of finished goods and work-in-progress (W1)		12,000
Raw materials and consumables (W2)	310,000	
Other external charges	80,000	
Staff costs (200 + 100)	300,000	
Other operating charges	20,000	
		(710,000)
		202,000

Working

		£
(W1)	Closing stock	
	Finished goods	80,000
	Work-in-progress	62,000
	Opening stock	
	Finished goods	(60,000)
	Work-in-progress	(70,000)
	Increase	12,000
(W2)	Raw materials	
	Opening stock	40,000
	Purchases	300,000
	Closing stock	(30,000)
		310,000

9 The directors' report

The company's annual report and accounts must include a **directors' report**. The information to be disclosed is set out in **Sch 7 CA85**. A checklist of the requirements is given here.

Checklist of requirements

KEY POINT

The company's annual report and accounts must include a **directors' report.**

Principal activities. The principal activities of the company or group together with any changes in those activities during the financial year.

Business review. A fair review of the activities of the company or group during the year and the position at the end of it.

Post balance sheet events. Important events affecting the company or group which have occurred since the end of the year.

Future developments. An indication of likely future developments in the business.

Research and development. An indication of the activities of the company or group in the field of research and development.

Dividend. The amount which the directors recommend to be paid as dividends.

Asset values. Significant differences between the balance sheet value and market value of freehold or leasehold interests in land.

Use of financial instruments. The financial risk management policies of the company, and its exposure to each category of financial risk, unless such information is not material to an assessment of the company.

Directors. The names of those who were directors of the company at any time during the financial year.

Interests of directors. For each director who holds office at the end of the year, disclose the following (nil figures should be given if no interest exists):

- number of shares held
- amount of debentures held
- options for shares or debentures.

The information should be given for the following dates:

- at the beginning of the financial year, or on the date of appointment if appointed during the year
- at the end of the financial year.

Purchase of own shares. Where a company purchases its own shares, or acquires its own shares by forfeiture or in any other manner, there must be disclosure of:

- number and nominal value of shares purchased
- amount paid
- reasons for purchases
- percentage of called-up share capital which they represent.

Disabled employees. If the average number of the company's UK employees exceeds 250, a statement of its policy:

- for giving full and fair consideration to applications for employment made by disabled persons, having regard to their particular aptitudes and abilities
- for continuing the employment of, and for arranging appropriate training for, employees of the company who have become disabled persons during the period when they were employed by the company
- for the training, career development and promotion of disabled persons employed by the company.

Employee involvement. If the average number of the company's UK employees exceeds 250, a statement of its policy for:

- providing employees systematically with information on matters of concern to them as employees
- consulting employees or their representatives on a regular basis so that the views of employees can be taken into account in making decisions which are likely to affect their interests
- encouraging the involvement of employees in the company's performance through an employees' share scheme or by some other means
- achieving a common awareness on the part of all employees of the financial and economic factors affecting the performance of the company.

Donations. Disclose the total of political and charitable donations if the total is in excess of £200. The total must be split between those for charitable purposes and those for political purposes.

In respect of political donations only, disclose for each donation of more than £200:

- the name of the party or organisation concerned
- the amount given.

Creditor payment policy. Plcs, and any large private company whose parent is a plc, must disclose their payment policy for their suppliers. The directors must state, for the financial year *following* that covered by the annual report, whether it is the company's policy to follow any code or standard on payment practice. If so, the name of the code/standard must be given, together with information on how a copy can be obtained. If not, it must state its policy.

The directors must also state whether it is the company's policy to:

- settle the terms of payment with suppliers when agreeing the terms of each transaction
- ensure that suppliers are made aware of the terms of payment
- abide by the terms of payment.

The directors must also state the following figure, expressed in days:

$$\frac{\text{Amount owed to trade creditors at the year end}}{\text{Amount invoiced by suppliers during the year}} \times 365$$

Approval. The board of directors must approve the directors' report and authorise either a director or the company secretary to sign the directors' report on behalf of the board.

The items listed above are the minimum required to meet the requirements of **CA85.** It is common practice for other matters to be disclosed in the directors' report although not required by law (e.g. the reappointment of auditors at the next annual general meeting). There is no particular order of these matters which must be followed to meet legal requirements.

There are further disclosure requirements which apply to special category companies such as banks and insurance companies. There are further disclosure requirements under **Stock Exchange regulations**.

ACTIVITY **3**

Do the following items require disclosure in the directors' report, and if so, how? Jot down notes to explain your answers.

- Overseas plc exported half of its turnover of £400,000.
- Charitable donations of £500 were made, of which £400 was to Oxfam.

Feedback to this activity is at the end of the chapter.

10 Small and medium-sized companies

10.1 Introduction

Under **CA85**, as amended by **CA89** and statutory instruments, there is a distinction between requirements in relation to the accounts prepared by a small or medium company for circulation to its members, and those which it files with the **Registrar of Companies**.

Small and medium companies (as defined below) may file 'abbreviated' accounts with the Registrar of Companies.

Small or medium companies are not required to state in their full accounts whether the accounts have been prepared in accordance with applicable accounting standards. They are, however, still required to send a full set of accounts to their members (but see below).

10.2 Criteria

A company qualifies as small or medium if, for the financial year in question and the immediately preceding financial year, it is within the limits of at least two of the following three criteria:

Size criteria	*Small*	*Medium*
Balance sheet total (i.e. total assets)	£2,800,000	£11,400,000
Turnover*	£5,600,000	£22,800,000
Average number of employees	50	250

* *adjust pro rata where period is more or less than 12 months.*

KEY POINT

Balance sheet total, **turnover** and **average number of employees** are the three criteria on which company size is judged. A company must be within the limits of two of the three criteria to qualify as 'small' or 'medium'.

Having once qualified as small or medium, a company does not cease to qualify unless it fails to satisfy the conditions for two consecutive years, in which case it ceases to qualify in the second such year. For example, a company which satisfies the criteria for a small company in, say, 20X2 and 20X3, but not in 20X4, may still file small company accounts in 20X4. If in 20X5 it still does not satisfy the criteria for a small company (but does for a medium company) it may file medium company accounts (but not small company accounts) in 20X5.

10.3 Exemptions and abbreviations permitted for small companies

KEY POINT

Small companies are not required to produce a **directors' report**, or **profit and loss account**. An **abbreviated balance sheet** with limited notes is allowed.

Exemptions and abbreviations permitted for **small companies** include the following:

1 A **directors' report** is not required.

2 A **profit and loss account** is not required.

3 An '**abbreviated balance sheet**' is allowed. This need contain only the items preceded by capital letters or roman numerals in the formats in Sch 4 CA85. This means that the subheadings preceded by arabic numerals need not be shown.

4 Only a limited number of notes to the accounts.

5 Comparative figures are required for 3 and 4 above.

10.4 Exemptions and abbreviations permitted for medium companies

KEY POINT

Medium companies are required to produce a **full directors' report** and **balance sheet**, but an **abbreviated profit and loss account** is allowed.

Exemptions and abbreviations permitted for **medium companies** include the following:

- A full directors' report is required.
- An abbreviated profit and loss account is allowed which begins with the item 'gross profit or loss'. This is done by combining the following items:

  Using Format 1 – combine items 1, 2, 3 and 6.

  Using Format 2 – combine items 1, 2, 3, 4 and 5.
- A full balance sheet is required.
- A full set of notes is required, except that the particulars of turnover attributable to different classes of business and geographical markets need not be disclosed.

A company is not entitled to file abbreviated accounts if it is:

- a **public** company
- a **banking** or **insurance** company
- an **authorised person** under the **Financial Services and Markets Act 2000**
- a member of a group containing any such company.

10.5 Responsibility of directors and auditors

KEY POINT

Where abbreviated accounts are filed, the auditors must provide a **special report**, stating that the company is entitled to deliver abbreviated accounts and that the accounts have been properly prepared.

When abbreviated individual accounts are filed with the Registrar of Companies, they must be signed by directors of the company and include a statement by the directors, above their signatures, that they have relied on the exemptions for individual accounts on the ground that the company is entitled to be treated as a small or medium company, as the case may be. Where abbreviated group accounts are filed, the directors' statement must also include a reference to this fact.

Where abbreviated accounts are filed, the auditors must provide a **special report**, stating that the company is entitled to deliver abbreviated accounts and that the accounts have been properly prepared. Where the full accounts have been qualified, the auditors' report on the full accounts must also be attached.

10.6 Small company statutory accounts

KEY POINT

Classification as a small company entitles a company to reduce the extent of disclosure in its **annual reports for members**. These modifications apply to the **notes to the accounts** and **the directors' report**.

Classification as a small company also entitles a company to reduce the extent of disclosure in its **annual reports for members**. This set of rules considerably reduces the amount of disclosure required, both in the financial statements and in the directors' report.

Details are given below. There is no need to learn the reduced disclosures, but you need to have an appreciation of their extent.

In the balance sheet, the items preceded by letters and roman numerals are unchanged and must still be disclosed. However, many of the sub-items preceded by arabic numerals can be aggregated together and renamed as appropriate. In the profit and loss account there are no changes to the standard formats. What has changed is the level of disclosure in the notes to the accounts.

Modifications to the notes to the accounts

The notes relating to the following may be omitted:

- debentures
- split of freehold, long leasehold and short leasehold within land and buildings
- provision for taxation and other particulars of tax
- particulars of long-term debts (terms of repayment, rate of interest, security, etc.)
- proposed and paid dividends
- separate statement of certain items of income and expenditure, i.e.
  - interest payable
  - auditors' remuneration
- particulars of staff (numbers, emoluments, etc.)
- breakdown of aggregate amount of directors' emoluments
- turnover and geographical analysis.

Modifications to the directors' report

The following information need not be given:

- fair review of business and amount to be paid as dividend
- employee involvement
- post balance sheet events
- likely future developments
- research and development activities
- asset values.

ACTIVITY **4**

State whether a company with the following results could file small or medium accounts in the years 20X6 to 20X9:

	Balance sheet total	*Turnover*	*Average number of employees*
	£000	£000	
20X5	2,600	5,000	45
20X6	2,700	5,500	48
20X7 (15 months)	3,400	6,900	49
20X8	3,600	5,900	52
20X9	3,900	6,200	52

Feedback to this activity is at the end of the chapter.

10.7 Other criteria that may be used to identify a small business

The current definition of a 'small company' is based on size. However, many people would argue that it is not size alone that makes a small company different from a large company.

Large companies are often publicly quoted companies, owned by a large number of outside investors. They are managed by directors who may not even own shares and who are accountable to the shareholders. The overriding objective of a large company is to maximise the return to the investors by maximising profit.

Small companies are almost always private companies. They are often owned and managed by the same people. The objective of a small company is usually to make sufficient profit to support the owners and their dependants. Beyond that it may seek to maximise profit, but may equally well have an interest in minimising profits above a certain level, for tax reasons.

The requirements of Financial Reporting Standards are mainly designed to satisfy the information needs of the owners of large companies, that is, external investors. Many recent accounting standards have had the objective of protecting external investors from the consequences of 'creative accounting' by the directors.

The main users of small company financial statements are not normally external investors, but the Inland Revenue, lenders and potential lenders (often high street banks) and the owner/managers themselves. Increasingly it is being argued that the extensive disclosures required by accounting standards are irrelevant to small companies. The recognition and measurement criteria used by large companies may not be appropriate and may even be positively unhelpful to owner/managers of small companies, who often have little specialist accounting knowledge.

10.8 Financial Reporting Standard for Smaller Entities (FRSSE)

KEY POINT

The ASB made an important concession to small companies by issuing the **Financial Reporting Standard for Smaller Entities** (**FRSSE**).

In addition to the various exemptions available under the Companies Acts, small companies are exempt from the requirements of FRS 1 *Cash flow statements* and from some of the requirements of SSAP 13 *Accounting for research and development* and SSAP 25 *Segmental reporting.*

The ASB has now acknowledged that many of the provisions of existing accounting standards are not relevant to smaller entities. In 1997 it made a further and more important concession to small companies by issuing the Financial Reporting Standard for Smaller Entities (FRSSE).

The FRSSE is a comprehensive standard containing the measurement and disclosure requirements in existing accounting standards and UITF Abstracts that are relevant to most smaller entities, in a simplified form. It is revised and updated from time to time to reflect the issue of new FRSs.

Scope

KEY POINT

The FRSSE applies to 'small' companies. 'Small' companies may choose to comply with the FRSSE rather than with the 'full' set of accounting standards and UITF Abstracts.

The FRSSE applies to:

- companies incorporated under companies legislation and entitled to the exemptions available for small companies when filing accounts with the Registrar of Companies
- entities that would have come into the above category had they been companies incorporated under companies legislation.

Compliance with the FRSSE is optional. An entity that chooses to comply with the FRSSE is exempt from all other accounting standards and UITF Abstracts.

True and fair view

KEY POINT

The FRSSE requires that financial statements should present a **true and fair view** of the results for the period and of the **state of affairs** at the end of the period.

The FRSSE requires that financial statements should present a **true and fair view** of the results for the period and of the **state of affairs** at the end of the period. To achieve such a view, regard should be had to the substance of any arrangement or transaction into which the entity has entered. To determine the substance of a transaction, it is necessary to identify whether the transaction has given rise to new assets or liabilities for the reporting entity and whether it has changed the entity's existing assets or liabilities.

Therefore, the requirement to present a true and fair view is explicitly linked with the requirement to have regard to the substance of transactions.

Measurement

The measurement bases required are the same as those in existing standards, but they have been simplified. For example:

- for a finance lease, an asset and liability should normally be stated at fair value (SSAP 21 requires them to be stated at the present value of the minimum lease payments)
- finance charges on finance leases may be charged on a straight line basis (SSAP 21 normally requires the actuarial method or the sum of the digits method).

Disclosure

KEY POINT

Under the FRSSE, many disclosures are not required. A statement should be made if accounts have been prepared in accordance with the FRSSE.

The financial statements should state that they have been prepared in accordance with the FRSSE. Many disclosures currently required under existing accounting standards are not required by the FRSSE. Examples of disclosures not required include the following:

- analysis of turnover, costs and results into continuing operations, acquisitions and discontinued operations (FRS 3)
- note of historic cost profits and losses and reconciliation of movements in shareholders' funds (FRS 3)
- analysis of stocks into raw materials, work in progress and finished goods (SSAP 9)
- amounts of research and development expenditure charged to the profit and loss account and movements on deferred development expenditure (SSAP 13).

In addition, entities complying with the FRSSE do not have to make most of the disclosures required under FRS 19 *Deferred tax* and SSAP 21 *Accounting for leases and hire purchase contracts.*

Groups

The FRSSE applies to small groups (as defined by the Companies Acts). Under the Companies Acts, small groups are not required to prepare consolidated accounts, but may choose to do so. The FRSSE does not cover consolidated accounts and therefore small groups preparing consolidated financial statements are required to comply with the accounting practices and disclosure requirements in FRSs 2, 6, 7, 9 and 10 in their present form.

Cash flow statements

The FRSSE encourages, but does not require, small entities to prepare cash flow statements. It has been argued that a cash flow statement is of limited value for small companies because:

- if transactions are normally straightforward, a cash flow statement adds little to the picture already given by the profit and loss account and the balance sheet
- the gap between the period-end and the date on which the financial statements are finalised may be so long that the usefulness of cash flow information is limited
- managers in small businesses are well aware of the need to manage cash effectively.

The argument for requiring small companies to prepare a cash flow statement is that management of cash is crucial in small, as well as large, businesses. Potential lenders and other users of the financial statements believe that a cash flow statement provides a useful focus for discussion with management as well as a reference point for subsequent more detailed analysis that they might require.

11 Operating and financial review (OFR)

11.1 Introduction

DEFINITION

An **Operating and Financial Review (OFR)** is a clear and balanced analysis by the directors of the strategic position and direction of their business.

KEY POINT

RS1 provides a framework within which Directors can review the business in the most appropriate manner.

KEY POINT

The OFR assists **members** to assess the current and future performance of their business.

In May 2005 the ASB issued Reporting Standard (RS) 1 'The Operating and Financial Review'. This standard was developed in response to the Government's proposals for a statutory OFR. RS1 supersedes the ASB's 2003 statement of best practice.

11.2 Scope

RS1 applies to all UK quoted companies and to any other entity preparing an 'operational and financial review'. There is no legal requirement to prepare and OFR in the Republic of Ireland. The OFR is specifically prepared for the members (shareholders) of the company, **not** for the investors in general. This is to limit the extent of directors' liability to third parties.

11.3 Principles and objectives

Directors' view of the business

The OFR reflects the directors' view of the business. It should be a clear and balanced analysis of its strategic position and direction, and it should help members to assess those strategies and their potential to succeed.

Prepared for members

The information in the OFR will focus on members' needs. The OFR may also be of interest to other user groups.

Forward looking

The OFR should identify those trends and factors that help members to assess current and future performance. Members should be warned that some of this information cannot be verified, and they should be made aware of any uncertainties underpinning this information. Previous predictions should also be discussed and assessed.

Complement and supplement the financial statements

The OFR should complement the financial statements (FS) by providing useful financial and non-financial information not found in the FS. It will supplement the FS by providing additional information and explanation of amounts in the FS.

Comprehensive and understandable

The OFR should include all information that might reasonably be expected to influence significantly the assessment made by members.

Balanced and neutral

The OFR shall deal even-handedly with favourable and unfavourable information.

Comparable over time

The information in an OFR shall be sufficient to assess the OFRs published previously. Directors may also wish to consider OFRs prepared by similar companies.

11.4 Key disclosures

(a) the nature of the business, including a description of the market, competitive and regulatory environment in which the entity operates, and the entity's objectives and strategies;

(b) the development and performance of the business, both in the financial year under review and in the future;

(c) the resources, principal risks and uncertainties and relationships that may affect the entity's long-term value; and

(d) position of the business including a description of the capital structure, treasury policies and objectives and liquidity of the entity, both in the financial year under review and the future.

11.5 Key performance indicators

The OFR includes information on a range of matters, including employees, environmental matters, social and community issues, etc. 'Key Performance Indicators' (KPIs) are used to assess performance in these areas. Whereas Directors choose which KPI to use, they should disclose its definition, calculation and purpose, along with the source of the data used.

11.6 Framework and guidelines

The OFR sets out a framework within which Directors can formulate their own review. However, the ASB was conscious that Directors would need some help in preparing the OFR.

Therefore, RS1 includes 'Implementation Guidance' covering examples from noise infringement at airports to employee health and safety.

Conclusion

The format and content of the published accounts of limited companies are regulated by the Companies Act 1985. This requires the use of standard formats for the profit and loss account and balance sheet.

Small companies are allowed to disclose less in their published accounts to shareholders than other companies. Small and medium companies may file less detailed accounts with the Registrar.

SELF-TEST QUESTIONS

1. What is the difference between items preceded by letters, Roman numerals and Arabic numerals in the statutory balance sheets? (2.1)
2. State the four items that must be disclosed separately as the components of current assets on the balance sheet. (2.1)
3. What is the minimum number of directors who must sign a company's individual balance sheet? (2.3)
4. Define provisions. (4.7)
5. State the wordings of the first five lines in a Format 1 statutory profit and loss account. (6.1)
6. How are staff costs analysed in the notes to the profit and loss account? (7.4)
7. What three aspects of a company's employment policy towards disabled persons must be disclosed in the directors' report? (9)
8. Define a small company for the purposes of deciding whether a company can file an abbreviated balance sheet. (10.2)
9. What is the FRSSE? (10.8)
10. Which companies must include an Operating and Financial Review in their financial statements? (11.2)

EXAM-TYPE QUESTION

Slamometer Ltd

Slamometer Ltd, which has traded for many years, has an authorised and issued capital of 60,000 5.6% preference shares of £1 and 140,000 ordinary shares of £1, all of which are fully paid. The company also has in issue £20,000 9% debenture stock redeemable on 31 December 20X9.

The following draft profit and loss account for the year ended 31 March 20X4 has been prepared:

	£	£
Profit on trading		71,570
Interest received (gross)		
Imperial Chemical Industries plc		630
Latches Ltd (a private company)		280
		72,480

Less:		
Debenture interest	1,800	
Preference dividend	3,360	
Corporation tax under-provided for previous year	870	
		6,030
		66,450

The following further information is relevant:

(1) Total sales for the year were £1,013,000.

(2) Profit on trading is calculated after charging:

	£
Distribution costs	152,571
Raw materials	366,238
Manufacturing overheads	159,302
Wages of production employees	98,789
Salaries of sales staff	56,400
Depreciation of factory	4,000
Depreciation on plant and machinery	7,300
Office rent	2,300
Management remuneration	91,100
Auditors' remuneration	1,500
Legal and accounting charges	620
Interest on bank overdraft	1,310

(3) Management remuneration comprises the general manager's salary of £11,000 and the following directors' remuneration:

	Salary	*Fee*
	£	£
A – Chairman	–	11,500
B – Managing Director	23,000	500
C – Finance Director	17,000	500
D – Sales Director	14,800	500
E – Production Director	12,000	300

(4) The debenture interest and preference dividend were both paid on 31 March 20X4.

(5) Corporation tax on the profits of the year ended 31 March 20X4 is estimated at £32,000, based on a rate of 25%.

(6) The balances on the company's reserves on 31 March 20X3 were as follows:

	£
Share premium account	6,100
Plant replacement reserve	40,000
Retained profits	51,700

(7) The ordinary share capital of £140,000 includes 15,000 shares issued in June 20X3 at a premium of 30p each.

(8) During March 20X4 the directors decided to propose an ordinary dividend of 12% for the year and to transfer £10,000 to plant replacement reserve.

Required:

Prepare the profit and loss account of Slamometer Ltd for the year ended 31 March 20X4 in a form which complies with the Companies Act, together with a schedule showing the movements in reserves during the year. Ignore the requirement to show accounting policies. **(20 marks)**

For the answer to this question, see the 'Answers' section at the end of the book.

FEEDBACK TO ACTIVITY 1

Small plc
Balance sheet as at 31 March 20X5

	£	£
Fixed assets:		
Tangible assets (b)		157,760
Current assets:		
Stocks	160,000	
Debtors (c)	180,000	
Cash at bank and in hand	90,000	
	430,000	
Creditors: amounts falling due within one year (d)	220,000	
Net current assets		210,000
Total assets less current liabilities		367,760
Creditors: amounts falling due after more than one year (e)		50,000
		317,760
Capital and reserves:		
Called up share capital (f)		200,000
Profit and loss account (g)		117,760
		317,760

The accounts were approved by the directors on ....

Signed: A Director

Notes to the balance sheet

(a) **Statement of accounting policies**

- The accounts have been prepared in accordance with applicable UK accounting standards.
- Depreciation
  - Leasehold factory – 2% on cost.
  - Plant and machinery – depreciation is calculated on the reducing balance method at a rate of 20% p.a. Assets acquired during the year are charged with a full year's depreciation.
- Stock
  - Stock has been valued at the lower of cost and net realisable value.

(b) **Tangible assets**

	Long leasehold property £	*Plant and machinery* £	*Total* £
Cost:			
At 1 April 20X4	200,000	80,000	280,000
Additions	–	10,000	10,000
Disposals	–	(16,000)	(16,000)
At 31 March 20X5	200,000	74,000	274,000

Accumulated depreciation:			
At 1 April 20X4	76,000	30,000	106,000
Eliminated on disposals		(3,200)	(3,200)
Amount provided (W1)	4,000	9,440	13,440
At 31 March 20X5	80,000	36,240	116,240
Net book value:			
at 31 March 20X5	120,000	37,760	157,760
at 31 March 20X4	124,000	50,000	174,000

***Note*:** future capital expenditure:

	£
contracted for but not provided in the accounts	5,000

Tutorial note:
This note is an example of some detailed disclosure requirements that can be tested. You will not fail an exam if you do not know such detailed points but the more that is known, the more 'bonus' marks you will pick up.

(c) **Debtors**

	£
Trade debtors	100,000
Prepayments and accrued income	80,000
	180,000

(d) **Creditors: amounts falling due within one year**

	£
Debenture loan	10,000
Trade creditors	170,000
Proposed dividend	40,000
	220,000

(e) **Creditors: amounts falling due after more than one year**
This consists of 6% debenture stock repayable at par by five equal annual drawings commencing 31 December 20X6. £10,000 is payable more than five years from the balance sheet date. The debenture stock is secured.

(f) **Called up share capital**

	Authorised	*Allotted fully paid*
	£	£
Ordinary shares of £1 each	250,000	200,000

(g) **Profit and loss account**

	£
Retained profit as at 1 April 20X4	61,000
Add: Retained profit for the year (W3)	56,760
Retained profit as at 31 March 20X5	117,760

Workings

		£		£
(W1)	Depreciation			
	Leasehold factory 2% of £200,000			4,000
	Plant and machinery			
	NBV b/d	50,000		
	Additions	10,000		
	Disposals at NBV	(12,800)		
	Depreciation	20% × 47,200	=	9,440
				13,440
(W2)	Disposal of plant			
	Proceeds			12,000
	Cost	16,000		
	Less: Depreciation	3,200		
				12,800
				800
(W3)	Profit for year per TB			111,000
	Less: Depreciation (W1)	13,440		
	Loss on sale (W2)	800		
	Proposed dividend (20% × 200,000)	40,000		
				54,240
				56,760

FEEDBACK TO ACTIVITY **2**

1 and 3 require disclosure in notes to the profit and loss account.

2 would require disclosure only if the amount were exceptional for the company concerned.

4 requires disclosure in notes to the profit and loss account.

5 does not require disclosure.

6 does not require disclosure.

FEEDBACK TO ACTIVITY **3**

- No. CA85 requires no information with regard to exports.
- Charitable donations £500

(detail not required).

FEEDBACK TO ACTIVITY **4**

20X6 – Small.

20X7 – Small (turnover should be pro-rated to 12 months, i.e. £5,520,000).

20X8 – Meets medium criteria. However, only change if the company fails to satisfy small company criteria for two consecutive years. Therefore can file small company accounts.

20X9 – Medium.

Chapter 11

TAXATION IN FINANCIAL STATEMENTS

CHAPTER CONTENTS

1 Corporation tax

2 The accounting treatment of unfranked receipts and payments

3 FRS 16 *Current tax*

4 SSAP 5 *Accounting for value added tax*

5 Deferred taxation – timing differences

6 Alternative methods and bases of providing for deferred tax

7 FRS 19 *Deferred tax*

This chapter looks at the way in which taxation is dealt with in the financial statements. This is largely a matter of presentation, as the calculation of the actual corporation tax charge is outside the scope of this paper. For the purpose of published financial statements, there are three main categories of tax: current tax, value added tax and deferred tax.

Current tax includes corporation tax, income tax and tax credits on certain kinds of investment income. Mastering this is largely a matter of learning some simple double entry bookkeeping and understanding the rationale behind it. Accounting for value added tax is not often examined at this level and, again, you should concentrate on the basic principles.

Deferred tax is not a tax as such. Some items of income and expenditure are taxed in different accounting periods from the ones in which they are recognised in the financial statements. Deferred tax is a way of dealing with these timing differences. You will need to be able to calculate the provision for deferred tax, account for it and disclose it correctly in the financial statements and, as always, be able to explain the reasoning behind your calculations.

Objectives

By the time you have finished this chapter you should be able to:

- account for current taxation in accordance with FRS 16
- record entries relating to corporation tax in the accounting records
- apply the requirements of SSAP 5
- explain the effect of timing differences on accounting and taxable profits
- outline the principle of accounting for deferred tax
- outline the requirements of FRS 19
- calculate and record deferred tax amounts in the financial statements.

1 Corporation tax

1.1 The UK system of corporation tax

KEY POINT

Corporation tax is payable by companies on their **taxable profits**, **capital gains** and their **other income**.

Corporation tax is payable by companies on their **taxable profits**, **capital gains** and their **other income**.

Taxable profits are not the same amount as the **accounting profits** as:

- certain expenditure is not allowed as tax deductible
- **depreciation** is replaced by capital allowances
- **dividend income** from other UK companies is not taxable.

Under the UK tax rules, 'large' companies (defined as those with profits chargeable to corporation tax of more than £1.5 million) must pay their corporation tax in four quarterly instalments based on their anticipated profits for the current year.

Small and medium-sized companies pay their corporation tax liability nine months after the end of their accounting period.

1.2 Recording entries relating to corporation tax in the accounting records

The double entry for the corporation tax charge for the year is as follows:

	£	£
Dr Profit and loss account	X	
Cr Corporation tax account		X

KEY POINT

Although the tax payable is only an estimate and often referred to as a **corporation tax provision** it should be included in **creditors** and not under provisions.

Although the tax payable is only an estimate and often referred to as a **corporation tax provision** it should be included in **creditors** and *not* under provisions.

If the estimate is wrong, the under- or over-provision is dealt with by increasing or decreasing the following year's tax charge.

Although this relates to a prior year, it is *not* a prior year adjustment as it is simply a revision of an accounting estimate.

The notes to the profit and loss account will disclose the adjustment where it is material.

KEY POINT

If the estimate is wrong, the under or over provision is dealt with by increasing or decreasing the following year's tax charge.

Example

	£
Corporation tax provision at 31 May 20X5	316,000
Corporation tax charge at 30% for year ended 31 May 20X6	383,500
Corporation tax paid on 28 February 20X6	263,000

Corporation tax account

	£		£	£
Bank (paid)	263,000	Balance b/d		316,000
		P&L a/c		
		Charge for year	383,500	
		Less: Over provision £(316,000 – 263,000)	(53,000)	
Balance c/d	383,500			330,500
	646,500			646,500

Profit and loss account for the year ended 31 May 20X6

Extract	£
Profit on ordinary activities before taxation	X
Taxation	(330,500)
Profit on ordinary activities after taxation	X

Notes to the financial statements

Taxation

	£
UK corporation tax (at 30%)	383,500
Over provision in previous year	(53,000)
	330,500

1.3 The relationship between taxation and dividends

KEY POINT

Dividends are **appropriations** of profit, so are not tax deductible.

As dividends are **appropriations** of profit, it follows that they are not deductible as **expenses** in arriving at the corporation tax charge. This is why dividends are shown **after** taxation in the published profit and loss account.

2 The accounting treatment of unfranked receipts and payments

2.1 The company as a collecting agent

KEY POINT

A company acts as a **collecting agent** for the **Inland Revenue** for **income tax** on loan stock and debenture interest, royalties, covenants and annuities.

A company acts as a **collecting agent** for the **Inland Revenue** for **income tax** on certain payments. It deducts tax on certain payments that it makes to third parties, and must pay this to the Inland Revenue on the fourteenth day after the end of the quarter in which the payment is made. Payments by companies which are made under deduction of income tax at source are:

- loan stock and debenture interest
- patent and mineral output royalties
- covenants
- annuities.

2.2 Unfranked investment income (UFII)

DEFINITION

Unfranked investment income is income net of income tax paid.

A company in receipt of debenture interest will receive it net of 20% income tax which the paying company will have deducted at source. This income is known as **unfranked investment income**.

	£	£
Dr Cash (net receipt)	X	
Cr Debenture interest received		X

It follows that the company (which suffers corporation tax, not income tax) may reclaim the income tax deducted at source from the Inland Revenue. The double entry is to gross up the receipt using an income tax account.

	£	£
Dr Income tax account	X	
Cr Debenture interest received		X

The gross debenture interest is therefore credited to profit and loss account.

2.3 Recording transactions involving receipts and payments

KEY POINT

Where a company both pays interest and receives unfranked investment income, it should account for the difference between the **interest paid** and **received**.

Where a company both pays interest and receives unfranked investment income, it should adopt one of the following procedures:

- Income tax on the **excess of interest paid** over **interest received** is paid to the Inland Revenue. If this is unpaid at the year end, it forms part of the tax creditor.
- Income tax on the **excess of interest received** over **interest paid** is repayable to the company. This is done by offset against the corporation tax (CT) liability.

Example

	£
Loan interest received (gross)	28,000
Loan interest paid (gross)	48,000

Income tax is deducted at 20%.

The income tax account is as follows:

Income tax account

	£		£
Interest received account (20% × £28,000)	5,600	Interest paid account (20% × £48,000)	9,600
Balance c/d	4,000		
	9,600		9,600

£4,000 is subsequently paid to the Inland Revenue.

EXAM HINT

Questions will give the **gross** amount of interest unless there is a specific mention that the sum referred to is a net amount.

Note: In computational questions in the exam, the question will give the **gross** amount of interest unless there is a specific mention that the sum referred to is a net amount. This is because the information given is normally in the form of a trial balance and the above entries will have already been made.

3 FRS 16 *Current tax*

DEFINITION

Current tax is the amount of tax estimated to be payable or recoverable in respect of the taxable profit or loss for a period.

Taxable profit or loss is the profit or loss for the period upon which taxes are assessed.

3.1 The basic principles

The objective of FRS 16 is to ensure that reporting entities recognise current taxes in a consistent and transparent manner.

Current tax is the amount of tax estimated to be payable or recoverable in respect of the taxable profit or loss for a period, along with adjustments to estimates in respect of previous periods.

Taxable profit or loss is the profit or loss for the period, determined in accordance with the rules established by the tax authorities, upon which taxes are assessed.

Standard accounting practice

- **Current tax** should be recognised in the profit and loss account for the period.
- The exception to this is where a gain or loss has been directly recognised in the statement of total recognised gains and losses (**STRGL**). Tax attributable to that gain or loss must also be recognised in the STRGL.
- Current tax should be measured at the amounts expected to be paid (or recovered) using the tax rates and laws that have been enacted or substantively enacted by the balance sheet date.

3.2 Dividends and interest

KEY POINT

FRS 16 requires that dividends and interest should be recognised at an amount that includes **withholding taxes** and excludes **attributable tax credits**.

FRS 16 requires that outgoing dividends paid or proposed, incoming dividends, interest payable or receivable and other income receivable should be recognised at an amount that:

- includes any **withholding taxes**
- excludes **attributable tax credits**.

Withholding tax suffered on income should be taken into account as part of the tax charge.

DEFINITION

Withholding tax is tax on dividends or other income that is deducted by the payer of the income and paid to the tax authorities wholly on behalf of the recipient.

Withholding tax is tax on dividends or other income that is deducted by the payer of the income and paid to the tax authorities wholly on behalf of the recipient.

The recipient suffers tax on the **gross** amount of the income (i.e. the dividend or interest including the withholding tax). Therefore it is appropriate to 'gross up' the amount payable or receivable in the profit and loss account so that it includes the withholding tax deducted.

At present, dividends from UK companies are not subject to withholding tax.

FRS 16 does not specifically mention UK income tax on debenture interest and similar items (see above). However, this appears to fall within the definition of a withholding tax. The practical effect of this is that items received or paid under deduction of income tax must be included in the profit and loss account at the **gross** amount.

DEFINITION

A **tax credit** is given under UK tax legislation to the recipient of a dividend from a UK company.

A **tax credit** is given under UK tax legislation to the recipient of a dividend from a UK company. The credit is given to acknowledge that the income out of which the dividend has been paid has already been charged to tax in the company that earned it.

As the recipient of a dividend from a UK company has no further tax to pay and cannot reclaim the tax credit it would not be logical to recognise it in the profit and loss account.

3.3 Income and expenses subject to non-standard rates of tax

Some transactions are deliberately structured so that some or all of the income or expenditure is **non-taxable** or taxable at a different rate from the standard rate. This structure makes the transaction profitable. Examples include some leasing transactions and advances and investments made by financial institutions. One possible method of presenting these transactions in the profit and loss account is to 'gross up' to reflect the notional amount of tax that would have been payable if the transaction had been taxable on a different basis. Note that 'grossing up' only affects the presentation of the profit and loss account, not the actual amount of tax payable.

KEY POINT

FRS 16 states that income and expenses (other than dividends, interest and similar items) should be included in the pre-tax results on the basis of amounts **actually receivable or payable**.

FRS 16 states that income and expenses other than dividends, interest and similar items should be included in the pre-tax results on the basis of the income and expenses **actually receivable or payable**. No adjustment should be made to reflect a notional amount of tax that would have been paid or relieved in respect of the transaction if it had been taxable, or allowable for tax purposes, on a different basis.

'Grossing up' is prohibited because it fails to reflect the true nature of the transactions that have occurred in the period.

3.4 Disclosure of current tax

An Appendix to FRS 16 illustrates the required disclosures.

Tax on profit on ordinary activities (note to the profit and loss account)

	£000	£000
UK corporation tax		
Current tax on income for the period	X	
Adjustments in respect of prior periods	X	
	X	
Double taxation relief	(X)	
		X
Foreign tax		
Current tax on income for the period	X	
Adjustments in respect of prior periods	X	
		X
Tax on profit on ordinary activities		X

CA85 and FRS 3 require disclosure of special circumstances affecting the tax liability in respect of profits, income or capital gains for the current year or succeeding years.

A similar analysis note is required if any current tax is recognised in the STRGL.

Investment income

- Dividends received from UK companies are shown **net** (i.e. the actual cash amount received).
- Unfranked investment income (e.g. interest received) is shown **gross** (i.e. inclusive of income tax).
- Any income received subject to a withholding tax is shown **gross** (i.e. inclusive of the withholding tax).

Annual charges

Annual charges (e.g. debenture interest payable) are shown **gross**.

Dividends paid and proposed

Paid and proposed dividends are are charged to equity at the **net** amount.

ACTIVITY **1**

Apricot Ltd had trading profits of £500,000 for the year ended 31 December 20X1. The estimated tax liability for the year is £165,000. During the year to 31 December 20X1 the following transactions occurred.

- Payment of corporation tax of £160,000 for the year ended 31 December 20X0. The actual amount provided in the accounts for that year was £155,000.
- Receipt of a dividend of £30,000 from another UK company.
- Dividend of £138,000 proposed for the year on 29 December 20X1. This was paid on 31 March 20X2.

Required

Prepare the relevant extracts from the financial statements for the year ended 31 December 20X1. The tax credit relating to dividends from UK companies is 10/90 of the net amount.

Feedback to this activity is at the end of the chapter.

3.5 Published accounts questions involving taxation

EXAM HINT

Deal with the profit and loss account entries before the computation of the balance sheet liabilities.

The treatment of taxation in published accounts often causes considerable difficulties for students. The entries required will vary depending upon the information given, but a general approach is given below which should be sufficient for most questions. The main point to remember is to deal with the profit and loss account entries before the computation of the balance sheet liabilities.

Example

Simple Ltd has estimated its corporation tax liability for the year ended 31 December 20X8 at £180,000, based on taxable profits of £600,000. The corporation tax rate is 30%.

Extract from the trial balance as at 31 December 20X8

	Dr	*Cr*
	£	£
Sales		1,500,000
Cost of sales, distribution and admin. expenses	900,000	
Taxation		3,000

Deal with profit and loss account entries

Profit and loss account for the year ended 31 Dec 20X8

	£	£
Sales		1,500,000
Costs		900,000
Profit on ordinary activities before taxation		600,000
Taxation:		
UK corporation tax for the year	180,000	
Over-provision in prior year	(3,000)	
		177,000
Profit on ordinary activities after taxation		423,000

Tutorial note

The taxation figure in the trial balance must be the difference between last year's provision and the amount subsequently paid.

The amount is cleared to the profit and loss account:

Dr Taxation account
Cr Profit and loss

Deal with balance sheet entries

The only item which affects the balance sheet in this example is the provision for the year (£180,000).

The entry is:

	£	£
Dr. Profit and loss – tax charge	180,000	
Cr. Balance sheet – tax creditor		180,000

This will be shown separately under 'Creditors: amounts falling due within one year'.

Example

Extract from trial balance of More Complex Ltd as at 31 December 20X8

	Dr £	*Cr* £
Sales		1,500,000
Cost of sales, distribution and admin. expenses	950,000	
Taxation: (last year's provision £20,000; agreed liability £22,500)	2,500	
Interim dividend	22,500	
Dividend received		8,000
Deferred taxation (provision at 1 January 20X8)		30,000

Additional information:

- The tax provision for the year on ordinary operations is estimated at £170,000.
- The corporation tax rate is 30% and tax credits are available at $\frac{10}{90}$ of dividends received.
- The transfer to the deferred taxation provision for the year is £15,000 (a charge to the profit and loss account).
- The directors are not proposing a final dividend.

Complete the profit and loss account

Profit and loss account for the year ended 31 Dec 20X8

	£	£
Sales		1,500,000
Costs		950,000
		550,000
Investment income		8,000
Profit on ordinary activities before taxation		558,000
Taxation:		
UK corporation tax for the year	170,000	
Under-provision in prior year	2,500	
Deferred taxation	15,000	
		187,500
Profit for the financial year		370,500
Dividends charged to equity		22,500

Deal with balance sheet entries

A working should be set up to record the entries made from the profit and loss account to the balance sheet.

	Current tax liability £	*Deferred tax* £
Per trial balance	–	30,000
From profit and loss:		
– tax section	170,000	15,000
Year end balance	170,000	45,000

4 SSAP 5 *Accounting for value added tax*

4.1 Accounting treatment

KEY POINT

VAT is collected at **each stage** of the production and distribution chain.

VAT is a form of indirect taxation levied on most goods and services. Although it is eventually borne by the final consumer, VAT is collected at each stage of the production and distribution chain.

The majority of traders act as collection agents (unpaid) for HM Customs and Excise, accounting on a quarterly basis for VAT levied on their sales (or outputs), less VAT suffered on their purchases (or inputs).

KEY POINT

A VAT account should be opened, which acts as a personal account with **HM Customs and Excise**.

The simplest way in which this operation can be reflected in the books of account is by opening a VAT account which acts as a personal account with HM Customs and Excise. The VAT account is debited with all VAT suffered on inputs and credited with all VAT charged on outputs. The balance on the account will, therefore, represent the amount due to or from HM Customs and Excise. Entries in the account will be made as follows:

VAT suffered on inputs:

Dr Purchases account with cost excluding VAT
Dr VAT account with VAT
    Cr Supplier's account with cost including VAT

VAT charged on outputs:

Dr Customer's account with sales price including VAT
    Cr Sales account with sales price excluding VAT
    Cr VAT account with VAT

Payments over to Customs and Excise:

Dr VAT account
    Cr Cash book

Refunds of excess VAT made by Customs and Excise:

Dr Cash book
    Cr VAT account

Example

A trader's purchase and sales analysis shows the following information for the last quarter of his financial year:

	£
Taxable inputs	211,500
Taxable outputs	302,143

Both figures include VAT at 17.5%. During this time he paid £17,550 in settlement of the previous quarter's return.

Draft the VAT account to record these transactions (to the nearest £).

Solution

VAT account (a personal account with HM Customs and Excise)

	£		£
VAT on inputs:		VAT on outputs:	
Purchases		Balance b/d	17,550
(17.5/117.5 × £211,500)	31,500	Sales	
Cash paid	17,550	(17.5/117.5 × £302,143)	45,000
Balance c/d	13,500		
	62,550		62,550
		Balance b/d	13,500

Note: As the balance on this account represents a normal trade liability, it can be included in creditors on the balance sheet. It would only require separate disclosure in exceptional circumstances.

4.2 Taxable, zero-rated and exempt items

A clear distinction needs to be made between the treatment of traders in taxable items (which may be standard-rated or zero-rated), and exempt items as follows.

Taxable items: standard-rated

Because traders in standard-rated items are charged VAT on their purchases and can pass it on to their customers in sales, they do not suffer it as an expense. Consequently, VAT should have **no effect** on the profit and loss account. The only exceptions to this rule are non-deductible inputs, such as motor cars and certain business entertaining expenses. Because VAT on these items cannot be recovered, it should be included as part of the cost of the items.

KEY POINT

For traders whose supplies are taxable (either standard-rated or zero-rated), VAT will have no effect on the profit and loss account, other than in exceptional cases where input VAT is non-recoverable (e.g. on the purchase of a car, or expenditure on entertaining).

Taxable items: zero-rated

These include exports, food, books, newspapers, children's clothes, travel fares and construction. Traders in these items do not charge VAT on outputs, but can recover VAT on their inputs. Therefore, again, VAT should have no effect on the profit and loss account.

Exempt (i.e. non-taxable) items

These include land transactions, insurance premiums, postal and health services, betting, education and small businesses. Although such traders do not charge VAT on their outputs, they have no right (unlike zero-rated traders) to recover VAT on their inputs. In such cases, the irrecoverable VAT will be added to the trader's costs.

KEY POINT

Turnover should exclude VAT on taxable outputs.

4.3 Standard accounting practice

SSAP 5 requires the following treatment:

- **Turnover** shown in the profit and loss account should exclude VAT on taxable outputs (see also para 95 Sch 4 CA85).
- **Irrecoverable VAT** on fixed assets and other items disclosed separately in published accounts (e.g. capital commitments) should be included in their cost.

ACTIVITY **2**

A company trading in goods which are subject to VAT at standard rate (17.5%) has a total sales figure of £2,156,780 including VAT.

What figure for turnover should be disclosed in its published accounts?

Feedback to this activity is at the end of the chapter.

5 Deferred taxation – timing differences

5.1 What is deferred taxation?

KEY POINT

Deferred taxation is a basis of allocating tax charges to particular accounting periods.

Deferred taxation is a basis of allocating tax charges to particular accounting periods. The key to deferred taxation lies in the two quite different concepts of profit:

- the **accounting profit** (or the **reported profit**), which is the figure of profit before tax, reported to the shareholders in the published accounts
- the **taxable profit**, which is the figure of profit on which the Inland Revenue base their corporation tax calculations.

These two figures of profit are unlikely to be the same. The two areas of difference are as follows.

KEY POINT

Certain types of income and expenditure are recognised in **different periods** for accounting and taxation purposes.

Timing differences

Certain types of income and expenditure are recognised in **different periods** for the purposes of financial accounts on the one hand, and taxation on the other. **Timing difference** items *reverse* themselves over a period of time. These timing differences are the essence of the problem of deferred taxation.

Permanent differences

KEY POINT

Deferred taxation is *not* concerned with permanent differences.

Certain items taken into account for the purposes of the financial accounts are **disallowable** or **non-taxable**. Such **permanent differences** are quite distinct from timing differences. An example of a permanent difference is disallowable entertaining expenditure, which is charged against the accounting profit in the period in which it is incurred, but is never allowed against taxable profit. It is not simply a matter of deciding in which accounting period the item is to be recognised, as is the case with timing differences. Permanent difference items do not *reverse* themselves over a period of time. Deferred taxation is *not* concerned with permanent differences.

An important example of a permanent difference would be depreciation provided on buildings for which an industrial buildings allowance was not available, e.g. on a shop or office building.

5.2 Types of timing difference

Timing differences arise from four main sources as follows.

Short-term timing differences

KEY POINT

Short-term timing differences arise from the use of the receipts and payments basis for tax purposes, and the accruals basis for the published accounts.

These arise from the use of the **receipts and payments** basis for tax purposes and the **accruals** basis for the published accounts. Such timing differences are said to **originate** in the accounting period when accrued in the accounts and then **reverse**, normally in the following period when allowed or charged for taxation purposes.

Examples are:

- provisions for repair and maintenance made in the accounts but not allowed for tax purposes until the expenditure is incurred
- general bad debt provisions, allowed for tax purposes only when they become specific.

Fixed asset timing differences

KEY POINT

A timing difference arises where the **capital allowances** available in the tax computations are not equal to the related depreciation.

A timing difference arises where the capital allowances available in the tax computations are not equal to the related depreciation. Such differences are said to **originate** when this inequality occurs, and to **reverse** at some time in the future. Originating timing differences may give rise to deferred tax liabilities or deferred tax assets. Obviously, timing differences must originate *before* they can reverse.

Revaluation surpluses on fixed assets

These arise because the actual taxation liability does not arise until the gain is realised on disposal. The differences **originate** in the year of revaluation and **reverse** in the year of disposal.

FRS 19 states, however, that deferred tax should not be recognised on a fixed asset revaluation unless there is a commitment to sell the asset.

Losses

A loss for tax purposes can be available to relieve future profits.

5.3 The purpose of deferred taxation

KEY POINT

Full **deferred tax accounting** eliminates the effect of timing differences so that the tax charge reported to the shareholders is in direct relation to the reported profit.

If the tax charge shown in the profit and loss account were based on the tax actually payable, then the tax charge shown in the published accounts would not bear any relation to the accounting profit, solely because of the way the Inland Revenue allows or requires revenue or expenditure to be allocated to various periods for tax purposes. Full **deferred tax accounting** eliminates the effect of timing differences in such a way that the tax charge reported to the shareholders is in direct relation to the reported profit.

Remember that deferred taxation does not take account of permanent differences which, if of a material nature, will cause a **distortion** between the tax charge and the accounting or reported profit. This may well require explanation by way of a note to the shareholders.

Example

A company makes a profit of £100,000 (after depreciation but before taxation) each year. The company buys an asset in year 1 costing £40,000 and claims a 25% writing down allowance on the reducing balance each year. Depreciation policy is to write off the cost of the asset over five years, on a straight line basis. The rate of corporation tax is 30%.

You are required to calculate the balance on deferred tax at the end of each of the first six years.

Solution

Calculation for taxation purposes

	Year 1	*Year 2*	*Year 3*	*Year 4*	*Year 5*	*Year 6*
	£	£	£	£	£	£
Profit after depreciation before taxation (reported profit)	100,000	100,000	100,000	100,000	100,000	100,000
Add: Depreciation	8,000	8,000	8,000	8,000	8,000	-
	108,000	108,000	108,000	108,000	108,000	100,000
Less: Capital allowances	10,000	7,500	5,625	4,219	3,164	2,373
Taxable profit	98,000	100,500	102,375	103,781	104,836	97,627
Corporation tax payable at 30%	29,400	30,150	30,712	31,134	31,451	29,288

Calculation of deferred taxation

			Deferred tax account	*Memorandum re double entry*	
	£	£	£		£
Year 1					
Capital allowances	10,000				
Depreciation	8,000				
	2,000				
Originating timing difference		2,000			
Charged at 30%			600	Dr Profit and loss account	600
				Cr Deferred tax account	600
Balance on deferred tax account at year end – liability			600		
Year 2					
Capital allowances	7,500				
Depreciation	8,000				
Reversing timing difference		(500)			
Credited at 30%			(150)	Dr Deferred tax account	150
				Cr Profit and loss account	150
Balance on deferred tax account at year end – liability			450		

Year 3

Capital allowances	5,625			
Depreciation	8,000			
	(2,375)			
Reversing timing difference		(1,500)		
Credited at 30%			(450)	Dr Deferred tax account 712
Originating timing difference		(875)		Cr Profit and loss account 712
Credited at 30%			(262)	
		(2,375)		
Balance on deferred tax account at year end – asset			(262)	

Year 4

Capital allowances	4,219			
Depreciation	8,000			
Originating timing difference		(3,781)		
Credited at 30%			(1,134)	Dr Deferred tax account 1,134 Cr Profit and loss account 1,134
Balance on deferred tax account at year end – asset			(1,396)	

Year 5

Capital allowances	3,164			
Depreciation	8,000			
Originating timing difference		(4,836)		
Credited at 30%			(1,451)	Dr Deferred tax account 1,451 Cr Profit and loss account 1,451
Balance on deferred tax account at year end – asset			(2,847)	

Year 6

Capital allowances	2,373			
Depreciation	-			
Reversing timing difference		2,373		
Charged at 30%			712	Dr Profit and loss account 712 Cr Deferred tax account 712
Balance on deferred tax account at year end – asset			(2,135)	

Summary of tax charges reported to the shareholders in the published accounts

	Year 1	*Year 2*	*Year 3*	*Year 4*	*Year 5*	*Year 6*
	£	£	£	£	£	£
Reported profit	100,000	100,000	100,000	100,000	100,000	100,000
Corporation tax charge	29,400	30,150	30,712	31,134	31,451	29,288
Deferred tax charge/(credit)	600	(150)	(712)	(1,134)	(1,451)	712
Total tax charge	30,000	30,000	30,000	30,000	30,000	30,000

The total tax charge is 30% of the reported profit each year. If **deferred tax** were ignored, the tax charge would fluctuate between £29,288 and £31,451 even though the reported profit was constant over the six years.

In this example there are no **permanent differences**. If there had been, then the tax charge would have been distorted, and would no longer have been 30% of the reported profit.

The entry in Year 3 perhaps needs some explanation. In the year, depreciation exceeds capital allowances. There is thus a **reversal** of the timing differences which **originated** in Year 1. However, the amount by which depreciation exceeds capital allowances in Year 3 (£2,375) is greater than the originating timing difference which remains at the beginning of Year 3 (£1,500). Therefore, not only has the originated timing difference completely reversed, a new originating timing difference of £875 (£2,375 – £1,500) has arisen. This time, however, it originates due to depreciation exceeding capital allowances. It recognises a future tax *saving* that will arise.

6 Alternative methods and bases of providing for deferred tax

6.1 The deferral and liability/accrual methods of accounting for deferred taxation

KEY POINT

The two methods of accounting for deferred taxation are the **liability** or **accrual** method, and the **deferral** method.

There are two methods of dealing with deferred taxation:

- the **liability** or **accrual** method
- the **deferral** method (of which there are several variants).

The methods differ as to the treatment of changes in the tax rate, and of reversing timing differences which were created when the rate was different from the current rate.

Under the **liability method**, deferred tax is calculated at the rate of tax that it is estimated will be applicable when the timing differences reverse. Usually the current tax rate is used as the best estimate, unless changes in tax rates are known in advance. As a result, deferred tax provisions are revised to reflect changes in tax rates. Thus, the tax charge or credit for the period may include adjustments of accounting estimates relating to prior periods.

The **deferral method** shows deferred tax at the amount of the benefit to the company, in historic cost terms, of being able to defer taxation. Under this method the deferred taxation account records the originating timing differences at the rates of taxation in operation when those originating timing differences occurred. Unlike the liability method, no adjustment is made to the existing deferred taxation account when changes in taxation rates occur.

FRS 19 requires the use of the liability method in the sense that it requires deferred tax to be measured at the tax rates expected to apply on reversal, based on tax rates and laws that have been enacted or substantively enacted (i.e. passed by the House of Commons in the UK) by the balance sheet date.

KEY POINT

There are three possible bases for computing deferred tax: nil provision; full provision; and partial provision.

6.2 The advantages and disadvantages of the bases used for recording deferred taxation

There are three principal bases in theory for computing deferred tax:

- nil provision
- full provision
- partial provision.

Nil provision

KEY POINT

The '**nil provision**' basis is based on the principle that only tax payable in respect of a period should be charged in that period.

The '**nil provision**' or 'flow through' basis is based on the principle that only the current tax payable in respect of a period should be charged in that period. No provision for deferred tax is made.

Nil provision is straightforward and objective. Its supporters have argued that the taxation liability arises from taxable profits rather than from accounting profits. Whether or not timing differences reverse depends on future transactions and future profits. Some commentators argue that nil provision takes account of tax planning (i.e. the extent to which the company can manage the amount and timing of income and expenditure).

However, nil provision can result in large fluctuations in the tax charge (which have already been illustrated in the above example). For this reason, it has been consistently rejected by standard setters.

Full provision

KEY POINT

The '**full provision**' basis is based on the principle that financial statements for a period should recognise the tax effects of all transactions occurring in that period.

The '**full provision**' basis, as required by FRS 19, is based on the principle that financial statements for a period should recognise the tax effects, whether current or deferred, of all transactions occurring in that period.

The advantages of the full provision method are as follows.

- It is straightforward to apply and objective.
- It has the effect of smoothing out distortions in the tax charge caused by timing differences. This means that it may provide more useful information for users of the financial statements because it is easier to make comparisons.
- Full provision matches the tax liability against the revenue to which it relates.
- Deferred tax is like a valuation adjustment reflecting the change in value of an entity's assets and liabilities arising from its tax position. For example, claiming accelerated capital allowances on a fixed asset means that the asset is worth less than another asset that is still fully tax-deductible. This change in value should be recognised.
- It is consistent with international practice.

The disadvantages of the full provision method are as follows.

- It may lead to the build up of large balances which never **crystallise**. These may distort key performance measures. ***Note:*** crystallisation refers to the changing of a **provision** (for deferred tax) into a **liability** (for corporation tax).
- It could be argued that full provision is inconsistent with the ASB's Statement of Principles (because a liability is an **obligation** to transfer benefits).

KEY POINT

The '**partial provision**' basis requires that deferred tax should be accounted for in respect of the net amount by which payment of tax may be temporarily deferred or accelerated by reversible timing differences.

Partial provision

The '**partial provision**' basis requires that deferred tax should be accounted for in respect of the net amount by which it is probable that any payment of tax will be temporarily deferred or accelerated by the operation of timing differences which will reverse in the foreseeable future without being replaced.

The old SSAP 15 required the use of the partial provision basis.

The advantages of partial provision are as follows.

- It recognises that, if an enterprise is not expected to reduce the scale of its operations significantly, it will sometimes have what amounts to a hard core of timing differences, so that the payment of some tax will be permanently deferred or accelerated.
- It may provide information which has predictive value (because it reflects the amounts that the entity is likely to pay in practice).

The disadvantages of partial provision are as follows.

- It takes account of the tax consequences of future transactions, but not the transactions themselves. This has the effect (for example) that credit is taken in the current period for tax relief expected to be available in respect of fixed assets that have not yet been recognised in the financial statements. This contravenes the accruals concept.
- It takes into account future transactions to which the reporting entity is not yet committed. This is inconsistent with the ASB's belief (contained in the Statement of Principles) that items should only be recognised where they arise from past transactions or commitments.
- It relies on forecasts of future expenditure and is therefore time consuming and subjective to apply.
- It is inconsistent with international practice.

7 FRS 19 *Deferred tax*

7.1 The requirements of FRS 19

KEY POINT

FRS 19 *Deferred tax* requires **full provision for deferred tax**.

The UK found itself increasingly out on a limb with SSAP 15, since that standard required partial provision for deferred tax, while international accounting overwhelmingly favoured full provision. In December 2000, the ASB therefore issued FRS 19 *Deferred tax* in the interests of international harmonisation. FRS 19 requires full provision for deferred tax.

FRS 19 requires deferred tax (except as stated below) to be recognised on all timing differences that have originated but not reversed by the balance sheet date. Deferred tax should not be recognised on permanent differences.

Deferred tax **should** therefore be recognised on:

- accelerated capital allowances (i.e. capital allowances taken in excess of depreciation charged at the balance sheet date)
- accruals for pension costs that will be deductible for tax purposes only when paid
- elimination of unrealised intra-group profits on consolidation

- unrelieved tax losses
- other sources of short-term timing differences.

Deferred tax **should not** be recognised when:

- a fixed asset is revalued without there being any commitment to sell the asset
- the gain on sale of an asset is rolled over into replacement assets
- the remittance of a subsidiary, associate or joint venture's earnings would cause tax to be payable, but no commitment has been made to the remittance of the earnings.

KEY POINT

Deferred tax assets should be recognised to the extent that they are regarded as **recoverable**.

Deferred tax assets should be recognised to the extent that they are regarded as recoverable, i.e. on the basis of all available evidence, it is more likely than not that there will be suitable taxable profits in the future from which the future reversal of the underlying timing differences can be deducted.

Example of calculation of deferred tax charges

ABC plc is a highly profitable company. At 31 December 20X5 the accounts NBV of fixed assets ranking for capital allowances exceeds tax WDV by £750,000, but the company has hitherto not provided for deferred tax.

The company has produced the following forecast resulting from likely capital expenditure over the next few years:

Year	*Capital allowances*	*Depreciation*	*Timing differences Originating*	*Reversal*
	£'000	£'000	£'000	£'000
20X6	1,600	1,400	200	
20X7	1,750	1,600	150	
20X8	1,100	1,670		570

20X9 onwards – capital allowances are likely to be well in excess of depreciation.

You are required to show the deferred tax charges in the profit and loss account, and the provisions required in the balance sheet, for each year 20X5 to 20X8 under FRS 19.

Assume that there are no other timing differences to be considered and that the tax rate is 30%.

Solution

Full provision

Year	*Accumulated timing differences*	*Tax rate*	*Provision required*
	£'000		£'000
20X5	750	30%	225
20X6	750 + 200 = 950	30%	285
20X7	950 + 150 = 1,100	30%	330
20X8	1,100 - 570 = 530	30%	159

The charge or credit in the profit and loss account for deferred tax is the balancing figure required to reach the closing required provision from the opening provision.

Year	*Charge/(credit) required*
	£'000
20X5	225
20X6	285 – 225 = 60
20X7	330 – 285 = 45
20X8	159 – 330 = (171)

Alternatively, the profit and loss account charge or credit each year can be calculated by applying the tax rate to the timing difference arising in the year for 20X6 to 20X8.

7.2 Discounting deferred tax assets and liabilities

KEY POINT

The ASB permits (but does not require) entities to adopt a policy of **discounting deferred tax assets and liabilities**.

One criticism of the full provision basis is that large provisions can be set up which are not expected to reverse for a long time. The ASB has reacted to this by permitting (but not requiring) entities to adopt a policy of discounting deferred tax assets and liabilities.

If a policy of discounting is adopted, the discount period will be the number of years between the balance sheet date and the date on which the timing difference is expected to reverse. The discount rate used should be the post-tax yield to maturity on government bonds with similar maturity dates and currencies.

7.3 Disclosure requirements

KEY POINT

Deferred tax is normally shown in the profit and loss account under 'tax on profit or loss on ordinary activities'.
Deferred tax liabilities are shown under 'provisions for liabilities'.

Balance sheet

- Deferred tax assets should be classified as debtors, as a separate subheading of debtors where material.
- Deferred tax liabilities should be classified as provisions for liabilities.

Deferred tax debit and credit balances should be offset if, and only if, they relate to taxes levied by the same tax authority and arise in the same taxable entity or in a group of taxable entities where the tax losses of one entity can reduce the taxable profits of another.

Profit and loss account

Deferred tax for the period should be recognised in the profit and loss account under the heading 'tax on profit or loss on ordinary activities', except to the extent that it is attributable to a gain or loss that has been recognised directly in the statement of total recognised gains and losses when it should also be recognised directly in that statement.

Conclusion

FRS 16 requires that outgoing dividends paid or proposed, incoming dividends, interest payable or receivable and other income receivable should be recognised at an amount that:

- includes any withholding taxes
- excludes attributable tax credits.

Deferred taxation arises due to timing differences and the need to apply the accruals concept of matching revenues with the full costs of earning those revenues.

FRS 19 requires the use of the full provision basis i.e., provide deferred tax generally on all timing differences that have originated but not reversed by the balance sheet date.

SELF-TEST QUESTIONS

1 What is the double entry to record the corporation tax charge for the year? (1.2)
2 What is unfranked investment income? (2.2)
3 Define current tax. (3.1)
4 At what amount should incoming dividends be recognised in the profit and loss account, according to FRS 16? (3.2)
5 How should irrecoverable VAT (e.g. on motor cars), be dealt with? (4.3)
6 What are permanent differences? (5.1)
7 What is the purpose of deferred tax? (5.3)
8 Deferred tax can be calculated using the liability method or the deferral method. Which is required by FRS 19? (6.1)
9 What are the three possible bases for computing deferred tax? (6.2)
10 On which timing differences should deferred tax be recognised? (7.1)

PRACTICE QUESTIONS

Question 1: Dewar Ltd

Dewar Ltd has issued share capital of £500,000 in shares of £1 each and makes up its accounts to 31 December of each year. You are provided with the following information.

- On 1 January 20X6 the company's liability for corporation tax was £120,000 (estimated on the profits of the year ended 31 December 20X5).
- During the year ended 31 December 20X6, this liability was agreed at £115,000.
- On 1 January 20X6 the provision for deferred tax was £40,000.
- During the year ended 31 December 20X6, the company received a dividend from a UK company of £15,000.
- An interim dividend of 5p per share was paid on 30 June 20X6 and in December 20X6 the directors proposed a final dividend of 10p per share for the year ended 31 December 20X6.
- Operating profit for the year ended 31 December 20X6 was £300,000.
- The liability for corporation tax based on the profits for the year ended 31 December 20X6 was estimated to be £90,000.
- It has been decided that the provision for deferred tax is to be increased by £25,000.
- All timing differences are in respect of accelerated capital allowances.
- The rate of corporation tax is 30% and the tax credit rate is 10/90.

Required:

(a) Prepare the profit and loss account for the year ended 31 December 20X6, including notes, in so far as the information allows. **(8 marks)**

(b) Prepare relevant extracts from the balance sheet at 31 December 20X6, including notes, in so far as the information allows. **(7 marks)**

(Total: 15 marks)

Question 2: H plc

The Chief Accountant of H plc is in the process of drafting the annual report for the year ended 31 October 20X0. He is currently preparing the note in respect of deferred tax.

The deferred taxation account had a credit balance of £1.5 million at 31 October 20W9. All of these amounts arose in respect of the difference between depreciation and capital allowances.

During the year ended 31 October 20X0, the company charged £18.0 million in depreciation and claimed £20.8 million in capital allowances.

The current tax charge for the year is £4.7m.

Assume a corporation tax rate of 30% throughout.

Required:

(a) Explain the purpose of deferred taxation. **(5 marks)**

(b) Explain the accounting requirements of FRS 19 *Deferred tax*. **(5 marks)**

(c) Prepare notes in respect of deferred taxation for H plc. These should be in a form suitable for publication. **(5 marks)**

(Total: 15 marks)

The answers to these questions can be found in the 'Answers' section at the end of the book.

FEEDBACK TO ACTIVITY 1

Profit and loss account for the year ended 31 December 20X1 (extract)

	£
Operating profit	500,000
Investment income received	30,000
Profit on ordinary activities before taxation	530,000
Tax on profit on ordinary activities (Note)	(170,000)
Profit on ordinary activities after taxation	360,000
Dividends proposed – charged to equity	(138,000)

Note to the profit and loss account: Tax on profit on ordinary activities

	£
UK corporation tax:	
Current tax on income for the period	165,000
Adjustments in respect of prior periods	5,000
	170,000

Balance sheet at 31 December 20X1 (extract)

	£
Creditors: Amounts falling due within one year:	
Taxation	165,000
Proposed dividends	138,000

FEEDBACK TO ACTIVITY 2

The VAT-exclusive figure should be given:

$$\frac{100}{117.5} \times £2,156,780 = £1,835,557$$

Chapter 12

STOCK AND LONG-TERM CONTRACTS

CHAPTER CONTENTS

1 Stock valuation

2 Long-term contract work in progress

3 Accounting for long-term contracts

This chapter begins by revising the principles of stock valuation. It then introduces the new topic of accounting for long-term contracts, also covered by SSAP 9. Long-term contracts were touched upon in the chapter on revenue recognition; here we study the actual accounting treatment of long-term contracts. This may appear complicated at first. The most important thing to grasp is that in accounting for long-term contracts you are attempting to allocate turnover and profits to the accounting periods in which they are earned, in other words, to apply the accruals concept.

Objectives

By the time you have finished this chapter you should be able to:

- review the principles of stock valuation covered in Paper 1.1
- define a long-term contract and describe why recognising profit before completion is generally considered to be desirable
- describe the ways in which attributable profit may be measured
- calculate and disclose the amounts to be shown in the financial statements for long-term contracts.

1 Stock valuation

1.1 Lower of cost and net realisable value

KEY POINT

Stocks are valued at the **lower** of **cost** and **net realisable value**.

The basic rule is that stocks are valued at the lower of cost and net realisable value.

Cost

'**Cost**' for SSAP 9 means all costs incurred in bringing items of stock to their present location and condition (cost of purchase and costs of conversion).

DEFINITIONS

Cost for SSAP 9 means all costs incurred in bringing items of stock to their present location and condition.

Cost of purchase comprises purchase price including direct costs less **trade discounts**, **rebates** and **subsidies**.

Cost of conversion comprises costs specifically attributable to units of production and **overheads**.

Net realisable value is the actual or estimated **selling price** less **completion costs**.

Cost of purchase comprises purchase price including **import duties**, **transport** and **handling costs** and any other directly attributable costs, less **trade discounts**, **rebates** and **subsidies**.

Cost of conversion comprises:

- costs which are specifically attributable to units of production, e.g. **direct labour**, **direct expenses** and **subcontracted work**
- **production overheads**
- other **overheads**, if any, attributable in the particular circumstances of the business to bringing the product or service to its present location and condition.

Production overhead to be included is based on the normal level of activity.

Net realisable value

Actual or estimated **selling price** less all **costs to complete** (including all costs to be incurred in marketing, selling and distribution).

1.2 Valuation methods

KEY POINT

Acceptable valuation methods include **FIFO**, **unit cost**, **average cost** and in certain circumstances **standard cost** and **adjusted selling price**. **LIFO**, **replacement cost** and **base cost** are unacceptable methods under **SSAP 9**.

Acceptable under SSAP 9:

- FIFO
- unit cost
- average cost.

In certain circumstances:

- standard cost
- adjusted selling price.

Unacceptable under SSAP 9:

- LIFO
- replacement cost
- base cost.

1.3 Disclosure

KEY POINT

The lower of **cost/NRV** of the stock or groups of similar items should be disclosed under **raw materials**, **work in progress**, **finished goods** and **payments on account**.

Lower of **cost/NRV** of the separate items of stock or of groups of similar items.

Classify according to **CA85** headings as follows:

- raw materials
- work in progress
- finished goods and goods for resale
- payments on account.

ACTIVITY **1**

Value the following items of stock.

1 Materials costing £12,000 bought for processing and assembly for a profitable special order. Since buying these items, the cost price has fallen to £10,000.

2 Equipment constructed for a customer for an agreed price of £18,000. This has recently been completed at a cost of £16,800. It has now been discovered that, in order to meet certain regulations, conversion with an extra cost of £4,200 will be required. The customer has accepted partial responsibility and agreed to meet half the extra cost.

Feedback to this activity is at the end of the chapter.

2 Long-term contract work in progress

2.1 Definition of a long-term contract

DEFINITION

SSAP 9 defines a **long-term contract** as one where the time taken to complete the contract is such that the contract falls into different accounting periods.

SSAP 9 defines a **long-term contract** as 'a contract entered into for the design, manufacture or construction of a single substantial asset or the provision of a service (or of a combination of assets or services which together constitute a single project) where the time taken substantially to complete the contract is such that the contract activity falls into different accounting periods'.

2.2 Why is it desirable to recognise profit before completion of a contract?

Long-term contracts cause special problems due to their length of time relative to accounting periods. As they extend across accounting periods, we need some method of recording turnover, cost of sales and profit over the life of the contract.

Example

A company enters into a long-term contract which runs for twelve months from 1 July 20X7. Total costs on the contract are expected to amount to £300,000 and the total contract price is £1,000,000. The company prepares accounts to 31 December each year.

Assume that no profit is recognised until the contract is complete. At 31 December 20X7, costs of £200,000 have been incurred.

If the costs of £200,000 are treated as work in progress and included as an asset on the balance sheet, this gives rise to a profit of £Nil for the year ended 31 December 20X7, but a profit of £700,000 for the year ended 31 December 20X8.

KEY POINT

Turnover, cost of sales and profit need recording over the life of the long-term contract, otherwise a **true and fair view** of company activities may not be shown.

Given that a large proportion of the work was carried out in 20X7, this treatment does not give a true and fair view of the activities of the company.

In addition, we need to recognise the nature of the assets and liabilities that arise during the contract period. The assets will change in nature from stocks to debtors (amounts recoverable on contracts). This change results in detailed accounting procedures and disclosure requirements.

SSAP 9 applies the accruals concept to long-term contract accounting by requiring entities to recognise the attributable profit in the profit and loss account as the contract progresses. Another way of looking at accounting for long-term contracts is that it applies the accretion method to account for revenue and profits (discussed in Chapter 3). This is appropriate because revenue is earned over a period of time, rather than at a particular point in time.

2.3 Problems with SSAP 9 and profit smoothing

KEY POINT

Profit smoothing involves manipulating the profit figure in the financial statements by setting up assets or liabilities in the balance sheet and releasing these amounts to the profit and loss account over time.

Many 'creative accounting' practices use '**profit smoothing**'. Profit smoothing involves manipulating the profit figure in the financial statements by setting up assets or liabilities in the balance sheet and releasing these amounts to the profit and loss account over time. As you will see in a later chapter before the issue of FRS 12 on provisions, a common method of profit smoothing involved setting up a **provision for possible future expenditure**. This was then taken to the profit and loss account artificially to enhance profits in subsequent accounting periods.

Although there are sound reasons for recognising profit on long-term contracts before they are completed, it could be argued that SSAP 9 provides opportunities for profit smoothing. This is because allocating turnover and profit to accounting periods can only be a **subjective** exercise.

KEY POINT

Methods of calculating the profit earned to date on a long-term contract may be based on the **proportion** of **total costs incurred** or **work certified** to the total contract value.

For example, in practice, there are a number of different methods of calculating the proportion of profit earned to date on a long-term contract. The most commonly used methods are based on the **proportion of total costs incurred** to date or the **proportion of work certified** to the total value of the contract, but other calculations (for example, on a time basis) are also possible. SSAP 9 does not prescribe a method.

Even if SSAP 9 did require a particular method to be used, there would still be a certain amount of subjectivity, because the calculation must be based on estimated figures. For example, the total cost to be incurred cannot be known for certain until the contract is actually completed.

In addition, profit smoothing could also arise because SSAP 9 states that no profit can be recognised until the profitable outcome of the contract can be assessed with reasonable certainty. This is prudent, but means that preparers of accounts must use judgement to determine the point at which the outcome of a contract is reasonably certain. This depends on the individual circumstances of the contract and the business.

As we will see, SSAP 9 is based on the traditional view of the accounting process. It applies the concepts of **matching** and **prudence** to allocate profit to accounting periods. The amounts 'left over' from the matching process are assets and liabilities, such as long-term contract work in progress, trade debtors, trade creditors and provisions for losses. To some extent it is in conflict with the ASB's 'balance sheet' approach, which takes changes in assets and liabilities as the starting point for revenue recognition.

2.4 Standard accounting practice

The relevant parts of SSAP 9 are set out in full below together with some definitions. We will then see how the amounts to be shown in the financial statements are calculated.

The standard accounting practice for long-term contracts is as follows:

KEY POINT

The attributable profit should be recognised in the profit and loss account as the difference between the reported turnover and related costs for the contract.

- Long-term contracts should be assessed on a contract by contract basis and reflected in the profit and loss account by recording turnover and related costs as contract activity progresses. Turnover is ascertained in a manner appropriate to the stage of completion of the contract, the business and the industry in which it operates.
- Where it is considered that the outcome of a long-term contract can be assessed with reasonable certainty before its conclusion, the prudently calculated attributable profit should be recognised in the profit and loss account as the difference between the reported turnover and related costs for that contract.

KEY POINT

The amount by which recorded turnover is in excess of payments on account should be classified as '**amounts recoverable on contracts**' in the balance sheet.

- Long-term contracts should be disclosed in the balance sheet as follows:
  - the amount by which recorded turnover is in excess of payments on account should be classified as '**amounts recoverable on contracts**' and separately disclosed within debtors
  - the balance of payments on account (in excess of amounts matched with turnover, and offset against long-term contract balances) should be classified as payments on account and separately disclosed within creditors
  - the amount of long-term contracts, at costs incurred, net of amounts transferred to cost of sales, after deducting foreseeable losses and payments on account not matched with turnover, should be classified as '**long-term contract balances**' and separately disclosed within the balance sheet heading 'Stocks'.

KEY POINT

The amount of long-term contracts, at costs incurred net of amounts transferred to cost of sales (after deducting foreseeable losses and payments on account not matched with turnover) should be classified as '**long-term contract balances**' in the balance sheet.

- The balance sheet note should disclose separately the balances of:
  - net cost less foreseeable losses, and
  - applicable payments on account.
- The amount by which the provision or accrual for foreseeable losses exceeds the costs incurred (after transfers to cost of sales) should be included within either provisions for liabilities and charges or creditors as appropriate.

2.5 Definitions

DEFINITION

Attributable profit is that part of the total profit currently estimated to arise over the duration of the contract that fairly reflects the profit attributable to that part of the work performed at the accounting date.

The following terms are defined in SSAP 9:

Attributable profit: that part of the total profit currently estimated to arise over the duration of the contract, after allowing for estimated remedial and maintenance costs and increases in costs so far as not recoverable under the terms of the contract, that fairly reflects the profit attributable to that part of the work performed at the accounting date. (There can be no attributable profit until the profitable outcome of the contract can be assessed with reasonable certainty.)

Foreseeable losses: losses which are currently estimated to arise over the duration of the contract (after allowing for estimated remedial and maintenance costs and increases in costs so far as not recoverable under the terms of the contract). This estimate is required irrespective of:

- whether or not work has yet commenced on such contracts
- the proportion of work carried out at the accounting date
- the amount of profits expected to arise on other contracts.

Payments on account: all amounts received and receivable at the accounting date in respect of contracts in progress.

2.6 Measuring turnover

KEY POINT

Turnover and related costs should be recorded in the profit and loss account as contract activity progresses.

Turnover is not defined in SSAP 9. However Appendix 1 to SSAP 9 states that turnover (ascertained in a manner appropriate to the industry, the nature of the contracts concerned and the contractual relationship with the customer) and **related costs** should be recorded in the profit and loss account as contract activity progresses. Turnover may sometimes be ascertained by reference to valuation of the work carried out to date. In other cases, there may be specific points during a contract at which individual elements of work done with separately ascertainable sales values and costs can be identified and appropriately recorded as turnover (e.g. because delivery or customer acceptance has taken place). For examination purposes, **turnover** is likely normally to represent the **value of work done** or **certified as done**.

EXAM HINT

For exam purposes, **turnover** is likely normally to represent the **value of work done** or **certified as done**.

2.7 Measuring attributable profit

KEY POINT

SSAP 9 states that **attributable profit** should reflect the proportion of work carried out at the balance sheet date and take account of any known inequalities of profitability in the various stages of the contract.

SSAP 9 does not prescribe a method of arriving at **attributable profit**, although it does state that it should reflect the proportion of work carried out at the balance sheet date and take account of any known inequalities of profitability in the various stages of the contract. Possible methods of calculating it include:

1 turnover to date less cost to date
2 work certified as a proportion of total contract price × total estimated profit
3 cost to date as a proportion of total estimated cost × total estimated profit.

Method 1 does not normally reflect the proportion of work carried out at the balance sheet date. Methods 2 and 3 are most commonly used in practice. **Exam questions normally specify the method that is to be used.**

If a contract is expected to make a loss, the whole of the loss must be recognised in the profit and loss account immediately.

2.8 Ongoing contracts for services

SSAP 9 deals with long term contracts for the provision of a **single** asset or service. It does not address the provision of services on an ongoing basis. For example, a company might have a contract to provide staff to a client as and when needed over a period of twelve months. Should revenue be deferred until the twelve months is up, or can revenue be claimed as the service is provided?

UITF Abstract 40 states that where a seller's contractual obligations are performed gradually over time, revenue should be recognised as contract activity progresses. Revenue claimed will reflect the seller's partial performance of its contractual obligations. It is inappropriate to defer recognition until the contract is complete.

So, in this case the company will claim income as staff are provided to the client in accordance with the provisions in SSAP 9 for long term contracts.

There are two exceptions to this rule. If an ongoing contract falls into two or more distinguishable phases that can be valued reliably, then each phase should be treated as a separate transaction. If the right to consideration depends upon a critical event beyond the control of the seller, then revenue will be deferred until the event occurs.

ACTIVITY **2**

The following amounts relate to a long-term contract:

	£
Selling price	150,000
Cost to date	(60,000)
Estimated cost to complete	(30,000)
Estimated total profit	60,000
Work certified to date	110,000

Calculate attributable profit using each of the three methods outlined above.

Feedback to this activity is at the end of the chapter.

3 Accounting for long-term contracts

3.1 Comprehensive example

Example

Bloggs Builders undertake a three-year contract to build a bridge for £1 million. The following information applies at the end of Years 1, 2 and 3:

	Value of work done	*Costs*	*Payments on account Received*	*Invoiced*
	£000	£000	£000	£000
Year 1				
To date	200	210	150	160
To complete (estimated)	800	Not known	-	-
Year 2				
To date	500	550	535	570
To complete (estimated)	500	390	-	-
Year 3				
To date (completed)	1,000	955	1,000	1,000

You are required to show how this information would be reflected in the accounts for each of the three years. (Attributable profit is to be calculated based on the value of work done to date as a proportion of the total contract value.)

Procedure

A contract account accumulates the various costs incurred on each contract. By the end of Year 1 the account will look as follows:

Contract account

	£		£
Bank/cash for:			
Materials	X		
Labour, etc.	X		
	210,000		

Because a contract can continue for some time, there is normally provision for the contractor to invoice the customer for parts of the contract (often on a monthly or quarterly basis). The part invoices are known as **progress payments**. They are credited to a progress payments account (it is thus a type of sales account) and debited to debtors.

By the end of Year 1, the account will look as follows:

Progress payments account

	£		£
		Debtors	X
			X
			160,000

Debtors are recorded in the normal way:

Debtors

	£		£
Progress payments account	160,000	Cash	150,000
		Balance c/d	10,000
	160,000		160,000

At the end of Year 1 a decision is required as to whether to take a proportion of profit. As the costs to completion are unknown at this stage, the profitable outcome cannot be assessed with reasonable certainty. Thus there can be no attributable profit.

The **value of work done** (given in the example) is recorded in the accounts:

Dr: Progress payments	£200,000	
Cr: Profit and loss account		£200,000

The contract account is closed off to the trading account up to the amount of recorded turnover.

Contract account

	£		£
Costs	210,000	Trading account	200,000
		Balance c/d (closing stock)	10,000
	210,000		210,000

Progress payments account

	£		£
Trading account	200,000	Debtors	160,000
		Balance c/d	40,000
	200,000		200,000

Relevant extracts from the accounts at the end of Year 1 are as follows:

Profit and loss account

	£000	£000
Turnover		200
Opening stock	-	
Purchases	210	
Closing stock (bal. fig.)	(10)	
Cost of sales		200
Gross profit		-

Balance sheet

	£000
Stock:	
Net cost	10
Debtors:	
Amounts recoverable on contracts	40
Progress payments receivable (debtor)	10

Year 2

Contract account

		£			£
(1)	Balance b/d year 1	10,000	(4)	Trading account	
(2)	Costs in year 2			(see workings)	270,000
	(550 – 210)	340,000		Balance c/d	80,000
		350,000			350,000

Progress payments account

		£			£
(1)	Balance b/d year 1	40,000	(2)	Debtors (570 – 160)	410,000
(3)	Trading account				
	(500 – 200)	300,000			
	Balance c/d	70,000			
		410,000			410,000

Debtors

		£			£
(1)	Balance b/d	10,000	(2)	Cash (535 – 150)	385,000
(2)	Progress payments			Balance c/d	35,000
	account	410,000			
		420,000			420,000

Accounts extracts at the end of Year 2 are as follows:

Profit and loss account

	£000	£000
Turnover (500 – 200)		300
Opening stock	10	
Purchases (550 – 210)	340	
Closing stock (bal. fig.)	(80)	
Cost of sales		270
Gross profit (see working)		30

Balance sheet

	£000
Stock:	
Net cost	80
Applicable payments on account	(70)
Debtors:	
Progress payments receivable	35

Working

At this stage the profitable outcome of the contract can be foreseen. The attributable profit is calculated as follows:

	£000
Contract price	1,000
Costs incurred	(550)
Estimated costs to complete	(390)
Anticipated total profit	60

Based on value of work done, the contract is 50% complete (500/1,000). Therefore, the attributable profit is £30,000 (£60,000 × 50%).

Note on the sequence of entries

The numbers in the ledger accounts record the sequence of entries. At the end of the year the turnover figure (given in the example) can be transferred to the trading account from the progress payments account. The transfer of costs from the contract account to the trading account should be computed in **reverse**, i.e.

- compute attributable profit (£30,000)
- deduct profit from turnover, giving cost of sales (£270,000).

Year 3

Contract account

	£		£
Balance b/d	80,000	Trading account	485,000
Costs in year 3 (955 – 550)	405,000		
	485,000		485,000

Progress payments account

	£		£
Trading account	500,000	Balance b/d	70,000
		Debtors (1,000 – 570)	430,000
	500,000		500,000

Profit and loss account

	£000	£000
Turnover (1,000 – 500)		500
Opening stock	80	
Purchases (955 – 550)	405	
Closing stock	(-)	
Cost of sales		485
Gross profit		15

Tutorial note

The total profit on the contract is as follows:

	£000
Contract price	1,000
Costs	955
Total profit	45

This profit is recognised as follows:

Year 1	-
Year 2	30
Year 3	15
	45

3.2 Contract accounts – summary of entries

During the accounting period, the following journal entries are required:

1 Expenses incurred

Debit	*Credit*	*With*
Contract account	Creditors/Cash	Expenses (labour, materials, sub-contractors' charges, site expenses, overheads, depreciation, etc.)

2 Invoices issued to customers

Debit	*Credit*	*With*
Customer's account	Progress payments invoiced	Invoices issued

3 Cash received from customers

Debit	*Credit*	*With*
Cash	Customer's account	Cash received

4 At the year end accruals and prepayments

Debit	*Credit*	*With*
Contract account	Accruals	Any accruals
Prepayments	Contract account	Any prepayments or stock of unused materials

5 At the year end calculate profit to be taken this year

Debit	*Credit*	*With*
Progress payments invoiced	Profit and loss account	Turnover for the year (probably the work certified for the year)
Profit and loss account	Contract account	Costs matched against turnover (probably the balancing figure of turnover less attributable profit)

KEY POINT

For contract accounts, SSAP 9 accounting requirements involve **stocks**, **debtors**, **creditors** and **provisions for liabilities and charges or creditors**.

3.3 Contract accounts – summary of disclosure requirements

SSAP 9 has been criticised by some commentators for scattering entries around the different sections of the balance sheet, rather than concentrating on reporting figures within stocks. The following balance sheet items are involved:

- **stocks** – costs incurred, net of transfers to cost of sales
- **debtors** – the amount by which the recognised turnover exceeds the payments on account
- **creditors** – excess payments on account received
- **provisions for liabilities and charges or creditors** – the amount by which the provision for future losses exceeds the costs incurred (after transfers to cost of sales).

SSAP 9 requires that the balance sheet note for stocks should disclose separately:

Net cost less foreseeable losses	X
Applicable payments on account	(X)
	—
Balance of long-term contracts (within stocks)	X
	—

3.4 Second example

Example

On 1 July 20X4 Buildem Ltd signed a £300,000 contract to build a new studio for Midlands TV. The following information is relevant to this contract:

	In 20X4	*In 20X5*
	£	£
Expenditure		
Labour	24,000	31,000
Materials	47,300	58,600
Site expenses	8,450	12,500
Hire of plant	5,750	1,400
Plant purchased 1 July 20X4	36,000	-
Progress payments invoiced		
(based on work certified)	100,000	200,000
Cash received from Midlands TV	90,000	180,000

(1) Accrued expenses and stocks of unused materials at 31 December 20X4 amounted to £800 and £1,700 respectively.
   - Overheads are allocated between contracts at 10% of labour costs.
   - Plant is depreciated at 25% pa straight line on cost.
   - A rectification provision of 4% of the contract price is set aside at the end of each contract.

(2) The profitable outcome of the contract was apparent on 31 December 20X4. Estimated costs to completion on 31 December 20X4 were £103,500.

(3) The contract was completed on 31 August 20X5 and Midlands TV paid the 10% retention money on 1 March 20X6. During January 20X6 £10,000 was incurred on maintenance expenditure.

(4) The figure for progress payments invoiced is to be taken as the value of work performed for the turnover figure in the profit and loss account.

Show the necessary ledger entries in the books of Buildem Ltd and the relevant profit and loss account and balance sheet extracts at 31 December 20X4 and 20X5.

Solution

20X4 entries are shown separately from 20X5 and 20X6 to emphasise the entries being made for each year.

Studio contract account

20X4		£	20X4		£
	Labour	24,000			
	Materials	47,300			
	Site expenses	8,450			
	Hire of plant	5,750			
	Overheads (10% × £24,000)	2,400	31 Dec	Trading account (see P&L a/c)	65,000
31 Dec	Depreciation (6/12 × 25% × £36,000)	4,500		Stocks c/d	1,700
	Accruals c/d	800		Work in progress c/d (balance)	26,500
		93,200			93,200

Progress payments account

20X4		£	20X4		£
31 Dec	Trading account	100,000		Midlands TV account debtor	100,000

Midlands TV account

20X4		£	20X4		£
	Progress payments account	100,000		Cash	90,000
				Balance c/d	10,000
		100,000			100,000

Calculation of attributable profit to date at 31 December 20X4

	£	£
Contract price		300,000
Less:		
Costs to date £(93,200 – 1,700)	91,500	
Estimated costs to complete	103,500	
		195,000
Estimated total profit		105,000

Tutorial note

There is a case for adding the rectification provision as an additional expected cost, i.e. reducing estimated total profit by £300,000 × 4% = £12,000.

Attributable profit for 20X4:

$$\frac{\text{Work certified}}{\text{Contract price}} \times \text{estimated total profit, i.e. } \frac{£100,000}{£300,000} \times £105,000 = £35,000$$

Profit and loss account for the year ended 31 December 20X4

	£
Turnover (given)	100,000
Cost of sales (bal. fig.)	65,000
Profit (calculated)	35,000

Balance sheet extract as at 31 December 20X4

	£	£	£
Fixed assets:			
Plant	36,000	(4,500)	31,500
Current assets:			
Stock:			
Raw materials		1,700	
Long-term contract balances – net cost	26,500		
Less: Applicable payments on account	Nil		
		26,500	
		28,200	
Debtors:			
Progress payments receivable		10,000	
		38,200	
Creditors: amounts falling due within one year			
Accruals		800	
			37,400
			68,900

Studio contract account

20X5		£	20X5		£
	Stock b/d	1,700		Accruals b/d	800
	Work in progress b/d	26,500			
	Labour	31,000			
	Materials	58,600			
	Site expenses	12,500			
	Hire of plant	1,400			
	Overheads (10% × £31,000)	3,100			
31 Dec	Depreciation (8/12 × 25% × £36,000)	6,000	31 Dec	Trading account (balance)	152,000
	Rectification (4% × £300,000) provision c/d	12,000			
		152,800			152,800

Studio contract account, continued

20X6			20X6		
	Maintenance expenditure	10,000		Provision b/d	12,000
	Profit and loss account (balance)	2,000			
		12,000			12,000

Progress payments account

20X5		£	20X5		£
31 Dec	Trading account	200,000		Midlands TV account debtor	200,000

Midlands TV account

20X5		£	20X5		£
	Balance b/d	10,000		Cash	180,000
	Progress payments account	200,000		Balance c/d	30,000
		210,000			210,000
20X6			20X6		
	Balance b/d	30,000		Cash	30,000

Profit and loss account for the year ended 31 December 20X5

	£
Turnover (given)	200,000
Cost of sales (remaining costs in contract account)	152,000
Profit (bal. fig.)	48,000
Depreciation $4/12 \times 25\% \times 36{,}000$	3,000

(Plant would continue to suffer a depreciation charge on other contracts.)

Balance sheet extract as at 31 December 20X5

	£	£
Fixed assets:		
Contract plant, at cost		36,000
Less: Accumulated depreciation (4,500 + 6,000 + 3,000)		13,500
		22,500
Current assets:		
Debtors – progress payments receivable	30,000	
Creditors – amounts falling due within one year		
Rectification provision	12,000	
		18,000
		40,500

Conclusion

Stocks and work in progress other than long-term contracts should be stated at the lower of cost and net realisable value.

Long-term contracts should be assessed on a contract-by-contract basis and attributable profit recognised in the profit and loss account. Losses on long-term contracts should be recognised immediately.

SELF-TEST QUESTIONS

1 What is the basic rule in SSAP 9 regarding stock valuation? (1.1)

2 Define cost of conversion. (1.1)

3 Which methods of stock valuation are acceptable under SSAP 9? (1.2)

4 Why is it desirable to recognise profit before the completion of a long term contract? (2.2)

5 How should long term contracts be disclosed in the balance sheet? (2.4)

6 How can turnover on contract activity be measured in practice? (2.6)

7 Give two possible methods of measuring attributable profit. (2.7)

8 If a contract is expected to make a loss, how should this be treated in the financial statements? (2.7)

EXAM-TYPE QUESTION

G Ltd

G Ltd is a company specialising in the construction of sophisticated items of plant and machinery for clients in the engineering industry. Details of two contracts outstanding at 30 September 20X5 (the balance sheet date) are as follows:

Contract with H Ltd

This contract was started on 1 January 20X5 and is expected to be complete by 31 March 20X6. The total contract price was fixed at £20 million and the total costs to be incurred originally estimated at £15 million, occurring evenly over the contract. The contract has been certified by experts as being 60% complete by 30 September 20X5. Due to inefficiencies caused by industrial relations difficulties in the summer of 20X5, the actual costs incurred on the contract in the period 1 January 20X5 to 30 September 20X5 were £10 million. However, the management is confident that these problems will not recur and that the remaining costs will be in line with the original estimate. In accordance with the payment terms laid down in the contract, G Ltd invoiced H Ltd for an interim payment of £10 million on 31 August 20X5. The interim payment was received from H Ltd on 31 October 20X5.

Contract with I Ltd

This contract was started on 1 April 20X5 and was expected to be complete by 31 December 20X5. The total contract price was fixed at £10 million and the total contract costs were originally estimated at £8 million. However, information received on 15 October 20X5 suggested that the total contract costs would in fact be £11 million. The contract was certified by experts as being $^2/_3$ complete by the year end and the costs actually incurred by G Ltd in respect of this contract in the period to 30 September 20X5 were £7.5 million. No progress payments are yet due under the payment terms specified in the contract with I Ltd.

Required:

(a) Explain the principles which are used to establish the timing of recognition of profits/losses on long-term contracts.

You should assume that recognition of profits/losses takes place in accordance with the provisions of SSAP 9 *Stocks and long-term contracts* and should refer to fundamental accounting concepts, where relevant.

(10 marks)

(b) Compute, separately for *each* of the contracts with H Ltd and I Ltd:

- the amount of turnover and cost of sales that will be recognised in the profit and loss account of G Ltd for the year ended 30 September 20X5
- the contract balances (including nil balances, if appropriate) that will be shown at 30 September 20X5 on the following accounts:
  - long-term contract work-in-progress
  - amounts recoverable on contracts
  - provision for losses
  - trade debtors. **(10 marks)**

For the answer to this question, see the 'Answers' section at the end of the book.

FEEDBACK TO ACTIVITY **1**

1 Value at £12,000. £10,000 is irrelevant. The rule is lower of cost or net realisable value, not lower of cost or replacement cost. Since the materials will be processed before sale there is no reason to believe that net realisable value will be below cost.

2 Value at net realisable value, i.e. £15,900, as this is below cost (NRV = contract price of £18,000 less the company's share of modification cost, £2,100).

FEEDBACK TO ACTIVITY **2**

1 **Turnover – cost**

150,000 – 60,000 = £90,000

2 **Work certified as a proportion of total contract price × total estimated profit**

$$\frac{110,000}{150,000} \times 60,000 = £44,000$$

3 **Cost to date as a proportion of total estimated cost × total estimated profit**

$$\frac{60,000}{90,000} \times 60,000 = £40,000$$

Chapter 13

REPORTING FINANCIAL PERFORMANCE

CHAPTER CONTENTS

1 The requirements of FRS 3

2 Classification of items

3 The statement of total recognised gains and losses (STRGL)

4 Other FRS 3 notes

5 Prior period adjustments

This chapter covers an important accounting standard: FRS 3 *Reporting financial performance.*

FRS 3 requires entities to disclose detailed information about financial performance in the profit and loss account and in a second statement: the statement of total recognised gains and losses. These disclosures are intended to help users of the financial statements to look behind the net profit figure and to understand the different components of an entity's performance.

Objectives

By the time you have finished this chapter you should be able to:

- explain the need for an accounting standard in this area
- discuss the importance of identifying and reporting the results of discontinuing operations
- distinguish between extraordinary and exceptional items
- prepare a profit and loss account in accordance with the requirements of FRS 3
- explain the contents and purpose of the statement of total recognised gains and losses
- describe and prepare the other notes required by FRS 3
- define and account for prior period adjustments.

1 The requirements of FRS 3

1.1 The need for a standard

KEY POINT

FRS 3 discourages the practice of '**creative accounting**' and encourages a view of company performance which is not based solely on profit.

FRS 3, issued in October 1992, radically reformed the presentation of the profit and loss account and added a new primary statement to the annual financial statements, the **statement of total recognised gains and losses (STRGL)**. In addition, it virtually eradicated extraordinary items and changed the earnings per share calculation.

There were two main reasons for the issue of FRS 3.

'Creative accounting'

Profit on ordinary activities is regarded as the most important measure of company performance. It forms the basis of two important ratios used by investors, earnings per share (EPS) and the price earnings ratio.

Extraordinary items are large, unusual items that arise from events or transactions that fall outside the ordinary activities of the business and are not expected to recur. Before FRS 3 was issued, profit on ordinary activities did not include extraordinary items. Instead, these items were reported '**below the line**', i.e. after profit on ordinary activities after taxation. This was because profit on ordinary activities was believed to give important information to the users of accounts which would be distorted by the inclusion of extraordinary items.

The result of this was that companies could and did improve the user's view of their performance by treating large items of expense as extraordinary and large items of unusual income as exceptional items, '**above the line**'.

Better information for users of financial statements

The ASB wanted to improve the information about financial performance given by the financial statements. In particular, it wanted to encourage users of accounts to concentrate less on profit on ordinary activities after taxation and instead to look at the performance of the company as a whole. It believed that the financial performance of many organisations was too complex to be summarised in a single indicator.

1.2 Objective of FRS 3

KEY POINT

The objective of the FRS is to require companies to highlight a range of important components of financial performance. All gains and losses are included in the profit and loss account or the **STRGL**.

The objective of the FRS is to require companies to highlight a range of important components of financial performance, to aid users in understanding the performance achieved by a reporting entity in a period, and to assist them in forming a basis for their assessment of future results and cash flows.

It attempts to achieve the objective by requiring that all gains and losses recognised in the financial statements for the period be included in the profit and loss account or the STRGL.

Gains and losses may be excluded from the profit and loss account only if their exclusion is specifically permitted or required to be taken directly to reserves by an accounting standard or by law.

1.3 Format of the profit and loss account

KEY POINT

The format of the profit and loss account is **layered** to highlight a number of components of financial performance.

A layered format is to be used for the profit and loss account to highlight a number of important components of financial performance:

1 results of continuing operations (including the results of acquisitions)

2 results of discontinued operations

3 profits or losses on the sale or termination of an operation, costs of a fundamental reorganisation or restructuring and profits or losses on the disposal of fixed assets

4 extraordinary items (in very rare circumstances).

Note: Exceptional items will comprise the items listed in 3 above, which are disclosed separately on the face of the profit and loss account, and other items which are disclosed separately by way of note only (and are thus within the normal operations).

A sample format is shown below:

Profit and loss account for the year ended 30 June 20X3

	Continuing operations 20X3	*Acquisitions 20X3*	*Discontinued operations 20X3*	*Total 20X3*	*Total 20X2 as restated*
	£m	£m	£m	£m	£m
Turnover	550	50	175	775	690
Cost of sales	(415)	(40)	(165)	(620)	(555)
	—	—	—	—	—
Gross profit	135	10	10	155	135
Net operating expenses	(85)	(4)	(25)	(114)	(83)
Less: 20X2 provision			10	10	
	—	—	—	—	—
Operating profit	50	6	(5)	51	52
Profit on sale of properties	9			9	6
Provision for loss on operations to be discontinued					(30)
Loss on disposal of discontinued operations			(17)	(17)	
Less: 20X2 provision			20	20	
	—	—	—	—	—

Profit on ordinary activities before interest	59	6	(2)	63	28
Interest payable				(18)	(15)
Profit on ordinary activities before taxation				45	13
Tax on profit on ordinary activities				(14)	(4)
Profit on ordinary activities after taxation				31	9
Minority interests				(2)	(2)
Extraordinary items (included only to show positioning)				-	-
Profit for the financial year				29	7
Dividends				(8)	(1)
Retained profit for the financial year				21	6
Earnings per share				39p	10p

1.4 Continuing and discontinued operations

KEY POINT

The analysis between **continuing operations**, **acquisitions** and **discontinued operations** should be disclosed to the level of operating profit.

The analysis between continuing operations, acquisitions (as a component of continuing operations) and discontinued operations should be disclosed to the level of operating profit. The analysis of turnover and operating profit is the **minimum** disclosure required in this respect on the **face** of the profit and loss account.

The example above thus provides more than the minimum disclosure. The minimum disclosures could be shown as follows:

	20X3	*20X3*	*20X2 as restated*
	£m	£m	£m
Turnover			
Continuing operations	550		500
Acquisitions	50		
	600		
Discontinued operations	175		190
		775	690
Cost of sales		(620)	(555)
Gross profit		155	135
Net operating expenses		(104)	(83)
Operating profit			
Continuing operations	50		40
Acquisitions	6		
	56		
Discontinued operations	(15)		12
Less: 20X2 provision	10		
		51	52

***Notes*:**

- In either example, as the full statutory headings have not been shown, a note to the accounts needs to show an analysis of the statutory cost headings between continuing operations, acquisitions (as a component of continuing operations) and discontinued operations.
- The analysis in respect of continuing operations, acquisitions and discontinued operations is required only to the profit before interest level. This is because interest payable is usually a reflection of a company's overall financing policy, involving both equity and debt funding considerations on a group wide basis, rather than an aggregation of the particular types of finance allocated to individual segments of the reporting entity's operations. Any allocation of interest would involve a considerable degree of subjectivity that could leave the user uncertain as to the relevance and reliability of the information.
- The comparative figures should be based on the status of an operation in the financial statements of the period under review and should, therefore, include in the continuing category only the results of those operations included in the current period's continuing operations. The comparative figures appearing under the heading 'continuing operations' may include figures which were shown under the heading of acquisitions in that previous period. No reference needs to be made to the results of those acquisitions, since they do not need to be presented separately in the current year.

The comparative figures for discontinued operations will include both amounts relating to operations discontinued in the previous period and amounts relating to operations discontinued in the period under review, which in the previous period would have been included as part of continuing operations.

The analysis of comparative figures between continuing and discontinued operations is not required on the face of the profit and loss account.

1.5 Definition of discontinued operations

The analysis of the figures in the profit and loss account is intended to enable users of the financial statements to predict the future performance of entities.

Continuing operations (including acquisitions) are the basis for the company's future; it is these operations which must generate the cash flows to pay the dividends to support the share price in the future. Users of accounts have to be able to identify these operations separately so that they can form an opinion on the company's future prospects.

This means that the results of **discontinued operations** must also be identified as a separate component of the period's results.

DEFINITION

Discontinued operations are those that are sold or terminated and that satisfy four conditions.

Discontinued operations are those that are sold or terminated and that satisfy all of the following conditions:

1 The sale or termination is completed either in the period or before the earlier of three months after the commencement of the subsequent period and the date on which the financial statements are approved.

2 If a termination, the former activities have ceased permanently.

3 The sale or termination has a material effect on the nature and focus of the reporting entity's operations, and represents a material reduction in its operating facilities resulting either from its withdrawal from a particular market (whether class of business or geographical) or from a material reduction in turnover in the reporting entity's continuing markets.

4 The assets, liabilities, results of operations and activities are clearly distinguishable, physically, operationally and for financial reporting purposes.

Operations not satisfying all these conditions are classified as continuing.

Note the timing restriction. If the termination is not completed within the time stated, the turnover and costs of the operations remain in continuing operations.

This does *not* mean, however, that an exceptional item should not be shown in respect of the actual profit/loss or anticipated loss on disposal. This point is discussed below after the definition of exceptional items has been considered.

Note also part 3 of the definition. The nature and focus of a reporting entity's operations refers to the positioning of its products or services in their markets including the aspects of both quality and location. For example, if a hotel company which had traditionally served the lower end of the hotel market sold its existing chain and bought luxury hotels then, while remaining in the business of managing hotels, the group would be changing the nature and focus of its operations. A similar situation would arise if the same company were to sell its hotels in (say) the United States and buy hotels in Europe.

The regular sales and replacements of material assets which are undertaken by a company as part of the routine maintenance of its portfolio of assets should not be classified as discontinuances and acquisitions. In the example, the sale of hotels and the purchase of others within the same market sector and similar locations would be treated as wholly within continuing operations.

2 Classification of items

2.1 Exceptional items

Exceptional items are material items which derive from events or transactions that fall within the ordinary activities of the reporting entity and which individually or, if of a similar type, in aggregate, need to be disclosed by virtue of their size or incidence if the financial statements are to give a true and fair view.

DEFINITION

Exceptional items are material items which individually or in aggregate, need to be disclosed by virtue of their size or incidence if the financial statements are to give a true and fair view.

All exceptional items, other than those stated below, should be included under the statutory format headings to which they relate. They should be separately disclosed by way of note or, where it is necessary in order that the financial statements give a true and fair view, on the face of the profit and loss account.

There are in effect two types of exceptional items: those that are exceptional but are still included in the statutory format headings, and those which are separately identified.

The view of the ASB is that exceptional items should not be transferred to a single heading of 'exceptional', because profit before exceptional items could then become the focus of financial statement presentations, with the implication that no exceptional items are expected in the future.

2.2 Items to be shown separately

KEY POINT

Profits or losses on the **sale of an operation** or **disposal of a fixed asset**, or the cost of **restructuring** should be **shown separately**.

The following items, including provisions in respect of such items, should be shown separately on the face of the profit and loss account, after operating profit and before interest:

- profits or losses on the sale or termination of an operation
- costs of a fundamental reorganisation or restructuring
- profits or losses on the disposal of fixed assets.

Each of the three specific items will be examined in turn.

KEY POINT

FRS 3 imposes restrictions on the use of **provisions** for losses arising from **the sale or termination of an operation**.

Profit or losses on the sale or termination of an operation

The '**sale or termination of an operation**' is not defined in FRS 3. It encompasses but is not restricted to the term '**discontinued operation**'. Thus the item may be part of continuing operations or discontinued operations and therefore needs to be disclosed under its correct heading. It is likely to be an exceptional item as well.

Often the sale or termination straddles two accounting periods. In the first period a **provision** may be required for losses expected to arise in the following period (under the prudence concept). However, there has been much criticism in recent years on the 'excessive' use of provisions by companies and thus FRS 3 imposes the following restrictions.

- A provision should not be made unless the company is demonstrably committed to the sale or termination, e.g. public announcement of specific plans has been made, or a binding contract for sale has been entered into after the balance sheet date.
- The provision should cover only:
  - direct costs of the sale or termination
  - operating losses up to the sale date
  - less anticipated trading profits (if any).

Example

X plc has a calendar year end. On 30 October 20X7 the board of directors decide to withdraw from a market which has been a significant part of the company's existing business. Plans are disclosed to the workforce on 30 November with termination set at 31 March 20X8.

Actual and projected results of the operation are as follows:

	Actual to 31 December 20X7 £000	*Projected to 31 March* 20X8 £000
Sales	45,000	8,000
Operating costs	44,000	12,000
Redundancy and other costs		3,000

The accounts for the year ended 31 December 20X7 are expected to be approved by 18 March 20X8.

In the accounts for the year ended 31 December 20X7 the operation is not classified as a discontinued operation (due to the timing of the date on which the accounts are approved). A provision should however be disclosed (as an exceptional item) totalling:

	£000
Projected loss	4,000
Redundancy and other costs	3,000
	7,000

If, in the 20X8 accounting period, actual results of the operation are:

	£000
Sales	9,400
Operating costs	11,600
Redundancy and other costs	3,000

the profit and loss account for the year ended 31 December 20X8 would show:

	Continuing operations 20X8	*Discontinued operations 20X8*	*Continuing operations 20X7*	*Discontinued operations 20X7*
	£000	£000	£000	£000
Turnover	X	9,400	X	45,000
Operating costs:	X	(11,600)		(44,000)
Less: 20X7 provision		4,000		
Operating profit	X	1,800		1,000
Provision for loss on operations to be discontinued				(7,000)
Loss on termination of discontinued operation		(3,000)		
Less: 20X7 provision		3,000		
Profit (loss) on ordinary activities before taxation	X	1,800		(6,000)

KEY POINT

Only a reorganisation or restructuring having a **material effect** on the nature and focus of the company's operation qualifies for separate disclosure.

Costs of a fundamental reorganisation

As the title of this item implies, only a reorganisation or restructuring having a **material effect** on the nature and focus of the company's operation qualifies for separate disclosure. This item will therefore be classified as exceptional as well.

Disposals of fixed assets

This heading is not intended to include profits and losses that are no more than marginal adjustments to depreciation previously charged.

KEY POINT

If an asset has previously been revalued, FRS 3 **standardises** the method of computation of the profit or loss on its disposal.

If an asset has previously been revalued, FRS 3 **standardises** the method of computation of the profit or loss. FRS 3 requires two adjustments to be made where a fixed asset which had previously been revalued is sold. These are computed as follows:

- difference between proceeds of sale and book value at date of sale – dealt with through the profit and loss account (this is also required by FRS 15.
- amount previously included under revaluation surplus – this now becomes a realised profit but should not be dealt with as part of the reported profit for the year.

2.3 Extraordinary items and ordinary activities

DEFINITION

Extraordinary items are material items possessing a high degree of abnormality which arise from events or transactions that fall **outside** the ordinary activities of the reporting entity and which are not expected to recur.

Ordinary activities are any activities which are undertaken by a reporting entity as part of its business and such related activities in which the reporting entity engages in furtherance of, incidental to, or arising from, these activities.

Extraordinary items are material items possessing a high degree of abnormality which arise from events or transactions that fall outside the ordinary activities of the reporting entity and which are not expected to recur. They do not include exceptional items, nor do they include prior period items merely because they relate to a prior period.

The ASB did not change the definition of extraordinary items when issuing FRS 3. Instead, it defined ordinary activities so widely that it is difficult to imagine any item that might fall outside them.

Ordinary activities are any activities which are undertaken by a reporting entity as part of its business and such related activities in which the reporting entity engages in furtherance of, incidental to, or arising from, these activities. Ordinary activities include the effects on the reporting entity of any event in the various environments in which it operates, including the political, regulatory, economic and geographical environments, irrespective of the frequency or unusual nature of the events.

No examples of extraordinary items are given in FRS 3. Indeed the ASB contemplated removing extraordinary items completely but did not do so because company law includes extraordinary items in the profit and loss account formats.

To emphasise the change Sir David Tweedie, then Chairman of the ASB stated: 'Martians walking down the street will be extraordinary, everything else is exceptional.'

2.4 Earnings per share

KEY POINT

Earnings per share is now calculated including extraordinary items.

Another route by which the ASB has reduced the importance of extraordinary items is by changing the definition of EPS.

Earnings are now to be calculated including the effects of extraordinary items (Earnings per share will be dealt with in more detail in a later chapter of this text).

ACTIVITY **1**

Do the following situations meet the definition of discontinued operations as defined by FRS 3?

1 X plc, an office furniture and equipment manufacturer, runs separate divisions of approximately equal size for the two activities. It has now decided to sell the less profitable equipment division and use the funds received to expand the furniture division by growth and acquisition. The decision to sell was made in October 20X5 and the sale was completed on 21 March 20X6. The accounts for the year 20X5 were approved on 15 March 20X6.

2 Y plc as a result of an economic recession has suffered a downturn in demand and now has productive overcapacity. In order to reduce costs, Y plc has decided to transfer production into one of its two factories and to 'moth-ball' the other factory. This decision was made in April 20X3 and the transfer was completed in August 20X3. The company has a September year end.

3 Z plc, a printing company, also carries out specialised book binding. This part of the business is carried out in a separate workshop and comprises approximately 0.5% of the total assets of the company and contributes approximately the same proportion of profits.

During 20X4 Z plc sold the bookbinding business to a consortium of the workforce and sold the workshop to the local council. The profit arising from this transaction amounted to £100,000 on profits of £2,400,000 for 20X4.

Feedback to this activity is at the end of the chapter.

3 The statement of total recognised gains and losses (STRGL)

3.1 The purpose of the statement

The STRGL is a **primary statement**, i.e. it is required for a true and fair view.

As the name suggests, this statement brings together **all the gains and losses** for the period, including items which do not pass through the profit and loss account.

KEY POINT

The STRGL is a **primary statement**, required for a true and fair view, which brings together all gains and losses for the period.

The STRGL reflects the ASB's concept of financial performance, as discussed in the Statement of Principles. The financial performance of an entity comprises the return it obtains on the resources it controls, the components of that return and the characteristics of those components. In other words, performance is wider than simply profit, it also includes items such as changes in the value of assets and gains and losses on currency translation.

KEY POINT

The Statement of Principles reflects performance as **comprehensive income** by defining gains and losses in terms of changes in net assets.

This is the concept of '**comprehensive income**'. Financial performance is effectively the change in the ownership interest, other than as a result of contributions from owners and distributions to owners. The Statement of Principles reflects performance as comprehensive income by defining gains and losses in terms of changes in net assets (the balance sheet based approach).

The STRGL highlights items that are taken straight to **reserves**, rather than passing through the profit and loss account. Before the issue of FRS 3, these items were often 'hidden' in reserve movements and it was often difficult for users to appreciate their impact upon the company's overall financial performance.

For example, revaluation gains cannot be taken to the profit and loss account, because they are unrealised, but nevertheless they may form an important part of a company's overall performance. The STRGL shows the effect of revaluations and other items such as prior period adjustments.

The STRGL is not intended to reflect the realisation of gains recognised in previous periods nor does it deal with transfers between reserves.

3.2 Illustrative STRGL

Example

An illustrative STRGL is shown below:

Statement of total recognised gains and losses
for the year ended 30 June 20X3

	20X3	*20X2 as restated*
	£m	£m
Profit for the financial year	27	7
Unrealised surplus on revaluation of properties	4	6
Unrealised (loss)/gain on trade investment	(3)	7
	—	—
Total recognised gains and losses relating to the year	28	20
		—
Prior year adjustment (as explained in note X)	(10)	
	—	
Total gains and losses recognised since last annual report	18	
	—	

4 Other FRS 3 notes

4.1 Two further statements

FRS 3 requires two other statements to be shown as **notes** to the accounts. The second of these notes, '**Historic cost profits and losses**' must, however, be presented immediately following the profit and loss account or the STRGL.

4.2 Reconciliation of movements in shareholders' funds

KEY POINT

FRS 3 requires a statement of the **reconciliation of movements in shareholders' funds**.

The reconciliation of movements in shareholders' funds brings together the performance of the period, as shown in the STRGL, with all the other changes in shareholders' funds in the period, including capital contributed by or repaid to shareholders.

FRS 3 requires this statement since the change in financial position of an entity can only be fully understood when all changes in shareholders' funds are reported, not just those shown in the STRGL.

Example

Reconciliation of movements in shareholders' funds for the year ended 30 June 20X3

	20X3	*20X2 as restated*
	£m	£m
Profit for the financial year	27	7
Dividends	(8)	(1)
	19	6
Other recognised gains and losses relating to the year (net)	1	18
New share capital subscribed	20	1
Net addition to shareholders' funds	40	25
Opening shareholders' funds (originally £375m before deducting prior year adjustment of £10m)	365	340
Closing shareholders' funds	405	365

4.3 Reserve note

KEY POINT

CA85 requires disclosure of all movements in reserves, in the form of a **reserve note**.

CA85 requires disclosure of all movements in reserves, in the form of a reserve note. The reserve note provides additional information as it discloses the movements on each separate reserve and between reserves.

Example

	Share premium account	*Revaluation reserve*	*Profit and loss account*	*Total*
	£m	£m	£m	£m
At beginning of year as previously stated	44	200	120	364
Prior year adjustment			(10)	(10)
At beginning of year as restated	44	200	110	354
Premium on issue of shares (nominal value £7 million)	13			13
Transfer from profit and loss account of the year			21	21
Transfer of realised profits		(14)	14	0
Decrease in value of trade investment		(3)		(3)
Surplus on property revaluations		4		4
At end of year	57	187	145	389

KEY POINT

The note of **historic cost profits and losses** presents the profits or losses of companies that have revalued assets on a more comparable basis with those of entities that have not.

4.4 Note of historic cost profits and losses

The note of historic cost profits and losses is a memorandum item, the primary purpose of which is to present the profits or losses of companies that have revalued assets on a more comparable basis with those of entities that have not. It is an abbreviated restatement of the profit and loss account which adjusts the reported profit or loss, if necessary, so as to show it as if no asset revaluation had been made. FRS 3 requires this statement to help users of accounts to compare the results of different companies, some of which revalue their assets and some of which do not.

Example

Note of historic cost profits and losses for the year ended 30 June 20X3

	20X3	*20X2 as restated*
	£m	£m
Reported profit on ordinary activities before taxation	45	13
Realisation of property revaluation gains of previous years	9	10
Difference between a historic cost depreciation charge and the actual depreciation charge of the year calculated on the revalued amount	5	4
Historic cost profit on ordinary activities before taxation	59	27
Historic cost profit for the year retained after taxation, minority interests, extraordinary items and dividends	35	20

ACTIVITY **2**

Phibbs plc

The following figures have been calculated for Phibbs plc for the year ended 31 December 20X9, together with comparatives for the previous year.

	20X9	*20X8*
	£m	£m
Profit before tax	50	35
Tax	(12)	(7)
Profit for the financial year	38	28
Dividends	(18)	(15)
Retained profit	20	13
Unrealised surplus on revaluation of property	2	1
Opening shareholders' funds	220	204
Share capital issued during the year		
Par value	10	3
Premium	2	1
Additional depreciation charged on property revaluations (i.e. over and above what would have been charged on their historic cost)	3	2

You are required to draft the following statements for Phibbs plc for inclusion in the 20X9 accounts:

- statement of total recognised gains and losses
- reconciliation of movements in shareholders' funds
- note of historic cost profits and losses.

Feedback to this activity is at the end of the chapter.

5 Prior period adjustments

5.1 Definition of prior period adjustments

DEFINITION

Prior period adjustments are material adjustments applicable to prior periods arising from changes in accounting policies or from the correction of fundamental errors.

Prior period adjustments are material adjustments applicable to prior periods arising from changes in accounting policies or from the correction of fundamental errors. They do not include normal recurring adjustments or corrections of accounting estimates made in prior periods.

The cumulative effect of the adjustments has to be noted at the foot of the STRGL (see above).

Prior period adjustments are rare. An entity may change its accounting policy only if the new policy will give a fairer presentation of its results and of its financial position. To be fundamental, an error must be so significant that it destroys the **true and fair view** and hence the validity of the financial statements.

KEY POINT

Corrections and adjustments to **estimates** made in prior periods, and modifications of **existing accounting treatments** are not classed as prior period adjustments.

The following are *not* prior period adjustments and should be dealt with in the profit and loss account of the period in which they are identified:

- corrections and adjustments to estimates made in prior periods (e.g. provisions for doubtful debts)
- modifications of an existing accounting treatment which are necessary because the entity is undertaking different transactions.

FRS 3 requires the following accounting treatment:

- restate the **comparative figures** for the preceding period in the primary statements and the notes
- adjust the **opening balance of reserves** for the cumulative effect of the adjustments. This adjustment should be clearly disclosed in the reserves note and should also be disclosed in the reconciliation of movements in shareholders' funds
- disclose the effect of **prior period adjustments** on the results for the preceding period where practicable
- disclose the **cumulative effect of the adjustments** at the foot of the STRGL for the current period.

Example

Harry plc was incorporated on 1 January 20X5. In the accounts for the first three years, development costs were carried forward as an intangible asset in the balance sheet. During 20X8 the directors decided that a change in accounting policy was appropriate for 20X8 and succeeding years that all development costs should be written off as incurred. The following information is available.

Development costs

Year	*Incurred during year*	*Transfer from development costs account to profit & loss account*
	£000	£000
20X5	500	-
20X6	800	200
20X7	900	320

The 20X7 financial statements showed:

	£000
Retained profits b/f	2,800
Retained profit for the year	1,600
Retained profits c/f	4,400

The retained profit for 20X8 after charging the actual development costs for the year was £1.8m.

Show how the change in accounting policy should be reflected in the statement of movements in reserves (including comparative figures) for the year ended 31 December 20X8. Ignore taxation.

Solution

If the new accounting policy had been in place since the company started, the additional charges for development expenditure in the profit and loss account of each year would have been:

	£000
20X5	500
20X6 (800 – 200)	600
20X7 (900 – 320)	580
	1,680

The statement of movements in reserves in the 20X8 financial statements would therefore appear as follows:

	20X8 £000	*20X7* £000
Retained profits b/f		
As previously reported	4,400	2,800
Prior year adjustment	(1,680)	(1,100)
As restated	2,720	1,700
Retained profits for the year	1,800	1,020
Retained profits c/f	4,520	2,720

Conclusion

FRS 3 is concerned with the presentation of the primary performance statements: the profit and loss account and the statement of total recognised gains and losses (STRGL). It requires results to be analysed between continuing operations, acquisitions and discontinued operations. It also contains requirements governing the disclosure of exceptional items and requires the preparation of a note of historic cost profits and losses and a reconciliation of shareholders' funds.

This additional information is intended to highlight a range of components of financial performance rather than encouraging a focus on one earnings figure.

SELF-TEST QUESTIONS

1. Why was FRS 3 issued? (1.1)
2. Define a discontinued operation. (1.5)
3. Which three items must be separately disclosed as exceptional items on the face of the profit and loss account? (2.2)
4. How should the profit or loss on disposal of a fixed asset be calculated? (2.2)
5. How does the STRGL reflect 'comprehensive income'? (3.1)
6. Which items are separately disclosed in the reconciliation of movements in shareholders' funds? (4.2)
7. What is the purpose of the note of historic cost profits and losses? (4.4)
8. When do prior period adjustments arise? (5.1)

EXAM-TYPE QUESTION

David plc

David plc is a diversified company that has operated in four main areas for many years. Each of these activities has usually contributed approximately one quarter of the company's annual operating profit.

During the year ended 31 December 20X3, the company disposed of its glass-making division and reorganised the other three divisions. These changes involved large numbers of redundancies.

The company's chief accountant has prepared the following summary:

Analysis of costs and revenues, year ended 31 December 20X3

	Glass-making	*Other divisions*
	£000	£000
Turnover	150	820
Operating expenses	(98)	(470)
Redundancies	(100)	(30)
Fees associated with closure/reorganisation	(27)	(12)
Losses on disposal of fixed assets	(78)	(19)

The company also incurred interest charges of £37,000 during the year.
The tax charge for the year has been estimated at £24,000.
The directors have proposed a dividend of £30,000.

The company financed the closure and reorganisation by means of a share issue which raised £180,000. Shareholders' funds at the beginning of the year were made up as follows:

	£000
Share capital (including share premium)	400
Revaluation reserve	160
Profit and loss account	670
	1,230

The balance on the revaluation reserve arose when the company valued the land occupied by the properties used in its retail division. In view of recent developments, it has been decided that this reserve should be reduced to £90,000.

'The objective of [Financial Reporting Standard 3] is to require entities ... to highlight a range of important components of financial performance to aid users in understanding the performance achieved by a reporting entity in a period and to assist them in forming a basis for their assessment of future results and cash flows.' (FRS 3, paragraph 1.)

'A layered format is to be used for the profit and loss account to highlight a number of important components of financial performance:

(i) results of continuing operations ...

(ii) results of discontinued operations

(iii) profits or losses on the sale or termination of an operation, costs of a fundamental reorganisation or restructuring and profits or losses on the disposal of fixed assets

(iv) extraordinary items.' (FRS 3, Summary, paragraph (b).)

Required:

(a) Explain why *each* of the above components is needed in order to assess a business's future results and cash flows. **(12 marks)**

(b) Prepare an outline profit and loss account for the year ended 31 December 20X3 for David plc in a form suitable for publication. **(8 marks)**

(c) Prepare a reconciliation of movements in shareholders' funds for David plc in accordance with the requirements of FRS 3. **(5 marks)**

(Total: 25 marks)

For the answer to this question, see the 'Answers' section at the end of the book.

FEEDBACK TO ACTIVITY **1**

1 This situation meets three of the four criteria laid down by FRS 3 but fails to meet the timing restriction. FRS 3 states that the sale should be completed before the earlier of three months after commencement of the subsequent period and the date on which the financial statements are approved.

2 This would not be treated as a discontinued operation as the activities have not ceased permanently. The purpose of this decision is to reduce productive capacity temporarily until there is an upturn in the market.

3 This situation appears to meet the FRS 3 criteria for discontinued operations except that the loss of this part of the business will have no material effect on the operations of Z plc. Therefore it will not be treated as a discontinued operation. (The size of the profit arising on the sale is not taken into account in the FRS 3 criteria.)

FEEDBACK TO ACTIVITY **2**

Phibbs plc

Statement of total recognised gains and losses for the year ended 31 December 20X9

	20X9	*20X8*
	£m	£m
Profit for the financial year	38	28
Unrealised surplus on revaluation of property	2	1
Total recognised gains and losses relating to the year	40	29

Reconciliation of movements in shareholders' funds for the year ended 31 December 20X9

	20X9	*20X8*
	£m	£m
Profit for the financial year	38	28
Dividends	(18)	(15)
	20	13
Other recognised gains and losses relating to the year (net)	2	1
New share capital subscribed	12	4
Net addition to shareholders' funds	34	18
Opening shareholders' funds	220	204
Closing shareholders' funds	254	222

Note of historic cost profits and losses for the year ended 31 December 20X9

	20X9	*20X8*
	£m	£m
Reported profit before taxation	50	35
Difference between a historic cost depreciation charge and the actual depreciation charge for the year calculated on the revalued amount	3	2
Historic cost profit before taxation	53	37
Historic cost profit for the year retained after taxation and dividends	23	15

Chapter 14

RELATED PARTIES AND SEGMENTAL REPORTING

CHAPTER CONTENTS

1 Related parties

2 FRS 8 *Related party disclosures*

3 SSAP 25 *Segmental reporting*

This final chapter deals with two accounting standards that each require additional disclosures in the financial statements: FRS 8 *Related party disclosures* and SSAP 25 *Segmental reporting*.

As their titles suggest, FRS 8 requires entities to disclose the existence of relationships and transactions with related parties, while SSAP 25 requires entities to analyse turnover, results and net assets between different classes of business and different geographical markets. The purpose of these disclosures is to provide users of the financial statements with information that helps them to appraise the financial performance and position of an entity.

Objectives

By the time you have finished this chapter you should be able to:

- define and apply the definition of related parties in accordance with FRS 8
- describe the potential to mislead users when related party transactions are included in a company's financial statements
- adjust financial statements for the effects of non-commercial related party transactions
- describe the disclosure requirements for related party transactions
- discuss the usefulness and problems associated with the provision of segmental information
- define a reportable segment and the information that is to be reported
- prepare segmental reports in accordance with SSAP 25
- assess the performance of a company based on the information contained in its segmental report.

1 Related parties

1.1 Definition

DEFINITION

Two or more parties are **related parties** when at any time during the period: one party controls or influences the other party or the parties are subject to common control or common influence from the same source.

1 Two or more parties are **related parties** when at any time during the financial period:

- one party has **direct** or **indirect control** of the other party; or
- the parties are subject to **common control** from the same source; or
- one party has **influence over the financial and operating policies** of the other party to an extent that that other party might be inhibited from pursuing at all times its own separate interests; or
- the parties, in entering a transaction, are subject to **influence from the same source** to such an extent that one of the parties to the transaction has subordinated its own separate interests.

2 For the avoidance of doubt, the following are related parties of the reporting entity:

- its ultimate and intermediate **parent** undertakings, **subsidiary** undertakings, and **fellow subsidiary** undertakings
- its **associates** and **joint ventures**
- the **investor** or **venturer** in respect of which the reporting entity is an associate or a joint venture
- **directors** of the reporting entity and the directors of its ultimate and intermediate parent undertakings
- **pension funds** for the benefit of employees of the reporting entity or of any entity that is a related party of the reporting entity.

3 The following are presumed to be related parties of the reporting entity unless it can be demonstrated that neither party has influenced the financial and operating policies of the other in such a way as to inhibit the pursuit of separate interests:

- the **key management** of the reporting entity and the key management of its parent undertaking or undertakings
- a **person owning** or able to **exercise control over 20 per cent** or more of the voting rights of the reporting entity, whether directly or through nominees
- each **person acting in concert** in such a way as to be able to exercise control or influence over the reporting entity
- an **entity managing or managed by** the reporting entity under a management contract.

4 Additionally, because of their relationship with certain parties that are, or are presumed to be, related parties of the reporting entity, the following are also presumed to be related parties of the reporting entity:

- **members of the close family** of any individual falling under parties mentioned in **1** to **3** above
- **partnerships**, **companies**, **trusts** or other entities in which any individual or member of the close family in **1** to **3** above has a controlling interest.

DEFINITION

A **related party transaction** is the transfer of assets or liabilities or the performance of services by, to or for a related party irrespective of whether a price is charged.

The definition concludes by stating that this list is not intended to be exhaustive.

A **related party transaction** is the transfer of assets or liabilities or the performance of services by, to or for a related party irrespective of whether a price is charged.

1.2 Transactions between related parties

KEY POINT

Transactions between related parties may not be on arm's length terms, and so **disclosure** is important in order to keep users of financial statements informed.

When transactions take place between related parties, they may not be on arm's length terms. Disclosure of the existence of such transactions, and of the relationships underlying them, gives important information to users of financial statements.

One striking example of the need for disclosure is that related party transactions have been a feature of a number of financial scandals in recent years, many of which have had in common the dominance of the company by a powerful chief executive who was also involved with the related party.

More generally, transactions between related parties – e.g. companies in the same group – are now a common feature of business operations. Disclosure of these transactions, some of which may not have been at arm's length, together with information about the underlying relationship, gives the user of accounts an important indication of their significance to the operating results and financial position of the reporting company. For the same reasons, disclosure is called for where transactions take place with a wide range of other related parties – e.g. directors, associates, pension funds and key management.

1.3 Distortion of financial statements

KEY POINT

A related party relationship can affect the **financial position** and **operating results** of an enterprise.

A related party relationship can affect the financial position and operating results of an enterprise in a number of ways.

- Transactions may be entered into with a related party which **may not have occurred** if the relationship did not exist, e.g. a company may sell a large proportion of its production to its parent company, where it might not have found an alternative customer if the parent company had not purchased the goods.
- Transactions may be entered into with a related party **on terms different** from those with an unrelated party, e.g. the terms under which a subsidiary leases equipment to another subsidiary of a common parent may be imposed by the common parent and might vary significantly from one lease to another because of circumstances entirely unrelated to market prices for similar leases; indeed, the terms may be such that no financial consideration passes between the parties.
- Transactions with third parties **may be affected** by the existence of the relationship, e.g. two enterprises in the same line of business may be controlled by a common party that has the ability to increase the volume of business done by each.

Example

The summary financial statements of Turner Ltd are shown below:

Profit and loss account for the year ended 31 December 20X4

	£000
Turnover	5,400
Cost of sales	(3,490)
Gross profit	1,910
Operating expenses	(1,008)
Retained profit for the year	902

Balance sheet at 31 December 20X4

	£000	£000
Fixed assets		4,212
Current assets		
Stocks	974	
Debtors	940	
Bank	36	
	1,950	
Creditors: Amounts falling due within one year		
Trade creditors	(1,160)	
		790
		5,002
Capital and reserves		5,002

Turner Ltd is a member of a group and during the year it entered into the following transactions with other companies in the group.

- On 1 October 20X4, Turner Ltd purchased materials costing £495,000 from Ravel Ltd and paid for these materials on 31 January 20X5. Turner Ltd had sold all these materials by the year end. If the transaction had been at arm's length, Ravel Ltd would have charged £540,000 for these materials and would have imposed its normal credit collection period of two months from the date of sale.
- On 1 December 20X4, Turner Ltd sold goods to Bell Ltd for £900,000 and received payment immediately. If the transaction had been at arm's length, Turner Ltd would have charged the commercial price of £675,000 and would have allowed three months' credit.

How have these transactions affected the view given by the financial statements of Turner Ltd?

Solution

The profit and loss account and balance sheet can be adjusted in order to reflect the situation had the transactions occurred on normal commercial terms.

Profit and loss account for the year ended 31 December 20X4

	£000
Turnover (5,400 – (900 – 675))	5,175
Cost of sales (3,490 + (540 – 495))	(3,535)
Gross profit	1,640
Operating expenses	(1,008)
Retained profit for the year	632

Balance sheet at 31 December 20X4

	£000	£000
Fixed assets		4,212
Current assets		
Stocks	974	
Debtors (940 + 675)	1,615	
	2,589	
Creditors: Amounts falling due within one year		
Bank overdraft (36 – 900 – 540)	1,404	
Trade creditors (1,160 – 495)	665	
	2,069	
		520
		4,732
Capital and reserves		4,732

The effect is clearest if we calculate key ratios based on the figures before and after the adjustments.

	Original	*Adjusted*
Return on capital employed (ROCE)	18%	13%
Gross profit margin	35%	32%
Current ratio	1.7	1.3
Debtors collection period	64 days	114 days
Creditors payment period	121 days	69 days

Without the favourable trading transactions, Turner Ltd would have had a lower gross profit and significant cash flow problems. This information would be particularly important to anybody attempting to compare Turner Ltd with other companies that might not have been able to take advantage of such relationships.

1.4 CA85 and Stock Exchange requirements concerning related party transactions

The CA85 provisions dealing with related parties are mainly concerned with directors and persons connected to directors (which can include companies).

KEY POINTS

If a company has a 'significant contract' with one of its directors, there is a need for disclosure if the director has a '**material interest**'.

Loans to a director from a company are generally illegal.

A circular to shareholders is required if, for example, there is an acquisition or disposal of assets between the company and a **Class 4 party** (i.e. a director or substantial shareholder).

If a company has a 'significant contract' with one of its directors, there is a need for disclosure if the director has a '**material interest**'. 'Material' is decided by the other directors (or the auditor if they cannot decide).

Loans to a director from a company are illegal except for sums up to £5,000 or if they are funds for business expenditure (there needs to be prior approval by members).

The Stock Exchange has numerous provisions relating to transactions between a company and its directors or substantial shareholders. They are referred to as **Class 4 parties**. Basically, a circular to shareholders is required if, for example, there is an acquisition or disposal of assets between the company and a Class 4 party.

The requirements of the Stock Exchange are extensive and are quite effective in reducing the amount of related party transactions that occur. However, they only apply to listed companies. For the reasons discussed above, the ASB considered that an accounting standard was necessary.

2 FRS 8 *Related party disclosures*

2.1 Possible approaches to related party transactions

There are two ways in which it is possible to deal with transactions between related parties.

- **Adjust** the financial statements to reflect the transaction as if it had occurred with an independent third party and record the transaction at the corresponding arm's length price. However, as a study by the Accountants International Study Group states, 'it often is impossible to establish what would have been the terms of any non-arm's length transaction had it been bargained on an arm's length basis, because no comparable transactions may have taken place and, in any event, the transaction might never have taken place at all if it had been bargained using different values'.
- As a result of the above difficulty, accounting standards internationally have concentrated on the **disclosure** of related party transactions and relationships.

During the development of the standard it was proposed that only **abnormal** transactions should be disclosed. FRS 8 does not draw this distinction since, in its view, when transactions with related parties are material in aggregate, they are of interest whether or not they are made at arm's length. This view coincides with current international treatment.

KEY POINT

FRS 8 *Related party disclosures* requires that financial statements disclose:

- information on related party transactions
- the name of the party controlling the reporting entity.

2.2 Requirements of FRS 8

FRS 8 *Related party disclosures* was issued in October 1995. It requires that financial statements disclose:

- information on related party transactions
- the name of the party controlling the reporting entity and, if different, that of the ultimate controlling party, whether or not any transactions between the reporting entity and those parties have taken place.

2.3 Control and influence

The terms **control** and **influence** are central to the definition of related parties. In establishing whether or not a related party relationship exists, it is often necessary to consider **common control** and **common influence**.

The definition of control is very similar to that found in FRS 2.

DEFINITIONS

Control is the ability to direct the financial and operating policies of an entity with a view to gaining economic benefit from its activities.

Influence is not defined, but is explained in FRS 2 as having a less certain outcome than is the case with control.

Control is the ability to direct the financial and operating policies of an entity with a view to gaining economic benefit from its activities.

Two subsidiaries of the same parent company would obviously be under **common control** and would therefore be related parties. Common control would also exist where both parties are subject to control from boards having a controlling nucleus of directors in common. For example, the directors of A Ltd are X, Y and Z. The directors of B Ltd are W, X and Y. A Ltd and B Ltd are related parties.

Influence is not defined. The explanation to the FRS states that while control brings with it the ability to cause the controlled party to subordinate its separate interests, the exercise of influence has a less certain outcome.

The FRS gives some examples of situations where there may be **common influence** but where a related party relationship does **not** necessarily exist:

- two entities are both associated companies of the same investor
- one party is subject to control and another party is subject to influence from the same source (for example, if A has a subsidiary B and an associate C, that situation in itself would not make B and C related parties)
- two entities have a director in common.

In order for there to be a related party relationship in these and similar situations, one or both parties must have **subordinated their own separate interests** in entering into a transaction.

2.4 Identifying related parties

In order to identify related parties it is necessary to apply the definition in FRS 8. There are many situations in which it is obvious that a related party relationship exists. For example, a subsidiary is clearly a related party of a parent.

In more complicated situations it may be necessary to consider whether the parties are included in the list in parts **2** to **4** of the definition given at the start of this chapter, **and** to consider the basic principle of control and influence. What actually happens within a relationship in practice is often important.

ACTIVITY **1**

X plc is an 80% owned subsidiary of T plc. The directors of X are A, B, C and D. Which of the following are related parties of X plc?

(a) V Ltd, which is not part of the T plc group, but of which A is a director.

(b) Y, who owns 20% of the shares in X plc.

(c) K, the financial controller of X plc (who is not a director).

(d) M, the common law wife of the chairman of B plc, a company in the T plc group.

Feedback to this activity is at the end of the chapter.

2.5 Types of transaction

Transactions between related parties are a normal feature of business. FRS 8 gives some examples:

- purchases or sales of goods (finished or unfinished)
- purchases or sales of property and other assets
- rendering or receiving of services, e.g. accounting, management, engineering or legal services

- agency arrangements
- leasing arrangements, e.g. allowing the use of an asset, whether for a rental or not
- transfer of research and development
- licence agreements
- finance (including loans and equity contributions in cash or in kind)
- guarantees or collaterals
- management contracts.

DEFINITIONS

Transactions are **material** when their disclosure might reasonably be expected to influence decisions made by the users of general purpose financial statements.

***Note*:** Disclosure is required of **all material** related party transactions.

Transactions are **material** when their disclosure might reasonably be expected to influence decisions made by the users of general purpose financial statements.

2.6 Disclosures

KEY POINTS

Where the reporting entity is controlled by another party, there should be **disclosure** of the **related party relationship**.

Where the reporting entity has undertaken transactions with a related party, information about these transactions should also be disclosed.

Disclosure of control

Where the reporting entity is controlled by another party, there should be disclosure of the related party relationship and, if different, that of the ultimate controlling party. If either of these is not known, that fact should be disclosed.

These disclosures must be made whether or not any transactions have taken place between the controlling parties and the reporting entity.

Disclosure of transactions and balances

Financial statements should disclose material transactions undertaken with a related party by the reporting entity. Disclosure should be made irrespective of whether a price is charged. The disclosure should include:

- the names of the transacting related parties
- a description of the relationship between the parties
- a description of the transactions
- the amounts involved
- any other elements of the transactions necessary for an understanding of the financial statements
- the amounts due to or from related parties at the balance sheet date and provisions for doubtful debts due from such parties at that date
- amounts written off in the period in respect of debts due to or from related parties.

Transactions with related parties may be disclosed on an aggregated basis (aggregation of similar transactions by type of related party) unless disclosure of an individual transaction, or connected transactions, is necessary for an understanding of the impact of the transactions on the financial statements of the reporting entity or is required by law.

2.7 Exemptions

KEY POINT

Certain transactions do not have to be disclosed:

- **intra-group** items that have been eliminated on consolidation
- **pension contributions** paid to a pension fund
- **emoluments** in respect of services as an employee of the reporting entity.

Certain transactions do not have to be disclosed as follows:

- in the consolidated financial statements, of intra-group items that have been eliminated on consolidation
- items in the parent's own financial statements, where these are presented with the consolidated financial statements
- items in the financial statements of subsidiaries, provided that at least 90% of their voting rights are controlled within the group and provided that the consolidated financial statements have been published
- **pension contributions** paid to a pension fund
- **emoluments** in respect of services as an employee of the reporting entity.

Note: The existence of the relationship would still have to be disclosed.

Relationships and transactions with the following do not have to be disclosed:

- providers of finance
- utility companies
- government departments and their sponsored bodies
- customers, suppliers, franchisers, distributors and general agents with whom the entity transacts a significant volume of business.

ACTIVITY **2**

Montgomery Ltd has entered into the following transactions during the financial year.

(a) It made sales totalling £500,000 to Cavendish Ltd, a 90% subsidiary.

(b) It sold a property which was included in the accounts at a valuation of £1,000,000 to Mr Carlisle, the brother-in-law of one of the directors, for £750,000.

(c) It paid a salary totalling £55,000 to Mrs Shirley, the personnel manager. Mrs Shirley is married to the managing director of Cavendish Ltd.

(d) It purchased design services worth £500 from Blythe and Co. Blythe and Co is a partnership set up by three design students. One of the partners is the niece of the chairman of Montgomery Ltd.

The directors intend to take advantage of the exemption from preparing consolidated accounts on the grounds that Montgomery Ltd is a small company as defined by the Companies Act 1985.

Which of these transactions would be required to be disclosed in the financial statements of Montgomery Ltd under FRS 8?

Feedback to this activity is at the end of the chapter.

3 SSAP 25 *Segmental reporting*

3.1 Why segmental information is useful

KEY POINT

The purpose of **segmental information** is to provide information about enterprises which carry on several classes of business or operate in several geographical areas.

Many enterprises carry on several classes of business or operate in several geographical areas, with different rates of profitability, different opportunities for growth and different degrees of risk. Consider a company with three business segments that have operating profits and losses as follows:

	£000
Business segment A	1,000
Business segment B	250
Business segment C	(500)
	750

Obviously, information about each of the three segments is much more useful than the total profit figure of £750,000.

The purpose of segmental information is to provide information to assist the readers of financial statements:

- to appreciate more thoroughly the results and financial position of the enterprise by permitting a better understanding of the enterprise's past performance and thus a better assessment of its future prospects
- to be aware of the impact that changes in significant components of a business may have on the business as a whole.

3.2 Determining reportable segments

The directors identify the **reportable segments** having regard to differences in:

- return on capital employed
- risk
- rate of growth
- potential for future development for both classes of business and geographical areas.

All significant segments should be identified as reportable segments.

DEFINITION

A segment is **significant** if:

- third party turnover is 10% or more of the total third party turnover
- its segment result is 10% or more of the combined result of all segments in profit, or in loss
- its net assets are 10% or more of the total net assets.

A segment is **significant** if:

- third party turnover is 10% or more of the total third party turnover; or
- its segment result is 10% or more of the combined result of all segments in profit, or in loss (whichever is greater, i.e. do not net off profits and losses to a net profit figure of say £20,000 and use £2,000 as a significance test when total profits might be £5.02m and losses total £5.00m); or
- its net assets are 10% or more of the total net assets.

The directors should review the definitions annually and redefine them when appropriate.

3.3 Classes of business

DEFINITION

A **class of business** is defined as a distinguishable component of an entity that provides a separate product or service or a separate group of related products or services.

A **class of business** is defined as a distinguishable component of an entity that provides a separate product or service or a separate group of related products or services.

To identify reportable **classes of business**, directors should consider the following factors:

- nature of products or services
- nature of production processes
- markets in which products or services are sold
- the distribution channels for the products (e.g. are the items sold by retail or mail order?)
- the manner in which the entity's activities are organised
- any separate legislative framework relating to part of the business (e.g. a bank or insurance company).

3.4 Geographical segments

DEFINITION

A **geographical segment** is a geographical area comprising an individual country or group of countries in which an entity operates or to which it supplies products or services.

A **geographical segment** is a geographical area comprising an individual country or group of countries in which an entity operates or to which it supplies products or services.

The analysis of **geographical segments** should help the users to assess the extent to which the operations are subject to factors such as:

- expansionist or restrictive economic climates
- stablc or unstablc political rcgimcs
- exchange control regulations
- exchange rate fluctuations.

KEY POINT

If an entity has two or more classes of business or operates in two or more geographical segments, it should make specific disclosures about each class of business or geographical segment.

KEY POINT

The standard distinguishes between **origin** of turnover and **destination** of turnover.

3.5 Standard disclosures

If an entity has two or more classes of business or operates in two or more geographical segments it should:

- define its **classes of business** and **geographical segments** in its financial statements
- for each class of business and geographical segment, disclose:
  - **turnover**, distinguishing turnover derived from external customers and turnover derived from other segments
  - **result** before tax, minority interests and extraordinary items
  - **net assets**.

The standard distinguishes:

- **origin** of turnover – the geographical segment from which products or services are supplied
- **destination** of turnover – the geographical segment to which products or services are supplied.

The geographical segmentation of turnover should be done by origin and also by destination where the latter is materially different.

Results should normally be given before interest, unless the interest income or expense is central to the business, when the result should be given after interest.

The net assets should normally be non-interest bearing unless the results are after interest, in which case the interest-bearing assets and liabilities should be included.

Segmental information should be presented on the basis of the consolidated financial statements.

3.6 Reconciliation

The total of the amounts disclosed by segment should agree with the total in the financial statements. If it does not, the reporting entity should provide a reconciliation between the two figures. Reconciling items should be properly identified and explained.

3.7 Comparatives

Comparatives should be provided. If a change is made to the definitions of the segments or to the accounting policies that are adopted for reporting segmental information, the nature of the change should be disclosed.

3.8 Scope

The standard applies to any entity that:

- is a plc or has a plc subsidiary; or
- is a banking or insurance company; or
- exceeds the criteria multiplied by 10 for defining a medium-sized company.

All other entities are encouraged to apply the provisions of the accounting standard.

If the directors consider that disclosure of any information required by the standard would be seriously prejudicial to the interests of the reporting entity, the information need not be disclosed.

3.9 Proforma

The appendix to SSAP 25 provides an illustrative example for guidance only. Part of this is shown below:

Class of business	*Industry A*		*Industry B*		*Other*		*Group*	
	20X1	*20X0*	*20X1*	*20X0*	*20X1*	*20X0*	*20X1*	*20X0*
	£000	£000	£000	£000	£000	£000	£000	£000
Turnover								
Total sales	33,000	30,000	42,000	38,000	26,000	23,000	101,000	91,000
Inter-segment sales	(4,000)	–	–	–	(12,000)	(14,000)	(16,000)	(14,000)
Sales to third parties	29,000	30,000	42,000	38,000	14,000	9,000	85,000	77,000
Profit before taxation								
Segment profit	3,000	2,500	4,500	4,000	1,800	1,500	9,300	8,000
Common costs							(300)	(300)
Operating profit							9,000	7,700
Net interest							(400)	(500)
							8,600	7,200
Group share of the profits before taxation of associated undertakings	1,000	1,000	1,400	1,200	–	–	2,400	2,200
Group profit before taxation							11,000	9,400
Net assets								
Segment net assets	17,600	15,000	24,000	25,000	19,400	19,000	61,000	59,000
Unallocated assets							3,000	3,000
							64,000	62,000
Group share of net assets of associated undertakings	10,200	8,000	8,800	9,000	–	–	19,000	17,000
Total net assets							83,000	79,000

Common costs refer to costs where allocation between segments could mislead. Likewise, the segmental disclosure of net assets might include unallocated assets.

Geographical segments	*United Kingdom*		*North America*		*Far East*		*Other*		*Group*	
	20X1	*20X0*	*20X1*	*20X0*	*20X1*	*20X0*	*20X1*	*20X0*	*20X1*	*20X0*
	£000	£000	£000	£000	£000	£000	£000	£000	£000	£000
Turnover										
Turnover by destination										
Sales to third parties	34,000	31,000	16,000	14,500	25,000	23,000	10,000	8,500	85,000	77,000
Turnover by origin										
Total sales	38,000	34,000	29,000	27,500	23,000	23,000	12,000	10,500	102,000	95,000
Inter-segment sales	–	–	(8,000)	(9,000)	(9,000)	(9,000)	–	–	(17,000)	(18,000)
Sales to third parties	38,000	34,000	21,000	18,500	14,000	14,000	12,000	10,500	85,000	77,000

ACTIVITY **3**

Medicine plc is a large international company operating in three main business sectors – pharmaceuticals, agricultural chemicals and industrial chemicals. It also operates in three main geographical areas – the UK, Europe and the USA. You are given the following information:

1 The total net assets are £10,529 million. Included in this amount is a net amount of £1,450 million which relates to interest bearing assets and liabilities.

2 Of the remaining net assets, £3,026 million and £4,540 million relate to pharmaceuticals and agricultural chemicals respectively. The geographical analysis of net operating assets is £6,263 million in the UK, £1,609 million in Europe, with the remainder being in the USA.

3 The total turnover, by destination of sales, is £15,001 million. This includes £5,000 million in the UK and £4,590 in Europe.

4 The profit on ordinary activities before taxation is £2,707 million, after £200,000 interest payable.

5 The industrial analysis of profit is £1,495 million in pharmaceuticals, £1,360 million in agricultural chemicals, with the remainder in industrial chemicals.

6 The geographical analysis of profit is £1,150 million in the United Kingdom, £1,301 million in Europe and the remainder in the USA.

7 The industrial analysis of turnover is £6,500 million in pharmaceuticals, £1,700 million in industrial chemicals with the balance being in agricultural chemicals.

Show the disclosure required by SSAP 25 for this information.

Feedback on this activity is at the end of the chapter.

3.10 Problems associated with the provision of segmental information

KEY POINT

One of the **weaknesses of SSAP 25** is that directors are able to circumvent it. They need not disclose any information if they believe that it would be prejudicial to the entity's interests.

One of the weaknesses of SSAP 25 is that directors are able to circumvent it. They need not disclose any information if they believe that it would be prejudicial to the entity's interests. For example, directors may resist disclosing segmental information on the grounds that it will provide information to competitors.

They may also believe that the costs of providing the information outweigh the usefulness to users of the financial statements.

Other criticisms of the standard can be made as follows.

- The class and geographical segment split is decided by the directors. Arguably, this provides too much flexibility. It also means that segmental information is only useful for comparing the performance of the same entity over time, not for comparing the performance of different entities.

  However, it is difficult to envisage the incorporation of hard and fast rules in a standard. Each company is different and judgements have to be made under any system. Also the standard does give guidance regarding what constitutes a significant segment.
- Common costs may be allocated to different segments on whatever basis the directors believe is reasonable. This can lead to arbitrary allocation of these costs.
- The basis of transfer pricing between group companies need not be disclosed. This limits the usefulness of the segmental information provided because profitability of different segments can be manipulated by means of intra-group trading.
- Although SSAP 25 states that net assets to be disclosed are normally non-interest bearing net assets, it does not define them. Because the standard does not explicitly

state that the figure to be disclosed should be based on the year-end position, it is possible to disclose net assets based on the average position during the year.

- There is no guidance on how to treat exceptional items. As these are part of results before tax, they should in theory be allocated between segments. However, some entities analyse their segmental results before exceptional items.
- SSAP 25 does not address the effect of changes within a group on the segmental results. However, FRS 3 requires that 'where an acquisition, sale or termination has a material impact on a major business segment this should be disclosed and explained'.

3.11 Interpreting segmental information

KEY POINT

It is possible to compute **return on capital employed** (ROCE), **profit margin** and **asset turnover** for each segment, based on the segmental information disclosed.

It is possible to compute return on capital employed (ROCE), profit margin and asset turnover for each segment, based on the segmental information disclosed. This provides information on the profitability, efficiency and overall performance of each segment.

However, it may be difficult to compute valid ratios for each segment under SSAP 25 as:

- common costs may or may not be included in the segment result (this is a decision of the directors)
- net assets may have an element of commonality across segments
- segment results may be distorted by transfer pricing policies.

Conclusion

FRS 8 requires the disclosure of related party relationships where the reporting entity is controlled by another party. Material transactions with a related party must also be disclosed.

SSAP 25 requires large companies to prepare and present segmental information in addition to that required by CA85. Turnover, results and net assets must be analysed by class of business and geographically. Again, the objective is to provide additional information to users of the financial statements.

SELF-TEST QUESTIONS

1. What is a related party transaction? (1.1)
2. How can related party transactions affect the view given by the financial statements? (1.3)
3. In general, what information about related parties must be disclosed in the financial statements? (2.2)
4. When two parties are under common influence, what must have happened for a related party relationship to exist? (2.3)
5. When is a related party transaction material? (2.5)
6. When is a segment significant? (3.2)
7. Define a class of business. (3.3)
8. Under SSAP 25, what information must be disclosed where an entity has two or more classes of business? (3.5)
9. To which types of entity does SSAP 25 apply? (3.8)
10. What are the main weaknesses of SSAP 25? (3.10)

EXAM-TYPE QUESTIONS

Question 1: Ace plc

FRS 8 *Related party disclosures* was issued in October 1995. Prior to its existence, there were specific requirements for related party disclosures contained in the 1985 Companies Act and the Listing Rules of the London Stock Exchange.

On 1 April 20X7, Ace plc owned 75% of the equity share capital of Deuce Ltd and 80% of the equity share capital of Trey Ltd. On 1 April 20X8, Ace plc purchased the remaining 25% of the equity shares of Deuce Ltd. In the two years ended 31 March 20X9, the following transactions occurred between the three companies:

1 On 30 June 20X7 Ace plc manufactured a machine for use by Deuce Ltd. The cost of manufacture was £20,000. The machine was delivered to Deuce Ltd for an invoiced price of £25,000. Deuce Ltd paid the invoice on 31 August 20X7. Deuce Ltd depreciated the machine over its anticipated useful economic life of five years, charging a full year's depreciation in the year of purchase.

2 On 30 September 20X8, Deuce Ltd sold some goods to Trey Ltd at an invoiced price of £15,000. Trey Ltd paid the invoice on 30 November 20X8. The goods had cost Deuce Ltd £12,000 to manufacture. By 31 March 20X9, Trey Ltd had sold all the goods outside the group.

3 For each of the two years ended 31 March 20X9, Ace plc provided management services to Deuce Ltd and Trey Ltd. Ace plc did not charge for these services in the year ended 31 March 20X8 but in the year ended 31 March 20X9 decided to impose a charge of £10,000 per annum to each company. The amounts of £10,000 are due to be paid by each company on 31 May 20X9.

Required:

(a) Explain why related party disclosures are needed and why FRS 8 was considered necessary, given the existing requirements of the 1985 Companies Act and the Listing Rules of the London Stock Exchange. **(6 marks)**

(b) Summarise the related party disclosures which will be required in respect of transactions 1 to 3 above for BOTH of the years ended 31 March 20X8 and 31 March 20X9 in the financial statements of Ace plc, Deuce Ltd and Trey Ltd.

(14 marks)

You may assume that Ace plc presents consolidated financial statements for BOTH of the years dealt with in the question. **(Total: 20 marks)**

Question 2: Innovations plc

Innovations plc is preparing a segmental report to include with its financial accounts prepared for the year ended 30 June 20X9.

The relevant information given below is based on the consolidated figures of Innovations plc and its subsidiaries. Associate company information is not shown.

	20X9	*20X8*
	£000	£000
Sales to customers outside the group by the Fruit Growing division	12,150	13,500
Sales to customers outside the group by the UK companies	27,000	24,300
Sales not derived from Fruit Growing, Canning or Bureau activities	2,700	1,350
Sales made to customers outside the group by the Canning Division	17,550	13,095
Assets used by the US companies	32,400	24,300

Assets not able to be allocated to Fruit Growing, Canning or Bureau activities	13,500	11,003
Assets used by Fruit Growing Division	33,750	32,400
Sales by the Canning Division to other group members	2,970	3,105
Assets used by the Bureau Service	18,765	17,563
Assets used by the UK Companies	43,200	40,500
Sales by the Fruit Growing Division to other group members	1,485	1,688
Sales not allocated to the UK, US or other areas	2,700	1,350
Sales made by group to other areas of the world	1,350	1,215
Expenses not allocated to UK, US or other areas	4,590	3,834
Sales to customers outside the group by US Companies	6,750	5,130
Expenses not allocated to Fruit Growing, Canning or Bureau Service	5,130	4,104
Sales by US Companies to group members	2,160	1,215
Sales to customers outside the group for Bureau Service	5,400	4,050
Sales made by UK companies to other group members	2,700	1,890
Assets used by Canning Division	40,500	33,750
Assets used by Group in other areas	18,360	19,683
Assets not allocated to UK, US or other areas	12,555	10,233
Segmental net operating profit by industry		
Fruit Growing	2,565	3,375
Canning	4,725	3,600
Bureau	412	540
Consolidated segmental net operating profit	7,695	6,750
Segmental net operating profit by geographical area		
UK	5,130	4,590
US	2,430	1,890
Other areas	270	405
Consolidated segmental net operating profit by geographical area	7,150	6,480

Required:

(a) State briefly:

(i) the case for segmental reporting

(ii) the case against segmental reporting. **(4 marks)**

(b) Draft an industry and geographical segmental report for inclusion in the annual report to give the maximum information to the shareholders.

(16 marks)

(Total: 20 marks)

For the answers to these questions, see the 'Answers' section at the end of the book.

FEEDBACK TO ACTIVITY **1**

(a) V Ltd and X plc are subject to common influence from A, but V Ltd is not a related party unless one or both companies have subordinated their own separate interests in entering into a transaction. (This assumes that A is the only director to serve on both boards; if there were a common nucleus of directors, a related party relationship would almost certainly exist.)

(b) Y is almost certainly not a related party. According to the definition Y is presumed to be a related party, but the existence of a parent company means that Y is unlikely to be able to exert influence over X plc in practice.

(c) K may be a related party, despite the fact that he or she is not a director. A financial controller would probably come within the definition of key management (i.e. 'those persons in senior positions having authority or responsibility for directing or controlling the major activities and resources of the reporting entity'). The issue would be decided by the extent to which K is able to control or influence the policies of the company in practice.

(d) M may be a related party. B plc and X plc are under common control and M falls within the definition of close family of a related party of B plc. (Close family means 'those family members, or members of the same household, who may be expected to influence, or be influenced by, that person in their dealings with the reporting entity.') M is not a related party if it can be demonstrated that she has not influenced the policies of X plc in such a way as to inhibit the pursuit of separate interests.

FEEDBACK TO ACTIVITY **2**

(a) Sales to the subsidiary must be disclosed. Although this is an intra-group transaction and would normally be exempt from disclosure, Montgomery Ltd does not prepare consolidated accounts and therefore cannot take advantage of the exemption.

(b) The sale of the property is clearly a related party transaction and must be disclosed. Mr Carlisle falls within the definition of 'close family' of a director.

(c) Mrs Shirley's salary need not be disclosed. Although Mrs Shirley may be a related party, the payment of emoluments is specifically exempt from disclosure.

(d) Blythe and Co probably falls within the definition of a related party as this includes partnerships and other entities in which any member of the 'close family' of a related party has a controlling interest. It could be argued that the purchase need not be disclosed on the grounds that the sum of £500 is unlikely to be material in the context of the financial statements of Montgomery Ltd. However, FRS 8 states that in some situations the materiality of a transaction should be considered, not only in relation to the reporting entity, but of the other party to the transaction. As £500 is almost certainly material to Blythe and Co, the spirit of FRS 8 suggests that this transaction should be disclosed.

FEEDBACK TO ACTIVITY 3

Classes of business	*Net assets*	*Turnover*	*Profit*
	£m	£m	£m
Pharmaceuticals	3,026	6,500	1,495
Agricultural chemicals	4,540	6,801	1,360
Industrial chemicals	1,513	1,700	52
Net operating assets	9,079		
Net non-operating assets	1,450		
	10,529	15,001	
Operating profit			2,907
Net interest payable			(200)
Profit on ordinary activities before taxation			2,707

Geographical areas	*Net operating assets*	*Turnover*	*Profit*
	£m	£m	£m
United Kingdom	6,263	5,000	1,150
Europe	1,609	4,590	1,301
USA	1,207	5,411	456
	9,079	15,001	2,907

Chapter 15
SHARE CAPITAL AND RESERVES

CHAPTER CONTENTS

1 FRS 25: *Financial Instruments: Disclosure and Presentation*
2 FRS 26: *Financial Instruments: measurement*
3 The issue and reorganisation of capital
4 Recording the transactions involving the redemption/ purchase of shares
5 The rules relating to the distribution of profits

This chapter brings together a number of topics connected with a limited company's share capital and reserves.

Capital instruments are issued to raise finance. They may be in the form of shares or loan stock or have characteristics of both. They have become increasingly important in recent years as companies devise increasingly sophisticated ways of financing their activities. We start this chapter with consideration of two of the latest Financial Reporting Standards, FRS 25 and FRS 26 which deal with the disclosure, presentation and measurement of financial instruments. The requirement of these FRSs, particularly FRS 26 may seem complex, but the areas that are relevant to the Paper 2.5 syllabus are fairly limited so concentrate on these.

Next, we look at changes in a company's capital structure, both in terms of the legal requirements and the accounting entries. In most cases, dealing with the purchase and redemption of a company's own shares is a matter of applying the rules in the Companies Act and learning the double entry bookkeeping involved.

Lastly, the chapter deals with calculating a limited company's distributable profit, which is not necessarily the same as its accumulated reserves. Again, the Companies Act contains detailed rules which must be understood and applied.

Objectives

By the time you have finished this chapter you should be able to:

- explain the need for an accounting standard on capital instruments
- apply the requirements of FRS 25 and FRS 26
- explain and apply the general requirements to purchase or redeem shares (including redemption out of capital)
- discuss the advantages of companies being able to redeem shares
- define and discuss the Companies Act's rules relating to profits available for distribution
- calculate the profits available for distribution of public and private companies.

1 FRS 25: *Financial Instruments: Disclosure and Presentation*

1.1 Introduction

In recent years there has been a huge growth worldwide in the variety and complexity of financial instruments in international financial markets. In 1993 FRS 4: *Capital Instruments* was issued in order to deal with the presentation, disclosure and measurement of financial instruments. However in line with the UK move to align domestic accounting standards with International Accounting Standards in December 2004 the ASB issued FRS 25: *Financial Instruments: Disclosure and Presentation* and FRS 26: *Financial Instruments: Measurement,* (IASs 32 and 39 respectively) which have superseded FRS 4.

KEY POINT

FRS 25 deals with the relatively simple matters of disclosure and presentation.

FRS 25 is the first part of the ASB's project to regulate financial instruments. It deals with the relatively simple matters of disclosure and presentation. Excluded from its scope are:

- interests in subsidiaries, associates or joint ventures
- employers' rights and obligations under employee benefit plans
- contracts for contingent consideration in a business combination
- obligations under insurance contracts
- share based payments.

The more complicated topic of the recognition and measurement of financial instruments in the balance sheet and income statement is dealt with in FRS 26.

1.2 Definitions

DEFINITIONS

A **financial instrument** is any contract that gives rise to both a financial asset of one entity and a financial liability or equity instrument of another entity

- A **financial instrument** is any contract that gives rise to a financial asset of one entity and a financial liability or equity instrument of another entity.
- A **financial asset** is any asset that is:
  - cash
  - a contractual right to receive cash or another financial asset from another entity
  - a contractual right to exchange financial instruments with another entity under conditions that are potentially favourable;
  - a contract that will or may be settled in the entity's own equity instrument
  - an equity instrument of another entity.
- A **financial liability** is any liability that is a contractual obligation:
  - to deliver cash or another financial asset to another entity; or
  - to exchange financial instruments with another entity under conditions that are potentially unfavourable
  - that will or may be settled in the entity's own equity instruments.
- An **equity instrument** is any contract that evidences a residual interest in the assets of an entity after deducting all of its liabilities.
- **Fair value** is the amount for which an asset could be exchanged, or a liability settled, between knowledgeable, willing parties in an arm's length transaction.

DEFINITIONS

An **equity instrument** is any contract that evidences a residual interest in the assets of an entity after deducting all of its liabilities.

1.3 Liabilities and equity

KEY POINT

The **substance** of a financial instrument may differ from its **legal form**.

The substance of a financial instrument may differ from its legal form. Some financial instruments take the legal form of equity but are liabilities in substance. Others may combine features associated with equity and features associated with liabilities.

FRS 25 requires the classification of a financial instrument, or its component parts, as a liability or as equity according to the substance of the contractual arrangement.

KEY POINT

When a financial instrument gives rise to a **contractual obligation** on the part of the issuer to deliver cash or another financial asset, it is a **financial liability**.

When no such contractual obligation exists, it is an **equity instrument**.

The critical feature in differentiating a **financial liability** from an equity instrument is the existence of a **contractual obligation** on one party to the financial instrument (the issuer) either to deliver cash or another financial asset to the other party (the holder) or to exchange another financial instrument with the holder under conditions that are potentially unfavourable to the issuer. When such a contractual obligation exists, that instrument meets the definition of a financial liability regardless of the manner in which the contractual obligation will be settled. A restriction on the ability of the issuer to satisfy an obligation, such as lack of access to foreign currency or the need to obtain approval for payment from a regulatory authority, does not negate the issuer's obligation or the holder's right under the instrument.

When a financial instrument does not give rise to a contractual obligation on the part of the issuer to deliver cash or another financial asset or to exchange another financial instrument under conditions that are potentially unfavourable, it is an **equity instrument**. Although the holder of an equity instrument may be entitled to receive a pro-rata share of any dividends or other distributions out of equity, the issuer does not have a contractual obligation to make such distributions.

1.4 Redeemable preference shares

When a preference share provides for mandatory redemption by the issuer for a fixed or determinable amount at a fixed or determinable future date, or gives the holder the right to require the issuer to redeem the share at or after a particular date for a fixed or determinable amount, the instrument meets the definition of a financial liability and is classified as such.

1.5 Classification of compound instruments by the issuer

KEY POINT

A **compound instrument** is one which has both a liability and an equity component, e.g. a convertible bond.

A **compound instrument** is one which has both a liability and an equity component. For example, the value of a convertible bond consists of a liability component – the bond – and an equity component – the value of the right to convert in due course to equity.

The economic effect of issuing convertible bonds is substantially the same as the simultaneous issue of a debt instrument with an early settlement provision and warrants to purchase shares.

All such compound instruments must be shown in the balance sheet with the liability and equity elements **separated**.

Example

An enterprise issues 20,000 convertible bonds at the start of Year 1. The bonds have a three-year term, and are issued at par with a face value of £100 per bond, giving total proceeds of £2,000,000. Interest is payable annually in arrears at a nominal annual interest rate of 6%. Each bond is convertible at any time up to maturity into 25 ordinary shares.

When the bonds are issued, the prevailing market interest rate for similar debt without conversion options is 9%.

Residual valuation of equity component

Under this approach, the liability component is valued first, and the difference between the proceeds of the bond issue and the fair value of the liability is assigned to the equity component. The present value of the liability component is calculated using a discount rate of 9%, the market interest rate for similar bonds having no conversion rights, as shown:

	£		
Present value of the principal £2,000,000 payable at the end of three years	1,544,000		
Present value of the interest £120,000 payable annually in arrears for three years	303,720		
Total liability component	1,847,720		
Equity component (balancing figure)	152,280		
Proceeds of the bond issue	£2,000,000		
Discounting factors at 9%:		1 year	0.917
		2 years	0.842
		3 years	0.772

Balance sheet (extracts):

	£
Capital and reserves:	
Equity: conversion rights	152,280
Non-current liabilities:	
Long-term borrowings: convertible bonds	1,847,720

1.6 Interest, dividends, losses and gains

KEY POINT

The accounting treatment of interest, dividends, losses and gains relating to a financial instrument follows the accounting treatment of the instrument itself.

The accounting treatment of interest, dividends, losses and gains relating to a financial instrument follows the accounting treatment of the instrument itself. In other words, interest, dividends, losses and gains attributable to a financial instrument or part of a financial instrument classified as a financial liability must be reported in the profit and loss account as expense or income, while distributions to holders of a financial instrument classified as equity must be debited direct to equity.

Therefore if a redeemable preference share is classified as a liability in the balance sheet then the dividend is treated just as interest on other liabilities would be and is an expense in the profit and loss account.

1.7 Offsetting of a financial asset and a financial liability

KEY POINT

In common with all FRS rules on offsetting, a financial asset and a financial liability may only be **offset** in very limited circumstances.

In common with all ASB rules on offsetting, a financial asset and a financial liability may only be offset in very limited circumstances. The net amount may only be reported when the enterprise:

- has a legally enforceable right to set off the amounts; and
- intends either to settle on a net basis or to realise the asset and settle the liability simultaneously.

1.8 Disclosure

The purpose of the disclosures required by FRS 25 is to provide information that will enhance understanding of the significance of on-balance-sheet and off-balance-sheet financial instruments to an entity's financial position, performance and cash flows and assist in assessing the amounts, timing and certainty of future cash flows associated with those instruments.

KEY POINT

FRS 25 encourages enterprises to provide a discussion of the extent to which financial instruments are used, the associated risks and the business purposes served.

In addition to providing specific information about particular financial instrument balances and transactions, enterprises are encouraged to provide a discussion of the extent to which financial instruments are used, the associated risks and the business purposes served. A discussion of management's policies for controlling the risks associated with financial instruments, including policies on matters such as hedging of risk exposures, avoidance of undue concentrations of risk and requirements for collateral to mitigate credit risks, provides a valuable additional perspective that is independent of the specific instruments outstanding at a particular time. Some enterprises provide such information in a commentary that accompanies their financial statements rather than as part of the financial statements.

2 FRS 26: *Financial Instruments: Measurement*

2.1 Introduction

FRS 26 *Financial Instruments: measurement* was issued by the ASB in December 2004 and is implements the measurement and hedge accounting requirements of IAS 39. However FRS 26 does not include the de-recognition provisions of IAS 39 and the ASB will be bringing forward proposals to deal with these provisions.

2.2 Initial recognition

KEY POINT

An entity should recognise a financial asset or a financial liability on its balance sheet only when it becomes a party to the contractual provisions of the instrument.

An entity should recognise a financial asset or a financial liability on its balance sheet when, and only when, it becomes a party to the contractual provisions of the instrument.

As examples of this principle:

- an unconditional receivable should be recognised as an asset when the enterprise becomes a party to the contract so that it has a legal right to receive cash
- a forward contract is recognised as an asset or liability on the commitment date, rather than waiting until the closing date when the exchange actually takes place.

2.3 Measurement

FRS 26 requires that:

- all derivatives and all financial assets and financial liabilities that are held for trading are measured at fair value with changes in those fair values recognised immediately in the profit and loss account
- all loans and receivables held as assets and all financial assets that are being held to maturity by the reporting entity are to be measured at cost-based amounts
- all other financial assets ('available-for-sale financial assets') to be measured at fair value with profits and losses measured immediately in the statement of total recognised gains and losses
- all other financial liabilities to be measured at cost-based amounts.

There are two exceptions to this:

- the entity can choose to measure at fair value any financial asset or financial liability that would otherwise be measured at a cost-based amount, as long as this choice is made on initial recognition. If this fair value option is chosen all changes in fair value should be recognised immediately in the profit and loss account;
- the requirements may be modified by the use of hedge accounting techniques.

2.4 Measurement of financial liabilities

The requirements of FRS 26 are largely beyond the scope of the Paper 2.5 syllabus but you may be required to value debt issues. After initial recognition an enterprise should measure all financial liabilities, other than liabilities held for trading and derivatives that are liabilities, at amortised cost using the effective interest rate method.

Example

The effective interest rate method calculates annual amortisation using the effective interest rate (i.e. the internal rate of return) of a financial asset or financial liability. It is similar to the actuarial method used in lease accounting to value finance leases. Consider the example below.

Debt is issued for £1,000. The debt is redeemable at £1,250. The term of the debt is five years and interest is paid at 5.9% p.a.

The debt would initially be recognised at £1,000. The total finance cost of the debt is the difference between the payments required by the debt which total £1,545 ((5 × £59) + £1,250) and the proceeds of £1,000, that is £545. The effective rate of interest on the debt can be calculated to be 10% p.a.

The movements on the carrying amount of the debt over its term would be as follows:

Year	*Balance at beginning of year*	*Finance cost for year (10%)*	*Cost paid during year*	*Balance paid end of year*
1	1,000	100	(59)	1,041
2	1,041	104	(59)	1,086
3	1,086	109	(59)	1,136
4	1,136	113	(59)	1,190
5	1,190	119	(1,250 + 59)	-
		545		

The amounts carried forward at each year end represent the amortised cost valuation to be shown in the balance sheet.

The carrying amount of the debt (amortised cost) is the net proceeds, plus finance charges recognised in the accounts, less payments made.

Tutorial note: In the exam, the question will either tell you the effective annual rate of interest (10% in the example above) or you will be allowed to apportion the total finance costs on a straight line basis (£545 ÷ 5 = £109 p.a. in the example above).

2.5 Gains and losses on remeasurement to fair value

A gain or loss on a financial asset or financial liability classified as 'at fair value through profit or loss' must be recognised in profit or loss.

For other items:

- dividends receivable from an available-for-sale equity instrument are recognised in profit or loss
- interest charged or credited using the effective interest rate method is a finance cost recognised in the profit and loss account

ACTIVITY **1**

An enterprise issues 2,000 convertible bonds at the start of Year 1. The bonds have a three-year term, and are issued at par with a face value of £1,000 per bond, giving total proceeds of £2,000,000. Interest is payable annually in arrears at a nominal annual interest rate of 6%. Each bond is convertible at any time up to maturity into 250 ordinary shares.

When the bonds are issued, the prevailing market interest rate for similar debt without conversion options is 9%.

Immediately after the bonds were issued, they were recognised in the balance sheet (in accordance with FRS 25) at the following amounts:

	$
Equity component	152,280
Liability component	1,847,720

How will the bonds be recognised in the financial statements at the end of Year 1?

Feedback to this activity is at the end of the chapter.

3 The issue and reorganisation of capital

3.1 Introduction

KEY POINT

To account properly for changes in a company's capital, the **commercial need** for the change and the relevant **company law** must be understood.

In order to account properly for changes in the capital of a company or for the reorganisation of the existing capital, two areas need to be understood:

- the relevant areas of **company law**
- the **commercial considerations** which have brought about the need for change.

If this background is known, then the debits and credits are understandable. Do not learn the provisions at this stage, but refer back to this section when studying the examples in the next section.

3.2 Company law – capital changes

KEY POINT

Categories of company capital include: **authorised share capital**, **issued share capital** and **called up share capital**.

Authorised, issued and called up capital

The distinction between these terms is as follows:

- **Authorised share capital** is the amount of share capital which a company is authorised to issue, e.g. £100 divided into 100 shares of £1 each.
- **Issued share capital** is the nominal amount of the share capital actually issued at any time, e.g. £100 authorised capital of which 50 £1 shares have been issued.
- **Called up share capital** is the aggregate amount of the calls made on its shares (whether or not those calls have been paid), together with any share capital paid up without being called and any share capital to be paid on a specified future date under the terms of allotment.

The original authorised capital of a company is stated in its **memorandum and articles of association**. Subsequently, the company may wish to increase or to reduce its authorised and/or issued capital.

KEY POINT

A company may increase its issued and authorised share capital and reduce its unissued shares. Issued share capital may be reduced by issuing **redeemable shares**, **purchasing own shares**, or through a **capital reduction scheme**.

Increase of capital

This expression covers two situations:

- Increase of the **issued share capital** up to the authorised amount. In the illustration above, the issued share capital could be increased by allotting and issuing the available 50 unissued £1 shares. This is a simple operation which the company itself effects by the appropriate procedure.
- Increase of the **authorised share capital**, which may be accompanied by an increase in the issued share capital. A company may increase its authorised share capital if so authorised by its articles.

The expression 'increase of share capital' usually denotes an increase of authorised share capital.

Reduction of capital

The company may cancel unissued shares in the same way (see above) as it can increase its unissued shares. But if it wishes to reduce its *issued* share capital, there are various means available:

- **capital reduction scheme**: S135 CA85
- power of a company to issue **redeemable shares**: Ss159 and 160 CA85
- purchase by a company of its **own shares**: S162 CA85
- **redemption** or **purchase** out of capital: S171 CA85.

Capital reduction schemes are not examinable at this level. The statutory provisions for the other three means of reducing capital are covered below.

3.3 How shares may be redeemed

KEY POINT

Where shares are redeemed wholly or partly out of profits available for appropriation, an amount equal to the excess of the nominal value of the shares redeemed over the proceeds of any fresh issue of shares must be transferred to a **capital redemption reserve**.

The restrictions on the issue and redemption of **redeemable shares** (of any type) are:

- the issue of redeemable shares must be authorised by the company's articles
- redeemable shares can only be issued when there are other issued shares which are not redeemable
- shares cannot be redeemed unless they are fully paid, and redemption may be made only out of profits otherwise available
- these available profits are the accumulated appropriated profits; however, redemption may also be paid for from the proceeds of a fresh issue of shares made for the purposes of the redemption, or a combination of both methods.

Where shares are redeemed wholly or partly out of profits available for appropriation, an amount equal to the excess of the nominal value of the shares redeemed over the proceeds of any fresh issue of shares must be transferred to a **capital redemption reserve**. This reserve may only be used subsequently to make a bonus issue of shares.

The capital redemption reserve does not have to replace any premium payable on redemption. Except as detailed below, any premium on redemption must be provided out of distributable profits.

KEY POINT

Where the shares to be redeemed were issued at a premium and a fresh issue of shares is made for the purposes of the redemption, any premium payable on redemption may be charged against the **share premium account**.

Where the shares to be redeemed were issued at a premium and a fresh issue of shares is made for the purposes of the redemption, any premium payable on redemption may be charged against the **share premium account**. The premium so charged cannot exceed the lower of:

- the premium received on the issue of the shares now being redeemed
- the current balance of the share premium account, including any premium on the new share issue
- the proceeds of the fresh issue.

The premium on any redeemable preference shares issued before S160 CA85 came into effect may be charged against the share premium account up to the balance on that account.

3.4 The power of companies to purchase their own shares

Any limited company may, if authorised to do so by its articles, purchase its own shares (including redeemable shares), subject to the same conditions as apply to the redemption of redeemable shares, except that the terms and manner of purchase need not be determined by the articles.

The procedure prescribed for the purchase of shares varies according to whether or not the purchase takes place through a recognised Stock Exchange.

An off-market purchase

An **off-market purchase** must be in pursuance of an interim contract of purchase, approved in advance by a **special resolution** of the company. The contract, or a memorandum thereof, must have been available for inspection by members for 15 days before the meeting and at the meeting at which it is approved.

KEY POINT

An **off-market purchase** of a company's own shares must be in pursuance of an interim contract of purchase approved in advance by a **special resolution** of the company.

A **market purchase** cannot be made unless the purchase has been authorised by an **ordinary resolution**.

Market purchase

A company cannot make a **market purchase** of its shares on a recognised Stock Exchange unless the purchase has been authorised by an **ordinary resolution** of the company. Such resolutions must specify the maximum number of shares that may be purchased, the maximum and minimum prices to be paid and the date the authority expires.

For both types of purchase there are detailed requirements for notice to the registrar and disclosure in the directors' report.

The main advantage to a company of being able to purchase its shares and then cancel them is that it provides a means of using surplus capital and enabling the remaining shareholders to acquire a larger percentage interest in the company. This could be particularly useful to private companies with a small number of shareholders where one of them dies, retires or leaves the service of the company. The other shareholders may be unable or unwilling to purchase his shares themselves, but can arrange for the company to do so.

3.5 Redemption or purchase out of capital

In addition to the above choices, a private company may, if authorised by its articles, **redeem** or **purchase its shares out of capital**. However, this is only to the extent that the purchase or redemption price exceeds available distributable profits and the proceeds of a new share issue.

DEFINITION

Permissible capital payment (PCP): the amount by which the purchase or redemption cost exceeds the amount of distributable profits plus the proceeds of any new share issue.

The Act refers to the **permissible capital payment** (**PCP**). This is the amount by which the purchase or redemption cost exceeds the amount of distributable profits plus the proceeds of any new share issue.

KEY POINT

If the total of the **PCP** plus proceeds of a **new share issue** is **less** than the nominal value of the shares redeemed, the difference is transferred to **capital redemption reserve**; if it is **more** than the nominal value of the shares redeemed, the excess may be used to reduce the:

- **capital redemption reserve**
- **share premium account**
- **fully paid share capital**
- **revaluation reserve.**

The difference between the PCP and the nominal value of the shares redeemed is dealt with as follows.

- If the total of PCP plus proceeds of a new share issue is less than the nominal value of the shares redeemed, the difference is transferred to **capital redemption reserve**.
- If the total of PCP plus proceeds of a new share issue is more than the nominal value of the shares redeemed, the excess may be used to reduce any of the following:
  - **capital redemption reserve**
  - **share premium account**
  - **fully paid share capital**
  - **revaluation reserve**.

There are, in addition, safeguards both for members and for creditors.

- The purchase or redemption must be authorised by special resolution (with voting restrictions on intending vendors).
- Directors must make a statutory declaration specifying the amount of the payments and stating that, in their opinion, the company could pay all existing debts, after the capital payment, and will be able to pay its debts throughout the ensuing year.
- The directors' declaration must be supported by the auditor stating that he has enquired into the company's affairs and considers that the amount specified in the declaration conforms to the requirements and that the opinion expressed by the directors is not unreasonable.

3.6 Recent changes to the law

The traditional position as set out in the CA85 is that shares acquired on a purchase of own shares must be cancelled. This rule was relaxed by the Companies (Acquisition of Own Shares) (Treasury Shares) Regulations 2003 which permit a listed company to purchase up to 10% of their own shares and then hold them in treasury (i.e. hold them as an investment, when they are then known as treasury shares). Treasury shares can subsequently be resold for cash, cancelled or transferred to an employee's share scheme.

Detailed requirements of the Regulations

- The shares held in treasury must be listed in the UK, traded on the Alternative Investment Market, or listed or traded on equivalent European markets.
- The aggregate nominal value of treasury shares at any one time must not exceed 10% of the nominal value of the company's issued share capital.
- The rights attending to treasury shares (e.g. voting rights and the rights to receive dividends) are generally suspended, though the right to participate in a bonus issue is preserved.
- Shares which are to be held in treasury must be purchased by a company out of distributable profits, not from the proceeds of a new issue of shares.
- Where the proceeds of sale of treasury shares are less than or equal to the price paid for them by the company, the proceeds are treated as realised profit. Where the proceeds of sale exceed the purchase price, the amount equalling the purchase price is treated as realised profit and the excess is credited to the share premium account.

3.7 Reorganisation of capital structure – commercial considerations

KEY POINT

Without altering their total capital requirements, companies can **restructure** to improve the mix of **capital types** and the timing of **funds availability**.

Companies undertake restructuring to improve the mix of different types of capital and the timing of availability of funds.

This can be done without altering the total capital requirement. The specific objects of reorganisation may be one or more of the following:

- to reduce the net of tax cost of borrowing
- to repay borrowing sooner or later
- to improve security of finance
- to make investing in the company more attractive
- to improve the image of the company to third parties
- to tidy up the balance sheet.

3.8 The advantages of redeemable shares

KEY POINT

Companies may issue **redeemable shares** to increase their attractiveness to **investors** or to facilitate **employee share schemes**. Redemption or purchase of own shares can be used to return a company to **private ownership** or to return surplus cash to shareholders.

There are many reasons why companies may wish to issue and redeem redeemable shares, or to purchase their own shares, as follows:

- Reduction in share capital increases earnings per share and return on capital employed. This makes the company more attractive to potential **lenders** and **investors**.
- Shares may be redeemed in order to buy out dissident shareholders.
- Redeemable shares may be attractive to potential private company shareholders as they provide an opportunity to **invest** in a company without being committed to that investment in the long term. (There is normally a very limited market for private company shares.)
- It enables companies to reduce total dividend payments while maintaining or increasing the level of dividend to individual shareholders. This means that more earnings are available for capital investment which leads to **growth**.

- Many companies now operate **employee share schemes**. Redeemable shares may be bought back when employees leave the company.
- Shares may be redeemed at a discount where the market price is low.
- Redemption or purchase of own shares may be used to take the company out of the public market and back into **private ownership**.
- Redemption or purchase of own shares provides an efficient means of returning surplus cash to the shareholders.

4 Recording the transactions involving the redemption/purchase of shares

4.1 Approach

The previous section has summarised the legal provisions for reorganising capital, and outlined the commercial rationale. Examples of the accounting implications are shown in this section.

KEY POINT

If shares are redeemed out of **profits**, account for the cash **inflow** from any issue of shares made to **finance the redemption first**. Account for the cash **outflow** through a **redemption account**. Calculate the required transfer to the **capital redemption reserve.**

The legal provisions in this area are complex but the accounting entries are more straightforward, providing the redemption/purchase is tackled in a logical way. In summary the steps are as follows:

1. If a private limited company, decide whether the redemption is out of **profits** or **capital**.
2. If out of **profits**, account for the cash **inflow** from any issue of shares made to **finance the redemption first**. This is necessary as the balance on share premium account needs to be established before the redemption takes place.
3. Account for the cash **outflow** for the redemption and the transfer of the nominal value of the shares redeemed through a **redemption account**.
4. Decide whether any of the balance in the redemption account (the balance will represent the premium on redemption) can be charged against **share premium**.
5. Calculate the required transfer to the **capital redemption reserve**.

Example

The summarised balance sheet of C plc is as follows:

	£
Net assets	100,000
Ordinary shares of £1	20,000
Share premium	10,000
Revaluation reserve	15,000
Profit and loss account	55,000
	100,000

C plc purchases 5,000 of its shares on the stock market for £30,000 as it does not have suitable opportunities for investment of surplus funds and it regards its share price as being relatively low at the present time.

The shares were originally issued at a premium of 50p per share and are cancelled after the purchase.

Solution

Steps 1 and 2 are not applicable (the company is a plc and there is no fresh issue).

	£
Redemption price	30,000
NV of shares redeemed	5,000
Premium on redemption	25,000

As no fresh issue, premium of £25,000 must go to profit and loss account.

Transfer to capital redemption reserve

	£
NV of shares redeemed	5,000
Less: Proceeds of fresh issue of shares	Nil
	5,000

Working

Profit and loss account

	£
Original balance	55,000
Less: Premium on redemption	(25,000)
To capital redemption reserve	(5,000)
	25,000

Tutorial note

The premium on redemption must come from distributable profits as there is no fresh issue of shares.

KEY POINT

Capital can be returned to shareholders provided that the **creditors' buffer** is not reduced.

4.2 Reasons for provisions

The reason for these legal provisions is to protect the rights of creditors. Capital can be returned to shareholders provided that the fund of assets available to pay creditors (the creditors' buffer) is not reduced as a result of the redemption/purchase of shares.

	Before purchase of shares £	*After purchase of shares* £
Net assets	100,000	70,000
Less: Reduction of assets if maximum dividend paid to shareholders (balance on profit and loss account)	55,000	25,000
Creditors' buffer	45,000	45,000

Despite the return of capital, the creditors' buffer remains the same amount because the legal provisions reduce the amount of distributable profits.

Example

C plc (with the opening balance sheet above) redeems 25% of its ordinary shares for £30,000. It finances the redemption by issuing £30,000 10% preference shares.

The ordinary shares were originally issued at a premium of 50p per share.

Balance sheet after the redemption

	£
Net assets £(100 + 30 – 30)	100,000
Ordinary shares £(20 – 5)	15,000
Preference shares	30,000
Share premium	7,500 (W2)
Revaluation reserve	15,000
Profit and loss account	32,500 (W3)
	100,000

Workings

(W1) **Transfer to capital redemption reserve**

	£	£
NV of shares redeemed		5,000
Less: Proceeds of fresh issue of shares		(30,000)
∴ No transfer to capital redemption reserve		

(W2) **Share premium account**

	£	£
Original balance		10,000
Less: Lowest of		
Proceeds of fresh issue	30,000	
Original premium on shares now being redeemed 5,000 × 50p	2,500	
Current balance on share premium account	10,000	
		(2,500)
		7,500

Tutorial notes

The premium offset against share premium is effectively the lowest of three figures:

- the proceeds of the fresh issue of shares
- the original premium on issue
- the balance on share premium, i.e. a negative balance on share premium account is not allowed.

(W3) **Profit and loss account**

	£
Original balance	55,000
Less: Premium on redemption to the extent not set off against share premium £(25,000 – 2,500)	(22,500)
	32,500

As fresh capital of £30,000 has replaced old capital of £30,000, the creditors' buffer should be maintained without any transfers to capital redemption reserve.

In this case, the creditors' buffer actually increases as most of the premium on redemption reduces distributable profits even though new capital has come in to replace the old.

4.3 Redemption out of capital

KEY POINT

Only **private companies** may **redeem shares** out of **capital**.

Only **private companies** may **redeem shares** out of **capital** and even then the redemption will be firstly out of distributable profits and a fresh issue of shares. So the first step is to consider whether a payment has or has not been made out of capital.

Example

Wessex Ltd issued 20,000 £1 ordinary shares and 6,000 £1 redeemable A ordinary shares several years ago at par. The A ordinary shares are now to be redeemed at a total cost of £7,000. Distributable reserves amount to £5,400. There is to be no new share issue.

Is the payment a PCP out of capital?

	£
Total redemption cost	7,000
Distributable profits	5,400
PCP	1,600

As the redemption cost is greater than the available distributable profits, the redemption is partly out of capital.

The journal entries are as follows:

	Dr £	*Cr* £
(1) A ordinary share capital	6,000	
Distributable profits	1,000	
Bank		7,000
Being redemption of A ordinary shares at a premium totalling £1,000.		
(2) Distributable profits	4,400	
Capital redemption reserve		4,400
Being transfer to capital redemption reserve of excess of nominal value of shares over PCP.		

Share capital and non-distributable reserves consist of the following:

	Before redemption £	*After redemption* £
Ordinary shares	20,000	20,000
A ordinary shares	6,000	
Capital redemption reserve		4,400
	26,000	24,400

The £1,600 reduction is the amount of the PCP.

Journal entry 2 can alternatively be calculated by reference to the PCP. The company law provisions (dealt with earlier) state that if the total of the PCP plus proceeds of a share issue is less than the nominal value of the shares redeemed, the difference is transferred to capital redemption reserve:

	£
Nominal value of shares redeemed	6,000
PCP	1,600
Capital redemption reserve	4,400

KEY POINT

Payments out of capital must be made after the proceeds of a **fresh issue** and **distributable profits** have been used up.

The main point to grasp with the payment out of capital provisions is that, although a payment out of capital is allowed, the redemption must, to the extent that they are available, come out of the proceeds of a **fresh issue** of shares made to finance the redemption, and **distributable profits**.

4.4 UITF Abstract 37 *Purchases and sales of own shares*

Following the issue of the Treasury Shares Regulations described earlier, the UITF issued Abstract 37 to regulate the accounting for the purchase and subsequent sale of treasury shares.

A company's holding of its own shares does not satisfy the definition of an asset, since there is no prospective receipt of future economic benefits. Therefore, in principle, a holding of own shares is a reduction of ownership interest that should be reported as an adjustment to shareholders' funds rather than as an asset. Transactions in own shares should be reported in the statement of movements in shareholders' funds; there is no gain or loss to be reported in the profit and loss account or STRGL.

Once these principles have been accepted, the rules in Abstract 37 follow logically.

- Amounts paid for an entity's own shares should be deducted from shareholders' funds, not shown as an asset on the balance sheet
- No gain or loss should be recognised in the profit and loss account or STRGL on the purchase, sale or cancellation of an entity's own shares
- Amounts paid or received for the purchase or sale of an entity's own shares should be reported separately in the reconciliation of movements in shareholders' funds.

5 The rules relating to the distribution of profits

5.1 Distributable profit

It is a basic principle of company law that a company with limited liability may not return capital to members except by the proper and **strictly regulated** procedure of **reduction of capital** or a **liquidation**. The principle is designed to safeguard the rights of creditors to be paid what is owing to them before capital is returned to members.

KEY POINT

A limited liability company may not return capital to members except by the proper and **strictly regulated** procedure of **reduction of capital** or a **liquidation.**

This principle underlies many specific rules such as the treatment of share premiums as a capital reserve, the rule that the redemption of redeemable shares is possible only out of the proceeds of a fresh issue of new shares or from distributable profits, and the restrictions imposed on the purchase by a company of its own shares.

It follows from the principle of conservation of subscribed capital that dividends may only be paid out of profits. The principle cannot, of course, safeguard the company from a loss of capital by unprofitable trading or unwise investment.

Apart from the legal rules imposed on companies by the CA85, there are a number of practical constraints on dividend policy.

- If the company becomes **insolvent** and goes into liquidation, the directors and others may be **liable for defrauding creditors**.
- **Dividends require cash**. There are practical limits on what can be borrowed to finance dividend payments. The accounts will, after the event at least, reveal the depletion of liquid assets.
- The articles of association may restrict payment of dividends, e.g. by limiting distributions to those of trading profit (thereby excluding profits arising from sale of fixed assets).
- The commercial standing and credit rating of a company depend to some extent on financial prudence and some retention of profits for expansion.

5.2 Profits available for dividend: rules for all companies

KEY POINT

Profits available for dividend are accumulated, realised profits, so far as not previously utilised (whether by distribution or capitalisation), less accumulated, realised losses, so far as not previously written off.

All companies, including private companies, are prohibited from paying dividends (making a distribution) except out of profits available for that purpose.

Profits available for dividend are accumulated, realised profits, so far as not previously utilised (whether by distribution or capitalisation), less accumulated, realised losses, so far as not previously written off: **S263 (3) CA85.**

This definition permits the distribution as dividend of a capital profit, i.e. a surplus over book value realised on sale of a fixed asset. But the key words are:

- **accumulated** – which means that the balance of profit or loss from previous years must be brought into account in the current period
- **realised** – which prohibits the inclusion of unrealised profits arising for example from the revaluation of fixed assets retained by the company.

There are the following detailed rules in CA85.

- A provision made in the accounts is a realised loss.
- A revaluation surplus is an unrealised profit.
- If fixed assets are revalued and, as a result, more has to be provided for depreciation than would have been necessary if the original value had been retained, the additional depreciation may be treated as part of the realised profit for dividend purposes. This effectively means the depreciation based on the revaluation surplus can be added back notionally to the profit and loss account for the determination of realised profits. This adjustment can be put through the accounts as a transfer between reserves.
- On the disposal of a revalued asset any unrealised surplus or loss on valuation immediately becomes realised.
- If there is no available record of the original cost of an asset, its cost may be taken as the value put on it in the earliest available record.
- If it is impossible to establish whether a profit or a loss brought forward was realised or unrealised, any such profit may be treated as realised and any such loss as unrealised.

ACTIVITY **2**

A Ltd purchased freehold land and buildings on 30 June 20X4 for £200,000 (land £60,000, buildings £140,000). The net book value of the buildings at 31 December 20X7 is £121,386. On 1 January 20X8 the land was revalued to £75,000 and the buildings to £135,000. Depreciation on buildings is computed at 4% reducing balance. Accounts are prepared on a calendar year basis.

Show the revaluation reserve for the year to 31 December 20X8.

Feedback to this activity is at the end of the chapter.

5.3 Revaluation deficits

KEY POINT

CA85 stipulates that a **provision** in the accounts is a **realised loss**, and a **revaluation deficit** is an **unrealised loss**.

Company legislation has enshrined in law the principles of distributable profits and losses decided in a series of court cases in the late nineteenth and early twentieth centuries. These principles were, in part, based on sound accounting concepts. However, in the treatment of provisions for losses on assets, the judgements of the courts were very difficult to reconcile with any accounting principles.

CA85 stipulates the following.

- A **provision** made in the accounts is a **realised loss**. A revaluation deficit is a provision for a loss in value and is therefore a realised loss.
- If a **revaluation deficit** arises on a revaluation of all fixed assets (or on a revaluation of all fixed assets except for goodwill) the revaluation deficit is an **unrealised loss**.

Consequently, where a company undertakes a partial revaluation of fixed assets, a deficit on one asset is a realised loss and cannot therefore be offset against a surplus on another asset (an unrealised profit) for the purposes of arriving at distributable profits. This is despite the fact that all surpluses and deficits can be accounted for in the revaluation reserve.

KEY POINT

Deficits arising from a partial revaluation are to be treated as **unrealised losses**, provided that the aggregate value of the **fixed assets** which have not been revalued is not less than their **aggregate book value**.

A partial remedy to this problem is contained in CA85. Deficits arising on an asset where there has been a partial revaluation of the assets are to be treated as unrealised losses provided that:

- the directors have 'considered' the **aggregate value** of the **fixed assets** which have not been revalued at the date of the partial revaluation
- the directors are satisfied that the aggregate value is not less than their **aggregate book value**
- a note to the accounts states the above two facts.

Example

X Ltd has the following balance sheet

	£000
Net assets	300
Share capital	100
Share premium	50
Revaluation reserve	70
Profit and loss account	80
	300

Two of the company's assets were revalued during the year, one giving rise to a surplus of £100,000, the other to a deficit of £30,000.

The profits available for distribution as dividend are as follows:

	£000
Net realised profits - profit and loss account	80
Less: Realised losses - revaluation deficit	(30)
	50

If all the company's assets had been revalued or the directors had 'considered' the value of the assets not revalued, the revaluation deficit would be unrealised and therefore the profits available for distribution would be £80,000.

5.4 Revaluation surpluses

KEY POINT

Revaluation surpluses are unrealised profits in the accounting period in which the revaluation takes place.

Revaluation surpluses are unrealised profits in the accounting period in which the revaluation takes place. The only exception to this rule is where the same asset was:

- previously revalued giving rise to a deficit
- the deficit was treated as a realised loss. In such a case, the revaluation surplus will be a realised profit to the extent that it makes good the realised loss. It should be noted that company law does not specify this but best accounting practice would require this treatment.

It should also be remembered that revaluation surpluses can eventually become realised profits when the asset is either depreciated or sold.

5.5 Development expenditure

KEY POINT

S269 CA85 states that **development costs** shown as an asset in the accounts are to be treated as a **realised loss**, unless there are **special circumstances** (e.g. expenditure carried forward under SSAP 13).

CA85 has special rules for **development costs** if they are not written off in the year in which the expenditure is incurred but carried forward as intangible assets. Whilst the legislation allows such intangible expenditure to be carried forward, on the grounds of prudence S269 CA85 states that development costs shown as an asset in the accounts are to be treated as a **realised loss**.

Therefore, they must be deducted from the accounting profits when determining distributable profits.

However, the legislation allows an exception to this, if:

- there are **special circumstances** justifying the directors in deciding that the amount is not to be treated as a realised loss
- the note to the accounts required by paragraph 20 Schedule 4 (reasons for showing development costs as an asset) states that the amount is not to be so treated and explains the circumstances relied upon to justify the decision of the directors to that effect.

The special circumstances are satisfied if the expenditure is carried forward under the provisions of SSAP 13 (see later chapter in this text.).

The only practical effect of this provision is to require a statement in the notes to the accounts. It should also be noted that if the expenditure is not treated as a realised loss in the year of expenditure, it will be a realised loss when written off in future years.

5.6 Profits available for dividend: additional rules for public companies

KEY POINT

A public company may not pay a dividend unless its **net assets** are at least equal to the aggregate amount of its **called-up share capital** and **undistributable reserves**.

In addition to the rules set out above, a public company may not pay a dividend unless its **net assets** are at least equal to the aggregate amount of its **called-up share capital** and **undistributable reserves**. It may not pay a dividend so as to reduce its net assets below that aggregate amount: S264 CA85. It must maintain its called up share capital and undistributable reserves.

Undistributable reserves are:

- share premium account
- capital redemption reserve
- unrealised profits (less unrealised losses unless previously written off)
- any other reserve which the company is prohibited from distributing by any statute or by its memorandum or articles of association.

The effect of this provision is that any excess of unrealised losses over unrealised profits must be deducted from realised profits in arriving at the amount available for distribution.

Example

A public company X plc has the following balance sheet:

	£000
Net assets	115
Share capital	100
Unrealised profits	60
Unrealised losses	(80)
Realised profits	35
	115

Net assets must not be reduced below:	
Share capital	100
Undistributable reserves	-
	100
i.e. Maximum distribution is £15,000, being:	
Realised profits	35
Less: Excess of unrealised losses over unrealised profits	(20)
	15

For a private company, the maximum distribution would be £35,000.

5.7 Relevant accounts: S270 CA85

KEY POINT

The **relevant accounts** are usually the latest audited accounts as laid before general meeting as required by **S270 CA85**.

The basis of calculation of what is available for dividend is the relevant accounts.

1 Usually the **relevant accounts** are the latest audited annual accounts laid before the company in general meeting as required by **S270 CA85**.

   When the annual accounts are the basis of calculation, the rules are as follows.

   – The accounts must have been properly prepared and also audited.

   – The report of the auditors must either be unqualified or, if qualified, accompanied by a statement by the auditors as to whether in their opinion the subject of their qualification is material to the determination of distributable profits. In this context, an unqualified report is one which states without qualification that the accounts have been properly prepared.

2 If figures derived from the latest annual accounts would preclude the payment of a dividend, interim accounts may be used, but they must be such as are necessary to enable a reasonable judgement to be made.

3 If the company has not yet produced its first annual accounts, interim accounts (as described in 2 above) may be used.

When annual accounts are used under 1, or interim accounts are used under 2 or 3 above, they must be properly prepared, i.e. they must comply with the various rules on statutory accounts and they must give a true and fair view. It is not necessary, however, that they should deal with matters which are not material to the dividend rules. In case 3, the auditors must report whether in their opinion the accounts have been properly prepared.

5.8 Pre-incorporation profits

KEY POINTS

Pre-incorporation profits are profits made by a company before it is legally incorporated.

Pre-incorporation profits are **not distributable**, but they increase the **capital worth** of the shareholders' investment.

Pre-incorporation profits are profits made by a company before it is legally incorporated. These may arise because the shareholders/directors who form the company are slow in sorting out the necessary paperwork and commence trading prior to incorporation.

In such a situation any profits made by the company are **not distributable** as legally the company did not exist. Profits, however, have been made and are due to the shareholders. They are thus put to a **capital reserve**, i.e. they increase the **capital worth** of the shareholders' investment.

For example, a company starts trading on the 1 January, is incorporated on 31 March and computes profits in the first year to 31 December as £60,000.

If we assume profits accrue evenly over the period, £15,000 is transferred from profit and loss account to capital reserve. £45,000 remains as distributable.

ACTIVITY 3

Scraper Ltd
Balance sheet as at 30 November 20X3

	Cost/valuation	*Dep'n*	*NBV*	
	£	£	£	£
Fixed assets				
Freehold properties	194,400	14,400	180,000	
Vehicles	300,000	60,000	240,000	
Fixtures and fittings	28,000	12,000	16,000	
				436,000
Current assets				
Stock		395,000		
Debtors		176,000		
Cash		232,000		
			803,000	
Creditors – amounts due less than 1 year				
Trade creditors		112,000		
Hire purchase creditors		89,100		
Bank overdraft		17,043		
			218,143	
Net current assets				584,857
Total assets less current liabilities				1,020,857
Creditors – amounts due more than 1 year				
10% debentures (convertible 20X6)		100,000		
Other creditors including tax		174,857		
				274,857
Net assets				746,000
Capital and reserves				
Share capital				400,000
Share premium account				50,000
Capital redemption reserve				100,000
Revaluation deficit				(130,000)
General reserve				70,000
Profit and loss account				256,000
				746,000

Note: the revaluation deficit results from a reappraisal on 30 November 20X3 of the fixed asset register of fixtures and fittings within one of the London properties. One of the properties was revalued from £30,000 to £124,400 on 1 December 20X2. There was no general programme of revaluation. The gain on the freehold has been netted off against the loss on revaluation of fixtures.

Depreciation on the freehold properties was £3,888 p.a. calculated at 2% of valuation cost.

The directors consider that the value of the assets not revalued is at least equal to their book value.

Calculate the distributable profits for Scraper Ltd as at 30 November 20X3:

- on the basis that Scraper Ltd is a private company
- on the basis that Scraper Ltd is a public company.

Feedback to this activity is at the end of the chapter.

Conclusion

FRS 25 and FRS 26 dealing with the disclosure, presentation and measurement of financial instruments have only recently been issued and have superseded FRS 4. Although they deal with complex issues the ones that are relevant to this syllabus are fairly straightforward.

A company may redeem or purchase its shares. It must protect the rights of creditors by creating a non-distributable capital redemption reserve (CRR) if the proceeds from the issue of new capital have been insufficient for this purpose.

A company's distributable profits are accumulated realised profits less accumulated realised losses. There are further restrictions for a public company, which must not pay a dividend unless its net assets are at least equal to the aggregate of its called up share capital and undistributable reserves.

SELF-TEST QUESTIONS

1 How should redeemable preference shares normally be classified? (1.4)

2 How should convertible bonds be shown in the balance sheet? (1.5)

3 How is the finance cost accounted for where debt has been issued? (2.5)

4 When shares are redeemed, what is the amount that must be transferred to the capital redemption reserve? (3.3)

5 Why might a company wish to purchase its own shares? (3.4)

6 What is the permissible capital payment (PCP)? (3.5)

7 What is the reason for the transfer to the capital redemption reserve? (4.3)

8 Define profits available for dividend. (5.2)

9 Is a provision a realised or unrealised loss? (5.2)

10 If a company revalues its fixed assets, how is the additional depreciation treated for the purpose of calculating distributable profits? (5.2)

EXAM-TYPE QUESTIONS

Question 1: Short plc

On 1 October 20X3, Short plc issued 10 million £1 preference shares at par, incurring issue costs of £100,000. The dividend payable on the preference shares was a fixed 4% per annum, payable on 30 September each year in arrears. The preference shares were redeemed on 1 October 20X8 at a price of £1.35 per share. The effective finance cost of the preference shares was 10%. The balance sheet of the company on 30 September 20X8, the day before the redemption of the preference shares, was as follows:

	£ million
Net assets	199.0
Ordinary share capital (non-redeemable)	100.0
Redeemable preference shares	13.5
Share premium account	25.8
Profit and loss account	59.7
	199.0

Required:

(a) Explain:

- how the total finance cost of the preference shares should be allocated to the profit and loss account over their period of issue
- where in the profit and loss account the finance cost should be reported
- where the preference shares should be disclosed in the balance sheet
- the nature of any supporting information which is required to be disclosed in the notes to the financial statements regarding the preference shares.

Your answer should refer to the provisions of relevant Accounting Standards. **(8 marks)**

(b) Calculate the finance cost in respect of the preference shares for *each* of the five years ended 30 September 20X8. **(7 marks)**

(c) Assuming no changes *other than those caused by the redemption of the preference shares*, prepare the balance sheet of Short plc at 1 October 20X8. You should give an explanation for any changes to any of the headings or any new headings which are required. **(5 marks)**

(Total: 20 marks)

Question 2: LED Ltd

LED Ltd is a private company, which maintains its accounting records on a computerised system. The financial director has decided that the company will redeem all of the preference shares of the company at a premium of 10% in accordance with the original terms of redemption. In order to assist with the redemption, a new issue of 5,000 £1 ordinary shares at £1.25 will be made and a bank overdraft limit of £10,000 has been negotiated. The redeemable preference shares were originally issued at par value and the preference dividend has been paid up to date.

The financial director has asked your advice on how to treat this matter in the financial statements. He realises that the current redemption plan would reduce the capital of the company and he wondered whether this was possible under the Companies Acts.

The current draft balance sheet (drafted before the requirements of FRS 25 were brought in) of LED Ltd is as follows:

LED Ltd
Draft balance sheet as at 30 November 20X4

	£	£
Sundry fixed assets		20,000
Sundry net current assets	25,000	
Cash	5,000	
		30,000
		50,000
Ordinary shares of £1 each		25,000
7% Redeemable preference shares of £1 each		12,500
Share premium account		7,500
Profit and loss account		5,000
		50,000

Required:

(a) Explain to the financial director the conditions and safeguards which must be fulfilled when a private company redeems shares out of capital. **(6 marks)**

(b) Explain the reasons why these conditions and safeguards relating to private companies have been introduced. **(4 marks)**

(c) Prepare the revised balance sheet of LED Ltd assuming the planned redemption of preference shares takes place. **(6 marks)**

(Total: 16 marks)

For the answers to these questions, see the 'Answers' section at the end of the book.

FEEDBACK TO ACTIVITY **1**

The equity component continues to be valued at $152,280 in the balance sheet.

The liability component is valued at amortised cost, as required by FRS 26:

	$
At beginning of year	1,847,720
Interest at 9%	166,295
Less: interest paid	(120,000)
	1,894,015

A finance charge of $166,295 is reported in the income statement.

FEEDBACK TO ACTIVITY **2**

The entries to the revaluation reserve should be:

	£
Re land	15,000
Re buildings £(135,000 – 121,386)	13,614
	28,614

The depreciation charge for the year ended 31 December 20X8 = 4% × £135,000 = £5,400. This amount is the charge to P&L account (FRS 15) although CA85 requires only the historic cost depreciation (4% × £121,386 = £4,855).

To show the realised part of the revaluation reserve, a transfer from the reserve to distributable reserves may be made.

Revaluation reserve

	£
Balance at 1 January 20X8	28,614
Transfer to distributable reserves £(5,400 – 4,855)	545
Balance at 31 December 20X8	28,069

FEEDBACK TO ACTIVITY 3

Distributable profits calculated on basis that Scraper Ltd is a private company:

	£	£
Profit and loss account		256,000
Add: Depreciation on revalued amount of:		
Freehold 2% of £194,400	3,888	
2% of cost £100,000	2,000	
		1,888
		257,888
General reserve		70,000
Available for distribution		327,888

If Scraper Ltd was a public company:

'Private' company rules		327,888
Less excess unrealised losses over unrealised profits		
Revaluation deficit (130,000 + 94,400)	224,400	
Revaluation surplus (94,400 – 1,888)	92,512	
		131,888
Distributable profit		196,000

Tutorial notes:

1 The revaluation deficit is an unrealised loss. Although there was only a partial revaluation, the directors have 'considered' the value of all the assets.

2 The alternative calculation compares net assets to share capital and undistributable reserves and can be used as a check:

Net assets before dividend		746,000
Share capital	400,000	
Share premium	50,000	
Capital redemption reserve	100,000	
		550,000
Distributable profit		196,000

Chapter 16
FIXED ASSETS – TANGIBLE

CHAPTER CONTENTS

1 FRS 15 *Tangible fixed assets*

2 Valuation of fixed assets

3 Depreciation

4 SSAP 4 *Accounting for government grants*

5 SSAP 19 *Accounting for investment properties*

6 UITF Abstract 5 *Transfers from current assets to fixed assets*

This chapter covers the requirements of the three main accounting standards that deal with tangible fixed assets:

- FRS 15 *Tangible fixed assets*
- SSAP 4 *Accounting for government grants*
- SSAP 19 *Accounting for investment properties.*

The most important of these is FRS 15. You should already be familiar with accounting for fixed assets and depreciation. However, FRS 15 also addresses several other important topics: the initial measurement of fixed assets, capitalisation of borrowing costs, and revaluation of fixed assets.

An entity may receive government grants to cover certain types of expenditure, including the cost of fixed assets. Accounting for grants is covered by SSAP 4.

An investment property, as its name suggests, is a property held as an investment, rather than for use in the normal operations of a business. Investment properties are treated differently from other tangible fixed assets and SSAP 19 sets out the required accounting treatment.

Objectives

By the time you have finished this chapter you should be able to:

- define the initial cost of a fixed asset and apply the definition
- describe, and be able to identify, subsequent expenditures that may be capitalised
- state and appraise the effects of FRS 15's rules for the revaluation of fixed assets
- account for gains and losses on the disposal of revalued assets
- calculate depreciation
- apply the provisions of SSAP 4
- discuss why the treatment of investment properties should differ from other properties
- apply the requirements of SSAP 19.

1 FRS 15 *Tangible fixed assets*

1.1 Introduction

DEFINITION

Tangible fixed assets are assets that have physical substance and are held for use in the production or supply of goods or services, for rental to others, or for administrative purposes on a continuing basis in the reporting entity's activities (FRS 15).

Tangible fixed assets are assets that have physical substance and are held for use in the production or supply of goods or services, for rental to others, or for administrative purposes on a continuing basis in the reporting entity's activities (FRS 15).

Fixed assets have the fundamental characteristic that they are held with the object of earning revenue by their *use*, not by their resale.

1.2 Initial measurement of fixed assets

An entity may acquire fixed assets by purchasing them, or by constructing them. Occasionally they may be donated to an entity (for example, if the entity is a charity).

FRS 15 states that a tangible fixed asset should initially be measured at its **cost**.

In principle, an asset's cost is its purchase price, *less* any trade discounts or rebates, *plus* any further costs directly attributable to bringing it into working condition for its intended use.

KEY POINT

Costs in purchasing a fixed asset may include **stamp duty**, **legal fees**, **delivery** and handling costs and **installation** costs. If the asset was constructed, costs may include **material**, **labour**, architects' **fees** and **overheads**.

Costs that might be incurred by an entity in purchasing a fixed asset include:

- stamp duty and other duties
- legal fees
- delivery and handling costs
- installation costs.

If the entity constructed the fixed asset, rather than buying it, it might incur other costs:

- materials costs
- labour costs
- architects' fees
- direct overheads (e.g. power).

Only those costs that are directly attributable to bringing the asset into working condition for its intended use should be included in its measurement.

FRS 15 also states the following.

KEY POINT

Capitalisation of attributable costs should cease when physical construction is complete.

The initial carrying amount of **donated assets** should be the current value at the date received.

- **Capitalisation** of directly attributable costs should cease when substantially all the activities that are necessary to get the tangible fixed asset ready for use are complete, even if the asset has not yet been brought into use. A tangible fixed asset is ready for use when its **physical construction** is complete.
- The costs associated with a start up or **commissioning** period should be included in the cost of the tangible fixed asset only where the asset is available for use but incapable of operating at normal levels without such a start up or commissioning period.

  For example, a machine has to be run in and tested before it can be used for producing goods. The costs associated with this *are included* in the cost of the machine.

  After the machine has been run in, there is a further period during which it is operated below its capacity. The machine is capable of operating at full capacity, but demand for the product it makes has not yet built up. Costs associated with this period *cannot be included* in the cost of the machine.
- The initial carrying amount of tangible fixed assets received as gifts and donations by charities should be the **current value** of the assets at the date that they are received.

Example

An entity incurred the following costs in constructing a building for its own use:

	£000
Purchase price of land	250,000
Stamp duty	5,000
Legal fees	10,000
Site preparation and clearance	18,000
Materials	100,000
Labour (period 1 April 20X7 to 30 September 20X8)	150,000
Architect's fees	20,000
General overheads	30,000
	583,000

The following information is also relevant.

- Material costs were greater than anticipated. On investigation, it was found that material costing £10 million had been spoiled and therefore was wasted and a further £15 million was incurred as a result of faulty design work.
- As a result of these problems, work on the building ceased for a fortnight during October 20X7 and it is estimated that approximately £9 million of the labour costs relate to this period.
- The building was completed on 1 July 20X8 and occupied on 1 September 20X8.

You are required to calculate the cost of the building that will be included in tangible fixed asset additions.

Solution

Only those costs which are directly attributable to bringing the asset into working condition for its intended use should be included. Therefore, administration and other general overhead costs cannot be included. FRS 15 also states that **abnormal costs should not be included** in the cost of a fixed asset. Abnormal costs include costs caused by design errors, industrial disputes, idle capacity, wasted materials and production delays.

The amount included in tangible fixed assets is computed as follows:

	Total	*Exclude*	*Include*
	£000	£000	£000
Purchase price of land	250,000		250,000
Stamp duty	5,000		5,000
Legal fees	10,000		10,000
Site preparation and clearance	18,000		18,000
Materials (Note 1)	100,000	25,000	75,000
Labour ((150,000 × 3/18) + 9,000) (Note 2)	150,000	34,000	116,000
Architect's fees	20,000		20,000
General overheads	30,000	30,000	–
	583,000	89,000	494,000

KEY POINT

Fixed assets should initially be measured at cost. Only those costs that are directly attributable to bringing the asset into working condition for its intended use should be included in its measurement.

Notes:

1 The costs of spoiled material and faulty design are abnormal costs.

2 Labour costs are only included for the period to 1 July 20X8. The building was available for use on that date, regardless of the fact that it was not actually in use until three months later. The £9 million labour cost incurred during the period of the stoppage is an abnormal cost and is also excluded.

1.3 Finance costs

KEY POINT

Whether or not finance (interest) costs should be included in the cost of a tangible fixed asset is arguable and is **optional**.

Interest on borrowings is often a very significant cost of acquiring or constructing an asset. Opinion is divided on whether or not finance costs should be included in the cost of a tangible fixed asset. Property companies are the most significant advocates of capitalisation – indeed, most of them capitalise interest on loans used to finance the construction of properties. Many supermarket chains have also capitalised finance costs relating to the construction of large 'superstores'.

Arguments for capitalising finance costs

- Finance costs are just as much a cost of constructing a tangible fixed asset as other directly attributable costs.
- Capitalising finance costs results in a tangible fixed asset cost that more closely matches the market price of completed assets. Treating the finance cost as an expense distorts the choice between purchasing and constructing a tangible fixed

asset. Capitalisation also means that users of the financial statements can more easily compare companies which construct their fixed assets themselves and those which purchase them from third parties.

- The accounts are more likely to reflect the true success or failure of projects involving the construction of assets.
- Failure to capitalise borrowing costs means that profits may be reduced in periods when fixed assets are acquired. This is misleading as capital investment should increase profits in the long term.

Arguments against capitalising finance costs

- Borrowing costs are incurred in support of the whole of the activities of an enterprise. Any attempt to associate borrowing costs with a particular asset is necessarily arbitrary.
- Capitalisation of borrowing costs results in the same type of asset having a different carrying amount, depending on the method of financing adopted by the enterprise.
- Treating borrowing costs as a charge against income results in financial statements giving more comparable results from period to period. This provides a better indication of the future cash flows of an enterprise. Interest remains a period cost of financing the business and its treatment should not change merely as a result of the completion of a tangible fixed asset.
- Capitalisation leads to higher tangible fixed asset costs, which are more likely to exceed the recoverable amount of the asset.

Standard accounting practice

KEY POINT

Only **directly** attributable finance costs should be capitalised and these should **not exceed** the total cost incurred.

Capitalisation should begin when costs are **being incurred**, should be **suspended** when activity is interrupted, and **ceased** on asset completion.

Capitalisation of finance costs is optional. FRS 15 does, however, set out rules that must be followed if interest is capitalised.

- Only finance costs that are **directly attributable** to the construction of a tangible fixed asset should be capitalised as part of the cost of that asset.
- The total amount of finance costs capitalised during a period should not exceed the total amount of finance costs incurred during that period.
- Capitalisation should begin when:
  - finance costs are being incurred
  - expenditures for the asset are being incurred
  - activities that are necessary to get the asset ready for use are in progress.
- Capitalisation should be **suspended** during extended periods in which active development is **interrupted.**
- Capitalisation should **cease** when substantially all the activities that are necessary to get the tangible fixed asset ready for use are complete.

Disclosures

KEY POINT

When finance costs are capitalised, the accounting policy, the amount capitalised, the finance costs recognised in the profit and loss account and the interest rate used must be disclosed.

Where finance costs are capitalised, the following disclosures are required:

- the accounting policy adopted
- the aggregate amount of finance costs included in the cost of tangible fixed assets
- the amount of finance costs capitalised during the period
- the amount of finance costs recognised in the profit and loss account during the period
- the capitalisation (interest) rate used to determine the amount of finance costs capitalised during the period.

Given that capitalisation of borrowing costs is optional, FRS 15 provides users of the financial statements with information to help them to compare the financial statements of different entities.

ACTIVITY **1**

On 1 January 20X5, X Ltd began to construct a supermarket. It purchased a leasehold interest in the site for £25 million. The construction of the building cost £9 million and the fixtures and fittings cost £6 million. The construction of the supermarket was completed on 30 September 20X5 and it was brought into use on 1 January 20X6.

X Ltd borrowed £40 million in order to finance this project. The loan carried interest at 10% per annum. It was repaid on 30 June 20X6.

X Ltd capitalises borrowing costs where this is permitted by accounting standards.

You are required to calculate the total amount to be included in fixed assets in respect of the development at 31 December 20X5.

Feedback to this activity is at the end of the chapter.

1.4 Subsequent expenditure

KEY POINT

Subsequent expenditure can only be capitalised if it **enhances** an asset or if it relates to **restoration** or **replacement** of a component of the asset.

As well as the initial cost of acquiring a fixed asset, an entity may also incur additional costs in relation to the asset during its life. There are two categories of subsequent expenditure:

- expenditure to **maintain** or **service** the asset (an **expense** of the period)
- expenditure to **improve** or **upgrade** the asset (effectively an **addition** to fixed assets).

FRS 15 sets out three circumstances in which subsequent expenditure should be capitalised:

- where it provides an **enhancement** of the economic benefits of the tangible fixed asset in excess of its previously assessed standard of performance, e.g.:
  - modification of an item of plant to extend its useful economic life or increase its capacity
  - upgrading machine parts to achieve a substantial improvement in the quality of output
- where a component of the tangible fixed asset that has been treated separately for depreciation purposes and depreciated over its individual useful economic life is **replaced** or **restored**
- where it relates to a major inspection or overhaul of a tangible fixed asset that restores the economic benefits of the asset that have been consumed by the entity and have already been reflected in depreciation.

All other subsequent expenditure must be recognised in the profit and loss account as it is incurred.

2 Valuation of fixed assets

2.1 Introduction

CA85 allows tangible fixed assets to be carried either at **historic cost** or at a **valuation**. Many entities take advantage of this rule and revalue some of their fixed assets (normally properties). Other entities continue to carry fixed assets at historic cost.

KEY POINT

The ASB wishes to encourage the use of **current value** in financial statements as it believes that this provides relevant information to users.

There are strong arguments for carrying assets at **current values**, which are mainly related to the disadvantages of using historic cost. The ASB wishes to encourage the use of **current value** in financial statements as it believes that this provides relevant information to users. However, until the issue of FRS 15 there was no accounting standard that gave guidance on revaluation.

This has led to the following problems:

- valuations were not kept up to date (particularly if property prices are falling)
- entities tended to '**cherry pick**', i.e. revalue certain assets and not others
- some entities did not depreciate revalued fixed assets.

2.2 The basic rules

KEY POINT

Revaluation of fixed assets is **optional**. If one tangible fixed asset is revalued, all tangible fixed assets of the same **class** must be revalued.

- Revaluation of fixed assets is **optional**.
- If one tangible fixed asset is revalued, all tangible fixed assets of the same **class** must be revalued. (This means that it is now impossible to 'cherry pick', for example, by revaluing some freehold properties and not others.)
- Where an entity adopts a policy of revaluation, it need not be applied to all classes of tangible fixed assets held by the entity.

A **class of tangible fixed assets** is a category of tangible fixed assets having a similar nature, function or use in the business of the entity.

In practice, a class of tangible fixed assets might be determined by the CA85 balance sheet formats, for example: land and buildings; plant and machinery; and fixtures, fittings, tools and equipment. However, narrower classes are allowed, for example: specialised properties; non-specialised properties; and short leasehold properties.

DEFINITIONS

A **class of tangible fixed assets** is a category of tangible fixed assets having a similar nature, function or use in the business of the entity.

The **current value** of a tangible fixed asset is the lower of replacement cost and recoverable amount.

Recoverable amount is the higher of net realisable value and value in use.

- The carrying amount of a revalued fixed asset should be its **current value** at the balance sheet date.

The **current value** of a tangible fixed asset is the lower of replacement cost and recoverable amount.

The definition of current value is consistent with the value to the business model set out in the Statement of Principles. This is also known as **deprival value**.

Recoverable amount is the higher of net realisable value and value in use.

2.3 Frequency and basis of valuation

Frequency

FRS 15 does not insist on annual revaluations, but instead requires the following:

- Non-specialised properties:
  - a full valuation at least every **five years** with an interim valuation in **Year 3** or in other years where there has been a material change in value; *or*
  - full valuation on a rolling basis over five-year cycles with an interim valuation on the remaining portfolio where there has been a material change in value.
- Specialised properties: valuation **at least every five years** and in the intervening years where there has been a material change in value.
- Other tangible fixed assets:
  - annual valuation where market comparisons or appropriate indices exist; *otherwise*
  - valuation at least every five years and in the intervening years where there has been a material change in value.

DEFINITION

An **internal valuer** is a director, officer or employee of the entity. An **external valuer** is not an internal valuer and does not have a significant financial interest in the entity.

Five-yearly valuations should be carried out by a qualified external or internal valuer. If an internal valuer is used, the valuation should be reviewed by a qualified external valuer.

An **internal valuer** is a director, officer or employee of the entity. An **external valuer** is not an internal valuer and does not have a significant financial interest in the entity.

Basis

KEY POINT

The basis for valuation depends on whether the property is **specialised**, **non-specialised** or **surplus** to requirements.

The following valuation bases should be used for revalued properties that are not impaired:

- **Non-specialised properties**: existing use value plus directly attributable acquisition costs if material. Disclose open market value where this is materially different.
- **Specialised properties**: depreciated replacement cost.
- **Properties surplus to an entity's requirements**: open market value less expected direct selling costs where these are material.

Tangible fixed assets other than properties should be valued using **market value**, where possible. Where market value is not obtainable, **depreciated replacement cost** should be used.

ACTIVITY **2**

A company revalues its buildings and decides to incorporate the revaluation into its financial statements.

Extract from the balance sheet at 31 December 20X7:

	£000
Buildings:	
Cost	1,200
Depreciation	144
	1,056

The building is revalued at 1 January 20X8 at £1,400,000. Its useful economic life is 40 years at that date.

You are required to show the relevant extracts from the final accounts at 31 December 20X8.

Feedback to this activity is at the end of the chapter.

2.4 Reporting gains and losses on revaluation

Gains

KEY POINT

A **revaluation gain** cannot be recognised in the profit and loss account because it is not yet **realised** and so should normally be recognised in the **STRGL**.

CA85 states that the profit and loss account should only include **realised gains**. A **revaluation gain** cannot be recognised in the profit and loss account because it is not yet realised (it will only be realised when the asset is sold).

Revaluation gains should normally be recognised in the **STRGL**, which includes all gains and losses incurred by an entity for a period, regardless of whether or not they are realised.

Losses

KEY POINT

Revaluation losses caused by consumption of economic benefits should be recognised in the profit and loss account, others should be recognised in the STRGL.

A **revaluation loss** may be caused either:

- by a fall in prices (e.g. a slump in the property market); or
- by consumption of economic benefits (e.g. physical damage or deterioration; this is similar to depreciation).

Unless there is evidence to the contrary, it is assumed that a loss is caused by a fall in prices.

- Revaluation losses that are caused by a clear consumption of economic benefits should be recognised in the **profit and loss account**.
- Other revaluation losses should normally be recognised in the **STRGL** until the carrying amount reaches its **depreciated historic cost**. Thereafter they should be recognised in the profit and loss account.

ACTIVITY **3**

A property costing £500,000 was purchased on 1 January 20X4 and is being depreciated over its useful economic life of 10 years. It has no residual value. At 31 December 20X4 the property was valued at £540,000 and at 31 December 20X5 it was valued at £350,000.

How should these revaluations be treated in the accounts for the years ended 31 December 20X4 and 31 December 20X5?

Feedback to this activity is at the end of the chapter.

2.5 Reporting gains and losses on disposal

KEY POINT

The profit or loss on **disposal of a revalued fixed asset** should be accounted for in the profit and loss account of the period in which the disposal occurs.

The profit or loss on disposal is the difference between the net sale proceeds and the carrying amount.

Realised revaluation gains can be transferred to the profit and loss account reserve.

The profit or loss on **disposal of a revalued fixed asset** should be calculated as the difference between the net sale proceeds and the carrying amount. It should be accounted for in the profit and loss account of the period in which the disposal occurs.

The gain or loss on revaluation has already been included in the accounts (in the STRGL) when the asset was revalued. If the profit or loss on disposal were based on the original cost of the asset, the gain or loss on revaluation would be recognised twice.

Note, however, that if there has been a gain on revaluation, it is now realised. When revaluation gains are realised they can be transferred from the revaluation reserve to the profit and loss account reserve. This transfer does not affect the profit for the year.

ACTIVITY **4**

A property costing £750,000 was purchased on 1 January 20X4 and is being depreciated over its useful economic life of 10 years. It has no residual value.

At 31 December 20X4 the property was valued at £810,000. There was no change to its useful economic life.

On 31 December 20X6 the property was sold for £900,000.

What is the profit or loss on disposal?

Feedback to this activity is at the end of the chapter.

2.6 Disclosures where assets have been revalued

For each class of revalued assets, disclose:

- name and qualifications of the valuer(s)
- bases of valuation
- date and amount of the valuation
- depreciated historic cost
- whether the valuer(s) is (are) internal or external
- if the valuation has not been updated because the directors are not aware of any material change, a statement to that effect
- date of the last full valuation (if not in the current period).

3 Depreciation

3.1 Introduction

DEFINITION

Depreciation is the measure of the cost or revalued amount of the economic benefits of the tangible fixed asset that have been consumed during the period.

Depreciation is the measure of the cost or revalued amount of the economic benefits of the tangible fixed asset that have been consumed during the period.

There is a note to the main definition as follows:

Consumption includes the wearing out, using up or other reduction in the useful economic life of a tangible fixed asset whether arising from use, effluxion of time or obsolescence through either changes in technology or demand for the goods and services produced by the asset.

3.2 Depreciable amount

DEFINITIONS

The **depreciable amount** is the cost or revalued amount of a tangible fixed asset less its residual value.

Residual value is the net realisable value of an asset at the end of its useful economic life.

The **useful economic life** of a tangible fixed asset is the period over which the entity expects to derive economic benefit from it.

FRS 15 requires that the depreciable amount of a tangible fixed asset should be allocated on a systematic basis over its useful economic life.

The **depreciable amount** is the cost (or revalued amount) of a tangible fixed asset less its residual value.

Residual value is the net realisable value of an asset at the end of its useful economic life.

The **useful economic life** of a tangible fixed asset is the period over which the entity expects to derive economic benefit from it.

The depreciation method used should reflect as fairly as possible the pattern in which the asset's economic benefits are consumed by the entity.

The depreciation charge for each period should be recognised as an expense in the profit and loss account unless it is permitted to be included in the carrying amount of another asset (for example, where it is part of development expenditure that is capitalised).

Depreciation is an application of the accruals concept rather than a means of measuring value. FRS 15 does not prescribe a particular method of depreciation.

3.3 Change in method

KEY POINT

A change from one method of providing depreciation to another is permissible only on the grounds that the new method will give a fairer presentation of the results.

A change from one method of providing depreciation to another is permissible only on the grounds that the new method will give a fairer presentation of the results and of the financial position.

This does not constitute a change in accounting policy. The carrying amount of the tangible fixed asset is depreciated using the revised method over the remaining useful economic life, beginning in the period in which the change is made.

3.4 Assets that have two or more major components

KEY POINT

Where a tangible fixed asset comprises two or more major components, each should be **depreciated separately** over its individual useful economic life.

Where a tangible fixed asset comprises two or more major components with substantially different useful economic lives, each component should be **depreciated separately** over its individual useful economic life.

Some assets require substantial expenditure every few years for overhauling and restoring major components. Examples include:

- replacing the lining of a blast furnace
- dry docking a ship
- replacing the roof of a building.

Previously, some entities dealt with this situation by setting up a provision for the expenditure, but FRS 12 *Provisions, contingent liabilities and contingent assets* has now prohibited this treatment (FRS 12 is discussed in a later chapter). Instead, the expenditure is capitalised and depreciated separately over its individual useful economic life.

Note that this kind of subsequent expenditure can only be capitalised if the asset is treated as separate components for depreciation purposes. Where a fixed asset is not accounted for as several different components, this kind of subsequent expenditure must be treated as normal repairs and maintenance and charged to the profit and loss account as it is incurred.

ACTIVITY **5**

An aircraft cost £1.5 million and has a useful economic life of 10 years. It is required by law to be overhauled every three years. The cost of the overhaul is estimated at £150,000. How should the cost of the overhaul be treated in the accounts?

Feedback to this activity is at the end of the chapter.

3.5 Depreciation of revalued assets

KEY POINT

Tangible fixed assets must be reviewed for **impairment** annually if they are not depreciated or if their remaining useful economic life is more than 50 years.

FRS 15 states the following about the **depreciation of revalued assets**.

- Subsequent expenditure on a tangible fixed asset that maintains or enhances the previously assessed standard of performance of the asset does not negate the need to charge **depreciation**.
- When either:
  - a tangible fixed asset is not depreciated on the grounds that the charge would be **immaterial** (either because of the length of the estimated remaining useful economic life or because the estimated residual value of the tangible fixed asset is not materially different from the carrying amount of the asset); or
  - the estimated remaining useful economic life of the tangible fixed asset **exceeds 50 years**,

  the asset should be **reviewed for impairment**, in accordance with FRS 11 (covered in a later chapter), at the end of each reporting period. (This does not apply to non-depreciable land.)

These requirements are designed to deal with two particular problems. We have already looked at the first of these, the treatment of subsequent expenditure.

The other problem is non-depreciation of revalued assets. In the past, many entities did not charge depreciation on revalued properties on the grounds that the assets were being maintained or refurbished regularly so that the economic life of the property was limitless. This treatment has been common in the hotel, brewing, public house and retail sectors.

It was widely expected that FRS 15 would require that all fixed assets were depreciated. However, the ASB has recognised that in rare cases, some tangible fixed assets may have very long useful economic lives. Entities can still avoid charging depreciation on the grounds that the charge is **immaterial**, but they must carry out annual **impairment reviews** as per FRS 11. This is likely to discourage non-depreciation as impairment reviews can be time consuming, complicated and costly and may result in reduced profits (if an impairment loss has to be recognised in the profit and loss account).

3.6 Transfers between reserves when an asset has been revalued

KEY POINT

It has become normal practice to make an annual **reserve transfer** equal to the difference between depreciation on the revalued amount and depreciation on the original cost.

When assets are carried at a valuation, FRS 15 states that depreciation must be based on the revalued amount and that the whole charge must pass through the profit and loss account. In theory, it is possible to split the depreciation charge between reserves. Only depreciation charged on historic cost passes directly through the profit and loss account while depreciation on the difference between cost and valuation is set against the revaluation reserve. This practice is known as 'split depreciation' and it is not acceptable.

However, it has become normal practice to make an annual reserve transfer equal to the difference between depreciation on the revalued amount and depreciation on the original cost. The illustrative examples included in FRS 3 adopt this treatment, thereby legitimising it.

ACTIVITY 6

Suggs Ltd sold one of its freehold properties on 30 June 20X4 (the last day of its accounting year). You are provided with the following information:

- Retained profit for the year, after charging depreciation on the above property, but before dealing with the gain on sale, is £797,000.
- Reserves at 30 June 20X3 comprised:

Profit and loss account	£1,852,000
Revaluation reserve	£937,000

-

	£
Original cost of property sold	700,000
Depreciation charged to date of revaluation (£700,000 × 2% = £14,000 pa for five years)	70,000
NBV at valuation	630,000
To revaluation reserve	270,000
Revaluation	900,000
Depreciation charge from date of revaluation to date of sale (£900,000 ÷ 45 = £20,000 pa for four years)	80,000
NBV at date of sale	820,000

- Annual transfers between the revaluation reserve and the profit and loss account have been made of the profits realised due to the additional depreciation charge.
- The property was sold for £932,000.

You are required to show the relevant extract from the profit and loss account and the reserves of Suggs Ltd for the year ended 30 June 20X4.

Feedback to this activity is at the end of the chapter.

3.7 Review of useful economic life and residual value

KEY POINT

Useful economic life should be **reviewed** at the end of each reporting period and revised if expectations are significantly different from previous estimates.

Useful economic life should be reviewed at the end of each reporting period and revised if expectations are significantly different from previous estimates. If a useful economic life is revised, the carrying amount of the asset at the date of revision should be depreciated over the revised remaining useful economic life.

Where the residual value is material it should be reviewed at the end of each reporting period to take account of reasonably expected technological changes based on prices prevailing at the date of acquisition (or revaluation). Any change should be accounted for prospectively over the asset's remaining useful economic life.

ACTIVITY **7**

An asset was purchased for £100,000 on 1 January 20X5 and is being depreciated over 5 years to a residual value of £10,000.

A general review of asset lives was undertaken and at 31 December 20X7 the remaining useful economic life was estimated at 7 years. Residual value was nil.

Calculate the depreciation charge for the year ended 31 December 20X7 and subsequent years.

Feedback to this activity is at the end of the chapter.

3.8 Disclosure

KEY POINT

FRS 15 requires the depreciation methods and rates used, and the useful economic lives to be disclosed, together with the effect of any change in method or useful economic life.

As well as the disclosures required by CA85 (see Chapter 6) FRS 15 requires the following disclosures for each class of tangible fixed assets:

- the depreciation methods used
- the useful economic lives or the depreciation rates used
- total depreciation charged for the period
- the effect of a change in useful economic lives or residual value in the period, where material.

Where there has been a change in the depreciation method used in the period, the effect should be disclosed, if material. The reason for the change should also be disclosed.

3.9 Evaluation of FRS 15

KEY POINT

FRS 15 discourages **creative accounting** and **cherry picking**. However, revaluing fixed assets is **optional** and **non-depreciation of revalued fixed assets** has not been prohibited.

On the whole, FRS 15 has been welcomed by users and preparers of financial statements.

- The requirement for regular revaluations has undoubted advantages in that it increases the comparability of financial statements and reduces opportunities for 'creative accounting'. (For example, many entities revalued assets during the 1980s and continued to use those valuations in their financial statements, despite the fact that property values subsequently fell.)
- The requirement to revalue all assets within a class means that entities will not be able to 'cherry pick' certain assets for revaluation while carrying others at historic cost. This will also increase comparability between entities.

However, there are some potential problems.

- Entities still have the choice of whether to revalue fixed assets, meaning that financial statements of different entities may still not be comparable. The ASB has accepted that enforcing the use of current values would not be practical, given that there is widespread resistance to the idea of current value accounting. Disclosures enable users to assess the effect of revaluations on the financial performance and position of an entity.
- The most controversial aspect of FRS 15 has probably been its failure to prohibit non-depreciation of revalued fixed assets (although it discourages the practice by requiring impairment reviews). Many commentators are concerned that this failure will lead to 'creative accounting' abuses.
- The ASB wishes to encourage the use of current values, as this provides relevant information to users of the financial statements. However, a few commentators fear that some entities could revert to using historic cost in order to avoid costly annual revaluations and the other disadvantages associated with using current values (for example, the higher depreciation charge and the requirement to 'report the bad news as well as the good' if market values fall).

4 SSAP 4 *Accounting for government grants*

4.1 Introduction

DEFINITIONS

Government is widely defined to include national government and all tiers of local and regional government. It also includes EC bodies.

Grants include cash or transfers of assets.

SSAP 4 was originally introduced following the advent of **regional development grants** under the Industry Act 1972. These grants were often related to capital expenditure and thus a standard was necessary to state how the grant should be accounted for.

Since the issue of SSAP 4, the variety of forms of government assistance available to industry has greatly increased: many are discretionary in nature both as to whether they are given at all and as to the amount given. Frequently, the terms on which grants are given do not make clear precisely the expenditure to which they are related. The problem facing accountants today is thus how to relate grants to **specific expenditure**.

Government is widely defined to include national government and all tiers of local and regional government. It also includes EC bodies.

Grants include cash or transfers of assets.

4.2 General principles

KEY POINT

Providing the conditions for receipt have been complied with, grants should be recognised in the profit and loss account so as to match them with the related expenditure.

Grants should not be recognised in the profit and loss account until the conditions for receipt have been complied with and there is reasonable assurance that the grant will be received. (This is **prudent**.)

Subject to this condition, grants should be recognised in the profit and loss account so as to match them with the expenditure towards which they are intended to contribute. (Application of the **accruals concept**.)

4.3 Revenue grants

KEY POINT

If the grant is paid when evidence is produced that certain **expenditure** has been incurred, or other **objectives** met, then it should be matched with that expenditure, or the costs of achieving the objective.

In the absence of evidence to the contrary, grants should be assumed to contribute towards the expenditure that is the basis for their payment. The explanatory foreword illustrates this principle by stating that if the grant is paid when evidence is produced that certain expenditure has been incurred, the grant should be matched with that expenditure.

However, if the grant is paid on a different basis, for example achievement of a non-financial objective, such as the creation of a specified number of new jobs, the grant should be matched with the identifiable costs of achieving that objective.

4.4 Alternative feasible ways of treating capital-based government grants received

Grants for fixed asset purchases should be recognised over the expected useful lives of the related assets.

KEY POINT

SSAP 4 permits either **writing off** the grant against asset cost and **depreciating the reduced cost**, or treating the grant as a **deferred credit** transferring a portion to revenue each year offsetting the higher depreciation charge on the original cost.

SSAP 4 permits two treatments. The explanatory foreword states that both treatments are acceptable in principle and capable of giving a true and fair view:

1 **write off** the grant against the cost of the fixed asset and **depreciate the reduced cost**

2 treat the grant as a **deferred credit** and transfer a portion to revenue each year, so offsetting the higher depreciation charge on the original cost.

Method 1 is obviously far simpler to operate. Method 2, however, has the advantage of ensuring that assets acquired at different times and in different locations are recorded on a uniform basis, regardless of changes in government policy.

However, CA85 requires that fixed assets should be stated at purchase price and this is defined as actual price paid plus any additional expenses. Legal opinion on this matter is that companies should not deduct grants from cost. Thus method 1 should only be adopted by unincorporated bodies, but in practice a large number of companies continue to use the method which contravenes CA85.

There are compelling arguments in favour of the deferred credit approach, not least being that it is difficult to reconcile the deduction from asset approach with the specific requirements of Sch 4 CA85. SSAP 4 continues to permit both treatments.

The two ways of dealing with capital grants are shown in the following example.

Example

A company opens a new factory in a development area and receives a government grant of £15,000 in respect of capital equipment costing £100,000. It depreciates all plant and machinery at 20% p.a. straight-line.

Show the balance sheet extracts to record the grant in the first year under methods 1 and 2 above.

Solution

1 Write off against asset:

Balance sheet extract

	£
Fixed assets:	
Plant and machinery at cost (100 – 15)	85,000
Less: Depreciation (20% × 85)	17,000
	68,000

2 Deferred credit:

Government grant deferred credit account

	£		£
Profit and loss a/c transfer for year: 20% × £15,000	3,000	Cash grant	15,000
Balance c/d	12,000		
	15,000		15,000
		Balance b/d	12,000

Balance sheet extract

	£
Fixed assets:	
Plant and machinery at cost	100,000
Less: Depreciation	20,000
	80,000
Deferred income:	
Government grant	12,000

4.5 Other grants

Purpose of grant	*Recognise in profit and loss account*
To give immediate financial support	When receivable
To reimburse previously incurred costs	When receivable
To finance general activities over a period	In relevant period
To compensate for a loss of income	In relevant period

4.6 Provisions and contingent liabilities

KEY POINT

If there is an obligation to repay the grant, and the repayment is probable it should be treated in accordance with FRS 12.

The SSAP's explanatory foreword states that enterprises should consider regularly whether there is a likelihood of a **breach of conditions** on which the grant was made. If such a breach has occurred or appears likely to occur, the likelihood of having to make a **repayment** should be considered.

If there is an obligation to repay the grant and the repayment is probable, then it should be provided for in accordance with the requirements of FRS 12. It should be accounted for by being set off against any **unamortised deferred income** relating to the grant. Any excess should be immediately charged to profit and loss account.

ACTIVITY 8

A Ltd has been awarded government assistance in the form of a training grant. Suggest three ways in which the grant could be accounted for.

Feedback to this activity is at the end of the chapter.

4.7 Disclosure

KEY POINT

The effects of grants on the profit and loss and deferred income accounts, and the accounting policy used should be disclosed.

The following information should be disclosed:

- accounting policy
- effects of government grants:
  - amount credited to profit and loss account
  - balance on deferred income account
- if other forms of government assistance have had a material effect on the results:
  - the nature
  - an estimate of those effects
- potential liabilities to repay grants should if necessary be disclosed in accordance with FRS 12.

5 SSAP 19 *Accounting for investment properties*

5.1 Introduction

Under the general requirements of FRS 15, all fixed assets having a finite useful life should be subject to a depreciation charge. Investment property companies objected to this requirement and as the ASC conceded they had reasonable grounds for objecting, SSAP 19 *Accounting for investment properties* was issued, providing a solution to the problem of investment property accounting. It should be looked at as an addition to FRS 15.

DEFINITION

An **investment property** is an interest in land and/or buildings in respect of which construction work and development have been completed, and which is being held for its investment potential.

Definition of an investment property

An **investment property** is an interest in land and/or buildings:

- in respect of which construction work and development have been completed; and
- which is being held for its investment potential, any rental income being negotiated at arm's length.

The following are exceptions from the definition:

- a property which is owned and occupied by a company for its own purposes is not an investment property
- a property let to and occupied by another group company is not an investment property for the purposes of its own accounts or the group accounts.

5.2 Why do investment properties need a different accounting treatment?

KEY POINT

Investment properties are not held for consumption within the operations of the business, so to the user of the financial statements the most important information about such assets relates to their **current value**.

SSAP 19 justifies the different accounting treatment for investment properties on the following grounds. Such assets are not held for consumption within the operations of the business but are held as investments. Therefore to the user of the financial statements, the most relevant information about such assets relates to their **current value**. Calculation of depreciation in such circumstances does not benefit the user from either a balance sheet perspective or a profit and loss account perspective, as the asset is not consumed in the business operations.

Another way of justifying the special treatment is that the disposal of such an asset would not materially affect the trading operations of the business; it therefore cannot be relevant to depreciate such items.

5.3 Standard accounting practice

KEY POINT

Investment properties should not be depreciated. The balance sheet should show **the open market value**, and changes in value should be taken to the **STRGL**.

Investment properties should not be subject to periodic charges for depreciation on the basis set out in FRS 15. However, properties held on **lease** should be **depreciated** on the basis set out in FRS 15 at least over the period when the unexpired term is 20 years or less.

Investment properties should be included in the balance sheet at their **open market value**.

The names of the persons making the valuation, or particulars of their qualifications, should be disclosed together with the bases of valuation used by them. If a person making a valuation is an employee or officer of the company or group which owns the property, this fact should be disclosed.

Changes in the value of investment properties should not be taken to the profit and loss account but should be taken to the **STRGL** (being a movement on an **investment revaluation reserve**), unless a deficit on an individual investment property is expected to be permanent. In this case it should be charged in the profit and loss account of the period.

Example

Industrial Ltd produces accounts to 31 December. On 1 January 20X8 it moved from its factory in Bolton to a new purpose-built factory in Rochdale (expected life of fifty years). The old premises were available for letting from 1 January 20X8 and a lease was granted on 30 September 20X8 to B Ltd at an annual rental of £8,000. A valuation of the old premises at 31 December 20X8 was £160,000.

Extracts from the balance sheet as at 31 December 20X7 were as follows:

Fixed assets	*Cost*	*Depreciation*	*NBV*
	£	£	£
Land and buildings:			
Old premises	200,000	80,000	120,000
New premises	450,000		450,000

Show the relevant balance sheet entries at 31 December 20X8.

Solution

Extracts from the balance sheet as at 31 December 20X8 are:

Fixed assets	*Cost*	*Depreciation*	*NBV*
	£	£	£
Land and buildings	450,000	9,000	441,000
Investment property at valuation			160,000
Reserves			
Investment revaluation reserve (160,000 – 120,000)			40,000

5.4 Treatment of annual valuations

SSAP 19 regards the total investment property revaluation reserve as being available to cover temporary deficits.

Example

Newline Investment Co Ltd purchased three investment properties on 31 December 20X1, and the following valuations have been made during the period to 31 December 20X4:

	31 Dec 20X1	*31 Dec 20X2*	*31 Dec 20X3*	*31 Dec 20X4*
	£000	£000	£000	£000
Property A	200	180*	120*	120
Property B	300	330	340	310**
Property C	400	440	450	450
Total	900	950	910	880

* deficit expected to be temporary
** deficit expected to be permanent

Show the balance on the investment revaluation reserve for each balance sheet date.

Solution

The investment revaluation reserve would be disclosed for the various years as follows:

	Year ended 31 December 20X2	20X3	20X4
	£000	£000	£000
Balance b/d	Nil	50	10
Net revaluation	50	(40)	–
Balance c/d	50	10	10

The permanent deficit of £30,000 arising on property B in the year ended 31 December 20X4 will be charged through the profit and loss account.

ACTIVITY 9

State whether the following are investment properties and, if so, whether they should be depreciated:

1 A freehold property bought for its investment potential and leased to an associated company at an arm's length rental.
2 A leasehold property let to a third party. The leasehold has 18 years to run.
3 An office building owned and occupied by the same company.
4 A leasehold property with 24 years left to run which is let to a subsidiary at an arm's length rental.

Feedback to this activity is at the end of the chapter.

5.5 The validity and legality of SSAP 19

KEY POINT

The requirement of SSAP 19 not to depreciate is in conflict with the requirement of CA85 to depreciate assets with a finite useful life. SSAP 19 states that the treatment is necessary to show a **true and fair view** and so the overriding provisions of CA85 are invoked.

The legality of SSAP 19 is questioned as the requirement not to depreciate is in conflict with the requirement of CA85 to depreciate all fixed assets with a finite useful life.

SSAP 19 states, however, that the treatment is necessary in order to show a **true and fair view** and thus use is made of the overriding provisions of CA85 to show such a true and fair view.

Some commentators continue to argue that SSAP 19 does not represent a valid treatment and is merely an example of the ASC giving way to the demands of property investment companies which have very high values of assets relative to profits. This is mainly due to the fact that an investment is made in property in order to make not only returns of income (i.e. rent) but also capital (when the property is eventually sold). These companies argue that, since the annual changes in the value of the properties are not reflected in the profit and loss account (as they are unrealised), to charge depreciation against the 'income' part of the overall profit anticipated is unreasonable.

6 UITF Abstract 5 *Transfers from current assets to fixed assets*

6.1 The issue

KEY POINT

To counter companies avoiding charging the profit and loss account with **write-downs to net realisable value**, when assets are transferred from current assets to fixed assets, the transfer should be made at the lower of cost and net realisable value.

Where it is decided to retain a current asset for use on a continuing basis in the company's activities, it becomes a fixed asset and the question arises as to the appropriate transfer value. Of particular concern is the possibility that companies could avoid charging the profit and loss account with **write-downs to net realisable value** by transferring the relevant assets from current assets to fixed assets at above net realisable value and then charging any subsequent write-down to revaluation reserve.

6.2 UITF consensus

Where assets are transferred from current to fixed, the transfer should be made at the lower of cost and net realisable value at the date of transfer. Fixed asset accounting rules then apply subsequent to the transfer.

Conclusion

FRS 15 requires that:

- a tangible fixed asset should initially be measured at its cost
- where tangible fixed assets are revalued, the valuation should be kept up to date
- tangible fixed assets should be depreciated over their estimated useful economic lives
- the useful economic lives and residual values of tangible fixed assets should be reviewed annually and revised where necessary.

SSAP 4 states that government grants should be matched with the expenditure to which they contribute. Where a company receives a grant towards the cost of a fixed asset, the grant should be taken to a deferred income account (a creditor) and should be released to the profit and loss account as income over the useful economic life of the asset to which it relates.

Investment properties meeting the definition in SSAP 19 are not depreciated. Instead they are included in the balance sheet at their open market value.

SELF-TEST QUESTIONS

1 How are tangible fixed assets measured on initial recognition? (1.2)

2 When can an entity capitalise subsequent expenditure? (1.4)

3 If an entity adopts a policy of revaluation, must all tangible fixed assets be revalued? (2.2)

4 If an entity adopts a policy of revaluation, how often must a full valuation be carried out? (2.3)

5 What is the useful economic life of a fixed asset? (3.2)

6 Is a change in the method of depreciation a change in accounting policy? (3.3)

7 Is it possible for an entity not to depreciate its tangible fixed assets? (3.5)

8 What are the two possible methods of accounting for a capital grant? (4.4)

9 What is an investment property? (5.1)

10 How are investment properties accounted for in the financial statements? (5.3)

EXAM-TYPE QUESTION

Trent plc

Trent plc is a quoted company that owns a large number of hotels throughout the UK. The company's latest trial balance at 31 December 20X0 contains the following balances:

	£000	£000
Hotel buildings:		
Cost	490,000	
Depreciation to date		46,200
Hotel fixtures and fittings:		
Cost	18,000	
Depreciation to date		9,400

- During the year the company spent a total of £12m on a new hotel and purchased new fixtures for £7m. These acquisitions have been included in the relevant trial balance totals.
- Hotels are to be depreciated by 2% of cost, and fixtures and fittings by 25% of the reducing balance, with a full year's depreciation to be charged in the year of acquisition or revaluation.

During the year, the company's external auditors expressed some concern that a large proportion of the hotels were several years old and yet none had ever been professionally valued. The directors were unsure whether there was a material difference between market valuations and net book values, and commissioned a valuation on three of the company's oldest hotels in order to see whether a more detailed valuation might prove useful.

	Original cost £000	*Depreciation to* *31.12.20X0* £000	*Market value at* *31.12.20X0* £000	*Estimated useful life at* *31.12.20X0* Years
Hotel A	800	180	1,300	50
Hotel B	700	120	850	30
Hotel C	1,000	140	650	40

- During the year ended 31 December 20X1 the directors are planning to start a major programme of repairs and refurbishment on the company's hotels. Over a five-year period the buildings will be checked to ensure that they are structurally sound, and they will be repaired wherever necessary. Preliminary investigations suggest that some of the hotels will not achieve their expected useful lives if the company does not invest in this preventive maintenance. The company will also redecorate the hotels and replace most of the furniture in the bedrooms and restaurants. The redecoration will create a new corporate image for all of Trent plc's hotels that will improve the company's marketing and promotion.

Required:

(a) Prepare the note that will appear in the financial statements in respect of tangible fixed assets. **(7 marks)**

The directors are keen to evaluate the effects of the revaluation of the hotels. They have asked for some further analyses and reports.

Required:

(b) Calculate the effects of the revaluation on the depreciation charge on the three hotels for the year ended 31 December 20X1, assuming that a full year's depreciation is charged on the revalued amounts **(3 marks)**

(c) Calculate the balance which would appear on the revaluation reserve in respect of the revalued hotels. **(3 marks)**

The directors regard the company's hotels as assets which generate both income and capital gains. Two of the hotels which were valued are appreciating in value. The company has sold hotels in the past in order to realise such gains.

Required:

(d) Explain whether it would be feasible for the directors to justify charging no depreciation, on the grounds that their hotels tend to increase in value or are held as investment properties. Your answer should refer to accounting concepts and to relevant accounting standards. **(7 marks)**

(e) The directors are keen to capitalise the costs of the programme of repairs and refurbishment. You are required to describe the factors which will have to be considered in deciding whether this will be acceptable from an accounting point of view. Your answer should refer to accounting concepts and to the relevant accounting standards as appropriate. **(5 marks)**

(Total: 25 marks)

For the answer to this question, see the 'Answers' section at the end of the book.

FEEDBACK TO ACTIVITY **1**

Total amount to be included in fixed assets at 31 December 20X5:

	£m
Lease	25
Building	9
Fittings	6
Interest capitalised (40 × 10% × 9/12)	3
	43

Only 9 months' interest can be capitalised, because FRS 15 states that capitalisation of borrowing costs must cease when the asset is substantially complete.

No depreciation is charged, because the supermarket is not brought into use until 1 January 20X6.

FEEDBACK TO ACTIVITY 2

The relevant extracts from the final accounts at 31 December 20X8 are as follows:

Profit and loss account (extract)	£000
Depreciation (1,400 ÷ 40)	35
Notes: Tangible fixed assets: Buildings	
Cost at 1 January 20X8	1,200
Revaluation	200
Valuation at 31 December 20X8	1,400
Accumulated depreciation at 1 January 20X8	144
Revaluation	(144)
Charge for year (1,400,000 ÷ 40)	35
Accumulated depreciation at 31 December 20X8	35
Net book value at 31 December 20X8 (1,400,000 – 35,000)	1,365
Net book value at 1 January 20X8	1,056
Notes: Reserves	
Revaluation reserve (1,400 – 1,056)	344

EXAM HINT

Note the presentation of the fixed asset note carefully; it is often examined. The double entry on revaluation is:

	£000	£000
Dr Fixed asset cost	200	
Dr Accumulated depreciation	144	
Cr Revaluation reserve		344

The accumulated depreciation account is cleared to the revaluation reserve because that depreciation is no longer relevant. After the asset is revalued, depreciation is based on the carrying amount (i.e. £1,400,000) and the asset is depreciated over its remaining useful economic life from the date of the revaluation.

Over the 40-year life of the revalued asset, the balance on the revaluation reserve will become realised. This is normally accounted for by annual transfer between reserves, from revaluation reserve to profit and loss account reserve, of the amount becoming realised each year (£344,000 ÷ 40 = £8,600 p.a. in the example above).

FEEDBACK TO ACTIVITY 3

Year ended 31 December 20X4: a revaluation gain of £90,000 is reported in the STRGL.

Year ended 31 December 20X5: a revaluation loss of £130,000 occurs and is dealt with as follows:

	£000
STRGL (480 – 400) (W)	80
Profit and loss account	50
	130

Working

	£000
Cost at 1 January 20X4	500
Less: depreciation (500 ÷ 10)	(50)
	450
Revaluation gain	90
Valuation at 31 December 20X4	540
Less: depreciation (540 ÷ 9)	(60)
	480
Revaluation loss	(130)
Valuation at 31 December 20X5	350
Depreciated historic cost at 31 December 20X5 (500 – 100)	400

FEEDBACK TO ACTIVITY 4

Profit on disposal

	£000	£000
Sales proceeds		900
Valuation at 31 December 20X4	810	
Less: depreciation ((810 ÷ 9)× 2)	(180)	
Net book value		(630)
Profit and loss account		270

FEEDBACK TO ACTIVITY 5

The overhaul costs of £150,000 are depreciated separately from the rest of the aircraft, so that depreciation of £50,000 is charged each year until the next overhaul. When the expenditure is incurred, at the end of the three-year period, it is capitalised and depreciated over the three years until the next major overhaul.

The balance of £1,350,000 is depreciated over ten years. The annual depreciation charge is £185,000 (£135,000 relating to the aircraft and £50,000 relating to the overhaul costs).

FEEDBACK TO ACTIVITY 6

- Set up a proforma profit and loss account with extracts of the relevant items to be disclosed.
- Profit on sale of property will be the difference between sale proceeds and NBV at date of sale.
- Retained earnings will be as given plus the gain on sale of property.

Profit and loss account for the year

	£
Operating profit	X
Profit on sale of property (932 – 820)	112,000
Tax, dividends, etc.	X
Retained (797 + 112)	909,000

- Calculate the transfer to be made from the revaluation reserve of the amount realised on the sale of the property. This will comprise the original amount taken to the reserve on revaluation less annual transfers re the additional depreciation charge.

Working

Transfer re sale

	£
To revaluation reserve at date of revaluation	270,000
Less: Previously realised 4 × (20,000 – 14,000)	24,000
	246,000

- Prepare a statement of reserves showing all movements on both the profit and loss account and the revaluation reserve. Transfers need to be made from the revaluation reserve of annual amounts realised due to the additional depreciation charge, and the amount realised due to the sale of the property.

	Profit and loss account	*Revaluation reserve*
	£	£
Balance at 1 July 20X3	1,852,000	937,000
Retained profit for year	909,000	
Transfer re additional depreciation charge (20,000 – 14,000)	6,000	(6,000)
Sale of property	246,000	(246,000)
Balance at 30 June 20X4	3,013,000	685,000

FEEDBACK TO ACTIVITY **7**

The depreciation charge is calculated as follows:

	£
Net book value at 31 December 20X6 (100,000 – 36,000)	64,000
Annual depreciation charge (64,000 ÷ 8)	8,000

Note that the estimated remaining life is seven years from 31 December 20X7, but this information is used to compute the current year's charge as well.

FEEDBACK TO ACTIVITY **8**

SSAP 4 requires that grants should be matched with expenditure to which it is intended to contribute. Hence A Ltd could account for the training grant as follows:

- match it against direct training costs
- match it against employee salary costs over the period of time training takes place.
- take it to profit and loss account over the estimated period during which A Ltd or the employees are expected to benefit from the training.

FEEDBACK TO ACTIVITY **9**

1 This is an investment property. An associated company is not a group company. The property should not be depreciated under SSAP 19.

2 This is an investment property. As the lease has less than 20 years to run it should be depreciated.

3 This is not an investment property as it is used by the company for the purposes of its own business.

4 This is not an investment property as it is occupied by a group company.

Chapter 17

FIXED ASSETS – GOODWILL AND INTANGIBLE ASSETS

CHAPTER CONTENTS

1 Problems of accounting for goodwill

2 Intangible assets

3 FRS 10 *Goodwill and intangible assets*

4 SSAP 13 *Accounting for research and development*

5 FRS 11 *Impairment of fixed assets and goodwill*

This chapter considers accounting for intangible fixed assets. It covers three standards:

- FRS 10 *Goodwill and intangible assets*
- SSAP 13 *Accounting for research and development*
- FRS 11 *Impairment of fixed assets and goodwill.*

SSAP 13 should already be familiar to you from your earlier studies. You should also be aware of the basic principles of accounting for goodwill. At this level, you will study the topic of goodwill and intangible assets in more depth.

This chapter also covers how to deal with the situation when a fixed asset suffers a loss in value, known as an impairment.

Objectives

By the time you have finished this chapter you should be able to:

- discuss the nature and possible accounting treatments of goodwill
- distinguish between goodwill and other intangible assets
- describe the accounting treatment for intangible assets
- describe the circumstances in which negative goodwill arises and its subsequent accounting treatment and disclosure
- describe and apply the requirements of SSAP 13
- define the recoverable amount of an asset and define impairment losses
- identify circumstances that may indicate that an impairment has occurred
- describe what is meant by an income generating unit
- state the basis on which impairment losses should be allocated
- allocate a given impairment loss to the assets of an income generating unit.

1 Problems of accounting for goodwill

1.1 Nature of goodwill

DEFINITION

Goodwill is the difference between the value of a business as a whole and the aggregate of the fair values of its separable net assets.

Goodwill is the difference between the value of a business as a whole and the aggregate of the fair values of its separable net assets. Goodwill may exist because of any combination of a number of possible factors: reputation for quality or service; technical expertise; possession of favourable contracts; good management and staff.

DEFINITIONS

Purchased goodwill is the difference between the cost of an acquired entity and the aggregate of the fair values of that entity's identifiable assets and liabilities.

FRS 10 contains the following definitions:

- Purchased goodwill is the difference between the cost of an acquired entity and the aggregate of the fair values of that entity's identifiable assets and liabilities.
- **Identifiable assets and liabilities** are the assets and liabilities of an entity that are capable of being disposed of or settled separately, without disposing of a business of the entity.

Identifiable assets and liabilities are the assets and liabilities of an entity that are capable of being disposed of or settled separately, without disposing of a business of the entity.

Fair value is the amount at which an asset or liability could be exchanged in an arm's length transaction between informed and willing parties, other than in a forced or liquidation sale.

FRS 10 does not include a definition of fair value, but FRS 7 defines it as follows:

- **Fair value** is the amount at which an asset or liability could be exchanged in an arm's length transaction between informed and willing parties, other than in a forced or liquidation sale.

There is an important distinction between purchased and non-purchased goodwill (sometimes called inherent goodwill or internally generated goodwill).

Purchased goodwill arises when one business acquires another as a going concern. The term therefore includes goodwill arising on the inclusion of a subsidiary or associated company in the consolidated accounts.

Purchased goodwill will be recognised within the accounts because at a specific point in time the fact of purchase has established a figure of value for the business as a whole which can be compared with the fair value of the individual net assets acquired. The difference will be incorporated in the accounts of the acquiring company as the cost of the acquisition.

KEY POINT

As purchased goodwill has a limited life, it should be **amortised**.

Purchased goodwill has a limited life: as time passes the reputation, for instance, of the business under its former owners ceases to have any value because potential customers begin to form a view of its performance under the present ownership. Purchased goodwill ought, therefore, to be **amortised**.

KEY POINT

Unless a business changes hands, goodwill can only be **estimated subjectively** and will not be recognised in the accounts.

Goodwill exists in any successful business. However, if the business has never changed hands, this goodwill will not be recognised in the accounts because no event has occurred to identify its value. Without a purchase, it can only be **subjectively estimated**. This is inherent goodwill.

Of course, a business which has acquired another and has thus purchased goodwill, may then build up inherent goodwill of its own, but only the former will be reflected in the accounts.

KEY POINT

There is no universally accepted method of accounting for goodwill. Accounting methods tend to result in inconsistencies.

There is no universally accepted method of accounting for goodwill. The ASB itself summed up the problem in a Discussion Paper as follows:

> *Purchased goodwill is ... an accounting anomaly. Every method of accounting for it results in inconsistencies with other aspects of financial reporting.*

Despite these problems, purchased goodwill arises from a distinct transaction that must be accounted for.

1.2 The advantages and disadvantages of each of the methods of accounting for goodwill

In this section, the principal ways of accounting for **purchased goodwill** in the past are listed, together with the major arguments for and against each of them.

Carry as an asset, amortised over useful life through the profit and loss account

Arguments for:

- Goodwill is an asset on which capital has been expended in exchange for benefits which will materialise in future periods. Although different in quality and character from other assets, it does exist and can be purchased or sold, and as such it should be treated as an asset.
- The expense of acquiring purchased goodwill should be matched against the extra earnings generated from its acquisition.
- Amortisation reflects the replacement of purchased goodwill with inherent goodwill over a period of time.

KEY POINT

This method recognises purchased goodwill as an asset (but not inherent goodwill). **Amortisation** reflects the replacement of **purchased** goodwill with **inherent** goodwill, but the amortisation period is arbitrary.

Arguments against:

- Comparability is lost when one type of goodwill ('purchased') is treated as an asset while another ('non-purchased') is not recognised as an asset.
- The life of goodwill is indeterminate, and even if determined, a single event may drastically alter that life. Any amortisation period is therefore too arbitrary to be realistic.

Eliminate against reserves on acquisition

Arguments for:

- Goodwill is not an asset in the normal sense of the word; it is not **independently realisable** and many of the factors contributing to it are beyond the control of management. Thus it is not prudent to carry goodwill as an asset in the balance sheet and, as a once-and-for-all expense of acquisition, it should be written off as it arises.
- Goodwill will usually be worthless in a forced liquidation.

Arguments against:

KEY POINT

Elimination is **inconsistent** with the treatment of other fixed assets, which must be **capitalised** and **depreciated** or **amortised**.

- Since consideration has been given, clearly an asset existed. If so, then it would seem excessively prudent to write it off immediately.
- It is assumed that the accounts are prepared on a **going concern basis**, which renders the point about the worth of goodwill in a forced liquidation irrelevant.
- Elimination is **inconsistent** with the treatment of other fixed assets, which must be **capitalised** and **depreciated** or **amortised**.

Carry as a permanent asset unless diminution in value (impairment) becomes evident

Arguments for:

- Purchased goodwill does not lose value with the passage of time as it should be maintained in the normal course of business.
- Following the principles of FRS 15, that depreciation should be provided on the cost less the net realisable value of an asset, if the goodwill is maintained then net realisable value will be equal to or exceed cost so that no write-off will be appropriate.
- The expenditure incurred in the normal course of business to generate inherent goodwill is charged to profit and loss. If purchased goodwill is also depreciated, there will be a double charge.

KEY POINT

The permanent asset method does not recognise that purchased goodwill is **consumed** and replaced by inherent goodwill. **CA85** requires purchased goodwill to be treated as an asset subject to depreciation.

Arguments against:

- Purchased goodwill is not maintained, but is **consumed** over a period of time and replaced by newly generated inherent goodwill which is not accounted for.
- The residual value of purchased goodwill is nil; it is the inherent goodwill by which it has been replaced which is subsequently valued.
- The expense of maintaining inherent goodwill is a normal trading charge falling on any business; the depreciation of purchased goodwill is the consequence of a business acquisition.
- This method is also contrary to **CA85**, which requires purchased goodwill of an individual company to be treated as an asset subject to depreciation.

The dangling debit

Under this approach, goodwill is shown as a deduction from the subtotal of share capital and reserves.

KEY POINT

The '**dangling debit**' approach shows goodwill as a deduction from the subtotal of share capital and reserves. This is contrary to CA85.

Advocates of the '**dangling debit**' approach argue that goodwill is not an asset in the normal sense of the word, having no objective value. Goodwill arises only because of the accounting conventions of double entry bookkeeping, and should be presented in such a way as to balance the accounts without creating any accounting entries. The dangling debit gives the fullest possible disclosure and allows the user of accounts to treat it in any way considered appropriate. Investment analysts normally disregard goodwill, and the dangling debit presenting goodwill outside the normal framework of results is in line with this approach.

This method has been rejected on the grounds of **ambiguity**; it is writing off goodwill against reserves while implying that the goodwill remains available as a form of asset. In addition, it is **contrary to CA85**, which presents goodwill as a fixed asset in the statutory formats.

The separate write-off reserve

KEY POINT

The **separate write-off reserve** method develops the dangling debit approach, by avoiding problems with the CA 85.

This is a development of the dangling debit approach and is designed to overcome the legal problems associated with the dangling debit.

A reserve is created and named as a '**goodwill write-off reserve**' or something similar. The goodwill is then charged against this reserve leaving a negative balance equivalent in amount to the goodwill. It is thus effectively the same as the dangling debit approach and thus the same advantages and disadvantages apply. However, as it is a reserve, it can be argued that the CA85 problems have been overcome.

1.3 Goodwill from the viewpoint of management and users of the financial statements

The previous sections have set out the conceptual arguments for and against each of the main methods of accounting for purchased goodwill. The three main methods of accounting for positive purchased goodwill also have practical advantages and disadvantages for management and for users of the financial statements.

The viewpoint of management

KEY POINT

Capitalisation and amortisation results in reduced profits.

Preparers of accounts have tended to resist **capitalisation and amortisation of goodwill**, because amortisation results in reduced profits. Opponents of amortisation have also argued that, where large sums are spent on maintaining and developing the value of an acquired business, a requirement to amortise a significant part of the investment over an arbitrary period has no economic meaning.

KEY POINT

Carrying goodwill as a **permanent asset** avoids reducing profits through **amortisation** and the **elimination of reserves**. However, **impairment reviews** will be necessary, which may be subjective, time-consuming and costly.

The main alternative, **elimination against reserves**, also has disadvantages. Immediate elimination of goodwill gives the impression that the acquirer's net worth has been depleted or even eliminated. A 'weak' balance sheet may result in the company being perceived as a 'target' in takeover bids and may make it difficult for the company to raise finance.

Carrying **goodwill in the balance sheet indefinitely**, unless there is an impairment in value, recognises that purchased goodwill is neither an identifiable asset like other assets, nor an immediate loss in value. It also avoids the reduction of profits through an amortisation charge and the elimination of reserves. However, to establish whether there has been an impairment in value it is necessary to carry out an **impairment review**. This relies on forecasts of future cash flows and may be subjective. Impairment reviews may also be time-consuming and costly.

The viewpoint of users of the financial statements

Immediate elimination against reserves has disadvantages for users of the financial statements.

- If goodwill is not included in the assets on which a return must be earned, management is not **held accountable** for the amount that it has invested in goodwill.
- Costs attributed to building up internally generated goodwill are offset against profits in the profit and loss account. The costs of purchased goodwill are not charged in the profit and loss account. This means that companies that grow by **acquisition** may appear to be more profitable than those that grow **organically**.

KEY POINT

If goodwill is carried as an asset, management performance is easier to judge, but it must then either be amortised or reviewed for impairment in value – both subjective approaches.

If goodwill is carried as an asset in the balance sheet, users are better able to judge the performance of management. Although purchased goodwill is not in itself an asset, it is part of a larger asset, the investment in another business. Including goodwill as an asset reflects management's success (or otherwise) in maintaining its value and generating a return from its investment.

However, if goodwill is carried in the balance sheet, it must either be amortised or reviewed for impairment in value. Both these approaches rely on the judgement of management and can only be **subjective**.

2 Intangible assets

2.1 Introduction

DEFINITION

Intangible assets are non-financial fixed assets that do not have physical substance but are identifiable and are controlled by the entity through custody or legal rights.

Intangible assets are non-financial fixed assets that do not have physical substance but are identifiable and are controlled by the entity through custody or legal rights.

Intangible assets may comprise **brands**, **patents**, **licences**, **publishing titles**, **franchises**, **quotas** and other types of asset. Some intangible assets, such as **brands**, are very similar in nature to goodwill, so that it can be difficult to distinguish between them. The important difference between goodwill and intangible assets is that an identifiable intangible asset **can be disposed of separately without disposing of the business of the entity**. If this is not the case, it is effectively part of goodwill.

KEY POINT

A **brand** is wider than a '**trade name**' because if a brand is purchased, the acquisition often involves the acquisition of many of the supporting functions which make the brand produce profits.

The term 'brand' is difficult to define precisely. The constituents of a brand include a recognised name, a product or range of products, an established operation and market position, marketing and other specialist know-how, and trading connections.

It is a wider term than '**trade name**' because, if a brand is purchased, the acquisition often involves the acquisition of many of the supporting functions which make the brand produce profits.

Thus a brand is a combination of factors expected to produce enhanced earnings just like goodwill. This analysis is further supported by the fact that brands and goodwill are commonly valued using earnings multiples.

2.2 The problem

The accounting treatment of intangible assets has been the subject of controversy in recent years. To understand the problem it is necessary to consider the context which gave rise to it.

Some companies, following an acquisition, assigned fair values to intangible assets of various types rather than to goodwill. Companies who made such a classification avoided having to apply the treatment required for accounting for goodwill to the assets thus identified. Until the issue of FRS 10 in 1997, there was no accounting standard dealing with intangible assets other than development expenditure and so intangible assets could be carried forward in the balance sheet indefinitely without mandatory review.

There was the possibility that it would become widespread practice to incorporate similar assets in the balance sheet by revaluation rather than by acquisition. The balance sheet would thus include 'home-grown' intangibles, as well as those which had been acquired at a known cost or an assigned fair value.

2.3 Arguments for and against including brands and similar intangible assets in the balance sheet

No one would deny that intangible assets are of real economic value to businesses, and in certain industry sectors, they are of overwhelming importance to the success of the enterprise. However, by their nature many intangible assets have characteristics which cause accounting difficulty.

Arguments for inclusion:

KEY POINT

Including intangible assets in the balance sheet reflects the **real value** of the business; results in accounting **consistency**; increased **earnings** and **net asset value** per share, and reduced **gearing**.

- Including intangible assets in the balance sheet reflects the '**real**' value of the business.
- Since goodwill and development costs may be capitalised, capitalising other intangibles results in **consistency** of accounting treatment.
- It would result in increased **earnings** per share, increased **net asset value** per share and reduced **gearing**.
- It would provide useful information to users of the accounts.
- Realistic asset values are believed to discourage potential takeover bids.

Arguments against inclusion:

KEY POINT

Arguably, including intangible assets in the balance sheet does not reflect real value, as this depends on the market's **perception of future performance**. Many intangibles cannot be measured at a monetary value with sufficient **reliability**.

- The balance sheet cannot possibly reflect the 'real' (or market) value of a business, as this depends on the market's **perception of its future performance**, not on the current value of its assets.
- Many intangibles cannot be measured at a monetary value with sufficient **reliability**. According to the Statement of Principles, they should therefore not be recognised as assets.
- Even if it were possible to arrive at a valuation, this would be time-consuming, costly and inherently subjective.

3 FRS 10 *Goodwill and intangible assets*

3.1 Why was a new accounting standard necessary?

FRS 10 was issued in December 1997 and replaced SSAP 22 *Accounting for goodwill*. Most commentators regarded SSAP 22 as unsatisfactory because it permitted a choice between two different accounting treatments. Entities chose the accounting treatment which gave the most favourable view of earnings and net assets. The preferred alternative, **immediate elimination against reserves**, was criticised for two main reasons:

- it gave the impression that the acquirer's **net worth** had been **depleted** or **eliminated**
- the financial statements **overstated** the **rate of return** on acquired investments.

In addition, there was clearly a need for an accounting standard which dealt with other intangible fixed assets as well. The similarities between goodwill and certain intangible assets such as brand names made it appropriate to consider the two together.

KEY POINT

The objective of FRS 10 is to ensure that capitalised goodwill and intangible assets are charged in the profit and loss account and sufficient information is disclosed to enable users to determine their impact.

3.2 Objective

The objective of FRS 10 is to ensure that:

- capitalised goodwill and intangible assets are charged in the profit and loss account in the periods in which they are depleted; and
- sufficient information is disclosed in the financial statements to enable users to determine the impact of goodwill and intangible assets on the financial position and performance of the reporting entity.

Note that the FRS applies to all intangible assets with the exception of:

- oil and gas exploration and development costs
- research and development costs (already covered by SSAP 13)
- any other intangible assets that are specifically addressed by another accounting standard.

KEY POINT

Internally generated goodwill should not be capitalised. Positive purchased goodwill should be included in the balance sheet as an intangible fixed asset.

3.3 Goodwill

- Positive purchased goodwill should be capitalised and classified as an intangible fixed asset on the balance sheet.
- Internally generated goodwill should not be capitalised.

3.4 Other intangible assets

FRS 10 recognises that there are many types of intangible asset. Although some intangible assets are very similar to goodwill, some can be readily identified and reliably valued.

KEY POINT

An intangible asset purchased separately from a business should be capitalised at its **cost**. An intangible asset acquired with a business should be capitalised **separately** from goodwill if its value can be measured reliably.

- An intangible asset purchased separately from a business should be capitalised at its cost.

Examples of assets which might be purchased separately from a business include copyrights, patents and licences.

- An intangible asset acquired as part of the acquisition of a business should be capitalised separately from goodwill if its value can be measured reliably on initial recognition. It should initially be recorded at its fair value.
- If its value cannot be measured reliably, an intangible asset purchased as part of the acquisition of a business should be subsumed within the amount of the purchase price attributable to goodwill.

Most purchased brand names are likely to be subsumed within goodwill, but the ASB has not specifically prohibited their recognition.

KEY POINT

Internally generated intangible assets may be recognised if they can be reliably valued.

- An internally developed intangible asset may be capitalised only if it has a readily ascertainable market value.

In practice, very few internally generated intangibles have a readily ascertainable market value. The ASB does not believe that it is possible to determine a market value for unique intangible assets such as brands and publishing titles, and so the recognition of internally generated brand names is effectively prohibited.

This treatment of internally generated intangible assets is consistent with the treatment of internally generated goodwill. If it is accepted that internally generated goodwill is never recognised because it cannot be valued objectively, it follows that internally generated brand names should not be recognised either.

ACTIVITY 1

How should the following intangible assets be treated in the financial statements?

- A publishing title acquired as part of a subsidiary company.
- A licence to market a new product.

Feedback to this activity is at the end of the chapter.

3.5 Amortisation

KEY POINT

FRS 10 requires that intangible assets are treated in the same way as goodwill.

Once they have been recognised, FRS 10 requires that intangible assets are treated in exactly the same way as goodwill. There are two reasons for this as follows:

- Even if assets such as brand names are not part of goodwill, they are so similar to goodwill that they should be accounted for in the same way.
- If intangibles must be treated in the same way as goodwill, there is no longer any advantage in separately recognising brand names and similar assets.

KEY POINT

Where goodwill and intangible assets are regarded as having limited useful economic lives, they should be amortised on a systematic basis. The straight line method of amortisation should normally be used.

Standard accounting practice

- Where goodwill and intangible assets are regarded as having **limited useful economic lives**, they should be amortised on a systematic basis over those lives.
- There is a rebuttable presumption that the useful economic lives of purchased goodwill and intangible assets are limited to **20 years** or less.
- A residual value may be assigned to an intangible asset only if the residual value can be measured reliably. No residual value may be assigned to goodwill.
- The **straight line** method of amortisation should normally be used unless another method can be demonstrated to be more appropriate.
- The useful economic lives of goodwill and intangible assets should be reviewed at the end of each reporting period and revised if necessary.

3.6 Where useful economic life is longer than 20 years

In most cases, goodwill and intangible assets will probably be amortised over a period of less than 20 years. However, FRS 10 does recognise that they may occasionally have longer useful economic lives or that their lives may even be indefinite.

KEY POINT

Goodwill and intangible assets should normally be amortised over a period of 20 years or less, but may be amortised over a longer period provided that certain conditions are met.

They should not be amortised if they are regarded as having indefinite lives.

A useful economic life may be regarded as longer than 20 years or indefinite if:

- the durability of the acquired business or intangible asset can be demonstrated and justifies estimating the useful economic life to exceed 20 years
- the goodwill or intangible asset is capable of continued measurement (so that annual impairment reviews will be feasible).

Where goodwill and intangible assets are regarded as having indefinite useful economic lives, they should not be amortised.

Note: CA85 does not allow purchased goodwill or intangible assets to be carried indefinitely as assets in the balance sheet. If goodwill and intangible assets are not amortised, it will be necessary to make the additional disclosures required by FRS 18, as the 'true and fair view override' will be invoked.

3.7 Impairment reviews

KEY POINT

Where goodwill and intangible assets are amortised over more than 20 years, **impairment reviews** are required at the end of **each** reporting period.

Where goodwill and intangible assets are amortised over 20 years or less

Impairment reviews are required:

- at the end of the **first full financial year** following the acquisition; and
- in other periods if events or changes in circumstances indicate that the carrying value may not be recoverable.

Where goodwill and intangible assets are amortised over more than 20 years

Impairment reviews are required:

- at the end of **each** reporting period.

If the review indicates that there has been a diminution in value, the goodwill and intangible assets must be written down accordingly. The revised carrying value should be amortised over the current estimate of the remaining useful economic life (unless the asset is not being amortised because it has an indefinite life). This is similar to the treatment of tangible fixed assets where there has been a diminution in value.

Impairment reviews should be carried out in accordance with the requirements of FRS 11 *Impairment of fixed assets and goodwill*, which is covered later in this chapter.

3.8 Negative goodwill

KEY POINT

Negative goodwill arises where an entity is purchased for less than the total fair values of its identifiable net assets.

Most purchased goodwill is positive goodwill, i.e. the price paid for the entity is more than the total fair values of the net assets acquired. Negative goodwill arises where an entity is purchased for less than the total fair values of its identifiable net assets. This may occur for a number of reasons; for example, a business may be sold at a bargain price because the vendor needs to achieve a quick sale. Alternatively, the purchase price of a business may be reduced to take account of future reorganisation costs or probable future losses.

The possible methods of accounting for negative goodwill in theory are as follows.

Recognise negative goodwill immediately as a gain in the profit and loss account or the statement of total recognised gains and losses (STRGL)

The rationale for this treatment is that negative goodwill arises from a bargain purchase. The value of the business acquired is not less than the fair values of its net assets and therefore the purchaser has made a gain.

Arguments against:

- Recognition in the profit and loss account contravenes CA85 as the gain is not realised until the assets acquired are depreciated or sold.
- Recognition in STRGL treats the negative goodwill as a revaluation gain, but recognition of a gain on non-monetary assets before they are realised is inconsistent with the requirements of other accounting standards.
- Not all negative goodwill arises from bargain purchases; some is attributable to expected future losses and therefore should not be treated as an immediate 'gain'.

Take negative goodwill to a capital reserve

The main argument for this treatment is that negative goodwill is not a liability or deferred income in the normal sense of the word and therefore it should not be treated as such.

The main argument against this treatment is that it artificially inflates reserves and shareholders' funds. Negative goodwill does not represent an actual reserve, and therefore should not be treated as one.

Eliminate negative goodwill against the fair value of assets acquired

Arguments for:

- It is consistent with the principle that assets should initially be recognised at cost.
- It helps to prevent unrealistically high fair values being assigned to assets whose values are very subjective. True bargain purchases are uncommon and cost may represent a realistic estimate of fair value.

Arguments against:

- Fair values can be different from cost, and stating assets acquired at lower than their fair values would be inconsistent with FRS 7.
- This method cannot be used where negative goodwill is attributable to future losses.

Include negative goodwill on the balance sheet and release to the profit and loss account over the periods expected to benefit

The rationale for this treatment is that it matches negative goodwill with the costs that gave rise to it. It can be used for all negative goodwill, including that attributable to future losses.

The main argument against this method is that any 'amortisation' of negative goodwill is bound to be subjective.

3.9 Accounting for negative goodwill

KEY POINT

FRS 10 requires that negative goodwill should be recognised on the face of the balance sheet immediately below the goodwill heading.

FRS 10 requires the following accounting treatment.

- Negative goodwill should be recognised and separately disclosed on the face of the balance sheet, immediately below the goodwill heading and followed by a subtotal showing the net amount of the positive and negative goodwill.
- Negative goodwill up to the fair values of the non-monetary assets (e.g. fixed assets) acquired should be recognised in the profit and loss account in the periods in which the non-monetary assets are recovered, whether through depreciation or sale.
- Any negative goodwill in excess of the fair values of the non-monetary assets acquired should be recognised in the profit and loss account in the periods where the benefit is expected to be felt.

Example

On 1 January 20X8 D plc acquired the whole of the share capital of E Ltd for £120,000. The summarised balance sheet of E Ltd at fair values at the date of acquisition is as follows:

	£
Fixed assets (5 years life remaining)	140,000
Stocks	35,000
Other current assets	12,000
Current liabilities	(27,000)
	160,000

What is the credit for negative goodwill in the profit and loss account for the year ended 31 December 20X8?

Solution

Negative goodwill arising is £160,000 – £120,000 = £40,000.

This is less than the fair value of non-monetary assets acquired (fixed assets and stocks totalling £140,000 + £35,000 = £175,000), so there is no excess goodwill. Negative goodwill is therefore credited in the periods in which the non-monetary assets are recovered. Assuming that the fixed assets are depreciated on a straight line basis and that all the opening stock is sold during 20X8, the non-monetary assets recovered in 20X8 are:

	£
Fixed assets (£140,000 ÷ 5)	28,000
Stocks	35,000
	63,000

The credit for the year therefore $\frac{63{,}000}{175{,}000} \times$ £40,000 = £14,400.

3.10 Disclosures

Recognition and measurement

- Describe the method used to value intangible assets.
- Disclose the following information separately for positive goodwill, negative goodwill and each class of intangible asset included on the balance sheet:
  - cost or revalued amount at the beginning of the financial period and at the balance sheet date
  - the cumulative amount of provisions for amortisation and impairment at the beginning of the financial period and at the balance sheet date
  - a reconciliation of the movements
  - the net carrying amount at the balance sheet date.

- Disclose the profit or loss on each material disposal of a previously acquired business or business segment.

Amortisation

- Disclose methods and periods of amortisation of goodwill and intangible assets and the reasons for choosing those periods.
- Disclose details of changes in amortisation period or method.
- Disclose grounds for amortising goodwill or intangible assets over a period that exceeds 20 years (if applicable).

Negative goodwill

- Disclose the periods in which negative goodwill is being written back in the profit and loss account.
- Where negative goodwill exceeds the fair values of the non-monetary assets, the amount and source of the 'excess' negative goodwill and the periods in which it is being written back should be explained.

4 SSAP 13 *Accounting for research and development*

4.1 Introduction

KEY POINT

SSAP 13 defines three broad areas of activity: **pure (or basic) research, applied research** and **development.**

The term **research and development** can be used to cover a wide range of activity. SSAP 13 defines three broad areas of activity as follows:

- **Pure (or basic) research**: experimental or theoretical work undertaken primarily to acquire new scientific or technical knowledge for its own sake rather than directed towards any specific aim or application.
- **Applied research:** original or critical investigation undertaken in order to gain new scientific or technical knowledge and directed towards a specific practical aim or objective.
- **Development:** use of scientific or technical knowledge in order to produce new or substantially improved materials, devices, products or services, to install new processes or systems prior to the commencement of commercial production or commercial applications, or to improve substantially those already produced or installed. Development is therefore concerned with using **existing** knowledge to introduce new products or processes.

4.2 Classification of costs

KEY POINT

Research and development costs include costs of **materials**, **employment**, **depreciation** of equipment and **overheads**.

Expenditure on research and development does not consist only of the salaries of scientists or the cost of test tubes. Many costs can properly be regarded as being incurred for research and development purposes. These include the following:

- costs of **materials**
- salaries, wages, and other **employment costs** of workers involved in research and development
- **depreciation** of scientific and other equipment, and land and buildings
- a proportion of **overhead** costs
- related costs, such as patents, licence fees, etc.

4.3 Accounting problems

The problems in accounting for research and development revolve around two of the fundamental accounting concepts: **accruals** and **prudence**.

Pure and applied research

KEY POINT

Pure and applied research expenditure should be written off **as incurred**.

Under the **accruals concept**, income is matched with the costs involved in generating that income. Yet how can expenditure on pure and applied research be matched with any particular period's income? There may be no direct benefit from the expenditure, or it may benefit many periods. Expenditure on pure and applied research can, therefore, be regarded as part of the continuing cost of running the business. Since no one period can be expected to benefit more than another, such expenditure should be written off **as incurred**. Carrying expenditure forward to future periods would conflict not only with the **accruals concept**, but with **prudent accounting practice**.

Development expenditure

In the case of development expenditure, it is likely that future income, or future cost reduction, can be directly attributable to a development project. An example of this is a car manufacturer who is developing a new model of car. He is incurring costs now, in the expectation that they will be recovered from future sales of the car. On the accruals basis, such expenditure should not be written off against the current year's income, but carried forward and set against income from the project in future years.

KEY POINT

SSAP 13 concludes that **development expenditure** should normally be written off as incurred, but *may* be carried forward provided that certain conditions are met.

However, prudence dictates that it is impossible to determine whether future benefits will arise from a development project unless the project and its related expenditure are clearly identifiable. SSAP 13 therefore concludes that development expenditure should normally be written off as incurred, but may be carried forward in certain circumstances.

SSAP 13 requirements

KEY POINT

Fixed assets required for research and development activities should be capitalised and depreciated through the profit and loss account.

The cost of **fixed assets** acquired or constructed in order to provide facilities for research and development activities over a number of accounting periods should be capitalised and written off over their useful lives through the profit and loss account.

Expenditure on **pure and applied research** (other than that referred to in the previous paragraph) should be written off in the year of expenditure through the profit and loss account.

Development expenditure should be written off in the year of expenditure, except in the following circumstances, when it may be deferred to future periods:

- there is a clearly defined project
- the related expenditure is separately identifiable
- the outcome of such a project has been assessed with reasonable certainty as to:
  - its technical feasibility
  - its ultimate commercial viability, considered in the light of factors such as likely market conditions (including competing products), public opinion, and consumer and environmental legislation
- the aggregate of the deferred development costs, any further development costs, and related production, selling and administration costs is reasonably expected to be exceeded by related future sales or other revenues
- adequate resources exist, or are reasonably expected to be available, to enable the project to be completed and to provide any consequential increases in working capital.

In the foregoing circumstances, development expenditure may be deferred to the extent that its recovery can reasonably be regarded as assured.

KEY POINT

If an accounting policy of deferral is adopted, it must be applied to all development projects that meet the criteria.

If an accounting policy of deferral of development expenditure is adopted, it should be applied to all development projects that meet the criteria above.

Development expenditure may also be carried forward where companies enter into a firm contract to carry out development work on behalf of third parties on such terms that the related expenditure is to be fully reimbursed. Such expenditure should be included in work-in-progress.

4.4 Further problems with development expenditure

If development expenditure is deferred to future periods, three further problems arise which we shall consider in turn.

1 How and when should the expenditure be written off?

The aim in carrying forward such expenditure is to match it against future benefits arising from the developed product. This can be in the form either of revenue from the sale of the product, or of reduced costs from improved production processes.

Deferred development expenditure should be matched against benefits in a sensible and consistent manner. It is not enough to write off the expenditure over an arbitrary number of years: writing off should start when the product begins to be produced commercially.

KEY POINT

If development costs are deferred to future periods, they should be **amortised**.

If development costs are deferred to future periods, they should be amortised. Amortisation should commence with the commercial production or application of the product, service, process or system. It should be allocated on a systematic basis to each accounting period, by reference to either the sale or the use of the product, service, process or system or the period over which these are expected to be sold or used.

Example

Improve plc has deferred development expenditure of £600,000 relating to the development of New Miracle Brand X. It is expected that the demand for the product will stay at a high level for the next three years. Annual sales of 400,000, 300,000 and 200,000 units respectively are expected over this period. Brand X sells for £10.

There are two possibilities for writing off the development expenditure

- Write off in equal instalments over the three-year period, i.e. £200,000 p.a.
- Write off in relation to total sales expected (900,000 units).

			£
Year 1	$\frac{400,000}{900,000} \times £600,000$	=	266,667
Year 2	$\frac{300,000}{900,000} \times £600,000$	=	200,000
Year 3	$\frac{200,000}{900,000} \times £600,000$	=	133,333

2 What should be done if circumstances surrounding the project change?

KEY POINT

Development expenditure should only be **carried forward** if there is a reasonable chance of setting it against income in the future.

Development expenditure should only be carried forward if there is a reasonable chance of setting it against income in the future, i.e. if the conditions mentioned above are met. If circumstances change, it may be necessary to write off the expenditure at once, on the basis of prudent accounting.

This can occur in a number of situations, including:

- the arrival of possible competing products
- changes in the general economic climate
- changes in legislation, such as consumer or environmental changes.

If brought-forward development expenditure is written off, it should not be regarded as a charge against prior years' profits.

Deferred development expenditure should be reviewed at the end of each accounting period. Where the circumstances that justified deferral of the expenditure no longer apply, or are considered doubtful, the expenditure, to the extent to which it is considered to be irrecoverable, should be written off immediately project by project.

3 How should development expenditure be shown in the accounts?

KEY POINT

The accounting policy on **research and development expenditure** should be stated; the total amount charged in the profit and loss account disclosed, together with movements on deferred expenditure.

- The accounting policy on research and development expenditure should be stated and explained.
- The total amount of research and development expenditure charged in the profit and loss account should be disclosed, analysed between the current year's expenditure and amounts amortised from deferred expenditure.
- Movements on deferred development expenditure and the amount carried forward at the beginning and the end of the period should be disclosed. Deferred development expenditure should be disclosed under intangible fixed assets in the balance sheet.

The requirement to disclose the expenditure charged in the profit and loss account does *not* apply to 'small' unquoted companies. A small company for this purpose is one which satisfies the criteria (multiplied in each case by ten) for defining a medium-sized company under the CA85 abbreviated accounts provisions. Thus all quoted companies and large unquoted companies have to disclose the information.

An example of an appropriate **note to the balance sheet** would be as follows:

	£000	£000
Deferred development expenditure 1/1/X1		320
Expenditure incurred in the period	70	
Expenditure amortised in the period	(64)	
	—	
		6
		—
Deferred development expenditure 31/12/X1		326
		—

The **profit and loss account** or a note to the profit and loss account would disclose the *total* amount of research and development expenditure.

	£000
Research and development expenditure:	
Expenditure in year charged	130
Development expenditure amortised	64
	—
	194
	—

The £130,000 does not include the £70,000 appearing in the balance sheet note, as it has not been charged in the profit and loss account.

5 FRS 11 *Impairment of fixed assets and goodwill*

5.1 Why was a new accounting standard needed?

DEFINITION

Impairment is a reduction in the recoverable amount of a fixed asset or goodwill below its carrying amount.

Impairment is a reduction in the recoverable amount of a fixed asset or goodwill below its carrying amount.

It is accepted practice that a fixed asset should not be carried in financial statements at more than its recoverable amount, but there has been very little guidance as to how recoverable amount should be identified or measured.

CA85 requires provision to be made for permanent diminutions in the value of fixed assets, but does not include guidance as to:

- what constitutes a permanent (as opposed to a temporary) diminution
- the way in which diminutions should be presented in the financial statements.

SSAP 12 (the predecessor of FRS 15) required that, where there was a permanent diminution in value, the asset should be immediately written down to its recoverable amount and then depreciated over its remaining useful economic life. This meant that in most cases the diminution was charged immediately to the profit and loss account and was effectively treated as additional depreciation. However, the issue is more complicated where a fixed asset has been revalued.

Example

An asset costing £100,000 was purchased on 1 January 20X1 and has a useful economic life of 10 years. On 1 January 20X3 it was revalued to £150,000. On 1 January 20X5 it was estimated that the recoverable amount of the asset was only £100,000.

How could this impairment be treated in the financial statements for the year ended 31 December 20X5?

Solution

The asset's revalued amount has been depreciated over two years when the impairment comes to light. The amount of the asset's impairment is therefore (£150,000 – (£150,000 / 8 × 2) – £100,000) = £12,500.

There are several possibilities. In theory (provided that the asset is not an investment property), the preparers of the financial statements could decide not to recognise the impairment on the grounds that it is temporary, but this would be unlikely to give a true and fair view.

In practice, there are two options:

Treat the impairment as a fall in value

Dr: Revaluation reserve	£12,500
Cr: Fixed assets	£12,500

The impairment is recorded in the STRGL, but does not affect the profits for the year. This is similar to the treatment of a temporary diminution required by SSAP 19.

Treat the impairment as additional depreciation.

Dr: Depreciation expense	£12,500
Cr: Accumulated depreciation	£12,500

This is similar to the treatment of a permanent diminution required by SSAP 19 and results in a charge to the profit and loss account for the year.

From this we can see that lack of guidance reduces the comparability of financial statements. In addition, impairment losses would not always be recognised as soon as they occurred.

The need for guidance on how to calculate and recognise impairment became more urgent with the issue of recent accounting standards.

- FRS 10 *Goodwill and intangible assets* requires annual impairment reviews where goodwill and intangible assets have a useful life exceeding 20 years.
- FRS 15 *Tangible fixed assets* requires annual impairment reviews where:
  - no depreciation charge is made on the grounds that it would be immaterial, or
  - the estimated remaining useful economic life of an asset is more than 50 years.

5.2 Scope of FRS 11

KEY POINT

FRS 11 applies to **purchased goodwill** recognised in the balance sheet and to all fixed assets except investment properties and investments.

FRS 11 applies to purchased goodwill that is recognised in the balance sheet and to all fixed assets except:

- investment properties as defined by SSAP 19
- fixed assets falling within the scope of FRSs 25 and 26 (e.g. investments).

Note that FRS 11 applies to investments in subsidiaries, associates and joint ventures because these are outside the scope of FRSs 25 and 26.

5.3 The basic principle

DEFINITION

Recoverable amount is the higher of the amounts that can be obtained from selling the asset (net realisable value) or using the asset (value in use).

DEFINITION

Net realisable value is the amount at which an asset could be disposed of, less any direct selling costs.

DEFINITION

Value in use is the present value of the future cash flows obtainable as a result of an asset's continued use, including those resulting from its ultimate disposal.

Impairment is measured by comparing the carrying value of the asset with its recoverable amount. If the carrying amount exceeds the recoverable amount, the asset is impaired and should be written down. (Note that this effectively abolishes the distinction between temporary and permanent diminutions in value by treating all diminutions as permanent.)

- **Recoverable amount** is the higher of the amounts that can be obtained from selling the asset (net realisable value) or using the asset (value in use).
- **Net realisable value** is the amount at which an asset could be disposed of, less any direct selling costs.
- **Value in use** is the present value of the future cash flows obtainable as a result of an asset's continued use, including those resulting from its ultimate disposal.

This is the same principle as **deprival value** and the definitions are based on the value to the business model in the ASB's Statement of Principles. The reasoning behind it is that, when a fixed asset becomes impaired, the decision must be made as to whether to continue to use it or to sell it. This decision is based on the cash flows that can be generated by following each course of action, so that an entity will not continue to use the asset if it can realise more cash by selling it and vice versa. This means that when an asset is stated at the higher of net realisable value or value in use it is recorded at its greatest value to the entity.

ACTIVITY 2

The following information relates to three assets:

	A	*B*	*C*
	£000	£000	£000
Net book value	100	150	120
Net realisable value	110	125	100
Value in use	120	130	90

- What is the recoverable amount of each asset?
- Calculate the impairment provision for each of the three assets.

Feedback to this activity is at the end of the chapter.

5.4 When should an impairment review be carried out?

KEY POINT

Impairment reviews are not required unless events or circumstances change indicating that the carrying amount may not be recoverable, or when required by FRS 10 or FRS 15.

An impairment review is *not* required unless:

- events or changes in circumstances indicate that the carrying amount of an asset may not be recoverable; or
- when required by FRS 10 or by FRS 15.

Indications that assets may have become impaired include:

- a current period operating loss in the business in which the fixed asset or goodwill is involved or a net cash outflow from the operating activities of the business, combined with either past or expected future operating losses or net cash outflows from operating activities

- a significant decline in a fixed asset's market value during the period
- evidence of obsolescence or physical damage to the fixed asset
- a significant adverse change in the business or the market in which the fixed asset or goodwill is involved (e.g. the entrance of a major competitor)
- a commitment by management to undertake a significant reorganisation
- a major loss of key employees
- a significant increase in market interest rates or other market rates of return that are likely to affect materially the fixed asset's recoverable amount.

5.5 Net realisable value

KEY POINT

The **net realisable value** (disposal amount less direct costs of sale) of an asset that is traded on an active market should be based on **market value**.

The net realisable value of an asset that is traded on an active market should be based on **market value**.

Net realisable value is the amount at which an asset could be disposed of, less any direct selling costs. Direct selling costs might include:

- legal costs
- stamp duty
- costs relating to the removal of a sitting tenant (in the case of a building).

Redundancy and reorganisation costs (e.g. following the sale of a business) are **not** direct selling costs.

5.6 Value in use

EXAM HINT

In the examination, you are likely to be given the figure for value in use.

KEY POINT

There are two steps to the **value in use** calculation:

- estimate **future cash flows**
- **discount** them to arrive at their **present value**.

Value in use is the present value of the future cash flows obtainable as a result of an asset's continued use. In the examination, you are likely to be given the figure for value in use, but you should understand how it is calculated.

There are two steps to the calculation:

1 estimate **future cash flows**

2 **discount** them to arrive at their **present value**.

Where possible, value in use should be estimated for individual assets. However, it may not always be possible to identify cash flows arising from individual fixed assets. If this is the case, value in use is calculated for income generating units (groups of assets that produce independent income streams).

Income generating units are identified by dividing the total income of the entity into as many largely independent income streams as is reasonably practicable (see below).

Estimates of future cash flows should be:

- based on reasonable and supportable assumptions
- consistent with the most up-to-date budgets and plans that have been formally approved by management
- based on the assumption that there will be a steady or declining growth rate for the period beyond that covered by formal budgets and plans.

The discount rate used to arrive at the present value of the expected future cash flows should be the rate of return that the market would expect from an equally risky investment.

5.7 Income generating units

DEFINITION

Income generating units are groups of assets, liabilities and goodwill that generate income largely independently of the entity's other income streams.

An **income generating unit** is a group of assets, liabilities and associated goodwill that generates income that is largely independent of the reporting entity's other income streams. The assets and liabilities include those directly involved in generating the income and an appropriate portion of those used to generate more than one income stream.

Income generating units should be as small as is reasonably practicable, but the income stream underlying the future cash flows of the unit should be largely independent of other income streams of the entity and should be capable of being monitored separately.

Where there is a large number of small income generating units, it may be appropriate to consider groups of units together.

Example

An entity has a chain of restaurants, each of which is an individual income generating unit. Impairment of individual restaurants is unlikely to be material, but a material impairment may occur if a number of restaurants are affected together by the same economic factors.

In practice, income streams can often be identified by reference to major products or services and unique intangible assets that generate income independently of each other, such as brands.

5.8 Allocating impairment losses

KEY POINT

Impairment losses should be allocated first to **goodwill**, then to other **intangible assets** followed by **tangible assets**.

Sometimes it may be obvious that specific assets are impaired (for example, they may be known to be damaged or obsolete). Otherwise, the loss is allocated to the assets in the income generating unit in the following order:

1 **goodwill**

2 other **intangible assets**

3 **tangible assets** (on a pro-rata or more appropriate basis).

This means that the loss is allocated to assets with the most **subjective valuations** first.

No intangible asset with a readily **ascertainable market value** should be written down below its net realisable value.

No tangible asset with a **net realisable value** that can be measured reliably should be written down below its net realisable value.

ACTIVITY **3**

An impairment loss of £60,000 arises in connection with an income generating unit. The carrying amount of the assets in the income generating unit, before the impairment, is as follows:

	£000
Goodwill	20
Patent (with no market value)	10
Tangible fixed assets	40
	70

How is the impairment loss allocated?

Feedback to this activity is at the end of the chapter.

5.9 Recognising impairment losses in the financial statements

Assets carried at historic cost

Impairment losses are recognised in the profit and loss account. The impairment is effectively treated as additional depreciation.

Assets which have been revalued

KEY POINT

Impairment losses are normally recognised in **STRGL** if the asset has been **revalued** and the impairment is not due to a consumption of economic benefits. Otherwise impairment losses are recognised in the profit and loss account.

Impairment losses are normally recognised in the STRGL until the carrying value of the asset falls below depreciated historic cost. Impairments below depreciated historic cost are recognised in the profit and loss account. The impairment is treated as a downward revaluation.

Where a fixed asset has been revalued but the impairment is caused by a clear consumption of economic benefits (e.g. because it is damaged) the loss is recognised in the profit and loss account. This type of impairment is treated as additional depreciation, rather than as a loss in value.

Revision of useful economic life

The remaining useful economic life and residual value of the asset should be reviewed and revised if necessary. The revised carrying amount should be depreciated over the revised estimate of the remaining useful economic life.

Notice that these rules are the same as the rules for recognising revaluation gains and losses (FRS 15).

ACTIVITY **4**

At 1 January 20X7 a fixed asset had a carrying value of £20,000, based on its revalued amount, and a depreciated historic cost of £10,000. An impairment loss of £12,000 arose in the year ended 31 December 20X7.

How should this loss be reported in the financial statements for the year ended 31 December 20X7?

Feedback to this activity is at the end of the chapter.

5.10 Presentation and disclosure

KEY POINT

Impairment losses recognised in the **profit and loss account** should be included within operating profit under the appropriate heading. Impairment losses recognised in the **STRGL** should be disclosed separately on the face of that statement.

- Impairment losses recognised in the **profit and loss account** should be included within operating profit under the appropriate statutory heading. They should be disclosed as an exceptional item if appropriate.
- Impairment losses recognised in the **STRGL** should be disclosed separately on the face of that statement.

In the notes to the financial statements in the accounting periods after the impairment, the impairment loss should be treated as follows.

- For assets held on a **historic cost** basis, the impairment loss should be included within cumulative depreciation: the cost of the asset should not be reduced.
- For revalued assets held at a **market value**, the impairment loss should be included within the revalued carrying amount.
- For revalued assets held at **depreciated replacement cost**, an impairment loss charged to the profit and loss account should be included within cumulative depreciation: the carrying amount of the asset should not be reduced; an impairment loss charged to the STRGL should be deducted from the carrying amount of the asset.

Other required disclosures include:

- the discount rate applied (where the impairment loss is based on value in use)
- the reason for any reversal of an impairment loss recognised in a previous period, including any changes in the assumptions upon which the calculation of recoverable amount is based.

Conclusion

FRS 10 requires that positive purchased goodwill is included in the balance sheet as an intangible fixed asset. Other intangible assets may be included in the balance sheet if they can be reliably valued. Goodwill and intangible assets should normally be amortised over a period of 20 years or less, but may be amortised over a longer period or maintained in the balance sheet indefinitely provided that certain conditions are met.

SSAP 13 allows a choice of accounting treatment for development costs provided that specific conditions are met. They may be written off to the profit and loss account as they are incurred, or carried forward as an intangible asset and amortised. Pure and applied research expenditure must be written off as an expense in the period in which it is incurred.

FRS 11 requires that fixed assets and goodwill are not carried at a value above their recoverable amount. Recoverable amount is the higher of net realisable value and value in use.

SELF-TEST QUESTIONS

1 Define goodwill. (1.1)

2 What are the arguments for including intangible assets such as brands in the balance sheet? (2.3)

3 How should internally generated goodwill be treated in the financial statements? (3.3)

4 Why are intangible fixed assets and goodwill treated in a similar way once they have been recognised? (3.5)

5 What is the maximum period that can normally be taken as the useful economic life of purchased goodwill? (3.5)

6 What is development expenditure? (4.1)

7 What are the conditions that must be met before development expenditure can be deferred? (4.3)

8 What is the recoverable amount of a fixed asset? (5.3)

9 When must an entity carry out an impairment review? (5.4)

10 How are impairment losses recognised in the financial statements? (5.9)

PRACTICE QUESTION

Goodwill characteristics

1 List three possible methods of accounting for purchased goodwill and briefly state the arguments in favour of each of the three. **(6 marks)**

2 What are the main characteristics of goodwill which distinguish it from other intangible assets? To what extent do you consider that these characteristics should affect the accounting treatment of goodwill?

State your reasons. **(7 marks)**

(Total: 13 marks)

EXAM-TYPE QUESTION

Calver plc

The objective of FRS 11, *Impairment of fixed assets and goodwill,* is to ensure that fixed assets and goodwill are recorded in the financial statements at no more than their recoverable amount and that any resulting impairment loss is measured and recognised on a consistent basis.

Required:

(a) Explain the reasons why the Accounting Standards Board felt it necessary to introduce FRS 11 *Impairment of fixed assets and goodwill.* **(5 marks)**

(b) Explain the reasoning behind the definition of **recoverable amount** contained within FRS 11. **(3 marks)**

A division of Calver plc has the following fixed assets, which are stated at their carrying amounts at 31 December 20X8:

	£m	£m
Intangible assets:		
Goodwill		45
Patent		25
		70
Tangible assets:		
Freehold land and buildings	320	
Plant and machinery	110	
		430
		500

Because these assets are used to produce a specific product, it is possible to identify the cash flows arising from their use. The management of Calver plc believes that the value of these assets may have become impaired, because a major competitor has developed a superior version of the same product. As a result, sales are expected to fall.

The following additional information is relevant.

- The freehold land and buildings are carried at a valuation. Their depreciated historical cost is £265 million at 31 December 20X8. All other fixed assets are carried at historic cost.
- The intangible fixed assets do not have a market value. It is estimated that the freehold land and buildings could be sold for £270 million and the plant and machinery could be sold for £50 million, net of direct selling costs.
- The value in use of the assets has been calculated as £385.3 million.

Required:

(c) Calculate the impairment loss that will be recognised in the accounts of Calver plc. **(4 marks)**

(d) Explain how this loss will be treated in the financial statements for the year ended 31 December 20X8. **(8 marks)**

(Total: 20 marks)

For the answers to these questions, see the 'Answers' section at the end of the book.

FEEDBACK TO ACTIVITY 1

- The answer depends on whether the asset can be valued reliably. Although the ASB believes that unique intangible assets cannot have a market value, it acknowledges that there are techniques that can be used for estimating values indirectly (e.g. indicators based on multiples of turnover). If this is possible, the title will be recognised at its fair value, otherwise it will be treated as part of goodwill.
- Assuming that the licence has been purchased separately from a business, it should be capitalised at cost.

FEEDBACK TO ACTIVITY 2

The recoverable amounts for each asset are as follows:

- A: £120,000
- B: £130,000
- C: £100,000

The impairment provisions of each asset are as follows:

- A: Nil
- B: £20,000
- C: £20,000

FEEDBACK TO ACTIVITY 3

The impairment loss is allocated as follows:

	Before impairment	*Loss*	*After impairment*
	£000	£000	£000
Goodwill	20	(20)	–
Patent (with no market value)	10	(10)	–
Tangible fixed assets	40	(30)	10
	70	(60)	10

FEEDBACK TO ACTIVITY 4

Assuming that the loss is not a reduction in the service potential of the asset, a loss of £10,000 will be recognised in the STRGL and the remaining loss of £2,000 will be recognised in the profit and loss account.

Chapter 18

LIABILITIES – PROVISIONS, CONTINGENT LIABILITIES AND CONTINGENT ASSETS

CHAPTER CONTENTS

1 **FRS 12 *Provisions, contingent liabilities and contingent assets***

2 **Post balance sheet events**

This chapter concentrates on an important standard, FRS 12 *Provisions, contingent liabilities and contingent assets*. FRS 12 sets out the precise circumstances in which provisions should be recognised and contingent assets and liabilities disclosed in the financial statements. It is one of the standards that is based very heavily on the ASB's Statement of Principles, so the best way to approach it is to concentrate on the principles behind the detailed requirements.

The chapter also covers FRS 21 *Events after the balance sheet date* which has now replaced SSAP 17 on this topic.

Objectives

By the time you have finished this chapter you should be able to:

- explain why an accounting standard on provisions is necessary
- define provisions, legal and constructive obligations, past events and the transfer of economic benefits
- state when provisions may and may not be made, and how they should be accounted for
- explain how provisions should be measured
- define contingent assets and liabilities and describe their accounting treatment
- be able to identify and account for: warranties/guarantees, onerous contracts, environmental and similar provisions
- discuss the validity of making provisions for future repairs or refurbishments.

1 FRS 12 *Provisions, contingent liabilities and contingent assets*

DEFINITIONS

FRS 12 defines provisions as liabilities of uncertain timing or amount.

A **liability** is an obligation to transfer economic benefits as a result of past transactions or events. **Uncertainty** distinguishes provisions from other liabilities.

1.1 What is a provision?

CA85 defines provisions as 'amounts retained as **reasonably necessary** for the purpose of providing for any liability the nature of which is clearly defined and which is either **likely** to be incurred, or certain to be incurred but **uncertain** as to amount or as to the date on which it will arise'.

Provisions may be made for items such as environmental liabilities, reorganisation costs, litigation and future losses. Although 'provisions' are often made for items such as depreciation and doubtful debts, strictly speaking these are not provisions, but normal accounting estimates.

The FRS 12 definition is as follows.

- A **provision** is a liability of uncertain timing or amount.

This definition means that provisions are a sub-class of **liabilities**.

- A **liability** is an obligation to transfer economic benefits as a result of past transactions or events. **Uncertainty** is what distinguishes a provision from another type of liability (such as a trade creditor or an accrued expense).

Note: The FRS 12 definition is narrower than the CA85 definition. For a provision to be recognised under FRS 12, there must be an **obligation** to incur expenditure.

1.2 The problem

KEY POINT

Until the issue of FRS 12, there was no accounting standard covering provisions.

Until the issue of FRS 12, there was no accounting standard covering the general topic of provisions. This led to various problems as follows.

- Provisions were often recognised as a result of an **intention** to make expenditure, rather than an **obligation** to do so.
- Several items could be aggregated into one large provision that was reported as an exceptional item (the 'big bath').
- Inadequate disclosure meant that in some cases it was difficult to ascertain the significance of the provisions and any movements in the year.

Example

Shortly before the end of 20X1, the Board of Directors of a company decides to carry out a reorganisation. A provision for reorganisation costs is set up. However, the Board is not committed to the plan and early in 20X2 the decision is reversed.

The directors expect that the company will make losses in the years 20X2 and 20X3. Therefore the provision becomes a provision for future losses and is released to the profit and loss account in 20X2 and 20X3, in each case artificially turning a loss into a small profit.

'Creative accounting' such as this was often justified on grounds of prudence.

FRS 12 was issued to prevent abuses such as this and to ensure that users of the financial statements are provided with sufficient information to understand the nature, timing and amount of provisions.

1.3 Contingent liabilities and contingent assets

DEFINITION

Contingent liabilities are: possible **obligations** arising from past events to be confirmed by the occurrence of uncertain future events; or present obligations arising from past events that are not recognised.

A **contingent liability** is:

- a possible obligation that arises from past events and whose existence will be confirmed only by the occurrence of one or more uncertain future events not wholly within the entity's control; or
- a present obligation that arises from past events but is not recognised because:
  - it is not probable that a transfer of economic benefits will be required to settle the obligation; or
  - the amount of the obligation cannot be measured with sufficient reliability.

DEFINITION

Contingent assets are possible **assets** arising from past events to be confirmed by the occurrence of uncertain future events.

A **contingent asset** is a possible asset that arises from past events and whose existence will be confirmed only by the occurrence of one or more uncertain future events not wholly within the entity's control.

Example

A common example of contingencies arises in connection with legal action. If Company A sues Company B because it believes that it has incurred losses as a result of Company B's faulty products, then Company B may be liable for damages. Whether or not the damages will actually be paid depends on the outcome of the case. Until this is known, Company B has a contingent **liability** and Company A has a contingent **asset**.

Contingencies do not include normal accounting estimates. For example, although the correctness of a provision for doubtful debts will be confirmed (or otherwise) by uncertain future events, it is not a contingent liability.

1.4 Recognition

KEY POINT

A provision should only be **recognised** when: an entity has a **present obligation**; a transfer of economic benefits is probable, and a reliable estimate can be made of the amount of the obligation.

Provisions

A provision should only be recognised when:

- an entity has a present obligation (legal or constructive) as a result of a past event
- it is probable that a transfer of economic benefits will be required to settle the obligation
- a reliable estimate can be made of the amount of the obligation.

DEFINITION

A **legal obligation** derives from a **contract** or **legislation**.

A **legal obligation** is an obligation that derives from:

- a **contract**
- **legislation**
- other operation of **law**.

DEFINITION

A **constructive obligation** derives from an entity's actions which create **valid expectations** that it will **accept** or **discharge** certain **responsibilities**.

A **constructive obligation** is an obligation that derives from an entity's actions where:

- by an established pattern of past practice, published policies or a sufficiently specific current statement, the entity has indicated to other parties that it will accept certain **responsibilities;** and
- as a result, the entity has created a **valid expectation** on the part of those other parties that it will discharge those responsibilities.

The idea of an obligation implies that action is **unavoidable** and that there is **no alternative**.

KEY POINT

FRS 12 explains that a past event gives rise to a present obligation if it is **more likely than not** that a present obligation exists at the balance sheet date. A transfer of economic benefits is probable if it is **more likely than not** to occur.

FRS 12 explains the following.

- A past event gives rise to a present obligation if, taking account of all available evidence, it is **more likely than not** that a present obligation exists at the balance sheet date.
- A transfer of economic benefits is regarded as probable if it is **more likely than not** to occur.
- Only in extremely rare cases will it not be possible to make a reliable estimate of the obligation.

Entities often settle liabilities by a transfer of economic benefits in the form of cash (for example, to pay for goods and services). However, an entity could have an obligation to transfer economic benefits other than cash. For example, it could have to repair or replace goods that are the subject of guarantees or warranties, to rectify damage to the environment caused by its activities, or to perform services.

KEY POINT

Contingent liabilities should not be recognised.

Contingent liabilities

Contingent liabilities should not be recognised in the balance sheet itself. They should be disclosed in a note unless the possibility of a transfer of economic benefits is remote.

Contingent assets

KEY POINT

Contingent assets should not be recognised unless a gain is virtually certain (as then they are not contingencies).

Contingent assets should not be recognised, as this could result in the recognition of profit that may never be realised. If the possibility of an inflow of economic benefits is probable they should be disclosed.

Only if a gain is virtually certain should it be recognised (because it cannot then be a contingency).

ACTIVITY **1**

How should the following items be treated in the financial statements?

1 A manufacturer gives warranties at the time of sale to purchasers of its product. Under the terms of the contract for sale the manufacturer undertakes to make good manufacturing defects that become apparent within three years from the date of sale. On past experience it is probable that there will be some claims under the warranties.

2 A retail store has a policy of refunding purchases by dissatisfied customers, even though there is no legal obligation to do so. Its policy of making refunds is generally known.

3 During 20X1, A gives a guarantee of certain borrowings of B, whose financial condition at that time is sound.

4 New laws have been passed that require an entity to fit smoke filters to its factories by 30 June 20X2. At 31 December 20X1 (the balance sheet date) the entity has not yet fitted the smoke filters.

Feedback to this activity is at the end of the chapter.

1.5 Measurement

General rules

KEY POINT

Recognised provisions should be the **best estimate** of the expenditure required to settle the **present obligation** at the balance sheet date.

- The amount recognised as a provision should be the **best estimate** of the expenditure required to settle the present obligation at the balance sheet date. (This is the amount that an entity would pay to settle the obligation at the balance sheet date or to persuade a third party to assume it.)
- In measuring a provision, an entity should take into account:
  - the risks and uncertainties surrounding the event (but uncertainty does not justify the creation of excessive provisions or overstatement of liabilities)
  - future events (e.g. technological developments) where there is sufficient objective evidence that they will occur.
- Where the effect of the time value of money is material (for example, where a liability will be settled in several years' time), the amount of a provision should be discounted. A risk-free rate should be used.
- Provisions should be reviewed at each balance sheet date and adjusted to reflect the current best estimate. They should be reversed if the transfer of economic benefits is no longer probable.
- A provision should only be used for expenditures for which it was originally recognised. (This requirement effectively prevents entities from using 'big bath accounting'.)

Reimbursements

DEFINITION

A **reimbursement** is an amount received from a third party to pay part or all of the expenditure required to settle a provision.

A **reimbursement** is an amount received from a third party to pay part or all of the expenditure required to settle a provision (for example, through an insurance contract).

- A reimbursement should be recognised only when it is virtually certain to be received.
- The reimbursement should be treated as a separate asset (i.e. it should not be netted off against the provision to which it relates).
- In the profit and loss account, the expense relating to a provision may be presented net of the income recognised for a reimbursement.

KEY POINT

Methods of measuring uncertainties include analysing by '**expected value**' and considering a range of outcomes.

Methods of measuring uncertainties

Methods of measuring uncertainties include:

- **weighting** the cost of all probable outcomes according to their **probabilities** ('**expected value**')
- considering a range of possible outcomes.

Expected value: example

An entity sells goods with a warranty covering customers for the cost of repairs of any defects that are discovered within the first two months after purchase. Past experience suggests that 90% of the goods sold will have no defects, 5% will have minor defects and 5% will have major defects. If minor defects were detected in all products sold, the cost of repairs would be £10,000; if major defects were detected in all products sold, the cost would be £100,000.

The **expected value** of the cost of repairs is £5,500 ((5% × 10,000) + (5% × 100,000)).

Possible outcomes: example

An entity has to rectify a serious fault in an item of plant that it has constructed for a customer.

In this case, the most likely outcome is that the repair will succeed at the first attempt at a cost of £400,000, but a provision for £500,000 is recognised because there is a significant chance that a further attempt will be necessary.

The most likely outcome may be the best estimate of the liability, but other possible outcomes must be considered. Where other possible outcomes are either mostly higher or mostly lower than the most likely outcome, the best estimate will be a higher or lower amount.

1.6 Future operating losses

KEY POINT

Provisions should not be recognised for **future operating losses** unless this is required by another accounting standard.

Provisions should not be recognised for future operating losses.

But FRS 12 only covers provisions which are not covered by another accounting standard. This means that there are still situations in which entities are required to make provisions for future losses (e.g. discontinued operations (FRS 3), foreseeable losses on long-term contracts (SSAP 9)).

1.7 Onerous contracts

DEFINITION

An **onerous contract** is a contract in which the unavoidable costs of meeting the obligation exceed the economic benefits expected to be received under it. A provision should be recognised for the **present obligation**

An **onerous contract** is a contract in which the unavoidable costs of meeting the obligation exceed the economic benefits expected to be received under it.

An example: a lease contract for a property that is no longer required and where the lease cannot be cancelled.

If an entity has an onerous contract, a provision should be recognised for the **present obligation** under the contract (for example, for the best estimate of unavoidable lease payments).

1.8 Restructuring

DEFINITION

Restructuring is a programme either to change the **scope** of the business or the manner in which it is conducted.

A **restructuring** is a programme that is planned and controlled by management and materially changes either:

- the scope of a business undertaken by an entity; or
- the manner in which that business is conducted.

Examples of restructuring are as follows:

- sale or termination of a line of business
- the closure of business locations in a country or region, or the relocation of business activities from one country or region to another
- changes in management structure, for example, eliminating a layer of management
- fundamental reorganisations that have a material effect on the nature and focus of the entity's operations.

When does an entity have an obligation to restructure?

KEY POINT

Provisions for restructuring costs can only be recognised where an entity has a **constructive obligation** to carry out the restructuring.

Provisions for restructuring costs can only be recognised where an entity has a **constructive obligation** to carry out the restructuring. A Board decision on its own is *not* sufficient to create an obligation.

This requirement is designed to prevent entities from recognising provisions where there is only an **intention to restructure** and also from making unnecessary provisions which can then be used artificially to enhance profits in subsequent periods. However, critics of the ASB have argued that in practice most Boards of Directors do not take decisions to restructure lightly.

KEY POINT

A **constructive obligation** to **restructure** arises only when the entity has a detailed formal plan for the restructuring and has raised a **valid expectation** that it will implement the plan.

A constructive obligation to restructure arises only when the entity:

- has a detailed formal plan for the restructuring, identifying at least:
  - the business or part of the business concerned
  - the principal locations affected
  - the location, function, and approximate number of employees who will be compensated for terminating their services
  - the expenditures that will be undertaken
  - when the plan will be implemented
- has raised a valid expectation in those affected that it will carry out the restructuring by starting to implement the plan or announcing its main features to those affected by it.

For an entity to have an obligation to sell an operation there must be a binding sale agreement.

Expenses of restructuring

KEY POINT

A **restructuring provision** should include only the **direct expenditures** arising from the restructuring.

A restructuring provision should include only the direct expenditures arising from the restructuring, which are those that are both:

- necessarily entailed by the restructuring
- not associated with the ongoing activities of the entity.

The provision should not include costs that relate to the future conduct of the business, such as the cost of:

- retraining or relocating staff who will continue with the business
- marketing
- investment in new systems and distribution networks.

ACTIVITY **2**

On 1 December 20X8 the board of an entity decided to close down a division on 31 March 20X9. On 31 January 20X9 a detailed plan for closing down the division was agreed; letters were sent to customers informing them of the decision and redundancy notices were sent to the staff of the division.

Should a provision be recognised in the accounts for the year ended 31 December 20X8?

Feedback to this activity is at the end of the chapter.

1.9 Future repairs and refurbishments

KEY POINT

Before FRS 12 was issued, it was usual for entities to set up provisions for **future expenditure**. FRS 12 ensures that provisions are not recognised unless they meet the definition of a **liability**. FRS 12 does not regard future refurbishment expenditure as a liability.

Some fixed assets need substantial expenditure every few years for major refits or refurbishment and the replacement of major components. Before FRS 12 was issued, it was usual for entities to set up provisions for the future expenditure. This was justified by the prudence concept: provision must be made for all known liabilities at the balance sheet date.

The rules in FRS 12 are designed to ensure that provisions are not recognised unless they meet the definition of a liability and the recognition criteria set out in the Statement of Principles:

- there must be a present obligation as a result of a past event (so that the provision meets the definition of a liability)
- the transfer must be probable (i.e. sufficient evidence exists that there is a liability)
- it must be possible to make a reliable estimate of the amount (i.e. the liability can be measured at a monetary amount with sufficient reliability).

FRS 12 does not regard future refurbishment expenditure as a liability. For example, suppose that an airline is required by law to overhaul its aircraft once every three years. Because the overhaul is required by law, at first sight it appears that there is an obligation and therefore a liability. However, the ASB argues that the airline has an alternative to incurring the expenditure – it could sell the aircraft. Instead, the entity should capitalise the cost of the expenditure when it is incurred and depreciate it over the three-year period. This matches the expenditure with the accounting periods in which it is effectively incurred. (This has already been discussed in an earlier chapter.)

1.10 FRS 12 and prudence

Entities are now not allowed to recognise provisions in many situations where they would probably have done so in the past. This should have the advantage of preventing many of the abuses that have taken place in the past, such as '**big bath**' accounting.

KEY POINT

Critics claim FRS 12 contravenes the concept of **prudence**. The ASB views prudence as a **desirable** quality of information rather than a **fundamental** concept.

However, critics of the ASB have claimed that FRS 12 contravenes the fundamental concept of **prudence**. For example, in Activity 1 above, an entity is required to fit smoke filters to its factories. Before the issue of FRS 12, it would probably have been argued that the cost of the filters is a known liability and should be provided. Under FRS 12, because the new law has not come into force at the balance sheet date, there is no past event giving rise to a present obligation and therefore there can be no provision.

The ASB views prudence as a **desirable** quality of financial information, rather than as a **fundamental** concept, as we saw in Chapter 1. It is not appropriate to use prudence as a reason for creating excessive provisions, or deliberately overstating liabilities or losses.

ACTIVITY 3

A furnace has a lining that needs to be replaced every five years for technical reasons. At the balance sheet date, the lining has been in use for three years.

How should the cost of replacing the lining be treated in the accounts?

Feedback to this activity is at the end of the chapter.

1.11 Disclosure

Provisions

KEY POINT

Disclosure is required for each class of **provision**, and each class of **contingent liability** and **asset**.

For each class of provision, disclose:

- carrying amount at the beginning and end of the period
- additional provisions made in the period
- amounts used during the period
- unused amounts reversed during the period

- effect of discounting during the period
- a brief description of the nature of the obligation and expected timing of any resulting transfers of economic benefit
- an indication of the uncertainties about the amount or timing of those transfers of economic benefit
- the amount of any expected reimbursement.

Contingent liabilities

For each class of contingent liability (unless remote), disclose:

- an estimate of its financial effect
- an indication of the uncertainties relating to the amount or timing of any outflow
- the possibility of any reimbursement.

Contingent assets

For contingent assets (only where probable), disclose:

- a brief description of their nature
- where practicable, an estimate of their financial effect.

1.12 Summary

A **provision** is a **liability** of **uncertain** timing or amount. A provision should only be recognised when:

- an entity has a **present obligation** as a result of a **past event**
- it is probable that a **transfer of economic benefits** will be required
- a **reliable estimate** can be made of the amount of the obligation.

The amount recognised as a provision should be the **best estimate** of the expenditure required to settle the present obligation at the balance sheet date.

2 Post balance sheet events

2.1 Introduction

DEFINITIONS

Post balance sheet events are those events which occur between the balance sheet date and the date on which the financial statements are approved by the board of directors.

Adjusting events are post balance sheet events which provide evidence of conditions existing at the balance sheet date.

Non-adjusting events are post balance sheet events which concern conditions that arose after the balance sheet date.

Suppose the year end of a company is 31 December 20X7 and the directors approve the financial statements at a board meeting held on 22 March 20X8. Certain events occurring during the intervening period will provide information which will help in preparing the financial statements.

- **Post balance sheet events** are those events, both favourable and unfavourable, which occur between the balance sheet date and the date on which the financial statements are approved for issue by the board of directors.
- **The date on which the financial statements are approved by the board of directors** is the date the board of directors formally approves a set of documents as the financial statements. In respect of unincorporated enterprises, the date of approval is the corresponding date. In respect of group accounts, the date of approval is the date when the group accounts are formally approved by the board of directors of the parent company.

These post balance sheet events fall into two categories: **adjusting events** and **non-adjusting events**.

- **Adjusting events** are post balance sheet events which provide additional evidence of conditions existing at the balance sheet date.
- **Non-adjusting events** are post balance sheet events which concern conditions that arose after the balance sheet date.

2.2 Adjusting events

For example, bad debts arising one or two months after the balance sheet date may help to quantify the bad debt provision as at the balance sheet date. **Adjusting events** may, therefore, affect the amount at which items are stated in the balance sheet.

Examples include the following:

- the bankruptcy of a customer that confirms the amount of a bad or doubtful debt
- the sale of stock after the balance sheet date that confirms that net realisable value is lower than cost
- the settlement of a court case that confirms that a liability existed at the balance sheet date
- amounts received or receivable in respect of insurance claims which were being negotiated at the balance sheet date.

2.3 Non-adjusting events

These are events arising after the balance sheet date but which, unlike those events above, do *not* concern conditions existing at the balance sheet date. Such events will not, therefore, have any effect on items in the balance sheet or profit and loss account. However, in order to prevent the financial statements from presenting a misleading position, some form of additional disclosure is required if the events are material, usually by way of a note indicating what effect the events would have had on the year end balance sheet.

KEY POINT

Adjusting events give rise to changes in the accounts figures. **Non-adjusting events** are disclosed by way of note.

Examples of non-adjusting events include the following:

- the issue of new share or loan capital
- major changes in the composition of the company (for example, acquisitions of new businesses)
- financial consequences of losses of fixed assets or stock as a result of fires or floods.

2.4 'Window dressing'

KEY POINT

'**Window dressing**' refers to the practice of entering into certain transactions before the year end and reversing those transactions after the year end.

'Window dressing' refers to the practice of entering into certain transactions before the year end and reversing those transactions after the year end. Thus, no real transaction has occurred (i.e. no substance, only legal form) but the balance sheet reflects the transaction (as it primarily records the legal form of assets and liabilities). The hoped-for effect is to improve the appearance of the balance sheet.

Example

UK Finance plc is concerned that it has over-lent to customers in the year to 31 December 20X8 and that its ratio of liquid assets to total assets is too low. It thus arranges a loan of £40 million from another company in December. The loan is repaid in January. Balance sheet extract (a) refers to the balance sheet if the transaction had not been entered into; extract (b) shows the actual balance sheet at the year end.

	(a)	(b)
	£m	£m
Liquid assets	10	50
Investments:		
Advances to customers	200	200
Fixed assets	20	20

Less: Creditors:		
amounts falling due within one year	(10)	(50)
Total assets less current liabilities	220	220
$\frac{\text{Liquid assets}}{\text{Total assets less current liabilities}}$	$\frac{10}{220} \times 100$	$\frac{50}{220} \times 100$
	= 4.5%	= 22.7%

Clearly (b) looks better if an accepted measure of security/solvency is a 'liquidity' ratio such as that calculated above.

SSAP 17 (the accounting standard preceding FRS 21) specifically required that details of window dressing transactions must be disclosed in a note to the accounts. FRS 21 contains no such requirement, but disclosure would still be required if it were necessary to give a true and fair view of the financial position.

2.5 Standard accounting practice – FRS 21

KEY POINT

FRS 21 *Events after the balance sheet date* requires that **adjusting** material post balance sheet events be recognised in financial statements. Non-adjusting events should be disclosed where material.

FRS 21 *Events after the balance sheet date* requires the following.

- Financial statements should be prepared on the basis of conditions existing at the balance sheet date.
- A material post balance sheet event requires changes in the amounts to be recognised in financial statements where:
  - it is an adjusting event; or
  - it indicates that application of the going concern concept is not appropriate.
- A material post balance sheet event should be disclosed where it is a non-adjusting event of such materiality that its non-disclosure would affect the ability of the users of financial statements to reach a proper understanding of the financial position.
- In respect of each post balance sheet event which is required to be disclosed under the previous paragraph, the following information should be stated by way of notes in financial statements:
  - the nature of the event; and
  - an estimate of the financial effect, or a statement that it is not practicable to make such an estimate.
- The date on which the financial statements are authorised for issue and who gave that authorisation should be disclosed in the financial statements.

ACTIVITY **4**

How should the following matters be dealt with?

1 When drafting the final accounts, a company's accountant includes a figure of £2,000 as the net realisable value of damaged items of stock.

The cost of these items was £3,000, and the normal selling price would be £4,000. Between the balance sheet date and the approval of the accounts the items are sold for £3,100.

2 A company is engaged in the construction of its own factory. The estimated value on completion is £200,000; costs to date are £80,000; and at the balance sheet date, expected further costs to completion were £90,000.

After the balance sheet date serious defects – which must have existed unnoticed for some time – are discovered in the foundations of the building, necessitating partial demolition and rebuilding at an estimated cost of £70,000 (in addition to the estimated further costs to completion of £90,000).

Feedback to this activity is at the end of the chapter.

2.6 Proposed dividends

Long-standing accounting practice in the UK has been to show proposed dividends as a current liability in the balance sheet, even if the directors' decision to declare the dividend was taken after the balance sheet date. This practice was sanctioned by SSAP 17, the standard preceding FRS 21. SSAP 17 listed proposed dividends as a special example of an adjusting event.

Accounting academics have never been happy with this practice. A liability should only be recognised in the balance sheet if there is an obligation at the balance sheet date. If the directors have not met to decide on the level of a final ordinary dividend by the balance sheet date, then there is no liability to be included in the balance sheet. This is the key difference between SSAP 17 and FRS 21.

KEY POINT

Proposed ordinary dividends are only a liability at the year end if they were declared prior to the year end.

FRS 21 requires that, if dividends on equity shares are declared after the balance sheet date, then these dividends cannot be recognised as a liability at the balance sheet date. If they are declared after the balance sheet date but before the financial statements are authorised for issue, then they should be disclosed in a note.

The situation with preference dividends is slightly different. By issuing preference shares, the company is committed to paying the preference dividends each year. Therefore, a liability for preference dividends will exist at the balance sheet date, even if the directors have not yet formally met to approve the payment of the dividends.

2.7 Directors' report

KEY POINT

CA85 requires the **directors' report** to contain particulars of important events which occurred since the end of that year.

Para 6 Sch 7 CA85 requires the directors' report to contain:

- particulars of any important events affecting the company or any of its subsidiaries which have occurred since the end of that year
- an indication of likely future developments in the business of the company and of its subsidiaries.

Conclusion

FRS 12 requires that provisions should only be recognised when:

- an entity has a present obligation as a result of a past event
- it is probable that a transfer of economic benefits will be required
- a reliable estimate can be made of the amount of the obligation.

The amount recognised as a provision should be the best estimate of the expenditure required to settle the present obligation at the balance sheet date.

FRS 21 requires that adjusting post balance sheet events should lead to changes in the amounts recognised in the financial statements, while non-adjusting events should be disclosed in a note.

SELF-TEST QUESTIONS

1. What were the problems that led to the issue of FRS 12? (1.2)
2. What is a contingent liability? (1.3)
3. When should a provision be recognised? (1.4)
4. How should a provision be measured? (1.5)
5. Can provisions be recognised for future operating losses? (1.6)
6. What is an onerous contract? (1.7)
7. What information should be disclosed about contingent liabilities? (1.11)
8. There are two types of post balance sheet event. What are they? (2.1)
9. Should a proposed ordinary dividend be recognised as a liability at the balance sheet date? (2.6)
10. What information about post balance sheet events must be disclosed in the directors' report? (2.7)

EXAM-TYPE QUESTION

Rowsley plc

Rowsley plc is a company that carries out many different activities. It is proud of its reputation as a 'caring' organisation and has adopted various ethical policies towards its employees and the wider community in which it operates. As part of its Annual Report, the company publishes details of its environmental policies, which include setting performance targets for activities such as recycling, controlling emissions of noxious substances and limiting use of non-renewable resources.

The finance director is reviewing the accounting treatment of various items prior to the signing of the accounts for the year ended 31 March 20X9. All four items are material in the context of the accounts as a whole. The accounts are to be approved by the directors on 30 June 20X9.

(a) On 15 February 20X9 the board of Rowsley plc decided to close down a large factory in Derby. The board is trying to draw up a plan to manage the effects of the reorganisation, and it is envisaged that production will be transferred to other factories, mainly in Wales. The factory will be closed on 31 August 20X9, but at 31 March this decision had not yet been announced to the employees or to any other interested parties. Costs of the reorganisation have been estimated at £45 million. **(6 marks)**

(b) During December 20X8 a division of the company moved from Buckingham to Sunderland in order to take advantage of regional development grants. It holds its main premises in Buckingham under an operating lease, which runs until 31 March 20Y1. Annual rentals under the lease are £10 million. The company is unable to cancel the lease, but it has let some of the premises to a charitable organisation at a nominal rent. The company is attempting to rent the remainder of the premises at a commercial rent, but the directors have been advised that the chances of achieving this are less than 50%. **(6 marks)**

(c) During the year to 31 March 20X9, a customer started legal proceedings against the company, claiming that one of the food products that it manufactures had caused several members of his family to become seriously ill. The company's lawyers have advised that this action will probably not succeed. **(3 marks)**

(d) The company has an overseas operation that is involved in mining precious metals. These activities cause significant damage to the environment, including deforestation. The company expects to abandon the mine in eight years time. The mine is situated in a country where there is no environmental legislation obliging companies to rectify environmental damage and it is very unlikely that any such legislation will be enacted within the next eight years. It has been estimated that the cost of cleaning the site and re-planting the trees will be £25 million if the re-planting were successful at the first attempt, but it will probably be necessary to make a further attempt, which will increase the cost by a further £5 million. **(5 marks)**

Required:

Explain how each of the items (a) to (d) above should be treated in the financial statements for the year ended 31 March 20X9.

(Total: 20 marks)

For the answer to this question, see the 'Answers' section at the end of the book.

FEEDBACK TO ACTIVITY 1

These items are taken from the Appendix to FRS 12. For each of the items, ask the following two questions:

- Is there a present obligation as the result of a past event?
- Is a transfer of economic benefits in settlement probable?

A provision is recognised if the answer to both questions is yes.

1 Present obligation? – Yes. The past (obligating) event is the sale of the product, which gives rise to a legal obligation (under the contract).

Transfer of benefits probable? – Yes. There will probably be claims for the warranties.

Conclusion – Recognise a provision.

2 Present obligation? – Yes. The past event is the sale of the product, which gives rise to a constructive obligation.

Transfer of benefits probable? – Yes.

Conclusion – Recognise a provision.

3 Present obligation? – Yes. The giving of the guarantee has given rise to a legal obligation.

Transfer of benefits probable? – No.

Conclusion – Do not recognise a provision. Disclose the guarantee as a contingent liability unless the probability of having to honour it is remote.

4 Present obligation? – No. The obligating event would be either the fitting of the filters (which has not happened) or the illegal operation of the factory without the filters (which has not happened because the filters are not yet legally required).

Conclusion – Do not recognise a provision.

FEEDBACK TO ACTIVITY 2

No provision should be recognised. There was no present obligation at the balance sheet date. The obligating event is the announcement of the plan, which creates a constructive obligation. This did not take place until after the balance sheet date.

FEEDBACK TO ACTIVITY 3

No obligation to replace the furnace lining exists independently of the entity's future actions. There is a realistic alternative to incurring the expenditure – the entity could decide not to continue operating the furnace, or could sell it.

Conclusion – No provision should be recognised. Instead, the cost of the furnace lining should be capitalised once incurred and depreciated over five years.

FEEDBACK TO ACTIVITY 4

1 The valuation in the accounts should be adjusted to £3,000, i.e. cost, since net realisable value has, in the event, turned out to be greater than cost. This is an adjusting post balance sheet event.

2 This is an adjusting post balance sheet event. There is an anticipated loss on the factory of £40,000 (value £200,000; less costs to date £80,000; less estimated further costs £160,000). The asset should, therefore, be valued at £40,000 (costs to date £80,000; less attributable loss £40,000).

Chapter 19

ACCOUNTING FOR THE SUBSTANCE OF TRANSACTIONS

CHAPTER CONTENTS

1 FRS 5 *Reporting the substance of transactions*

2 Application notes

This chapter covers an important standard, FRS 5 *Reporting the substance of transactions*. FRS 5 was issued in response to problems caused by complex transactions (including 'creative accounting' abuses). It requires reporting entities to reflect the substance of transactions in their financial statements, rather than their strict legal form.

The requirements of FRS 5 are based on the definitions of assets and liabilities and the recognition criteria in the ASB's Statement of Principles. Therefore, the best way to approach its requirements is to concentrate on the principles underpinning them.

Objectives

By the time you have finished this chapter you should be able to:

- explain the importance of recording the substance rather than the legal form of transactions
- describe the features which may indicate that the substance of transactions may differ from their legal form
- explain and apply the principles in FRS 5
- recognise the substance of transactions in general and specifically account for:
  - stock sold on sale or return/consignment stock
  - sale and repurchase/leaseback agreements
  - factoring of debtors.

1 FRS 5 *Reporting the substance of transactions*

1.1 Introduction

FRS 5 was issued in April 1994. Its main thrust is to ensure that financial statements report the substance of transactions and not merely their legal form. The view held by the ASB is that, before the issue of the FRS, users could be left unaware of the total assets employed in a business and of its overall financing. Detailed disclosure in the notes is no substitute for inclusion in the accounts.

1.2 How have companies tried to keep items off the balance sheet?

KEY POINT

Companies have tried to keep items off the balance sheet by **leasing assets**, non-consolidation of **controlled non-subsidiaries**, **window dressing** and **complex arrangements** in which the accounting entries were unclear.

'Reporting the **substance of transactions**' is a reaction to the practice of '**off balance sheet financing**' which became popular in the 1980s. As the term indicates, the most widely recognised effect is the omission of liabilities from the balance sheet. However, the assets being financed are also excluded, with the result that the resources of the company and its financing are understated.

Ways in which companies have tried to keep items off the balance sheet in the past include the following.

Leasing of assets

Prior to the issue of SSAP 21 leases were not capitalised, i.e. the asset and its related financial commitment were not shown on the lessee's balance sheet.

Controlled non-subsidiaries

Prior to CA89 and FRS 2 under the old, looser definition of a subsidiary, companies could control other companies but, as they were not technically subsidiaries, they were not consolidated in the group accounts. The effect of **non-consolidation** is that the assets and liabilities of the subsidiary are not included within the total assets and liabilities of the group.

After CA89, companies became more ingenious in arranging their affairs so that off balance sheet arrangements continued to occur in entities which were not classified as subsidiaries under the new legislation. FRS 5 tackles these issues.

Window dressing

Companies may enter into transactions shortly before the year end to 'improve' the look of the balance sheet. These transactions reverse shortly after the year end.

Innovations in the financial markets

A number of (often complex) arrangements were developed for which the accounting entries were not immediately obvious. It was the growth in these arrangements which resulted in the determination of the ASB to issue an accounting standard on the substance of transactions. We refer to some of these innovations in our coverage of the standard below.

ACTIVITY **1**

Note down two or three reasons companies use to justify off balance sheet financing schemes.

Feedback on this activity is at the end of the chapter.

1.3 General principles of FRS 5

FRS 5 sets out general principles covering the following:

- the **scope** of the standard
- how to determine the **substance** of a transaction
- whether any resulting assets and liabilities should be included in the balance sheet
- at what point there should be changes in **previously recognised assets**
- what **disclosures** are necessary
- whether any '**vehicle**' companies incorporated into a transaction should be consolidated
- under what circumstances a '**linked**' presentation is appropriate.

KEY POINT

The FRS refers to seven specific transaction types: **consignment stock**, **sale and repurchase** agreements, **factoring**, **securitised assets**, **loan transfers**, **Private Finance Initiative** contracts and **revenue recognition**.

The FRS also contains application notes showing how its proposals are to be applied to seven specific transaction types: **consignment stock**, **sale and repurchase** agreements, **factoring**, **securitised assets**, **loan transfers**, **Private Finance Initiative** contracts and **revenue recognition**.

1.4 Scope of the standard

KEY POINT

The main **exclusions** relate to financing arrangements such as **forward contracts**, **futures**, **foreign exchange** and **interest rate swaps**.

Certain transactions are **excluded** from the standard because of the special nature of the transactions. The main exclusions relate to financing arrangements such as **forward contracts**, **futures**, **foreign exchange** and **interest rate swaps**, which are covered by *FRS 25: Financial Instruments: Disclosure and Presentation.*

Where the general principles of the standard seem to apply to an asset or liability which is subject to the requirements of a more specific standard (e.g. SSAP 9 covers stocks), the specific requirements of the other standard apply.

1.5 Determining the substance of a transaction

KEY POINT

Features of transactions whose substance is not readily apparent are the separation of the **legal title** of an item; the **linking** of transactions with others, and the inclusion of **options**.

Common features of transactions whose substance is not readily apparent are:

- separation of the **legal title** to an item from the ability to enjoy the principal benefits and exposure to the principal risks associated with it
- **linking of a transaction** with one or more others in such a way that the commercial effect cannot be understood without reference to the series as a whole
- inclusion in a transaction of one or more **options** whose terms make it highly likely that the option will be exercised.

A key step in determining the substance of a transaction is to identify its effect on the **assets** and **liabilities** of the entity.

Assets are, broadly, rights or other access to future economic benefits controlled by an entity. Liabilities are, broadly, an entity's obligations to transfer economic benefits.

Risk often indicates which party has an asset. Risk is important, as the party which has access to benefits (and hence an asset) will usually also be the one to suffer or gain if the benefits ultimately differ from those expected.

These points are considered in detail in the ASB's Statement of Principles.

1.6 Inclusion of assets and liabilities in the balance sheet

KEY POINT

Assets or liabilities should be **included** when there is **evidence** for their existence and they can be **measured** reliably. Assets should **cease to be recognised** when an entity has no access to the benefits and its risk is **immaterial**.

Assets and liabilities should be **included** in the balance sheet where there is both:

- sufficient **evidence** that an asset or liability exists; and
- the asset or liability can be **measured** at a monetary amount with sufficient reliability.

1.7 Transactions in previously recognised assets

An asset should **cease to be recognised** only where two conditions are both fulfilled:

- the entity retains no significant access to material benefits; and
- any risk the entity retains is **immaterial** in relation to the variation in benefits likely to occur in practice.

1.8 Disclosures

KEY POINT

Disclosure of a transaction should be sufficiently detailed to enable the user of the financial statements to understand its commercial effect.

Disclosure of a transaction should be sufficiently detailed to enable the user of the financial statements to understand its commercial effect.

A transaction may need to be disclosed whether or not it results in additional assets and liabilities being recognised. Where assets or liabilities are recognised but their nature differs from that of items usually found under the relevant balance sheet heading, the differences should be explained. For example, certain assets may not be available for use as security for liabilities.

To the extent that a transaction has not resulted in the recognition of assets or liabilities, it is still necessary to consider whether disclosure of its nature and effect is required in order to give a **true and fair view**. For example, the transaction may give rise to guarantees or other obligations.

1.9 Quasi-subsidiaries

Some off balance sheet financing arrangements include the use of another entity (a '**vehicle**') to house certain assets and liabilities. Normally, the arrangement will be structured so that the vehicle does not meet the legal definition of a subsidiary. Where the commercial effect is no different from that which would result were the vehicle a subsidiary, the vehicle will meet FRS 5's definition of a '**quasi-subsidiary**'.

DEFINITION

A **quasi-subsidiary** is a company, trust, partnership or other vehicle that, though not fulfilling the definition of a **subsidiary**, is directly or indirectly controlled by the reporting entity and gives rise to benefits for that entity that are in substance no different from those that would arise were the vehicle a subsidiary.

A **quasi-subsidiary** is a company, trust, partnership or other vehicle that, though not fulfilling the definition of a **subsidiary**, is directly or indirectly controlled by the reporting entity and gives rise to benefits for that entity that are in substance no different from those that would arise were the vehicle a subsidiary.

In identifying quasi-subsidiaries, we need to look at the benefits arising from the net assets of the 'vehicle'. Evidence of which party gains these benefits is given by which party is exposed to the risks inherent in them.

Where an entity has a quasi-subsidiary, the quasi-subsidiary should be included in consolidated accounts in the same way as if it were a subsidiary.

Where one or more quasi-subsidiaries are included in consolidated financial statements, this fact should be disclosed. A summary of the financial statements of each quasi-subsidiary should be disclosed in the notes to the financial statements.

1.10 Linked presentation and offset

Parts of FRS 5 are responding to comments requesting certain assets and liabilities to be linked together (i.e. the gross amount of assets and liabilities are shown but are also netted off) or offset (i.e. only the net amount shown).

Linked presentation

KEY POINT

Linked presentation is available for certain **non-recourse finance** arrangements involving selling an asset to a third party.

Linked presentation is available for certain **non-recourse finance** arrangements. Non-recourse finance involves selling an asset such as a debtor to a third party. Provided the seller does not have to make any payments to the purchaser if the debtor does not eventually pay the debt, the seller no longer has an asset (i.e. the debtor) as it does not meet the recognition criteria in the FRS (all significant benefits and risks have been transferred).

In some non-recourse finance arrangements, however, an entity retains significant benefits and risks associated with a specific item, but the maximum loss it can suffer is limited to a fixed monetary amount. In such circumstances, a 'linked' presentation is required to present the nature of such an arrangement.

Example

Extract from balance sheet:

	£	£
Debtor	80,000	
Less: Non-returnable amounts received on sale of debtor	80,000	–

Pressure for the above approach came from certain financial institutions (e.g. banks) which wanted to show their gross 'assets' (e.g. mortgages advanced) even though they had passed on the assets, in this particular form, to another entity.

Offset

KEY POINT

The FRS allows **offset** when the items do not constitute 'separate assets and liabilities'.

Offsetting of an asset and liability is generally not allowed, but here also the FRS is attempting to respond to special cases. It allows offset when the items do not constitute 'separate assets and liabilities'. Its main area of use would be certain types of bank balances and overdrafts.

Example

X plc has a bank overdraft of £50,000 at the Anytown branch of Northbank and a credit balance of £10,000 on another account at the same branch. The bank has a legal right of set-off between the two balances.

Extract from balance sheet:

	£
Bank overdraft	40,000

1.11 Companies Act 1985

The CA 85 contains a general requirement for directors, when determining the appropriate accounting for items, to have regard to the substance of the reported transaction, in accordance with generally accepted accounting principles or practice. Thus the Act is confirming the main objective of FRS 5.

The Act also prohibits assets from being set off against liabilities, and income from being set off against expenditure, confirming the general rule in FRS 5.

2 Application notes

2.1 Introduction

Detailed application notes are included in FRS 5 dealing with:

- **consignment stock**
- **sale and repurchase** agreements
- **factoring of debts**
- **securitised assets**
- **loan transfers**
- **Private Finance Initiative** (PFI) and similar contracts
- **revenue recognition**.

The notes are meant to clarify, rather than to override, the general principles of the FRS but they are mandatory. The note on revenue recognition has already been discussed earlier in this text, so is not covered here.

2.2 Consignment stock

DEFINITION

Consignment stock is stock held by one party but legally owned by another on terms which give holders the right to sell the stock or an option to return it unsold to the legal owner.

Consignment stock is stock held by one party but legally owned by another on terms which give holders the right to sell the stock in the normal course of business, or at their option, to return it unsold to the legal owner.

Legal title may pass when one of a number of events has occurred, for example when the dealer has held the stock for a specified period such as six months, or when the dealer has sold the goods. The sales price may be determined at the date of supply, or it may vary with the length of the period between supply and purchase, or it may be the manufacturer's factory price at sale.

Other terms of such arrangements can include a requirement for the dealer to pay a deposit, and responsibility for insurance. The arrangement should be analysed to determine whether the dealer has in substance acquired the stock before the date of transfer of legal title.

KEY POINT

Whoever bears the slow movement risk should recognise the stock on the balance sheet.

FRS 5 states that the key factor will be who **bears the risk** of slow moving stock. The risk involved is the cost of financing the stock for the period it is held. In a simple arrangement where stock is supplied for a fixed price that will be charged whenever the title is transferred and there is no deposit, the manufacturer bears the slow movement risk. If, however, the price to be paid increases by a factor that varies with interest rates and the time the stock is held, then the dealer bears the risk. If the price charged to the dealer is the manufacturer's list price at the date of sale, then again the risks associated with the stock fall on the manufacturer. Whoever bears the slow movement risk should recognise the stock on the balance sheet.

Consignment stock arrangements are most common in the **motor trade**.

Example

On 1 January 20X6 Gillingham plc, a manufacturer, entered into an agreement to provide Canterbury plc, a retailer, with machines for resale. Under the terms of the agreement Canterbury plc pays a fixed rental per month for each machine that it holds and also pays the cost of insuring and maintaining the machines. The company can display the machines in its showrooms and use them as demonstration models.

When a machine is sold to a customer, Canterbury plc pays Gillingham plc the factory price at the time the machine was originally delivered. All machines remaining unsold six months after their original delivery must be purchased by Canterbury plc at the factory price at the time of delivery.

Gillingham plc can require Canterbury plc to return the machines at any time within the six month period. In practice, this right has never been exercised. Canterbury plc can return unsold machines to Gillingham plc at any time during the six month period, without penalty. In practice, this has never happened.

At 31 December 20X6 the agreement is still in force and Canterbury plc holds several machines which were delivered less than six months earlier. How should these machines be treated in the accounts of Canterbury plc for the year ended 31 December 20X6?

Solution

The key issue is whether Canterbury plc has purchased the machines from Gillingham plc or whether they are merely on loan.

It is necessary to determine whether Canterbury plc has the benefits of holding the machines and is exposed to the risks inherent in those benefits.

Gillingham plc can demand the return of the machines and Canterbury plc is able to return them without paying a penalty. This suggests that Canterbury plc does not have the automatic right to retain or to use them.

Canterbury plc pays a rental charge for the machines, despite the fact that it may eventually purchase them outright. This suggests a financing arrangement as the rental could be seen as loan interest on the purchase price. Canterbury plc also incurs the costs normally associated with holding stocks.

The purchase price is the price at the date the machines were first delivered. This suggests that the sale actually takes place at the delivery date. Canterbury plc has to purchase any stocks still held six months after delivery. Therefore the company is exposed to slow payment and obsolescence risks. Because Canterbury plc can return the stocks before that time, this exposure is limited.

It appears that both parties experience the risks and benefits. However, although the agreement provides for the return of the machines, in practice this has never happened.

Conclusion: the machines are assets of Canterbury plc and should be included in the balance sheet.

2.3 Sale and repurchase agreements

KEY POINT

Sale and repurchase agreements are arrangements under which assets are sold by one party to another on terms that may provide for the seller to repurchase the assets.

Sale and repurchase agreements are arrangements under which assets are sold by one party to another on terms that provide for the seller to repurchase the assets in certain circumstances. The sale may be at market value or at some agreed percentage of market value. The repurchase arrangement may take a number of forms, for example, a commitment on the part of the seller, an option granted to the seller to require resale (a **call option**) or an option granted to the buyer to require repurchase (a **put option**). The arrangements often contain provisions to enable the seller to make use of the asset during its ownership by the buyer.

The repurchase price may be variable (depending on the original price and the period during which the asset has been held by the purchaser), agreed at the time of repurchase or subject to market price movements. The repurchase price may also be designed to permit the purchaser to recover incidental holding costs if these do not continue to be met by the seller.

FRS 5 states that the key question is whether the commercial effect is that of a sale or of a secured loan. A **secured loan transaction** will usually have the following features:

- the seller will secure access to all future benefits inherent in the asset, often through **call options**
- the buyer will secure adequate return on the purchase (interest on the loan, often through adjustment of the repurchase price) and appropriate protection against loss in value of the asset bought, often through **put options**.

The analysis should look at all features of the agreement that are likely to have a commercial effect in practice.

Sale and repurchase arrangements are common in **property development** and in **maturing whisky stocks**.

Example

X plc has sold a building to Z Ltd, an investment company, for £1m when the current market value was £2m. X can repurchase the property at any time within the next three years for the original selling price (£1m) plus a sum, added quarterly, based on the bank base lending rate plus 2%. How should X plc account for this transaction?

Solution

The substance of this deal is a secured loan from Z to X, with the expectation being that X will exercise its option to repurchase the building. No sale should therefore be recognised; the £1m is a loan received from Z Ltd.

ACTIVITY **2**

Bright plc operates a large hotel which it sold to Dim plc on 30 June 20X0 for its then market value of £12,000,000. Consider each of the four possible conditions attached to the sale given below and analyse the transaction.

(a) Bright plc leases the hotel from Dim plc at a nominal rental and agrees to repurchase the freehold for £25,000,000 on 1 July 20Y0.

(b) Bright plc leases the hotel from Dim plc at a market rental and Dim plc grants Bright plc an option to repurchase the hotel for £15,000,000 on 1 July 20Y0.

(c) Bright plc leases the hotel from Dim plc at a market rental and Dim plc grants Bright plc an option to repurchase the hotel for £5,000,000 on 1 July 20Y0.

(d) Bright plc leases the hotel from Dim plc at a market rental and agrees to repurchase the freehold at market value on 1 July 20Y0.

In each case, is the transaction a sale or a secured loan?

Feedback to this activity is at the end of the chapter.

2.4 Sale and leaseback

KEY POINT

If a sale and leaseback results in a **finance lease**, the substance of the transaction is a **loan** secured on the asset, rather than a sale.

A sale and repurchase agreement can be in the form of a **sale and leaseback**. If this is the case, the first step is to determine whether the lease is an operating lease or a finance lease according to the rules in SSAP 21.

If the lease is a **finance lease**, the lessee (the original owner of the asset) retains the risks and benefits attaching to the asset. This means that the substance of the transaction is a **loan** secured on the asset, rather than a sale. The asset remains in the balance sheet at its original value and the amount received on the sale is treated as a lease creditor. The lease payments are treated in the usual way, i.e. they are allocated between interest and repayment of capital.

2.5 Debt factoring

KEY POINT

If a factoring arrangement leads to the receipt of cash earlier than would have been the case, the seller has in substance received either a loan on the security of his debtors, or receipts that are credited to reduce a debtor.

Factoring of debts is a well-established method of obtaining finance. In most forms of factoring, debts are sold to the factor, but the latter's degree of control over, and responsibility for, those debts will vary from one arrangement to another. A significant accounting question is only likely to arise where the factoring arrangement leads to the receipt of cash earlier than would have been the case had the debts been unfactored. If this is so, the question to be answered is whether the seller has in substance received either a loan on the security of his debtors, or receipts that are appropriately credited to reduce a debtor.

If the seller is in essence a borrower, and the factor a lender, then the arrangements will be such as to provide that the seller pays the equivalent of interest to the factor on the timing difference between amounts received by him from the factor and those collected by the factor from the debtor. Such payment would be in addition to any other charges.

FRS 5 states that the key factor in the analysis will be who **bears the risk** (of slow payment) and the benefit (of early payment) by the debtor. If the finance cost reflects events subsequent to transfer, then the transfer is likely to be equivalent to obtaining finance because the seller is bearing the risks and rewards of the debtor. If the cost is determined when the transfer is made, with no other variable costs, then it is likely to be a straightforward sale.

The risk of bad debts is unlikely to be relevant to the analysis, as the exposure to such risk is agreed between the seller and the factor and charges will reflect this, just as in a normal credit insurance contract.

Example

On 1 January 20X6 Lewis plc entered into an agreement with Factoring plc whereby it transferred title to its debtors to Factoring plc subject to a reduction in bad debts based on past experience. Lewis plc received a payment of 90% of the total of net debtors. Under the terms of the agreement, the company had the right to a future sum, the amount of which depended on whether and when the debtors paid. Factoring plc had the right of recourse against Lewis plc for any additional losses up to an agreed maximum amount.

At 31 December 20X6, title had been transferred to debtors with an invoice value of £10 million less a bad debt provision of £300,000 and Lewis plc was subject under the agreement to a maximum potential debit of £100,000 to cover losses.

What is the appropriate accounting treatment for this transaction in the balance sheet of Lewis plc at 31 December 20X6?

Solution

As Lewis plc retains the risk of slow payment and bad debts, the substance of the transaction is that of a financing arrangement and the company has not disposed of the debtors.

Under the terms of the factoring agreement, finance will be repaid only from the proceeds generated by the debtors. There appears to be no possibility of any claim against Lewis plc being made other than against proceeds generated from the debtors. The finance appears to be non-returnable. There is only recourse for losses up to a fixed amount. These are indications that linked presentation is appropriate.

Balance sheet (extract)

	£m	£m
Current assets		
Gross debts (after providing for bad debts)	9.7	
Less: non returnable proceeds		
((90% × 9.7) – 0.1)	(8.63)	
		1.07
Cash		8.73
Creditors: amounts falling due within one year		
Recourse under factored debts		0.1

Conclusion

FRS 5 requires entities to recognise the substance of transactions rather than their legal form. In order to identify the substance of a transaction it is necessary to determine whether the assets or liabilities of the entity have changed as a result of entering into the transaction. The party to a transaction that suffers the risks and rewards attaching to an asset normally controls the asset, whether or not it legally owns it.

SELF-TEST QUESTIONS

1 Give four examples of ways in which companies have tried to keep assets and liabilities off the balance sheet. (1.2)

2 What are common features of transactions whose substance is not readily apparent? (1.5)

3 In general terms, how is the substance of a transaction determined? (1.5)

4 When should assets and liabilities be recognised in the balance sheet? (1.6)

5 What are the general disclosure requirements of FRS 5? (1.8)

6 What is a quasi-subsidiary? (1.9)

7 When is linked presentation used? (1.10)

8 What is consignment stock? (2.2)

9 What is a sale and repurchase agreement? (2.3)

10 How is a sale and leaseback treated in the financial statements? (2.4)

EXAM-TYPE QUESTION

D Ltd

FRS 5 *Reporting the substance of transactions* requires that a reporting entity's financial statements should report the substance of the transactions into which it has entered. FRS 5 states that in order to determine the substance of a transaction it is necessary to identify whether the transaction has given rise to new assets or liabilities for the reporting entity and whether it has changed the entity's existing assets or liabilities.

D Ltd has three principal activities. These are the sale of motor vehicles (both new and second-hand), the provision of spare parts for motor vehicles, and the servicing of motor vehicles.

During the financial year ended 31 August 20X6, the company has entered into a type of business transaction not previously undertaken by it. With effect from 1 January 20X6, D Ltd entered into an agreement whereby it received motor vehicles on a consignment basis from E plc, a large manufacturer. The terms of the arrangement were as follows.

- On delivery, the stock of vehicles remains the legal property of E plc.
- Legal title to a vehicle passes to D Ltd either when D Ltd enters into a binding arrangement to sell the vehicle to a third party, or six months after the date of delivery by E plc to D Ltd.

- At the date legal title passes, E plc invoices D Ltd for the sale of the vehicles. The price payable by D Ltd is the normal selling price of E plc at the date of delivery, increased by 1% for every complete month the vehicles are held on consignment by D Ltd. Any change in E plc's normal selling price between the date of delivery and the date legal title to the goods passes to D Ltd does not change the amount payable by D Ltd to E plc.
- At any time between the date of delivery and the date legal title passes to D Ltd, the company (D Ltd) has the right to return the vehicles to E plc provided they are not damaged or obsolete. D Ltd does not have the right to return damaged or obsolete vehicles. If D Ltd exercises this right of return then a return penalty is payable by D Ltd as follows:

Time since date of delivery	*Penalty as a percentage of invoiced price**
Three months or less	50%
Three to four months	75%
More than four months	100%

* i.e. the price that would otherwise be payable by D Ltd if legal title to the vehicles had passed at the date of return.

- E plc has no right to demand return of vehicles on consignment to D Ltd unless D Ltd becomes insolvent.

The managing director suggests that the vehicles should be shown as an asset of D Ltd only when title passes, and the purchase price becomes legally payable.

Required:

(a) Explain how (under the principles established in FRS 5) an asset or liability is identified, and when an asset or liability should be recognised and should cease to be recognised, in the financial statements of a business. **(12 marks)**

(b) Evaluate, in the light of the principles you have explained in (a), the correctness or otherwise of the managing director's suggested accounting treatment for the new transaction. **(8 marks)**

(Total: 20 marks)

FEEDBACK TO ACTIVITY 1

Companies have put forward a number of reasons to justify the use of off balance sheet financing schemes:

- to maintain a level of gearing similar to their counterparts in other countries (having regard to comparable permissible borrowing levels)
- to maintain the share price on the basis that the market would place a lower value on a listed company whose borrowings are considered by the analysts to be high
- to maintain return on capital employed by keeping the asset and the related liability off the balance sheet until the asset starts to produce income
- in groups of companies to keep activities which have different characteristics (e.g. high gearing ratios) separate (by keeping them off the balance sheet) in order not to distort the financial ratios of the remainder of the group.

FEEDBACK TO ACTIVITY 2

(a) Bright plc will receive the benefit of any increase in the value of the hotel and also bears the risk of any falls in the value of the hotel. The transaction is effectively that of a secured loan being taken out against the hotel with the repurchase price of £25,000,000 representing a repayment of the original sum advanced plus interest.

(b) Bright plc will benefit from any increase in the hotel's value, but does not run the risk of having to buy the hotel if its value is less than £25,000,000. It would appear that the hotel has been sold and in return Bright plc has received £12,000,000 plus the option. However, if Bright plc only operates the one hotel it may be necessary commercially for the company to exercise its option of repurchase on 1 July 20Y0. If this is the case then, once again, the sale is effectively a secured loan on the hotel.

(c) In this instance Bright plc is virtually obliged to repurchase the hotel given that the option is well below the hotel's current market value. The benefits and risks associated with any increase or fall in the value of the hotel all rest with Bright plc. The transaction is a secured loan.

(d) Bright plc has agreed to repurchase the hotel freehold at its market value on 1 July 20Y0 and could gain or lose depending on whether the market value of the hotel has risen or fallen. However these are not the risks of ownership as Bright plc will lose if the value of the hotel increases, that is, it does not receive the benefits associated with owning the asset. The transaction is a sale.

Chapter 20

HIRE PURCHASE AND LEASING

CHAPTER CONTENTS

1 Explanation of credit and leasing agreements
2 Finance leases and operating leases
3 Recording operating leases in the books of the lessee
4 Recording finance leases in the books of the lessee
5 Recording leases in the books of the lessor

This chapter covers the appropriate accounting treatment for assets that are used by a business but where payment for the asset is spread over time. In some cases, such as finance leases, the user of the asset will never become the owner of the asset.

There is a fair amount of new terminology and accounting entries for you to consider. The most important thing to grasp is the main principle: account for the substance of the arrangement. That is, treat a finance lease as if the business has purchased an asset and taken on a loan to finance the purchase.

The chapter also covers the transactions from the point of view of the business providing the asset – the lessor or HP trader. This area may be new to you and should be studied carefully. Most exam questions, however, concentrate on the user of the asset and not the supplier.

Objectives

By the time you have finished this chapter you should be able to:

- distinguish between a hire purchase contract and a lease
- describe and apply the method of determining a lease type
- explain the effect on the financial statements of a finance lease being incorrectly treated as an operating lease
- account for operating leases in financial statements
- account for finance leases in the financial statements of lessor and lessee
- outline the principles of SSAP 21 and its main disclosure requirements.

1 Explanation of credit and leasing agreements

1.1 Introduction

It is important to distinguish between the different types of agreement whereby payment can be made on extended terms so that the appropriate means of accounting can be considered.

DEFINITION

Under a **hire purchase agreement**, goods are supplied on hire to customers on terms that, once an agreed number of instalments have been paid, they may exercise an option to purchase the goods for a nominal sum.

1.2 Hire purchase

Under a **hire purchase agreement**, goods are supplied on hire to customers on terms that, once an agreed number of instalments have been paid, they may exercise an option to purchase the goods for a nominal sum. Until the option is exercised, the goods remain the legal property of the supplier.

As the goods remain the property of the seller until the option to purchase is exercised, the seller may repossess the goods for non-payment of instalments, although a court order is required for repossession once one-third of the hire purchase price has been paid.

If we accounted for the legal form of the transaction, the asset would not be treated as an asset in the accounts of the user of the item until all payments had been made. However, as the substance of the transaction is the purchase of an asset financed over time, an HP item is recorded as an asset from the date of the agreement in the books of the 'buyer'.

KEY POINT

Under a hire purchase agreement, until the **option to purchase** is exercised, goods remain the legal property of the supplier.

Treating the goods as a fixed asset in the books of the buyer creates an accounting problem in that the total amounts payable under the agreement exceed the price which would have been paid on a normal sale for credit or cash.

The solution for the buyer is to record the asset at its 'cash price' and any excess is treated as interest which is charged to profit and loss account over the life of the agreement.

1.3 Credit sale agreement

KEY POINT

A **credit sale agreement** is a contract for the sale of goods, whereby the price is paid by instalments. Since ownership passes on delivery to the buyer, the seller's only remedy on default by the buyer is to sue for the outstanding instalments; he cannot recover the goods.

A **credit sale agreement** is a contract for the sale of goods, whereby the price is paid by instalments. Since ownership passes on delivery to the buyer, the seller's only remedy on default by the buyer is to sue for the outstanding instalments; he cannot recover the goods.

Credit sale agreements are treated in a similar way to hire purchase in the books of the buyer.

In the books of the seller, the transaction is treated as a sale at the date of the agreement, but the proceeds need to be split between 'normal' proceeds, i.e. those that would have been receivable on a cash sale, and the interest element. The difference between 'normal' proceeds and cost is a trading profit which is taken to the profit and loss account in the accounting period in which the agreement is entered into. The interest element is spread over the life of the agreement in the profit and loss account and recorded as interest receivable.

1.4 Lease agreements

KEY POINT

Under a **lease agreement**, a customer agrees to hire goods, normally for a fixed minimum period with rights of renewal. The goods remain the property of the hirer throughout the period.

Under a **lease agreement**, a customer agrees to hire goods, normally for a fixed minimum period with rights of renewal. The goods remain the property of the original owner throughout the period. Lease agreements can involve a finance lease, a long-term arrangement where the rights and responsibilities in the asset pass to the user (lessee), or an operating lease, a short-term arrangement where such rights remain with the owner (lessor).

In substance a finance lease is similar to a hire purchase transaction, as the lessee treats the asset as if it is his own property. The lease is recorded as a **fixed asset** in the lessee's books. We will see later how this is achieved.

The lessor will treat the transaction as if he has made a loan to the lessee which, initially, will be represented by the cost of providing the asset for the use of the lessee. This loan will be reduced over a period of time by the 'capital' element of the rental payments made by the lessee. The 'income' elements of the rentals will constitute interest income to be recorded in the profit and loss account over the period of the 'loan'.

KEY POINT

Of all the agreements which require payment for the use of an asset over a period of time, it is only for **operating leases** that the user of the asset does not record the asset as a fixed asset in his books.

An **operating lease** will, however, be treated as a fixed asset in the books of the **lessor**, as it is contemplated that the lessor will be hiring out the asset to more than one person. The lessee does not treat the asset as a fixed asset and the rentals paid are expenses to be charged in the profit and loss account.

Of all the agreements which require payment for the use of an asset over a period of time, it is only for operating leases that the user of the asset does not record the asset as a fixed asset in his books.

2 Finance leases and operating leases

2.1 Lease agreements

KEY POINT

Lease agreements can be either **finance leases** or **operating leases**.

The impetus for the issue of SSAP 21 *Accounting for leases and hire purchase contracts* was the need to change the accounting treatment of leases.

As mentioned earlier, lease agreements can be either finance leases, where the rights and responsibilities of ownership (though not the legal title) pass to the user, or operating leases where such rights remain with the owner.

2.2 Substance over form

KEY POINT

Finance leases give rights over the use of assets for a period which covers all or a substantial part of their useful life, so failure to capitalise such leases could distort comparisons between companies (e.g. **return on capital employed** and **gearing**).

Finance leases give rights over the use of assets for a period which covers all or a substantial part of their useful life. Such leases are effectively an alternative to hire purchase and loan financing, so failure to capitalise such leases would give rise to a disparity of accounting treatments which could distort comparisons between companies. In particular, comparisons could be misleading of:

- **return on capital employed**
- **gearing**.

Return on capital employed normally reduces, and gearing normally increases, when leases are included in the balance sheet.

The treatment of finance leases is an example of the application of substance over form.

KEY POINT

Substance over form requires that transactions and other events should be accounted for and presented in accordance with their substance and financial reality and not merely with their legal form.

Substance over form requires that transactions and other events should be accounted for and presented in accordance with their substance and financial reality and not merely with their legal form.

Substance over form is at the heart of SSAP 21.

- Under a finance lease, the lessee acquires substantially all the benefits of use of an asset for the substantial majority of its useful economic life. The lessee also takes on the risks of ownership – repairs, maintenance and insurance. A finance lease is therefore similar to the purchase of an asset on credit terms.
- Under a finance lease, the lessor is providing finance and obtaining a return on his investment.

2.3 Identifying finance leases

DEFINITION

A **finance lease** is a lease that transfers substantially all the risks and rewards of ownership of an asset to the lessee.

A **finance lease** is defined as a lease that transfers substantially all the risks and rewards of ownership of an asset to the lessee.

There are a number of features which indicate whether or not a lease is a finance lease. The most important of these is the '90% test'.

The '90% test'

It should be presumed that a lease is a finance lease if, at the inception of the lease, the present value of the minimum lease payments amounts to substantially all (90% or more) of the fair value of the leased asset. To decide whether this is the case it is necessary to complete the following steps:

Step		*Comment*
1	Calculate minimum lease payments (MLPs) inclusive of initial payment.	MLPs = minimum payments plus any residual amounts guaranteed by lessee.
2	Discount (1) to determine the present value of the MLPs.	Discount rate is normally the rate of interest implicit in the lease.
3	Calculate fair value of asset at beginning of lease.	Fair value = arm's length price less any government grants receivable by lessor.
4	Presumption is satisfied if (2) amounts to 90% or more of (3).	

Other tests

A finance lease **transfers the risks and rewards of ownership to the lessee**. SSAP 21 states that even if a lease meets the '90% test' it should not be treated as a finance lease if it can be demonstrated that this transfer is not the case. Similarly, even if a lease fails the '90% test' it should be classified as a finance lease if it can be demonstrated that the lease does in fact transfer the risks and rewards of ownership to the lessee.

However, SSAP 21 uses the words 'in exceptional circumstances' and this has caused problems. If a leased asset and the related creditor are brought into the balance sheet, gearing normally increases significantly, meaning that investors and lenders may view the company as a much riskier prospect. Therefore, lease agreements are often deliberately structured so that the minimum lease payments are 88% or 89% of the fair value of the leased asset, and so the lease is technically an operating lease.

KEY POINT

A lease is probably a **finance** lease if the lessee is able to use the asset for most of its useful economic life and is responsible for repairing and insuring it; the asset is specialised, or there is an option of a secondary lease term.

A lease is probably a finance lease if:

- the lessee is able to use the asset for all or most of its useful economic life (as if the lessee owned the asset: look at the length of the lease term)
- the lessee is responsible for repairing and insuring the asset (the lessee has the risk of breakdown or theft)
- the nature of the asset is specialised so that only the lessee can use it
- there is an option for a secondary lease term at a nominal rent (if so, the lessee is reasonably certain to exercise it, with the effect that the lessee has the asset for its useful economic life).

ACTIVITY **1**

Warner Ltd leases an asset which has a useful economic life of five years. It could be purchased outright for £16,500. The rate of interest implicit in the lease is 10%.

Five annual rentals of £3,956 are payable in advance. Warner Ltd is responsible for the maintenance of the equipment.

Is the lease an operating lease or a finance lease?

Feedback to this activity is at the end of the chapter.

3 Recording operating leases in the books of the lessee

KEY POINT

Rentals under operating leases should be charged to the profit and loss account on a straight-line basis over the term of the lease.

3.1 Accounting treatment

Rentals under operating leases should be charged to the profit and loss account on a straight-line basis over the term of the lease, unless another systematic and rational basis is more appropriate. Any difference between amounts charged and amounts paid should be adjusted to debtors or creditors.

KEY POINT

Lessees should disclose the payments which they are committed to make during the next year, analysed between years in which the commitment expires. Operating lease rentals should be charged as an expense in the profit and loss account.

3.2 Disclosure – operating leases

Obligations under operating leases

In respect of operating leases, the lessee should disclose the payments which they are committed to make during the next year, analysed between those in which the commitment expires: within that year; in the second to fifth years inclusive; and over five years from the balance sheet date. The commitments in respect of leases of land and buildings should be shown separately from those of other operating leases.

Profit and loss account

Total operating lease rentals should be charged as an expense in the profit and loss account – split between hire of plant and machinery rentals and other operating leases.

Example

At 31 December 20X2 the company had annual commitments under non-cancellable operating leases as set out below:

	Land and buildings	*Other*
	£	£
Operating leases which expire:		
Within one year	x	x
In the second to fifth years inclusive	x	x
Over five years	x	x

This disclosure does not require the total sums which will actually be paid in future, but merely for how long a particular lease will require payments. For example, a company uses two offices, both leased:

Lease A expires in 3 years – annual rental £30,000
Lease B expires in 45 years – annual rental £20,000

The disclosure would be:

Land and buildings

	£
Operating leases which expire:	
In the second to fifth years inclusive	30,000
Over five years	20,000
Total annual commitment as at the current year-end	50,000

4 Recording finance leases in the books of the lessee

4.1 Initial entries

KEY POINT

At the start of the lease, the **present value** of the MLPs should be included as a **fixed asset**; the obligation to pay rentals should be included as a **liability**.

At the start of the lease:

- the **present value** of the MLPs should be included as a **fixed asset**, subject to depreciation
- the obligation to pay rentals should be included as a **liability**.

In practice, the fair value of the asset or its cash price will often be a sufficiently close approximation to the present value of the MLPs and therefore can be used instead.

4.2 Depreciation

KEY POINT

The related fixed asset should be depreciated over the shorter of the **useful economic life** or the **lease term**.

The related fixed asset should be depreciated over the shorter of:

- the **useful economic life** of the asset (as in FRS 15)
- the **lease term.**

The lease term is essentially the period over which the lessee has the use of the asset. It includes:

- the primary (non-cancellable) period

- any secondary periods during which the lessee has the contractual right to continue to use the asset, provided that it is reasonably certain at the outset that this right will be exercised.

4.3 Payment of rentals and allocation of finance charges

KEY POINT

Rental payments should be split between **finance charges** (P&L expense) and **repayments** (reducing balance sheet liabilities).

There are three main methods of allocating finance charges: **actuarial**, **sum of the digits**, and **straight-line**.

Each individual rental payment should be split between:

- finance charge (an expense in the profit and loss account)
- repayment of obligation to pay rentals (thus reducing the balance sheet liability).

Over the period of the lease, the total finance charge is the amount by which the rentals paid to the lessor exceed the present value of the MLPs.

How should finance charges be allocated over the term of the lease? The basic aim is to allocate the charge in such a way as to produce a reasonably constant periodic rate of return on the remaining balance of liability. There are three main methods:

- **actuarial** method
- **sum of the digits** (rule of 78) method
- **straight-line** method.

Of the above methods the actuarial method gives the most accurate result.

KEY POINT

The **actuarial** method allocates interest at a constant rate on the outstanding amount.

4.4 The actuarial method

The **actuarial method** allocates interest at a constant rate on the outstanding amount.

Example

A company has a choice. It can buy an asset for cash at a cost of £5,710 or it can lease it by way of a finance lease. The terms of the lease are as follows:

- The primary period is for four years from 1 January 20X2 with a rental of £2,000 p.a. payable on the 31 December each year.
- The lessee has the right to continue to lease the asset after the end of the primary period for an indefinite period, subject only to a peppercorn (nominal) rent.
- The lessee is required to pay all repair, maintenance and insurance costs as they arise.
- The interest rate implicit in the lease is 15%.

The lessee estimates the useful economic life of the asset to be eight years. Depreciation is provided on a straight-line basis.

Solution

Step 1

Is the lease a finance lease?

Referring to the steps in the table shown earlier in this chapter:

1 MLPs = 4 × £2,000 = £8,000

2 Present value of MLPs:

From discount tables take the factor for the present value of four annual sums, the first receivable at the end of the first year:

£2,000 × 2.855 = £5,710

3 Fair value of asset is £5,710.

4 Present value of MLPs is more than 90% of the asset's fair value.

The lease is therefore a finance lease.

Step 2

The asset is shown in the balance sheet at £5,710 (subject to depreciation).

Depreciation is over eight years (presumably there is no residual value to the asset at the end of eight years).

Annual depreciation charge = 1/8 × £5,710 = £714

Step 3

The liability is shown in the balance sheet at £5,710 but is subsequently reduced by the capital portion of the leasing payments.

The total finance charge is £(8,000 – 5,710) = £2,290. The allocation of this to each rental payment, and the consequent capital sum outstanding, is calculated as follows:

Period (year ended 31 December)	*Capital sum at start of period*	*Finance charge at 15% p.a.*	*Subtotal*	*Rental paid*	*Capital sum at end of period*
	£	£	£	£	£
20X2	5,710	856	6,566	(2,000)	4,566
20X3	4,566	685	5,251	(2,000)	3,251
20X4	3,251	488	3,739	(2,000)	1,739
20X5	1,739	261	2,000	(2,000)	-
		2,290		8,000	

Step 4

The effect on the financial statements of the lessee may be summarised as follows:

Profit and loss account			*Balance sheet*			
				Obligation		
Year ended 31 December	*Finance charge*	*Dep'n*	*Fixed asset (NBV)*	*Total*	*Non-current*	*Current*
	£	£	£	£	£	£
20X2	856	714	4,996	4,566	3,251	1,315
20X3	685	714	4,282	3,251	1,739	1,512
20X4	488	714	3,568	1,739	-	1,739
20X5	261	714	2,854	-	-	-
20X6	-	714	2,140	-	-	-
20X7	-	714	1,426	-	-	-
20X8	-	714	712	-	-	-
20X9	-	712	-	-	-	-
	2,290	5,710				

The finance charge each year is a constant periodic rate of return (15%) on the remaining balance of liability, e.g. £856 is 15% of £5,710.

KEY POINT

The **sum of the years'** digits method distributes interest in proportion to the reducing balance outstanding.

4.5 The sum of the years' digits method

The total interest charge contained in the agreement is distributed over the life of the agreement arithmetically in proportion to the reducing balances outstanding.

ACTIVITY **2**

£234 interest is charged on a hire purchase agreement spread over twelve instalments.

Calculate the interest charge included in each instalment, using the sum of the years' digits method.

Feedback to this activity is at the end of the chapter.

KEY POINT

The **straight-ine method** apportions finance charges **equally** over the period of the lease.

4.6 The straight-line method

The finance charges are apportioned equally over the period of the lease. For example, in the activity above, the finance charge would be £19.50 for each of the 12 years.

The straight-line method does not produce a reasonably constant periodic rate of return on the remaining balance of liability and therefore it should not be used unless the lease is 'small'.

4.7 Summary of bookkeeping entries

At the **inception** of the lease:

- Dr Fixed assets: Cost
- Cr Lease creditor

with the present value of the minimum lease payments/fair value of the leased asset.

At the **end** of each period of the lease:

- Dr Depreciation expense (profit and loss account)
- Cr Fixed assets: accumulated depreciation

with the depreciation charge for the period.

As each **rental is paid**:

- Dr Lease creditor
- Cr Cash

with the rental paid, and

- Dr Interest expense (profit and loss account)
- Cr Lease creditor

with the finance charge.

KEY POINT

Disclose either the **gross** amount of assets held under a finance lease (for each class) or the **net** amount under finance leases.

4.8 Disclosure

For disclosure purposes finance leases and hire purchase agreements are treated in the same way.

Balance sheet: assets

There is a choice of disclosure for assets. Either:

- show by each major class of asset the **gross** amounts of assets held under a finance lease and related accumulated depreciation; or
- integrate the finance lease assets with owned fixed assets and disclose the **net** amount of assets held under finance leases.

Balance sheet: obligations under finance leases

The amounts of obligations related to finance leases (net of finance charges allocated to future periods) should be disclosed separately from other obligations and liabilities, either on the face of the balance sheet or in the notes to the accounts.

KEY POINT

Obligations related to finance leases should be disclosed separately either on the face of the balance sheet or in the notes.

These net obligations under finance leases should then be analysed between amounts payable in the next year, amounts payable in the second to fifth years inclusive from the balance sheet date, and the aggregate amounts payable thereafter. This analysis may be presented either:

1 separately for obligations under finance leases

2 where the total of these items is combined on the balance sheet with other obligations and liabilities, by giving the equivalent analysis of the total in which it is included.

KEY POINT

Depreciation and aggregate finance charges for the period should be disclosed in respect of finance leases.

If the analysis is presented according to 1 above, a lessee may, as an alternative to analysing the net obligations, analyse the gross obligations, with future finance charges being separately deducted from the total.

Profit and loss account

The total **depreciation** charge and the **aggregate finance** charges for the period in respect of finance leases should be disclosed.

Example

Using the earlier illustration and the calculations under the actuarial method (see above) the following disclosure would be appropriate:

Extracts from balance sheet

	31 Dec 20X2
	£
Assets:	
Leased property under finance leases	5,710
Less: Accumulated depreciation	714
	4,996

Alternatively, the above figures could be included within the overall totals of fixed assets, and merely the NBV of £4,996 would be disclosed.

Extracts from balance sheet

	£
Liabilities:	
Non-current obligations under finance leases	3,251
Current obligations under finance leases	1,315
	4,566

The above figures may be disclosed separately on the face of the balance sheet or aggregated with other items (e.g. bank loans and overdrafts). In the latter situation the notes to the accounts would reveal the above figures.

Notes to the accounts – obligations under finance leases

The future minimum lease payments to which the company is committed as at 31 December 20X2 are:

	£
Amounts payable next year	2,000
Amounts payable in the second and third years	4,000
	6,000
Less: Finance charges allocated to future periods	1,434
	4,566

An alternative disclosure would be:

The future net obligations to which the company is committed as at 31 December 20X2 are:

	£
Amounts due within one year	1,315
Amounts due in the second and third years	3,251
	4,566

Notes to the accounts – profit and loss account

Profit is stated after charging:

	£
Depreciation of owned assets	X
Depreciation of assets held under finance leases (and hire purchase contracts – if relevant)	714
Finance charges payable:	
Finance leases (and hire purchase contracts)	856
Hire of plant and machinery – operating leases	X
Hire of other assets – operating leases	X

Extract from statement of accounting policies

Where assets are financed by leasing agreements that give rights approximating to ownership ('finance leases'), the assets are treated as if they had been purchased outright at the present value of the total rentals payable during the primary period of the lease. The corresponding leasing commitments are shown as obligations to the lessor.

Charges are made to the profit and loss account in respect of:

- depreciation – which is provided on a straight-line basis over the economic useful life of the asset
- the total finance charge – which is allocated over the primary period of the lease using the actuarial method.

ACTIVITY 3

P Ltd entered into a five-year lease on 1 January 20X3 for a machine with a fair value of £20,000. Rentals are £5,200 p.a. payable in advance, and the residual value at the end of the lease is calculated as £4,200 which will be returned to P Ltd.

P Ltd is responsible for insurance and maintenance costs. The rate of interest implicit in the lease is 15.15%. You are required to show the allocation of finance charges on a sum of the digits basis and on an actuarial basis and comment on the result.

Feedback to this activity is at the end of the chapter.

5 Recording leases in the books of the lessor

5.1 Introduction

KEY POINT

Finance leases are equivalent to the provision of finance. Operating leases should be accounted for by capitalising and depreciating the leased asset.

From the viewpoint of the lessor, the substance over form argument regards a finance lease as being equivalent to the provision of finance, rather than the hiring out of a fixed asset. Conversely an operating lease should be accounted for by capitalising and depreciating the leased asset.

The two types of lease may be compared as follows:

	Finance leases	*Operating leases*
Balance sheet	Net investment in finance lease (i.e. a debtor)	Property held for operating leases (cost less depreciation)
Profit and loss account	Finance income (allocated on basis which gives constant periodic return on net cash investment)	Rental income (straight-line basis) Depreciation

5.2 Accounting for finance leases

KEY POINT

SSAP 21 requires receivables to be carried on a balance sheet at an amount based on the **net investment in the lease**. Conversely it requires that profit recognition should normally be based on the lessor's **net cash investment** (NCI).

SSAP 21 deals with calculating the carrying value of finance lease receivables and with lessors' profit recognition. The rentals paid by the lessee should be apportioned by the lessor between:

- gross earnings (i.e. the lessor's interest earned)
- repayment of capital.

It requires receivables to be carried on a balance sheet at an amount based on the **net investment in the lease**. The net investment in a lease is initially the cost of the asset to the lessor, less any government or other grants receivable (i.e. the fair value). Over the period of the lease the net investment in the lease (i.e. the carrying value of the receivables) will therefore be the fair value of the asset less those portions of the rentals which are apportioned as a repayment of capital.

Conversely, SSAP 21 requires that profit recognition should normally be based on the lessor's **net *cash* investment** (NCI), which is based on the funds that the lessor has invested in the lease. This is different from the net investment in the lease because there are a number of other cash flows which affect the lessor in addition to those which affect net investment. In particular, tax cash flows are an important component of the NCI.

KEY POINT

For the purposes of profit recognition the total gross earnings should normally be allocated to accounting periods to give a **constant periodic rate of return** on the lessor's NCI in the lease in each period.

For the purposes of profit recognition the total gross earnings should normally be allocated to accounting periods to give a **constant periodic rate of return** on the lessor's NCI in the lease in each period.

The standard permits a reasonable approximation to be made in arriving at the constant periodic rate of return. Hence there are a number of different methods of profit recognition which may comply with the standard.

The two most precise methods (the '**after tax**' methods) are the **actuarial method after tax** and the **investment period** method, but the calculations involved are rather complicated.

EXAM HINT

Think of lessor accounting as the mirror image of the entries made in the lessee's accounts.

Instead the '**pre-tax**' methods already looked at in lessee accounting (i.e. the **straight-line** method, the **sum of the digits** method and the **actuarial** method) will usually give an acceptable answer for lessor accounting as well.

A particular exam question will specify the method to be used, but it will help if you think of lessor accounting as being the mirror image of the entries made in the lessee's accounts. However, the examiner has stated in the Syllabus Guidance Notes that the net cash investment method will not be examined. Therefore, any lessor accounting is likely to be made quite simple, if it appears in the examination.

Example

The lessor in the example of the actuarial method above will account for the leased asset as follows:

- confirm that the terms of the lease satisfy the conditions to be a finance lease (as above)
- recognise the £5,710 value of the asset as a receivable (debtor), 'investment in finance lease'

- recognise the finance income receivable each year on the same basis that the lessee recognised the finance charge payable.

Year	*Finance income receivable*
	£
20X2	856
20X3	685
20X4	488
20X5	261
	2,290

At the end of the primary period of the lease, the total lease payments received (4 × £2,000) will exactly equal the original receivable (£5,710) plus the total finance income recognised (£2,290).

5.3 Accounting for hire purchase contracts

KEY POINT

In the case of **hire purchase**, profit recognition should also be based on NCI. The allocation of **gross earnings** based on net investment will in most cases be a suitable approximation to allocation based on NCI.

In the case of **hire purchase**, profit recognition should also, in principle, be based on NCI. However, since the tax capital allowances under a hire purchase contract are claimed by the hirer, the finance company's NCI is often not significantly different from its net investment. Thus, again, the allocation of gross earnings (i.e. finance charges) based on net investment will in most cases be a suitable approximation to allocation based on NCI.

This will have the result that, again, the entries in the finance company's accounts will be a mirror image of the entries in the hirer's accounts if the hirer is using the actuarial method before tax.

5.4 Presentation in accounts

KEY POINT

SSAP 21 requires disclosure of the net investment in finance leases and hire purchase contracts at each balance sheet date. The amounts should be described as **receivables**.

SSAP 21 requires disclosure of the net investment in finance leases and hire purchase contracts at each balance sheet date. The amounts should be described as **receivables**. Whereas in lessee accounting the figures in respect of leases and hire purchase contracts may be aggregated, in the case of lessors and finance companies, the amounts in respect of each should be shown separately.

For companies subject to Sch 4 CA85, the net investment in finance leases and hire purchase contracts should be included in current assets under the heading 'debtors' and described as 'finance lease receivables' and/or 'hire purchase receivables' as appropriate. It should be analysed in the notes to the accounts between those amounts receivable within one year and those amounts receivable thereafter.

A suitable form of disclosure would be as follows:

Balance sheet as at 31 December 20X7

	20X7	*20X6*
Current assets:	£	£
Finance lease and hire purchase receivables	1,200	1,100

Notes to the accounts

(1) The amounts receivable under finance leases and hire purchase contracts comprise:

	20X7	*20X6*
	£	£
Finance leases	900	820
Hire purchase contracts	300	280
	1,200	1,100

(2) Included in the total receivables is £900 (20X6 £850) which falls due after more than one year.

KEY POINT

SSAP 21 requires that the gross amounts and accumulated depreciation of assets held for use in operating leases should be disclosed.

SSAP 21 requires that the gross amounts (i.e. original cost or revaluation) and accumulated depreciation of assets held for use in operating leases should be disclosed. This information could be incorporated into tables showing the amounts for other fixed assets, or could be shown as a separate table. It is recognised that, for banks, assets held for use in operating leases are different in nature from a bank's infrastructure (e.g. its own premises). Hence it may not be appropriate to combine assets held for use in operating leases with a bank's infrastructure for capital adequacy purposes.

5.5 Manufacturer/dealer lessor

A manufacturer or dealer may offer customers the option of either outright purchase or rental of an asset. The rental option is a means of encouraging sales and may be packaged to appear attractive, e.g. cars sold with 0% finance option.

The question then arises as to whether the total profit on a transaction is split into a trading profit (and thus recognised at the date the agreement is signed) plus finance income (spread over the lifetime of the agreement).

KEY POINT

A manufacturer or dealer/lessor should not recognise a selling profit under an operating lease. The selling profit under a finance lease should be restricted to the excess of the fair value of the asset over the cost, less grants.

SSAP 21 states the following:

> *'A manufacturer or dealer/lessor should not recognise a selling profit under an operating lease. The selling profit under a finance lease should be restricted to the excess of the fair value of the asset over the manufacturer's or dealer's cost less any grants receivable by the manufacturer or dealer towards the purchase, construction or use of the asset.'*

The fair value of the asset can be taken to be the cash selling price, as long as the credit terms reflect a reasonable level of interest. However where, for example, a car dealer is offering 0% finance deals, it is not reasonable to record all the profit as trading profit and no finance income. Clearly the trader in this situation is reducing the fair value of the car. An approach that could be taken in this situation is to discount the lease payments using a reasonable estimate of the implicit rate of interest. The PV of the MLPs thus becomes the fair value for determining trading profit.

Conclusion

SSAP 21 defines a finance lease as a lease that transfers substantially all the risks and rewards of ownership to the lessee. An operating lease is a lease other than a finance lease. Assets leased under finance leases are included on the balance sheet of the lessee and the related liability is included in creditors.

A lessor should record amounts receivable under finance leases as a debtor. Assets leased under operating leases remain as fixed assets in the lessor's balance sheet.

SELF-TEST QUESTIONS

1 Which accounting concept underpins the requirements of SSAP 21? (2.2)

2 What is a finance lease? (2.3)

3 How can a finance lease be distinguished from an operating lease in practice? (2.3)

4 How are operating leases treated in the financial statements of the lessee? (3.1)

5 What are the three methods of allocating the finance cost when a lessee is accounting for a finance lease? (4.3)

6 How are obligations under finance leases disclosed in the accounts of the lessee? (4.8)

7 How are gross earnings allocated to accounting periods when accounting for a finance lease in the accounts of a lessor? (5.2)

8 How are amounts receivable under finance leases disclosed in the balance sheet of a lessor? (5.4)

PRACTICE QUESTION

Jones plc

Jones plc is considering acquiring on 1 January 20X7 the use of a major piece of heavy agricultural plant, the Vinnie, which has a useful economic life of 8 years with nil residual value. The cost of the Vinnie would be £600,000 if it were bought for cash. Jones plc has employed a firm of consultants, Cly Vallon and Co, who are experienced in high value purchases of this type, to recommend a range of financing options. Their suggestions are as follows, all transactions being with Backward Bust plc.

Option A

Enter an HP agreement for the Vinnie. The rentals would be £100,000 per annum for four years, with a deposit of £100,000 payable immediately. At the end of the four-year period, Jones plc would have the option to purchase the Vinnie for £200,000.

Option B

Enter an eight-year lease for the Vinnie, with lease rentals of £110,000 payable annually in advance.

Option C

Enter a four-year lease for the Vinnie, with lease rentals of £150,000 payable annually in advance, and with an optional secondary period of three years at rentals of 60%, 40% and 20% of the annual rental in the primary period. Maintenance and insurance are to be the responsibility of Jones plc but Backward Bust plc has negotiated a guaranteed trade-in with the manufacturer at £166,000 if Jones plc returns the Vinnie after four years and does not take up the secondary period. The rate of interest implicit in the lease is 13.5%. The Vinnie would be worthless at the end of the secondary lease period if it was taken up.

Required:

(a) Prepare a memorandum for the finance director of Jones plc setting out the amounts to be included in the balance sheet and profit and loss account of Jones plc at 31 December 20X7 under each of the three options, explaining briefly the justification for the treatments you have adopted. **(10 marks)**

(b) State briefly (without calculations) how the three alternatives would be treated in Backward Bust plc's accounts for the year ended 31 December 20X7.

(4 marks)

(Total: 14 marks)

EXAM-TYPE QUESTION

P Ltd

P Ltd is an engineering company which invests heavily in plant and equipment. Due to poor cashflow in recent years the majority of this investment has been financed by loans. Consequently, the gearing ratio of P Ltd has increased to an unacceptably high level. However, the requirement for new plant and equipment for the business remains as high as ever.

One of the assistant accountants of P Ltd suggests that one way to obtain the additional plant required, without increasing the gearing ratio by further borrowings, would be to lease the plant rather than buy it. Accordingly, the assistant accountant obtains details concerning the possibility of leasing an item of plant required by P Ltd on 1 October 20X5.

These are as follows:

- The cost to purchase the plant outright would be £2 million. The plant would have a five-year life, with no residual value.
- The plant can be leased on a five-year lease with 20 quarterly payments (in arrears) of £122,320. P Ltd would be responsible for the repairs and maintenance to the asset during the lease term, and would have an option to purchase the asset for £1 at the end of the lease term.

The board of directors is considering the principle of switching from outright purchase of plant to leasing. The directors are attracted by the suggestions of the assistant accountant that the leasing option will have beneficial effects on the gearing of the company when compared with outright purchase.

Required:

(a) Draft a memorandum to the assistant accountant responding to their suggestion that leasing the asset will have no effect on the gearing ratio of P Ltd. Your memorandum should refer to the provisions of any relevant accounting standards. **(8 marks)**

(b) Prepare extracts from the financial statements of P Ltd for the year ending 31 December 20X5 showing the effect of the leased asset on the profit and loss account and the balance sheet. Interest on finance leases is allocated using the sum of the digits method. **(12 marks)**

(Total: 20 marks)

For the answers to these questions, see the 'Answers' section at the end of the book.

FEEDBACK TO ACTIVITY **1**

Discounting the lease payments using a rate of 10% gives us the following result:

Year	*Discount factor*	£
1	1	3,956
2	0.909	3,596
3	0.826	3,268
4	0.751	2,971
5	0.683	2,702
Net present value		16,493

This is 99.9% of the fair value of the asset. The lease term is five years, which is the same as the useful economic life of the asset. The lessee bears the cost of maintaining the equipment.

Conclusion: The lease is a finance lease.

FEEDBACK TO ACTIVITY **2**

The sum of the years' digits for 12 instalments is:

12 + 11 + 10 + 9 + 8 + 7 + 6 + 5 + 4 + 3 + 2 + 1 = 78

The interest is spread as follows:

Instalment no.	*Relevant fraction*		*Interest charge per instalment (£)*
1	12/78	x £234	36
2	11/78	x £234	33
3	10/78	x £234	30
4	9/78	x £234	27
5	8/78	x £234	24
6	7/78	x £234	21
7	6/78	x £234	18
8	5/78	x £234	15
9	4/78	x £234	12
10	3/78	x £234	9
11	2/78	x £234	6
12	1/78	x £234	3
Total	1		234

FEEDBACK TO ACTIVITY 3

Calculate the finance charge.

	£
5 × £5,200	26,000
Fair value	20,000
Finance charge	6,000

Allocate finance charge on a sum of the digits basis.

$$\text{Finance charge p.a.} = \frac{\text{Number of rentals not yet due} \times \text{total finance charge}}{\text{Sum of number of rentals}}$$

Year	*No of rentals not yet due*		*Finance charge*
			£
20X3	4	6,000 / 10	2,400
20X4	3		1,800
20X5	2		1,200
20X6	1		600
20X7	-		
	10		6,000

Allocate finance charge on an actuarial basis.

Year	*Capital*	*Lease payment*	*Capital outstanding*	*Finance charge @ 15.15%*	*Capital at year end*
	£	£	£	£	£
20X3	20,000	5,200	14,800	2,242	17,042
20X4	17,042	5,200	11,842	1,794	13,636
20X5	13,636	5,200	8,436	1,278	9,714
20X6	9,714	5,200	4,514	686	5,200
20X7	5,200	5,200	-	-	-

Tutorial note

Where the lease term is relatively short and the interest rate is not too high, the two methods of interest allocation produce very similar results.

Chapter 21

EARNINGS PER SHARE

CHAPTER CONTENTS

1 Earnings per share

2 The requirements of FRS 22 regarding EPS

3 Diluted earnings per share

4 Presentation and disclosure of earnings per share

5 Significance of the different EPS figures

Earnings per share is an important figure to the users of listed company accounts. It is a widely used measure of a company's performance, particularly over a number of years. Its calculation is stipulated in detail by FRS 22. You should ensure that you can perform the calculations and that you understand the principles behind them.

Objectives

By the time you have finished this chapter you should be able to:

- explain the importance of earnings per share
- define earnings and the basic number of shares
- calculate earnings per share in accordance with FRS 22
- explain the relevance of diluted earnings per share
- calculate diluted earnings per share.

1 Earnings per share

1.1 The need for a standard for earnings per share

KEY POINT

The figure '**earnings per share**' (**EPS**) is used to compute the major stock market indicator of performance, the **Price Earnings ratio** (**PE ratio**).

The figure '**earnings per share**' (**EPS**) is used to compute the major stock market indicator of performance, the **Price Earnings ratio** (**PE ratio**). The calculation is as follows:

$$\text{PE ratio} = \frac{\text{Market value of share}}{\text{EPS}}$$

Rightly or wrongly, the stock market places great emphasis on a company's PE ratio and therefore a standard form of measurement of EPS is required.

Because EPS is widely regarded as the most important indicator of a company's performance, it is important that users of the financial statements are able to compare the EPS of different entities and are able to compare the EPS of the same entity in different accounting periods. FRS 22 achieves comparability by defining earnings and by prescribing methods for determining the number of shares to be included in the calculation of earnings per share. It also requires standard presentation and disclosures, so that users can look behind the headline figure and analyse it further.

1.2 The trend of EPS as a performance indicator

KEY POINT

The **trend in EPS** may be a more accurate performance indicator than the **trend in profit**.

Although EPS is based on profit on ordinary activities after taxation, the **trend in EPS** may be a more accurate performance indicator than the **trend in profit**.

EPS measures performance from the perspective of investors and potential investors. It shows the amount of earnings available to each ordinary shareholder, so that it indicates the potential return on individual investments. This is particularly useful information if there are also preference shareholders, as they are entitled to receive a fixed dividend out of profit before an ordinary dividend can be paid.

FRS 3 *Reporting financial performance* was discussed in an earlier chapter. FRS 3 virtually abolished extraordinary items and also changed the definition of earnings per share so that it included all items of income and expense in the profit and loss account. As a result, the trend of both profits and standard EPS (based on profit on ordinary activities after taxation) may be distorted by 'one off' gains and losses, for example, on the disposal of property or as a result of reorganisations.

2 The requirements of FRS 22 regarding EPS

2.1 Computation of the basic EPS

DEFINITION

Earnings per share is the net profit or loss for the period attributable to ordinary shareholders divided by the weighted average number of ordinary shares outstanding in the period.

Earnings per share (in pence) =

$$\frac{\text{net profit or loss for the period attributable to ordinary shareholders}}{\text{weighted average number of ordinary shares outstanding in the period}}$$

The net profit or loss attributable to ordinary shareholders is the net profit or loss after deducting preference dividends and other appropriations in respect of preference shares.

Therefore the earnings figure should be taken in the profit after:

- minority interests
- tax, and
- preference dividends

are deducted.

If the preference shares are cumulative preference shares then the preference dividends are deducted whether or not the dividend has been declared.

2.2 Scope of FRS 22

FRS 22 applies only to public companies. Private companies that voluntarily disclose earnings per share must also comply with FRS 22.

2.3 Shares in issue

Where several classes of shares are in issue, the earnings should be apportioned according to dividend rights.

2.4 When to include shares in the calculation

KEY POINT

Where there has been an issue of shares during the period, these are normally included in the weighted average number of shares.

Where there has been an issue of shares during the period, these shares are normally included in the weighted average number of shares from the date consideration is receivable, which is generally the date of their issue. For example:

- ordinary shares issued in exchange for cash are included from the date when cash is receivable
- ordinary shares issued as a result of the conversion of a debt instrument are included as of the date that interest ceases to accrue
- ordinary shares issued as part of the purchase consideration for an acquisition are included as of the date of the acquisition

2.5 Issue of shares at full market price during the period

Earnings should be apportioned over the weighted average equity share capital (i.e. taking account of when shares are issued during the year).

Example

A company issued 200,000 shares at full market price (£3.00) on 1 July 20X8.

Relevant information

	20X8	*20X7*
Ordinary profit attributable to the ordinary shareholders for the year ending 31 December	£550,000	£460,000
Number of ordinary shares in issue at 31 December	1,000,000	800,000

Calculation of earnings per share

$$20X7 = \frac{£460{,}000}{800{,}000} = 57.5p$$

$$20X8 = \frac{£550{,}000}{800{,}000 + (\frac{1}{2} \times 200{,}000)} = 61.11p$$

KEY POINT

Where there is an issue of shares at full market price during the year use the earnings figure for the period without adjustment, but divide by the average number of shares weighted on a time basis.

Since the 200,000 shares have only contributed finance for half a year, the number of shares is adjusted accordingly. Note that the solution is to use the earnings figure for the period without adjustment, but divide by the average number of shares weighted on a time basis.

2.6 Capitalisation or bonus issues

When there has been an event that has changed the number of ordinary shares outstanding without a corresponding change in resources (inflow or outflow of cash), the comparative earnings per share figure should also be adjusted.

KEY POINT

When there is a bonus issue(or capitalisation issue), the comparative earnings per share figure should also be adjusted.

Example

A company makes a bonus issue (also known as a capitalisation issue or stock dividend) of one new share for every five existing shares held on 1 July 20X8.

Relevant information

	20X8	*20X7*
Ordinary profit attributable to the ordinary shareholders for the year ending 31 December	£550,000	£460,000
Number of ordinary shares in issue at 31 December	1,200,000	1,000,000

Calculation of earnings per share in 20X8 accounts

$$20X7 = \frac{£460{,}000}{1{,}200{,}000} = 38.33p$$

$$20X8 = \frac{£550{,}000}{1{,}200{,}000} = 45.83p$$

In the 20X7 accounts, the EPS for the year would have appeared as 46p (£460,000 ÷ 1,000,000). In the example above, the computation has been reworked from scratch. However, to make the changes required it would be simpler to adjust directly the EPS figures themselves.

Since the old calculation was based on dividing by 1,000,000 while the new is determined by using 1,200,000, it would be necessary to multiply the EPS by the first and divide by the second. The fraction to apply is, therefore,

$$\frac{1{,}000{,}000}{1{,}200{,}000} \text{ or } \frac{5}{6}$$

Consequently: $46p \times \frac{5}{6} = 38.33p$.

Given that the bonus issue has not increased the assets in the company, the market value of each share would be expected to be only 5/6 of the former price, since for every five shares previously held, the shareholder now has six.

Assuming a pre-issue market price of £3.00, five shares would have a market value of £15.00. After the issue six shares would, other things being equal, have the same value. Therefore, one share would have a theoretical post-issue price of £15.00 ÷ 6 = £2.50. The new EPS could in consequence equally well have been calculated by multiplying the old EPS by the theoretical new share price divided by the actual old price:

$$\frac{£2.50}{£3.00} = \frac{5}{6}$$

Since there are now six shares in issue for every five previously held, the number of shares after the issue is similarly:

$$1{,}000{,}000 \times \frac{6}{5} = 1{,}200{,}000$$

or alternatively:

$$1{,}000{,}000 \times \frac{£3.00}{£2.50} = 1{,}200{,}000$$

These interrelationships are important when considering a rights issue.

ACTIVITY 1

Dorabella plc had the following capital and reserves on 1 April 20X1:

	£000
Share capital (£1 ordinary shares)	7,000
Share premium	900
Revaluation reserve	500
Profit and loss account	9,000
Shareholders' funds	17,400

Dorabella plc makes a bonus issue, of one share for every seven held, on 31 August 20X2.

Dorabella plc's results are as follows:

	20X3	20X2
	£000	£000
Profit after tax and minority interests	1,150	750
Dividends	(500)	(450)
	650	300

Calculate EPS for the year ending 31 March 20X3, together with the comparative EPS for 20X2 that would be presented in the 20X3 accounts.

Feedback on this activity is at the end of the chapter.

2.7 Rights issues

KEY POINT

Rights issues are normally below full market price and so combine the characteristics of **issues at full market price** and **bonus issues**.

KEY POINT

To determine weighted average capital where there has been a rights issue: adjust for the bonus element then calculate the weighted average capital as usual.

Rights issues present special problems, because they are normally below full market price and therefore combine the characteristics of issues at full market price and bonus issues as above. Determining the weighted average capital, therefore, involves two steps as follows:

1 Adjust for bonus element in rights issue, by multiplying capital in issue before the rights issue by the following fraction:

$$\frac{\text{Actual cum rights price}}{\text{Theoretical ex rights price}}$$

2 Calculate the weighted average capital in the issue as above.

Example

A company issued one new share for every two existing shares held by way of rights at £1.50 per share on 1 July 20X8. Pre-issue market price was £3.00 per share.

Relevant information

	20X8	*20X7*
Ordinary profit attributable to the ordinary shareholders for the year ending 31 December	£550,000	£460,000
Number of ordinary shares in issue at 31 December	1,200,000	800,000

Calculation of earnings per share

20X7: Original per 20X7 accounts: $\frac{£460,000}{800,000} = 57.5p$

Adjusted for rights issue: $57.5p \times \frac{2.50}{3.00} = 47.92p$

20X8: Based on weighted average number of shares:

1st half-year:

– actual in issue 800,000

– adjusted for bonus element $800,000 \times \frac{3.00}{2.50} = 960,000$

2nd half-year:

– actual in issue, including bonus element: 1,200,000

Therefore, EPS $= \frac{£550,000}{(960,000 + 1,200,000) \div 2} = 50.92p$

Notes on solution

(1) 20X7

Pre-rights, two shares would be worth £6.00. Ex-rights, three shares would theoretically be worth £6.00 + £1.50 = £7.50, or £2.50 each. The appropriate fraction for the adjustment of comparatives is, therefore, £2.50 divided by £3.00.

The revised EPS figure could have been obtained by dividing the earnings figure of £460,000 by a share number adjusted for the bonus element, i.e.:

$$800,000 \times \frac{3.00}{2.50} = 960,000$$

$$(\frac{£460,000}{960,000} = 47.92p)$$

(2) 20X8

The calculation must take account of the quasi-capitalisation. The share number used must, therefore, reflect the bonus element for the whole year and the increase in the fund of capital from the half year.

(3) Relationship of rights issue to issue at full market price and capitalisation

Each of the examples used a pre-issue share price of £3.00. Both the rights issue and the issue at full market price raised £600,000 from shareholders. However, after the rights issue there were 1,200,000 shares in issue, whereas following the issue at full market value there were only 1,000,000.

If the latter had been followed immediately by a capitalisation (bonus issue) to bring the number of shares issued up to 1,200,000, the EPS figures would have become:

20X7 $= 57.5p \times \frac{2.50}{3.00} = 47.92p$

20X8 $= 61.11p \times \frac{2.50}{3.00} = 50.92p$

These are, as would be expected, the same as those calculated for the rights issue.

ACTIVITY 2

On 31 December 20X1 the issued share capital of X plc consisted of 4,000,000 ordinary shares of 25p each, and the shares were quoted at 100p. On 1 January 20X2 the company made a rights issue in the proportion of 1 for 4 at 50p per share. Its trading results for the two years were as follows:

	Year ended 30 June	
	20X1	*20X2*
	£	£
Net profit after taxation	400,000	425,000

Show the calculation of EPS to be presented in the final accounts in 20X2 (including the comparative figure).

Feedback to this activity is at the end of the chapter.

3 Diluted earnings per share

3.1 Introduction

As well as basic earnings per share, FRS 22 requires entities to disclose diluted earnings per share. To calculate diluted earnings per share, the net profit attributable to ordinary shareholders and the weighted average number of shares outstanding are adjusted for the effect of all dilutive potential ordinary shares.

DEFINITION

A **potential ordinary share** is a financial instrument or other contract that may entitle its holder to ordinary shares.

A **potential ordinary share** is a financial instrument or other contract that may entitle its holder to ordinary shares.

Examples of potential ordinary shares:

- convertible debt
- convertible preference shares
- share warrants and options
- rights granted under employee share schemes
- rights to ordinary shares that are conditional upon the satisfaction of conditions.
- Use is often made of potential share issues at a future date as an inducement to purchase fixed interest stock or to reward management.

KEY POINT

Diluted earnings per share shows to what extent the amount available for ordinary dividends per share would have been affected if all the **potential ordinary shares** had been issued.

Diluted earnings per share shows to what extent the amount available for ordinary dividends per share would have been affected if all the potential ordinary shares had been issued.

To calculate diluted earnings per share:

- the net profit or loss for the period attributable to ordinary shareholders is adjusted for:
  - dividends on potential shares (e.g. on convertible preference shares)
  - interest (e.g. on convertible debt)
  - any other changes in income and expense that would result from the conversion
- the weighted average number of ordinary shares that would be issued if all the potential ordinary shares were converted under the most dilution possible is added to the weighted number of ordinary shares. (Potential ordinary shares should be assumed to have been converted at the beginning of the period, or, if they were not in existence at the beginning of the period, the date of issue.)

EXAM HINT

Convertible debt, convertible preference shares, options and **warrants** are the types of potential ordinary share that you are most likely to meet in the exam.

Convertible debt, convertible preference shares, options and **warrants** are the types of potential ordinary share that you are most likely to meet in the exam.

3.2 Convertibles

The principles of **convertible debt** and **convertible preference shares** are similar and will be dealt with together.

Example

On 1 April 20X1, the company issued by way of rights or otherwise £1,250,000 8% convertible unsecured debt for cash at par. Each £100 nominal of the loan stock will be convertible in 20X6/20X9 into the number of ordinary shares set out below:

- On 31 December 20X6   124 shares
- On 31 December 20X7   120 shares
- On 31 December 20X8   115 shares
- On 31 December 20X9   110 shares

Relevant information

Issued share capital:

- £500,000 in 10% cumulative preference shares of £1
- £1,000,000 in ordinary shares of 25p = 4,000,000 shares

Corporation tax is 45%.

Trading results for the years ended 31 December were as follows:

	20X2	*20X1*
	£	£
Profit before interest and tax	1,100,000	991,818
Interest on 8% convertible unsecured loan stock	100,000	75,000
Profit before tax	1,000,000	916,818
Corporation tax	450,000	412,568
Profit after tax	550,000	504,250

Calculation of earnings per share

	20X2	*20X1*
Basic earnings per share	£	£
Profit after tax	550,000	504,250
Less: Preference dividend	50,000	50,000
Earnings	500,000	454,250
Earnings per share based on 4,000,000 shares	12.5p	11.4p
Diluted earnings per share		
Earnings as above	500,000	454,250
Add: Interest on the convertible unsecured debt	100,000	75,000
Less: Corporation tax	45,000	33,750
	55,000	41,250
Adjusted earnings	555,000	495,500
Earnings per share based on 5,550,000 shares (20X1 – 5,162,500)	10p	9.6p

Notes

(1) Up to 20X5 the **maximum** number of shares issuable after the end of the financial year will be at the rate of 124 shares per £100, viz: 1,550,000 shares, making a total of 5,550,000.

(2) The weighted average number of shares issued and issuable for 20X1 would have been one-quarter of 4,000,000 plus three-quarters of 5,550,000, i.e. 5,162,500.

3.3 Options and warrants

KEY POINT

Shares issued on the exercise of an **option** or **warrant** are split into the number that would have been issued if shares had been bought at fair value, and the remainder, which are treated like a bonus issue.

The total number of shares issued on the exercise of the **option** or **warrant** is split into two:

- the number of shares that would have been issued if the cash received had been used to buy shares at **fair value** (using the average price of the shares during the period)
- the remainder, which are treated like a **bonus issue** (i.e. as having been issued for no consideration).

The number of shares issued for no consideration is added to the number of shares when calculating the diluted earnings per share.

Example

On 1 January 20X7 a company issues 1,000,000 share options. The net profit for the year is £500,000 and the company already has 4,000,000 ordinary shares in issue at that date.

During the year to 31 December 20X7 the average fair value of one ordinary share was £3 and the exercise price for the shares under option was £2.

Solution

Basic earnings per share: $\frac{£500{,}000}{4{,}000{,}000} = 12.5p$

Diluted earnings per share:	
Number of ordinary shares in issue	4,000,000
Number of shares under option	1,000,000
Number of shares that would have been issued at fair value: (1,000,000 × 2/3)	(666,667)
	4,333,333

Earnings per share: $\frac{£500{,}000}{4{,}333{,}333} = 11.5p$

3.4 The effect on diluted EPS of the order in which dilutive factors are allowed for

KEY POINT

The order in which dilutive factors are allowed for can affect the diluted EPS that is calculated.

The order in which dilutive factors are allowed for can affect the diluted EPS. This is because a factor which, taken on its own, is dilutive, may in fact be anti-dilutive.

Definition Antidilution is defined in FRS 22 as an increase in earnings per share or a reduction in loss per share resulting from the assumption that potential ordinary shares are issued.

Example

Earnings – Net profit attributable to ordinary shareholders	£10,000,000
Ordinary shares outstanding	2,000,000
Average fair value of one ordinary share during year	£75

Potential ordinary shares

Options	100,000 with exercise price of £60
Convertible preference shares	800,000 shares entitled to a cumulative dividend of £8 per share. Each preference share is convertible to 2 ordinary shares.
5% convertible bond	nominal amount £100,000,000. Each £1,000 bond is convertible to 20 ordinary shares. There is no amortisation of premium or discount affecting the determination of interest expense.
Tax rate	40%

Increase in earnings attributable to ordinary shareholders on conversion of potential ordinary shares

		Increase in earnings £	*Increase in number of ordinary shares*	*Earnings per incremental share* £
Options				
Increase in earnings		nil		
Incremental shares issued for no consideration	100,000 – (100,000 x 60)/75		20,000	nil
Convertible preference shares				
Increase in net profit	8 × £800,000	6,400,000		
Incremental shares	2 × 800,000		1,600,000	4.00
5% convertible bonds				
Increase in net profit	100,000,000 × 5% × (1–0.4)	3,000,000		
Incremental shares	100,000 × 20		2,000,000	1.50

These calculations allow us to place the three dilutive factors in order. Dealing with the most dilutive first we have:

Computation of diluted earnings per share

	Net profit attributable £	*Ordinary shares*	*Per share* £	
As reported	10,000,000	2,000,000	5.00	
Options		20,000		
	10,000,000	2,020,000	4.95	Dilutive
5% convertible bonds	3,000,000	2,000,000		
	13,000,000	4,020,000	3.23	Dilutive
Convertible preference shares	6,400,000	1,600,000		
	19,400,000	5,620,000	3.45	Anti-dilutive

Since diluted earnings per share is increased when taking the convertible preference shares into account (from £3.23 to £3.45), the convertible preference shares are anti-dilutive and are ignored in the calculation of diluted earnings per share, which is required to be the worst possible figure. Therefore, diluted earnings per share is £3.23.

To understand the reasoning behind the ordering, it is necessary to realise that the lower the incremental EPS, the greater the dilutive effect.

If a different order had been taken the final EPS figure of £3.45 would have stayed the same but the lower figure of £3.23 would not have emerged, as the following calculation demonstrates:

	Net profit attributable	*Ordinary shares*	*Per share*
	£		£
As reported	10,000,000	2,000,000	5.00
Convertible pref. shares	6,400,000	1,600,000	
	16,400,000	3,600,000	4.56
5% convertible bonds	3,000,000	2,000,000	
	19,400,000	5,600,000	3.46
Options	–	20,000	
	19,400,000	5,620,000	3.45

Potential ordinary shares should be included in the calculation of diluted EPS when their conversion to ordinary shares would decrease **net profit from continuing operations**, rather than 'net profit'. This means that items relating to discontinued operations, the effects of changes in accounting policies and correction of fundamental errors would all be excluded.

4 Presentation and disclosure of earnings per share

4.1 Presentation

KEY POINT

Basic and **diluted** earnings per share should be presented on the face of the profit and loss account for each class of ordinary share, and with **equal prominence**.

- Basic and diluted earnings per share should be presented on the face of the profit and loss account for each class of ordinary share.
- Basic and diluted earnings per share must be presented with equal prominence.
- Basic and diluted earnings per share should be presented even if the amounts are negative (i.e. a loss per share).

4.2 Additional disclosures

KEY POINT

For both **basic** and **diluted** earnings per share, the amounts used as **numerators** and the weighted average number of ordinary shares used as the **denominator** should be disclosed.

The following information should be disclosed for both **basic** and **diluted** earnings per share:

- the amounts used as **numerators** and a reconciliation of those amounts to the net profit or loss for the period
- the weighted average number of ordinary shares used as the **denominator** and a reconciliation of the denominators to each other.

If an **alternative measure** of earnings per share is also disclosed (as permitted by FRS 3) this should be:

- calculated using the weighted average number of ordinary shares determined in accordance with **FRS 22**
- presented **consistently** over time

- if the component of the profit and loss account used for earnings for this calculation is not a line item in the profit and loss account then a reconciliation should be provided between the component and the line item
- should be presented in the notes to the financial statements not on the face of the profit and loss account

5 Significance of the different EPS figures

5.1 Basic EPS

Standard calculation per FRS 22

The standard calculation reflects the earnings performance of the company taking into account all costs and revenues that have occurred during the year.

Other measures

KEY POINT

Alternatives to the FRS 14/FRS 3 calculation include **IIMR headline earnings**, as defined by the Institute of Investment Management and Research (IIMR).

FRS 3 and FRS 22 permit alternative EPS figures to be calculated at different levels of profit. Possible alternatives to the FRS 22/FRS 3 calculation include:

- **IIMR headline earnings** (basic earnings adjusted for profits and losses on sales and terminations, profits and losses on the sale of fixed assets, amortisation of goodwill and other unusual items; it includes exceptional items that are not required to be disclosed separately)
- excluding exceptional items
- excluding discontinued operations.

5.2 Diluted EPS

KEY POINT

Diluted EPS shows what the current year's EPS would be if all the dilutive potential ordinary shares in issue had been converted. It is a measure of past performance. It is only of limited use as a prediction of future EPS.

Diluted EPS shows what the current year's EPS would be if all the dilutive potential ordinary shares in issue had been converted. Because it always has to be disclosed, it can be used to assess trends in past performance.

In theory, diluted EPS serves as a warning to equity shareholders that the return on their investment may fall in future periods. However, diluted EPS as currently required by FRS 22 is not intended to be forward looking but is an additional past performance measure. For example, when calculating diluted EPS where there are warrants or options, fair value is based on the average price of an ordinary share for the period, rather than the market price at the period end. Therefore, diluted EPS is only of limited use as a prediction of future EPS.

5.3 Limitations of EPS as a performance measure

KEY POINT

The **limitations** of EPS are that it does not take account of **inflation**, and being based on **historic information**, does not necessarily have predictive value.

Although EPS is believed to have a real influence on the market price of shares, it has several important **limitations** as a **performance measure**.

- It does not take account of **inflation**. Apparent growth in earnings may not be real growth.
- It is based on **historic information** and therefore it does not necessarily have predictive value. High earnings and growth in earnings may be achieved at the expense of investment which may generate increased earnings in the future.
- An entity's earnings are affected by the choice of its accounting policies. Therefore it may not always be appropriate to compare the EPS of different companies.

Conclusion

FRS 22 requires that all listed companies calculate and disclose earnings per share. It sets out the way in which earnings per share should be calculated in different situations, for example, where there has been a bonus issue or a rights issue during the year.

Where there are dilutive potential ordinary shares, diluted earnings per share must also be calculated and disclosed.

SELF-TEST QUESTIONS

1 What is the price earnings ratio? (1.1)

2 How is the basic EPS calculated? (2.1)

3 Which companies must comply with FRS 22? (2.2)

4 Does a bonus issue reduce or increase EPS? (2.6)

5 What is the ratio used in a rights issue to adjust for the bonus element of the rights? (2.7)

6 What is a potential ordinary share? (3.1)

7 Give three examples of situations in which there may be potential ordinary shares. (3.1)

8 Where there are options or warrants, how is the weighted average number of potential shares calculated? (3.3)

9 Where should earnings per share be presented in the financial statements? (4.1)

10 Give three possible alternatives to the standard earnings per share calculation. (5.1)

EXAM-TYPE QUESTION

Earnit plc

Earnit plc is a listed company. The issued capital of the company at 1 April 20X4 was as follows:

- 500 million equity shares of 50p each
- 100 million £1 preference shares, redeemable at a premium on 31 March 20X9. The effective finance cost of these shares in the financial statements at 31 March 20X4 was £10 million.

Extract from the consolidated profit and loss account of Earnit plc for the year ended 31 March 20X5 showed:

	£ million
Turnover	250
Cost of sales	(130)
Gross profit	120
Other operating expenses	(40)
Operating profit	80
Exceptional gain	10
Interest payable	(25)
Profit before taxation	65
Taxation	(20)
Profit after taxation	45
Appropriations of profit (see note)	(26)
Retained profit	19

Note: appropriations of profit:

• to preference shareholders	11
• to equity shareholders	15
	26

The company has a share option scheme in operation. The terms of the options are that option holders are permitted to purchase 1 equity share for every option held at a price of £1.50 per share. At 1 April 20X4, 100 million share options were in issue. On 1 October 20X4, the holders of 50 million options exercised their option to purchase, and 70 million new options were issued on the same terms as the existing options. During the year ended 31 March 20X5, the average market price of an equity share in Earnit plc was £2.00.

There were no changes to the number of shares or share options outstanding during the year ended 31 March 20X5 other than as noted in the previous paragraph.

Required:

(a) Compute the basic and diluted earnings per share of Earnit plc for the year ended 31 March 20X5. Comparative figures are NOT required. **(10 marks)**

(b) Explain to a holder of equity shares in Earnit plc the usefulness of both the figures you have calculated in part (a). **(10 marks)**

(Total: 20 marks)

For the answer to this question, see the 'Answers' section at the end of the book.

FEEDBACK TO ACTIVITY **1**

The number of shares to be used in the EPS calculation for both years is 7,000,000 + 1,000,000 = 8,000,000.

The EPS for 20X2 is $\frac{750,000}{8,000,000} \times 100$ pence = 9.38 pence

The EPS for 20X3 is $\frac{1,150,000}{8,000,000} \times 100$ pence = 14.38 pence

FEEDBACK TO ACTIVITY **2**

Past earnings per share (comparative figure)

Because the rights issue contains a bonus element, the past earnings per share figures should be adjusted by the factor:

$$\frac{\text{Theoretical ex rights price}}{\text{Actual cum rights price}}$$

Consider a holder of 100 shares:

			£
Prior to rights issue 100 shares worth	100	× 100p	= 100.00
Taking up rights 25 shares cost	25	× 50p	= 12.50
	125		112.50

i.e. theoretical ex rights price of each share is $\frac{£112.50}{125}$ = 90p

Last year, reported earnings per share were $\frac{£400,000}{4,000,000}$ = 10p

Applying the correction factor to calculate adjusted comparative figure of earnings per share:

$$10\text{p} \times \frac{\text{Theoretical ex rights price}}{\text{Actual cum rights price}} = 10\text{p} \times \frac{90}{100} = 9\text{p}$$

Current earnings per share

Number of shares 1 July 20X1 to 31 December 20X1 (as adjusted):

$$4,000,000 \times \frac{\text{Actual cum rights price}}{\text{Theoretical ex rights price}} \times \frac{6 \text{ months}}{12 \text{ months}}$$

i.e. $4{,}000{,}000 \times \frac{100}{90} \times \frac{6}{12}$	= 2,222,222 shares
Number of shares 1 January 20X2 to 30 June 20X2 (actual):	
$\frac{6}{12} \times 5{,}000{,}000$	= 2,500,000 shares
Total adjusted shares for year	4,722,222 shares
∴ Earnings per share = $\frac{£425{,}000}{4{,}722{,}222}$	= 9p per share

Chapter 22

ANALYSIS AND INTERPRETATION OF FINANCIAL STATEMENTS

CHAPTER CONTENTS

1 Interpreting financial information
2 Calculating useful ratios from company or group financial statements
3 Profitability ratios
4 Short-term financial stability
5 Long-term financial stability
6 Investors' ratios
7 Producing written reports on the position and progress of companies
8 Trend analysis
9 The effect of accounting policies
10 Interpreting current cost and current purchasing power accounts
11 The limitations of ratio analysis

This chapter concentrates on ratio analysis. You should already know how to calculate most of the ratios covered here. At this level most of the available marks in a question are awarded for comment and analysis, rather than the calculations themselves.

Although ratio analysis is a useful tool, it is important to remember that it does have significant limitations. It does not necessarily take account of the effect of inflation, nor does it take account of the effect of the use of different accounting policies by companies. These and other limitations are discussed in this chapter.

Objectives

By the time you have finished this chapter you should be able to:

- calculate useful financial ratios for single company or group financial statements
- analyse and interpret ratios to give an assessment of a company's performance
- discuss the effect that changes in accounting policies or the use of different accounting policies between companies can have on the ability to interpret performance
- discuss how the interpretation of current cost accounts or current purchasing power accounts would differ from that of historic cost accounts
- discuss the limitations in the use of ratio analysis for assessing corporate performance, outlining other information that may be of relevance.

1 Interpreting financial information

1.1 Horizontal analysis

KEY POINT

A **horizontal analysis** compares the current year's financial statements with the previous year.

The most straightforward method of analysing financial statements is simply to compare the current year with the previous year and to note and rationalise any significant changes. This is known as '**horizontal analysis**', but its formal title is hardly important as it amounts to the application of basic common sense. It is a form of 'inter temporal' analysis, i.e. a comparison between accounting periods.

The line by line comparison must be performed whilst also considering:

- the change in **turnover**
- the relevance of anything else you may know about the company.

In practice, an analyst will find any other information in the directors' report, in the chairman's report, or in press cuttings about the company or the industry in which it operates.

In an exam question, this other information is usually found in the opening lines of the question, where you will be told:

- what the company does
- why you are being asked to interpret the accounts.

Further information is then usually provided in the notes following on from the numerical information.

EXAM HINT

A good exam answer should consider all the additional information in the question.

You must ensure that your answer makes best use of this additional information. In a good answer all of the points will be referred to and used to rationalise the observed trends.

Any change in turnover underpins the analysis. Assuming a 30% increase in turnover, we might predict a 30% increase in everything else in the profit and loss account. Balance sheet changes, for example in stocks and debtors, may be rationalised in the same way. The following sections are intended to prompt some ideas for the profit and loss account.

1.2 Gross profit

KEY POINT

If **gross profit** has not increased in line with **turnover**, the reasons need to be established.

If **gross profit** has not increased in line with turnover, you need to establish why not. Is the discrepancy due to:

- increased '**purchase**' **costs**: if so are the costs under the company's control (i.e. does the company manufacture the goods sold)
- **stock write-offs** (likely where the company operates in a volatile market place, such as fashion retail); or
- other costs being allocated to cost of sales – for example, research and development expenditure?

The other information in the question should provide some clues.

1.3 Operating profit

KEY POINT

In considering **operating profit**, remember that costs can be either fixed (or semi-fixed) or variable.

By the time you have reached **operating profit**, there are many more factors to consider. If you are provided with a breakdown of expenses you can use this for further line by line comparisons. Bear in mind that:

- some costs are fixed or semi-fixed (for example property costs) and therefore not expected to change in line with turnover
- other costs are variable (for example, packing and distribution, and commission).

ACTIVITY **1**

In arriving at operating profit, various significant items which may affect the analysis may have been included. List some examples.

Feedback to this activity is at the end of the chapter.

1.4 Profit before tax

In moving from operating profit to **profit before tax**, two items appear:

- **investment income**
- **interest payable**.

It is unlikely that either of these will move in line with turnover. However, a simple year on year comparison may highlight other changes, such as:

- changes in holdings of investments
- leasing charges
- increased borrowings.

These figures may tie in with the balance sheet. Check them against:

- the **investments held** (both fixed and current)
- the level of **borrowings** (particularly the bank overdraft).

1.5 Profit after tax

It is useful to compute the 'rate' of tax by comparing the tax charge to the profits before tax. The rate should be fairly constant from year to year. The company's policy for providing deferred tax may also be relevant.

1.6 Dividends

Dividends should be compared to the previous year. Even when profit for the year has declined, a fall in dividends for a plc is an extremely worrying sign. Major companies usually try to avoid this where at all possible.

2 Calculating useful ratios from company or group financial statements

2.1 Introduction

Ratio analysis is a more sophisticated technique for analysing financial statements. It is the next step after the so-called horizontal analysis.

In general, ratio analysis should only be used in answering exam questions where the question specifically calls for use of ratios.

KEY POINT

The principal analytical ratios are **ROCE**, **profit margin**, **current** or **quick ratio** and **gearing ratio**.

For example, the question might state 'using the principal analytical ratios'. In this case the following should be calculated:

- **return on capital employed**
- **profit margin** (e.g. gross profit to sales)
- **current** or **quick ratio**
- **gearing ratio**.

Very often the question gives no indication of which ratios to calculate, in which case you must make a choice.

2.2 Choice of ratios

KEY POINT

There are three broad classes of ratio: **profitability**, **financial** and **investment**.

The variety of ratios that could be calculated is vast, so it is important to restrict the calculations by being selective. The ratios chosen should be the key ones relevant to the requirements of the question. These may be further limited by the available information (i.e. there may be some you are simply unable to calculate). This point is considered further below.

Ratios can be classified into three main groups, which are summarised in the table below:

Type	*Reflect*	*Examples*
Profitability	Performance of company and its managers, including the efficiency of asset usage	ROCE Gross profit % Stock turnover Debtors and creditors days
Financial	Financial structure and stability of the company	Gearing Current and liquidity ratios
Investment	Relationship of the number of ordinary shares and their price to the profits, dividends and assets of the company	EPS P/E ratio Dividend yield Dividend cover Net assets per share

The managers of the company are likely to be concerned about all aspects of the company and therefore may want to know about all of the key ratios in each category.

Shareholders or potential investors are concerned primarily with the investment ratios, though certain financial stability and profitability measures are also likely to be of interest (for example, gearing and ROCE).

Creditors are most likely to be concerned about financial stability, though a bank, acting as a major source of finance, will usually also look at profitability.

2.3 Commenting on the ratios

EXAM HINT

Most of the marks in an exam question will be for sensible, well explained and accurate comments on the key ratios.

Ratios are of limited use on their own, thus most of the marks in an exam question will be available for sensible, well explained and accurate comments on the key ratios.

If you doubt that you have anything to say, the following points should serve as a useful checklist:

- What does the ratio literally mean?
- What does a change in the ratio mean?
- What is the norm?
- What are the limitations of the ratio?

2.4 Further information required

EXAM HINT

An exam question could ask you to interpret given information, then ask what further information you require.

Any analyst in practice will be limited in the analysis he can perform by the amount of information available. He is unlikely to have access to all the facts which are available to a company's management.

In the exam the information which can be provided about a company in any one question will be limited. Part 1 of such a question could well ask you to interpret the available information, while part 2 could easily ask you to state what further information you require.

3 Profitability ratios

3.1 Return on capital employed (ROCE)

KEY POINT

ROCE is a key **business objective** and reflects the **earning power** of the business.

The absolute figure of profit earned is not, in itself, the whole story since the size of the business earning that profit may vary enormously. It is significant to consider the size of the profit figure relative to the size of the business, size being expressed in terms of the quantity of capital employed by that business.

The return on capital employed is the ratio which measures this relationship. It is a key **business objective**, and is thus the key ratio in assessing financial achievement. It reflects the **earning power** of the business operations.

$$\textbf{Return on capital employed (ROCE)} = \frac{\text{Profit}}{\text{Capital employed}} \times 100\%$$

ROCE is also known as the **primary ratio** because it is often the most important measure of profitability.

The ratio shows how efficiently a business is using its resources. If the return is very low, the business may be better off realising its assets and investing the proceeds in a high interest bank account! (This may sound extreme, but should be considered particularly for a small, unprofitable business with valuable assets such as freehold property.) Furthermore, a low return can easily become a loss if the business suffers a downturn.

KEY POINT

The two main factors affecting ROCE are **profitability of sales** and the rate of **asset utilisation**.

Two main factors affect ROCE:

- **profitability of sales**
- rate of **asset utilisation**.

Note that the product of these two gives the return on capital employed:

$$\frac{\text{Operating profit}}{\text{Sales}} \times \frac{\text{Sales}}{\text{Operating assets}} = \frac{\text{Operating profit}}{\text{Operating assets}} = \text{ROCE}$$

or:

Operating Profit Margin × Asset Turnover = ROCE

Once calculated, ROCE should be compared with:

- **previous years' figures** – provided there have been no changes in accounting policies, or suitable adjustments have been made to facilitate comparison (note, however that the effect of not replacing fixed assets is that their value will decrease and ROCE will increase)
- **company's target ROCE** – where the company's management has determined a target return as part of its budget procedure, consistent failure by a part of the business to meet the target may make it a target for disposal
- **the cost of borrowings** – if the cost of borrowing is say 10% and ROCE 7%, then further borrowings will reduce EPS unless the extra money can be used in areas where the ROCE is higher than the cost of borrowings
- **other companies in same industry** – care is required in interpretation, since there may be:
  - different accounting policies, e.g. research and development expenditure, stock valuation and depreciation
  - different ages of plant – where assets are written down to low book values the ROCE will appear high
  - leased assets which may not appear in the balance sheet at all. (SSAP 21 requires assets held under finance leases to be on the balance sheet but not those held under operating leases.)

ACTIVITY 2

A company has revalued its fixed assets during the most recent accounting period. How will this affect the calculation of ROCE?

Feedback to this activity is at the end of the chapter.

Alternative calculations

Return on capital employed can be calculated in a number of different ways.

One version is the return on shareholders' equity, which is more relevant for existing or prospective shareholders than management.

$$\text{Return on equity} = \frac{\text{Profit after interest and after preference dividends}}{\text{Ordinary share capital + reserves}} \times 100\%$$

Profit may be before or after tax. After tax is a more accurate reflection of profits (management should seek to minimise tax). However, deferred tax provisions can be subjective, so profit before tax may be more objective.

The other commonly used ROCE is:

$$\text{Overall return} = \frac{\text{Operating profit}}{\text{Share capital + reserves + all borrowings}} \times 100\%$$

This is used by managers assessing performance.

Further points

- **Treatment of associates and investments**: where the profit excludes investment income, the balance sheet carrying amounts for associates and investments should be excluded from the capital employed.

  This gives an accurate measure of trading performance. If associates and investments are not excluded, the overall profit figure should include income from investments and associates.

- **Purchased goodwill** may be being amortised over an unrealistically long period. Some analysts are suspicious of any goodwill and eliminate it before carrying out their detailed analysis.
- **Large cash balances** are not contributing to profits and some analysts therefore deduct them from capital employed (to compare operating profits with operating assets). However, it is usually acceptable not to make this adjustment as ROCE is a performance measure and management have decided to operate with that large balance.

3.2 Gross profit percentage

Gross profit percentage is:

$$\frac{\text{Gross profit}}{\text{Turnover}} \times 100\%$$

KEY POINT

Gross profit percentage is the sales margin and is expected to be reasonably constant.

This is the margin that the company makes on its sales.

It is expected to remain reasonably constant. Since the ratio consists of a small number of components, a change may be traced to a change in:

- **selling prices** – normally deliberate though sometimes unavoidable, for example because of increased competition
- **sales mix** – often deliberate
- **purchase cost** – including carriage or discounts
- **production cost** – materials, labour or production overheads
- **stock** – errors in counting, valuing or cut-off, stock shortages.

KEY POINT

Inter-company comparison of margins can be useful but it is important to look at businesses within the same sector.

Inter-company comparison of margins can be very useful but it is especially important to look at businesses within the same sector. For example, food retailing is able to support low margins because of the high volume of sales. A manufacturing industry would usually have higher margins.

Low margins usually suggest poor performance but may be due to expansion costs (launching a new product) or trying to increase market share. Lower margins than usual suggest scope for improvement.

Above average margins are usually a sign of good management although unusually high margins may make the competition keen to join in and enjoy the 'rich pickings'.

A **trading profit margin** is:

$$\frac{\text{Trading profit}}{\text{Turnover}} \times 100\%$$

KEY POINT

The **trading profit margin** is affected by **depreciation**, which can be subjective, requiring care when making comparisons.

This is affected by more factors than the gross profit margin but it is equally useful and if the company does not disclose a cost of sales (perhaps using format 2) it may be used on its own in lieu of the gross profit percentage.

One of the many factors affecting the trading profit margin is **depreciation**, which is open to considerable subjective judgement. Inter-company comparisons should be made after suitable adjustments to align accounting policies.

3.3 Stock turnover

Stock turnover is defined as:

$$\frac{\text{Cost of sales}}{\text{Stocks}} = \text{times p.a.}$$

This yields a multiple expressed as, say, 10 times per annum. If format 2 is used, then simply compare turnover and stocks, though bear in mind that this is also affected by the margin achieved by the company.

An alternative is to express the stock turnover as so many days stock:

$$\frac{\text{Stocks}}{\text{Cost of sales}} \times 365 \text{ days}$$

KEY POINT

Sometimes an **average stock turnover** is calculated, based on average stock levels.

Sometimes an average (based on the **average stock**) is calculated which has a smoothing effect but may dampen the effect of a major change in the period.

KEY POINT

An increasing stock turnover period is usually a warning signal.

An increasing number of days (or a diminishing multiple) implies that stock is turning over less quickly. This is usually regarded as a bad sign because:

- it may reflect lack of demand for the goods
- it may reflect poor stock control, with its associated costs such as storage and insurance
- it may ultimately lead to stock obsolescence and related write-offs.

However, it may not necessarily be bad where:

- management are buying stock in larger quantities to take advantage of trade discounts
- management have increased stock levels to avoid stockouts
- the increase is slight and due to distortion of the ratio caused by comparing a year end stock figure with cost of sales for a year of increasing growth.

KEY POINT

Stock turnover varies greatly with the nature of the business.

Stock turnover ratios vary enormously with the nature of the business. For example, a fishmonger selling fresh fish would have a stock turnover period of 1–2 days, whereas a building contractor may have a stock turnover period of 200 days. Manufacturing companies may have a stock turnover ratio of 60–100 days; this period is likely to increase as the goods made become larger and more complex.

For large and complex items (for example rolling stock or aircraft) there may be sharp fluctuations in stock turnover according to whether delivery took place just before or just after the year end.

A manufacturer should take into consideration:

- **reliability of suppliers**: if the supplier is unreliable it is prudent to hold more raw materials
- **demand**: if demand is erratic it is prudent to hold more finished goods.

3.4 Debtors turnover

Debtors turnover is defined as:

$$\frac{\text{Trade debtors}}{\text{Turnover}} \times 100\%$$

This can be expressed as a percentage or more commonly as a number of days:

$$\frac{\text{Trade debtors}}{\text{Turnover}} \times 365 \text{ days}$$

The trade debtors used may be a year-end figure or the average for the year. Where an average is used to calculate a number of days, the ratio is the average number of days' credit taken by customers.

For cash-based businesses like supermarkets, debtors days is unlikely to exceed 1 as there are no true credit sales.

KEY POINT

The **debtors turnover** should be compared with the stated **credit policy** of the business.

For other businesses, the result should be compared with the stated **credit policy**. A period of 30 days or 'at the end of the month following delivery' are common credit terms.

Increasing debtors days is usually a bad sign as it suggests lack of proper credit control. However, it may be due to:

- a deliberate policy to extend the stated credit period to attract more trade
- one major new customer being allowed different terms.

Falling debtors days is usually a good sign, though it could indicate that the company is suffering a cash shortage.

The debtors days ratio can be distorted by:

- using year-end figures which do not represent average debtors
- debt factoring which results in very low debtors
- other credit finance agreements such as hire purchase, where there is insufficient analysis of turnover (HP debtors should be shown separately) to calculate proper ratios.

3.5 Creditors days

Creditors days is usually expressed as:

$$\frac{\text{Trade creditors}}{\text{Purchases}} \times 365 \text{ days}$$

and represents the credit period taken by the company from its suppliers. An average of trade creditors may also be used.

Where purchases are not known, cost of sales is used or, failing that, sales.

KEY POINT

A long credit period may represent a source of **free finance**, but may also indicate **liquidity problems**.

The ratio is always compared to previous years. Once again there are two main contrasting points:

- A long credit period may be good as it represents a source of **free finance**.
- A long credit period may indicate that the company is unable to pay more quickly because of **liquidity problems**.

Note that if the credit period is long:

- the company may develop a poor reputation as a slow payer and may not be able to find new suppliers
- existing suppliers may decide to discontinue supplies
- the company may be losing out on worthwhile cash discounts.

4 Short-term financial stability

4.1 Introduction

Two ratios are used to measure a business's ability to meet its own short-term liabilities. These are:

- current or working capital ratio:

$$\frac{\text{Current assets}}{\text{Current liabilities}}$$

- liquidity, acid test or quick assets ratio:

$$\frac{\text{Current assets} - \text{stock}}{\text{Current liabilities}}$$

It is not usually appropriate to calculate both ratios when answering a time-pressured exam question, as trends in the ratios are likely to be similar.

As a general rule calculate only the current ratio unless the company has slow-moving stocks (for example in the construction industry), in which case calculate the quick ratio instead.

4.2 Current ratio

KEY POINT

The **current ratio** measures the adequacy of current assets to meet the company's short-term liabilities.

The **current ratio** measures the adequacy of current assets to meet the company's short term liabilities. It reflects whether the company is in a position to meet its liabilities as they fall due.

Traditionally, a current ratio of 2 or higher was regarded as appropriate for most businesses to maintain creditworthiness. However, more recently a figure of 1.5 is regarded as the norm.

A higher figure should be regarded with suspicion as it may be due to:

- high levels of **stocks and debtors** (check working capital management ratios)
- high **cash levels** which could be put to better use (for example by investing in fixed assets).

The current ratio should be looked at in the light of what is normal for the business. For example, supermarkets tend to have low current ratios because:

- there are no trade debtors
- there is usually very tight cash control as there will be considerable investment in developing new sites and improving sites.

It is also worth considering:

- availability of further **finance**, for example is the overdraft at the limit? – very often this information is highly relevant but is not disclosed in the accounts
- **seasonal nature** of the business – one way of doing this is to compare the interest charges in the profit and loss account with the overdraft and other loans in the balance sheet; if the interest rate appears abnormally high, this is probably because the company has had higher levels of borrowings during the year
- **long-term liabilities**, when they fall due and how will they be financed
- nature of the **stocks** – where stocks are slow moving, the quick ratio probably provides a better indicator of short-term liquidity.

4.3 Quick ratio

KEY POINT

The **quick** or **acid test ratio** shows whether the company has sufficient resources to settle its liabilities.

This is also known as the **acid test ratio** because, by eliminating stocks from current assets, it provides the acid test of whether the company has sufficient resources (debtors and cash) to settle its liabilities. Norms for the quick ratio range from 1 to 0.7.

Like the current ratio it is relevant to consider the nature of the business (again supermarkets have very low quick ratios).

Sometimes the **quick ratio** is calculated on the basis of a six-week time frame (i.e. the quick assets are those which will turn into cash in six weeks; quick liabilities are those which fall due for payment within six weeks). This basis would usually include the following in **quick assets**:

- bank, cash and short-term investments
- trade debtors

thus excluding prepayments and stocks.

Quick liabilities would usually include:

- bank overdraft which is repayable on demand
- trade creditors, tax and social security
- proposed dividends.

Corporation tax liabilities may be excluded.

When interpreting the quick ratio, care should be taken over the status of the **bank overdraft**. A company with a low quick ratio may actually have no problem in paying its creditors if sufficient overall overdraft facilities are available.

KEY POINT

Both the current and quick ratio may be distorted by **window dressing**.

Both the current and quick ratio may be distorted by **window dressing;** for example, if the current ratio is 1.4 and trade creditors are paid just before the year end out of positive cash balances, the ratios improve as follows:

	Before	*Repayment of £400 trade creditors*	*After*
Current assets	£1,400	–£400	£1,000
Current liabilities	£1,000	–£400	£600
Current ratio	1.4		1.7

5 Long-term financial stability

5.1 Introduction

KEY POINT

When assessing **long-term stability, gearing, financial balance** and **overtrading** should be considered.

The main points to consider when assessing the longer-term financial position are:

- **gearing**
- **financial balance**
- overtrading**.**

5.2 Gearing

'**Gearing**' is the relationship between a company's equity capital (known as residual return capital) and reserves, and its fixed return capital.

DEFINITION

'**Gearing**' is the relationship between a company's equity capital and reserves and its fixed return capital. A company has **high gearing** when a high proportion of its capital is in the form of **preference shares, debentures** or **loan stock**.

A company is **highly geared** if it has a substantial proportion of its capital in the form of preference shares or debentures or loan stock.

A company is said to have **low gearing** if only a small proportion of its capital is in the form of preference shares, debentures or loan stock.

A company financed entirely by equity shares has **no gearing**.

The importance of gearing can be illustrated by an example as follows:

ACTIVITY **3**

Two companies, A plc and B plc, both have capital of £10,000. A plc has it all in the form of equity shares of £1 each; B plc has 5,000 £1 equity shares and £5,000 of 10% debentures.

Both companies earn operating profits of £5,000 in year 1 and £2,000 in year 2. Tax is assumed at 35% and the dividend paid is 10p per share each year.

The capital position is therefore as follows:

	A plc	*B plc*
	£	£
Shares	10,000	5,000
Debentures	-	5,000
	10,000	10,000

What is the EPS in each year?

Feedback to this activity is at the end of the chapter.

5.3 Effects of gearing

The effects of gearing can be seen to be as follows:

- Debenture interest is an allowable deduction **before taxation**, whereas dividends are paid out of profits **after taxation**; Company B has consistently higher retained profits than Company A.
- Earnings of a highly geared company are more sensitive to profit changes; this is shown by the following table:

Company	*A plc*	*B plc*
Change in profit before interest and taxation	–60%	–60%
Change in earnings	–60%	$-66\frac{2}{3}\%$

The reason for the fluctuation is obviously the element of debenture interest which must be paid regardless of profit level.

This more than proportionate change in earnings is important in relation to the share price of the companies. Many investors value their shares by applying a multiple (known as the P/E ratio) to the earnings per share. Applying a multiple of, say, 10 to the EPS disclosed above would indicate share valuations as follows:

Company	*A plc*		*B plc*	
Year	1	2	1	2
Share price	£3.25	£1.30	£5.85	£1.95

KEY POINT

The **share price** of a highly geared company will often be more volatile than a company with lower gearing.

Thus the **share price** of a highly geared company will often be more volatile than a company with only a small amount of gearing.

Not all companies are suitable for a highly geared structure. A company must have two fundamental characteristics if it is to use gearing successfully.

Relatively stable profits

Debenture interest must be paid whether or not profits are earned. A company with erratic profits may have insufficient funds in a bad year with which to pay debenture interest. This would result in the appointment of a receiver and possibly the liquidation of the company.

Suitable assets for security

Most issues of loan capital are secured on some or all of the company's assets which must be suitable for the purpose. A company with most of its capital invested in fast depreciating assets or stocks subject to rapid changes in demand and price would not be suitable for high gearing.

KEY POINT

Companies suited to high gearing are those with **stable profits**, and **assets** to pledge as security.

The classic examples of companies that are suited to high gearing are those in property investment and the hotel/leisure services industry. These companies generally enjoy relatively **stable profits** and have assets which are highly suitable for charging. Nonetheless, these are industries that could be described as cyclical.

Companies not suited to high gearing would include those in the extractive industries and high-tech industries where constant changes occur. These companies could experience erratic profits and would generally have inadequate **assets** to pledge as security.

There are two methods commonly used to express gearing as follows:

1 Debt/equity ratio

$$\frac{\text{Loans} + \text{preference share capital}}{\text{Ordinary share capital} + \text{reserves} + \text{minority interest}}$$

This is more sensitive than 2.

2 Percentage of capital employed represented by borrowings

Total capital is loans, preference share capital, ordinary share capital, reserves and minority interests.

5.4 Interest cover

This ratio emphasises the cover (or security) for interest payable.

$$\textbf{Interest cover} = \frac{\text{Profit before interest and tax}}{\text{Interest payable}}$$

5.5 Overtrading

KEY POINT

Overtrading arises where a company expands its turnover fairly rapidly without securing additional long-term capital adequate for its needs.

Overtrading arises where a company expands its turnover fairly rapidly without securing additional long-term capital adequate for its needs. The symptoms of overtrading are:

- **stocks** increasing, possibly more than proportionately to sales
- **debtors** increasing, possibly more than proportionately to sales
- **cash and liquid assets** declining at a fairly alarming rate
- **creditors** increasing rapidly.

The above symptoms simply imply that the company has expanded without giving proper thought to the necessity to expand its capital base. It has consequently continued to rely on its creditors and probably its bank overdraft to provide the additional finance required. It will reach a stage where creditors will withhold further supplies and bankers will refuse to honour further cheques until borrowings are reduced. The problem is that borrowings cannot be reduced until sales revenue is earned, which in turn cannot be achieved until production is completed, which in turn is dependent upon materials being available and wages paid. Overall result – deadlock and rapid financial collapse!

This is a particularly difficult stage for any small to medium company. They have reached a stage in their life when conventional creditor and overdraft facilities are being stretched to the maximum, but they are probably too small to manage a flotation. In many cases, by proper planning, the company can arrange fixed-term loan funding from the bank rather than relying exclusively on overdraft finance.

6 Investors' ratios

6.1 Earnings per share (EPS)

The calculation of EPS was covered in an earlier chapter.

KEY POINT

Earnings per share (EPS) is a primary profitability measure. An increasing EPS is a good sign.

EPS is used primarily as a measure of profitability, so an increasing EPS is seen as a good sign. EPS is also used to calculate the price earnings ratio which is dealt with below.

The limitations of EPS may be listed as follows.

- In times of rising prices EPS will increase as profits increase. Thus any improvement in EPS should be viewed in the context of the effect of price level changes on the company's profits.
- Where there is a new share issue, the shares are included for, say, half of the year on the grounds that earnings will also increase for half of the year. However, in practice a new project does not begin generating normal returns immediately, so a new share issue is often accompanied by a decrease in EPS.
- EPS is dependent on an earnings figure which is a subjective measure. Some elements of that earnings figure are particularly subjective, such as movements on provisions.
- FRS 3 emphasises that one earnings figure should not be used as a key performance measure. This is to take far too simplistic an approach to performance analysis.

- EPS cannot be used as a basis of comparison between companies, as the number of shares in issue in any particular company is not related to the amount of capital employed. For example, two companies may have the same amount of capital employed but one company has 100,000 £1 shares in issue and reserves of £4,900,000. Another company may have 5 million 50p shares in issue and reserves of £2,500,000. If earnings are the same, EPS is different.
- EPS is an historical figure based on historic accounts. This is a disadvantage where it is used for a forward-looking figure such as the price earnings ratio. This is considered below.
- The diluted EPS (DEPS) is a theoretical measure of the effect of dilution on the basic EPS. There is no evidence to suggest that even the most sophisticated analysts use the DEPS. This is because of its hypothetical nature. In the past the DEPS has served as a warning to equity shareholders that their future earnings will be affected by diluting factors. Following the introduction of FRS 22, the DEPS will have less predictive value as it has become an additional measure of past performance. Thus, notes in the accounts relating to convertible loan stock, convertible preference shares and share options should all be analysed carefully.

KEY POINT

Price/earnings (P/E) ratio is the stock market measure most widely referred to. The higher the P/E ratio, the faster the growth the market is expecting in the company's future EPS.

6.2 Price/earnings ratio

This is the stock market ratio which is most widely referred to, also commonly described as an earnings multiple. It is calculated as the '**purchase of a number of years' earnings**' but it represents the market's consensus of the future prospects of that share. The higher the P/E ratio, the faster the growth the market is expecting in the company's future EPS. Correspondingly, the lower the P/E ratio the lower the expected future growth.

6.3 Dividend yield gross

This is the (gross) percentage of the dividend to the market price. The dividends are grossed up to show the amount including the tax credit (at the rate of 10% i.e. 10/90 of the net amount).

6.4 Dividend cover

This is the relationship between available profits (adjusted to exclude non-trading profits and losses) and the dividends payable out of the profits. The higher the dividend cover, the more likely it is that the current dividend level can be sustained in the future.

7 Producing written reports on the position and progress of companies

The syllabus requires the preparation and presentation of reports for a variety of users and purposes. This section summarises the general principles to follow.

The particular problems of producing written reports in the context of **inter-firm** and **inter-temporal comparisons** are detailed in the following sections.

In practice, there are several possible ways of setting out a report. Usually a report contains two basic sections:

1 main body, including conclusions

2 statistical appendices and supplementary statements which back up the comments or conclusions in 1 above.

EXAM HINT

In an exam answer, as it may not be practical to maintain a split report layout, it may be helpful to note the sections that would normally go in an appendix.

In an exam answer it may not be practical to maintain this split, in which case it is helpful to state by a particular section that it would normally go into an appendix.

The following is a suitable approach to setting out a report:

- **Index** to report.
- **Addressee, date and title.**
- **Introduction** – Introduce the reader to the aim or purpose of the report, for example 'Analysis of the accounts of X Ltd for the two years ended 31 December 20X8'.
- **Assumptions** – State key assumptions.
- **Information used** – State the source of the financial information included in the report. Mention the extent to which the report has been limited by specific instructions.
- **Conclusions** – State these as clearly as possible.

  Note: Some reports state the conclusions at the beginning of the report. This is a perfectly acceptable alternative to the above approach.
- **Appendices** – Containing detailed figures.

8 Trend analysis

KEY POINT

To appreciate the overall financial position or strength of a company or group, it is important to review the **trend of results**.

In order to appreciate the overall financial position or strength of a company or group, it is important to review the **trend of results**. By including a summary of the results of the company for the last few years within annual financial statements, the reader is shown how the company has arrived at its present position, and is thereby enabled to view the year's results in the context of the disclosed trend.

Published accounts give comparative information in two main areas as follows:

- the corresponding amounts for items shown in the balance sheet, profit and loss account and notes. Such amounts are required by the CA85 for virtually all items disclosed in the accounts
- any historical summary provided. Such summaries, which often take the form of five- or ten-year summaries, are not required by law, but have nevertheless become a common feature in the annual reports of listed companies. Historical summaries will usually be disclosed as information supplemental to the financial statements.

KEY POINT

It is important to consider any **change in accounting policy** during the summary period, and whether the summarised figures have been adjusted for **inflation**.

There are two important points to consider here.

- Have there been any **changes in accounting policies** during the period and, if so, have the summarised figures been restated?
- Have the summarised figures been adjusted for the effect of **inflation** and, if not, what adjustments are necessary in order to draw any conclusions from the information?

ACTIVITY 4

Explain why trends in accounting ratios may provide a more useful insight into an entity's financial performance and position than the latest financial statements taken on their own.

Feedback to this activity is at the end of the chapter.

9 The effect of accounting policies

9.1 Changes in accounting policy

KEY POINT

FRS 3 requires that a change in accounting policy is accompanied by **restated comparative figures** in the published accounts and summarised data.

If a company changes an accounting policy, it must have good reasons to make a change. FRS 3 states that a change in accounting policy can only be made if it will give a fairer presentation of the reporting entity's results and financial position. The company must also **restate comparative figures** in the published accounts and summarised five- or ten-year data for the new policy. Therefore the user of the accounts has some assurance in using the financial data.

However, the user must be aware of the extent to which policies are changed, as it is relatively easy for the directors to come up with 'good' reasons for making a change. It is not unlikely that the real reason for the change in policy is that the new policy puts the current results of the company in a more favourable light.

9.2 The use of different accounting policies between companies

KEY POINT

A limitation of ratio analysis is that different entities may adopt **different accounting policies**.

One of the major limitations of ratio analysis is that different entities may adopt **different accounting policies**, so ratios based on their accounts may not be strictly comparable.

There are still a few areas in which accounting standards permit a choice of accounting treatment. There are many others in which preparers of accounts are required to exercise judgement. The main ones are listed below.

9.3 Tangible fixed assets

KEY POINT

How entities account for **tangible fixed assets**, **development expenditure** and **leases** can affect ROCE, gearing and profits.

Entities may carry **tangible fixed assets** at **cost** or at a **valuation**. Revaluation must be applied consistently to all assets in the same class, but in practice classes are defined by the directors and very narrow definition is possible. A company that carries its assets at a valuation will normally have a lower ROCE and lower profits than an otherwise comparable company that carries its assets at historic cost (assuming that current value is higher than historic cost). However, gearing is reduced if assets are revalued upwards, making a company that adopts this policy appear to be a safer investment than an otherwise comparable company that does not.

Entities may choose whether or not to **capitalise interest on borrowings** made to construct fixed assets. Capitalisation strengthens the balance sheet (reducing gearing) but can reduce ROCE.

The choice of **depreciation method** can materially affect profits. This is left with the directors of a company provided it achieves the objectives of FRS 15. This involves an assessment of the useful economic life and the pattern of wearing out over that life (e.g. whether a straight line or reducing balance charge would be most appropriate). Because of this choice there is scope for manipulation.

Some companies do not charge depreciation on freehold properties on the grounds that high ongoing maintenance and refurbishment costs mean that estimated residual value is always kept at greater than cost and that the asset's life effectively becomes infinite. Although FRS 15 discourages this practice by requiring impairment reviews, it does not actually prohibit it.

In addition, a change of method or useful economic life, neither of which is dealt with as a prior period adjustment, can be used to adjust profits. For a change of method, the effect on *current period* profits has to be disclosed where material, but such a change can increase profits for many years to come.

9.4 Development expenditure

Development expenditure that meets the SSAP 13 criteria for deferral may either be **capitalised and amortised** or **written off** to the profit and loss account in the period in which it is incurred. Again, this choice could have a significant effect on ROCE, gearing and profits.

9.5 Leases

The main scope for manipulation here is with the misuse of the so-called **'90% test'**. Companies have used this to keep leased assets and their corresponding liabilities off the balance sheet and so improve ratios such as gearing.

10 Interpreting current cost and current purchasing power accounts

10.1 Current cost accounts

KEY POINT

Ratios based on **current cost accounts** (CCA) may provide more useful information than ratios based on **historic cost accounts** (HCA).

In many ways, ratios based on **current cost accounts** (CCA) may provide more useful information than ratios based on **historic cost accounts** (HCA).

- CCA accounts reflect **current asset values**. This means that ROCE is not distorted by out of date asset values and the 'real' return can be seen. Inter-company comparisons based on CCA accounts are likely to be more accurate because they circumvent the problems caused by the use of the modified historic cost convention (i.e. where some entities revalue fixed assets and others do not).
- CCA profits are stated after the operating capacity of the business has been maintained. This means that ratios based on CCA accounts normally give a more realistic picture of the 'true' performance of a company.

However, CCA accounts have some limitations and these should be borne in mind when interpreting ratios based on them.

- Valuation of assets is always **subjective**. In addition, it may be difficult to arrive at a current value for an asset which is unique or which is not traded in an active market. This subjectivity limits the usefulness of inter-company comparisons, especially comparisons between companies that do not operate in the same industry sector.
- CCA accounts show the effect of **specific price changes**, but not the effect of general **inflation**. Depreciation and cost of sales are restated, but general expenses, tax and interest are not. This should be taken into account when interpreting trends.
- The CCA profit and loss account is adjusted to reflect the effect of changes in the value of monetary working capital and the effect of gearing. These adjustments have been criticised as being arbitrary and some experts believe that the gearing adjustment is not theoretically sound. This raises the question as to whether CCA earnings can be interpreted as 'real' earnings.
- CCA profit is profit after maintaining the operating capacity of the business. This is not necessarily the 'real' return on shareholders' funds as this will also be affected by general inflation.

10.2 Current purchasing power accounts

KEY POINT

Ratios based on **current purchasing power accounts** may provide useful information as they adjust for inflation.

Ratios based on **current purchasing power accounts** (CPP) may also provide useful information.

- CPP accounts are adjusted for the general effect of inflation. This means that **inter-temporal comparisons** are more meaningful than those based on HCA information.
- CPP takes account of both realised and unrealised holding gains and therefore earnings and ROCE can be said to represent the 'real' return on shareholders' funds.
- CPP is more objective than CCA and therefore it can be argued that **inter-company comparisons** based on CPP accounts are more meaningful than those based on CCA and HCA information.

The main limitation of CPP is that it does not take account of specific price changes. This affects the interpretation of CPP accounts.

- CPP earnings and the information in the CPP profit and loss account are not necessarily relevant to a manufacturing business. It is possible for a business to make a profit under CPP and yet not have maintained its physical operating capacity.
- Asset values under CPP do not necessarily represent their current values or their value to the business. This means that ROCE and gearing may be distorted.

11 The limitations of ratio analysis

11.1 General limitations

KEY POINT

Accounting ratios must always be interpreted in relation to other contextual information.

Accounting ratios are a useful means of identifying significant relationships between different figures. However, they cannot be considered in isolation; they must always be interpreted in relation to other information, for example:

- **budgeted figures**
- **industry averages**
- **'ideal'** figures
- figures for a **similar business**
- **comparative figures** for the same business.

The chief limitations of the usefulness of ratio analysis are as follows.

- Although there are general guidelines (for example, the quick ratio should not normally be less than 1), there is no such thing as an 'ideal' ratio. A quick ratio of less than 1 would be acceptable in some businesses, but would be dangerously low for many others.
- Unless ratios are calculated on a uniform basis, from uniform data, comparisons can be very misleading.
- The accounting periods covered by the financial statements may not reflect representative financial positions. Many businesses produce accounts to a date on which there is a relatively low amount of trading activity. Retail organisations often have an end of February accounting date (after the peak pre-Christmas trading and the January sales). As a result, the items on a balance sheet are not representative of the items throughout the accounting period.

  Consider stock levels in a retail organisation. They may vary as shown in the following graph:

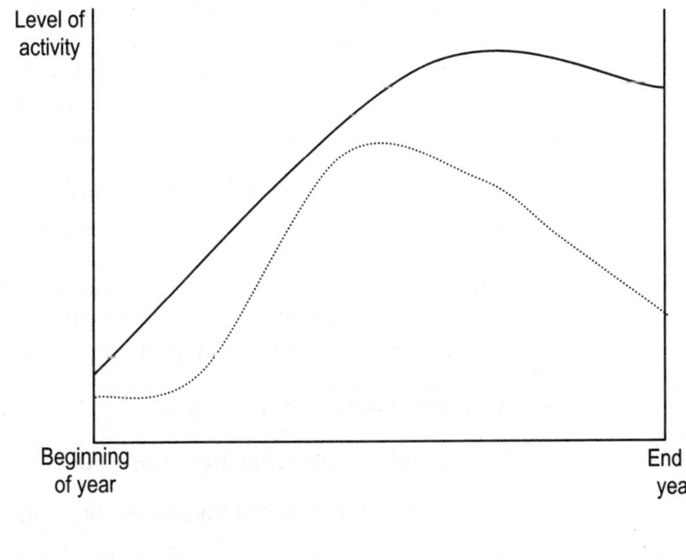

  Adding opening and closing stock and dividing by two will not produce a fair average.

- Ratios based on **historic cost accounts** do not give a true picture of trends from year to year. An apparent increase in profit may not be a 'true' increase, because of the effects of inflation.
- Financial statements only reflect those activities which can be expressed in money terms. They do not give a complete picture of the activities of a business.
- The application of accounting policies in the preparation of financial statements must be understood when attempting to interpret financial ratios.
- The earning power of a business may well be affected by factors which are not reflected in the financial statements. Thus, these do not necessarily represent a complete picture of a business, but only a collection of those parts which can be translated into money terms. For example, the size of the order book is normally ignored in financial statements.
- Ratios must not be used as the sole test of efficiency. Concentration on ratios by managers may inhibit the incentive to grow and expand, to the detriment of the long-term interests of the company.
- A few simple ratios do not provide an automatic means of running a company. Business problems usually involve complex patterns which cannot be solved solely by the use of ratios.

11.2 Inter-firm comparisons

KEY POINT

In comparing firms' ratios, care must be taken to ensure that the data is consistent.

It can be useful to compare ratios for an individual company with those of other firms in the same industry. However, comparing the financial statements of similar businesses can be misleading because:

- the businesses may use different accounting policies
- ratios may not be calculated according to the same formula (for example, there are several possible definitions of gearing and return on capital employed)
- large organisations can achieve **economies of scale** (e.g. by negotiating extended credit periods, or discounts for bulk buying with suppliers) while these measures may not be available to smaller businesses
- companies within the same industry can serve completely **different markets** and there may be differences in sales mix and product range. These can affect profitability and activity ratios such as profit margin and expenses to sales.

Conclusion

Ratio analysis is a technique for analysing and interpreting financial statements. Commonly used ratios include return on capital employed (ROCE), profit margin, asset turnover, current ratio, quick (acid test) ratio, earnings per share and gearing. When interpreting financial statements it is important to ask the following questions:

- Who are the users of the accounts?
- What decisions do they wish to make?
- What information is relevant for this purpose?

Although ratio analysis is a useful tool for interpreting financial statements, it has many limitations. Ratios should always be interpreted in the context of other information about the business involved, particularly the accounting policies adopted.

SELF-TEST QUESTIONS

1 What is horizontal analysis? (1.1)

2 What are the principal analytical ratios? (2.1)

3 In which ratios are investors most likely to be interested? (2.2)

4 Which two factors affect ROCE? (3.1)

5 How is the stock turnover ratio computed? (3.3)

6 What is the difference between the current ratio and the quick ratio? (4.1)

7 What is overtrading? (5.5)

8 What are the limitations of EPS as a measure of performance? (6.1)

9 Why do ratios based on CCA accounts often provide more useful information than ratios based on HCA accounts? (10.1)

10 What problems may arise from the choice of a particular year end for a company? (11.1)

EXAM-TYPE QUESTION

Wandafood Products

The following five-year summary relates to Wandafood Products plc, and is based on financial statements prepared under the historic cost convention.

	20X9	*20X8*	*20X7*	*20X6*	*20X5*
Financial ratios					
Profitability					
Margin $\frac{\text{Trading profit}}{\text{Sales}}$ %	7.8	7.5	7.0	7.2	7.3
Return on assets $\frac{\text{Trading profit}}{\text{Net operating assets}}$ %	16.3	17.6	16.2	18.2	18.3
Interest and dividend cover					
Interest cover $\frac{\text{Trading profit}}{\text{Net finance charges}}$ times	2.9	4.8	5.1	6.5	3.6
Dividend cover					
$\frac{\text{Earnings per ordinary share}}{\text{Dividend per ordinary share}}$ times	2.7	2.6	2.1	2.5	3.1
Debt to equity ratios					
$\frac{\text{Net borrowings}}{\text{Shareholders funds}}$ %	65.9	61.3	48.3	10.8	36.5
$\frac{\text{Net borrowings}}{\text{Shareholders funds plus minority interests}}$	59.3	55.5	44.0	10.1	33.9
Liquidity ratios					
Quick: $\frac{\text{Current assets less stock}}{\text{Current liabilities}}$ %	82.1	81.9	83.4	94.2	101.2
Current: $\frac{\text{Current assets}}{\text{Current liabilities}}$ %	133.6	130.3	142.2	178.9	174.7
Asset ratios					
$\frac{\text{Sales}}{\text{Net operating assets}}$ times	2.1	2.4	2.3	2.5	2.5
$\frac{\text{Sales}}{\text{Working capital}}$ times	8.6	8.0	7.0	7.4	6.2
Per share					
Earnings per share ... p	15.65	13.60	10.98	11.32	12.18
Dividends per share ... p	5.90	5.40	4.90	4.60	4.10
Net assets per share ... p	102.10	89.22	85.95	85.79	78.11

Net operating assets include tangible fixed assets, stock, debtors and creditors. They exclude borrowings, taxation and dividends.

Required:

Prepare a report on the company, clearly interpreting and evaluating the information given. Include comments on possible effects of price changes which may limit the quality of the report. **(30 marks)**

For the answer to this question, see the 'Answers' section at the end of the book.

FEEDBACK TO ACTIVITY 1

- Exceptional items.
- Depreciation of tangible fixed assets.
- Research and development (if not already dealt with in cost of sales).
- Advertising expenditure.
- Staff costs which may have risen in line with inflation.
- Amortisation of intangibles (including goodwill).
- Directors' emoluments.
- Government grants received.

The list above is not intended to be comprehensive, but it may serve as a source of ideas and it should prompt your own thoughts.

FEEDBACK TO ACTIVITY 2

Any upward revaluation of fixed assets causes a reduction in ROCE by:

- increasing the capital employed, and
- decreasing profits by a higher depreciation charge.

FEEDBACK TO ACTIVITY 3

	A plc		*B plc*	
	Year 1	*Year 2*	*Year 1*	*Year 2*
	£	£	£	£
Profit before tax and debenture interest	5,000	2,000	5,000	2,000
Debenture interest	-	-	500	500
			4,500	1,500
Taxation (35%)	1,750	700	1,575	525
Earnings	3,250	1,300	2,925	975
Dividend (10%)	1,000	1,000	500	500
Retained profits	2,250	300	2,425	475
Earnings per share	32.5p	13p	58.5p	19.5p

FEEDBACK TO ACTIVITY 4

Comparative figures for several years provide information about the way in which the performance and financial position of a business has changed over a period. For example, if a company has low liquidity ratios for a particular year, this would normally indicate liquidity problems. However, if low liquidity ratios are viewed in the context of a steadily improving trend, the picture is very different: the company is able to survive at this level, is overcoming its problems and is unlikely to go into receivership in the near future.

Trends in accounting ratios may provide information from which future performance can be predicted, particularly if the figures are very stable.

The extent to which amounts and ratios are stable or volatile can reveal a great deal. Ratios which are very volatile, or sudden changes in trends, may indicate that the company will experience problems in the future, even if performance is apparently improving.

Chapter 23

CASH FLOW STATEMENTS

CHAPTER CONTENTS

1 **FRS 1 *Cash flow statements***

2 **Classification of cash flows**

3 **Net debt, exceptional items and non-cash transactions**

4 **Scope of FRS 1**

5 **Usefulness of the cash flow statement**

6 **Interpretation of cash flow data**

The balance sheet and profit and loss account of a business give a good indication of how healthy it is financially and how successfully it is performing. But neither statement gives direct information about a crucial aspect in the stability and success of any business: namely, its ability to generate cash.

This chapter explains how to prepare a cash flow statement and covers the requirements of FRS 1 *Cash flow statements*. FRS 1 requires companies to publish a cash flow statement showing how cash inflows have been generated and how the cash has been spent.

Objectives

By the time you have finished this chapter you should be able to:

- prepare a cash flow statement for an individual company in accordance with FRS 1 (revised)
- appraise the usefulness of, and interpret the information in, a cash flow statement.

1 FRS 1 *Cash flow statements*

1.1 Objective of cash flow statements

FRS 1 requires 'large' reporting entities to include a **cash flow statement** in their financial statements.

The objective of FRS 1 is to ensure that reporting entities falling within its scope:

- report their cash generation and cash absorption for a period by highlighting the significant components of cash flow in a way that facilitates comparison of the cash flow performance of different businesses
- provide information that assists in the assessment of their liquidity, solvency and financial adaptability.

KEY POINT

Cash flow statements enable users of financial statements to assess the liquidity, viability and financial adaptability of entities.

Users of financial statements need information on the liquidity, viability and financial adaptability of entities. Deriving this information involves the user in making assessments of the future cash flows of the entity. Future cash flows are regarded (in financial management theory and increasingly in practice in large companies) as the prime determinant of the worth of a business.

To help to achieve the objective of cash flow reporting, FRS 1 requires that individual cash flows should be classified under certain standard headings according to the activity that gave rise to them. The **standard headings** required in a cash flow statement are:

- operating activities
- dividends from joint ventures and associates (relevant only for the cash flow statements of groups)
- returns on investments and servicing of finance
- taxation
- capital expenditure and financial investment
- acquisitions and disposals
- equity dividends paid
- management of liquid resources
- financing.

KEY POINT

Standard headings ensure that cash flows are reported in a form that highlights the significant components of cash flow and facilitates comparison.

The objective of the standard headings is to ensure that cash flows are reported in a form that highlights the significant components of cash flow and facilitates comparison of the cash flow performance of different businesses.

Cash flows relating to the management of liquid resources and financing can be combined under a single heading, provided that the cash flows relating to each are shown separately and separate subtotals are given.

Each cash flow should be classified according to the substance of the transaction giving rise to it. The substance of a transaction determines the most appropriate standard heading under which to report cash flows that are not specified in the standard categories.

1.2 Definitions

The definition of cash is central to the preparation and interpretation of cash flow statements.

DEFINITION

Cash is cash in hand and deposits repayable on demand, less **overdrafts** repayable on demand.

Cash is cash in hand and deposits repayable on demand with any qualifying financial institution, less overdrafts from any qualifying financial institution repayable on demand. Deposits are repayable on demand if they can be withdrawn at any time without notice and without penalty or if a maturity or period of notice of not more than 24 hours or one working day has been agreed. Cash includes cash in hand and deposits denominated in foreign currencies.

DEFINITION

An **overdraft** is a borrowing facility repayable on demand.

An **overdraft** is a borrowing facility repayable on demand that is used by drawing on a current account with a qualifying financial institution.

A **qualifying financial institution** is an entity that as part of its business receives deposits or other repayable funds and grants credits for its own account.

DEFINITION

Cash flow is an increase or decrease in an amount of cash.

Cash flow is an increase or decrease in an amount of cash.

The bottom line in the cash flow statement is the **total cash flow** for the period, in other words, the total increase or decrease in the amount of cash.

The practical effect of these definitions is that the cash flow statement reports inflows and outflows of 'pure' cash. Short-term deposits and loans are not included within the definitions.

Example

The following illustration is included in FRS 1. It shows a cash flow statement for a single company. It illustrates the standard headings and examples of items within the standard headings.

The illustration includes the reconciliations and notes required by FRS 1. The reconciliations may be shown adjoining the cash flow statement or in the notes. If they adjoin the cash flow statement they should be clearly labelled and kept separate.

Note 1 gives the components of the net cash flows reported under each heading. These can be shown on the face of the cash flow statement or in the notes.

XYZ Ltd
Cash flow statement for year ended 31 December 20X6

Reconciliation of operating profit to net cash inflow from operating activities

	£000
Operating profit	6,022
Depreciation charges	899
Increase in stocks	(194)
Increase in debtors	(72)
Increase in creditors	234
Net cash inflow from operating activities	6,889

Cash flow statement

Net cash inflow from operating activities	6,889
Returns on investments and servicing of finance (note 1)	2,999
Taxation	(2,922)
Capital expenditure (note 1)	(1,525)
	5,441
Equity dividends paid	(2,417)
	3,024
Management of liquid resources (note 1)	(450)
Financing (note 1)	57
Increase in cash	2,631

Reconciliation of net cash flow to movement in net debt (note 2)

Increase in cash in the period	2,631
Cash to repurchase debenture	149
Cash used to increase liquid resources	450
Change in net debt	3,230
Net debt at 1 Jan 20X6	(2,903)
Net funds at 31 Dec 20X6	327

Notes to cash flow statement

(1) Gross cash flows

	£000	£000
Returns on investments and servicing of finance		
Interest received	3,011	
Interest paid	(12)	
		2,999

Capital expenditure		
Payments to acquire intangible fixed assets	(71)	
Payments to acquire tangible fixed assets	(1,496)	
Receipts from sales of tangible fixed assets	42	
		(1,525)
Management of liquid resources		
Purchase of treasury bills	(650)	
Sale of treasury bills	200	
		(450)
Financing		
Issue of ordinary share capital		211
Repurchase of debenture loan		(149)
Expenses paid in connection with share issues		(5)
		57

(2) **Analysis of changes in net debt**

	At 1 Jan 20X6	*Cash flows*	*Other changes*	*At 31 Dec 20X6*
	£000	£000	£000	£000
Cash in hand, at bank	42	847		889
Overdrafts	(1,784)	1,784		
		2,631		
Debts due within 1 year	(149)	149	(230)	(230)
Debts due after 1 year	(1,262)		230	(1,032)
Current asset investments	250	450		700
Total	(2,903)	3,230	–	327

2 Classification of cash flows

2.1 Operating activities

Standard accounting practice

KEY POINT

A **reconciliation** between the operating profit and the net cash flow from operating activities should be given, disclosing separately the movements in stocks, debtors and creditors.

Cash flows from operating activities are in general the cash effects of transactions and other events relating to operating or trading activities. Net cash flow from operating activities represents the net increase or decrease in cash resulting from the operations shown in the profit and loss account in arriving at operating profit.

Operating cash flows may be reported in the cash flow statement on a net or gross basis.

A **reconciliation** between the operating profit (for non-financial companies this is normally profit before interest) reported in the profit and loss account and the net cash flow from operating activities should be given. This reconciliation should disclose separately the movements in stocks, debtors and creditors related to operating activities, and other differences between cash flows and profits.

KEY POINT

The **direct method** shows the actual operating cash receipts and payments that make up net cash flow from operating activities.
The **indirect method** starts with operating profit and adjusts it for non-cash items to reconcile it to the net cash flow from operating activities.

There are two possible methods for reporting net cash flow from operating activities:

- The **direct method** shows operating cash receipts and payments (including, in particular, cash receipts from customers, cash payments to suppliers and cash payments to and on behalf of employees), aggregating to the net cash flow from operating activities.
- The **indirect method** starts with operating profit and adjusts it for non-cash charges and credits to reconcile it to the net cash flow from operating activities.

A comparison of the two methods is shown below. The methods differ only as regards the derivation of the item 'Net cash inflow from operating activities'. Subsequent inflows and outflows in the rest of the cash flow statement are the same.

Direct method

Cash received from customers	15,424
Cash payments to suppliers	(5,824)
Cash paid to and on behalf of employees	(2,200)
Other cash payments	(511)
Net cash inflow from operating activities	6,889

Indirect method

Operating profit	6,022
Depreciation charges	899
Increase in stocks	(194)
Increase in debtors	(72)
Increase in creditors	234
Net cash inflow from operating activities	6,889

The principal advantage of the direct method is that it shows operating cash receipts and payments. Knowledge of the specific sources of cash receipts and the purposes for which cash payments were made in past periods may be useful in assessing future cash flows. However, the ASB does not believe at present that in all cases the benefits to users of this information outweigh the costs to the reporting entity of providing it and, therefore, has not required the information to be given.

KEY POINT

The principal advantage of the **direct method** is that it shows operating cash receipts and payments. The principal advantage of the **indirect method** is that it highlights the differences between operating profit and net cash flow from operating activities.

The principal advantage of the indirect method is that it highlights the differences between operating profit and net cash flow from operating activities. Many users of financial statements believe that such a reconciliation is essential to give an indication of the **quality** of the reporting entity's earnings. Some investors and creditors assess future cash flows by estimating future income and then allowing for accruals adjustments, so information about past accruals adjustments may be useful to help estimate future adjustments.

Accordingly, the FRS requires the cash flow statement to show the net cash flow from operating activities, supplemented by a reconciliation of operating profit for the period to the net cash flow from operating activities. The result is that reporting entities **must** give the information required by the indirect method and that they **may** also give the information required by the direct method.

2.2 Calculation of net cash flow from operating activities

Operating profit is computed using the **accruals concept**. Net cash flow from operating activities only records the cash inflows and outflows arising out of trading. **Net cash inflow** can be derived:

- from the accounting records of the entity by totalling the cash receipts and payments directly, or
- operating profit can be adjusted by the relevant amounts in the profit and loss account and the opening and closing balance sheets which represent the differences between cash flows and amounts accrued.

In most situations the latter approach is quicker and easier. It also results in the production of the reconciliation statement which is required.

KEY POINT

The main categories which form the reconciliation between operating profit and net cash flow are **depreciation**, **profit/loss on fixed asset disposal**, and changes in **debtors**, **stocks** and **creditors** on the balance sheet.

The main categories of items in the profit and loss account and on a balance sheet which form part of the reconciliation between operating profit and net cash flow from operating activities are as follows.

Depreciation

Depreciation is a book write-off of capital expenditure. Capital expenditure will be recorded under 'capital expenditure' at the time of the cash outflow. Depreciation therefore represents an *addition* to operating profit in deriving cash inflow.

Profit/loss on disposal of fixed asset

The cash inflow from a sale needs to be recorded under 'capital expenditure'. Following the issue of FRS 3, most profits and losses on disposal are no longer included in operating profit, but occasionally it may be necessary to adjust operating profit. A loss on disposal is added to operating profit; a profit on disposal is deducted from operating profit.

Balance sheet change in debtors

A sale once made creates income irrespective of the date of cash receipt. If the cash has not been received by the balance sheet date, however, there is no cash inflow from operating activities for the current accounting period. Similarly, opening debtors represent sales of a previous accounting period most of which will be cash receipts in the current period.

The *change* between opening and closing debtors will thus represent the adjustment required to move from operating profit to net cash inflow.

- An increase in debtors is a deduction from operating profit. More sales are not being received in cash in the current period than are being brought forward from the previous period.
- A decrease in debtors is an addition to operating profit.

Balance sheet change in stocks

Stock at the balance sheet date represents a purchase which has not actually been charged against current operating profits. Since cash was spent on its purchase or a creditor incurred, it does represent an actual or potential cash outflow.

- An increase in stocks is a deduction from operating profit in the same way as an increase in debtors.
- A decrease in stocks is an addition to operating profit.

Balance sheet change in creditors

A purchase represents the incurring of expenditure and a charge or potential charge to the profit and loss account. It does not represent a cash outflow until paid. To the extent that a purchase results in a charge to the profit and loss account:

- an increase in creditors between two balance sheet dates is an addition to operating profit
- a decrease in creditors is a deduction from operating profit.

If the purchase does not result in a charge to the profit and loss account in the current year, the corresponding creditor is not included in the reconciliation of operating profit to net cash inflow. For example, a fixed asset creditor is not included.

ACTIVITY **1**

A new business made operating profits of £300,000 in its first year. Extracts from the closing balance sheet are given below. Calculate the net cash inflow from operating activities.

	£
Debtors	125,000
Stocks	118,000
Creditors	135,000

An analysis of creditors showed:

	£
For raw materials	102,700
For fixed asset	12,000
For various expenses	13,500
Accruals	6,800

Feedback to this activity is at the end of the chapter.

2.3 Using the direct method to calculate cash flows from operating activities

KEY POINT

Reporting entities may use the **direct method** for reporting **net cash flow** from operating activities, in which case they must additionally disclose the reconciliation required by the indirect method.

Reporting entities may use the direct method for reporting net cash flow from operating activities. The relevant cash flows can be derived from:

- the accounting records of the entity, by totalling the cash receipts and payments directly; or
- the opening and closing balance sheets and profit and loss account for the year by constructing summary control accounts for:
  - sales (to derive cash received from customers)
  - purchases (to derive cash payments to suppliers)
  - wages (to derive cash paid to and on behalf of employees).

Example

The balance sheets of a business are as follows:

	Last year	*This year*
	£	£
Fixed assets	153,364	149,364
Stocks	–	–
Debtors	265,840	346,000
Cash	–	165,166
Creditors	(219,204)	(318,890)
	200,000	341,640
Share capital	200,000	200,000
Reserves	–	141,640
	200,000	341,640

Extracts from the profit and loss account for the year are as follows:

	£	£
Sales		1,589,447
Cost of sales:		
Purchases (no stocks)	1,021,830	
Wages and salaries	145,900	
Depreciation	84,000	
		(1,251,730)
Administration:		
Purchases	96,077	
Salaries	100,000	
		(196,077)
Operating profit and retained profit for the year		141,640

1 Creditors

	£	£
Creditors from purchases ledger:		
– re fixed assets	–	46,000
– other	210,564	258,240
PAYE/NI creditor	8,640	14,650

2 Purchase invoices relating to fixed assets totalling £80,000 have been posted to the purchase ledger during the year.

Prepare the cash flow statement using the direct method and a note reconciling operating profit to net cash inflow from operating activities.

Solution

Cash flow statement

	£
Operating activities	
Cash received from customers (W1)	1,509,287
Cash payments to suppliers (W2)	(1,070,231)
Cash paid to and on behalf of employees (W3)	(239,890)
Net cash inflow from operating activities	199,166
Capital expenditure	
Purchase of fixed assets (W4)	(34,000)
Increase in cash	165,166

Reconciliation of operating profit to net cash inflow from operating activities

	£
Operating profit	141,640
Depreciation charges	84,000
Increase in stock	–
Increase in debtors	(80,160)
Increase in creditors	53,686
Net cash inflow from operating activities	199,166

Workings

(W1) **Sales ledger control**

	£		£
Balance b/d – Debtors	265,840	Cash receipts	1,509,287
Sales	1,589,447	Balance c/d – Debtors	346,000
	1,855,287		1,855,287

(W2) **Purchases ledger control (excluding fixed asset purchases)**

	£		£
Cash paid (bal. fig.)	1,070,231	Balance b/d – Creditors	210,564
Balance c/d	258,240	Purchases	
		– cost of sales	1,021,830
		– administration	96,077
	1,328,471		1,328,471

(W3) **Wages control**

	£		£
Net wages and PAYE/NI		Balance b/d	
paid (bal. fig.)	239,890	PAYE and NI	8,640
Balance c/d		Cost of sales	145,900
PAYE and NI	14,650	Administration	100,000
	254,540		254,540

(W4) **Fixed asset expenditure**

Cash paid for fixed assets is 80,000 – 46,000 = £34,000. The £80,000 invoice agrees with the movement in fixed assets per the balance sheets.

Fixed assets (NBV)

	£		£
Balance b/d	153,364	Depreciation charge	84,000
Addition (bal. fig.)	80,000	Balance c/d	149,364
	233,364		233,364

2.4 Returns on investments and servicing of finance

KEY POINT

'Returns on investments and servicing of finance' are receipts resulting from the ownership of an investment and payments to providers of finance.

'**Returns on investments and servicing of finance**' are receipts resulting from the ownership of an investment and payments to providers of finance: non-equity shareholders (e.g. the holders of preference shares) and minority interests, excluding those items required to be classified under another heading.

Cash inflows from returns on investments and servicing of finance include:

- interest received, including any related tax recovered
- dividends received net of any tax credits.

Cash outflows from returns on investments and servicing of finance include:

- interest paid (even if capitalised), including any tax deducted and paid to the relevant tax authority
- cash flows that are treated as finance costs under FRS 26

- the interest element of finance lease rental payments
- dividends paid on non-equity shares of the entity.

The ASB believes that the presentation of net cash flow from operating activities should not be affected by the capital structure of the reporting entity. Thus payments resulting from the servicing of finance (e.g. interest and non-equity dividends paid) should be shown together.

KEY POINT

Cash flow from operating activities shown in the reconciliation of operating profit to net cash inflow is stated before interest receipts and payments.

Interest and dividend receipts for a trading company may arise from long-term investing activities, temporary investment of surplus funds or perhaps operating activities. The different categories would often be difficult to analyse and so the receipts are grouped together.

It follows from the above classification that cash flow from operating activities shown in the reconciliation of operating profit to net cash inflow is stated before interest receipts and payments.

2.5 Taxation

Standard accounting practice

KEY POINT

Cash flows should be shown net of any attributable **VAT** unless the tax is irrecoverable.

The cash flows included under this heading are cash flows to or from taxation authorities in respect of the reporting entity's revenue and capital profits. In practice, this is normally the amount paid for UK corporation tax.

Value Added Tax (VAT) is not included under this heading. Cash flows should be shown net of any attributable VAT unless the tax is irrecoverable. The net movement on the VAT account should normally be allocated to cash flows from operating activities (i.e. it is treated as a normal movement in working capital).

Computation of tax paid

KEY POINT

In many statements there will only be one tax figure shown: **UK corporation tax** paid.

In many statements there will only be one figure shown: the **UK corporation tax** paid in the year.

The creation of a taxation account recording all opening and closing tax balances relating to corporation tax is often the easiest way to derive the tax paid for the year.

ACTIVITY 2

Extracts from X Ltd's profit and loss account for the year ended 31 December 20X8 show:

	£	£
Turnover		X
Costs		X
Dividends received		100,000
Profit on ordinary activities before taxation		X
Taxation:		
Corporation tax	300,000	
Deferred tax	50,000	
		350,000
Dividends:		
Interim	96,000	
Final	240,000	
		336,000

Extracts from X Ltd's balance sheets are:

	31 December	
	20X7	*20X8*
	£	£
Creditors: amounts falling due within one year:		
Corporation tax	170,000	331,000
Provisions for liabilities and charges:		
Deferred tax	110,000	130,000

Calculate the amount of tax paid by X Ltd in the year.

Feedback to this activity is at the end of the chapter.

2.6 Capital expenditure and financial investment

KEY POINT

Cash flows included in '**capital expenditure and financial investment**' are those related to fixed assets (other than those required to be classified under '**acquisitions and disposals**').

The cash flows included in '**capital expenditure and financial investment**' are those related to the acquisition or disposal of any fixed asset other than one required to be classified under '**acquisitions and disposals**' and any current asset investment not included in liquid resources. (Acquisitions and disposals and liquid resources are explained below.)

If no cash flows relating to financial investment fall to be included under this heading, the caption may be reduced to '**capital expenditure**'.

Cash inflows from capital expenditure and financial investment include:

- receipts from sales or disposals of property, plant or equipment
- receipts from the repayment of the reporting entity's loans to other entities or sales of debt instruments of other entities other than receipts forming part of an acquisition or disposal or a movement in liquid resources.

Cash outflows from capital expenditure and financial investment include:

- payments to acquire property, plant or equipment (this includes the capital element of any finance lease payments – see earlier chapter on finance leases)
- loans made by the reporting entity and payments to acquire debt instruments of other entities other than payments forming part of an acquisition or disposal or a movement in liquid resources.

2.7 Acquisitions and disposals

KEY POINT

Cash flows included in '**acquisitions and disposals**' relate to the acquisition or disposal of any trade or business.

The cash flows included in '**acquisitions and disposals**' are those related to the acquisition or disposal of any trade or business, or of an investment in an entity that is, or, as a result of the transaction, becomes or ceases to be either an associate, a joint venture, or a subsidiary undertaking.

Cash inflows from acquisitions and disposals include:

- receipts from sales of investments in subsidiary undertakings, showing separately any balances of cash and overdrafts transferred as part of the sale
- receipts from sales of investments in associates or joint ventures
- receipts from sales of trades or businesses.

Cash outflows from acquisitions and disposals include:

- payments to acquire investments in subsidiary undertakings, showing separately any balances of cash and overdrafts acquired
- payments to acquire investments in associates and joint ventures
- payments to acquire trades or businesses.

It follows that this caption does not normally appear in the cash flow statement of a single company. The exception would be if a company had acquired or disposed of an unincorporated business during the period.

2.8 Equity dividends paid

KEY POINT

Cash outflows included in '**equity dividends paid**' are dividends paid on the reporting entity's equity shares.

The cash outflows included in '**equity dividends paid**' are dividends paid on the reporting entity's equity shares.

Equity dividends paid are reported separately from interest and preference dividends paid, to highlight the fact that payment of equity dividends is discretionary. In contrast, an entity has no discretion over the amount or the timing of interest payable and no discretion over the amount of preference dividends.

2.9 Management of liquid resources

DEFINITION

Liquid resources are current asset investments held as readily disposable stores of value.

The 'management of liquid resources' section should include cash flows in respect of liquid resources as defined below.

Liquid resources are current asset investments held as readily disposable stores of value.

A readily disposable investment is one that:

- is disposable by the reporting entity without curtailing or disrupting its business; and is either
- readily convertible into known amounts of cash at or close to its carrying amount; or
- traded in an active market.

KEY POINT

Short-term deposits, term deposits, government securities, loan stock, equities and **derivatives** might form part of an entity's liquid resources.

This definition does not specify the type of investment that would be classed as a liquid resource. Instead it has been drafted in general terms, in order to emphasise the liquidity of the investment and its function as a readily disposable store of value. In practice **term deposits**, **government securities**, **loan stock**, **equities** and **derivatives** might form part of an entity's liquid resources. **Short-term deposits** would also fall within the definition. Because of the requirement that they should be readily convertible into known amounts of cash at or close to their carrying amount, deposits that are more than one year from maturity on acquisition would not normally be classed as liquid resources.

Each entity should explain what it includes as liquid resources and any changes in its policy.

Cash inflows in management of liquid resources include:

- withdrawals from short-term deposits not qualifying as cash in so far as not netted (see below)
- inflows from disposal or redemption of any other investments held as liquid resources.

Cash outflows in management of liquid resources include:

- payments into short-term deposits not qualifying as cash in so far as not netted
- outflows to acquire any other investments held as liquid resources.

Cash inflows and outflows within the management of liquid resources may be netted against each other if they are due to short maturities and high turnover occurring from rollover or reissue (for example, short-term deposits).

This section of the cash flow statement is designed to provide information about the way that entities manage their cash and similar assets. It distinguishes cash flows in relation to cash management, from cash flows arising from other investment decisions (for example, the acquisition and disposal of fixed asset investments).

2.10 Financing

KEY POINT

Financing cash flows comprise receipts or repayments of principal from or to external providers of finance.

Financing cash flows comprise receipts or repayments of principal from or to external providers of finance.

Financing cash inflows include:

- receipts from issuing shares or other equity instruments
- receipts from issuing debentures, loans, notes and bonds and from other long-term and short-term borrowings (other than overdrafts).

Financing cash outflows include:

- repayments of amounts borrowed (other than overdrafts)
- the capital element of finance lease rental payments
- payments to reacquire or redeem the entity's shares
- payments of expenses or commissions on any issue of equity shares.

Example

Extracts from the opening and closing balance sheets of a company are as follows:

	31.12.20X8	*31.12.20X9*
	£000	£000
Creditors: amounts falling due after more than one year		
10% convertible unsecured loan stock	434	280
12% Debenture	–	158
Share capital and reserves:		
Ordinary shares of £1 each	150	296
8% convertible preference shares	30	30
Share premium	78	130

During the year the following events occurred.

- £48,000 of 10% convertible unsecured loan stock was converted into 16,000 ordinary shares; the remaining reduction represents the purchase and cancellation of the loan stock by the company for total consideration of £90,000.
- A bonus issue of one for five ordinary shares (in issue at beginning of the year) was made from share premium.
- A fresh issue of ordinary shares was made to provide further funds.

Prepare the financing section of the cash flow statement.

Solution

The financing section of the cash flow statement would appear as follows:

	£000	£000
Financing:		
Issue of debentures	158	
Issue of shares	150	
Purchase of loan stock	(90)	
	—	
Net cash inflow from financing		218

Working

Changes in financing during the year

	Ordinary share capital	*Pref. share capital*	*Share premium*	*Loans*
	£000	£000	£000	£000
Balance at 1 Jan 20X9	150	30	78	434
Conversion of loan stock	16		32	(48)
Issue of debentures				158
Bonus issue	30		(30)	
Purchase of loan stock				
– consideration				(90)
– par value (434 – 48 – 280) = 106				
– profit on repurchase (106 – 90)				(16)
Share issue (bal fig)	100		50	
Balance at 31 Dec 20X9	296	30	130	438

Tutorial note

The conversion of £48,000 nominal value of loan stock into £16,000 nominal value of shares means that the premium on issue of the shares is the difference between the two nominal values.

3 Net debt, exceptional items and non-cash transactions

3.1 Reconciliation of movements in net debt

KEY POINT

FRS 1 requires a reconciliation of the **movement of cash** in the period with the **movement in net debt**.

FRS 1 requires a note reconciling the **movement of cash** in the period with the **movement in net debt**. (An example of this reconciliation was illustrated earlier in the chapter.) This reconciliation can be given either adjoining the cash flow statement or in a note. If the reconciliation adjoins the cash flow statement, it should be clearly labelled and kept separate.

The objective of the reconciliation is to provide information that assists in the assessment of liquidity, solvency and financial adaptability.

DEFINITION

Net debt comprises the borrowings of the reporting entity, less cash and liquid resources.

Net debt comprises the borrowings of the reporting entity (comprising capital instruments classified as liabilities in accordance with FRS 25 *Financial Instruments: Disclosure and Presentation,* together with related derivatives and obligations under finance leases) less cash and liquid resources. Where cash and liquid resources exceed the borrowings of the entity, reference should be made to 'net funds' rather than to 'net debt'.

Therefore redeemable preference shares treated as liabilities under FRS 25 will be included in net debt.

The definition also excludes debtors and creditors. While these are short-term claims on and sources of finance for the entity, their main role is as part of the entity's trading activities. (Movements in debtors and creditors are dealt with as part of operating activities.)

The changes in net debt should be analysed from the opening to the closing component amounts, showing separately, where material, changes resulting from:

- the cash flows of the entity
- the acquisition or disposal of subsidiary undertakings
- other non-cash changes
- the recognition of changes in market value and exchange rate movements.

Where several balance sheet amounts or parts thereof have to be combined to form the components of opening and closing net debt, sufficient detail should be shown to enable the cash and other components of net debt to be traced back to amounts shown under the equivalent captions in the balance sheet. This is done by means of a note analysing net debt.

Example

Extracts from the opening and closing balance sheets of a company are as follows:

	31 Dec 20X8	*31 Dec 20X9*
	£000	£000
Current assets		
Investments – Government stock	118	74
Cash at bank	40	5
Creditors: amounts falling due within one year		
Loan	120	100
Overdraft	–	47
Creditors: amounts falling due after more than one year		
Loan	100	–

- The government stock consists of a number of holdings, all of which were made with a view to disposal by the company within two months of acquisition.
- The loan was originally made in December 20X8 with repayments required of £20,000 every two months.
- The overdraft is repayable on demand.

Show the cash flow for the year ended 31 December 20X9, the reconciliation of net cash flow to movement in net debt and the note analysing movements in net debt.

Solution

	£000
Decrease in cash for the year (40 – 5 + 47)	(82)
Reconciliation of net cash flow to movement in net debt (note)	
Decrease in cash in the period	(82)
Cash outflow from decrease in debt	120
Cash inflow from sale of liquid resources (118 – 74)	(44)
Change in net debt	(6)
Net debt at 1 January 20X9	(62)
Net debt at 31 December 20X9	(68)

Analysis of changes in net debt

	At 1 Jan 20X9	*Cash flows*	*Other changes*	*At 31 Dec 20X9*
	£000	£000	£000	£000
Cash at bank	40	(35)		5
Overdrafts	–	(47)		(47)
		(82)		
Debts due within 1 year	(120)	120	(100)	(100)
Debts due after 1 year	(100)		100	-
Current asset investments	118	(44)		74
Total	(62)	(6)	–	(68)

3.2 Exceptional items

Exceptional items in the profit and loss account

KEY POINT

Cash flows relating to **exceptional items** should be identified in the cash flow statement or in a note to it.

Where cash flows relate to items that are classified as **exceptional** in the profit and loss account, they should be shown under the appropriate standard headings according to the nature of each item. The cash flows relating to exceptional items should be identified in the cash flow statement or a note to it and the relationship between the cash flows and the originating exceptional item should be explained.

Discontinued operations and provisions

KEY POINT

Cash flows in respect of **provisions** are included in operating activities.

Reorganisation charges that are exceptional must be disclosed separately and explained.

Cash flows in respect of operating items relating to **provisions** are included in operating activities, even if the provision was not included in operating profit. Examples of such cash flows are redundancy payments falling under a provision for the termination of an operation or for a fundamental reorganisation or restructuring, and operating item cash flows provided for on an acquisition.

Exceptional cash flows

KEY POINT

Where cash flows are **exceptional**, sufficient disclosure should be given to explain their cause and nature.

Where cash flows are exceptional because of their size or incidence but are not related to items that are treated as exceptional in the profit and loss account, sufficient disclosure should be given to explain their cause and nature.

For a cash flow to be exceptional on the grounds of its size alone, it must be exceptional in relation to cash flows of a similar nature.

3.3 Major non-cash transactions

Standard accounting practice

Material transactions not resulting in movements of cash of the reporting entity should be disclosed in the notes to the cash flow statement if disclosure is necessary for an understanding of the underlying transactions.

KEY POINT

Material non-cash transactions should not be reported in a cash flow statement but disclosed separately.

Consideration for transactions may be in a form other than cash. The purpose of a cash flow statement is to report cash flows and **non-cash transactions** should, therefore, not be reported in a cash flow statement. However, to obtain a full picture of the alterations in financial position caused by the transactions for the period, separate disclosure of material non-cash transactions is also necessary.

Examples of non-cash transactions are:

- certain acquisitions and disposals of subsidiaries by a group
- finance leases
- certain changes in debt and equity.

3.4 HP and finance leases

KEY POINT

FRS 1 requires a split between the interest and capital elements of the rentals paid on **hire purchase** and **finance leases**.

Hire purchase and **finance leases** are accounted for by the lessee/purchaser capitalising the present value of the minimum lease payments. A liability and a corresponding asset are produced which do not reflect cash flows in the accounting period.

The cash flow statement records the cash flow, i.e. the rentals paid. As each rental represents a payment of interest and capital, FRS 1 requires a split between the two elements:

- the **interest element** shown under servicing of finance
- the **capital element** shown under financing.

The interest element will already be computed as it is charged (and disclosed in the financial statements) in arriving at profit before taxation. Deducting the interest charge from rentals paid provides the capital paid in the year.

Note that the above paragraph assumes that rentals are paid frequently, e.g. monthly, and there is thus effectively no/little difference between interest charged against profits for a 12-month period and interest within the rentals *paid* over a 12-month period. If the rental payment dates do not closely coincide with the end of an accounting period, it may be necessary to compute the interest element relating to rentals actually paid.

The non-cash flow elements of a finance lease may need to be disclosed:

- if the finance lease is of such significance that it is classified as a major non-cash transaction; and/or
- in the note reconciling the net cash flow to the movement in net debt (as the finance lease liability may have been aggregated with, for example, bank loans on the balance sheet).

Example

A company entered into a number of finance leases during the current year. There were no such leases in the previous year.

Extracts from balance sheets

	31 Dec 20X2	*31 Dec 20X1*
	£000	£000
Fixed assets:		
Leased property under finance lease	5,710	4,000
Less: Accumulated depreciation	1,714	1,000
	3,996	3,000
Liabilities:		
Non-current obligations under finance leases	3,251	2,645
Current obligations under finance leases	1,315	1,150
	4,566	3,795

Notes to the accounts – Profit and loss account for 20X2

Profit is stated after charging:

	£000
Depreciation of owned assets	2,300
Depreciation of assets held under finance leases	714
Finance charges payable:	
Finance leases	856
Interest	1,325
Hire of plant and machinery – operating leases	360
Hire of other assets – operating leases	190

Produce extracts from the cash flow statement as far as information is available.

Solution

Extract from cash flow statement for year ended 31 December 20X2

	£000
Returns on investments and servicing of finance:	
Interest element of finance lease rentals	(856)
Interest paid	(1,325)
Financing:	
Capital element of finance lease rentals (working)	(939)

Working

Note: Grouping the current and non-current obligations together and deriving new finance leases from the increase in fixed asset cost allows the capital element of the rentals to be computed as a balancing figure.

Operating leases are treated like any other expense.

Obligations under finance leases

	£000		£000
Capital element of rentals paid in year	939	Balance b/d Current and non current	3,795
Balance b/d Current and non current	4,566	New finance leases (from fixed asset increase)	1,710
	5,505		5,505

4 Scope of FRS 1

KEY POINT

'Small' companies are exempt from FRS 1.

FRS 1 applies to all financial statements intended to give a true and fair view of the financial position and profit or loss (or income and expenditure) except those of:

1. subsidiary undertakings where 90% or more of the voting rights are controlled within the group, provided that consolidated financial statements in which the subsidiary undertakings are included are publicly available
2. companies incorporated under companies legislation and entitled to the exemptions available in the legislation for small companies when filing accounts with the Registrar of Companies
3. entities that would have been in category 2 above if they were companies incorporated under companies legislation
4. mutual life assurance companies, pension funds, some open-ended investment funds and some building societies.

KEY POINT

FRS 1 exempts subsidiary undertakings where 90% or more of voting rights are controlled within its group.

FRS 1 exempts subsidiary undertakings where 90% or more of the voting rights in the subsidiary are controlled within its group. In this situation, it is likely that the liquidity, solvency and financial adaptability of the subsidiary will depend upon the group, rather than its own cash flows. Groups often have centralised cash management operations and cash balances can be moved around a group rapidly. For this reason, historical cash flow information of individual group companies does not always contribute to an assessment of future cash flows.

5 Usefulness of the cash flow statement

5.1 Advantages of the cash flow statement

KEY POINT

Cash flow statements have the advantage of providing information which is not available from balance sheets and profit and loss accounts.

A cash flow statement can provide information which is not available from balance sheets and profit and loss accounts.

- It may assist users of financial statements in making judgements on the amount, timing and degree of certainty of future cash flows.
- It gives an indication of the relationship between profitability and cash generating ability, and thus of the quality of the profit earned.
- Analysts and other users of financial information often, formally or informally, develop models to assess and compare the present value of the future cash flow of entities. Historical cash flow information could be useful to check the accuracy of past assessments.

- A cash flow statement in conjunction with a balance sheet provides information on liquidity, viability and adaptability. The balance sheet is often used to obtain information on liquidity, but the information is incomplete for this purpose as the balance sheet is drawn up at a particular point in time.
- Cash flow cannot easily be manipulated and is not affected by judgement or by accounting policies.

5.2 Limitations of the cash flow statement

KEY POINT

Cash flow statements should be used in conjunction with profit and loss accounts and balance sheets when making an assessment of future cash flows.

Cash flow statements should normally be used in conjunction with profit and loss accounts and balance sheets when making an assessment of future cash flows.

- Cash flow statements are based on historical information and therefore do not provide complete information for assessing future cash flows.
- There is some scope for manipulation of cash flows. For example, a business may delay paying creditors until after the year-end, or it may structure transactions so that the cash balance is favourably affected. It can be argued that cash management is an important aspect of stewardship and therefore desirable. However, more deliberate manipulation is possible (e.g. assets may be sold and then immediately repurchased). Following the issue of FRS 5 *Reporting the substance of transactions,* users of the financial statements will be alerted to the true nature of such arrangements.
- Cash flow is necessary for survival in the short term, but in order to survive in the long term a business must be profitable. It is often necessary to sacrifice cash flow in the short term in order to generate profits in the long term (e.g. by investment in fixed assets). A huge cash balance is not a sign of good management if the cash could be invested elsewhere to generate profit.

Neither cash flow nor profit provide a complete picture of a company's performance when looked at in isolation.

5.3 The strict cash approach

Cash is very narrowly defined in FRS 1 (revised). It does not include investments or short-term deposits, however liquid or near maturity. The effect of this definition is that the bottom line of the cash flow statement shows the increase or decrease in 'pure' cash for the period.

Under the original version of FRS 1, the cash flow statement showed the movement in cash and cash equivalents. Cash equivalents were defined as 'short term, highly liquid investments which are readily convertible into known amounts of cash without notice and which are within three months of maturity when acquired'.

This definition was widely criticised by commentators and by preparers of financial statements. In particular, the three-month limit was regarded as arbitrary. Deposits which in practice were used as part of treasury management had to be classified as investments, thus presenting a potentially misleading picture to users of the financial statements.

KEY POINT

In revising FRS 1, the ASB decided to use pure cash as the basis of the cash flows reported in the cash flow statement.

In revising FRS 1, the ASB decided to use pure cash as the basis of the cash flows reported in the cash flow statement. However, it has also introduced a section for cash flows relating to the management of liquid resources. It believes that this approach has the following advantages.

- It avoids an arbitrary cut-off point in the definition of cash equivalents.
- It distinguishes cash flows arising from accumulating or using liquid resources, from those for other investing activities.
- It provides information about an entity's treasury activities that was not previously available, to the extent that the instruments dealt in fell within the definition of cash equivalents.

5.4 The advantages and disadvantages of the direct and indirect methods

We have seen that the two methods which can be used to prepare the cash flow statement are the **direct** (gross) and **indirect** (net) methods.

Advantages of the direct method

- Information is shown which is not shown elsewhere in the financial statements.
- The method does show the true cash flows involved in the trading operations of the entity.

Disadvantage of the direct method

- There may be a significant cost in preparing the information, as it is not revealed elsewhere in the financial statements.

Advantages of the indirect method

- Used in conjunction with the note which reconciles operating profit to net cash flow from operating activities, the user can easily relate trading profits to cash flow and thus understand the 'quality' of the earnings made by the entity in the accounting period. Earnings are of a good quality if they are represented by real cash flows now or in the near future.
- There is a low cost in preparing the information.

Disadvantage of the indirect method

- There is a lack of information on the significant elements of trading cash flows.

6 Interpretation of cash flow data

6.1 Interpretation of the cash flow statement

Estimating future cash flows is very important in determining the solvency or otherwise of a business. The financial accounts are, of course, historical records, but they can provide some evidence of solvency. This section summarises the areas to consider.

KEY POINT

Points of interpretation in the cash flow statement should cover: cash generation from trading operations; dividend and interest payouts; capital expenditure and financial investment; management of liquid resources, and cash flow.

The cash flow statement should be reviewed first. Points to watch for within the various headings in the cash flow statement include the following.

Cash generation from trading operations

The figure should be compared to the operating profit. The reconciliation note to the cash flow statement is useful in this regard. Overtrading may be indicated by:

- high profits and low cash generation
- large increases in stock, debtors and creditors.

Dividend and interest payouts

These can be compared to cash generated from trading operations to see whether the normal operations can sustain such payments. In most years they should.

Capital expenditure and financial investment

The nature and scale of a company's investment in fixed assets is clearly shown.

Management of liquid resources and financing

The subtotal 'cash inflow/outflow before use of liquid resources and financing' indicates the financing required unless existing cash is available. The changes in financing (in pure cash terms) are clearly shown. There may be a note to the cash flow statement which links the inflows/outflows with the balance sheet movement. There may be significant non-cash flow changes in the capital structure of the business.

Gearing can be considered at this point.

Cash flow

The statement clearly shows the end result in cash terms of the company's activities in the year. Do not overstate the importance of this figure alone however. A decrease in cash in the year may be for very sound reasons (e.g. there was surplus cash last year) or may be mainly the result of timing (e.g. a new loan was raised just after the end of the accounting period).

To help in determining the future cash position, other areas of the published accounts should be considered as illustrated below.

6.2 Cash requirements

KEY POINT

When identifying whether or not the company has sufficient cash, consider existing loans, working capital, expenditure requirements and other commitments.

There are four areas to consider when identifying whether or not the company has sufficient cash.

Repayment of existing loans

All loans to be repaid in the next couple of years should be considered, including any convertible loans if the conversion rights are unlikely to be exercised.

Increase in working capital

If the business is expanding (making more sales), working capital will also need to increase. The extra cash needed to finance the expansion can easily be calculated by comparing working capital to sales:

$$\frac{\text{Stocks} + \text{debtors} - \text{creditors}}{\text{Turnover}} \times 100\%$$

Suppose this is 20% and turnover is currently £5m, a 10% increase in turnover requires finance of £0.1m (£5m × 10% × 20%) to increase the working capital.

Capital expenditure requirements

The notes to the financial statements should disclose capital expenditure contracted for. It is necessary to consider whether the company will have sufficient cash to meet this capital expenditure.

Other commitments

Contingent liabilities

Most contingent liabilities do not crystallise, but if the liabilities are very high their crystallisation can cause real problems for the company. Some analysts compare contingent liabilities with ordinary shareholders' funds to assess the materiality of those commitments. In particular, any sharp increases in the amounts involved should act as a warning.

Leasing commitments

If these are material, they should be carefully monitored in relation to the cash available. The accounts should disclose both finance lease commitments (for new leases where repayments have not commenced) and operating lease commitments.

KEY POINT

If there appears to be a **cash shortfall**, there are a number of measures a company should consider in preference to reducing dividends or its level of activity.

6.3 Cash shortfall

If there appears to be a **cash shortfall**, the company may have to take one or more of the following steps.

- Increase its overdraft (if it is not already at the limit).
- Increase its longer-term borrowings. Remember that the Articles often restrict the borrowings by reference to shareholders' funds, which may need to be artificially increased, for example by revaluing assets. Alternatively, the company may ask shareholders to pass a resolution changing the borrowing restriction.
- Raising money through a share issue (the company must have a good record of profitability and of dividend growth, and the share price must be high).
- Tightening credit and stock control, paying creditors later.
- Limiting capital expenditure.
- Entering into sale and leaseback arrangements (it will need some assets which are not already charged).
- Selling some assets (for example investments, or parts of the business which are less related to the main trade).
- Purchasing a cash-rich company by issuing shares in consideration.

The company should consider most of these measures in preference to:

- reducing **dividends**
- reducing its **level of activity**.

Conclusion

FRS 1 requires 'large' companies to include a cash flow statement in their published accounts. This shows the inflows and outflows of cash for an accounting period grouped under standard headings:

- operating activities
- returns on investments and servicing of finance
- taxation
- capital expenditure and financial investment
- acquisitions and disposals
- equity dividends paid
- management of liquid resources
- financing.

The bottom line in the cash flow statement is the total increase or decrease in the amount of cash for the period.

SELF-TEST QUESTIONS

1 What are the objectives of FRS 1? (1.1)

2 Define cash. (1.2)

3 What are the two permitted methods of reporting net cash flow from operating activities? (2.1)

4 What cash flows are included under returns on investments and servicing of finance? (2.4)

5 Why are equity dividends paid reported under a separate heading? (2.8)

6 What is a readily disposable investment? (2.9)

7 Two reconciliations are presented with the cash flow statement. One is the reconciliation of operating profit to net cash flow from operating activities. What is the other? (3.1)

8 How are major non-cash transactions dealt with in relation to the cash flow statement? (3.3)

9 Which companies are exempt from the requirements of FRS 1? (4)

10 What are the limitations of cash flow information? (5.2)

PRACTICE QUESTION

Solid plc

The summarised balance sheets of Solid plc at 31 December 20X7 and 20X8 are as follows:

	20X8	*20X7*
	£	£
Freehold property at cost	130,000	110,000
Plant and machinery at cost	151,000	120,000
Fixtures and fittings at cost	29,000	24,000
Stock	51,000	37,000
Debtors	44,000	42,800
Government stock	4,600	–
Cash at bank	11,400	200
	421,000	334,000
Issued share capital (ordinary shares)	150,000	100,000
Share premium	35,000	15,000
Profit and loss account	36,000	11,500
Debentures	30,000	70,000
Deferred taxation	18,000	11,000
Creditors	48,000	34,000
Bank overdraft	–	14,000
Corporation tax payable	15,000	10,500
Proposed dividends	20,000	10,000
Depreciation on plant and machinery	54,000	45,000
Depreciation on fixtures and fittings	15,000	13,000
	421,000	334,000

- There had been no disposal of freehold property in the year.
- A machine tool which had cost £8,000 (in respect of which £6,000 depreciation had been provided) was sold for £3,000, and fixtures which had cost £5,000 (in respect of which depreciation of £2,000 had been provided) were sold for £1,000. Profits and losses on those transactions had been dealt with through the profit and loss account.

- The government stock is a short-term investment traded in an active market.
- The corporation tax liability in respect of the year ended 31 December 20X7, amounting to £10,500, had been paid during the year.
- The profit and loss account charges in respect of tax were: current tax £12,500; deferred tax £9,500.
- The premium paid on redemption of debentures was £2,000, which has been written off to profit and loss account.
- The proposed dividend for 20X7 had been paid during the year.
- Interest received during the year was £450. Interest charged in the profit and loss account for the year was £6,400. Accrued interest of £440 is included in creditors at 31 December 20X7 (nil at 31 December 20X8).

Required:

Prepare a cash flow statement for the year ended 31 December 20X8, together with notes as required by FRS 1.

EXAM-TYPE QUESTION

Ozac plc

The following information relates to the draft financial statements of Ozac plc

Profit and loss account year to 30 September 20X9

	£'000	£'000
Turnover		3,536
Materials consumed	1,079	
Labour costs	758	
Production overheads	453	
Cost of sales		(2,290)
Gross profit		1,246
Selling and distribution costs	221	
Administration	252	
		(473)
Interest payable	(85)	
Dividends receivable	24	
		(61)
		712
Taxation		(210)
		502
Dividends		(350)
Retained profit for period		152

Ozac plc Balance Sheet as at:

	30 September 20X9:			*30 September 20X8:*		
Fixed assets:	*Cost*	*Depreciation*	*NBV*	*Cost*	*Depreciation*	*NBV*
Tangible:	£'000	£'000	£'000	£'000	£'000	£'000
Land and buildings	2,000	750	1,250	1,700	745	955
Plant	1,368	525	843	940	310	630
	3,368	1,275	2,093	2,640	1,055	1,585

Investments:				
Shares in unquoted company		800		nil
		2,893		1,585
Current assets:				
Stocks	758		628	
Debtors – all trade	260		194	
Dividend receivable	15		–	
Bank	22		–	
	1,055		822	
Creditors: amounts falling due within one year:				
Creditors – all trade	234		253	
Proposed dividends	200		180	
Taxation	251		204	
Government grants	125		75	
Overdraft	—		28	
	810		740	
Net current assets		245		82
Creditors: amounts falling due after more than one year:				
Deferred tax	252		141	
Government grants	220		160	
7% Debenture	968	(1,440)	nil	(301)
		1,698		1,366
Share capital and reserves:				
Ordinary shares of £1 each		1,100		1,000
Reserves:				
Share premium	180		100	
Profit and loss account	418	598	266	366
		1,698		1,366

Notes:

(i) Included in turnover are sales of £500,000 to Petrov, a company located in Bulgarussia. This figure consists of two separate sales transactions, both of which have been translated into sterling. The first transaction, translated at £200,000, was paid in Bulgas, the local currency. Ozac plc had difficulties in converting the Bulgas into sterling. Petrov's main activity relates to the extraction of crude oil, and as a result of previous exchange difficulties, it was agreed that Petrov would pay for the second transaction in barrels of oil. The spot rate for the crude oil at the date it was shipped to Ozac was £10 per barrel. Ozac plc later used the crude oil in one of its manufacturing processes.

(ii) All depreciation charges and a credit of £80,000 relating to the amortisation of government grants have been included in production overheads. There were no disposals of fixed assets during the year.

(iii) During the year 10,000 ordinary shares were issued to employees under the company's employee share purchase scheme. The market value of these shares was £50,000. This amount has been correctly recorded in share capital and share premium. The terms of the share scheme meant that the employees were required to contribute only the nominal value of the shares. The net cost to the company of this transaction has been included in labour costs.

(iv) On 1 October 20X8 Ozac plc issued a £1,000,000 7% Debenture at a discount of 5%. The debenture is redeemable on 30 September 20Y3 at a premium of 4%. Ozac plc has amortised the discount and premium on this financial instrument equally (straight-line) over its five-year life and included the amortisation charge in the interest payable figure.

(v) On 1 October 20X8 Ozac plc acquired 15% of the share capital of Tilzac Ltd, one of its major materials suppliers. It has treated this as a fixed asset investment. Ozac plc has recently received the financial statements of Tilzac Ltd for the year to 30 September 20X9. These show an interim dividend paid of £60,000 and proposed final dividend of £100,000. Ozac plc received an interim dividend from Tilzac Ltd in March 20X9, and has accrued for its share of the proposed dividend.

Required:

Prepare the Cash Flow Statement for Ozac plc for the year to 30 September 20X9.

(20 marks)

Note: The cash flow from operations must be prepared using the DIRECT METHOD; you are NOT required to prepare the reconciliation to operating profit nor the notes relating to net debt.

For the answers to these questions, see the 'Answers' section at the end of the book.

FEEDBACK TO ACTIVITY **1**

	£
Operating profit	300,000
Increase in stocks	(118,000)
Increase in debtors	(125,000)
Increase in creditors (135 – 12)	123,000
Net cash inflow from operating activities	180,000

FEEDBACK TO ACTIVITY **2**

Taxation account

	£		£
Tax paid (bal. fig.)	169,000	Balances b/d	
Balances c/d		Corporation tax	170,000
Corporation tax	331,000	Deferred tax	110,000
Deferred tax	130,000	Profit and loss:	
		Corporation tax	300,000
		Deferred tax	50,000
	630,000		630,000

There is sufficient information to compute the tax paid in the year directly, but it is often easier to compute tax as a balancing figure. All tax items are inserted into a tax account and the tax paid for the year emerges as the balancing figure on the account.

Answers to practice questions and exam-type questions

CHAPTER 1

PRACTICE QUESTION

DWS Ltd

(a)

DWS Ltd – Trading and profit and loss account for year ended 30 September 20X4

		£	£
Sales			188,000
Less: Returns inwards			(8,000)
			180,000
Opening stock		31,000	
Purchases	(115,000 + 1,200)	116,200	
Returns outwards		(6,000)	
Closing stock		(53,000)	
			(88,200)
Gross profit			91,800
Selling expenses		12,000	
Heat and light		8,000	
Wages and salaries	(14,000 + 1,500)	15,500	
Directors' fees	(5,000 + 3,600)	8,600	
Printing and stationery		6,000	
Telephone and fax	(6,000 – 1,000)	5,000	
Rent, rates and insurance	(4,000 – 1,000)	3,000	
Auditor's fees		3,500	
Bad debts written off		3,000	
Decrease in allowance for doubtful debts (W1)		(2,400)	
Bank charges accrued		4,000	
Depreciation of plant and machinery (W2)		12,500	
Depreciation of office equipment (W2)		9,600	
			(88,300)
Profit for the year before tax			3,500
Provision for corporation tax			(1,000)
Net profit after tax			2,500

(b) **Statement of movement in profit and loss account reserve**

		£
Balance at 1 October 20X3		34,000
Net profit for the year		2,500
Less:		
Interim dividend paid	2,000	
Proposed dividend	3,000	
		(5,000)
Transfer to general reserves		(10,000)
Profit and loss account c/fwd		21,500

(c)

DWS Ltd – Balance sheet at 30 September 20X4

		Cost £	*Depreciation* £	*Net* £
Fixed assets				
Plant and machinery		125,000	40,500	84,500
Office equipment		43,800	24,600	19,200
		168,800	65,100	103,700
Current assets				
Stock		53,000		
Debtors	(32,000 – 1,600)	30,400		
Prepayments	(3,000 (W3) + 2,000)	5,000		
Petty cash		1,000		
			89,400	
Current liabilities				
Creditors	(33,000 – 2,600)	30,400		
Accruals	(1,500 + 3,600 + 3,500)	8,600		
Overdraft		3,600		
Provision for corporation tax		1,000		
Proposed final dividend		3,000		
			46,600	
				42,800
				146,500
Capital and reserves				
Ordinary shares of 50p each				100,000
Share premium account				8,000
General reserve account	(7,000 + 10,000)			17,000
Profit and loss account balance				21,500
				146,500

Workings

(W1) Decrease in allowance for doubtful debts

	£
Debtors in trial balance	35,000
Bad debt written off	(3,000)
	32,000

£32,000 × 5% = £1,600, therefore decrease provision by £2,400

(W2) Depreciation

Plant and machinery: £125,000 × 10% = £12,500

Office equipment: (£45,000 – £1,200 – £15,000) × 33.33% = £9,600

(W3) Prepayments and suspense account

Adjustments to correct the errors discovered in note (vi) are:

	£	£
Debit purchases	1,200	
Credit office equipment		1,200
Debit bank	2,600	
Credit creditors		2,600

CHAPTER 3 EXAM-TYPE QUESTION

Revenue recognition

(a) **Critical event approach to revenue recognition**

- **Obtaining an order prior to manufacture**

  This would be an unlikely place for the critical event to occur. In the case of obtaining an order for a large or long-term contract, such an event is often very important and gives some measure of reassurance in matters such as job security and even going concern. However, as there would be so much uncertainty involved with regard to the final outcome of such contracts, it would not be prudent to recognise profit at this point.

- **Acquisition of goods or raw materials**

  For most industries this event is a routine occurrence that could not be considered as critical. However, where this is a very difficult task, perhaps due to the rarity or scarcity of materials, then it may be critical. A rare practical example of this is in the extraction of precious metals or gems, e.g. gold and diamond mining. Because gold is a valuable and readily marketable commodity the real difficulty in deriving income from it is obtaining it, so this becomes the critical event in such circumstances.

- **Production of goods**

  Again for most industries this is routine and not critical. There are some industries where, due to a long production period, revenues are recognised during the production or manufacturing period. The most common example of this is the treatment of long-term construction contracts under SSAP 9 *Stocks and long-term contracts*. A less well-known example of this 'accretion approach' is found where natural growth occurs, such as in the growing of timber. In this industry, market prices are available at various stages of growth and revenue could be recognised at these stages.

- **Obtaining an order for goods that are in stock**

  This is getting near to the point when most of the uncertainties in the cycle have either been resolved or are reasonably determinable. The sales/marketing department of a company would probably consider this as the critical event, however recognition is usually delayed until delivery.

- **Delivery/acceptance of the goods**

  For the vast majority of businesses this is the point at which revenue is recognised, and it usually coincides with the transfer of legal title to the goods. There are still some uncertainties at this point. For example, the goods may be faulty or the customer may not be able to pay for them. However, past experience can be used to quantify and provide for these possibilities with reasonable accuracy. Occasionally goods are delivered subject to a 'reservation of title' clause (e.g. as in the Romalpa case), however this is usually ignored for the purpose of revenue recognition.

- **Collection of cash**

  With the obvious exception of cash sales, revenue recognition would only be delayed to this point if collection was perceived to be particularly difficult or risky. Revenues (and profits) from high-risk credit sale agreements may be one example of this. Another possibility is sales made to risky overseas countries/customers, particularly if they are in non-convertible currencies.

- **After-sales service or warranties**

  This serves as a reminder that not all the risks and associated costs are resolved when cash is received. For some products such costs can be significant (e.g. in the supply of new motor vehicles or rectification work on long-term contracts); however, it is normally possible to estimate these costs and provide for them at the time of the sale. It would be unrealistic, and may cause distortions, if revenues were not recognised until such obligations had elapsed.

(b) **Statement of Principles approach to revenue recognition**

The Statement of Principles approaches revenue (and expense) recognition from a balance sheet perspective. Recognition of gains and losses takes place when there is an increase or decrease in equity other than from contributions to, or withdrawals of, capital. Thus increases in assets or reductions of liabilities result in gains (income); the opposite results in losses (expenses).

The Statement establishes three recognition criteria.

- An item must meet the definition of an 'element' within the Statement.
- There must be evidence that a change in the inherent asset or liability has occurred – for example, if the 'item' is a gain then this could arise because an increase in a 'defined' asset has occurred.
- The item can be measured in monetary terms and with sufficient reliability.

It also says that in a transaction involving the provision of services or goods for a net gain, the recognition criteria will be met on the occurrence of the critical event in the operating cycle involved.

This is expanded upon in the explanatory section of the Statement. For most types of transaction, the critical event in the operating cycle occurs when the entity providing the goods or services has fully performed. However, the critical event could occur at other times in the cycle and there could be more than one critical event. The critical event or events will depend on the circumstances involved:

- if the reporting entity has carried out all its obligations under an agreement except for a few minor acts of performance, the critical event will have occurred

- if a sale is contingent upon acceptance by the buyer, the critical event will not have occurred if the likelihood of the goods or services not being accepted is significant
- the reporting entity may be involved in performing a series of significant acts of performance over a period of time. As a result, the operating cycle might best be viewed as involving a series of critical events. A long-term contract to build an asset is usually an example of such an operating cycle. The gain that is expected to be earned on the contract as a whole will need to be allocated among the critical events.

Only items which meet the definitions of gains and losses should be reported in the statements of financial performance. Only realised items are reported in the profit and loss account. Unrealised gains and losses are reported in the statement of total recognised gains and losses.

(c) **Telecast Industries plc**

- **Warmer Cinemas plc**

  Although the 'performance' side of this contract is complete from Telecast Industries plc's point of view, the revenues are only earned as the film is shown. Therefore Telecast Industries plc should accrue for 15% of Warmer Cinemas plc's box office revenues from this film for the period 1 July 20X7 to the year end of 30 September 20X7. The only problems here would be prompt access to the relevant information from Warmer Cinemas plc and the possibility, which is probably remote, of a bad debt.

- **Big Screen Ltd**

  In this case the income is a fixed fee and not dependent on any future performance from either party to the contract. Therefore, applying the criteria in the Statement of Principles, Telecast Industries plc should recognise the whole of the £10,000 in the current year even though some of the screenings may take place after the year end.

- **Global Satellite plc**

  A traditional view of this contract may be that £4 million has been paid by Global Satellite plc to screen the film 10 times and Telecast Industries plc should therefore recognise £400,000 each time the film is screened. If this were the case, it would mean that none of the revenue would be recognised in the current year. However, if the ASB's principles described above are considered:

  - the film is complete and the rights to it are owned by Telecast Industries plc
  - a contract has been agreed
  - the consideration has been received
  - Telecast Industries plc have no significant future obligations to perform.

  This would appear to meet all of the criteria for revenue recognition and thus the whole of the £4 million should be recognised in the current year.

CHAPTER 4 — EXAM-TYPE QUESTION

Barty plc

(a) **The treatment of holding gains as a measure of business profit**

Holding gains are increases in the value of an asset while that asset is owned by a company. For example, a company might buy an item of stock for £100 and then later sell it for £180 when its replacement cost had gone up to £150. The holding gain of £50 is realised at the date of sale; the 'real' profit, or operating gain, on the disposal is £30.

There are several alternative possible accounting treatments for holding gains, both realised and unrealised. Conventional historic cost accounting ignores unrealised holding gains, and includes realised holding gains in the profit and loss account of the period in which the asset is disposed of. Current cost accounting, on the other hand, excludes realised holding gains on the disposals of stock items by making an adjustment against reported profits so that only operating gains are reported as profits.

The significance of the treatment of holding gains is therefore the enormous effect that such treatment will have on reported profits. Although earnings per share is not the only important indicator of financial performance, it is still the most important, and the exclusion of holding gains from earnings will materially depress earnings per share and may thereby reduce the share price.

(b) **Arguments for the recognition of holding gains**

The accruals concept would suggest that gains and losses should be recognised in the period in which they occurred, rather than being deferred. So investments would be shown on the balance sheet at their market value. As a separate issue, prudence might dictate that gains should be credited to reserves rather than to the profit and loss account, but the principle of revaluing investments in the balance sheet remains valid.

The objective of financial statements is set out in Chapter 1 of the Statement of Principles as being to provide useful information to a wide range of user groups. The current value of assets held is more relevant to the needs of users than the historic cost.

If holding gains are not recognised year-by-year, companies experiencing a bad year can flatter their reported profits by deciding to sell assets held for many years which have large unrealised holding gains. Often these assets may be immediately repurchased as a 'bed and breakfast' transaction. The profit generated on this deal does not reflect the genuine economic performance of the company in the period but under existing accounting practices may be all reported in the year of disposal.

In addition, asset-stripping hostile acquisitive companies will not be able to make money by breaking up target companies whose share prices do not reflect the real value of their underlying assets.

Arguments against the recognition of holding gains

The prudence concept seeks to prevent profits being included in the profit and loss account unless their realisation is reasonably certain. CA 1985 ensures that unrealised holding gains may not be recognised in the profit and loss account.

Subjectivity and uncertainty exist in trying to determine the current value of an asset at the balance sheet date. An advantage of deferring holding gains until the date of disposal is the avoidance of this uncertainty.

If holding gains are included in reported profits and distributed out of the business, the company will not be able to finance the replacement of its assets without raising new funds externally. Operating capital will not be maintained if a policy of maximum distributions is carried on.

(c) **Comments on the adjusted earnings statement**

Barty is a company which invests in property. As such it is a value-based company which is attempting to maximise the return to shareholders, primarily by long-term capital growth in the value of the investments.

The traditional profit and loss account concentrates on current revenue and matches the immediate return of the shareholders (i.e. dividends) with the rental income.

The adjusted earnings statement recognises that the shareholders are interested in both revenue and capital gains. As can be seen, the unrealised gains exceed the revenue profit which is to be expected from such a company.

The shareholders are also interested in the protection from general inflation of their investment in the company. The inflation adjustment of £520,000 is the amount needed to maintain the purchasing power of the shareholders' investment during the year. Their equity investment at the beginning of the year was £13m, and applying 4% inflation gives £520,000. The unrealised gains are comfortably protecting the shareholders' investment.

CHAPTER 5

PRACTICE QUESTIONS

Question 1: Different bodies

MEMORANDUM

To: The managing director

From: The management accountant

Date: X-X-20XX

Subject: Bodies involved in the standard setting process

The Financial Reporting Council (FRC)

The purpose of the FRC is to supervise the ASB, to carry out the strategic and policy reviews that are necessary and to ensure that the ASB is properly funded, leaving the ASB itself free to get on with its task of formulating accounting standards.

The chairman of the FRC is appointed jointly by the Secretary of State at the DTI and the Governor of the Bank of England. The other twenty or so members come from a range of users of accounts, namely the accounting bodies, the Stock Exchange and institutional investors.

The FRC meets three or four times a year and publishes an annual report of its activities.

The Accounting Standards Board (ASB)

The body now responsible for drafting and publishing accounting standards is the ASB. It has a full-time chairman and technical director, and eight other part-time members. The ASB issues standards on its own authority, requiring a two-thirds majority of its members to approve a standard before issue.

To date at the time of writing, the ASB has issued 27 Financial Reporting Standards (FRSs) as well as an FRS for smaller entities, and 35 Financial Reporting Exposure Drafts (FREDs), which will be converted into standards in due course. The ASB has also published a Statement of Principles under which accounts should be drawn up.

The ASB currently has the confidence of the accounting profession, although this has been tested by some of the ideas in the Statement of Principles, particularly the emphasis on the balance sheet. The ASB has also been criticised for downgrading traditional accounting concepts such as prudence.

The Financial Reporting Review Panel

During the 1980s some accountants became cynical about complying with accounting standards because there seemed to be no penalty for non-compliance. The Companies Act 1989 now requires companies to state explicitly whether they have complied with accounting standards.

The role of the Review Panel is therefore to examine any alleged material departures from accounting standards which either involve an issue of principle or might result in the accounts not giving a true and fair view. If the Panel wish to take a matter further, they will invite the company and its auditors to give evidence on the matter. If the Panel still believe that the accounts are defective, they can ask the company to publish revised accounts, or apply to the Court for an order to revise the accounts.

This power is still untested, since all companies so far approached by the Panel have agreed to revise their accounts. Commentators await an instance of the Panel's advice being tested in the courts.

One key example of the Panel's work to date was their success in forcing Trafalgar House plc to restate their accounts for the year to 30 September 1991. Trafalgar House had decided to reclassify certain current asset commercial properties as fixed assets before revaluing them downwards, so the £102.7m deficit on revaluation was charged against the revaluation reserve rather than the profit and loss account. Although the auditors had not qualified the accounts, the Panel took exception to this treatment and after the threat of court action, the directors agreed to write off the deficit against the £122.4m of pre-tax profits originally reported for the year.

The Urgent Issues Task Force (UITF)

The normal process of developing an accounting standard is long, while issues emerge frequently where it would be desirable for expert guidance to be available quickly from an authoritative source. The ASB therefore formed the UITF as a committee of the ASB to publish Abstracts of advice in areas where an accounting standard or a Companies Act provision exists, but where unsatisfactory or conflicting interpretations have developed or seem likely to develop.

At the time of writing, the UITF has so far issued 40 Abstracts, i.e. 40 separate statements stating how particular items should be dealt with in sets of accounts. For example, Abstract 5 prohibits the practice attempted by Trafalgar House described above. Where there are transfers of assets from current assets to fixed assets, they must be transferred at the lower of cost and net realisable value at the date of transfer, with any valuation difference being reflected in the profit and loss account. So the valuation must take place before the transfer, contrary to Trafalgar House's proposed treatment.

Question 2: FRRP

(a) The role of the Financial Reporting Review Panel (FRRP) has been described as that of the 'police force' of the UK accounting standard regime. The panel is responsible for investigating instances where published financial statements (particularly those of public and large private companies) do not comply with the relevant provisions of company law and accounting standards. The FRRP will be particularly concerned to investigate instances where alleged departures impair the truth and fairness of the view presented by the financial statements.

In instances where financial statements are found to be materially in breach of statutory and professional requirements, the FRRP may ask for the statements to be revised and reissued. The panel may also request that the matters in question be dealt with in a more acceptable way in subsequent periods.

The panel acts on matters drawn to its attention – currently it does not systematically review or monitor financial statements itself.

In practice, companies tend to comply with the panel's wishes (to avoid adverse publicity), but the panel has the power to seek a Court Order for non-compliant financial statements to be revised and reissued.

(b) FRS 15 requires depreciation to be charged so as to spread the net cost (or valuation) of a fixed asset fairly over its useful economic life. It appears that the policies adopted by S plc will not comply with this requirement. The properties are not depreciated until the final ten years of their lives. The effect will be to understate depreciation (overstate profit) in the early years of the life of a property – vice versa in the later years. This is likely to make it difficult for the user of the financial statements to assess the trend in the company's performance and difficult to compare S plc's performance with other companies which may adopt a more 'acceptable' depreciation policy.

Similar points can be made in respect of the policy on plant and equipment, but the distorting effect is likely to be less significant. The failure to charge depreciation in the year of acquisition will tend to overstate profit in that year, and understate profits in subsequent years.

The publication of the FRRP's findings (in the form of press notices) can be seen to have two beneficial effects:

- **Deterrent effect**. It is likely that making instances of non compliance by large companies public will encourage these companies to comply with relevant regulations in future periods. In addition public disclosure may encourage other companies to take steps to ensure that their financial statements comply with relevant statutory and professional requirements in all material respects.
- **Educational effect**. By publicising specific instances of non-compliance with accounting regulations, the FRRP is making available a pool of knowledge and experience. This will enable accountants, auditors, users of financial statements (and students) to distinguish more clearly between acceptable and unacceptable accounting treatments.

CHAPTER **6**

PRACTICE QUESTION

Subsidiary company

(a) **Definition of a subsidiary company**

S Ltd is a subsidiary of H Ltd if any of the following conditions apply:

1. The parent holds a majority of the rights to vote at general meetings of the undertaking/company on all or substantially all matters.
2. The parent is a member and has a right to appoint or remove directors having a majority of the rights to vote at board meetings of the undertaking/company on all or substantially all matters.
3. The parent is a member and has the right to control alone a majority of the rights to vote at general meetings of the undertaking/company pursuant to an agreement with other shareholders.
4. The parent has a right to exercise a dominant influence over the undertaking by virtue of provisions in the memorandum or articles or by a lawful contract.
5. The parent has the power to exercise, or actually exercises a dominant influence, or the parent and subsidiary undertaking are managed on a unified basis.

(b) **Problems with the old definition**

There were two main problems in the old definition as follows:

1. A situation may have arisen in which none of the conditions was fully satisfied and yet H had substantial influence over S. If a holding was not above 50% but was significant, the company may have been an associated company and the equity method of accounting would have been used. However, a holding of 50% or just below may have effectively given H control over S.
2. H may have held more than one half of the equity shares but was unable to exercise control fully due to the lack of voting rights. Equity shares could, for example, comprise ordinary A shares and non-voting B shares. H may have held more than half of the combined set but not half of the A shares.

In the new definition, situation 1 is likely to be covered (definition 5) and in situation 2 the company is not a subsidiary as no control exists.

CHAPTER 7 PRACTICE QUESTION

Pixie and Dixie

Pixie Ltd and its subsidiary
Group balance sheet as at 31 December 20X9

	£	£
Fixed assets (320,600 + 1,125)		321,725
Current assets (W2)	149,500	
Creditors: amounts falling due within one year		
Sundry	78,200	
Proposed dividends	20,000	
Minority dividends payable (W4)	1,465	
	99,665	
Net current assets		49,835
Total assets less current liabilities		371,560
Minority interests (W7)		(44,250)
		327,310
Capital and reserves		
Called up share capital		200,000
Profit and loss account (W6)		127,310
		327,310

Workings

(W1) **Shareholdings in Dixie Ltd**

	Ordinary	*Preference*
Group	75%	40%
Minority	25%	60%
	100%	100%

(W2) **Consolidated current assets**

	£
Pixie Ltd:	113,100
Dixie Ltd:	43,400
Less: Provision for unrealised profit on stock (W3)	(7,000)
	149,500

(W3) **Stock – unrealised profit**

	£
Stock held by Pixie purchased from Dixie	42,000
Unrealised profit $\frac{20}{120} \times 42,000$	7,000
Group share 75%	5,250
Minority interest 25%	1,750

Tutorial note

As the subsidiary recorded the original profit, the elimination must be shared between the group and the minority. This may be achieved if the unrealised profit is deducted from Dixie Ltd stock and reserves on the balance sheet working papers.

(W4) **Treatment of proposed dividends of Dixie Ltd**

	Ordinary	*Preference*	*Total*
	£	£	£
Proposed dividends	2,500	1,400	3,900
Less: Cancelled with dividends receivable by Pixie Ltd	(1,875)	(560)	(2,435)
Dividend payable to minority shareholders	625	840	1,465

(W5) **Goodwill**

	£	£
Cost of investment		73,000
Less: Share of net assets at acquisition		
Ordinary share capital	50,000	
Profit and loss account	20,000	
	70,000	
	× 75%	
		(52,500)
Preference share capital	40,000	
	× 40%	
		(16,000)
		4,500
Amortisation charge (4,500 ÷ 4 × 3)		(3,375)
		1,125

(W6) **Consolidated reserves**

	£
Pixie Ltd: Per question	120,000
Add: dividends receivable (W4)	2,435
	122,435
Dixie Ltd: 75% (38,000 – 7,000 (W3) – 20,000)	8,250
Less: Goodwill amortised	(3,375)
	127,310

(W7) **Minority interest**

Net assets of Dixie Ltd

	£	£
Ordinary share capital	50,000	
Profit and loss account (38,000 – 7,000)	31,000	
	81,000	
	× 25%	
		20,250
Preference share capital	40,000	
	× 60%	
		24,000
		44,250

CHAPTER 7

EXAM-TYPE QUESTION

Pillar plc

(a) **Consolidated balance sheet at 31 March 20X9**

	£000	£000
Fixed assets		
Intangible		
Software (W1)	2,400	
Goodwill (W2)	400	
		2,800
Tangible		
Property (720 + 1,080)	1,800	
Plant and equipment (W3)	3,096	
		4,896
Investments (214 + 252)		466
		8,162
Current assets		
Stocks (W4)	1,529	
Trade debtors (629 + 394)	1,023	
Cash and bank (24 + 18 cash in transit)	42	
	2,594	
Creditors: amounts falling due within one year		
Trade creditors (570 + 566)	1,136	
Operating overdraft	32	
Taxation (274 + 210)	484	
Proposed dividend – Pillar plc	120	
	1,772	

Net current assets		822
Total assets less current liabilities		8,984
Creditors: amounts falling due after more than one year		
Government grants (276 + 240)		(516)
		8,468
Share capital and reserves:		
Ordinary shares £1 each		2,400
Reserves		
Share premium	2,400	
Profit and loss account (W5)	3,174	
		5,574
		7,974
Minority interest (W6)		494
		8,468

Workings

(W1) **Software**

	Steeple Ltd's books	*Consolidated figures*	*Difference*
	£000	£000	£000
Capitalised amount	2,880	2,880	
Depreciation to 31 March 20X9	(360)	(480)	120 additional depreciation
Carrying value 31 March 20X9	2,520	2,400	

(W2) **Goodwill**

	£'000	£'000
Cost of investment		5,036
Less: share of net assets acquired:		
Share capital	1,800	
Share premium	600	
Profit and loss account	2,640	
	5,040	
Group share (90%)		(4,536)
		500
Less: amortisation (500 ÷ 5)		(100)
		400

(W3) **Plant and equipment**

Consolidation adjustment

	Steeple Ltd's books	*Consolidated figures*	*Difference*
	£000	£000	£000
Cost	240	200	40
Depreciation for year (10% on cost)	(24)	(20)	(4)
NBV at 31 March 20X9	216	180	36

Balance sheet:

	£000
Amounts per question (1,824 + 1,308)	3,132
Unrealised profit	(40)
Depreciation	4
	3,096

(W4) **Stock**

	£000
Amounts per question (863 + 672)	1,535
Unrealised profit in stock (30 × 25/125)	(6)
	1,529

(W5) **Group profit and loss account**

	£000	£000
Pillar plc		3,360
Steeple Ltd:		
At 31 March 20X9	2,706	
Additional depreciation: software	(120)	
Unrealised profit on plant	(36)	
Unrealised profit in stock	(6)	
	2,544	
At acquisition	(2,640)	
	(96)	
Group share (90%)		(86)
Less: goodwill		(100)
		3,174

(W6) **Minority interest**

	£000	£000
Share capital	1,800	
Share premium	600	
Profit and loss account (as above)	2,544	
	4,944	
MI share (10%)		494

(W7) **Elimination of current account:**

	£'000
Steeple Ltd's with Pillar plc per question	90
Deduct cash in transit regarding this balance	(18)
Adjusted figure to cancel	72

(b) The reasons why a parent company may not wish to consolidate a subsidiary can be broken down into two broad groups: (i) to improve the reported position of the group financial statements: and (ii) for the reasons, and in compliance with the Companies Acts/FRS 2 requirements.

Improvement of the financial position

The financial statements of a subsidiary could show any of the following:

- substantial operating losses
- a poor liquidity position
- high levels of borrowing (high gearing).

If a parent were to consolidate such a subsidiary, it would proportionately worsen the group position in the above areas. Thus a parent may prefer not to consolidate poorly performing subsidiaries.

Companies Act/FRS 2 requirements

Subsidiaries should/may be excluded from a parent's consolidated financial statements for the following reasons:

- Immateriality. The CA 85 permits an immaterial subsidiary to be excluded from consolidation, while FRS 2 contains no rules applying to immaterial items.
- The subsidiary operates under severe long-term restrictions. In effect the parent does not have full control over the subsidiary. The Companies Acts permit such exclusion, FRS 2 requires it
- Disproportionate expense or undue delay. The CA 85 permits exclusion on these grounds, while FRS 2 does not.
- The investment is held with a view to subsequent resale. Exclusion on these grounds is only permitted where a subsidiary has never been consolidated in the past.
- Differing activities. Some commentators believe that this exclusion exists (in theory at least) because it is argued that to add together the assets and liabilities of companies whose activities differ greatly could lead to consolidated financial statements that give a misleading impression (or not show a true and fair view). In practice the ASB have made it clear that they do not consider any activities so different as justify exclusion for this

reason. They feel 'differing activity' problems are overcome by the provision of segmental information.

It is apparent that the first group of reasons for non-consolidation is not permitted by the Companies Act/accounting standards, whereas the latter group is.

CHAPTER 8 PRACTICE QUESTION

N and S

Consolidated profit and loss account for the year ended 30 September 20X7

	£000
Sales	5,350
Cost of sales	2,715
Gross profit	2,635
Expenses	1,620
Profit on ordinary activities before taxation	1,015
Taxation	280
Profit on ordinary activities after taxation	735
Minority interests (W3)	80
Profit attributable to N plc	655
Dividends paid and proposed	450
Retained profit for the year	205
Reserves brought forward (W4)	702
Reserves carried forward (W5)	907

Tutorial note: In practice the dividends for the year would not be shown in the consolidated profit and loss account but in the statement of movement on reserves. However for tutorial purposes the payout has been maintained as per the original question.

Workings

Consolidation schedule

	N	*S*	*Adjusted*	*Consolidated*
	£000	£000	£000	£000
Sales	4,500	1,100	(250)	5,350
Cost of sales	2,320	620	(225)	2,715
Gross profit (W1)	2,180	480	(25)	2,635
Expenses	1,400	220		1,620
Taxation	200	80		280

(W1) **Unrealised profit in stock**

$\frac{25}{125} \times 250{,}000 \times ½ = £25{,}000$

Tutorial note

The unrealised profit is eliminated in full against the group as it is the parent company which originally recorded the profit.

(W2) **Dividends received by N from S**

	£000
Preference 20% × 20	4
Ordinary 60% × 80	48
All investment income is intra-group	52

(W3) **Minority interest**

	£000		*Minority interest* £000
Profit after taxation of S	180		
Preference dividend	20	80%	16
For ordinary shareholders	160	40%	64
			80

(W4) **Reserves brought forward**

	£'000
N	600
S 60% × (250 – 80)	102
	702

(W5) **Reserves carried forward**

	£'000
N	782
S 60% × (330 – 80)	150
Unrealised profit in stock provision carried forward	(25)
	907

EXAM-TYPE QUESTION

Greenhouse plc

(a) **Consolidated profit and loss account for the year ended 31 August 20X4**

	£000
Turnover (W1)	26,665
Cost of sales (W1)	(22,576)
Gross profit	4,089
Net operating expenses (W1)	(2,847)
Profit on ordinary activities before taxation	1,242
Tax on profit on ordinary activities (W3)	(364)
Profit on ordinary activities after taxation	878
Minority interests (W4)	(222)
Profit for financial year	656
Dividends	(30)
Retained profit for the financial year	626

Tutorial note: In practice the dividends for the year would not be shown in the consolidated profit and loss account but in the statement of movement on reserves. However for tutorial purposes the payout has been maintained as per the original question.

Workings

All workings are in £000.

(W1)

	Greenhouse	*Airedale*	*Inter Co*	*Total*
Sales	15,050	12,340	(725)	26,665
Cost of sales	12,679	10,622	(725)	22,576
Gross profit	2,371	1,718	–	4,089
Net operating expenses				
Distribution costs	1,042	824	–	1,866
Administrative expenses	946	307	60	1,313
Other operating income				
Dividend income	(280)	(64)	12 (W2)	(332)
Net operating expenses	1,708	1,067	72	2,847
Net profit	663	651	(72)	1,242

(W2) Inter-company dividend = 60% of 20 = 12

(W3) Tax on profit on ordinary activities

Greenhouse plc	268	
Airedale plc	96	
		364

(W4)

Minority interest	
Airedale plc net profit after tax	555
Minority interest 40% thereof	222

(b) **Group profit/loss account as at 31 August 20X4**

	£'000	£'000
Greenhouse plc profit/loss account at 1.9.X3		1,750
Airedale plc profit/loss account at 1.9.X3	1,600	
Less profit/loss account at acquisition	(1,400)	
	200	
Group share thereof 60%		120
Profit and loss for year		626
Amortisation of goodwill (300 × 2/5)		(120)
Group reserves at 31 August 20X4		2,376

CHAPTER 9 PRACTICE QUESTION

H, S and A

(a) **H Ltd and its subsidiary – Group profit and loss account for the year ended 31 December 20X5**

	£
Group operating profit	900,000
Share of operating profit of associated undertakings	35,000
Investment income	3,000
Profit on ordinary activities before taxation	938,000
Tax on profit on ordinary activities	467,500
Profit on ordinary activities after taxation	470,500
Minority interests	10,000
Profit attributable to members of the parent undertaking	460,500

Notes to profit and loss account

Statement of retained reserves

	Total £
Retained reserves at 1 January 20X5	2,072,300
Retained profit for the year	460,500
Dividends	(103,000)
Retained reserves at 31 December 20X5	2,429,800

Tax on profit on ordinary activities

	£
Corporation tax at x%	450,000
Associated undertaking	17,500
	467,500

(b) **Balance sheet extracts**

	31.12.X4 £	*31.12.X5* £
Interest in associated undertaking		
Group share of net assets (other than goodwill)	87,500	103,000

Tutorial note: Journal entry required in consolidated working papers is:

Dr: Investment in associate	£15,500	
Cr: Accumulated reserves		£15,500

Consolidation schedule

	H £	*S 80%* £	*Consolidation adjustments* £	*Total* £	*A 25%* £
Trading profit	800,000	100,000		900,000	
Share of profit				35,000	35,000
Investment income	3,000			3,000	
	803,000	100,000		938,000	
Tax	400,000	50,000		(450,000)	
Share of tax				(17,500)	(17,500)
	403,000	50,000		470,500	17,500
Minority interest 20% × 50,000		(10,000)		(10,000)	
		40,000		460,500	
Inter co dividend 25% × 8,000	2,000				(2,000)
Profit before dividend	405,000				
Dividend	103,000			103,000	
Retained for year	302,000	40,000		357,500	15,500

Workings

(W1) **Investment in associate**

	Acquisition	*31.12.X4*	*31.12.X5*
	£	£	£
Shares	250,000	250,000	250,000
Reserves	32,000	100,000	162,000
Net assets	282,000	350,000	412,000
Group share 25%	70,500	87,500	103,000
Cost of investment	81,200		
Goodwill – fully amortised	10,700		

(W2) **Reserves brought forward**

	£
Associate	
25% × (100,000 – 32,000)	17,000

	£
Group	
H	2,000,000
S 80% × (130,000 – 40,000)	72,000
Goodwill amortised	
S	(6,000)
A (W1)	(10,700)
	2,055,300

CHAPTER 9 EXAM-TYPE QUESTION

J plc

(a) **Working schedules**

1 and 2 J plc investment in P Ltd – 60% subsidiary

The fair value adjustment of £400,000 increases fixed assets, and 40% (£160,000) belongs to the minority interest. The 60% group share (£240,000) is pre-acquisition and is included in the goodwill calculation.

The revalued asset purchased in 20V9 is 10 years old on acquisition, so 50% of the increased value (£200,000) must be depreciated over the remaining life of 40 years, i.e. £5,000 p.a. This amount for 6 years 20W9 – 20X4 gives £30,000 to be deducted from the asset value, and apportioned between the group reserves (£18,000) and the minority interest (£12,000).

Goodwill calculation

			£000
Price			1,000
Net assets acquired	– Share capital	60% × 1,000 = 600	
	– Reserves	60% × 200 = 120	
	– Fair value adj.	60% × 400 = 240	(960)
Goodwill (written off over the five years to 20X3, so deduct from group reserves)			40

3 J plc investment in S Ltd – 30% associate

Goodwill calculation

			£000
Price			500
Net assets acquired	– Share capital	30% × 750 = 225	
	– Reserves	30% × 150 = 45	
			(270)
Goodwill, amortised over 5 years			230

This goodwill is amortised to the extent of £92,000 ($230 \times {}^{1}/_{5} \times 2$). This amount will reduce group reserves and will affect the value of the investment in associate shown in the consolidated balance sheet.

4 Intra-group profits

	£000
Unrealised profit on stocks of J plc = (£100,000 × $\frac{25}{125}$)	20

Reduce group stock by £20,000. Reduce group reserves by £12,000 (60% × £20,000) and minority interest by £8,000 (40% × £20,000).

	£000
Unrealised profit on stocks of S Ltd = (£80,000 × $\frac{25}{125}$)	16
30% group share (30% × £16,000)	4.8

Reduce investment in associate by £4,800. Reduce group reserves by £2,880 (60% × £4,800) and minority interest by £1,920 (40% × £4,800).

5 Goodwill

Already dealt with in 1 and 3 above.

6 Proposed dividends

Proposed dividends of P Ltd

Cancel £30,000 (60% × £50,000) of the proposed dividend as part of the consolidation, leaving £20,000 (40% × £50,000) to be included in other creditors, described as dividends due to the minority.

Proposed dividends of S Ltd

The group share of £7,500 (30% × £25,000) increases group reserves and debtors.

Final consolidation schedules

Minority interest in P Ltd

		£000
Share capital (40% × 1,000)		400.00
Reserves (40% × 885)		354.00
Fair value adjustment (40% × 400)		160.00
Share of stock profit adjustment	– J plc (40% × 20,000)	(8.00)
	– S Ltd (40% × 4,800)	(1.92)
Share of depreciation on fair value (40% × 30)		(12.00)
		892.08

Group reserves

		£000
Reserves of J plc		1,460.00
P Ltd – post acquisition profits 60% × (885 –200)		411.00
Dividend receivable from P Ltd		30.00
Dividend receivable from S Ltd		7.50
S Ltd post-acquisition profits		72.00
Goodwill of S Ltd written off		(92.00)
Goodwill of P Ltd written off		(40.00)
Group share of fair value depreciation		(18.00)
Group share of stock profit	– J plc (60% × 20,000)	(12.00)
	– S Ltd (60% × 4,800)	(2.88)
		1,815.62

Investment in associated undertaking

	£000			£000
Cost	500.0	or	Group share of net assets at balance sheet date	
Group share of post-acquisition profits	72.0		(30% × 1,140)	342.0
Unrealised profit on stock	(4.8)		Unrealised profit on stock	(4.8)
Goodwill written off	(92.0)		Goodwill not yet written off	138.0
Investment	475.2		Investment	475.2

(b)

J Group
Consolidated balance sheet at 31 December 20X4

		£000	£000
Fixed assets:			
Tangible assets	– Freehold property		3,570.00
	– Plant and machinery		1,170.00
Investments	– associated undertaking		475.20
			5,215.20
Current assets:			
Stocks		855.0	
Debtors		627.5	
Cash		170.0	
		1,652.5	

Creditors: amounts falling due within one year			
Bank overdraft		560.0	
Trade creditors		780.0	
Proposed dividends –	parent undertaking	200.0	
	– minority interests	20.0	
		1,560.0	
Net current assets			92.50
Total assets less current liabilities			5,307.70
Creditors: amounts falling due after more than one year			(600.00)
Net assets			4,707.70
Financed by:			
Capital	– Share capital		2,000.00
	– Profit and loss account		1,815.62
			3,815.62
Minority interests			892.08
			4,707.70

CHAPTER 10 EXAM-TYPE QUESTION

Slamometer Ltd

Profit and loss account for the year ended 31 March 20X4

Notes		£	£
	Turnover		1,013,000
	Cost of sales (W)		647,929
	Gross profit		365,071
	Distribution costs (W)	224,271	
	Administrative expenses (W)	67,920	
			292,191
			72,880
	Interest receivable	910	
(1)	Interest payable	(3,110)	
			(2,200)
(2)	Profit on ordinary activities before taxation		70,680
(5)	Tax on profit on ordinary activities		32,870
	Profit on ordinary activities after taxation		37,810

Movements in reserves

	Share premium account	*Plant replacement reserve*	*Retained profits*	*Total*
	£	£	£	£
Balance at 1 April 20X3	6,100	40,000	51,700	97,800
Profit after tax	–	–	37,810	17,650
Dividends			(20,160)	
Transfer	–	10,000	(10,000)	–
Premium on shares issued in year	4,500	–	–	4,500
Balance at 31 March 20X4	10,600	50,000	59,350	119,950

Notes to the accounts

(1) **Interest payable**

	£
Interest on bank overdraft	1,310
Interest on debenture loan	1,800
	3,110

(2) **The profit on ordinary activities is after charging**

	£
Depreciation	11,300
Staff costs	246,289
Auditors' remuneration	1,500

(3) **Staff costs**

	£
Wages and salaries	246,289

(4) **Directors' remuneration**

	£
Aggregate emoluments	80,100

(5) **Taxation**

	£
Corporation tax at 25%	32,000
Taxation under-provided in previous year	870
	32,870

(6) **Dividends**

	£
Preference dividend	3,360
Proposed ordinary dividend (£140,000 × 12%)	16,800
	20,160

Working

Classification of expenditure

	Cost of sales £	*Distribution costs* £	*Administrative expenses* £
Expenses per note 2			
Distribution costs		152,571	
Raw materials	366,238		
Manufacturing overheads	159,302		
Staff costs	98,789	56,400	11,000
Directors	12,300	15,300	52,500
Depreciation	11,300		
Office rent			2,300
Audit			1,500
Legal and accountancy			620
	647,929	224,271	67,920

Tutorial note

As the aggregate directors' emoluments are less than £200,000, there is no requirement to disclose the highest paid director's emoluments.

CHAPTER 11

PRACTICE QUESTION

Question 1: Dewar Ltd

(a) **Profit and loss account for the year ended 31 December 20X6**

	£000	£000
Operating profit		300
Investment income received		15
Profit on ordinary activities before taxation		315
Tax on profit on ordinary activities (note)		(110)
Profit on ordinary activities after taxation		205

Note to the profit and loss account: Tax on profit on ordinary activities

	£000
Corporation tax at 30% based on the profit for the year	90
Over-provision in respect of prior year (120 – 115)	(5)
Transfer to deferred taxation	25
	110

(b) **Balance sheet at 31 December 20X6 (extracts)**

	£000
Creditors: Amounts falling due within one year:	
Corporation tax	90
Dividends proposed	50
Provisions for liabilities (Note)	65

Note to the balance sheet: Provisions for liabilities

Deferred taxation

	£000
At 1 January 20X6	40
Charged to the profit and loss account	25
At 31 December 20X6	65

All deferred taxation relates to accelerated capital allowances.

Question 2: H plc

(a) Deferred taxation is a basis of allocating tax charges to particular accounting periods.

The key to deferred taxation lies in the two quite different concepts of profit: the accounting profit (the figure of profit before tax reported to the shareholders) and the taxable profit (the profit on which the Inland Revenue base their corporation tax calculations).

These two figures of profit are unlikely to be the same due to two areas of difference:

(i) timing differences: types of income and expenditure recognised in different periods for the purposes of financial accounts on the one hand, and taxation on the other;

(ii) permanent differences: items accounted for in the financial accounts which are disallowable or non-taxable.

Deferred taxation is not concerned with permanent differences but full deferred tax accounting eliminates the effect of timing differences so that the tax charge reported to shareholders is in direct relation to the reported profit.

One of the main reasons for deferral of tax is the availability of capital allowances in taxation computations which are different from the related depreciation charge in financial statements. The deferral period may be for several years, but the obligation to pay tax eventually cannot be escaped. This long term liability cannot be ignored, but must be brought into the accounts in the year the liability arises.

The liability reduces the profit for the year, and is also shown as a separate item under provisions in the balance sheet. Movements to and from the deferred tax account must also be disclosed. When the tax actually becomes due, the deferred tax account is debited with the amount. This process ensures that the accounting principle of accruals is adhered to, since the payment of tax is matched to the year to which it relates.

(b) FRS 19 *Deferred tax* requires that full provision should be made for deferred tax assets and liabilities arising from most types of timing differences including accelerated capital allowances, pension costs, unrelieved timing losses and short-term timing differences. However deferred tax should not be recognised on the revaluation of a fixed asset where there is no commitment to sell the asset or when the gain on the sale of an asset is rolled over into replacement assets.

Most deferred tax balances will be liabilities due to accelerated capital allowances. However if there is a deferred tax asset this is to be recognised to the extent that it is regarded as more likely than not that it will be recovered.

Due to the method of full provision being required by FRS 19 it is possible that large liabilities may build up on companies' balance sheets. Therefore FRS 19 permits the use of discounting of deferred tax balances to take account of the time value of money. If this policy is chosen then it should be followed for all deferred tax balances.

The tax rate that should be used to calculate deferred tax balances should be measured at the average tax rates expected to apply in the period in which the timing differences are expected to reverse based upon tax rates and laws that have been enacted by the balance sheet date.

Any net deferred tax liability should be shown on the balance sheet as a provision for liabilities. Any net deferred tax asset will be shown as part of debtors and shown as a separate sub-heading of debtors if it is material. In the profit and loss account the increase or decrease in the deferred tax balance for the period is shown as part of the tax charge for the year.

(c)

Deferred tax note	£m
Deferred tax balance at 1 November 20W9	1.50
Increase for the year (W1)	0.84
Deferred tax balance at 31 October 20X0	2.34
Tax charge	
Current tax	4.70
Deferred tax	0.84
	5.54

Working

(W1)

	£m	£m
Increase in provision		
Capital allowances	20.8	
Depreciation	18.0	
	2.8 × 30%	0.84

CHAPTER 12 EXAM-TYPE QUESTION

G Ltd

(a) **Recognition of profits/losses on long-term contracts**

A long-term contract is a contract where the time taken to complete the contract is such that the contract activity falls into different accounting periods. A long-term contract normally lasts for more than one year.

The legal form of a long-term contract is that no turnover or profit arises until the contract is complete. It could be argued that it would not be prudent to recognise profit until the contract is completed. However, this treatment would result in the profit and loss account reflecting the results relating to contracts that have been completed in the year, rather than the results relating to the activity of the company during the year.

Under the accruals concept, turnover should be set against the costs to which it relates. Turnover and costs should be matched with the accounting period in which they arise. The requirements of SSAP 9 apply the accruals concept to the accounting treatment of long-term contracts so that the profit and loss account reflects the results of contract activity in the period.

Reporting entities are required to recognise an appropriate proportion of contract value as turnover in the profit and loss account as the contract progresses. In practice, architects' certificates value the work completed and may be used to provide a figure for turnover. Turnover may also be calculated as a proportion of the work completed. Costs are matched with this turnover. The profit attributable to the contract work performed at the balance sheet date is recognised in the profit and loss account.

SSAP 9 sets out a number of rules for calculating attributable profit. The purpose of these rules is to apply the prudence concept. No profit may be recognised before the outcome of a contract can be assessed with reasonable certainty. Where a loss is expected on a contract as a whole, all the loss must be recognised as soon as it is foreseen. Attributable profit must be calculated on 'a prudent basis'.

Attributable profit is normally calculated as a proportion of the expected final profit. The proportion can be calculated on the basis of the percentage of total costs incurred to date or the percentage of the total contract price certified to date. The attributable profit taken must reflect any known inequalities of profitability in the various stages of a contract. The method applied must be used consistently.

SSAP 9 defines attributable profit as that part of the total profit currently estimated to arise over the duration of the contract, after allowing for estimated remedial and maintenance costs and increases in costs which are not recoverable.

Where unprofitable contracts are so material that they are expected to absorb a considerable part of the company's capacity for a substantial period, the related future administration overheads should be included in the provision for losses.

(b) **Contract with H Ltd**

Profit and loss account

	£000
Turnover (20,000 × 60%)	12,000
Cost of sales (15,000 × 60% + 1,000)	10,000
Attributable profit	2,000

Balance sheet

Stocks: long-term contract work in progress	
(10,000 – 10,000)	NIL
Debtors:	
Trade debtors	10,000
Amounts recoverable on contracts	
(12,000 – 10,000)	2,000
Provisions: losses on long-term contracts	NIL

Contract with I Ltd

Profit and loss account

Turnover (10,000 × 2/3)	6,700
Cost of sales (balancing figure)	7,700
Foreseeable loss	(1,000)

Balance sheet

Stocks: long-term contract work in progress	
(7,500 – 7,500)	NIL
Debtors:	
Trade debtors	NIL
Amounts recoverable on contracts	6,700
Provisions: losses on long-term contracts	
(7,700 – 7,500)	200

Information received after the balance sheet date regarding increased costs is an adjusting post-balance sheet event under FRS 21.

Working

Attributable profit/foreseeable losses

	H Ltd	*I Ltd*
	£000	£000
Contract price	20,000	10,000
Total costs (15 + 1)	16,000	11,000
Total profit/(loss)	4,000	(1,000)

Attributable profit on the contract with H Ltd:

$$\frac{\text{Turnover to date}}{\text{Price}} \times \text{estimated final profit } \frac{12{,}000}{20{,}000} \times 4{,}000 = £2{,}400{,}000$$

$$\frac{\text{Cost to date}}{\text{Total cost}} \times \text{estimated final profit} \frac{10{,}000}{16{,}000} \times 4{,}000 = £2{,}500{,}000$$

The contract account shows £2,000,000 and it is prudent to restrict attributable profit to this amount.

The whole of the foreseeable loss on the contract with I Ltd is taken immediately.

CHAPTER 13 EXAM-TYPE QUESTION

David plc

(a) FRS 3 lists four components of a profit and loss account which must be disclosed in a layered format:

- results of continuing operations

- results of discontinued operations
- profits/losses on the sale/termination of an operation, on a fundamental restructuring or on the disposal of fixed assets
- extraordinary items.

Each of these components is needed to assess a business's future results and cash flows for the following reasons:

- Continuing operations (including acquisitions) are the basis for the company's future; it is these operations which must generate the cash flows to pay the dividends to support the share price in the future. Readers of accounts have to be able to identify these operations separately so that they can form an opinion on the company's future prospects.
- If continuing operations must be identified separately, clearly the results of discontinued operations have to be stripped out as a separate component of the period's results. The profits or losses up to the date of sale or termination form part of the overall result out of which the dividend for that period will be paid, so a complete view of the activities of the business can only be achieved by showing both continuing and discontinued operations separately.
- The third category of items are particular sorts of exceptional items which FRS 3 requires to be shown on the face of the profit and loss account. Because of their exceptional size or incidence, they must be separately disclosed if the accounts are to give a true and fair view. They are not expected to recur regularly, but they are likely to be of such a size that readers of the accounts need to have these items highlighted to warn of their possible effects on future results and cash flows.
- Extraordinary items are defined as material abnormal items deriving from outside the ordinary activities and expected not to recur. FRS 3 makes it clear that such items are very rare indeed, if they exist at all. Certainly no accounts in practice have included extraordinary items since FRS 3 was published, so discussion here is a bit academic.

  However it is reasonable to say that readers of accounts should be warned separately of the existence of such items due to their material size and the effects that they might have on future results and cash flows.

(b) **David plc**

Outline profit and loss account for the year ended 31 December 20X3

	Continuing operations	*Discontinued operations*	*Total*
	£000	£000	£000
Turnover	820	150	970
Operating expenses	(470)	(98)	(568)
Operating profit	350	52	402
Closure and reorganisation costs	(42)	(127)	(169)
Losses on disposal of fixed assets	(19)	(78)	(97)
Profit on ordinary activities before interest	289	(153)	136
Interest payable			(37)
Profit on ordinary activities before taxation			99
Tax on profit on ordinary activities			(24)
Profit for the financial year			75

Tutorial note

The profit and loss account above has been drawn up as per example 2 in the illustrative examples at the end of FRS 3. It would also be possible to use example 1 and a vertical approach, but in the exam the columnar approach of example 2 is recommended since it is clearer.

(c) **David plc**

Reconciliation of movements in shareholders' funds in the year ended 31 December 20X3

	£000
Profit for the financial year	75
Dividends	(30)
	45
New share capital subscribed	180
Reduction in revaluation reserve (160-90)	(70)
Net addition to shareholders' funds	155
Opening shareholders' funds	1,230
Closing shareholders' funds	1,385

Tutorial note

This *pro forma* is also in the illustrative examples at the end of FRS 3.

CHAPTER 14

EXAM-TYPE QUESTIONS

Question 1: Ace plc

(a) **Why FRS 8 was considered necessary**

In theory, an entity controls its own resources and acts independently of its individual owners, managers and other people connected with it. Unless they have reason to believe otherwise, users of financial statements assume that the transactions included in the financial statements were undertaken on an arm's length basis. In practice, this is not always the case.

When transactions are arranged between related parties, they might not take place on the same terms that could have been obtained in a transaction with an external party. Transactions between related parties are often arranged to obtain a particular result desired by one or both of the parties. Therefore they can have a material effect on the position and performance of one or both parties. Unless users of the financial statements are made aware of the existence of related party relationships and transactions, the view given by the financial statements may be misleading.

Although the Companies Act 1985 and the Stock Exchange Listing Rules do contain requirements to disclose related party transactions, these are largely limited to transactions between directors and the company or group. The Accounting Standards Board (ASB) recognised that 'related party' relationships are not limited to those between a company and its directors. FRS 8 contains a much wider definition of 'related parties', which is based upon ideas of 'control', 'common control' and 'influence', rather than upon specific categories of people or organisations.

The main objective of the Companies Act and Stock Exchange disclosures is to ensure that shareholders can assess the stewardship of the directors. FRS 8 has a wider objective, which is to ensure that users of the financial statements are provided with information on which to base economic decisions. It extends the Companies Act requirements as entities must disclose all material related party transactions in the notes to the financial statements. When the reporting entity is controlled by another party, there must be disclosure of this relationship, regardless of whether any transactions have taken place.

Lastly, FRS 8 brings UK practice broadly into line with International Accounting Standards.

(b) **Disclosure of related party transactions**

The first step is to determine whether related party relationships existed between the three companies during each of the two accounting periods.

Year ended 31 March 20X8

Ace plc owns 75% of the equity share capital of Deuce Ltd and 80% of the equity share capital of Trey Ltd. This means that Ace plc is a related party of both subsidiaries, as it controls both of them. (An entity is presumed to be a related party of another entity if that entity owns more than 20% of its equity share capital.)

Deuce Ltd and Trey Ltd are related parties as they are under common control.

Year ended 31 March 20X9

Ace plc owns 100% of the equity share capital of Deuce Ltd and 80% of the equity share capital of Trey Ltd. Therefore all three companies are still related parties of each other. As Ace plc now owns over 90% of the equity shares in Deuce Ltd, Deuce Ltd need not disclose transactions with Ace plc.

Three sets of financial statements are relevant:

- the consolidated financial statements of Ace plc
- the individual financial statements of Deuce Ltd
- the individual financial statements of Trey Ltd.

Ace plc will not prepare individual company financial statements and so there is no distinction between the transactions of Ace plc and the transactions of the Ace Group.

Related party disclosures

The following details of each related party transaction are required:

- name of related party with which the transaction was made
- description of the relationship between the parties
- description of the transaction and the amounts involved (including the fair value of the transaction if this is different from the actual value)
- any amounts due to or from related parties at the year end (including any doubtful debts)
- any amounts written off related party debtors
- any other information necessary for an understanding of the transaction and its effect on the financial statements.

It is assumed that all related party transactions are material.

The transactions are summarised in the table below:

Year ended 31 March 20X8

	Ace plc: Consolidated financial statements	*Deuce Ltd*	*Trey Ltd*
(i) Sale of machine by Ace plc to Deuce Ltd	Disclose intra-group profit on sale of £5,000. Otherwise sale eliminated on consolidation.	Disclose purchase of machine from parent at £25,000 and depreciation charge of £5,000. No amounts outstanding at year end.	
(ii) Not applicable			
(iii) Management charges made by Ace plc to both Deuce Ltd and Trey Ltd	No disclosure: eliminated on consolidation	Disclose purchase of management services from parent at no charge.	Disclose purchase of management services from parent at no charge.

Year ended 31 March 20X9

	Ace plc: Consolidated financial statements	*Deuce Ltd*	*Trey Ltd*
(i) Sale of machine by Ace plc to Deuce Ltd	No disclosure as transaction completed.	Disclose depreciation charge of £5,000 on machine purchased from parent in previous year.	
(ii) Sale of goods by Deuce Ltd to Trey Ltd		Disclose sale of goods to Trey Ltd for £15,000 and profit of £3,000. No debt written off or outstanding at year end.	Disclose purchase of goods from Deuce Ltd for £15,000. No amounts outstanding at year end. All stock sold at year end.
(iii) Management charges made by Ace plc to both Deuce Ltd and Trey Ltd	No disclosure: eliminated on consolidation	No disclosure because more than 90% of equity share capital owned.	Disclose purchase of management services from parent for £10,000. Disclose £10,000 due to parent at year end.

Question 2: Innovations plc

(a) (i) The objectives of segmental reporting are to provide users with a greater level of information about the results and resources of a group than is available from the profit and loss account and balance sheet.

In addition, disclosure of this information by classes of business and geographical segments allows greater comparability between companies in the same industry.

The disclosure of inter-segment sales and profits also gives greater information on the total activities of the group, as the consolidated accounts only disclose transactions outside the group.

(ii) The additional information provided by groups may put them at a competitive disadvantage, especially with overseas companies which may not have to disclose this information.

The requirements of SSAP 25 allow the directors considerable flexibility in defining segments. This will reduce comparability.

The costs of providing this information may be high. Although management usually prepares this type of information for its own purposes, it may not be in a form suitable for publication in the financial statements.

(b) **Segmental report for Innovations plc for year ended 30 June 20X9**

Classes of business	***Fruit growing***		***Canning***		***Bureau***		***Group***	
	20X9	20X8	20X9	20X8	20X9	20X8	20X9	20X8
	£000	£000	£000	£000	£000	£000	£000	£000
Turnover								
Total sales	13,635	15,188	20,520	16,200	5,400	4,050	39,555	35,438
Inter-segment sales	1,485	1,688	2,970	3,105	-	-	4,455	4,793
Sales to 3rd parties	12,150	13,500	17,550	13,095	5,400	4,050	35,100	30,645
Unallocated sales							2,700	1,350
							37,800	31,995

Classes of business	***Fruit growing***		***Canning***		***Bureau***		***Group***	
	20X9	20X8	20X9	20X8	20X9	20X8	20X9	20X8
	£000	£000	£000	£000	£000	£000	£000	£000
Profit before taxation								
Segment profit	2,565	3,375	4,725	3,600	412	540	7,702	7,515
Inter-segment loss							(7)	(765)
							7,695	6,750
Common costs							(5,130)	(4,104)
Group operating profit							2,565	2,646
Net assets								
Segment net assets	33,750	32,400	40,500	33,750	18,765	17,563	93,015	83,713
Unallocated assets							13,500	11,003
Group net assets							106,515	94,716

Geographical segments	***UK***		***US***		***Other***		***Group***	
	20X9	*20X8*	*20X9*	*20X8*	*20X9*	*20X8*	*20X9*	*20X8*
	£000	£000	£000	£000	£000	£000	£000	£000
Turnover by origin								
Total sales	29,700	26,190	8,910	6,345	1,350	1,215	39,960	33,750
Inter-segment sales	2,700	1,890	2,160	1,215	-	-	4,860	3,105
Sales to 3rd parties	27,000	24,300	6,750	5,130	1,350	1,215	35,100	30,645
Unallocated sales							2,700	1,350
							37,800	31,995

Profit before taxation								
Segment profit	5,130	4,590	2,430	1,890	270	405	7,830	6,885
Inter-segment loss							(680)	(405)
							7,150	6,480
Common costs							(4,590)	(3,834)
Group operating profit							2,560	2,646
Net assets								
Segment net assets	43,200	40,500	32,400	24,300	18,360	19,683	93,960	84,483
Unallocated assets							12,555	10,233
Group net assets							106,515	94,716

CHAPTER 15

EXAM-TYPE QUESTION

Question 1: Short plc

(a) **Treatment of the preference shares**

FRS 25 Financial Instruments: Disclosure and Presentation sets out the required accounting treatment and disclosures in respect of the preference shares. As these are redeemable preference shares then according to FRS 25 they are to be treated as liabilities. The following points are relevant:

The finance charge must be allocated to accounting periods over the term of the preference shares at a constant rate on the carrying amount.

The finance charge should be included in the profit and loss account as part of the finance cost before the taxation charge.

The shares should be included as liabilities in the balance sheet, but described as preference shares. The amount at which they are stated is the opening balance, plus the finance cost for the period, less the dividends paid in the period.

(b) **Finance costs**

	Bal b/f	*Finance cost @ 10%*	*Cash paid*	*Bal c/f*
	£000	£000	£000	£000
Year ended 30 September:				
20X4	9,900	990	(400)	10,490
20X5	10,490	1,049	(400)	11,139
20X6	11,139	1,114	(400)	11,853
20X7	11,853	1,185	(400)	12,638
20X8	12,638	1,264	(400)	13,502

Net issue proceeds: 10,000,000 – 100,000 = £9,900,000.

Amount payable on redemption: 10,000,000 × £1.35 = £13,500,000. The difference is due to rounding.

(c) **Balance sheet at 1 October 20X8 (summary)**

	£m
Net assets (199 – 13.5)	185.50
Capital and reserves:	
Ordinary share capital (non-redeemable)	100.00
Share premium account	25.80
Capital redemption reserve	10.00
Profit and loss account (59.7 – 10)	49.70
	185.50

The net assets are reduced by cash of £13.5 million which has been used to redeem the shares. Because the shares are redeemed out of profits, the Companies Act requires £10m to be transferred from the profit and loss account reserve to a capital redemption reserve. This amount represents the nominal value of the shares redeemed.

Question 2: LED Ltd

(a) There are several conditions and safeguards which must be fulfilled before a private company can redeem shares out of capital. There are certain conditions set out in the Companies Act 1985 (the Act) which must be observed before even considering redemption. These involve ensuring that the transaction is permitted by the articles of association and is authorised by the shareholders. A special resolution must be passed by the company authorising the transaction. Further, the shares may not be redeemed if after redemption there are no shares in issue or only redeemable shares remain. If the shares to be redeemed are not fully paid up, then they may not be redeemed until paid up.

The redemption of a private company's shares out of capital is a significant event with many possible repercussions and so the Act states that after the special resolution has been passed, the company must publicise the authorisation in an official gazette and, either in a newspaper or individually, notify each creditor. Further, the directors must state that the company will be solvent after the redemption and during the next year. The auditor must report upon the reasonableness of the directors' assumptions.

The Act also gives guidance on the accounting requirements of the redemption. Once the shares are redeemed they must be cancelled and not reissued. Generally, the capital of the company must be maintained when shares are redeemed either by freezing an equivalent amount of distributable profits in a 'capital redemption reserve' or making it good from a fresh issue of shares made for the purposes of redemption. However, in the case of private companies, the rules are relaxed to allow a payment out of capital to the extent of the difference between the redemption cost and the distributable profits plus the proceeds of any fresh issue made for the purpose of the purchase. Often companies will give shareholders a premium when they are redeeming their shares. This premium is normally taken out of distributable profits although in certain circumstances it may be charged to the share premium account. These circumstances are as follows: if the redeemable shares had originally been issued at a premium and there is a fresh issue for the purposes of redemption, then the premium on redemption can be met out of the proceeds of the fresh issue up to the limit of the lesser of:

(i) the premium received originally on the shares now being redeemed; or

(ii) the current balance on the share premium account including any premium on the issue of the fresh issue of shares.

The rules relating to the redemption of private company shares out of capital are quite detailed but the Companies Act 1985 attempts to safeguard several parties by these rules.

(b) The Companies Act 1985 has laid down detailed rules to ensure that a company's permanent capital is maintained intact following a redemption or purchase of shares. In the case of a private company, the Act provides the company with a means of reducing its permanent capital without the formality and expense of undertaking a capital reduction scheme.

Obviously, this concession can be of great benefit to a family owned company where a member of the family wishes to realise their investment, but no other member of the family wishes to purchase the investment. The redemption or purchase of shares may result in a fall in the assets available to creditors and shareholders and therefore the Companies Act 1985 provides these safeguards in order to protect the creditors' interests.

The protection of creditors and shareholders is dependent upon the continuing solvency of the company and hence the requirement for the statutory declaration of solvency by the directors of the company.

(c)

Balance sheet – LED Ltd

(after redemption of shares)

	£	£
Sundry fixed assets		20,000
Sundry net current assets	25,000	
Bank overdraft	(2,500)	
		22,500
		42,500
Ordinary £1 shares		30,000
Share premium account		8,750
Capital redemption reserve		3,750
		42,500

Workings

	£
Cost of redemption	13,750
Less proceeds of new issue	(6,250)
Profit and loss account	(5,000)
Permissible capital payment	2,500

Share premium account

Balance per balance sheet	7,500
Plus premium on new issue of shares	1,250
	8,750

Profit and loss account

Balance per balance sheet	5,000
Less premium on redemption	(1,250)
Transfer to CRR	(3,750)
	–

Cash account

Balance per balance sheet	5,000
Add new issue of shares	6,250
Less payment on redemption	(13,750)
Bank overdraft	(2,500)

CHAPTER **16** EXAM-TYPE QUESTION

Trent plc

(a)

	Hotels £000	*Fixtures and fittings* £000	*Total* £000
Cost or valuation			
At 31 December 20W9	478,000	11,000	489,000
Additions	12,000	7,000	19,000
At 31 December 20X0	490,000	18,000	508,000
Depreciation			
At 31 December 20W9	46,200	9,400	55,600
Charge for year (W1)	9,800	2,150	11,950
At 31 December 20X0	56,000	11,550	67,550
Net book value			
At 31 December 20X0	434,000	6,450	440,450
At 31 December 20W9	431,800	1,600	433,400

Working

	£000
Depreciation (W1)	
hotels (490,000 × 2%)	9,800
fixtures and fittings ((18,000 – 9,400) × 25%)	2,150
	11,950

(b)

Current depreciation charge	£000
Hotel A (800 × 2%)	16
Hotel B (700 × 2%)	14
Hotel C (1,000 × 2%)	20
	50

Revised depreciation charge

Hotel A (1,300/50)	26.000
Hotel B (850/30)	28.333
Hotel C (650/40)	16.250
	70.583

The depreciation charge will increase by £20,583.

(c) **Revaluation:**

	£'000
Hotel A ((800 – 180) – 1,300)	680
Hotel B ((700 – 120) – 850)	270
Balance on revaluation reserve	950

(d) **Feasibility of charging no depreciation**

FRS 15 makes it quite clear that all tangible fixed assets with a finite useful economic life should be depreciated. Depreciation is not a reflection of any loss in value of the asset but an application of the matching concept. As the fixed assets are being used to earn income for the business, so a proportion of the cost of the fixed assets should be matched with this income as an expense in the profit and loss account.

The fact that the hotels are increasing in value is not a valid argument for not depreciating the assets. In the past some hotel chains have tended not to depreciate their hotels, on the grounds that they have high residual values and are subject to high levels of repairs and maintenance. However, under FRS 15 it will be harder to avoid charging depreciation and even if a hotel were not depreciated for any reason, then it would be subject to an impairment review, and a subsequent write off of any diminution in value.

The hotels cannot be treated as investment properties. SSAP 19 specifically states that if a property is to be regarded as an investment property then it must not be occupied or used by the owner, but held for its investment potential.

(e) **Capitalisation of repairs and refurbishment**

FRS 15 makes it clear that, in general, any expenditure on fixed assets should normally be recognised in the profit and loss account when it is incurred. FRS 15 gives only three specific circumstances when subsequent expenditure should be capitalised and in general terms these are when the expenditure enhances the economic benefits obtained from use of the asset.

The expenditure on the repairs seems to be necessary maintenance in order to maintain the hotels' useful lives, not in any way expenditure to enhance the hotels or extend their useful lives. Therefore this should be charged to the profit and loss account as an expense, in accordance with the matching concept.

It could be argued that the redecoration and new furniture do enhance the economic benefits of the hotels and therefore these expenses should be capitalised. However, the value of the old fixtures and fittings may need to be written off as well.

CHAPTER **17**

PRACTICE QUESTION

Goodwill characteristics

Tutorial note: For part 1 there is no requirement to refer to any accounting standard. Make sure you give the arguments for each method.

When answering part 2 consider other forms of intangible assets, e.g. development expenditure, patents, and consider how these types of items differ from goodwill. Remember to answer both parts of the question.

(1) **Methods of accounting for purchased goodwill**

Carry goodwill as an asset and amortise it over its estimated useful economic life through the profit and loss account.

This method recognises goodwill as an asset which, if the business is a going concern, is in principle no different from any other asset with a finite useful life. It has a 'cost' which should be written off over the periods that are expected to benefit from the existence of this goodwill.

Eliminate goodwill against reserves immediately on acquisition.

This method treats all goodwill, purchased and inherent (non-purchased), in a consistent manner. Purchased goodwill may, through effluxion of time, be replaced by inherent goodwill. Therefore consistent treatment of the two would appear to be appropriate.

Retain goodwill in the accounts indefinitely, unless an impairment in its value becomes evident.

The method does not require a subjective estimate of its useful life (for amortisation purposes). In addition, an asset for which consideration has been given continues to be disclosed in the balance sheet. This may be considered to be more informative than when it is eliminated as a 'reserve movement'.

(2) **The distinguishing characteristics of goodwill**

- It is a 'balancing figure'. Goodwill itself is not valued but a comparison is made between the fair value of the whole business and the fair value of the separable net assets of the business. It cannot be valued on its own.
- Goodwill cannot be disposed of as a separate asset.
- The factors contributing to the value of goodwill cannot be valued, e.g. how can one value the benefit of a experienced workforce?
- The value of goodwill is volatile – it can only be given a numerical value at the time of acquisition of the whole business.

If the characteristics listed above are considered to be material, goodwill can be considered to be unique and requiring special treatment. The argument in favour of the first method – amortisation – cannot be considered to be relevant. Because of this uniqueness it may be considered more appropriate either to eliminate it (therefore 'removing' the problem) as advocated in the second method, or effectively ignore it by leaving it untouched in the balance sheet, as advocated in the third method.

An alternative view is that these characteristics still label goodwill as an asset. If this argument is favoured, the amortisation method would be the most appropriate.

Thus, while these characteristics label goodwill as an asset, they do not lead automatically to a single acceptable method of accounting for goodwill.

CHAPTER 17 EXAM-TYPE QUESTION

Calver plc

(a) Why FRS 11 was necessary

FRS 11 was issued in response to a number of perceived problems as follows.

It is accepted practice that a fixed asset should not be carried in financial statements at more than its recoverable amount, i.e. the higher of the amount for which it could be sold and the amount recoverable from its future use. However, there was very little authoritative guidance as to how the recoverable amount should be identified or measured.

The Companies Act requires provision to be made for permanent diminutions in the value of fixed assets. There was no clear definition of what constituted a permanent (as opposed to a temporary) diminution.

There was uncertainty as to how diminutions should be presented in the financial statements, for example, were they to be treated as additional depreciation (which affected profits) or as downward revaluations (which did not)?

As a result of these problems, accounting practice was often inconsistent and there was a risk that impairments might occur without being recognised in the financial statements.

In December 1997 the ASB issued FRS 10 *Goodwill and intangible assets.* FRS 10 requires annual impairment reviews where goodwill and intangible assets have a useful life exceeding twenty years. FRS 15 *Tangible fixed assets* also requires impairment reviews to be performed under certain circumstances. These requirements increased the need for a new FRS on impairment.

(b) Recoverable amount

FRS 11 defines recoverable amount as the higher of net realisable value and value in use. Net realisable value is the amount at which an asset could be disposed of, less any direct selling costs. Value in use is the present value of the future cash flows obtainable as a result of an asset's continued use, including those resulting from its ultimate disposal.

The rationale behind these definitions is that, when a fixed asset becomes impaired, the decision must be made whether to continue to use it or to sell it. This decision is based on the cash flows that can be generated by following each course of action, so that an entity will not continue to use the asset if it can realise more cash by selling it and vice versa. This means that when an asset is stated at the higher of net realisable value or value in use it is recorded at its greatest value to the entity.

(c) Impairment loss

	£m
Carrying amount	500
Recoverable amount	(385)
Impairment loss	115

Recoverable amount is value in use (£385.3 million) as this is higher than net realisable value (W1).

(W1) **Net realisable value:**

	£m
Goodwill	–
Patent	–
Freehold land and buildings	270
Plant and equipment	50
	320

(d) **How the loss will be treated**

The impairment loss must be allocated to the various fixed assets in the following order: first, goodwill, second, other intangible assets; and finally to tangible assets, either pro-rata or on another more appropriate basis.

	Before impairment £m	*Impairment loss* £m	*After impairment* £m
Goodwill	45	(45)	–
Patent	25	(25)	–
Freehold land and buildings	320	(33) (W2)	287
Plant and machinery	110	(12) (W2)	98
	500	(115)	385

Because the freehold land and buildings have been revalued, and the loss does not relate to the consumption of economic benefits, the impairment is recognised in the statement of total recognised gains and losses until the carrying amount of the asset reaches its depreciated historical cost. The depreciated historical cost of the freehold land and buildings is £265 million, less than the new carrying amount of £287 million, and therefore the whole of the impairment of £33 million may be taken to the statement of total recognised gains and losses. The impairment must be separately disclosed on the face of the statement.

The remainder of the impairment loss (£82 million) must be recognised in the profit and loss account for the year. It must be included within operating profit under the appropriate statutory headings and may also need to be disclosed as an exceptional item.

In the notes to the financial statements, the loss on the freehold land and buildings is treated as a downward revaluation and included within the revalued carrying amount of fixed assets. The remaining impairment loss (on the intangible assets and on plant and machinery) is treated as additional depreciation. The cost of the assets is not reduced.

(W2)

The impairment loss of £115m must first be allocated to the goodwill (£45m) and the patent (£25m). This leaves £45m to be allocated pro rata to the tangible assets.

Loss on land and buildings = $\frac{320}{430} \times$ £45m = £33m

Loss on plant and machinery = $\frac{110}{430} \times$ £45m = £12m

EXAM-TYPE QUESTION

Rowsley plc

In all four cases, the key issue is whether or not a provision should be recognised. Under FRS 12 *Provisions, contingent liabilities and contingent assets*, a provision should only be recognised when:

- there is a present obligation as a result of a past event
- it is probable that a transfer of economic benefits will be required to settle the obligation
- a reliable estimate can be made of the amount of the obligation.

(a) **Factory closure**

As the factory closure changes the way in which the business is conducted (it involves the relocation of business activities from one part of the country to another) it appears to fall within the FRS 12 definition of a restructuring.

The key issue here is whether the company has an obligation to incur expenditure in connection with the restructuring. There is clearly no legal obligation, but there may be a constructive obligation. FRS 12 states that a constructive obligation only exists if the company has created valid expectations in other parties, such as employees, customers and suppliers, that the restructuring will actually be carried out. As the company is still drawing up a formal plan for the restructuring and no announcements have been made to any of the parties affected, there cannot be an obligation to restructure. A board decision alone is not sufficient. Therefore no provision should be made.

If the company starts to implement the restructuring or makes announcements to those affected before the accounts are approved by the directors, it may be necessary to disclose the details in the financial statements as required by FRS 21 *Events after the balance sheet date*. This will be the case if the restructuring is of such importance that non-disclosure would affect the ability of the users of the financial statements to reach a proper understanding of the company's financial position.

(b) **Operating lease**

The lease contract appears to be an onerous contract as defined by FRS 12 (i.e. the unavoidable costs of meeting the obligations under it exceed the economic benefits expected to be received under it).

Because the company has signed the lease contract, there is a clear legal obligation and the company will have to transfer economic benefits (pay the lease rentals) in settlement. Therefore the company should recognise a provision for the remaining lease payments. The company may recognise a corresponding asset in relation to the nominal rentals currently being received, if these are virtually certain to continue. (In practice, it is unlikely that this amount is material). As the chances of renting the premises at a commercial rent are less than 50%, no further potential rent receivable may be taken into account.

The financial statements should disclose the carrying amount at the balance sheet date, a description of the nature of the obligation and the expected timing of the lease payments, and the amount of any expected rentals receivable from sub-letting. If an asset is recognised in respect of any rentals receivable, this should also be disclosed.

(c) **Legal proceedings**

It is unlikely that the company has a present obligation to compensate the customer and therefore no provision should be recognised. However, there is a contingent liability. Unless the possibility of a transfer of economic benefits is remote, the financial statements should disclose a brief description of the nature of the contingent liability, an estimate of its financial effect and an indication of the uncertainties relating to the amount or timing of any outflow.

(d) **Environmental damage**

It is clear that there is no legal obligation to rectify the damage. However, through its published policies, the group has created expectations on the part of those affected that it will take action to do so. There is therefore a constructive obligation to rectify the damage and a transfer of economic benefits is probable.

The company must recognise a provision for the best estimate of the cost. As the most likely outcome is that more than one attempt at re-planting will be needed, the full amount of £30 million should be provided. The expenditure will take place some time in the future, and so the provision should be discounted at a pre-tax rate that reflects current market assessments of the time value of money and the risks specific to the liability.

The financial statements should disclose the carrying amount at the balance sheet date, a description of the nature of the obligation and the expected timing of the expenditure. The financial statements should also give an indication of the uncertainties about the amount and timing of the expenditure.

CHAPTER **19**

EXAM-TYPE QUESTION

D Ltd

Tutorial note: A straightforward question on FRS 5. The problem in part (b) is reasonably easy, but note the analysis. Following these steps should concentrate your mind and ensure some marks, even when the transaction is more complex than this.

(a) **Recognising assets and liabilities**

The central requirement of FRS 5 *Reporting the substance of transactions* is that entities should report the commercial substance of transactions in their financial statements, rather than their strict legal form. A key step in determining the substance of a transaction is to identify its effect on the assets and liabilities of the entity.

FRS 5 defines an asset as 'rights or other access to future economic benefits controlled by an entity as a result of past transactions or events'. Control is the ability to obtain the future economic benefits relating to an asset and to restrict the access of others to those benefits. This means that it is more than the management of an asset. In practice, an entity which has access to benefits usually suffers or gains if those benefits turn out to be different from those expected. The ability to obtain benefits also implies exposure to risks. Evidence of whether an entity has benefits (and therefore has an asset) is given by whether it is exposed to the risks inherent in those benefits.

A liability is defined as 'an obligation to transfer economic benefits as a result of past transactions or events'. If an entity cannot avoid an outflow of resources, it has a liability. The reason for the obligation may be legal or commercial (for example, an entity may have no realistic alternative to refunding the price of defective goods, even though there is no legal obligation to do so).

An asset or a liability should be recognised if there is sufficient evidence of its existence. Evidence of the existence of an asset or liability may include evidence that a future inflow or outflow of benefit will occur.

Assets and liabilities cannot be recognised unless they can be measured at a monetary amount with sufficient reliability. The fundamental concept of prudence is relevant here. A liability should be recognised where a reasonable estimate of the amount can be made. A greater level of reliability is necessary before an asset can be recognised.

Subsequent transactions may affect assets that have previously been recognised in the financial statements. For example, an asset may be financed by means of a sale and repurchase agreement. Provided that this does not result in any significant changes to the entity's rights to benefits and exposure to risks inherent in those benefits, it should continue to recognise the asset in its financial statements. (The entity may also need to recognise a liability for the finance.)

Where a transaction transfers to others all significant rights to benefits associated with an asset, and significant exposure to the risks inherent in those benefits, the entire asset should cease to be recognised.

(b) **Accounting treatment for the new transaction**

The managing director has suggested that the company recognises the vehicles only when title passes to it, which is to account for the strict legal form of the transaction. FRS 5 requires it to account for the commercial substance of the transaction, which may not be the same.

The key issue is whether D Ltd has the benefits and is exposed to the risks associated with the vehicles. If the company has the benefits and risks then it should recognise the vehicles in its financial statements.

The benefits normally associated with holding stock are:

- the right to sell the stock and obtain future cash flows
- insulation from increases in price charged by the manufacturer
- the right to use the stock.

The risks normally associated with holding stock are:

- the risk of making a loss on the sale
- slow movement (possibly with increased holding and financing costs)
- obsolescence.

D Ltd has the right to sell the vehicles, as E plc cannot normally demand their return (a benefit). The price at which it buys the vehicles depends on the date of delivery, not the date on which legal title passes (insulation from price rises – a benefit). D Ltd has the right to use the vehicles (a benefit).

E plc can demand the return of the vehicles if D Ltd becomes insolvent, but in practice, this is unlikely to happen.

D Ltd pays a penalty if it returns the vehicles to E plc. The size of the penalty means that D Ltd stands to lose a significant sum if it returns the vehicles (a risk). Although the transfer price rises by 1% for every complete month that the vehicles are held, this additional charge is effectively an interest charge (increased stock holding costs – a risk). D Ltd cannot return damaged or obsolete stock (a risk).

In this case, it is fairly clear that D Ltd has the benefits and is exposed to the risks associated with holding the vehicles as stock, even before legal title passes. In order to comply with the requirements of FRS 5, therefore, all vehicles held by the company at 31 August 20X6 must be included in the balance sheet as stock. This also means that there will be a corresponding liability to E plc included in current liabilities, representing the amount that will be paid for the stock plus any accrued finance charges.

CHAPTER 20

EXAM-TYPE QUESTION

Jones plc

(a) **MEMORANDUM**

To: Finance Director, Jones plc

From: ABC, Accountant

Date: XX-XX-XX

Accounting for lease/hire of 'Vinnie'

Option A

Owing to the size of the option to purchase, and to the fact that the hire term is substantially shorter than the Vinnie's useful economic life, SSAP 21 dictates that this arrangement (unusually for an HP agreement) should be accounted for as an operating lease.

Amounts in the financial statements should therefore be as follows:

Profit and loss account

	£
Hire of plant and machinery (W1)	125,000

Balance sheet

Prepayments and accrued income (W1)	75,000

Option B

The primary period of this lease is for the whole of the Vinnie's useful economic life. This lease must therefore be accounted for as a finance lease, as the risks and rewards of ownership have passed totally to the lessee. The sum of the years' digits method of allocating finance charges has been adopted. A straight line method would have been unacceptable due to the size of the lease, while actuarial methods could have been used as an alternative to sum of digits.

Amounts in the financial statements should therefore be as follows:

Balance sheet

Creditors: amounts falling due	*within one year* £	*after one year* £
Net obligation under finance leases (W2)	40,000	450,000
Accruals and deferred income (W2)	70,000	
Fixed assets, tangible		
Plant held under finance leases:		
Cost		600,000
Depreciation $\frac{600,000}{8}$		75,000

Profit and loss account

Depreciation on plant held under finance leases	75,000
Finance charges on finance leases (W2)	70,000

Option C

The contracted lease term is only for half of the useful economic life of the Vinnie and thus the risks and rewards of ownership have not passed to the lessee. Accordingly, Jones plc should account for this lease as an operating lease.

Amounts in the financial statements should therefore be:

Profit and loss account

	£
Hire of plant and machinery	150,000

(b) **Accounting treatments in Backward Bust plc's books**

Option A

The transaction would be treated as an operating lease. Therefore the balance sheet would show the plant as a tangible fixed asset, and the rentals receivable would be credited to profit and loss account. The deposit would be credited to profit and loss account over the four-year period on a straight-line basis.

Option B

The transaction would be treated as a finance lease. Thus the balance sheet would show as a current asset the capital amount outstanding under the lease, and the profit and loss account would be credited with the interest element of the lease rentals received.

Option C

All residual amounts are guaranteed to Backward Bust plc, although not necessarily by Jones plc. Backward Bust plc should therefore account for this transaction as a finance lease.

Workings

		£
(W1)	**Option A**	
	Total payment over lease term	500,000
	Profit and loss charge per annum (4 years)	125,000
	Amount paid 20X7	200,000
	Prepayment 31.12.X7	75,000

		£
(W2)	**Option B:** net obligation	
	Capitalised amount (fair value)	600,000
	Rentals 20X7	(110,000)
		490,000
	Finance charges in 20X7 rentals (as in advance)	–
	Net obligation	490,000
	Of which due within one year	
	Instalment 20X8	110,000
	Less finance charges 20X7	(70,000)
		40,000

Finance charges

	£
Minimum lease payments (8 × £110,000)	880,000
Fair value	(600,000)
Total	280,000

Allocated to 20X7 (sum of digits) $= \frac{7}{8(8-1)(\frac{1}{2})} \times £280,000$

= £70,000

Tutorial note

- To charge the full £200,000 paid under Option A to profit and loss account in 20X7 would be inappropriate as it would not follow the matching concept set out in SSAP 21 for operating leases.
- The '90% test' is totally unnecessary in Option B (which is just as well, as no information is given) because the risks and rewards of ownership, i.e. the rights to the undivided enjoyment of the leased asset, have passed to the lessee.
- The '90% test' could have been applied under Option C, but this would have been a waste of time as the lease is clearly an operating lease from useful economic life considerations. The maintenance and insurance are of peripheral importance.

For information:

Fair value = £600,000

PV of minimum lease payments = £501,188 (i.e. 83.5% of fair value).

CHAPTER 20 — EXAM-TYPE QUESTION

P Ltd

(a) ***MEMORANDUM***

To: Assistant Accountant

From: Chief Accountant

Subject: Leasing and the gearing ratio

Date: 22 November 20X5

SSAP 21 *Accounting for leases and hire purchase contracts* defines two types of lease: a finance lease and an operating lease.

A finance lease is a lease which transfers substantially all the risks and rewards of ownership of an asset to the lessee. A lease is presumed to be a finance lease if the present value of the minimum lease payments, including any initial payment, amounts to substantially all (90% or more) of the fair value of the leased asset. An operating lease is a lease other than a finance lease.

SSAP 21 requires that the financial statements reflect the commercial substance of lease agreements, rather than their strict legal form. Operating leases are treated as rental agreements, there is no effect on the balance sheet and therefore no effect on gearing. The commercial effect of a finance lease is that the lessee has raised a loan in order to acquire an asset, regardless of the fact that the lessee does not legally own the asset. Therefore the asset is included in fixed assets and depreciated over its estimated useful economic life. The capital element of future lease rentals is included in the balance sheet as a liability. Because of this treatment, a finance lease would have an adverse effect on the gearing ratio.

In theory, it would be possible to draft a lease agreement so that the lease failed the '90% test' and was therefore an operating lease. However, SSAP 21 states that a lease should be classified as a finance lease if it can be clearly demonstrated that substantially all the risks and rewards of ownership are transferred to the lessee. For example, the leasing agreement currently under consideration gives P Ltd the right to use the asset for most of its economic life and therefore should be treated as a finance lease. There are other indications that the lease is a finance lease. P Ltd is responsible for repairs and maintenance and has an option to purchase the asset at the end of the lease term.

FRS 5 *Reporting the substance of transactions* requires financial statements to reflect the economic substance of transactions, rather than their strict legal form. The effect of these two accounting standards is that leasing can no longer be used as 'off balance sheet' finance.

(b) **Balance sheet at 31 December 20X5 (extracts)**

	£
Tangible fixed assets: plant and machinery	1,900,000
Creditors: amounts falling due within one year	
Obligations under finance leases	340,480
Creditors: amounts falling due after more than one year	
Obligations under finance leases	1,579,714

Notes to the profit and loss account for the year ended 31 December 20X5

	£
Operating profit is stated after charging:	
Depreciation on leased assets	100,000
Interest payable and similar charges	
Finance leases (W1)	42,514

Notes to the balance sheet (extracts)

	£
Plant and machinery	
Tangible fixed assets	
Cost at 1 January 20X5	–
Additions	2,000,000
Cost at 31 December 20X5	2,000,000
Accumulated depreciation at 1 January 20X5	–
Charge for the year (2,000,000 × 3/12 ÷ 5)	100,000
Accumulated depreciation at 31 December 20X5	100,000
Net book value at 31 December 20X5	1,900,000
Obligations under finance leases (W2)	
Falling due within one year	340,480
Falling due within two to five years	1,579,714
	1,920,194

Workings

(W1) **Interest**

	£
Total payments (122,320 × 20)	2,446,400
Less: Fair value (taken as cost)	2,000,000
	446,400
Payable in year ended 31 December 20X5	
(20/210 × 446,400)	42,514
Payable in year ended 31 December 20X6	
((19 + 18 + 17 + 16)/210 × 446,400)	148,800

(W2) **Lease creditor**

	Balance b/d	*Interest*	*Repayment*	*Balance c/d*
	£	£	£	£
20X5	2,000,000	42,514	(122,320)	1,920,194
20X6	1,920,194	148,800	(489,280)	1,579,714

CHAPTER 21

EXAM-TYPE QUESTION

Earnit plc

(a) **Earnings per share for the year ended 31 March 20X5**

Basic:

$$\frac{34}{525} = 6.48 \text{ pence}$$

Diluted:

$$\frac{34}{552.5} = 6.15 \text{ pence}$$

Workings

(W1) **Basic earnings**

	£m
Profit after tax	45
Appropriation of profit to non-equity shareholders	(11)
	34

(W2) **Weighted average number of ordinary shares in issue:**

Date	*No of shares in issue* (million)	*Weighted average* (million)
1 April – 30 September	500 × 6/12	250
1 October – 31 March	550 × 6/12	275
		525

(W3) Weighted average number of potential ordinary shares

	Million	Million
Weighted average number of ordinary shares in issue (W2)		525.0
Number of shares under option:		
1 April – 30 September (100 × 6/12)	50.0	
1 October – 31 March (120 × 6/12)	60.0	
	110.0	
Number of shares that would have been issued at fair value (110 × 1.50/2.00)	(82.5)	
		27.5
		552.5

(b) **The usefulness of basic and diluted earnings per share to an equity shareholder**

Basic earnings per share measures the earnings (profit) in relation to each equity share and is regarded as a key measure of performance.

(i) FRS 22 *Earnings per share* sets out the method of calculation and required disclosures. Therefore shareholders can compare the return on their investment for the current period with previous periods. Shareholders can also compare the earnings underlying their investment with the earnings underlying investments in similar entities.

(ii) Earnings per share is used to calculate the price earnings ratio, which represents the market's view of the future prospects of a share. The price earnings ratio enables shareholders to judge the cost of a share relative to the earnings that it produces.

Diluted earnings per share alerts equity shareholders to the possibility that there may be additional equity shares in future periods as the result of the exercise of existing capital instruments such as options and warrants. If this is the case, their investment income may be reduced. This applies to Earnit plc, which has issued options for shares which are likely to be exercised (because the shares can be issued below the current market price). Diluted earnings per share shows the earnings per share if all the options were exercised. This is 5.1% lower than basic earnings per share and this indicates that there is a small risk associated with the shares.

The usefulness of earnings per share may be limited by the following factors.

1 It is not necessarily a predictor of future earnings because it is based on historical information. It only measures past performance. This also applies to diluted earnings per share as calculated in accordance with FRS 14 and for this reason it is only of limited use as a 'warning signal'.

2 The earnings figure is affected by an entity's choice of accounting policies. Therefore it may not always be appropriate to compare the earnings per share of different companies.

3 It does not take account of inflation. Apparent growth in earnings may not be true growth.

4 It only measures profitability, which is only one aspect of overall performance. In the longer term, cash flow, gearing and working capital management may be equally important influences on the return on an equity investment.

CHAPTER 22

EXAM-TYPE QUESTION

Wandafood Products

Tutorial note

- A typical interpretation question with the 'chore' of calculating the ratios removed.
- Use the grouping of the ratios as a guide to the format of your report.
- Remember to avoid repeating the data given in the question, and make sensible suggestions, including the need for more information.
- Make sure your answer includes comments on the effect of changing price levels on a 'trend analysis' of this type.

REPORT

To: Directors – Wandafood Products plc

From: AN Alyst – Certified Accountant

Date: X-X-20XX

Subject: **Interpretation and evaluation of five-year summary**

The following comments are based on a financial ratio analysis of the financial statements of Wandafood Products plc for the five-year period 20X5 to 20X9. The ratios and their method of computation are contained in the appendix to this report.

Tutorial note

- The appendix would contain the information given in the question.
- The ratios have been 'grouped' to aid interpretation – this report follows the same structure.

Profitability

The level of trading profit in relation to both sales and operating assets has remained relatively stable over the five-year period. The profit margin percentage declined in the early years of this period but has improved steadily since 20X7, reaching its peak in 20X9. Management should attempt to discover the reason for this trend, e.g. cost savings or increased selling price, and endeavour to maintain it. However, the level of profitability is now requiring the highest relative level of net operating assets. Management should be encouraged to make the optimum use of the assets available, but it is possible that the significant drop (over 7%) from 20X8 to 20X9 is the result of the acquisition of new assets which have yet to generate a return.

Interest and dividend cover

The interest cover has been very variable over the five-year period but does not appear to indicate any specific problem for the company. However, there is a constant downward trend from 20X6 and if this trend were to continue, the company may find it difficult to raise finance from lenders who use such a ratio as an indicator of a company's ability to meet its interest payments. Probably of more interest to such a group is the level of cash available to make such payments, making the liquidity ratios of more relevance.

The dividend cover indicates that in recent years the amount of earnings retained in the business for capital maintenance and expansion has increased. This may be as a result of prudent management, but the level of dividends must be maintained to give the owners (shareholders) a 'fair' return on their investment. This would be of particular interest to shareholders investing for periodic income not capital growth.

Debt to equity ratios

These ratios will be of interest to the lenders and shareholders considered in the previous section. The two ratios, one with and one without minority interests as part of equity, both follow the same pattern and the level of minority interests within the group has therefore probably been fairly constant.

These ratios, often referred to as 'gearing ratios' indicate that the relative amount of long-term finance provided by borrowings is increasing. This would account for the declining trend in interest cover discussed earlier. The level of gearing has become higher, such that 40% of long-term finance was provided by borrowings in 20X9 compared with only 10% in 20X6. This may be as a result of taking advantage of 'cheaper' long-term finance but management should take care; the higher the gearing, the riskier any investment in the company, particularly in periods of volatile profitability where fixed interest payments cannot be 'flexed' in line with the variable profit levels.

Liquidity ratios

These ratios are important indicators of the short-term viability of the company. It is important to remember that companies often go into receivership because of cash problems rather than a lack of profitability.

At present the company has insufficient liquid or near liquid assets to meet its current liabilities. This may initially be considered to show a sign of weakness in the company, but this position has existed since 20X6 and is therefore likely to be currently at an acceptable level. However, management must ensure that the position does not deteriorate. If it does, the company may find itself unable to continue to operate.

Asset ratios

The ratio of sales to net operating assets shows a slight decline. As mentioned earlier, this could be a result of increased investment in fixed assets but could also indicate falling relative sales. Management should ensure that any downtrend in 'real' sales levels is not allowed to continue.

The sales to working capital indicates a fall in the relative value of working capital. This is linked to the liquidity problem but indicates that there may be a more efficient use of the net current assets.

Per share

The three ratios indicate an improving earnings, dividends and net assets per share position. This may prove to be very useful if future long-term funds are to be requested from equity investors, either new shareholders or from current shareholders, by way of a rights issue. The ratio relating to net assets indicates that the company is perhaps financing additional assets by way of retained profits. The dividends per share have increased steadily which is a good management policy and the earnings per share have increased likewise.

Overall the position for shareholders looks favourable but it is necessary to consider these ratios in the light of the market prices of the shares during the five-year period. This would enable the calculation of the price/earnings (P/E) ratio, considered to be a very useful market indicator. The use of the share price would put these 'per share' ratios into a proper perspective.

Concluding remarks

In relation to some of the points made in this report, it is important that management consider the company's ratios in the light of those of other similar organisations. The company could consider participating in an inter-firm comparison scheme, which, while maintaining non-identification of participants, enables the comparison of the company's financial ratios with other similar companies and averages for that business sector.

Finally, the ratios used to compile this report have been calculated using information contained in financial statements prepared under the historic cost convention. It may be necessary to adjust some of the figures to reflect price level changes, particularly where one figure in the ratio is affected by inflation at a different rate to the other figure in the ratio. For example, some assets may require adjustment by reference to a specific index of price level changes while another would be adjusted using a general price index. This could materially affect the trend indicated by a ratio. It is generally advisable to attempt to express all the figures in the financial statements for the five years in pounds at the same date, perhaps based on the retail price index.

CHAPTER 23 PRACTICE QUESTION

Solid plc

Cash flow statement for the year ended 31 December 20X8

Reconciliation of operating profit to net cash inflow from operating activities

	£
Operating profit (W7)	75,450
Depreciation charges (W5)	19,000
Increase in stocks (51,000 – 37,000)	(14,000)
Increase in debtors (44,000 – 42,800)	(1,200)
Increase in creditors [48,000 – (34,000 – 440)]	14,440
Net cash inflow from operating activities	93,690

Cash flow statement

	£	£
Net cash inflow from operating activities		93,690
Returns on investments and servicing of finance:		
Interest received	450	
Interest paid (6,400 + 440)	(6,840)	
		(6,390)
Taxation:		
Corporation tax paid (W6)		(10,500)
Capital expenditure:		
Purchases of tangible fixed assets (W2)	(69,000)	
Receipts from sales of tangible fixed assets	4,000	
		(65,000)
Equity dividends paid		(10,000)
Net cash outflow before use of liquid resources and financing		1,800
Management of liquid resources:		
Purchase of government stock		(4,600)
Financing:		
Issue of share capital (50,000 + 20,000)	70,000	
Redemption of debentures	(42,000)	
		28,000
Increase in cash in the period		25,200

Reconciliation of net cash flow to movement in net debt (Note)

Increase in cash in the period	25,200
Cash outflow from redemption of debentures	42,000
Cash outflow from purchase of current asset investments	4,600
Change in net debt resulting from cash flows	71,800
Premium on redemption of debentures	(2,000)
Change in net debt for the period	69,800
Net debt at 1 January 20X8	(83,800)
Net debt at 31 December 20X8	(14,000)

***Note:* Analysis of changes in net debt**

	At 1 January 20X8	*Cash flows*	*Other changes*	*At 31 December 20X8*
	£	£	£	£
Cash at bank	200	11,200	-	11,400
Bank overdraft	(14,000)	14,000	-	-
Debentures	(70,000)	42,000	(2,000)	(30,000)
Current asset investments	-	4,600	-	4,600
Total	(83,800)	71,800	(2,000)	(14,000)

Workings

(W1) **Plant and machinery account – at cost**

	£		£
Balance b/d	120,000	Disposals a/c	8,000
Additions	39,000	Balance c/d	151,000
	159,000		159,000

(W2) **Fixtures and fittings account – at cost**

	£		£
Balance b/d	24,000	Disposals a/c	5,000
Additions	10,000	Balance c/d	29,000
	34,000		34,000

Fixed assets – additions summary

	£
Freehold property	20,000
Plant and machinery	39,000
Fixtures and fittings	10,000
	69,000

(W3) **Plant and machinery account – depreciation**

	£		£
Disposal a/c	6,000	Balance b/d	45,000
Balance c/d	54,000	Charge for year	15,000
	60,000		60,000

(W4) **Fixtures and fittings account – depreciation**

	£		£
Disposal a/c	2,000	Balance b/d	13,000
Balance c/d	15,000	Charge for year	4,000
	17,000		17,000

(W5) **Fixed assets disposals account**

	£		£
Plant cost	8,000	Plant depreciation	6,000
Fittings cost	5,000	Fittings depreciation	2,000
		Cash proceeds:	
		Plant	3,000
		Fittings	1,000
		Depreciation under-provided (bal. fig.)	1,000
	13,000		13,000

Depreciation – summary

	£
Plant	15,000
Fixtures	4,000
Disposals	1,000
	20,000

(W6) **Taxation**

The only figure relating to tax that requires computation for the cash flow statement is the total tax paid in the accounting period.

To determine the tax paid it is only necessary to insert all opening and closing balances relating to tax and the profit and loss account tax charge into a 'tax account'.

Tax account

	£		£
Cash paid (bal. fig.)	10,500	Balance b/d	
Balance c/d:		Deferred tax	11,000
Deferred tax	18,000	Corporation tax	10,500
Corporation tax	15,000	Profit and loss a/c	
		Deferred tax	9,500
		Corporation tax	12,500
	43,500		43,500

(W7) **Profit and loss account**

As the figure for operating profit is required, reconstruct the profit and loss account up to this figure.

Profit and loss account

	£	£
Operating profit (bal fig)		75,450
Loss on disposal of fixed assets		(1,000)
Interest received		450
Interest paid		(6,400)
Premium on redemption of debentures		(2,000)
		66,500
Taxation		
Corporation tax	12,500	
Deferred tax	9,500	
		(22,000)
		44,500
Dividends		(20,000)
Retained profit for year		24,500
Balance b/d		11,500
Balance c/d		36,000

CHAPTER 23 EXAM-TYPE QUESTION

Ozac plc

(a) **Cash flow statement for the year to 30 September 20X9**

Operating activities	£000	£000
Receipts from customers (W1)		3,170
Payments to suppliers (W2)		(928)
Payments to employees (W3)		(718)
Other cash operating expenses (W4)		(786)
Cash flow from operating activities		738
Returns on investments and servicing of finance		
Interest paid (W5)	(67)	
Investment income (W5)	9	
		(58)
Taxation (W6)		(52)
Capital expenditure (W7 728 + 800 – 190)		(1,338)
		(710)
Equity dividends paid (350 + 180 – 200)		(330
		(1,040)
Financing (W8)		1,090
Increase in cash (22 + 28)		50

Workings

(***Note:*** All figures in £000)

(W1) Receipts from customers:

Turnover	3,536
Adjust for debtors (260 – 194)	(66)
Non-cash adjustment – barter transaction	(300)
Cash receipts	3,170

(W2) Payments to suppliers:

Material consumed	1,079
Adjust for increase in stock (758 – 628)	130
Non-cash barter transaction	(300)
Reduction in creditors (253 – 234)	19
	928

(W3) Payments to employees:

Labour costs from question	758
Non-cash share issue cost (see W8)	(40)
	718

(W4) Other cash operating expenses:

Production overheads	453
Selling and distribution	221
Administration	252
Non-cash items:	
Depreciation (1,275 – 1,055)	(220)
Government grant	80
Cash paid	786

(W5) Returns on investments and servicing of finance:

Interest payable – from question	85
Amortisation of debenture discount and premium (below)	(18)
Cash flow for interest costs	67
Dividends from Tilzac Ltd (interim only – 15% of £60,000)	9

The discount on the issue of the debenture is £50,000 (5% of £1 million), and the premium is £40,000 (4% of £1 million). The total of these items (£90,000) is being amortised (straight-line) over five years. Therefore £18,000 (£90,000/5) has been included in interest payable and added to the net proceeds of £950,000 of the debenture to give the balance sheet carrying value of £968,000. This £18,000 is not a cash flow and must be adjusted for as above.

The cash flow statement should only include dividends actually received (the interim only), the accrual of the proposed final dividend from Tilzac Ltd is not a cash flow.

(W6) Taxation:

Charge to profit and loss account	210
Deferred tax (252 – 141)	(111)
Year end provisions (251 – 204)	(47)
Cash paid	52

(W7)	Capital expenditure:	
	Tangible fixed assets:	
	Cost c/f	3,368
	Cost b/f	(2,640)
	Additions for cash	728
	Purchase of fixed asset investment	800
	Government grants	
	Balance c/f (125 + 220)	345
	Amortised in year	80
	Balance b/f (75 + 160)	(235)
	Received in cash during year	190
(W8)	Financing:	
	Ordinary shares:	
	Increase in ordinary share capital (1,100 – 1,000)	100
	Increase in share premium (180 – 100)	80
	Non-cash element re share scheme (50 – 10)	(40)
	Cash received	140
	Debentures:	
	£1,000,000 issued at 95 (discount 5%)	950
		1,090

Index

A

Accounting period convention, 15
Abbreviated accounts, 194
Accounting for finance leases, 381
Accounting for hire purchase contracts, 382
Accounting for price level changes, 41
Accounting policies, 13, 415
Accounting principles, 15
Accounting standards, 58
Accounting Standards Board (ASB), 35, 51, 59, 60
Accounting Standards Committee (ASC), 58
Accretion approach, 35, 37
Accruals concept, 12, 33
Acid test ratio, 409
Acquisition costs, 135
Acquisitions (FRS 3), 243
Acquisitions and disposals, 433
Actuarial method, 376
Adjusted earnings statements, 50
Adjusting events, 353
Aggregation, 11, 162
Alternative rules, 163
Amortisation, 325, 329
Applied research, 333
Assets, 7, 36
Associated undertakings, 143
Attributable profit, 228, 229
Attributable tax credits, 208
Authorised share capital, 281

B

Balance sheet, 164
Balance sheet consolidation, 79
Basic EPS, 397
Big bath, 351
Bonus issues, 389
Brands, 327

C

Called up share capital, 176, 281, 292
Capital expenditure, 433
Capital maintenance concepts, 49, 51
Capital redemption, 282
Capitalising finance costs, 301
Cash, 424
Cash flow statements, 423
Cash shortfall, 444
Cherry picking, 310
Classification, 11
Collecting agent, 207
Companies Act 1989, 161
Company law, 57, 161
Comparability, 6
Completeness, 5
Compound instrument, 277
Comprehensive income, 23, 249
Conceptual framework, 1
Consignment stock, 363
Consistency, 6, 12
Consolidated accounts, 71
Consolidation working papers, 124
Construction obligation, 347
Contingent assets, 346
Contingent liabilities, 178, 313, 346
Continuing operations, 243
Contract accounts, 234
Contributions from owners, 8
Controlled non-subsidiaries, 360
Conventions, 12
Convertible loan stock, 393
Convertible preference shares, 393
Corporation tax, 205
Cost, 225
Counterbalancing liability, 85
Creative accounting, 62, 241
Credit sale agreement, 372
Creditors days, 408
Creditors: amounts falling due after more than one year, 175
Creditors: amounts falling due within one year, 174
Creditors' buffer, 286
Critical event approach, 37
Current accounts, 93
Currents assets, 172
Current cost accounting (CCA), 43, 45, 51
Current cost accounts, 416
Current liabilities, 172
Current operating performance concept, 23, 24
Current purchasing power accounting (CPP), 43, 44, 416
Current ratio, 409
Current tax, 208
Current values, 26

D

Dangling debit, 325
Debentures in a subsidiary company, 105
Debt factoring, 366
Debtors, 173
Debtors turnover, 407
Deferral and liability/accrual methods of accounting for deferred taxation, 218
Deferred taxation, 176, 214
Depreciation, 45, 46, 185, 307
Deprival method, 45
Deprival value, 25, 26
Derecognition, 10
Development, 333
Development expenditure, 292, 415
Diluted earnings per share, 392, 397
Direct method, 427
Directors' emoluments, 186
Directors' report, 192, 355
Disclosure, 6, 75, 361
Discontinued operations, 243
Discounting deferred tax assets and liabilities, 222
Discussion Paper, 62
Disposal of a revalued fixed asset, 306
Distributable profit, 289
Distributions to owners, 9
Dividend cover, 413
Dividend yield gross, 413
Dividends, 106, 208, 403

E

Earnings per share, 248, 387, 412
EC Directives, 58
EC Seventh Directive, 74
Elements of financial statements, 7
Entity concept, 72
Entity or accounting unit convention, 15

Equity dividends paid, 434
Equity instrument, 276
Equity method, 147
Estimation techniques, 13
Events after the balance sheet date, 354
Exceptional items, 188, 245, 438
Exchange value, 31
Excluded subsidiaries, 77
Exempt (i.e. non-taxable) items, 214
Exempt subsidiaries, 76
Extraordinary items, 241, 247

F

Fair value, 24, 132, 163, 324, 394
Faithful representation, 5
FIFO, 226
Finance leases, 372, 373, 438
Financial capital maintenance (FCM), 49, 52
Financial commitments, 178
Financial instrument, 276
Financial investment, 433
Financial Reporting Council (FRC), 59
Financial Reporting Exposure Draft (FRED), 62
Financial Reporting Review Panel (FRRP), 59, 60
Financial reporting standard for smaller entities (FRSSE), 197
Financial Reporting Standards (FRSs), 58
Financial statements, 3, 7
Financing cash flows, 435
Fixed assets, 46, 171
Foreseeable losses, 228
Format 1 – the vertical balance sheet, 164
FRS 1 Cash flow statements, 7, 423, 440
FRS 2 Accounting for subsidiary undertakings, 74
FRS 3 Reporting financial performance, 7, 241
FRS 5 Reporting the substance of transactions, 34, 359
FRS 7 Fair values in acquisition accounting, 28, 132
FRS 9 Associates and joint ventures, 144
FRS 8 Related party disclosures, 261
FRS 10 Goodwill and intangible assets, 28, 328
FRS 11 Impairment of fixed assets and goodwill, 28, 336
FRS 12 Provisions, contingent liabilities and contingent assets, 345
FRS 15 Tangible fixed assets, 29, 299
FRS 16 Current tax, 208
FRS 18 Accounting policies, 13
FRS 19 Deferred tax, 220
FRS 21 Events after the balance sheet date, 354
FRS 22 Earnings per share, 387, 413
FRS 25 Financial Instruments: Disclosure and Presentation, 275
FRS 26 Financial Instruments: measurement, 278
Full provision, 219
Fundamental reorganisation, 245
Future operating losses, 349

G

Gains, 8
Gearing, 410
General price changes, 52
Generally Accepted Accounting Practice (GAAP), 1
Geographical segments, 265
Going concern concept, 12
Goodwill, 80, 323, 329
Government grants, 311
Gross equity method, 152
Gross profit, 402
Gross profit percentage, 406
Group accounts, 72

H

Headline earnings, 397
Hire purchase, 371, 438
Historic cost accounting, 41, 42, 163, 416
Horizontal analysis, 401

I

IAS 32, 275
IAS 39 Financial instruments: Recognition and measurement, 278
IFRS 1 First-time adoption of International Financial Reporting Standards, 65
Impairment, 336
Impairment losses, 340
Impairment reviews, 330
Income from fixed asset investments, 187
Income generating units, 339
Increase of capital, 281
Indirect method, 442, 427
Intangible assets, 327
Intangible fixed assets, 168
Inter-company dividends, 119
Inter-company items, 93
Interest cover, 412
Interest payable, 187
Intermediate holding companies, 76
International Accounting Standards, 63
International Accounting Standards Board (IASB), 63
International Accounting Standards Committee (IASC), 63
International Financial Reporting Standards (IFRSs), 63
International Organisation of Securities Commissions, 64
Interpreting financial information, 401
Intra-group adjustments, 93
Intra-group interest, 132
Intra-group transactions, 127
Investment property, 314
Investments, 171, 173
Investors' ratios, 412
Issued share capital, 281

J

Joint arrangement, 146
Joint ventures, 146

L

Lease agreements, 372
Lessee, 374, 416
Liabilities, 8, 36, 345
Linked presentation, 362
Liquid resources, 434
Listing rules, 59
Long-term contracts, 35, 226, 230
Long-term financial stability, 410
Losses, 8

M

Manufacturer/dealer lessor, 383
Market purchase, 283
Materiality, 6, 164
Materiality convention, 16
Measurement, 27

Measurement of revenue, 31
Measurement systems, 51
Medium sized company accounts, 194
Merger accounting, 73
Minority interests, 85
Monetary items, 44

N

Negative goodwill, 135, 331
Net debt, 436
Net realisable value, 225, 338, 339
Neutrality, 5
Nil provision, 219
Non-adjusting events, 353
Non-cash transactions, 438
Non-equity shares, 436
Non-monetary items, 44
Note of historic cost profits and losses, 250
Notes to the balance sheet – current assets and liabilities, 172
Notes to the balance sheet – fixed assets, 168

O

Objectivity convention, 16
Off-market purchase, 282
Offset, 362
Offsetting of a financial asset and a financial liability, 278
Onerous contracts, 349
Operating activities, 426
Operating and Financial Review (OFR), 199
Operating leases, 372
Operating profit, 402
Options and warrants, 394
Ordinary activities, 247
Ordinary shares, 119
Ordinary shareholders, 102
Overdraft, 424
Overtrading, 412
Ownership interest, 8

P

Parent, 71
Partial provision, 220
Participating interest, 144
Partly-owned subsidiary, 96
Performance indicator, 387
Permissible capital payment (PCP, 283
Physical capital maintenance (PCM), 49
Policies, 13
Post balance sheet events, 352
Potential ordinary share, 392
Pre-acquisition dividends, 122
Preference shares, 102, 120
Pre-acquisition reserves, 82
Pre-incorporation profits, 293
Preference shares in subsidiaries, 102
Presentation of financial information, 10
Price/earnings ratio, 387, 413
Prior period adjustments, 188, 252
Production cost, 163
Profit after tax, 402
Profit and loss account – Format 1, 181
Profit and loss account – Format 2, 182
Profit before tax, 185, 402
Profit on ordinary activities before taxation, 184
Profit smoothing, 227
Profitability ratios, 404
Profits, 96
Proportional consolidation method, 147
Proposed dividends, 355
Provisions, 176, 313, 345
Prudence concept, 5, 12, 33
Purchase price, 163
Purchase their own shares, 282
Purchased goodwill, 323, 338
Pure (or basic) research, 333

Q

Qualitative characteristics of financial information, 4
Quasi-subsidiaries, 361
Quick ratio, 409

R

Ratio analysis, 403, 417
Real terms accounting, 50
Realisation principle, 33
Realised profits, 32
Realised revaluation gains, 306
Recognition, 10
Reconciliation of movements in shareholders' funds, 249
Recoverable amount, 338
Redeemable shares, 282
Redemption out of capital, 288
Reduction of capital, 281
Regulatory system of accounting, 57
Reimbursements, 348
Related parties, 257
Relevance, 5
Relevant accounts, 293
Reliability, 5
Reportable segments, 265
Research and development, 333
Reserves, 82, 177, 178, 275
Residual value, 307, 309
Restructuring, 245, 349
Retail Price Index (RPI), 44
Return on capital employed (ROCE), 404
Returns on investments and servicing of finance, 431
Revaluation deficits, 290
Revaluation gain, 305
Revaluation loss, 305
Revaluation of fixed assets, 303
Revaluation reserve, 177
Revaluation surpluses, 291
Revenue grants, 311
Revenue recognition, 31
Rights issues, 390

S

Sale and leaseback, 365
Sale and repurchase agreements, 364
Securities and Exchange Commission (SEC), 64
Segmental information, 264
Separate write-off reserve, 326
Share capital, 177, 275
Short-term financial stability, 408
Significant influence, 144
Small company statutory accounts, 196
Specific price changes, 52
SSAP 4 Accounting for government grants, 311
SSAP 5 Accounting for value added tax, 212
SSAP 9 Stocks and Long-term contracts, 37, 227
SSAP 13 Accounting for research and development, 333
SSAP 19 Accounting for investment properties, 313
SSAP 21 Accounting for leases and hire purchase contracts, 372
SSAP 25 Segmental reporting, 264

Staff costs, 187
Statement of Principles, 2, 73
Statement of total recognised gains and losses (STRGL), 241, 248
Statements of Standard Accounting Practice (SSAPs), 58
Statutory Instruments, 161
Stock Exchange, 59
Stock turnover, 406
Stock valuation, 225
Stocks, 172
Straight line method for interest, 378
Subsequent expenditure, 303
Subsidiary undertaking, 71, 74
Substance of a transaction, 33, 361
Substance over form convention, 16, 373
Sufficient evidence, 10
Sum of the years' digits method, 377

T

Tangible fixed assets, 170, 299, 415
Tax credit, 209
Tax on profit on ordinary activities, 188
Taxable items, 214
Taxable profit or loss, 208
Taxation, 432
Taxation provision, 176
Timing differences, 214
Transfers between current and fixed assets, 316
Treasury shares, 284, 289
Treasury Shares Regulations, 289
Trend analysis, 414
Trend information, 11
True and fair view, 58, 198

U

UITF Abstract 4 Presentation of long-term debtors in current assets, 62
UITF Abstract 5 Transfers from current assets to fixed assets, 316
UITF Abstract 15 Disclosure of substantial acquisitions, 75
UITF Abstract 37 Purchases and sales of own shares, 289
UITF Abstract 40 Revenue recognition and service contracts, 40
Understandability, 6
Undistributable reserves, 292
Unfranked investment income (UFII), 207
Unrealised profits, 96, 291
Urgent Issues Task Force (UITF), 59, 61
Useful economic life, 307, 309
Users of financial statements, 3

V

Valuation methods, 226
Value in use, 338, 339
VAT, 212

W

Warrants, 393
Wholly-owned subsidiary, 96
Window dressing, 353, 410
Withholding taxes, 208
Written reports, 413

Y

Yellow Book, 59

Z

Zero-rated, 214

FTC Foulks Lynch
A **Kaplan Professional** Company

STUDY TEXT REVIEW FORM
ACCA Paper 2.5 UK

Thank you for choosing this text for your ACCA professional qualification. As we are constantly striving to improve our products, we would be grateful if you could provide us with feedback about how useful you found this publication.

Name: ....

Address: ....

....

Email: ....

Why did you decide to purchase this Study Text?

- Have used them in the past ☐
- Recommended by lecturer ☐
- Recommended by friend ☐
- Saw advertising ☐
- Other (please specify)...

How do you study?

- At a college ☐
- On a distance learning course ☐
- Home study ☐
- Other (please specify)...

Within our ACCA range we also offer Exam Kits and Pocket Notes. Is there any other type of service/publication that you would like to see as part of the range?

- CD Rom with additional questions and answers ☐
- A booklet that would help you master exam skills and techniques ☐
- Space on our website that would answer your technical questions and queries ☐
- Other (please specify)...

During the past six month do you recall seeing/receiving any of the following?

- Our advertisement in *Student Accountant* magazine? ☐
- Our advertisement in any other magazine? (please specify) ☐

....

- Our leaflet/brochure or a letter through the post? ☐
- Other (please specify)...

Overall opinion of this Study Text

	Excellent	*Adequate*	*Poor*
Introductory pages	☐	☐	☐
Syllabus coverage	☐	☐	☐
Clarity of explanations	☐	☐	☐
Clarity of definitions and key terms	☐	☐	☐
Diagrams	☐	☐	☐
Activities	☐	☐	☐
Self-test questions	☐	☐	☐
Practice questions	☐	☐	☐
Answers to practice questions	☐	☐	☐
Layout	☐	☐	☐
Index	☐	☐	☐

If you have further comments/suggestions or have spotted any errors, please write them on the next page.

Please return this form to: The Publisher, FTC Foulks Lynch, FREEPOST NAT 17540, Wokingham RG40 1BR

Other comments/suggestions and errors

ftc
FTC Foulks Lynch
A **Kaplan Professional** Company

ACCA Order Form

Swift House, Market Place, Wokingham, Berkshire RG40 1AP, UK
Tel: +44 (0) 118 989 0629 Fax: +44 (0) 118 979 7455
Order online: www.financial-training.com
Email: publishing@financial-training.com

Examination Date: Dec 05 ☐ Jun 06 ☐ (please tick the exam you intend to take)		Study Text £26.00	Exam Kit Dec 05 £13.00	Exam Kit Jun 06 £14.00	Pocket Notes £10.00	Drill & Practice £10.00
Part 1						
1.1	Preparing Financial Statements (UK)	☐	☐	☐	☐	☐
1.1	Preparing Financial Statements (International)	☐	☐	☐	☐	☐
1.2	Financial Information for Management	☐	☐	☐	☐	☐
1.3	Managing People	☐	☐	☐	☐	N/A
Part 2						
2.1	Information Systems	☐	☐	☐	☐	N/A
2.2	Corporate & Business Law (English)	☐	☐	☐	☐	N/A
2.2	Corporate & Business Law (Scottish)	☐	N/A	N/A	N/A	N/A
2.3	Business Taxation – FA 2004	☐	☐	N/A	☐	N/A
2.3	Business Taxation – FA 2005	☐	N/A	☐	☐	N/A
2.4	Financial Management & Control	☐	☐	☐	☐	N/A
2.5	Financial Reporting (UK)	☐	☐	☐	☐	N/A
2.5	Financial Reporting (International)	☐	☐	☐	☐	N/A
2.6	Audit & Internal Review (UK)	☐	☐	☐	☐	N/A
2.6	Audit & Internal Review (International)	☐	☐	☐	☐	N/A
Part 3						
3.1	Audit & Assurance Services (UK)	☐	☐	☐	☐	N/A
3.1	Audit & Assurance Services (International)	☐	☐	☐	☐	N/A
3.2	Advanced Taxation – FA 2004	☐	☐	N/A	☐	N/A
3.2	Advanced Taxation – FA 2005	☐	N/A	☐	☐	N/A
3.3	Performance Management	☐	☐	☐	☐	N/A
3.4	Business Information Management	☐	☐	☐	☐	N/A
3.5	Strategic Business Planning & Development	☐	☐	☐	☐	N/A
3.6	Advanced Corporate Reporting (UK)	☐	☐	☐	☐	N/A
3.6	Advanced Corporate Reporting (International)	☐	☐	☐	☐	N/A
3.7	Strategic Financial Management	☐	☐	☐	☐	N/A
Research and Analysis Project Guide (supporting Oxford Brookes University BSc (Hons) in Applied Accounting)		☐				
Postage, Packaging and Delivery (per item):	**Note**: Maximum postage charged for UK orders is £15				**TOTAL**	

Study Texts and Exam Kits	*First*	*Each Extra*	**Pocket Notes and Drill & Practice**	*First*	*Each Extra*
UK	£5.00	£2.00	UK	£2.00	£1.00
Europe (incl Republic of Ireland and Channel Isles)	£7.00	£4.00	Europe (incl Republic of Ireland and Channel Isles)	£3.00	£2.00
Rest of World	£22.00	£8.00	Rest of World	£8.00	£5.00

Product Sub Total £.................. **Postage & Packaging £................** **Order Total £....................** **(Payments in UK £ Sterling)**

Customer Details

☐ Mr ☐ Mrs ☐ Ms ☐ Miss Other ....

Initials:.................................. Surname: ....

Address: ....

....

....

Postcode: ....

Delivery Address – if different from above

Address: ....

....

Postcode: ....

Telephone: ....

Email: ....

Fax: ....

Delivery please allow: United Kingdom – 5 working days
Europe – 8 working days
Rest of World – 10 working days

Payment

1 I enclose Cheque/Postal Order/Bankers Draft for £....................................

Please make cheques payable to '**The Financial Training Company Ltd**'.

2 Charge MasterCard/Visa/Switch/Delta no:

Valid from: Expiry date:

Issue no:

(Switch only) Verification No.

Signature: .... Date: ....

Declaration

I agree to pay as indicated on this form and understand that The Financial Training Company's Terms and Conditions apply (available on request).

Signature: .... Date: ....

Notes: All orders over 1kg will be fully tracked & insured. Signature required on receipt of order. Delivery times subject to stock availability. A telephone number or email address is required for orders that are to be delivered to a PO Box number.

ACCA
Approved Publisher

ftc

FTC Foulks Lynch

A **Kaplan Professional** Company

ACCA Distance Learning Enrolment Form

Surname First Name Mr / Miss / Mrs / Ms

Home Address

Post Code Country

Home Tel Office Tel

Mobile E-mail

Date of Birth ACCA Registration Number

Exam sitting: ☐ CBE ☐ December 2005 ☐ June 2006

EMPLOYER DETAILS (Sponsor must be UK based company)

Company Name

Manager's Name

Address

Post Code Country

Telephone Email

SPONSORED STUDENTS: EMPLOYER'S AUTHORISATION

If the above employer is responsible for the payment of fees, please complete the following:

As employer of the student for whom this form is completed, we are responsible for payment of fees due on receipt of the invoice in respect of the student named above and undertake to inform you in writing of any change to this arrangement. We understand that we are fully responsible for the payment of fees due in all circumstances including termination of employment or cancellation of course.

Purchase Order Number ______________________

Manager's Name ______________________

Manager's Signature ______________________ Date ______________

DATA PROTECTION ACT:

Your sponsor can be informed of your test results unless we are otherwise notified.

HOW TO ENROL:

By phone: If you are paying by credit card, please telephone +44 (0)113 200 6363

By post: Complete this enrolment form and return to:
FTC Foulks Lynch Distance Learning, 49 St Paul's Street, LEEDS LS1 2TE

By fax: Fax both sides of your completed enrolment form to +44 (0)113 243 0133

Distance Learning Courses include VAT and all materials. Add postage & packing – applicable to both Distance Learning options (for rates see below).		**Distance Learning**		**Distance Learning** (excluding Official ACCA Study Text applicable for the December 2005 and June 2006 examinations sittings only)	
		£	✓	£	✓
Part 1					
1.1	Preparing Financial Statements (UK)	114		88	
1.1	Preparing Financial Statements (International)	114		88	
1.2	Financial Information for Management	114		88	
1.3	Managing People	114		88	
Part 2					
2.1	Information Systems	114		88	
2.2	Corporate & Business Law	114		88	
2.3	Business Taxation	114		88	
2.4	Financial Management and Control	114		88	
2.5	Financial Reporting (UK)	114		88	
2.5	Financial Reporting (International)	114		88	
2.6	Audit & Internal Review (UK)	114		88	
2.6	Audit & Internal Review (International)	114		88	
Part 3 Options					
3.1	Audit & Assurance Services (UK)	114		88	
3.1	Audit & Assurance Services (International)	114		88	
3.2	Advanced Taxation	114		88	
3.3	Performance Management	114		88	
3.4	Business Information Management	114		88	
Part 3 Core					
3.5	Strategic Business Planning & Development	114		88	
3.6	Advanced Corporate Reporting (UK)	114		88	
3.6	Advanced Corporate Reporting (International)	114		88	
3.7	Strategic Financial Management	114		88	

FEES	£
Postage & Packing	£
Total	£

POSTAGE & PACKING
Distance Learning (per paper):
UK & NI £6, Europe & Channel Islands £15, Rest of World £40

DISTANCE LEARNING TERMS AND CONDITIONS OF ENROLMENT:

1. A completed enrolment form must be accompanied by the full fee or employer's authorisation.
2. Where an employer's authorisation is received, the full fees are payable within 30 days of the invoice date. The employer is responsible for the payment of fees due in all circumstances including termination of employment or cancellation of course. FTC reserves the right to charge interest on overdue accounts.
3. A deferral can be processed to the following exam sitting subject to a deferral fee of £25 if notified in writing. If new study materials are required due to syllabus changes or changes in Finance Acts, they will have to be paid for in addition to the deferral fee.
4. Refunds are only available on study materials returned within 14 days in a saleable condition.
5. Courses are not transferable between students.
6. Distance Learning fees include VAT and all materials but exclude any taxes or duties imposed by countries outside the UK.

METHODS OF PAYMENT:

☐ Please invoice my employer (details completed overleaf).
☐ I enclose a cheque made payable to The Financial Training Company Ltd. for £ ____________
Payments will only be accepted in UK Sterling.
☐ Please charge my Credit/Debit Card Number for the fees indicated above.

Valid from ☐☐☐☐ Expiry ☐☐☐☐ Solo/Switch Issue No ☐☐ Security Code ☐☐☐

I agree to the terms and conditions of enrolment which I have read.

Student Signature ______________________________ Date ________________